# LANGUAGE, CULTURE, AND SOCIETY

## A BOOK OF READINGS  SECOND EDITION

## BEN G. BLOUNT

*The University of Georgia*

**WAVELAND PRESS, INC.**

Prospect Heights, Illinois

For information about this book, write or call:
    Waveland Press, Inc.
    P.O. Box 400
    Prospect Heights, Illinois 60070
    (708) 634-0081

# TABLE OF CONTENTS

# I. FORMATIVE PERIOD
## 1910-1940s

# II. PARADIGM DEVELOPMENT
## 1950s-1970s

# III. DIRECTIONS
## 1980s-1990s

# Acknowledgments

Franz Boas, "Introduction to the Handbook of American Indian Language," *Bureau of American Ethnology Bulletin* 40, courtesy of the Smithsonian Institution.

Edward Sapir, "The Unconscious Patterning of Behavior in Society." Reprinted with permission of Mr. Philip Sapir, Editor-in-Chief, *The Collected Works of Edward Sapir*, published by Walter de Gruyter & Co. First published in *The Unconscious: A Symposium*, E. S. Drummer, ed., Alfred A. Knopf, publisher, 1927.

Edward Sapir, "Language." From the *Encyclopaedia of the Social Sciences*, Edwin A. Seligman, Editor-in-Chief, vol. 9, pp. 155–69. Copyright 1933, renewed 1961 by Macmillan Publishing Company. Reprinted with permission of Macmillan Publishing Company.

Benjamin Lee Whorf, "The Relation of Habitual Thought and Behavior to Language." From *Language, Culture, and Personality, Essays in Memory of Edward Sapir*, Leslie Spier, A. Irving Hallowell and Stanley S. Newman, eds., pp. 75–93. Published by the Sapir Memorial Publication Fund, 1941.

George Herbert Mead, "The Problem of Society: How We Become Selves." From *Movements of Thought in the Nineteenth Century*, Merritt H. Moore, ed. Published by the University of California Press, 1936.

George Herbert Mead, "Relation of Mind to Response and Environment." From *Mind, Self, and Society*, Charles W. Morris, ed. Published by the University of California Press, 1934.

Harry Hoijer, "The Sapir-Whorf Hypothesis." From *Language in Culture*, Harry Hoijer, ed. Published by the University of Chicago Press, 1954. Reprinted by permission of the author and The University of Chicago Press.

Charles O. Frake, "The Ethnographic Description of Cognitive Systems." From *Anthropology and Human Behavior*, T. Gladwin and W. Sturtevant, eds., pp. 72–85. Published by the Anthropological Society of Washington, 1962. Reprinted by permission of the Society.

Claude Lévi-Strauss, "Language and the Analysis of Social Laws." Chapter III of *Structural Anthropology* by Claude Lévi Strauss, translated by Claire Jacobson and Brooke Grundfest Schoepf. Copyright © 1963 by Basic Books Inc. Reprinted by permission of HarperCollins Publishers, Inc.

Brent Berlin, "Speculations on the Growth of Ethnobotanical Nomenclature." From *Language in Society*, vol. 1, no. 1, pp. 51–86, copyright 1972 by Cambridge University Press. Reprinted with permission of Cambridge University Press.

Michael Silverstein, "Shifters, Linguistic Categories and Cultural Description," originally published in *Meaning in Anthropology*, School of American Research Advanced Seminar Series. Copyright © 1987 by the School of American Research, Santa Fe, New Mexico.

Erving Goffman, "On Face-Work: An Analysis of Ritual Elements in Social Interaction." From *Psychiatry*, vol. 18, pp. 213–31, 1955. Reprinted by permission of Guilford Publications, Inc.

Dell Hymes, "The Ethnography of Speaking." From *Anthropology and Human Behavior*, T. Gladwin and W. Sturtevant, eds., pp. 13–53. Published by the Anthropological Society of Washington, 1962. Reprinted by permission of the Society.

John J. Gumperz, "Linguistic and Social Interaction in Two Communities." Reproduced by permission of the American Anthropological Association. From *American Anthropologist*, vol. 66, no. 6, Part 2, December 1964. Not for further reproduction.

Susan M. Ervin-Tripp, "Sociolinguistics." From *Advances in Experimental Social Psychology*, Leonard Berkowitz, ed., vol. 4, pp. 93–107. Copyright © 1969 by Academic Press, Inc. Reprinted with permission of the author and Academic Press.

Roy Turner, "Words, Utterances, and Activities." From *Understanding Everyday Life*, J. Douglas, ed., pp. 169–187. Published by Aldine de Gruyter, 1970. Reprinted with permission of the author.

Jane H. Hill, "The Grammar of Consciousness and the Consciousness of Grammar." Reproduced by permission of the American Anthropological Association. From *American Ethnologist*, vol. 12, no. 4, 1985. Not for further reproduction.

John A. Lucy, "Whorf's View of the Linguistic Mediation of Thought." From *Semiotic Mediation*, Elizabeth Mertz and Richard Parmentier, eds., pp. 73–97, 1985. Reprinted by permission of Academic Press.

Eugene Hunn, "Ethnoecology: The Relevance of Cognitive Anthropology for Human Ecology." From *The Relevance of Culture*, Morris Freilich, ed., pp. 143–160. Copyright 1989 by Greenwood Publishing Group, Inc., Westport, CT. Reprinted with permission of Greenwood Publishing Group.

Paul Kay, Brent Berlin and William Merrifield, "Biocultural Implications of Systems of Color Naming." Reproduced by permission of the American Anthropological Association. From *Journal of Linguistic Anthropology*, vol. 1, no. 1., June 1991. Not for further reproduction.

Elinor Ochs and Bambi Schieffelin, "Language Acquisition and Socialization: Three Developmental Stories and Their Implications." From *Culture Theory: Essays on Mind, Self, and Emotion*, Richard A. Shweder and Robert A. LeVine, eds., pp. 276–320. Copyright 1984 by Cambridge University Press. Reprinted with permission of Cambridge University Press.

Michael Silverstein, "Language and the Culture of Gender: At the Intersection of Structure, Usage, and Ideology." From *Semiotic Mediation*, Elizabeth Mertz and Richard Parmentier, eds., pp. 220–259, 1985. Reprinted by permission of Academic Press.

Ben G. Blount, "Parental Speech and Language Acquisition: An Anthropological Perspective." Reprinted by permission of Human Sciences Press. From *Pre- and Peri-Natal Psychology*, vol. 4, no. 4, 1990, pp. 319–337.

Charles Briggs and Richard Bauman, "Genre, Intertextuality, and Social Power." Reproduced by permission of the American Anthropological Association. From *Journal of Linguistic Anthropology*, vol. 2, no. 2, December 1992. Not for further reproduction.

# Preface

The first edition of this reader appeared in 1974, issued by Winthrop Publishers. Within a few years, all of the printed copies were sold, and the book went out of print. In the ensuing period, inquiries were received each year about the availability of the book, in particular to ask for a personal copy or for permission to photocopy the book. In virtually all of those cases, the story was the same; since copies of the reader were not available for students to purchase, at least one copy was needed to place on reserve in the university library. Students would then at least have access to the articles for assigned reading. What few personal copies existed were soon exhausted, and recourse to photocopying was necessary. Apparently the reader has filled a niche during the past two decades as required or recommended reading for language and culture courses.

The demand for the reader is clearly attributable to the continued importance of the articles reprinted in it. That is not surprising, since the articles were initially selected primarily because they are classics in the field of language, culture, and society. To one degree or another, they were major contributions at the time that they were originally published, and their importance has not substantially diminished with the passage of time. They continue to be cited in the literature. Care was also taken to ensure that the articles collectively span the entire historical period of language and culture studies in North America. The reader thus contains only articles that are viewed as pivotal in the historical development of the field of inquiry.

Overall, then, the readings provide a kind of capsule summary of the field, at least in terms of the concepts and themes that have given central definition to it historically. Although new issues and concerns inevitably arose as the field progressed, a number of the earlier topics have remained central, becoming more elaborated and clarified across the years. The concept of culture has been at the base of inquiry throughout, from its earliest formal definition by Edward B. Tylor in 1871 to the present. In language and culture studies, the view of culture has been first and foremost a cognitive one, that culture is knowledge, a system of information that is in speakers' heads, at least in large part. How the knowledge is represented has changed substantially, but the basic assumptions about what it is are still present. The idea that language is a fundamental part of culture has also been constant throughout, as has the idea that the study of language is a particularly important and revealing way to access culture and even thought itself. The latter idea is embedded in the so-called Sapir-Whorf hypothesis, that the habitual use of language influences the way its speakers view the world. The Sapir-Whorf hypothesis engenders discussion as lively today as it did when Edward Sapir and

Benjamin Lee Whorf wrote in the 1920s and 1930s. Other abiding issues related to language and to society can also be identified, but perhaps they are best left to the introductions of the various sections of the reader.

For students new to the subject matter of language, culture, and society, the articles in the first edition issue of the reader also gave identity to the authors who had played seminal roles in the development of the field. The particular stances and contributions could be related to the individuals who gave shape and definition to them.

The original edition of the reader contained 17 articles that were considered at that time to be classics, in effect to have been sufficiently important to still be widely read. In the twenty years since those assessments and selections were made, the field has continued to develop and change. The readings in the current edition of the book have been expanded to reflect developments of the past two decades. Twelve new selections have been added to cover the period from approximately 1970 to the present. The primary consideration in the addition of the new readings is to bring the book up to date, thus giving priority to the historical continuity of the field. While an effort was made to choose articles that meet the definition of "classic," the more recent the publication of the article, the less certain one can be about that status. Nonetheless, the articles published in the 1970s and 1980s have, to various degrees, achieved some prominence.

While 12 new articles were added to the book, five of the articles in the first edition were deleted. Although they remain important in the historical development of the field, they have become less central to current issues, prefiguring less in the directions that language, culture, and society studies are now going. The reader thus contains 24 articles, spanning the history of the field from approximately the beginning of the twentieth century to the present. Whether all of the readings equally will stand the test of time remains to be seen, but there is considerable consensus that they are all important publications in shaping the field as it has grown and expanded. An overview of the development of language, culture, and society can be gained from reading them, and it is hoped that the book will continue to serve that role for current and future generations of students.

# PART 1

# FORMATIVE PERIOD

1910-1940s

# INTRODUCTION

To use a passage from the work of Franz Boas to mark the beginning of studies on language, culture, and society is somewhat arbitrary. Language and culture studies have a history that goes far deeper than the beginning of twentieth century anthropology, which is when Boas began to exert his deep and lasting influence. The roots of the field are in the Philosophy of the Enlightenment of the eighteenth century, especially in the writings of Johann Gottfried Herder (1784–91). The topic of language in relation to human thought and history became a centerpiece in the nineteenth-century German historical idealism, in particular in the work of Wilhelm von Humboldt (1903–36). Readers interested in pursuing the history of language and culture from the late eighteenth into the early twentieth century can consult writings by Regna Darnell (1990), Dell Hymes (1983) and Konrad Koerner (1977, 1992).

To begin the modern era of language and culture studies with the work of Franz Boas is justifiable. The overwhelmingly dominant role of Boas in the development of anthropology in North America probably has no counterpart in history for any other academic discipline. Although anthropology was present in North America decades prior to Boas, he began the first department of anthropology in the United States, was responsible (directly or indirectly) for the beginnings of virtually all of the older, major departments of anthropology, and trained the first generation of academic anthropologists (see Stocking 1974 and Lesser 1981 for historical accounts). The subject matter of anthropology in the formative years was largely American Indians, and the objectives sought in their study was their origins, distribution, and genetic and cultural relatedness. The study of American Indian languages was an integral part of the larger research endeavor, much of it orchestrated by Franz Boas. His Introduction to the *Handbook of American Indian Languages* (1911) was a major contribution when it appeared, and as testament to its importance, it has been reprinted many times.

Boas's Introduction was not limited to linguistic and genetic aspects of American Indian languages. It contains many of the topics that continue to be of interest in language and culture studies to the present. In the section of the Introduction entitled "Linguistics and Ethnology," reprinted in the present reader, Boas was primarily concerned with the practical value of linguistics in collecting and analyzing ethnographic data, but that practical concern led him to consider one of the fundamental relationships between language and culture. Specifically, he concluded that without a knowledge of the language, an ethnographer would fail to grasp the content of a culture.

2

The key to the relationship of language and culture, as Boas saw it, was that linguistic categories are always unconscious and are therefore not subject to rationalization or secondary explanations which obscure true development and history. Speakers could not, in other words, alter and thereby distort linguistic categories and, by extension, culture. The identification of cultural traits through the "pure" medium of language was seen to guarantee to a greater degree the authenticity of any ethnographic account. In his emphasis on the unconscious nature of linguistic phenomena, Boas appeared to be developing the idea, later termed the Sapir-Whorf hypothesis, that unconscious linguistic forms condition cultural forms of behavior. He did not, however, arrive fully at that conclusion and in fact disavowed that determinacy between form and behavior existed: "It does not seem likely . . . that there is any direct relation between the culture of a tribe and the language they speak, except in so far as a certain state of culture is conditioned by morphological traits of the language" (1911:66).

Boas' reluctance to equate language and culture more strongly may have been due to his concern to separate race, language, and culture. Section I of the Introduction, "Race and Language" is included in the reader, primarily because of the historical importance of Boas' position on the issue of the relationship between language and culture at its most general level, i.e., the necessary relationships among race, language, and culture. The necessary relationships were of considerable practical and theoretical importance in the decades around the turn of the century, and Boas was instrumental in exposing the fallacy of assuming necessary relationships. He examined the possible permutations (for instance, language determines race and culture, race determines language and culture, and so on), demonstrating that none of them were binding and thus not necessary. The principal idea was to remove the determinacy of race on language and culture.

Note should be made that Boas' work was not directed toward a clarification of the role of society in regard to language and culture. He certainly was not oblivious to the social importance of speech genre, use of imagery, and metaphor in verbal performance, given his interests in folklore, but he did not develop a theory of society or of language and culture in society.

The concept of society is, however, clearly present and developed in the work of Edward Sapir, as is language and culture. In "The Unconscious Patterning of Behavior in Society," Sapir differentiated social from individual behavior on the basis of norms of conduct and perpetuation of tradition. Social behavior was seen as culturally organized and arranged aspects of individual behavior. Since the patterning of social behavior, however, is typically out of consciousness, Sapir saw the patterning as reflecting the underlying cultural patterns, and that is what was sought research-wise. Language was seen as subject to a similar contingency; its structure is largely unconsciously determined. Sapir viewed social behavior and language as distinct entities but with a common underlying base—society's tacit agreement to see and use them as symbols of reference. They both depended on a common underlying and unconscious pattern, which itself was a manifestation of culture.

Sapir did not appear to view the relationship between language and culture as directly functional. He noted that "Purely functional explanations of language, if valid, would lead us to expect either a far greater uniformity in linguistic expression than we actually find, or should lead us to discover strict relations of a functional nature between a particular form of language and the culture of the people using it. Neither of these expectations [is] fulfilled by the facts" (1927:127). In other words, according to Sapir the relationship could not be strongly functional because it would produce a kind of determinacy, for language and culture in general or for particular elements of a language and a culture, and no evidence for either level of determinacy had even been detected.

In the article "Language," Sapir presented a survey of language in terms of the major topics which linguists and anthropologists typically study. In order, he discussed phonetics, phonemics, psychological characteristics of language, language as a symbolic system, the origin of language, functions of language, language in socialization, classification of languages, linguistic change, and international languages. The two topics most relevant for our present concern are the functions of language and language in socialization. Sapir noted that language is rarely purely referential. Reference, the picking out and denoting of some object in the environment, is only one of many functions in the spoken language. The expressive function, for example, is usually present and obvious, to the extent that the mere content of speech does not serve to convince people of a speaker's intention as much as the expressive elements or components do. In other words, what is said usually does not matter as much as how it is said, a phenomenon of which Sapir was clearly aware. Sapir also observed that language has a specific socialization function, such as a unifying function among special interest groups (families, undergraduates, labor unions) and a rapport function at social gatherings (parties, conventions).

While Sapir's views on language, culture, and society were considerably more developed than were those of Boas, they were based on the same central idea, that language and social behavior were reflective of the underlying culture and that the study of their patterns was thus a way of studying culture without secondary interpretations and local rationalization of culture getting in the way and distorting its actual nature. Culture "seen" or "heard" directly, in this view, has been filtered through interpretation and is thus not an accurate reflection of what it actually is. To see what it actually is requires a discovery of the underlying patterning—a task that Sapir's student, Benjamin Lee Whorf, set for himself. Before turning to Whorf's work, however, some references for further reading on Sapir may be of interest to some readers. Sapir is widely recognized as one of the premier linguists in the history of the discipline, and as one would expect, there is both a large literature produced by him and by others about him and his contributions. His 1921 book, *Language*, can be profitably read today, and a useful collection of his writings can be found in Mandelbaum (1949). A ten-volume set of his writings was published to commemorate the hundredth year of his birth (published as the *Collected Works of Edward Sapir*, by Mouton de Gruyter Press). A series of his lectures on the psychology of culture has also been reconstructed and edited by Irvine (1994), and among the works appraising his contributions to linguistics and anthropology are Darnell (1990) and Koerner (1984).

Benjamin Lee Whorf did not write extensively, but in virtually all of his writings, he was concerned with the unconscious patterning of language and behavior, essentially with establishing the influence of linguistic patterns on thought and behavior. Whorf, far more than Sapir, however, has been misunderstood and roundly criticized for his views on language and culture. Whereas Whorf attempted to show that the patterns of grammar were related to the way that its speakers categorized and viewed the world, his efforts unfortunately have often been transformed into "the language a person speaks determines the way that person sees the world." That is a profound misreading of what Whorf was attempting to accomplish, as a careful reading of his article "The Relation of Habitual Thought and Behavior to Language" will show. What Whorf actually sought was a demonstration that the deeper patterns on which grammar itself was based would be reflected in the behavior of the speakers. The patterns would be habitual, that is, unconscious, and would predispose the holder or bearer of those patterns to apply them, again, unconsciously, to behavior and thus eventually the way the world was seen and interpreted. The common origin of the underlying patterns is what made the "results" similar, not that one pattern "determined" the other to the extent that the world could not be seen or experienced in any other way.

For further reading on Whorf and his scholarly contributions, the basic references are an edited collection by Carroll (1956) and a collection of articles about Whorf's work by Hoijer (1956). More recent interpretations of Whorf can be found in the collection of articles edited by Mertz and Parmentier (1985).

Sapir's and Whorf's interest in the relationship between patterns of language and cultural expressions of behavior came to be called the Sapir-Whorf hypothesis. Simply the fact that the complex of ideas was given a name indicates the sway that it held in the early part of this century. The interest, however, was not limited to the formative period of language and culture studies. The Sapir-Whorf hypothesis has been an abiding interest throughout the anthropological study of language and culture, up to the present day, as more recently published articles in this collection show.

The lineage of ideas from Boas to Sapir and to Whorf was constructed centrally around the concepts of language and culture. The concepts of society and social behavior were more taken for granted. Stated otherwise, society and social behavior were the dependent variables, and language and culture were the independent variables. If changes occur in the patterns of language (and thus of culture), then social behavior (and thus society) would be changed. Despite their relative neglect, social behavior and society are, of course, complex phenomena in their own right; and inquiry into their nature is also an interesting and worthwhile pursuit. Although language-and-culture anthropologists did not directly pursue those topics, they were the focus of inquiry in other intellectual lineages during the same historical period.

George Herbert Mead was a social psychologist and social philosopher whose primary interest was in the question of how individuals acquire social selves. He was a member of the "Chicago School" of sociology and philosophy at the University of Chicago, whose scholarly agendas were constructed around the theoretical issue of how individuals and society were related. The basic question was how individuals, as autonomous beings, acquire as a part of their self a societal component—that is, their social self—that allows them to interact as *social* beings. Mead's answer was that self is acquired through symbolic interactions, the process through which the subjective experiences of individuals are brought into objectivity by mutual acceptance of symbols. Although one might be interested in the origin of the symbols, the important point was that every individual is socialized into a system in which every member tacitly agrees to recognize the symbols as objective reality. Mead's ideas and proposals are developed in the article "The Problem of Society: How We Become Selves."

Language has a central position in the symbolic system as conceptualized by Mead: "Language is the means whereby individuals can indicate to one another what their responses to objects will be, and hence what the meanings of objects are . . ." (1934:114). Language is therefore a symbolic system firmly embedded in a social matrix, an interactional definition of language quite different from the more structural one used by Boas, Sapir, and Whorf. The fundamentally social nature of Mead's theory of society and self can be further seen in the second excerpt from his writings, "Relation of Mind to Response and Environment," His goal in that chapter was to explain how "Mind," the organization of mental activities, is basically a social phenomenon. To understand what Mead meant, we must start with his idea that the social environment was viewed as having meaning as a function of social activity. The meaning attached to any object or feature of the environment was seen as the result of an individual's control, mentally, over the organization of those features. The importance of language in that perspective lies in the increased control it provides over the organization of the social environment. A mutual interdependence was thus established between language and the field of Mind, both of which arose and developed with the social process, and that within the matrix of social interactions.

Mead's views on language, mind, and society had little direct impact on anthropological views of language, culture, and society during the formative period. They were, however, to heavily influence thought in that area during the next historical period, largely through the contributions of Erving Goffman. The two lines of intellectual development, one of language-and-culture and one of language-and-society, both merge and remain distinct lines of inquiry, as the readings in the second section of the reader will show. Readers interested in more of Mead's work should consult his posthumously edited book (Morris 1934) and an edited reader in social psychology (Manis 1972).

## REFERENCES

Boas, Franz.
1911 "Introduction." In *Handbook of American Indian Languages*, Part I. Pp. 1–83. Washington, D.C.: Government Printing Office.
Carroll, John B. ed.
1956 *Language, Thought, and Reality: Selected Writings of Benjamin Lee Whorf*. Cambridge, MA: MIT Press.
Darnell, Regna.
1990 *Edward Sapir: Linguist, Anthropologist, Humanist*. Berkeley: University of California Press.
Herder, Johann Gottfried.
1784–91 *Ideen zur Philosophie der Geschichte der Menschheit*. 4 vols. Riga: Johann Friedrich Hartknoch.
Hoijer, Harry, ed.
1956 *Language in Culture: Conference on the Interrelations of Language and Other Aspects of Culture*. Chicago: University of Chicago Press.
Humboldt, Wilhelm von.
1903–36 *Gesammelte Schriften. Herausgegeben von der Koniglichen Preusischen Akademie der Wissenschaften*. 17 vols. Berlin: B. Behr.
Hymes, Dell H.
1983 *Essays in the History of Linguistic Anthropology*. Amsterdam: John Benjamins.
Irvine, Judith T., ed.
1994 *The Psychology of Culture: A Course of Lectures*. The Hague: Mouton de Gruyter.
Koerner, E. F. Konrad.
1977 "The Humboldtian Trend in Linguistics." In *Descriptive and Historical Linguistics: Festschrift for Winfred P. Lehmann*. Paul J. Hopper, ed. Pp. 144–158. Amsterdam: John Benjamins.
1992 "The Sapir-Whorf Hypothesis: A preliminary History and a Bibliographic Essay." *Journal of Linguistic Anthropology* (2):173–198.
Koerner, E. F. Konrad, ed.
1984 *Edward Sapir: Appraisals of his Life and Work*. Amsterdam: John Benjamins.
Lesser, Alexander.
1981 "Franz Boas." In *Totems and Teachers: Perspectives on the History of Anthropology*, Sydel Silverman, ed. Pp. 1–33. New York: Columbia University Press.
Mandelbaum, David, ed.
1949 *Selected Writings of Edward Sapir in Language, Culture, and Personality*. Berkeley: University of California Press.

Manis, Jerome G., ed.
   1972   *Symbolic Interaction: A Reader in Social Psychology*. Boston: Allyn and Bacon.

Mertz, Elizabeth and Richard J. Parmentier, eds.
   1985   *Semiotic Mediation: Sociocultural and Psychological Perspectives*. Orlando: Academic Press.

Morris, Charles, ed.
   1934   *Mind, Self, and Society*. Berkeley: University of California Press.

Sapir, Edward.
   1921   *Language: An Introduction to the Study of Speech*. New York: Harcourt, Brace & Co.

   1927   "The Unconscious Patterning of Behavior in Society." In *The Unconscious: A Symposium*, E. S. Drummer, ed. New York: Knopf.

Stocking, George W., Jr., ed.
   1974   *A Franz Boas Reader: The Shaping of American Anthropology, 1883–1911*. New York: Basic Books.

# Introduction to the Handbook of American Indian Languages
## Franz Boas

## I. RACE AND LANGUAGE

### Early Attempts to Determine the Position of the American Race

When Columbus started on his journey to reach the Indies, sailing westward, and discovered the shores of America, he beheld a new race of man, different in type, different in culture, different in language, from any known before that time. This race resembled neither the European types, nor the negroes, nor the better-known races of southern Asia. As the Spanish conquest of America progressed, other peoples of our continent became known to the invaders, and all showed a certain degree of outer resemblance, which led the Spaniards to designate them by the term "Indios" (Indians), the inhabitants of the country which was believed to be part of India. Thus the mistaken geographical term came to be applied to the inhabitants of the New World; and owing to the contrast of their appearance to that of other races, and the peculiarities of their cultures and their languages, they came to be in time considered as a racial unit.

The same point of view still prevailed when the discoveries included more extended parts of the New World. The people with whom the Spaniards and Portuguese came into contact in South America, as well as the inhabitants of the northern parts of North America, all seemed to partake so much of the same characteristics, that they were readily classed with the natives first discovered, and were considered as a single race of mankind.

It was only when our knowledge of the Indian tribes increased, that differences between the various types of man inhabiting our continent became known. Differences in degree of culture, as well as differences in language, were recognized at an early time. Much later came a recognition of the fact that the Indians of our continent differ in type as much among themselves as do the members of other races.

As soon as investigators began to concern themselves with these questions, the problem of the position of the natives of America among the races of mankind came to be of considerable interest, and speculations in regard to their origin and relationships occur even in the early descriptions of the New World.

Among the earlier attempts we find particularly endeavors to prove that certain parts of the beliefs and customs of the Indians agree with those of the Old World. Such agreements were considered proof that the Indians belong to one of the races enumerated in biblical history; and the theory that they represent the lost tribes of Israel was propounded frequently, and has held its own for a long time. In a similar way were traced analogies between the languages of the New World and those of the Old World, and many investigators believe even now that they have established such relationships. Attempts were also made to prove similarities in appearance between the American races and other races, and thus to determine their position among the races of the Old World.

## Classifications based on Physical Type, Language, and Customs

The problems involved in the determination of the relations of the various races have been approached from two different points of view—either the attempt has been made to assign a definite position to a race in a classificatory system of the races of man, or the history of the race has been traced as far back as available data may permit.

The attempts to classify mankind are numerous. Setting aside the classifications based on biblical tradition, and considering only those that are based on scientific discussion, we find a number of attempts based on comparisons of the anatomical characteristics of mankind, combined with geographical considerations; others are based on the discussion of a combination of anatomical and cultural characteristics—traits which are considered as characteristic of certain groups of mankind; while still others are based primarily on the study of the languages spoken by people representing a certain anatomical type.

The attempts that have thus been made have led to entirely different results. Blumenback, one of the first scientists who attempted to classify mankind, first distinguished five races—the Caucasian, Mongolian, Ethiopian, American, and Malay. It is fairly clear that this Classification is based as much on geographical as on anatomical considerations, although the description of each race is primarily an anatomical one. Cuvier distinguished three races—the white, yellow, and black. Huxley proceeds more strictly on a biological basis. He combines part of the Mongolian and American races of Blumenback into one, assigns part of the South Asiatic peoples to the Australian type, and subdivides the European races into a dark and a light division. The numerical preponderance of the European types has evidently led him to make finer distinctions in this race, which he divides into the xanthochroic and melanochroic races. It would be easy to make subdivisions of equal value in other races. Still clearer is the influence of cultural points of view in classifications like those of Gobineau and Klemm (who distinguishes the active and passive races), according to the cultural achievements of the various types of man.

The most typical attempt to classify mankind from a consideration of both anatomical and linguistic points of view is that of Friederich Muller, who takes as the basic of his primary divisions the form of hair, while all the minor divisions are based on linguistic considerations.

## Relations between Physical Type, Language, and Customs

An attempt to correlate the numerous classifications that have been proposed shows clearly a condition of utter confusion and contradiction. If it were true that anatomical form, language, and culture are all closely associated, and that each subdivision of mankind is characterized by a certain bodily form, a certain culture, and a certain language, which can never become separated, we might expect that the results of the various investigations would show better agreement. If, on the other hand, the various phenomena which were made the leading points in the attempt at classification are not closely associated, then we may naturally expect such contradictions and lack of agreement as are actually found.

It is therefore necessary, first of all, to be clear in regard to the significance of anatomical characteristics, language, and culture, as characteristic of any subdivision of mankind.

It seems desirable to consider the actual development of these various traits among the existing races.

## Permanence of Physical Type; Changes in Language and Culture

At the present period we may observe many cases in which a complete change of language and culture takes place without a corresponding change in physical type. This is true, for instance, among the North American negroes, a people by descent largely African; in culture and language, however, essentially European. While it is true that certain survivals of African culture and language are found among our American negroes, their culture is essentially that of the uneducated classes of the people among whom they live, and their language is on the whole identical with that of their neighbors—English, French, Spanish, and Portuguese, according to the prevalent language in various parts of the continent. It might be objected that the transportation of the African race to America was an artificial one, and that in earlier times extended migrations and transplantations of this kind have not taken place.

The history of medieval Europe, however, shows clearly that extended changes in language and culture have taken place many times without corresponding changes in blood.

Recent investigations of the physical types of Europe have shown with great clearness that the distribution of types has remained the same for a long period. Without considering details, it may be said that an Alpine type can easily be distinguished from a north-European type on the one hand, and a south-European type on the other. The Alpine type appears fairly uniform over a large territory, no matter what language may be spoken and what national culture may prevail in the particular district. The central-European Frenchman, Germans, Italians, and Slavs are so nearly of the same type that we may safely assume a considerable degree of blood relationship, notwithstanding their linguistic differences.

Instances of similar kind, in which we find permanence of blood with far-reaching modifications of language and culture, are found in other parts of the world. As an example may be mentioned the Veddah of Ceylon, a people fundamentally different in type from the neighboring Singhalese, whose language they seem to have adopted, and from whom they have also evidently borrowed a number of cultural traits. Still other examples are the Japanese of the northern part of Japan, who are undoubtedly, to a considerable extent, Ainu in blood; and the Yukaghir of Siberia, who, while retaining to a great extent the old blood, have been assimilated in culture and language by the neighboring Tungus.

## Permanence of Language; Changes of Physical Type

While it is therefore evident that in many cases a people, without undergoing a considerable change in type by mixture, have changed completely their language and culture, still other cases may be adduced in which it can be shown that a people have retained their language while undergoing material changes in blood and culture, or in both. As an example of this may be mentioned the Magyar of Europe, who have retained their old language, but have become mixed with people speaking Indo-European languages, and who have, to all intents and purposes, adopted European culture.

Similar conditions must have prevailed among the Athapascans, one of the great linguistic families of North America. The great body of people speaking languages belonging to this linguistic stock live in the northwestern part of America, while other dialects are spoken by small tribes in California, and still others by a large body of people in Arizona and New Mexico. The relationship between all these dialects is so close that they must be considered as branches of one large group, and it must be assumed that all of them have sprung from a language once spoken over a continuous area. At the present time the people speaking these languages differ fundamentally in type, the inhabitants of the Mackenzie river region being quite different from the tribes of California, and these, again, differing from the tribes of New Mexico. The forms of culture in these different regions are also quite distinct; the culture of the California Athapascans resembles that of other Californian tribes, while the culture of the Athapascans of New Mexico and Arizona is influenced by that of other peoples of that area. It seems most plausible to assume in this case that branches of this stock migrated from one part of this large area to another, where they intermingled with the neighboring people, and thus changed their physical characteristics, while at the same time they retained their speech. Without historical evidence this process can not, of course, by proved. I shall refer to this example later on.

## Changes of Language and Type

These two phenomena—a retention of type with a change of language, and a retention of language with a change of type—apparently opposed to each other, are still very closely related, and in many cases go hand in hand. An example of this is, for instance, the distribution of the Arabs along the north coast of Africa. On the whole, the Arab element has retained its language; but at the same time intermarriages with the native races were common, so that the descendants of the Arabs have often retained the old language and have changed their type. On the other hand, the natives have to a certain extent given up their own languages, but have continued to intermarry among themselves and have thus preserved their type. So far as any change of this kind is connected with intermixture, both types of changes must always occur at the same time, and will be classed as a change of type or a change of language, as our attention is directed to the one people or the other, or, in some cases, as the one or the other change is more pronounced. Cases of complete assimilation without any mixture of the people involved seem to be rare, if not entirely absent.

## Permanence of Type and Language; Change of Culture

Cases of permanence of type and language and of change of culture are much more numerous. As a matter of fact, the whole historical development of Europe, from prehistoric times on, is one endless series of examples of this process, which seems to be much easier, since assimilation of cultures occurs everywhere without actual blood mixture, as an effect of imitation. Proof of diffusion of cultural elements may be found in every single cultural area which covers a district in which many languages are spoken. In North America, California offers a good example of this kind; for here many languages are spoken, and there is a certain degree of differentiation of type, but at the same time a considerable uniformity of culture prevails. Another case in point is the coast of New Guinea, where, notwithstanding strong local differentiations, a certain fairly characteristic type of culture prevails, which goes hand in hand with a strong differentiation of languages. Among more highly civilized peoples, the whole area which is under the influence of Chinese culture might be given as an example.

These considerations make it fairly clear that, at least at the present time, anatomical type, language, and culture have not necessarily the same fates; that a people may remain constant in type and language and change in culture;

that they may remain constant in type, but change in language; or that they may remain constant in language and change in type and culture. If this is true, then it is obvious that attempts to classify mankind, based on the present distribution of type, language, and culture, must lead to different results, according to the point of view taken; that a classification based primarily on type alone will lead to a system which represents, more or less accurately, the blood relationships of the people, which do not need to coincide with their cultural relationships; and that, in the same way, classifications based on language and culture do not need at all to coincide with a biological classification.

If this be true, then a problem like the much discussed Aryan problem really does not exist, because the problem is primarily a linguistic one, relating to the history of the Aryan languages; and the assumption that a certain definite people whose members have always been related by blood must have been the carriers of this language throughout history; and the other assumption, that a certain cultural type must have always belonged to this people—are purely arbitrary ones and not in accord with the observed facts.

## Hypothesis of Original Correlation of Type, Language, and Culture

Nevertheless, it must be granted, that in a theoretical consideration of the history of the types of mankind, or languages, and of cultures, we are led back to the assumption of early conditions during which each type was much more isolated from the rest of mankind than it is at the present time. For this reason, the culture and the language belonging to a single type must have been much more sharply separated from those of other types than we find them to be at the present period. It is true that such a condition has nowhere been observed; but the knowledge of historical developments almost compels us to assume its existence at a very early period in the development of mankind. If this is true, the question would arise, whether an isolated group, at an early period, was necessarily characterized by a single type, a single language, and a single culture, or whether in such a group different types, different languages, and different cultures may have been represented.

The historical development of mankind would afford a simpler and clearer picture, if we were justified in assuming that in primitive communities the three phenomena had been intimately associated. No proof, however, of such an assumption can be given. On the contrary, the present distribution of languages, as compared with the distribution of types, makes it plausible that even at the earliest times the biological units may have been wider than the linguistic units, and presumably also wider than the cultural units. I believe that it may be safely said that all over the world the biological unit is much larger than the linguistic unit: in other words, that groups of men who are so closely related in bodily appearance that we must consider them as representatives of the same variety of mankind, embrace a much larger number of individuals than the number of men speaking languages which we know to be genetically related. Examples of this kind may be given from many parts of the world. Thus, the European race—including under this term roughly all those individuals who are without hesitation classed by us as members of the white race—would include peoples speaking Indo-European, Basque, and Ural-Altaic languages. West African negroes would represent individuals of a certain negro type, but speaking the most diverse languages; and the same would be true, among Asiatic types, of Siberians; among American types, of part of the Californian Indians.

So far as our historical evidence goes, there is no reason to believe that the number of distinct languages has at any time been less than it is now. On the contrary, all our evidence goes to show that the number of apparently unrelated languages has been much greater in earlier times than at present. On the other hand, the number of types that have presumably become extinct seems to be rather small, so that there is no reason to suppose that at an early period there should have been a nearer correspondence between the number of distinct linguistic and anatomical types; and we are thus led to the conclusion that presumably, at an early time, each human type may have existed in a number of small isolated groups, each of which may have possessed a language and culture of its own.

However this may be, the probabilities are decidedly in favor of the assumption that there is no necessity to assume that originally each language and culture were confined to a single type, or that each type and culture were confined to one language: in short, that there has been at any time a close correlation between these three phenomena.

The assumption that type, language, and culture were originally closely correlated would entail the further assumption that these three traits developed approximately at the same period, and that they developed conjointly for a considerable length of time. This assumption does not seem by any means plausible. The fundamental types of man which are represented in the negroid race and in the mongoloid race must have been differentiated long before the formation of those forms of speech that are now recognized in the linguistic families of the world. I think that even the differentiation of the more important subdivisions of the great races antedates the formation of the existing linguistic families. At any rate, the biological differentiation and the formation of speech were, at this early period, subject to the same causes that are acting upon them now, and our whole experience shows that these causes act much more rapidly on language than on the human body. In this consideration lies the principal reason for the theory of lack of correlation of type and language, even during the period of formation of types and of linguistic families.

What is true of language is obviously even more true of culture. In other words, if a certain type of man migrated over a considerable area before its language assumed the form which can now be traced in related linguistic groups, and before its culture assumed the definite type the further development of which can now be recognized, there would be no possibility of ever discovering a correlation of type, language, and culture, even if it had ever existed; but it is quite possible that such correlation has really never occurred.

It is quite conceivable that a certain racial type may have scattered over a considerable area during a formative period of speech, and that the languages which developed among the various groups of this racial type came to be so different that it is now impossible to prove them to be genetically related. In the same way, new developments of culture may have taken place which are so entirely disconnected with older types that the older genetic relationships, even if they existed, can no longer be discovered.

If we adopt this point of view, and thus eliminate the hypothetical assumption of correlation between primitive type, primitive language, and primitive culture, we recognize that any attempt at classification which includes more than one of these traits can not be consistent.

It may be added that the general term "culture" which has been used here may be subdivided from a considerable number of points of view, and different results again might be expected when we consider the inventions, the types of social organization, or beliefs, as leading points of view in our classification.

## Artificial Character of All Classifications of Mankind

We recognize thus that every classification of mankind must be more or less artificial, according to the point of view selected, and here, even more than in the domain of biology, we find that classification can only be a substitute for the genesis and history of the now existing types.

Thus we recognize that the essential object in comparing different types of man must be the reconstruction of the history of the development of their types, their languages, and their cultures. The history of each of these various traits is subject to a distinct set of modifying causes, and the investigation of each may be expected to contribute data toward the solution of our problem. The biological investigation may reveal the blood-relationships of types and their modifications under social and geographical environment. The linguistic investigation may disclose the history of languages, the contact of the people speaking them with other people, and the causes that led to linguistic differentiation and integration; while the history of civilization deals with the contact of a people with neighboring peoples, as well as with the history of its own achievements.

•     •     •

## IV. LINGUISTICS AND ETHNOLOGY

It seems desirable to say a few words on the function of linguistic researches in the study of the ethnography of the Indians.

## Practical Need of Linguistic Studies for Ethnological Purposes

First of all, the purely practical aspect of this question may be considered. Ordinarily, the investigator who visits an Indian tribe is not able to converse with the natives themselves and to obtain his information first-hand, but he is obliged to rely more or less on data transmitted by interpreters, or at least by the help of interpreters. He may ask his question through an interpreter, and receive again through his mouth the answer given by the Indians. It is obvious that this is an unsatisfactory method, even when the interpreters are good; but, as a rule, the available men are either not sufficiently familiar with the English language, or they are so entirely out of sympathy with the Indian point of view, and understand the need of accuracy on the part of the investigator so little, that information furnished by them can be used only with a considerable degree of caution. At the present time it is possible to get along in many parts of America without interpreters, by means of the trade-jargons that have developed everywhere in the intercourse between the whites and the Indians. These, however, are also a very unsatisfactory means of inquiring into the customs of the natives because, in some cases, the vocabulary of the trade-languages is extremely limited, and it is almost impossible to convey information relating to the religious and philosophic ideas or to the higher aspects of native art, all of which play so important a part in Indian life. Another difficulty which often develops whenever the investigator works with a particularly intelligent interpreter is that the interpreter imbibes too readily the view of the investigator, and that his information, for this reason, is strongly biased, because he is not so well able to withstand the influence of formative theories as the trained investigator ought to be. Anyone who has carried on work with intelligent Indians will recall instances of this kind, where the interpreter may have formulated a theory based on the questions that have been put through him, and has interpreted his answers under the guidance of his preconceived notions. All this is so obvious that it hardly requires a full discussion. Our needs become particularly apparent when we compare the methods that we expect from any investigator of cultures of the Old World with those of the ethnologist who is studying primitive tribes. Nobody would expect authoritative accounts of the civilization of China or of Japan from a man who does not speak the languages readily, and who has not mastered their literatures. The student of antiquity is expected to have a thorough mastery of the ancient languages. A student of Mohammedan life in Arabia or Turkey would hardly be considered a serious investigator if all his knowledge had to be derived from second-hand accounts. The ethnologist, on the other hand, undertakes in the majority of cases to elucidate the innermost thoughts and feelings of a people without so much as a smattering of knowledge of their language.

It is true that the American ethnologist is confronted with a serious practical difficulty, for, in the present state of American society, by far the greater number of customs and practices have gone out of existence, and the investigator is compelled to rely upon accounts of customs of former times recorded from the mouths of the old generation who, when young, still took part in these performances. Added to this he is confronted with the difficulty that the number of trained investigators is very small, and the number of American languages that are mutually unintelligible exceedingly large, probably exceeding three hundred in number. Our investigating ethnologists are also denied opportunity to spend long continuous periods with any particular tribe, so that the practical difficulties in the way of acquiring languages are almost insuperable. Nevertheless, we must insist that a command of the language is an indispensable means of obtaining accurate and thorough knowledge, because much information can be gained by listening to conversations of the natives and by taking part in their daily life, which, to the observer who has no command of the language, will remain entirely inaccessible.

It must be admitted that this ideal aim is, under present conditions, entirely beyond our reach. It is, however, quite possible for the ethnographer to obtain a theoretical knowledge of native languages that will enable him to collect at least part of the information that could be best obtained by a practical knowledge of the language. Fortunately, the Indian is easily misled, by the ability of the observer to read his language, into thinking that he is also able to understand what he reads. Thus, in taking down tales or other records in the native language, and reading them to the Indians, the Indian always believes that the reader also understands what he pronounces, because it is quite inconceivable to him that a person can freely utter the sentences in his language without clearly grasping their meaning. This fact facilitates the initial stages of ethnographic information in the native languages, because, on the whole, the northern Indians are eager to be put on record in regard to questions that are of supreme interest to them. If the observer is capable of grasping by a rapid analysis the significance of what is dictated to him, even without being able to express himself freely in the native language, he is in a position to obtain much information that otherwise would be entirely unobtainable. Although this is wholly a makeshift, still it puts the observer in an infinitely better position than that in which he would be without any knowledge whatever of the language. First of all, he can get the information from the Indians first-hand, without employing an interpreter, who may mislead him. Furthermore, the range of subjects on which he can get information is considerably increased, because the limitations of the linguistic knowledge of the interpreter, or those of the trade-language, are eliminated. It would seem, therefore, that under present conditions we are more or less compelled to rely upon an extended series of texts as the safest means of obtaining information from the Indians. A general review of our ethnographic literature shows clearly how much better is the information obtained by observers who have command of the language, and who are on terms of intimate friendship with the natives, than that obtained through the medium of interpreters.

The best material we possess is perhaps contained in the naive outpourings of the Eskimo, which they write and print themselves, and distribute as a newspaper, intended to inform the people of all the events that are of interest. These used to contain much mythological matter and much that related to the mode of life of the people. Other material of similar character is furnished by the large text collections of the Ponca, published by the late James Owen Dorsey; although many of these are influenced by the changed conditions under which the people now live. Some older records on the Iroquois, written by prominent members of the tribe, also deserve attention; and among the most recent literature the descriptions of the Sauk and Fox by Dr. William Jones are remarkable on account of the thorough understanding that the author has reached, owing to his mastery of the language. Similar in character, although rendered entirely in English, are the observations of Mr. James Teit on the Thompson Indians.

In some cases is has been possible to interest educated natives in the study of their own tribes and to induce them to write down in their own language their observations. These, also, are much superior to English records, in which the natives are generally hampered by the lack of mastery of the foreign language.

While in all these cases a collector thoroughly familiar with the Indian language and with English might give us the results of his studies without using the native language in his publications, this is quite indispensable when we try to investigate the deeper problems of ethnology. A few examples will show clearly what is meant. When the question arises, for instance, of investigating the poetry of the Indians, no translation can possibly be considered as an adequate substitute for the original. The form of rhythm, the treatment of the language, the adjustment of text to music, the imagery, the use of metaphors, and all the numerous problems involved in any thorough investigation of the style of poetry, can be interpreted only by the investigator who has equal command of the ethnographical traits of the tribe and of their language. The same is true in the investigation of rituals, with their set, more or less poetic phrases, or in the investigation of prayers and incantations. The oratory of the Indians, a subject that has received much attention by ethnologists, is not adequately known, because only a very few speeches have been handed down in the original. Here, also, an accurate investigation of the method of composition and of the devices used to reach oratorical effect, requires the preservation of speeches as rendered in the original language.

There are also numerous other features of the life of the Indians which can not be adequately presented without linguistic investigation. To these belong, for instance, the discussion of personal, tribal, and local names. The translations of Indian names which are popularly known—like Sitting-Bull, Afraid-Of-His-Horse, etc.—indicate that names possess a deeper significance. The translations, however, are so difficult that a thorough linguistic knowledge is required in order to explain the significance adequately.

In all the subjects mentioned heretofore, a knowledge of Indian languages serves as an important adjunct to a full understanding of the customs and beliefs of the people whom we are studying. But in all these cases the service which language lends us is first of all a practical one—a means to a clearer understanding of ethnological phenomena which in themselves have nothing to do with linguistic problems.

## THEORETICAL IMPORTANCE OF LINGUISTIC STUDIES

### Language a Part of Ethnological Phenomena in General

It seems, however, that a theoretical study of Indian languages is not less important than a practical knowledge of them; that the purely linguistic inquiry is part and parcel of a thorough investigation of the psychology of the peoples of the world. If ethnology is understood as the science dealing with the mental phenomena of the life of the peoples of the world, human language, one of the most important manifestations of mental life, would seem to belong naturally to the field of work of ethnology, unless special reasons can be adduced why it should not be so considered. It is true that a practical reason of this kind exists, namely, the specialization which has taken place in the methods of philological research, which has progressed to such an extent that philology and comparative linguistics are sciences which require the utmost attention, and do not allow the student to devote much of his time to other fields that require different methods of study. This, however, is no reason for believing that the results of linguistic inquiry are unimportant to the ethnologist. There are other fields of ethnological investigation which have come to be more or less specialized, and which require for their successful treatment peculiar specialization. This is true, for instance, of the study of primitive music, of primitive art, and, to a certain extent, of primitive law. Nevertheless, these subjects continue to form an important part of ethnological science.

If the phenomena of human speech seem to form in a way a subject by itself, this is perhaps largely due to the fact that the laws of language remain entirely unknown to the speakers, that linguistic phenomena never rise into the consciousness of primitive man, while all other ethnological phenomena are more or less clearly subjects of conscious thought.

The question of the relation of linguistic phenomena to ethnological phenomena, in the narrower sense of the term, deserves, therefore, special discussion.

### Language and Thought

First of all, it may be well to discuss the relation between language and thought. It has been claimed that the conciseness and clearness of thought of a people depend to a great extent upon their language. The ease with which in our modern European languages we express wide abstract ideas by a single term, and the facility with which wide generalizations are cast into the frame of a simple sentence, have been claimed to be one of the fundamental conditions of the clearness of our concepts, the logical force of our thought, and the precision with which we eliminate in our thoughts irrelevant details. Apparently this view has much in its favor. When we compare modern English with some of those Indian languages which are most concrete in their formative expression, the contrast is striking. When we say *The eye is the organ of sight,* the Indian may not be able to form the expression *the eye,* but may have to define that the eye of a person or an animal is meant. Neither may the Indian be able to generalize readily the abstract idea of an eye as the representative of the whole class of objects, but may have to specialize by an expression like *this eye here.* Neither may he be able to express by a single term the idea of *organ,* but may have to specify it by an expression like *instrument of seeing,* so the whole sentence might assume a form like *An indefinite person's eye is his means of seeing.* Still, it will be recognized that in this more specific form the general idea may be well expressed. It seems very questionable in how far the restriction of the use of certain grammatical forms can really be conceived as a hindrance in the formulation of generalized ideas. It seems much more likely that the lack of these forms is due to the lack of their need. Primitive man, when conversing with his fellow-man, is not in the habit of discussing abstract ideas. His interests center around the occupations of his daily life; and where philosophic problems are touched upon, they appear either in relation to definite individuals or in the more or less anthropomorphic forms of religious beliefs. Discourses on qualities without connection with the object to which the qualities belong, or of activities or states disconnected from the idea of the actor or the subject being in a certain state, will hardly occur in primitive speech. Thus the Indian will not speak of goodness as such, although he may very well speak of the goodness of a person. He will not speak of a state of bliss apart from the person who is in such a state. He will not refer to the power of seeing without designating an individual who has such power. Thus it happens that in languages in which the idea of possession is expressed by elements subordinated to nouns, all abstract terms appear always with possessive elements. It is, however, perfectly conceivable that an Indian trained in philosophic thought would proceed to free the underlying nominal forms from the possessive elements, and thus reach abstract forms strictly corresponding to the abstract forms of our modern languages. I have made this experiment, for instance, with the Kwakiutl language of Vancouver Island, in which no abstract term ever occurs without its possessive elements. After some discussion, I found it perfectly easy to develop the idea of the abstract term in the mind of the Indian, who will state that the word without a possessive pronoun gives a sense, although it is not used idiomatically. I succeeded, for instance, in this manner, in isolating the terms for *love* and *pity,* which ordinarily occur only in possessive forms, like *his love for him* or *my pity for you.* That this view is correct may also be observed in languages in which possessive elements appear as independent forms, as, for instance, in the Siouan languages. In these, pure abstract terms are quite common.

There is also evidence that other specializing elements, which are so characteristic of many Indian languages, may be dispensed with when, for one reason or another, it seems desirable to generalize a term. To use the example of the Kwakiutl language, the idea *to be seated* is almost always expressed with an inseparable suffix expressing the place in which a person is seated, as *seated on the floor of the house, on the ground, on the beach, on a pile of things,* or *on a round thing,* etc. When, however, for some reason, the idea of the state of sitting is to be emphasized, a form may be used which expresses simply *being in a sitting posture.* In this case, also, the device for generalized expression is present, but the opportunity for its application arises seldom, or perhaps never. I think what is true in these cases is true of the structure of every single language. The fact that generalized forms of expression are not used does not prove inability to form them, but it merely proves that the mode of life of the people is such that they are not required; that they would, however, develop just as soon as needed.

This point of view is also corroborated by a study of the numeral systems of primitive languages. As is well known, many languages exist in which the numerals do not exceed two or three. It has been inferred from this that the people speaking these languages are not capable of forming the concept of higher numbers. I think this interpretation of the existing conditions is quite erroneous. People like the South American Indians (among whom these defective numeral systems are found), or like the Eskimo (whose old system of numbers probably did not exceed ten), are presumably not in need of higher numerical expressions, because there are not many objects that they have to count. On the other hand, just as soon as these same people find themselves in contact with civilization, and when they acquire standards of value that have to be counted, they adopt with perfect ease higher numerals from other languages and develop a more or less perfect system of counting. This does not mean that every individual who in the course of his life has never made use of higher numerals would acquire more complex systems readily, but the tribe as a whole seems always to be capable of adjusting itself to the needs of counting. It must be borne in mind that counting does not become necessary until objects are considered in such generalized form that their individualities are entirely lost sight of. For this reason it is possible that even a person who has a flock of domesticated animals may know them by name and by their characteristics without ever desiring to count them. Members of a war expedition may be known by name and may not be counted. In short, there is no proof that the lack of the use of numerals is in any way connected with the inability to form the concepts of higher numbers.

If we want to form a correct judgement of the influence that language exerts over thought, we ought to bear in mind that our European languages as found at the present time have been moulded to a great extent by the abstract thought of philosophers. Terms like *essence* and *existence,* many of which are now commonly used, are by origin artificial devices for expressing the results of abstract thought. In this they would resemble the artificial, unidiomatic abstract terms that may be formed in primitive languages.

Thus it would seem that the obstacles to generalized thought inherent in the form of a language are of minor importance only, and that presumably the language alone would not prevent a people from advancing to more generalized forms of thinking if the general state of their culture should require expression of such thought; that under these conditions the language would be moulded rather by the cultural state. It does not seem likely, therefore, that there is any direct relation between the culture of a tribe and the language they speak, except in so far as the form of the language will be moulded by the state of culture, but not in so far as a certain state of culture is conditioned by morphological traits of the language.

## Unconscious Character of Linguistic Phenomena

Of greater positive importance is the question of the relation of the unconscious character of linguistic phenomena to the more conscious ethnological phenomena. It seems to my mind that this contrast is only apparent, and that the very fact of the unconsciousness of linguistic processes helps us to gain a clearer understanding of the ethnological phenomena, a point the importance of which can not be underrated. It has been mentioned before that in all languages certain classifications of concepts occur. To mention only a few: we find objects classified according to sex, or as animate and inanimate, or according to form. We find actions determined according to time and place, etc. The behavior of primitive man makes it perfectly clear that all these concepts, although they are in constant use, have never risen into consciousness, and that consequently their origin must be sought, not in rational, but in entirely unconscious, we may perhaps say instinctive, processes of the mind. They must be due to a grouping of sense-impressions and of concepts which is not in any sense of the term voluntary, but which develops from quite different psychological causes. It would seem that the essential difference between linguistic phenomena and other ethnological phenomena is that the linguistic classifications never rise into consciousness, while in other ethnological phenomena, although the same unconscious origin prevails, these often rise into consciousness, and thus give rise to secondary reasoning and to reinterpretations. It would, for instance, seem very plausible that the fundamental religious notions —like the idea of the voluntary power of inanimate objects, or of the anthropomorphic character of animals, or of the existence of powers that are superior to the mental and physical powers of man—are in their origin just as little conscious as are the fundamental ideas of language. While, however, the use of language is so automatic that the opportunity never arises for the fundamental notions to emerge into consciousness, this happens very frequently in all phenomena relating to religion. It would seem that there is no tribe in the world in which the religious activities have not come to be a subject of thought. While the religious activities may have been performed before the reason for performing them had become a subject of thought, they attained at an early time such importance that man asked himself the reason why he performed these actions. With this moment speculation in regard to religious activities arose, and the whole series of secondary explanations which form so vast a field of ethnological phenomena came into existence.

It is difficult to give a definite proof of the unconscious origin of ethnic phenomena, because so many of them are, or have come to be, subjects of thought. The best evidence that can be given for their unconscious origin must be taken from our own experience, and I think it is not difficult to show that certain groups of our activities, whatever the history of their earlier development may have been, develop at present in each individual and in the whole people entirely sub-consciously, and nevertheless are most potent in the formation of our opinions and actions. Simple examples of this kind are actions which we consider as proper and improper, and which may be found in great numbers in what we call good manners. Thus table manners, which on the whole are impressed vigorously upon the child while it is still young, have a very fixed form. Smacking of the lips and bringing the plate up to the mouth would not be tolerated, although no esthetic or other reason could be given for their rigid exclusion; and it is instructive to know that among a tribe like the Omaha it is considered as bad taste, when invited to eat, not to smack one's lips, because this is a sign of appreciation of the meal. I think it will readily be recognized that the simple fact that these habits are customary, while others are not, is sufficient reason for eliminating those acts that are not customary, and that the idea of propriety simply arises from the continuity and automatic repetition of these acts, which brings about the notion that manners contrary to custom are unusual, and therefore not the proper manners. It may be observed in this connection that bad manners are always accompanied by rather intense feelings of displeasure, the psychological reason for which can be found only in the fact that the actions in question are contrary to those which have become habitual. It is fairly evident that in our table manners this strong feeling of propriety is associated with the familiar modes of eating. When a new kind of food is presented, the proper manner of eating which is not known, practically any habit that is not in absolute conflict with the common habits may readily establish itself.

The example of table manners gives also a fairly good instance of secondary explanation. It is not customary to bring the knife to the mouth, and very readily the feeling arises, that the knife is not used in this manner because in eating thus one would easily cut the lips. The lateness of the invention of the fork, and the fact that in many countries dull knives are used and that a similar danger exists of pricking the tongue or the lips with the sharp-pointed steel fork which is commonly used in Europe, show readily that this explanation is only a secondary rationalistic attempt to explain a custom that otherwise would remain unexplained.

If we are to draw a parallel to linguistic phenomena in this case, it would appear that the grouping of a number of unrelated actions in one group, for the reason that they cause a feeling of disgust, is brought about without any reasoning, and still sets off these actions clearly and definitely in a group by themselves.

On account of the importance of this question, it seems desirable to give another example, and one that seems to be more deeply seated than the one given before. A case of this kind is presented in the group of acts which we characterize as modest. It requires very little thought to see that, while the feelings of modesty are fundamental, the particular acts which are considered modest or immodest show immense variation, and are determined entirely by habits that develop unconsciously so far as their relation to modesty is concerned, and which may have their ultimate origin in causes of an entirely different character. A study of the history of costume proves at once that at different times and in different parts of the world it has been considered immodest to bare certain parts of the body. What parts of the body these are, is to a great extent a matter of accident. Even at the present time, and within a rather narrow range, great variations in this respect may be found. Examples are the use of the veil in Turkey, the more or less rigid use of the glove in our own society, and the difference between street costume and evening dress. A lady in full evening dress in a streetcar, during the daytime, would hardly appear in place.

We all are at once conscious of the intensity of these feelings of modesty, and of the extreme repugnance of the individual to any act that goes counter to the customary concepts of modesty. In a number of cases the origin of a costume can readily be traced, and in its development no considerations of modesty exert any influence. It is therefore evident that in this respect the grouping-together of certain customs again develops entirely unconsciously, but that, nevertheless, they stand out as a group set apart from others with great clearness as soon as our attention is directed toward the feelings of modesty.

To draw a parallel again between this ethnological phenomenon and linguistic phenomena, it would seem that the common feature of both is the grouping-together of a considerable number of activities under the form of a single idea, without the necessity of this idea itself entering into consciousness. The difference, again, would lie in the fact that the idea of modesty is easily isolated from other concepts, and that then secondary explanations are given of what is considered modest and what not. I believe that the unconscious formation of these categories is one of the fundamental traits of ethnic life, and that it even manifests itself in many of its more complex aspects; that many of our religious views and activities, of our ethical concepts, and even our scientific view, which are apparently based entirely on conscious reasoning, are affected by this tendency of distinct activities to associate themselves under the influence of strong emotions. It has been recognized before that this is one of the fundamental causes of error and of the diversity of opinion.

It seems necessary to dwell upon the analogy of ethnology and language in this respect, because, if we adopt this point of view, language seems to be one of the most instructive fields of inquiry in an investigation of the formulation of the fundamental ethnic ideas. The great advantage that linguistics offer in this respect is the fact that, on the whole, the categories which are formed always remain unconscious, and that for this reason the processes which lead to their formation can be followed without the misleading and disturbing factors of secondary explanations, which are so common in ethnology, so much so that they generally obscure the real history of the development of ideas entirely.

Cases are rare in which a people have begun to speculate about linguistic categories, and these speculations are almost always so clearly affected by the faulty reasoning that has led to secondary explanations, that they are readily recognized as such, and can not disturb the clear view of the history of linguistic processes. In America we find this tendency, for instance, among the Pawnee, who seem to have been led to several of their religious opinions by linguistic similarities. Incidentally such cases occur also in other languages, as, for instance, in Chinook mythology, where the Culture Hero discovers a man in a canoe who obtains fish by dancing, and tells him that he must not do so, but must catch fish with the net, a tale which is entirely based on the identity of the two words for *dancing,* and *catching with a net.* These are cases which show that Max Muller's theory of the influence of etymology upon religious concepts explains some of the religious phenomena, although, of course, it can be held to account for only a very small portion.

Judging the importance of linguistic studies from this point of view, it seems well worth while to subject the whole range of linguistic concepts to a searching analysis, and to seek in the peculiarities of the grouping of ideas in different languages an important characteristic in the history of the mental development of the various branches of mankind. From this point of view, the occurrence of the most fundamental grammatical concepts in all languages must be considered as proof of the unity of fundamental psychological processes. The characteristic groupings of concepts in American languages will be treated more fully in the discussion of the single linguistic stocks. The ethnological significance of these studies lies in the clear definition of the groupings of ideas which are brought out by the objective study of language.

There is still another theoretical aspect that deserves special attention. When we try to think at all clearly, we think, on the whole, in words; and it is well known that, even in the advancement of science, inaccuracy of vocabulary has often been a stumbling block which has made it difficult to reach accurate conclusions. The same words may be used with different significance, and by assuming the word to have the same significance always, erroneous conclusions may be reached. It may also be that the word expresses only part of an idea, so that owing to its use the full range of the subject-matter discussed may not be recognized. In the same manner the words may be too wide in their significance, including a number of distinct ideas the differences of which in the course of the development of the language were not recognized. Furthermore we find that, among more primitive tribes, similarities of sound are misunderstood, and that ideas expressed by similar words are considered as similar or identical, and that descriptive terms are misunderstood as expressing an identity, or at least close relationship, between the object described and the group of ideas contained in the description.

All these traits of human thought, which are known to influence the history of science and which play a more or less important role in the general history of civilization, occur with equal frequency in the thoughts of primitive man. It will be sufficient to give a few examples of these cases.

One of the most common cases of a group of views due to failure to notice that the same word may signify diverse objects, is that based on the belief of the identity of persons bearing the same name. Generally the interpretation is given that a child receives the name of an ancestor because he is believed to be a re-incarnation of the individuality of the ancestor. It seems, however, much more likely that this is not the real reason for the view connected with this custom, which seems due to the fact that no distinction is made between the name and the personality known under the name. The association established between name and individual is so close that the two seem almost inseparable; and when a name is mentioned, not only the name itself, but also the personality of its bearer, appears before the mind of the speaker.

Inferences based on peculiar forms of classification of ideas, and due to the fact that a whole group of distinct ideas are expressed by a single term, occur commonly in the terms of relationship of various languages; as, for instance, in our term *uncle,* which means the two distinct classes of father's brother and mother's brother. Here, also, it is commonly assumed that the linguistic expression is a secondary reflex of the customs of the people; but the question is quite often open in how far the one phenomenon is the primary one and the other the secondary one, and whether the customs of the people have not rather developed from the unconsciously developed terminology.

Cases in which the similarity of sound of words is reflected in the views of the people are not rare, and examples of these have been given before in referring to Max Muller's theory of the origin of religions.

Finally, a few examples may be given of cases in which the use of descriptive terms for certain concepts, or the metaphorical use of terms, has led to peculiar views or customs. It seems plausible to my mind, for instance, that the terms of relationship by which some of the eastern Indian tribes designate one another were originally nothing but a metaphorical use of these terms, and that the further elaboration of the social relations of the tribes may have been largely determined by transferring the ideas accompanying these terms into practice.

More convincing are examples taken from the use of metaphorical terms in poetry, which, in rituals, are taken literally, and are made the basis of certain rites. I am inclined to believe, for instance, that the frequently occurring image of *the devouring of wealth* has a close relation to the detailed form of the winter ritual among the Indians of the North Pacific coast, and that the poetical simile in which the chief is called the *support of the sky* has to a certain extent been taken literally in the elaboration of mythological ideas.

Thus it appears that from practical, as well as from theoretical, points of view, the study of language must be considered as one of the most important branches of ethnological study, because, on the one hand, a thorough insight into ethnology can not be gained without practical knowledge of language, and, on the other hand, the fundamental concepts illustrated by human languages are not distinct in kind from ethnological phenomena; and because, furthermore, the peculiar characteristics of languages are clearly reflected in the views and customs of the peoples of the world.

# The Unconscious Patterning of Behavior in Society

## Edward Sapir

We may seem to be guilty of a paradox when we speak of the unconscious in reference to social activity. Doubtful as is the usefulness of this concept when we confine ourselves to the behavior of the individual, it may seem to be worse than doubtful when we leave the kinds of behavior that are strictly individual and deal with those more complex kinds of activity which, rightly or wrongly, are supposed to be carried on, not by individuals as such, but by the associations of human beings that constitute society. It may be argued that society has no more of an unconscious than it has hands or legs.

I propose to show, however, that the paradox is a real one only if the term "social behavior" is understood in the very literal sense of behavior referred to groups of human beings which act as such, regardless of the mentalities of the individuals which compose the groups. To such a mystical group alone can a mysterious "social unconsciousness" be ascribed. But as we are very far from believing that such groups really exist, we may be able to persuade ourselves that no more especial kind of unconsciousness need be imputed to social behavior than is needed to understand the behavior of the individual himself. We shall be on much safer ground if we take it for granted that all human behavior involves essentially the same types of mental functioning, as well conscious as unconscious, and that the term "social" is no more exclusive of the concept "unconscious" than is the term "individual," for the very simple reason that the terms "social" and "individual" are contrastive in only a limited sense. We will assume that any kind of psychology that explains the behavior of the individual also explains the behavior of society in so far as the psychological point of view is applicable to and sufficient for the study of social behavior. It is true that for certain purposes it is very useful to look away entirely from the individual and to think of socialized behavior as though it were carried on by certain larger entities which transcend the psycho-physical organism. But this viewpoint implicitly demands the abandonment of the psychological approach to the explanation of human conduct in society.

It will be clear from what we have said that we do not find the essential difference between individual and social behavior to lie in the psychology of the behavior itself. Strictly speaking, each kind of behavior is individual, the difference in terminology being entirely due to a difference in the point of view.

If our attention is focused on the actual, theoretically measurable behavior of a given individual at a given time and place, we call it "individual," no matter what the physiological or psychological nature of that behavior may be. If, on the other hand, we prefer to eliminate certain aspects of such individual behavior from our consideration and to hold on only to those respects in which it corresponds to certain norms of conduct which have been developed by human beings in association with one another and which tend to perpetuate themselves by tradition, we speak of "social behavior." In other words, social behavior is merely the sum or, better, arrangement of such aspects of individual behavior as are referred to culture patterns that have their proper context, not in the spatial and temporal continuities of biological behavior, but in historical sequences that are imputed to actual behavior by a principle of selection.

We have thus defined the difference between individual and social behavior, not in terms of kind or essence, but in terms of organization. To say that the human being behaves individually at one moment and socially at another is as absurd as to declare that matter follows the laws of chemistry at a certain time and succumbs to the supposedly different laws of atomic physics at another, for matter is always obeying certain mechanical laws which are at one and the same time both physical and chemical according to the manner in which we choose to define its organization. In dealing with human beings, we simply find it more convenient for certain purposes to refer a given act to the psychophysical organism itself. In other cases the interest happens to lie in continuities that go beyond the individual organism and its functioning, so that a bit of conduct that is objectively no more and no less individual than the first is interpreted in terms of the non-individual patterns that constitute social behavior or cultural behavior.

It would be a useful exercise to force ourselves to see any given human act from both of these points of view and to try to convince ourselves in this way that it is futile to classify human acts as such as having an inherently individual or social significance. It is true that there are a great many organismal functions that it is difficult to think of in social terms, but I think that even here the social point of view may often be applied with success. Few social students are interested, for instance, in the exact manner in which a given individual breathes. Yet it is not to be doubted that our breathing habits are largely conditioned by factors conventionally classified as social. There are polite and impolite ways of breathing. There are special attitudes which seem to characterize whole societies that undoubtedly condition the breathing habits of the individuals who make up these societies. Ordinarily the characteristic rhythm of breathing of a given individual is looked upon as a matter for strictly individual definition. But if, for one reason or another, the emphasis shifts to the consideration of a certain manner of breathing as due to good form or social tradition or some other principle that is usually given a social context, then the whole subject of breathing at once ceases to be a merely individual concern and takes on the appearance of a social pattern. Thus, the regularized breathing of the Hindu Yogi, the subdued breathing of those who are in the presence of a recently deceased companion laid away in a coffin and surrounded by all the ritual of funeral observances, the style of breathing which one learns from an operatic singer who gives lessons on the proper control of the voice, are, each and every one of them, capable of isolation as socialized modes of conduct that have a definite place in the history of human culture, though they are obviously not a whit less facts of individual behavior than the most casual and normal style of breathing, such as one rarely imagines to have other than purely individual implications. Strange as it may seem at first blush, there is no hard and fast line of division as to class of behavior between a given style of breathing, *provided that it be socially interpreted,* and a religious doctrine or a form of political administration. This is not to say that it may not be infinitely more useful to apply the social mode of analysis of human conduct to certain cases and the individual mode of analysis to others. But we do maintain that such differences of analysis are merely imposed by the nature of the interest of the observer and are not inherent in the phenomena themselves.

All cultural behavior is patterned. This is merely a way of saying that many things that an individual does and thinks and feels may be looked upon not merely from the standpoint of the forms of behavior that are proper to himself as a biological organism but from the standpoint of a generalized mode of conduct that is imputed to society rather than to the individual, though the personal genesis of conduct is of precisely the same nature, whether we choose to call the conduct individual or social. It is impossible to say what an individual is doing unless we have tacitly accepted the essentially arbitrary modes of interpretation that social tradition is constantly suggesting to us from the very moment of our birth. Let anyone who doubts this try the experiment of making a painstaking report of the actions of a group of natives engaged in some form of activity, say religious, to which he has not the cultural key. If he is a skillful writer, he may succeed in giving a picturesque account of what he sees and hears, or thinks he sees and hears, but the chances of his being able to give a relation of what happens in terms that would be intelligible and acceptable to the natives themselves are practically nil. He will be guilty of all manner of distortion. His emphasis will be constantly askew. He will find interesting what the natives take for granted as a casual kind of behavior worthy of no particular comment, and he will utterly fail to observe the crucial turning points in the course of action that give formal significance to the whole in the minds of those who do possess the key to its understanding. This patterning or formal analysis of behavior is to a surprising degree dependent on the mode of apprehension which has been established by the tradition of the group. Forms and significances which seem obvious to an outsider will be denied outright by those who carry out the pattern; outlines and implications that are perfectly clear to these may be absent to the eye of the onlooker. It is the failure to understand the necessity of grasping the native patterning which is responsible for so much unimaginative and misconceiving description of procedures that we have not been brought up with. It becomes actually possible to interpret as base what is inspired by the noblest and even holiest of motives, and to see altruism or beauty where nothing of the kind is either felt or intended.

Ordinarily a cultural pattern is to be defined both in terms of function and of form, the two concepts being inseparably intertwined in practice, however convenient it may be to dissociate them in theory. Many functions of behavior are primary in the sense that an individual organic need, such as the satisfaction of hunger, is being fulfilled, but often the functional side of behavior is either entirely transformed or, at the least, takes on a new increment of significance. In this way new functional interpretations are constantly being developed for forms set by tradition. Often the true functions of behavior are unknown and a merely rationalized function may be imputed to it. Because of the readiness with which forms of human conduct lose or modify their original functions or take on entirely new ones, it becomes necessary to see social behavior from a formal as well as from a functional point of view, and we shall not consider any kind of human behavior as understood if we can merely give, or think we can give, an answer to the question "For what purpose is this being done?" We shall have also to know what is the precise manner and articulation of the doing.

Now it is a commonplace of observation that the reasoning intelligence seeks to attach itself rather to the functions than to the forms of conduct. For every thousand individuals who can tell with some show of reason why they sing or use words in connected speech or handle money, there is barely one who can adequately define the essential outlines of these modes of behavior. No doubt certain forms will be imputed to such behavior if attention is drawn to it, but experience shows that the forms discovered may be very seriously at variance with those actually followed and discoverable on closer study. In other words, the patterns of social behavior are not necessarily discovered by simple observation, though they may be adhered to with tyrannical consistency in the actual conduct of life. If we can show that normal human beings, both in confessedly social behavior and often in supposedly individual behavior, are reacting in accordance with deep-seated cultural patterns, and if, further, we can show that these patterns are not so much known as felt, not so much capable of conscious description as of naive practice, then we have the right to speak of the "unconscious patterning of behavior in society." The unconscious nature of this patterning consists not in some mysterious function of a racial or social mind reflected in the minds of the individual members of society, but merely in a typical unawareness on the part of the individual of outlines and demarcations and significances of conduct which he is all the time implicitly following. Jung's "racial unconscious" is neither an intelligible nor a necessary concept. It introduces more difficulties than it solves, while we have all we need for the psychological understanding of social behavior in the facts of individual psychology.

Why are the forms of social behavior not adequately known by the normal individual? How is it that we can speak, if only metaphorically, of a social unconscious? I believe that the answer to this question rests in the fact that the relations between the elements of experience which serve to give them their form and significance are more powerfully "felt" or "intuited" than consciously perceived. It is a matter of common knowledge that it is relatively easy to fix the attention on some arbitrarily selected element of experience, such as a sensation or an emotion, but that it is far from easy to become conscious of the exact place which such an element holds in the total constellations of behavior. It is easy for an Australian native, for instance, to say by what kinship term he calls so and so or whether or not he may undertake such and such relations with a given individual. It is exceedingly difficult for him to give a general rule of which these specific examples of behavior are but illustrations, though all the while he acts as though the rule were perfectly well known to him. *In a sense it is well known to him.* But this knowledge is not capable of conscious manipulation in terms of word symbols. It is, rather, a very delicately nuanced feeling of subtle relations, both experienced and possible. To this kind of knowledge may be applied the term "intuition," which, when so defined, need have no mystic connotations whatever. It is strange how frequently one has the illusion of free knowledge, in the light of which one may manipulate conduct at will, only to discover in the test that one is being impelled by strict loyalty to forms of behavior that one can feel with the utmost nicety but can state only in the vaguest and most approximate fashion. It would seem that we act all the more securely for our unawareness of the patterns that control us. It may well be that, owing to the limitations of the conscious life, any attempt to subject even the higher forms of social behavior to purely conscious control must result in disaster. Perhaps there is a far-reaching moral in the fact that even a child may speak the most difficult language with idiomatic ease but that it takes an unusually analytical type of mind to define the mere elements of that incredibly subtle linguistic mechanism which is but a plaything of the child's unconscious. Is it not possible that the contemporary mind, in its restless attempt to drag all the forms of behavior into consciousness and to apply the results of its fragmentary or experimental analysis to the guidance of conduct, is really throwing away a greater wealth for the sake of a lesser and more dazzling one? It is almost as though a misguided enthusiast exchanged his thousands of dollars of accumulated credit at the bank for a few glittering coins of manifest, though little, worth.

We shall now give a number of examples of patterns of social behavior and show that they are very incompletely, if at all, known by the normal, naive individual. We shall see that the penumbra of unconscious patterning of social behavior is an extraordinarily complex realm, in which one and the same type of overt behavior may have altogether distinct significances in accordance with its relation to other types of behavior. Owing to the compelling, but mainly unconscious, nature of the forms of social behavior, it becomes almost impossible for the normal individual to observe or to conceive of functionally similar types of behavior in other societies than his own, or in other cultural contexts than those he has experienced, without projecting into them the forms that he is familiar with. In other words, one is always unconsciously finding what one is in unconscious subjection to.

Our first example will be taken from the field of language. Language has the somewhat exceptional property that its forms are, for the most part, indirect rather than direct in their functional significance. The sounds, words, grammatical forms, syntactic constructions, and other linguistic forms that we assimilate in childhood have only value in so far as society has tacitly agreed to see them as symbols of reference. For this reason language is an unusually favorable domain for the study of the general tendency of cultural behavior to work out all sorts of formal elaborations that have only a secondary, and, as it were, "after the event" relevance to functional needs. Purely functional explanations of language, if valid, would lead us to expect either a far greater uniformity in linguistic expression than we actually find, or should lead us to discover strict relations of a functional nature between a particular form of language and the culture of the people using it. Neither of these expectations is fulfilled by the facts. Whatever may be true of other types of cultural behavior, we can safely say that the forms of speech developed in the different parts of the world are at once free and necessary, in the sense in which all artistic productions are free and necessary. Linguistic forms as we find them bear only the loosest relation to the cultural needs of a given society, but they have the very tightest consistency as aesthetic products.

A very simple example of the justice of these remarks is afforded by the English plural. To most of us who speak English the tangible expression of the plural idea in the noun seems to be a self-evident necessity. Careful observation of English usage, however, leads to the conviction that this self-evident necessity of expression is more of an illusion than a reality. If the plural were to be understood functionally alone, we should find it difficult to explain why we use plural forms with numerals and other words that in themselves imply plurality. "Five man" or "several house" would be just as adequate as "five men" or "several houses." Clearly, what has happened is that English, like all of the other Indo-European languages, has developed a feeling for the classification of all expressions which have a nominal form into singulars and plurals. So much is this the case that in the early period of the history of our linguistic family even the adjective, which is nominal in form, is unusable except in conjunction with the category of number. In many of the languages of the group this habit still persists. Such notions as "white" or "long" are incapable of expression in French or Russian without formal commitments on the score of whether the quality is predicated of one or several persons or objects. Now it is not denied that the expression of the concept of plurality is useful. Indeed, language that is forever incapable of making the difference between the one and the many is obviously to that extent hampered in its technique of expression. But we must emphatically deny that this particular kind of expression need ever develop into the complex formal system of number definition that we are familiar with. In many other linguistic groups the concept of number belongs to the group of optionally expressible notions. In Chinese, for instance, the word "man" may be interpreted as the English equivalent of either "man" or "men," according to the particular context in which the word is used. It is to be carefully noted, however, that this formal ambiguity is never a functional one. Terms of inherent plurality, such as "five," "all," or "several," or of inherent singularity, such as "one" or "my" in the phrase "my wife," can always be counted upon to render factually clear what is formally left to the imagination. If the ambiguity persists, it is a useful one or one that does not matter. How little the expression of our concept of number is left to the practical exigencies of a particular case, how much it is a matter of consistency of aesthetic treatment, will be obvious from such examples as the editorial "we are in favor of prohibition," when what is really meant is "I, John Smith, am in favor of prohibition."

A complete survey of the methods of handling the category of number in the languages of the world would reveal an astonishing variety of treatment. In some languages number is a necessary and well developed category. In others it is an accessory or optional one. In still others, it can hardly be considered as a grammatical category at all but is left entirely to the implications of vocabulary and syntax. Now the interesting thing psychologically about this variety of forms is this, that while everyone may learn to see the need of distinguishing the one from the many and has some sort of notion that his language more or less adequately provides for this necessity, only a very competent philologist has any notion of the true formal outlines of the expression of plurality, of whether, for instance, it constitutes a category comparable to that of gender or case, whether or not it is separable from the expression of gender, whether it is a strictly nominal category or a verbal one or both, whether it is used as a lever for syntactic expression, and so on. Here are found determinations of a bewildering variety, concerning which few even among the sophisticated have any clarity, though the lowliest peasant or savage head-hunter may have control of them in his intuitive repertoire.

So great are the possibilities of linguistic patterning that the languages actually known seem to present the whole gamut of possible forms. We have extremely analytic types of speech, such as Chinese, in which the formal unit of discourse, the word, expresses nothing in itself but a single notion of thing or quality or activity or else some relational nuance. At the other extreme are the incredibly complex languages of many American Indian tribes, languages of so-called polysynthetic type, in which the same formal unit, the word, is a sentence microcosm full of delicate formal elaborations of the most specialized type. Let one example do for many. Anyone who is brought up in English, even if he has had the benefit of some familiarity with the classical languages, will take it for granted that in such a sentence as "Shall I have the people move across the river to the east?" there is rather little elbow room for varieties of formal expression. It would not easily occur to us, for instance, that the notion of "to the east" might be conveyed not by an independent word or phrase but by a mere suffix in complex verb.

There is a rather obscure Indian language in northern California, Yana, which not only can express this thought in a single word, but would find it difficult to express it in any other way. The form of expression which is peculiar to Yana may be roughly analyzed as follows. The first element in the verb complex indicates the notion of several people living together or moving as a group from place to place. This element, which we may call the "verb stem," can only occur at the beginning of the verb, never in any other position. The second element in the complete word indicates the notion of crossing a stream or of moving from one side of an area to the other. It is in no sense an independent word, but can only be used as an element attached to a verb stem or to other elements which have themselves been attached to the verb stem. The third element in the word is similarly suffixed and conveys the notion of movement toward the east. It is one of a set of eight elements which convey the respective notions of movement toward the east, south, west, and north, and of movement from the east, south, west, and north. None of these elements is an intelligible word in itself but receives meaning only in so far as it falls into its proper place in the complexly organized verb. The fourth element is a suffix that indicates the relation of causality, that is, of causing one to do or be something, bring it about that one does or is in a certain way, treating one in such and such an indicated manner. At this point the language indulges in a rather pretty piece of formal play. The vowel of the verb stem which we spoke of as occupying the first position in the verb symbolized the intransitive or static mode of apprehension of the act. As soon as the causative notion is introduced, however, the verb stem is compelled to pass to the category of transitivized or active notions, which means that the causative suffix, in spite of the parenthetical inclusion of certain notions of direction of movement, has the retroactive effect of changing the vowel of the stem. Up to this point, therefore, we get a perfectly unified complex of notions which may be rendered "to cause a group to move across a stream in an easterly direction."

But this is not yet a word, at least not a word in the finished sense of the term, for the elements that are still to follow have just as little independent existence as those we have already referred to. Of the more formal elements that are needed to complete the word, the first is a tense suffix referring to the future. This is followed by a pronominal element which refers to the person singular, is different in form from the suffixed pronoun used in other tenses and modalities. Finally, there is an element consisting of a single consonant which indicates that the whole word, which is a complete proposition in itself, is to be understood in an interrogative sense. Here again the language illustrates an interesting kind of specialization of form. Nearly all words of the language differ slightly in form according to whether the speaker is a man speaking to a man or, on the other hand, is a woman or a man speaking to a woman. The interrogative form that we have just discussed can only be used by a man speaking to a man. In the other three cases the suffix in question is not used, but the last vowel of the word, which in this particular case happens to be the final vowel of the pronominal suffix, is lengthened in order to express the interrogative modality.

We are not in the least interested in the details of this analysis, but some of its implications should interest us. In the first place, it is necessary to bear in mind that there is nothing arbitrary or accidental or even curious about the structure of this word. Every element falls into its proper place in accordance with definitely formulable rules which can be discovered by the investigator but of which the speakers themselves have no more conscious knowledge than of the inhabitants of the moon. It is possible to say, for instance, that the verb stem is a particular example of a large number of elements which belong to the same general class, such as "to sit," "to walk," "to run," " to jump," and so on; or that the element which expresses the idea crossing from one side to another is a particular example of a large class of local elements of parallel function, such as "to the next house," "up the hill," "into a hollow," "over the crest," "down hill," "under," "over," "in the middle of," "off," "hither," and so on. We may quite safely assume that no Yana Indian ever had the slightest knowledge of classification such as these or ever possessed even an inkling of the fact that his language neatly symbolized classifications of this sort by means of its phonetic apparatus and by rigid rules of sequence and cohesion of formal elements. Yet all the while we may be perfectly certain that the relations which give the elements of the language their significance were somehow felt and adhered to. A mistake in the vowel of the first syllable, for instance, would undoubtedly feel to a native speaker like a self-contradictory form in English, for instance "five house" instead of "five houses" or "they runs" instead of "they run." Mistakes of this sort are resisted as any aesthetic transgression might be resisted—as being somehow incongruous, out of the picture, or, if one chooses to rationalize the resistance, as inherently illogical.

The unconscious patterning of linguistic conduct is discoverable not only in the significant forms of language but, just as surely, in the several materials out of which language is built, namely the vowels and consonants, the changes of stress and quantity, and the fleeting intonations of speech. It is quite an illusion to believe that the sounds and the sound dynamics of language can be sufficiently defined by more or less detailed statements of how the speech articulations are managed in a neurological or muscular sense. Every language has a phonetic scheme in which a given sound or a given dynamic treatment of a sound has a definite configurated place in reference to all the other sounds recognized by the language. The single sound, in other words, is in no sense identical with an articulation or with the perception of an articulation. It is, rather, a point in a pattern, precisely as a tone in a given musical tradition is a point in a pattern which includes the whole range of aesthetically possible tones. Two given tones may be physically distinguished but aesthetically identical because each is heard or understood as occupying the same formal position in the total set of recognized tones. In a musical tradition which does not recognize chromatic intervals "C sharp" would have to be identified with "C" and would be considered as a mere deviation, pleasant or unpleasant, from "C." In our own musical tradition the difference between "C" and "C sharp" is crucial to an understanding of all our music, and, by unconscious projection, to a certain way of misunderstanding all other music built on different principles. In still other musical traditions there are still finer intervalic differences recognized, none of which quite corresponds to our semitone interval. In these three cases it is obvious that nothing can be said as to the cultural and aesthetic status of a given tone in a song unless we know or feel against what sort of general tonal background it is to be interpreted.

It is precisely so with the sounds of speech. From a purely objective standpoint the difference between the *k* of "kill" and the *k* of "skill" is as easily definable as the, to us, major difference between the *k* of "kill" and the *g* of "gill" (of a fish). In some languages the *g* sound of "gill" would be looked upon, or rather would be intuitively interpreted, as a comparatively unimportant or individual divergence from a sound typically represented by the *k* of "skill," while the *k* of "kill," with its greater strength of articulation and its audible breath release, would constitute an utterly distinct phonetic entity. Obviously the two distinct *k* sounds of such a language and the two ways of pronouncing the *k* in English, while objectively comparable and even identical phenomena, are from the point of view of patterning utterly different. Hundreds of interesting and, at first blush, strangely paradoxical examples of this sort could be given, but the subject is perhaps too technical for treatment in this paper.

It is needless to say that no normal speaker has an adequate knowledge of these submerged sound configurations. He is the unconscious and magnificently loyal adherent of thoroughly socialized phonetic patterns, which are simple and self-evident in daily practice, but subtly involved and historically determined in actual fact. Owing to the necessity of thinking of speech habits not merely in overt terms but as involving the setting up of intuitively mastered relations in suitable contexts, we need not be surprised that an articulatory habit which is perfectly feasible in one set of relations becomes subjectively impossible when the pattern in which it is to be fitted is changed. Thus, an English-speaking person who is utterly unable to pronounce a French nasalized vowel may nevertheless be quite able to execute the necessary articulation in another context, such as the imitation of snoring or of the sound of some wild animal. Again, the Frenchman or German who cannot pronounce the "wh" of our American-English "why" can easily produce the same sound when he gently blows out a candle. It is obviously correct to say that the acts illustrated in these cases can only be understood as they are fitted into definite cultural patterns concerning the form and mechanics of which the normal individual has no adequate knowledge.

We may summarize our interpretation of these, and thousands of other, examples of language behavior by saying that in each case an unconscious control of very complicated configurations or formal sets is individually acquired by processes which it is the business of the psychologist to try to understand but that, in spite of the enormously varied psychological predispositions and types of conditioning which characterize different personalities, these patterns in their completed form differ only infinitesimally from individual to individual, in many cases from generation to generation. And yet these forms lie entirely outside the inherited biological tendencies of the race and can be explained only in strictly social terms. In the simple facts of language we have an excellent example of an important network of patterns of behavior, each of them with exceedingly complex and, to a large extent, only vaguely definable functions, which is preserved and transmitted with a minimum of consciousness. The forms of speech so transmitted seem as necessary as the simplest reflexes of the organism. So powerfully, indeed, are we in the grip of our phonetic habits that it becomes one of the most delicate and difficult tasks of the linguistic student to discover what is the true configuration of sounds in languages alien to his own. This means that the average person unconsciously interprets the phonetic material of other languages in terms imposed upon him by the habits of his own language. Thus, the naive Frenchman confounds the two sounds "s" of "sick" and "th" of "thick" in a single pattern point—not because he is really unable to hear the difference, but because the setting up of such a difference disturbs his feeling for the necessary configuration of linguistic sounds. It is as though an observer from Mars, knowing nothing of the custom we call war, were intuitively led to confound a punishable murder with a thoroughly legal and noble act of killing in the course of battle. The mechanism of projection of patterns is as evident in the one case as in the other.

Not all forms of cultural behavior so well illustrate the mechanics of unconscious patterning as does linguistic behavior, but there are few, if any, types of cultural behavior which do not illustrate it. Functional considerations of all kinds, leading to a greater degree of conscious control, or apparent control, of the patterns of behavior, tend to obscure the unconscious nature of the patterns themselves, but the more carefully we study cultural behavior, the more thoroughly we become convinced that the differences are but differences of degree. A very good example of another field for the development of unconscious cultural patterns is that of gesture. Gestures are hard to classify and it is difficult to make a conscious separation between that in gesture which is of merely individual origin and that which is referable to the habits of the group as a whole. In spite of these difficulties of conscious analysis, we respond to gestures with an extreme alertness and, one might almost say, in accordance with an elaborate and secret code that is written nowhere, known by none, and understood by all. But this code is by no means referable to simple organic responses. On the contrary, it is as finely certain and artificial, as definitely a creation of social tradition, as language or religion or industrial technology. Like everything else in human conduct, gesture roots in the reactive necessities

of the organism, but the laws of gesture, the unwritten code of gestured messages and responses, is the anonymous work of an elaborate social tradition.
Whoever doubts this may soon become convinced when he penetrates into the
significance of gesture patterns of other societies than his own. A Jewish or
Italian shrug of the shoulders is no more the same pattern of behavior·as the
shrug of a typical American than the forms and significant evocations of the
Yiddish or Italian sentence are identical with those of any thinkable English
sentence. The differences are not to be referred to supposedly deep-seated racial
differencs of a biological sort. They lie in the unconsciously apprehended builds
of the respective social patterns which include them and out of which they
have been abstracted for an essentially artificial comparison. A certain im-
mobility of countenance in New York or Chicago may be interpreted as a
masterly example of the art of wearing a poker face, but when worn by a
perfectly average inhabitant of Tokyo, it may be explainable as nothing more
interesting or important than the simplest and most obvious of good manners.
It is the failure to understand the relativity of gesture and posture, the degree
to which these classes of behavior are referable to social patterns which
transcend merely individual psychological significances, which makes it so easy
for us to find individual indices of personality where it is only the alien culture
that speaks.

In the economic life of a people, too, we are constantly forced to recognize
the pervasive influence of patterns which stand in no immediate relation to the
needs of the organism and which are by no means to be taken for granted in
a general philosophy of economic conduct but which must be fitted into the
framework of social forms characteristic of a given society. There is not only
an unconscious patterning of the types of endeavor that are classed as economic, there is even such a thing as a characteristic patterning of economic
motive. Thus, the acquirement of wealth is not to be lightly taken for granted
as one of the basic drives of human beings. One accumulates property, one
defers the immediate enjoyment of wealth, only in so far as society sets the pace
for these activities and inhibitions. Many primitive societies are quite innocent
of an understanding of the accumulation of wealth in our sense of the phrase.
Even where there is a definite feeling that wealth should be accumulated, the
motives which are responsible for the practice and which give definite form to
the methods of acquiring wealth are often signally different from such as we
can readily understand.

The West Coast Indians of British Columbia have often been quoted as a
primitive society that has developed a philosophy of wealth which is somewhat
comparable to our own, with its emphasis on "conspicuous waste" and on the
sacrosanct character of property. The comparison is not essentially sound. The
West Coast Indian does not handle wealth in a manner which we can recognize
as our own. We can find plenty of analogies, to be sure, but they are more
likely to be misleading than helpful. No West Coast Indian, so far as we know,
ever amassed wealth as an individual pure and simple, with the expectation of
disposing of it in the fullness of time at his own sweet will. This is a dream of

the modern European and American individualist, and it is a dream which not only brings no thrill to the heart of the West Coast Indian but is probably almost meaningless to him. The concepts of wealth and the display of honorific privileges, such as crests and dances and songs and names, which have been inherited from legendary ancestors are inseparable among these Indians. One cannot publicly exhibit such a privilege without expending wealth in connection with it. Nor is there much object in accumulating wealth except to reaffirm privileges already possessed, or, in the spirit of a parvenu, to imply the possession of privileges none too clearly recognized as legitimate by one's fellow tribesmen. In other words, wealth, beyond a certain point, is with these people much more a token of status than it is a tool for the fulfillment of personal desires. We may go so far as to say that among the West Coast Indians it is not the individual at all who possesses wealth. It is primarily the ceremonial patrimony of which he is the temporary custodian that demands the symbolism of wealth. Arrived at a certain age, the West Coast Indian turns his privileges over to those who are by kind or marriage connection entitled to manipulate them. Henceforth he may be as poor as a church mouse, without loss of prestige. I should not like to go so far as to say that the concepts of wealth among ourselves and among the West Coast Indians are utterly different things. Obviously they are nothing of the kind, but they are measurably distinct and the nature of the difference must be sought in the total patterning of life in the two communities from which the particular pattern of wealth and its acquirement has been extracted. It should be fairly clear that where the patterns of manipulation of wealth are as different as they are in these two cases, it would be a mere exercise of the academic imagination to interpret the economic activities of one society in terms of the general economy which has been abstracted from the mode of life of the other.

No matter where we turn in the field of social behavior, men and women do what they do, and cannot help but do, not merely because they are built thus and so, or possess such and such differences of personality, or must needs adapt to their immediate environment in such and such a way in order to survive at all, but very largely because they have found it easiest and aesthetically most satisfactory to pattern their conduct in accordance with more or less clearly organized forms of behavior which no one is individually responsible for, which are not clearly grasped in their true nature, and which one might almost say are as self-evidently imputed to the nature of things as the three dimensions are imputed to space. It is sometimes necessary to become conscious of the forms of social behavior in order to bring about a more serviceable adaptation to changed conditions, but I believe it can be laid down as a principle of far-reaching application that in the normal business of life it is useless and even mischievous for the individual to carry the conscious analysis of his cultural patterns around with him. That should be left to the student whose business it is to understand these patterns. A healthy unconsciousness of the forms of socialized behavior to which we are subject is as necessary to society as is the mind's ignorance, or better unawareness, of the workings of the viscera to the health of the body. In great works of the imagination, form is significant only in so far as we feel ourselves to be in its grip. It is unimpressive when divulged in the explicit terms of this or that simple or complex arrangement of known elements. So, too, in social behavior, it is not the overt forms that rise readily to the surface of attention that are most worth our while. We must learn to take joy in the larger freedom of loyalty to thousands of subtle patterns of behavior that we can never hope to understand in explicit terms. Complete analysis and the conscious control that comes with a complete analysis are at best but the medicine of society, not its food. We must never allow ourselves to substitute the starveling calories of knowledge for the meat and bread of historical experience. This historic experience may be theoretically knowable, but it dare never be fully known in the conduct of daily life.

# Language
## Edward Sapir

The gift of speech and a well ordered language are characteristic of every known group of human beings. No tribe has ever been found which is without language, and all statements to the contrary may be dismissed as mere folklore. There seems to be no warrant whatever for the statement which is sometimes made that there are certain people whose vocabulary is so limited that they cannot get on without the supplementary use of gesture so that intelligible communication between members of such a group becomes impossible in the dark. The truth of the matter is that language is an essentially perfect means of expression and communication among every known people. Of all aspects of culture, it is a fair guess that language was the first to receive a highly developed form and that its essential perfection is a prerequisite to the development of culture as a whole.

There are such general characteristics which apply to all languages, living or extinct, written or unwritten. In the first place, language is primarily a system of phonetic symbols for the expression of communicable thought and feeling. In other words, the symbols of language are differentiated products of the vocal behavior which is associated with the larynx of the higher mammals. As a mere matter of theory, it is conceivable that something like a linguistic structure could have been evolved out of gesture or other forms of bodily behavior. The fact that at an advanced stage in the history of the human race writing emerged in close imitation of the pattern of spoken language proved that language as a purely instrumental and logical device is not dependent on the use of articulate sound. Nevertheless, the actual history of man and a wealth of anthropological evidence indicate with overwhelming certainty that phonetic language takes precedence over all other kinds of communicative symbolism, all of which are, by comparison, either substitutive, like writing, or excessively supplementary, like the gesture accompanying speech. The speech apparatus which is used in the articulation of language is the same for all known peoples. It consists of the larynx, with its delicately adjustable glottal chords, the nose, the tongue, the hard and soft palate, the teeth, and the lips. While the orginial impulses leading to speech may be thought of as localized in the larynx, the finer phonetic articulations are chiefly due to the muscular activity of the tongue, an organ whose primary function has, of course, nothing whatever to do with sound production but which, in actual speech behavior, is indispensable for the development of emotionally expressive sound into what we call language. It is so indispensable, in fact, that one of the most common terms for "language" or "speech" is "tongue." Language is thus not a simple biological function even as regards the simple matter of sound production, for primary laryngeal patterns of behavior have had to be completely overhauled by the interference of lingual, labial, and nasal modifications before a "speech organ" was ready for work. Perhaps it is because this "speech organ" is a diffused and secondary network of physiological activities which do not correspond to the primary functions of the organs involved that language has been enabled to free itself from direct bodily expressiveness.

Not only are all languages phonetic in character; they are also "phonemic." Between the articulation of the voice into the phonetic sequence, which is immediately audible as a mere sensation, and the complicated patterning of phonetic sequences into such symbolically significant entities as words, phrases, and sentences there is a very interesting process of phonetic selection and generalization which is easily overlooked but which is crucial for the development of the specifically symbolic aspect of language. Language is not merely articulated sound; its significant structure is dependent upon the unconscious selection of a fixed number of "phonetic stations" or sound units. These are in actual behavior individually modifiable; but the essential point is that through the unconscious selection of sounds as phonemes, definite psychological barriers are erected between various phonetic stations, so that speech ceases to be an expressive flow of sound and becomes a symbolic composition with limited materials or units. The analogy with musical theory seems quite fair. Even the most resplendant and dynamic symphony is built up of tangibly distinct musical entities or notes which, in the physical world, flow into each other in an indefinite continuum but which, in the world of aesthetic composition and appreciation are definitely bounded off against each other so that they may enter into an intricate mathematics of significant relationships. The phonemes of a language are, in principle, distinct systems peculiar to the given language, and its words must be made up, in unconscious theory if not always in actualized behavior, of these phonemes. Languages differ very widely in their phonemic structure. But whatever the details of these structures may be, the important fact remains that there is no known language which has not a perfectly definite phonemic system. The difference between a sound and a phoneme can be illustrated by a simple example in English. If the word "matter" is pronounced in a slovenly fashion as in the phrase "What's the matter?" the t sound, not being pronounced with the proper amount of energy required to bring out its physical characteristics, tends to slip into a d. Nevertheless this phonetic d will not be felt as a functional d but as a variety of t of a particular type of expressiveness. Obviously the functional relation between the proper t sound of such a word as "matter" and its d variant is quite other than the relation of the t of such a word as "town" and the d of "down." In every known language it is possible to distinguish merely phonetic variations, whether expressive or not, from symbolically functional ones of a phonemic order.

In all known languages, phonemes are built up into distinct and arbitrary sequences which are at once recognized by speakers as meaningful symbols of reference. In English, for instance, the sequence g plus o in the word "go" is an unanalyzable unit and the meaning attaching to the symbol cannot be derived by relating to each other values which might be imputed to the g and to the o independently. In other words, while the mechanical functional units of language are phonemes, the true units of language as symbolism are conventional groupings of such phonemes. The size of these units and the laws of their mechanical structure vary widely in their different languages and their limiting conditions may be said to constitute the phonemic mechanics, or "phonology," of a particular language. But the fundamental theory of sound symbolism remains the same everywhere. The formal behavior of the irreducible symbol also varies within wide limits in the languages of the world. Such a unit may be either a complete word, as in the English example already given, or a significant element like the suffix ness of "goodness." Between the meaningful and unanalyzable word or word element and the integrated meaning of continuous discourse lies the whole complicated field of the formal procedures which are intuitively employed by the speakers of a language in order to build up aesthetically and functionally satisfying symbol sequences out of the theoretically isolable units. These procedures constitute grammar, which may be defined as the sum total of formal economies intuitively recognized by the speakers of a language. There seem to be no types of cultural patterns which vary more surprisingly and with a greater exuberance of detail than the morphologies of the known languages. In spite of endless differences of detail, however, it may justly be said that all grammars have the same degree of fixity. One language may be more complex or difficult grammatically than another, but there is no meaning whatever in the statement which is sometimes made that one language is more grammatical, or form bound, than another. Our rationalizations of the structure of our own language lead to a self-consciousness of speech and of academic discipline which are of course interesting psychological and social phenomena in themselves but have very little to do with the question of form in language.

Besides these general formal characteristics language has certain psychological qualities which make it peculiarly important for the student of social science. In the first place, language is felt to be a perfect symbolic system, in a perfectly homogeneous medium, for the handling of all references and meanings that a given culture is capable of, whether these be in the form of actual communications or in that of such ideal substitutes of communication as thinking. The content of every culture is expressible in its language and there are no linguistic materials whether as to content or form which are not felt to symbolize actual meanings, whatever may be the attitude of those who belong to other cultures. New cultural experiences frequently make it necessary to enlarge the resources of a language, but such enlargement is never an arbitrary addition to the materials and forms already present; it is merely a further application of principles already in use and in many cases little more than a metaphorical extension of old terms and meanings. It is highly important to realize that once the form of a language is established it can discover meanings for its speakers which are not simply traceable to the given quality of experience itself but must be explained to a large extent as the projection of potential meanings into the raw material of experience. If a man who has never seen more than a single elephant in the course of his life, nevertheless speaks without the slightest hesitation of ten elephants or a million elephants or a herd of elephants or of elephants walking two by two or three by three or of generations of elephants, it is obvious that language has the power to analyze experience into theoretically dissociable elements and to create that world of the potential intergrading with the actual which enables human beings to transcend the immediately given in their individual experiences and to join in a larger common understanding. This common understanding constitutes culture, which cannot be adequately defined by a description of those more colorful patterns of behavior in society which lie open to observation. Language is heuristic, not merely in the simple sense which this example suggests, but in the much more far-reaching sense that its forms predetermine for us certain modes of observation and interpretation. This means of course that as our scientific experience grows we must learn to fight the implications of language. "The grass waves in the wind" is shown by its linguistic form to be a member of the same relational class of experiences as "The man works in the house." As an interim solution of the problem of expressing the experience referred to in this sentence it is clear that the language has proved useful, for it has made significant use of certain symbols of conceptual relation, such as agency and location. If we feel the sentence to be poetic or metaphorical, it is largely because other more complex types of experience with their appropriate symbolisms of reference enable us to reinterpret the situation and to say, for instance, "The grass is waved by the wind" or "The wind causes the grass to wave." The point is that no matter how sophisticated our modes of interpretation become, we never really get beyond the projection and continuous transfer of relations suggested by the forms of our speech. After all, to say "Friction causes such and such a result" is not very different from saying "The grass waves in the wind." Language is at one and the same time helping and retarding us in our exploration of experience, and the details of these processes of help and hindrance are deposited in the subtler meanings of different cultures.

A further psychological characteristic of language is the fact that while it may be looked upon as a symbolic system which reports or refers to or otherwise substitutes for direct experience, it does not as a matter of actual behavior stand apart from or run parallel to direct experience but completely interpenetrates with it. This is indicated by the widespread feeling, particularly among primitive people, of that virtual identity or close correspondence of word and thing which leads to the magic of spells. On our own level it is generally difficult to make a complete divorce between objective reality and our linguistic symbols of reference to it; and things, qualities, and events are on the whole felt to be what they are called. For the normal person every experience, real or potential, is saturated with verbalism. This explains why so many lovers of nature, for instance, do not feel that they are truly in touch with it until they have mastered the names of a great many flowers and trees, as though the primary world of reality were a verbal one and as though one could not get close to nature unless one first mastered the terminology which somehow magically expresses it. It is this constant interplay between language and experience which removes language from the cold status of such purely and simply symbolic systems as mathematical symbolism or flag signaling. This interpenetration is not only an intimate associative fact; it is also a contextual one. It is important to realize that language may not only refer to experience or even mold, interpret, and discover experience, but that it also substitutes for it in the sense that in those sequences of interpersonal behavior which form the greater part of our daily lives speech and action supplement each other and do · each other's work in a web of unbroken pattern. If one says to me "Lend me a dollar," I may hand over the money without a word or I may give it with an accompanying "Here it is" or I may say "I haven't got it" or "I'll give it to you tomorrow." Each of these responses is structurally equivalent, if one thinks of the larger behavior pattern. It is clear that if language is in its analyzed form a symbolic system of reference, it is far from being merely that if we consider the psychological part that it plays in continuous behavior. The reason for this almost unique position of intimacy which language holds among all known symbolisms is probably the fact that it is learned in the earliest years of childhood.

It is because it is learned early and piecemeal, in constant association with the color and the requirements of actual contexts, that language, in spite of its quasi-mathematical form, is rarely a purely referential organization. It tends to be so only in scientific discourse, and even there it may be seriously doubted whether the ideal of pure reference is ever attained by language. Ordinary speech is directly expressive and the purely formal pattern of sounds, words, grammatical forms, phrases and sentences are always to be thought of as compounded by intended or unintended symbolisms of expression, if they are to be understood fully from the standpoint of behavior. The choice of words in a particular context may convey the opposite of what they mean on the surface. The same external message is differently interpreted according to whether the speaker has this or that psychological status in his personal relations, or whether such primary expressions as those of affection or anger or fear may inform the spoken words with a significance which completely transcends their normal value. On the whole, however, there is no danger that the expressive character of language will be overlooked. It is too obvious a fact to call for much emphasis. What is understood is that the quasi-mathematical patterns, as we have called them, of the grammarian's language, unreal as these are in a contextual sense, have, nevertheless, a tremendous intuitive vitality; and that these patterns, never divorced in experience from the expressive ones, are nevertheless easily separated from them by the normal individual. The fact that almost any word or phrase can be made to take on an infinite variety of meanings seems to indicate that in all language behavior there are intertwined, in enormously complex patterns, isolable patterns of two distinct orders. These may be roughly defined as patterns of reference and patterns of expression.

That language is a perfect symbolism of experience, that in the actual context of behavior it cannot be divorced from action and that it is the carrier of an infinitely nuanced expressiveness are universally valid psychological facts. There is a fourth general psychological peculiarity which applies more particularly to the languages of sophisticated peoples. This is the fact that the referential form systems which are actualized in language behavior do not need speech in its literal sense in order to preserve their substantial integrity. The history of writing is in essence the long attempt to develop an independent symbolism on the basis of graphic representation, followed by the slow and begrudging realization that spoken language is a more powerful symbolism than any graphic one can possibly be and that true progress in the art of writing lay in the virtual abandonment of the principle with which it originally started. Effective systems of writing, whether alphabetic or not, are more or less exact transfers of speech. The original language system may maintain itself in other and remoter transfers, one of the best examples of these being the Morse telegraph code. It is a very interesting fact that the principle of linguistic transfer is not entirely absent even among the unlettered peoples of the world. Some at least of the drum signal and horn signal systems of the West African natives are in principle transfers of the organizations of speech, often in minute phonetic detail.

Many attempts have been made to unravel the origin of language, but most of these are hardly more than exercises of the speculative imagination. Linguists as a whole have lost interest in the problem, and this for two reasons. In the first place, it has come to be realized that we have no truly primitive languages in a psychological sense, that modern researches in archaeology have indefinitely extended the time of man's cultural past and that it is therefore vain to go much beyond the perspective opened up by the study of actual languages. In the second place, our knowledge of psychology, particularly of the symbolic processes in general, is not felt to be sound enough or far-reaching enough to help materially with the problem of the emergence of speech. It is probable that the origin of language is not a problem that can be solved out of the resources of linguistics alone but that it is essentially a particular case of a much wider problem of the genesis of symbolic behavior and of the specialization of such behavior in the laryngeal region, which may be presumed to have had only expressive functions to begin with. Perhaps a close study of the behavior of very young children under controlled conditions may provide some valuable hints, but it seems dangerous to reason from such experiments to the behavior of pre-cultural man. It is more likely that the kinds of studies which are now in progress of the behavior of the higher apes will help to give us some idea of the genesis of speech. The most popular earlier theories were the interjectional and onomatopoetic theories. The former derived speech from involuntary cries of an expressive nature, while the latter maintained that the words of actual language are conventionalized forms of imitation of the sounds of nature. Both of these theories suffer from two fatal defects. While it is true that both interjectional and onomatopoetic elements are found in most languages, they are always relatively unimportant and tend to contrast somewhat with the more normal materials of language. The very fact that they are constantly being formed anew seems to indicate that they belong rather to the directly expressive layer of speech which intercrosses with the main level of referential symbolism. The second difficulty is even more serious. The essential problem of the origin of speech is not to attempt to discover the kinds of vocal elements which constitute the historical nucleus of language. It is rather to point out how vocal articulations of any sort could become dissociated from their original expressive value. About all that can be said at present is that while speech as a finished organization is a distinctly human achievement, its roots probably lie in the power of the higher apes to solve specific problems by abstracting general forms or schemata from the details of given situations; that the habit of interpreting certain selected elements in a situation as signs of a desired total one gradually led in early man to a dim feeling for symbolism; and that, in the long run and for reasons which can hardly be guessed at, the elements of experience which were most often interpreted in a symbolic sense came to be the largely useless or supplementary vocal behavior that must have often attended significant action. According to this point of view language is not so much directly developed out of vocal expression as it is an actualization in terms of vocal expression of the tendency to master reality, not by direct and ad hoc handling of this element but by the reduction of experience to familiar form. Vocal expression is only superficially the same as language. The tendency to derive speech from emotional expression has not led to anything tangible in the way of scientific theory and the attempt must now be made to see in language the slowly evolved product of a peculiar technique or tendency which may be called the symbolic one, and to see the relatively meaningless or incomplete part as a sign of the whole. Language, then, is what it is essentially, not because of its admirable expressive power but in spite of it. Speech as behavior is a wonderfully complex blend of two pattern systems, the symbolic and the expressive, neither of which could have developed to its present perfection without the interference of the other.

It is difficult to see adequately the functions of language, because it is so deeply rooted in the whole of human behavior that it may be suspected that there is little in the functional side of our conscious behavior in which language does not play its part. The primary function of language is generally said to be communication. There can be no quarrel with this so long as it is distinctly understood that there may be effective communication without overt speech and that language is highly relevant to situations which are not obviously of a communicative sort. To say that thought, which is hardly possible in any sustained sense without the symbolic organization brought by language, is that form of communication in which the speaker and the person addressed are identified in one person is not far from begging the question. The autistic speech of children seems to show that the purely communicative aspect of language has been exaggerated. It is best to admit that language is primarily a vocal actualization of the tendency to see realities symbolically, that it is precisely this quality which renders it a fit instrument for communication and that it is in the actual give and take of social intercourse that it has been complicated and refined into the form in which it is known today. Besides the very general function which language fulfills in the spheres of thought, communication, and expression which are implicit in its very nature, there may be pointed out a number of special derivatives of these which are of particular interest to students of society.

Language is a great force of socialization, probably the greatest that exists. By this is meant not merely the obvious fact that significant social intercourse is hardly possible without language but that the mere fact of a common speech serves as a peculiarly potent symbol of the social solidarity of those who speak the language. The psychological significance of this goes far beyond the association of particular languages with nationalities, political entities, or smaller local groups. In between the recognized dialect or language as a whole and the individualized speech of a given individual lies a kind of linguistic unit which is not often discussed by the linguist but which is of the greatest importance to social psychology. This is the subform of a language which is current among a group of people who are held together by ties of common interest. Such a group may be a family, the undergraduates of a college, a labor union, the underworld in a large city, the members of a club, a group of four or five friends who hold together through life in spite of differences of professional interest, and untold thousands of other kinds of groups. Each of these tends to develop peculiarities of speech which have the symbolic function of somehow distinguishing the group from the larger group into which its members might be too completely absorbed. The complete absence of linguistic indices of such small groups is obscurely felt as a defect or sign of emotional poverty. Within the confines of a particular family, for instance, the name "Georgy," having once been mispronounced "Doody" in childhood, may take on the latter form forever after; and this unofficial pronunciation of a familiar name as applied to a particular person becomes a very important symbol indeed of the solidarity of a particular family and of the continuance of the sentiment that keeps its members together. A stranger cannot lightly take on the privilege of saying "Doody" if the members of the family feel that he is not entitled to go beyond the degree of familiarity symbolized by the use of "Georgy" or "George." Again, no one is entitled to say "trig" or "math" who has not gone through such familiar and painful experiences as a high school or undergraduate student. The use of such words at once declares the speaker a member of an unorganized but psychologically real group. A self-made mathematician has hardly the right to use the word "math" in referring to his own interests because the student overtones of the word do not properly apply to him. The extraordinary importance of minute linguistic differences for the symbolization of psychologically real as contrasted with politically or sociologically official groups is intuitively felt by most people. "He talks like us" is equivalent to saying "He is one of us."

There is another important sense in which language is a socializer beyond its literal use as a means of communication. This is in the establishment of rapport between the members of a physical group, such as a house party. It is not what is said that matters so much as that something is said. Particularly where cultural understandings of an intimate sort are somewhat lacking among the members of a physical group it is felt to be important that the lack be made good by a constant supply of small talk. This caressing or reassuring quality of speech in general, even where no one has anything of moment to communicate, reminds us how much more language is than a mere technique of communication. Nothing better shows how completely the life of man as an animal made over by culture is dominated by the verbal substitutes for the physical world.

The use of language in cultural accumulation and historical transmission is obvious and important. This applies not only to sophisticated levels but to primitive ones as well. A great deal of the cultural stock in trade of a primitive society is presented in a more or less well defined linguistic form. Proverbs, medicine formulae, standardized prayers, folk tales, standardized speeches, song texts, genealogies are some of the more overt forms which language takes as a culture-preserving instrument. The pragmatic ideal of education, which aims to reduce the influence of standardized lore to a minimum and to get the individual to educate himself through as direct a contact as possible with the realities of his environment, is certainly not realized among the primitives, who are often as word-bound as the humanistic tradition itself. Few cultures perhaps have gone to the length of the classical Chinese culture or of the rabbinical Jewish culture in making the word do duty for the thing or the personal experience as the ultimate unit of reality. Modern civilization as a whole, with its schools, its libraries, and its endless stores of knowledge, opinion, and sentiment stored up in verbalized form, would be unthinkable without language made eternal as document. On the whole, we probably tend to exaggerate the differences between "high" and "low" cultures or saturated and emergent cultures in the matter of traditionally conserved verbal authority. The enormous differences that seem to exist are rather differences in the outward form and content of the cultures themselves than in the psychological relation which obtains between the individual and his culture.

In spite of the fact that language acts as a socializing and uniformizing force, it is at the same time the most potent single known factor for the growth of individuality. The fundamental quality of one's voice, the phonetic patterns of speech, the speed and relative smoothness of articulation, the length and build of the sentences, the character and range of the vocabulary, the scholastic consistency of the words used, the readiness with which words respond to the requirements of the social environment, in particular the suitability of one's language to the language habits of the persons addressed—all these are so many complex indicators of the personality. "Actions speak louder than words" may be an excellent maxim from the pragmatic point of view but betrays little insight into the nature of speech. The language habits of people are by no means irrelevant as unconscious indicators of the more important traits of their personalities, and the folk is psychologically wiser than the adage in paying a great deal of attention, willingly or not, to the psychological significance of a man's language. The normal person is never convinced by the mere content of speech but is very sensitive to many of the implications of language behavior, however feebly (if at all) these may have been consciously analyzed. All in all, it is not too much to say that one of the really important functions of language is to be constantly declaring to society the psychological place held by all of its members.

Besides this more general type of personality expression or fulfillment there is to be kept in mind the important role which language plays as a substitutive means of expression for those individuals who have a greater than normal difficulty in adjusting to the environment in terms of primary action patterns. Even in the most primitive cultures the strategic word is likely to be more powerful than the direct blow. It is unwise to speak too blithely of "mere" words, for to do so may be to imperil the value and perhaps the very existence of civilization and personality.

The languages of the world may be classified either structurally or genetically. An adequate structural analysis is an intricate matter and no classification seems to have been suggested which does justice to the bewildering variety of known forms. It is useful to recognize three distinct criteria of classification: the relative degree of synthesis or elaboration of the words of the language; the degree to which the various parts of a word are welded together; and the extent to which the fundamental relational concepts of the language are directly expressed as such. As regards synthesis, languages range all the way from the isolating type, in which the single word is essentially unanalyzable, to the type represented by many American Indian languages in which the single word is functionally often the equivalent of a sentence with many concrete references that would, in most languages, require the use of a number of words. Four stages of synthesis may be conveniently recognized: the isolating type, the weakly synthetic type, the fully synthetic type, and the polysynthetic type. The classical example of the first type is Chinese, which does not allow the words of the language to be modified by internal changes or the addition of prefixed or suffixed elements to express such concepts as those of number, tense, mode, case relation, and the like. This seems to be one of the more uncommon types of language and is best represented by a number of languages in eastern Asia. Besides Chinese itself, Siamese, Burmese, modern Tibetan, Annamite, and Khmer, or Cambodian, may be given as examples. The older view, which regarded such languages as representing a peculiarly primitive stage in the evolution of language, may now be dismissed as antiquated. All evidence points to the contrary hypothesis that such languages are the logically extreme analytic developments of more synthetic languages which because of processes of phonetic disintegration have had to reexpress by analytical means combinations of ideas originally expressed within the framework of the single word. The weakly synthetic type of language is best represented by the most familiar modern languages of Europe, such as English, French, Spanish, Italian, German, Dutch, and Danish. Such languages modify words to some extent but have only a moderate formal elaboration of the word. The plural formations of English and French, for instance, are relatively simple and the tense and modal systems of all the languages of this type tend to use analytic methods as supplementary to the older synthetic one. The third group of languages is represented by such languages as Arabic and the earlier Indo-European languages, like Sanskrit, Latin, and Greek. These are all languages of great formal complexity, in which classificatory ideas, such as sex gender, number, case relations, tense, and mood, are expressed with considerable nicety and in a great variety of ways. Because of the rich formal implications of the single word the sentence tends not to be so highly energized and ordered as in the first mentioned types. Lastly, the polysynthetic languages add to the formal complexity of the treatment of fundamental relational ideas the power to arrange a number of logically distinct, concrete ideas into an ordered whole within the confines of a single word. Eskimo and Algonquin are classical examples of this type.

From the standpoint of the mechanical cohesiveness with which the elements of words are united languages may be conveniently grouped into four types. The first of these, in which there is no such process of combination, is the isolating type already referred to. To the second group of languages belong all those in which the word can be adequately analyzed into a mechanical sum of elements, each of which has its more or less clearly established meaning and each of which is regularly used in all other words into which the associated notion enters. These are the so-called agglutinative languages. The majority of languages seem to use the agglutinative technique, which has the great advantage of combining logical analysis with economy of means. The Altaic language, of which Turkish is a good example, and the Bantu languages of Africa are agglutinative in form.

In the third type, the so-called inflective languages, the degree of union between the radical element or stem of the word and the modifying prefixes or suffixes is greater than in the agglutinative languages, so that it becomes difficult in many cases to isolate the stem and set it off against the accreted elements. More important than this, however, is the fact that there is more or less of a one-to-one correspondence between the linguistic elements and the notion referred to than in the agglutinative languages. In Latin, for instance, the notion of plurality is expressed in a great variety of ways which seem to have little phonetic connection with each other. For example, the final vowel or diphthong of *equi* (horses), *dona* (gifts), *mensae* (tables), and the final vowel and consonant of *hostes* (enemies) are functionally equivalent elements the distribution of which is dependent on purely formal and historical factors which have no logical relevance. Furthermore in the verb the notion of plurality is quite differently expressed, as in the last two consonants of *amant* (they love). It used to be fashionable to contrast in a favorable sense the "chemical" qualities of such inflective languages as Latin and Greek with the soberly mechanical quality of such languages as Turkish. But these evaluations may now be dismissed as antiquated and subjective. They were obviously due to the fact that scholars who wrote in English, French, and German were not above rationalizing the linguistic structure with which they were most familiar into a position of ideal advantage.

As an offshoot of the inflective languages may be considered a fourth group, those in which the processes of welding, due to the operation of complex phonetic laws, have gone so far as to result in the creation of patterns of internal change of the nuclear elements of speech. Such familiar English examples as the words "sing," "sang," "sung," "song" will serve to give some idea of the nature of these structures, which may be termed "symbolistic." The kinds of internal change which may be recognized are changes in vocalic quality, changes in consonants, changes in quantity, various types of reduplication or repetition, changes in stress accent, and, as in Chinese and many African languages, changes in pitch. The classical example of this type of language is Arabic, in which, as in the other Semitic languages, nuclear meanings are expressed by sequences of consonants, which have, however, to be connected by significant vowels whose sequence patterns establish fixed functions independent of the meanings conveyed by the consonantal framework.

Elaboration and technique of word analysis are perhaps of less logical and psychological significance than the selection and treatment of fundamental relational concepts for grammatical treatment. It would be very difficult, however, to devise a satisfactory conceptual classification of languages because of the extraordinary diversity of the concepts and classification of ideas which are illustrated in linguistic form. In the Indo-European and Semitic languages, for instance, noun classification on the basis of gender is a vital principle of structure; but in most of the other languages of the world this principle is absent, although other methods of noun classification are found. Again, tense or case relations may be formally important in one language, for example, Latin, but of relatively little grammatical importance in another, although the logical references implied by such form must naturally somehow be taken care of in the economy of the language as, for instance, by the use of specific words within the framework of the sentence. Perhaps the most fundamental conceptual basis of classification is that of the expression of fundamental syntactic relations as such versus their expression in necessary combination with notions of a concrete order. In Latin, for example, the notion of the subject of a predicate is never purely expressed in a formal sense, because there is no distinctive symbol for this relation. It is impossible to render it without at the same time defining the number and gender of the subject of the sentence. There are languages, however, in which syntactic relations are expressed purely, without admixture of implications of a nonrelational sort. We may speak therefore of pure relational languages as contrasted with mixed relational languages. Most of the languages with which we are familiar belong to the latter category. It goes without saying that such a conceptual classification has no direct relation to the other two types of classification which we have mentioned.

The genetic classification of languages is one which attempts to arrange the languages of the world in groups and subgroups in accordance with the main lines of historical connection, which can be worked out either on the basis of documentary evidence or of a careful comparison of the languages studied. Because of the far-reaching effect of slow phonetic changes and of other causes languages which were originally nothing but dialects of the same form of speech have diverged so widely that it is not apparent that they are but specialized developments of a single prototype. An enormous amount of work has been done in the genetic classification and subclassification of the languages of the world, but very many problems still await research and solution. At the present time it is known definitely that there are certain very large linguistic groups, or families, as they are often called, the members of which may, roughly speaking, be looked upon as lineally descended from languages which can be theoretically reconstructed in their main phonetic and structural outlines. It is obvious, however, that languages may so diverge as to leave little trace of their original relationship. It is therefore very dangerous to assume that languages are not, at last analysis, divergent members of a single genetic group merely because the evidence is negative. The only contrast that is legitimate is between languages known to be historically related and languages not known to be so related. Languages known to be related cannot be legitimately contrasted with languages known not to be related.

Because of the fact that languages have differentiated at different rates and because of the important effects of cultural diffusion, which have brought it about that strategically placed languages, such as Arabic, Latin, and English, have spread over large parts of the earth at the expense of others, very varied conditions are found to prevail in regard to the distribution of linguistic families. In Europe, for instance, there are only two linguistic families of importance represented today, the Indo-European languages and the Ugro-Finnic languages, of which Finnish and Hungarian are examples. The Basque dialects of southern France and northern Spain are the survivors of another and apparently isolated group. On the other hand, in aboriginal America the linguistic differentiation is extreme and a surprisingly large number of essentially unrelated linguistic families must be recognized. Some of the families occupy very small areas, while others, such as the Algonquin and the Athabaskan languages of North America, are spread over a large territory. The technique of establishing linguistic families and of working out the precise relationship of the languages included in these families is too difficult to be gone into here. It suffices to say that random word comparisons are of little importance. Experience shows that very precise phonetic relations can be worked out between the languages of a group and that, on the whole, fundamental morphological features tend to preserve themselves over exceedingly long periods of time. Thus modern Lithuanian is in structure, vocabulary and, to a large extent, even phonemic pattern very much the kind of a language which must be assumed as the prototype for the Indo-European languages as a whole.

In spite of the fact that structural classifications are, in theory, unrelated to genetic ones and in spite of the fact that languages can be shown to have influenced each other, not only in phonetics and vocabulary but also to an appreciable extent in structure, it is not often found that the languages of a genetic group exhibit utterly irreconcilable structures. Thus even English, which is one of the least conservative of Indo-European languages, has many far-reaching points of structure in common with as remote a language as Sanskrit in contrast, say, to Basque or Finnish. Again, different as are Assyrian, modern Arabic, and the Semitic languages of Abyssinia, they exhibit numerous points of resemblance in phonetics, vocabulary, and structure which set them off at once from, say, Turkish or the Negro languages of the Nile headwaters.

The complete rationale of linguistic change, involving as it does many of the most complex processes of psychology and sociology, has not yet been satisfactorily worked out, but there are a number of general processes that emerge with sufficient clarity. For practical purposes, inherent changes may be distinguished from changes due to contact with other linguistic communities. There can be no hard line of division between these two groups of changes because every individual's language is a distinct psychological entity in itself, so that all inherent changes are likely, at last analysis, to be peculiarly remote or subtle forms of change due to contact. The distinction, however, has great practical value, all the more so as there is a tendency among anthropologists and sociologists to operate far too hastily with wholesale linguistic changes due to external ethnic and cultural influences. The enormous amount of study that has been lavished on the history of particular languages and groups of languages shows very clearly that the most powerful differentiating factors are not outside influences, as ordinarily understood, but rather the very slow but powerful unconscious changes in certain directions which seem to be implicit in the phonemic systems and morphologies of the languages themselves. These "drifts" are powerfully conditioned by unconscious formal feelings and are made necessary by the inability of human beings to actualize ideal patterns in a permanently set fashion.

Linguistic changes may be analyzed into phonetic changes, changes in form, and changes in vocabulary. Of these the phonetic changes seem to be the most important and the most removed from direct observation. The factors which lead to these phonetic changes are probably exceedingly complex and no doubt include the operation of obscure symbolisms which define the relation of various age groups to each other. Not all phonetic changes, however, can be explained in terms of social symbolism. It seems that many of them are due to the operation of unconscious economies in actualizing sounds or combinations of sounds. The most impressive thing about internal phonetic change is its high degree of regularity. It is this regularity, whatever its ultimate cause, that is more responsible than any other single factor for the enviable degree of exactness which linguistics has attained as a historical discipline. Changes in grammatical form often follow in the wake of destructive phonetic changes. In many cases it can be seen how irregularities produced by the disintegrating effect of phonetic change are ironed out by the analogical spread of more regular forms. The cumulative effect of these corrective changes is quite sensibly to modify the structure of the language in many details and sometimes even in its fundamental features. Changes in vocabulary are due to a great variety of causes, most of which are of a cultural rather than of a strictly linguistic nature. The too frequent use of a word, for instance, may reduce it to a commonplace term, so that it needs to be replaced by a new word. On the other hand, changes of attitude may make certain words with their traditional overtones of meaning unacceptable to the younger generation, so that they tend to become obsolete. Probably the most important single source of changes in vocabulary is the creation of new words on analogies which have spread from a few specific words.

Of the linguistic changes due to the more obvious types of contact the one which seems to have played the most important part in the history of language is the "borrowing" of words across linguistic frontiers. This borrowing naturally goes hand in hand with cultural diffusion. An analysis of the provenience of the words of a given language is frequently an important index of the direction of cultural influence. Our English vocabulary, for instance, is very richly stratified in a cultural sense. The various layers of early Latin, mediaeval French, humanistic Latin and Greek, and modern French borrowings constitute a fairly accurate gauge of the time, extent, and nature of the various foreign cultural influences which have helped to mold the English civilization. The notable lack of German loan words in English until a very recent period, as contrasted with the large number of Italian words which were adopted at the time of the Renaissance and later, is again a historically significant fact. By the diffusion of culturally important words, such as those referring to art, literature, the church, military affairs, sport, and business, important transnational vocabularies have grown up which do something to combat the isolating effect of the large number of languages which are still spoken in the modern world. Such borrowings have taken place in all directions, but the number of truly important source languages is surprisingly small. Among the more important of them are Chinese, which has saturated the vocabularies of Korean, Japanese, and Annamite; Sanskrit, whose influence on the cultural vocabulary of central Asia, India, and Indo-China, has been enormous; Arabic, Greek, Latin, and French. English, Spanish, and Italian have also been of great importance as agencies of cultural transmission, but their influence seems less far-reaching than that of the languages mentioned above. The cultural influence of a language is not always in direct proportion to its intrinsic literary interest or to the cultural place which its speakers have held in the history of the world. For example, while Hebrew is the carrier of a peculiarly significant culture, actually it has not had as important an influence on other languages of Asia as Aramaic, a sister language of the Semitic stock.

The phonetic influence exerted by a foreign language may be very considerable, and there is a great deal of evidence to show that dialectic peculiarities have often originated as a result of the unconscious transfer of phonetic habits from the language in which one was brought up to that which has been adopted later in life. Apart, however, from such complete changes in speech is the remarkable fact that distinctive phonetic features tend to be distributed over wide areas regardless of the vocabularies and structures of the languages involved. One of the most striking examples of this type of distribution is found among the Indian languages of the Pacific coast of California, Oregon, Washington, British Columbia, and southern Alaska. Here are a large number of absolutely distinct languages belonging to a number of genetically unrelated stocks, so far as we are able to tell, which nevertheless have many important and distinctive phonetic features in common. An analogous fact is the distribution of certain peculiar phonetic features in both the Slavic languages and the Ugro-Finnic languages, which are unrelated to them. Such processes of phonetic diffusion must be due to the influence exerted by bilingual speakers, who act as unconscious agents for the spread of phonetic habits over wide areas. Primitive man is not isolated, and bilingualism is probably as important a factor in the contact of primitive groups as it is on more sophisticated levels.

Opinions differ as to the importance of the purely morphological influence exerted by one language on another in contrast with the more external type of phonetic and lexical influence. Undoubtedly such influences must be taken into account, but so far they have not been shown to operate on any great scale. In spite of the centuries of contact, for instance, between Semitic and Indo-European languages we know of no language which is definitely a blend of the structures of these two stocks. Similarly, while Japanese is flooded with Chinese loan words, there seems to be no structural influence of Chinese on Japanese.

A type of influence which is neither exactly one of vocabulary nor of linguistic form, in the ordinary sense of the word, and to which insufficient attention has so far been called, is that of meaning pattern. It is a remarkable fact of modern European culture, for instance, that while the actual terms used for certain ideas may vary enormously from language to language, the range of significance of these equivalent terms tends to be very similar, so that to a large extent the vocabulary of one language tends to be a psychological and cultural translation of the vocabulary of another. A simple example of this sort would be the translation of such terms as "Your Excellency" to equivalent but etymologically unrelated terms in Russian. Another instance of this kind would be the interesting parallelism in nomenclature between the kinship terms of affinity in English, French, and German. Such terms as "mother-in-law," "belle-mère," and "Schwiegermutter" are not, strictly speaking, equivalent either as to etymology or literal meaning but they are patterned in exactly the same manner. Thus "mother-in-law" and "father-in-law" are parallel in nomenclature to "belle-mère" and "beau-père" and to "Schwiegermutter" and "Schwiegervater."

These terms clearly illustrate the diffusion of a lexical pattern which in turn probably expresses a growing feeling of the sentimental equivalent of blood relatives and relatives by marriage.

The importance of language as a whole for the definition, expression, and transmission of culture is undoubted. The relevance of linguistic details, in both content and form, for the profounder understanding of culture is also clear. It does not follow, however, that there is a simple correspondence between the form of a language and the form of the culture of those who speak it. The tendency to see linguistic categories as directly expressive of overt cultural outlines, which seems to have come into fashion among certain sociologists and anthropologists, should be resisted as in no way warranted by the actual facts. There is no general correlation between cultural type and linguistic structure. So far as can be seen, isolating or agglutinative or inflective types of speech are possible on any level of civilization. Nor does the presence or absence of grammatical gender, for example, seem to have any relevance for our understanding of the social organization or religion or folklore of the associated peoples. If there were any such parallelism as has sometimes been maintained, it would be quite impossible to understand the rapidity with which culture diffuses in spite of profound linguistic differences between the borrowing and giving communities.

The cultural significance of linguistic form, in other words, lies on a much more submerged level than on the overt one of definite cultural pattern. It is only very rarely, as a matter of fact, that it can be pointed out how a cultural trait has had some influence on the fundamental structure of a language. To a certain extent this lack of correspondence may be due to the fact that linguistic changes do not proceed at the same rate as most cultural changes, which are on the whole far more rapid. Short of yielding to another language which takes its place, linguistic organization, largely because it is unconscious, tends to maintain itself indefinitely and does not allow its fundamental formal categories to be seriously influenced by changing cultural needs. If the forms of culture and language were, then, in complete correspondence with each other, the nature of the processes making for linguistic and cultural changes respectively would soon bring about a lack of necessary correspondence. This is exactly what is found as a mere matter of descriptive fact. Logically it is indefensible that the masculine, feminine, and neuter genders of German and Russian should be allowed to continue their sway in the modern world; but any intellectualist attempt to weed out these unnecessary genders would obviously be fruitless, for the normal speaker does not actually feel the clash which the logician requires.

It is another matter when we pass from general form to the detailed content of a language. Vocabulary is a very sensitive index of the culture of a people and changes of the meaning, loss of old words, the creation and borrowing of new ones are all dependent on the history of culture itself. Languages differ widely in the nature of their vocabularies. Distinctions which seem inevitable to us may be utterly ignored in languages which reflect an entirely different type of culture, while these in turn insist on distinctions which are all but unintelligible to us.

Such differences of vocabulary go far beyond the names of cultural objects such as arrow point, coat of armor, or gunboat. They apply just as well to the mental world. It would be difficult in some languages, for instance, to express the distinction which we feel between "to kill" and "to murder," for the simple reason that the underlying legal philosophy which determines our use of these words does not seem natural to all societies. Abstract terms, which are so necessary to our thinking, may be infrequent in a language whose speakers formulate their behavior on more pragmatic lines. On the other hand, the question of presence or absence of abstract nouns may be bound up with the fundamental form of the language; and there exist a large number of primitive languages whose structure allows of the very ready creation and use of abstract nouns of quality or action.

There are many language patterns of a special sort which are of interest to the social scientist. One of these is the tendency to create tabus for certain words or names. A very widespread custom, for instance, among primitive peoples is the tabu which is placed not only on the use of the name of a person recently deceased but of any word that is etymologically connected in the feeling of the speakers with such a name. This means that ideas have often to be expressed by circumlocutions, or that terms must be borrowed from neighboring dialects. Sometimes certain names or words are too holy to be pronounced except under very special conditions, and curious patterns of behavior develop which are designed to prevent one from making use of such interdicted terms. An example of this is the Jewish custom of pronouncing the Hebrew name for God, not as Yahwe or Jehovah but as Adonai, "My Lord." Such customs seem strange to us but equally strange to many primitive communities would be our extraordinary reluctance to pronounce obscene words under normal social conditions.

Another class of special linguistic phenomena is the use of esoteric language devices, such as passwords or technical terminologies for ceremonial attitudes or practices. Among the Eskimo, for instance, the medicine man has a peculiar vocabulary which is not understood by those who are not members of his guild. Special dialectic forms or otherwise peculiar linguistic patterns are common among primitive peoples for the texts of songs. Sometimes, as in Melanesia, such song texts are due to the influence of neighboring dialects. This is strangely analogous to the practice among ourselves of singing songs in Italian, French, or German rather than in English, and it is likely that the historical processes which have led to the parallel custom are of a similar nature. Thieves' jargon and secret languages of children may also be mentioned. These lead over into special sign and gesture languages, many of which are based directly on spoken or written speech; they seem to exist on many levels of culture. The sign language of the Plains Indians of North America arose in response to the need for some medium of communication between tribes speaking mutually unintelligible languages. Within the Christian church we may note the elaboration of gesture languages by orders of monks vowed to silence.

Not only a language or a terminology but the mere external form in which it is written may become important as a symbol of sentimental or social distinction. Thus Croatian and Serbian are essentially the same language but they are presented in very different outward forms, the former being written in Latin characters, the latter in the Cyrillic character of the Greek Orthodox church. This external difference, associated with a difference in religion, has of course the important function of preventing people who speak closely related languages or dialects but who wish for reasons of sentiment not to confound themselves in a larger unity from becoming too keenly aware of how much they actually resemble each other.

The relation of language to nationalism and internationalism presents a number of interesting sociological problems. Anthropology makes a rigid distinction between ethnic units based on race, on culture, and on language. It points out that these do not need to coincide in the least—that they do not, as a matter of fact, often coincide in reality. But with the increased emphasis on nationalism in modern times, the question of the symbolic meaning of race and language has taken on a new significance and, whatever the scientist may say, the layman is ever inclined to see culture, language, and race as but different facets of a single social unity which he tends in turn to identify with such political entities as England or France or Germany. To point out, as the anthropologist easily can, that cultural distributions and nationalities override language and race groups, does not end the matter for the sociologist, because he feels that the concept of nation or nationality must be integrally imaged in behavior by the nonanalytical person as carrying with it the connotation, real or supposed, of both race and language. From this standpoint it really makes little difference whether history and anthropology support the popular identification of nationality, language, and race. The important thing to hold on to is that a particular language tends to become the fitting expression of a self-conscious nationality and that such a group will construct for itself, in spite of all that the physical anthropologist can do, a race to which is to be attributed the mystic power of creating a language and a culture as twin expressions of its psychic peculiarities.

So far as language and race are concerned, it is true that the major races of man have tended in the past to be set off against each other by important differences of language. There is less point to this, however, than might be imagined, because the linguistic differentiations within any given race are just as far-reaching as those which can be pointed out across racial lines, yet they do not at all correspond to subracial units. Even the major races are not always clearly sundered by language. This is notably the case with the Malayo-Polynesian languages, which are spoken by peoples as racially distinct as the Malays, the Polynesians, and the Negroes of Melanesia. Not one of the great languages of modern man follows racial lines. French, for example, is spoken by a highly mixed population which is largely Nordic in the north, Alpine in the center, and Mediterranean in the south, each of these subraces being liberally represented in the rest of Europe.

While language differences have always been important symbols of cultural difference, it is only in comparatively recent times, with the exaggerated development of the ideal of the sovereign nation and with the resulting eagerness to discover linguistic symbols for this ideal of sovereignty, that language differences have taken on an implication of antagonism. In ancient Rome and all through mediaeval Europe there were plenty of cultural differences running side by side with linguistic ones, and the political status of Roman citizen or the fact of adherence to the Roman Catholic church was of vastly greater significance as a symbol of the individual's place in the world than the language or dialect he happened to speak. It is probably altogether incorrect to maintain that language differences are responsible for national antagonisms. It would seem to be much more reasonable to suppose that a political and national unit, once definitely formed, uses a prevailing language as a symbol of its identity, whence gradually emerges the peculiarly modern feeling that every language should properly be the expression of a distinctive nationality.

In earlier times there seems to have been little systematic attempt to impose the language of a conquering people on the subject people, although it happened frequently as a result of the processes implicit in the spread of culture that such a conqueror's language was gradually taken over by the dispossessed population. Witness the spread of the Romance languages and of the modern Arabic dialects. On the other hand, it seems to have happened about as frequently that the conquering group was culturally and linguistically absorbed and that their own language disappeared without necessary danger to their privileged status. Thus foreign dynasties in China have always submitted to the superior culture of the Chinese and have taken on their language. In the same way the Moslem Moguls of India, while true to their religion, made one of the Hindu vernaculars the basis of the great literary language of Moslem India, Hindustani. Definitely repressive attitudes toward the languages and dialects of subject peoples seem to be distinctive only of European political policy in comparatively recent times. The attempt of czarist Russia to stamp out Polish by forbidding its teaching in the schools and the similarly repressive policy of contemporary Italy in its attempt to wipe out German from the territory recently acquired from Austria are illuminating examples of the heightened emphasis on language as a symbol of political allegiance in the modern world.

To match these repressive measures, we have the oft repeated attempt of minority groups to erect their languages into the status of a fully accredited medium of cultural and literary expression. Many of these restored or semi-manufactured languages have come in on the wave of resistance to political or cultural hostility. Such are the Gaelic of Ireland, the Lithuanian of a recently created republic, and the Hebrew of the Zionists. Other such languages have come in more peacefully because of a sentimental interest in local culture. Such are the modern Provençal of southern France, the Plattdeutsch of northern

Germany, Frisian, and the Norwegian *landsmaal*. It is very doubtful whether these persistent attempts to make true culture languages of local dialects that have long ceased to be of primary literary importance can succeed in the long run. The failure of modern Provençal to hold its own and the very dubious success of Gaelic make it seem probable that, following the recent tendency to resurrect minor languages, there will come a renewed leveling of speech more suitably expressing the internationalism which is slowly emerging.

The logical necessity of an international language in modern times is in strange contrast to the indifference and even opposition with which most people consider its possibility. The attempts so far made to solve this problem, of which Esperanto has probably had the greatest measure of practical success, have not affected more than a very small proportion of the people whose international interest and needs might have led to a desire for a simple and uniform means of international expression, at least for certain purposes. It is in the less important countries of Europe, such as Czechoslovakia, that Esperanto has been moderately successful, and for obvious reasons.

The opposition to an international language has little logic or psychology in its favor. The supposed artificiality of such a language as Esperanto or any of the equivalent languages that have been proposed is absurdly exaggerated, for in sober truth there is practically nothing in these languages that is not taken from the common stock of words and forms which have gradually developed in Europe. Such an international language could, of course, have only the status of a secondary form of speech for distinctly limited purposes. Thus considered, the learning of a constructed international language offers no further psychological problem than the learning of any other language which is acquired after childhood through the medium of books and with the conscious application of grammatical rules. The lack of interest in the international language problem in spite of the manifest need for one is an excellent example of how little logic or intellectual necessity has to do with the acquirement of language habits. Even the acquiring of the barest smattering of a foreign language is imaginatively equivalent to some measure of identification with a people or a culture. The purely instrumental value of such knowledge is frequently nil.

Any consciously constructed international language has to deal with the great difficulty of not being felt to represent a distinctive people or culture. Hence the learning of it is of very little symbolic significance for the average person, who remains blind to the fact that such a language, easy and regular as it inevitably must be, would solve many of his educational and practical difficulties at a single blow. The future alone will tell whether the logical advantages and theoretical necessity of an international language can overcome the largely symbolic opposition which it has to meet. In any event it is at least conceivable that one of the great national languages of modern times, such as English or Spanish or Russian, may in due course find itself in the position of a *de facto* international language without any conscious attempt having been made to put it there.

# The Relation of Habitual Thought and Behavior to Language

## Benjamin Lee Whorf

> Human beings do not live in the objective world alone, nor alone in the world of social activity as ordinarily understood, but are very much at the mercy of the particular language which has become the medium of expression for their society. It is quite an illusion to imagine that one adjusts to reality essentially without the use of language and that language is merely an incidental means of solving specific problems of communication or reflection. The fact of the matter is that the "real world" is to a large extent unconsciously built up on the language habits of the group.... We see and hear and otherwise experience very largely as we do because the language habits of our community predispose certain choices of interpretation.
>
> —Edward Sapir

There will probably be general assent to the proposition that an accepted pattern of using words is often prior to certain lines of thinking and forms of behavior, but he who assents often sees in such a statement nothing more than a platitudinous recognition of the hypnotic power of philosophical and learned terminology on the one hand or of catchwords, slogans, and rallying cries on the other. To see only thus far is to miss the point of one of the important interconnections which Sapir saw between language, culture, and psychology, and succinctly expressed in the introductory quotation. It is not so much in these special uses of language as in its constant ways of arranging data and its most ordinary everyday analysis of phenomena that we need to recognize the influence it has on other activities, cultural and personal.

## THE NAME OF THE SITUATION AS AFFECTING BEHAVIOR

I came in touch with an aspect of this problem before I had studied under Dr. Sapir, and in a field usually considered remote from linguistics. It was in the course of my professional work for a fire insurance company, in which I undertook the task of analyzing many hundreds of reports of circumstances surrounding the start of fires, and in some cases, of explosions. My analysis was directed toward purely physical conditions, such as defective wiring, presence or lack

64

of air spaces between metal flues and woodwork, etc., and the results were presented in these terms. Indeed it was undertaken with no thought that any other significances would or could be revealed. But in due course it became evident that not only a physical situation *qua* physics, but the meaning of that situation to people, was sometimes a factor, through the behavior of the people, in the start of the fire. And this factor of meaning was clearest when it was a LINGUISTIC MEANING, residing in the name or the linguistic description commonly applied to the situation. Thus, around a storage of what are called "gasoline drums," behavior will tend to a certain type, that is, great care will be exercised; while around a storage of what are called "empty gasoline drums," it will tend to be different—careless, with little repression of smoking or of tossing cigarette stubs about. Yet the "empty" drums are perhaps the more dangerous, since they contain explosive vapor. Physically the situation is hazardous, but the linguistic analysis according to regular analogy must employ the word "empty," which inevitably suggests lack of hazard. The word "empty" is used in two linguistic patterns: (1) as a virtual synonym for "null and void, negative, inert," (2) applied in analysis of physical situations without regard to, e.g., vapor, liquid vestiges, or stray rubbish, in the container. The situation is named in one pattern (2) and the name is then "acted out" or "lived up to" in another (1), this being a general formula for the linguistic conditioning of behavior into hazardous forms.

In a wood distillation plant the metal stills were insulated with a composition prepared from limestone and called at the plant "spun limestone." No attempt was made to protect this covering from excessive heat or the contact of flame. After a period of use, the fire below one of the stills spread to the "limestone," which to everyone's great surprise burned vigorously. Exposure to acetic acid fumes from the stills had converted part of the limestone (calcium carbonate) to calcium acetate. This when heated in a fire decomposes, forming inflammable acetone. Behavior that tolerated fire close to the covering was induced by use of the name "limestone," which because it ends in "-stone" implies noncombustibility.

A huge iron kettle of boiling varnish was observed to be overheated, nearing the temperature at which it would ignite. The operator moved it off the fire and ran it on its wheels to a distance, but did not cover it. In a minute or so the varnish ignited. Here the linguistic influence is more complex; it is due to the metaphorical objectifying (of which more later) of "cause" as contact or the spatial juxtaposition of "things"—to analyzing the situation as "on" versus "off" the fire. In reality, the stage when the external fire was the main factor had passed; the overheating was now an internal process of convection in the varnish from the intensely heated kettle, and still continued when "off" the fire.

An electric glow heater on the wall was little used, and for one workman had the meaning of a convenient coathanger. At night a watchman entered and snapped a switch, which action he verbalized as "turning on the light." No light appeared, and this result he verbalized as "light is burned out." He could not see the glow of the heater because of the old coat hung on it. Soon the heater ignited the coat, which set fire to the building.

A tannery discharged waste water containing animal matter into an outdoor settling basin partly roofed with wood and partly open. This situation is one that ordinarily would be verbalized as "pool of water." A workman had occasion to light a blowtorch near by, and threw his match into the water. But the decomposing waste matter was evolving gas under the wood cover, so that the setup was the reverse of "watery." An instant flare of flame ignited the woodwork, and the fire quickly spread into the adjoining building.

A drying room for hides was arranged with a blower at one end to make a current of air along the room and thence outdoors through a vent at the other end. Fire started at a hot bearing on the blower, which blew the flames directly into the hides and fanned them along the room, destroying the entire stock. This hazardous setup followed naturally from the term "blower" with its linguistic equivalence to "that which blows," implying that its function necessarily is to "blow." Also its function is verbalized as "blowing air for drying," overlooking that it can blow other things, e.g., flames and sparks. In reality, a blower simply makes a current of air and can exhaust as well as blow. It should have been installed at the vent end to DRAW the air over the hides, then through the hazard (its own casing and bearings), and thence outdoors.

Beside a coal-fired melting pot for lead reclaiming was dumped a pile of "scrap lead"—a misleading verbalization, for it consisted of the lead sheets of old radio condensers, which still had paraffin paper between them. Soon the paraffin blazed up and fired the roof, half of which was burned off.

Such examples, which could be greatly multiplied, will suffice to show how the cue to a certain line of behavior is often given by the analogies of the linguistic formula in which the situation is spoken of, and by which to some degree it is analyzed, classified, and allotted its place in that world which is "to a large extent unconsciously built up on the language habits of the group." And we always assume that the linguistic analysis made by our group reflects reality better than it does.

## GRAMMATICAL PATTERNS AS INTERPRETATIONS OF EXPERIENCE

The linguistic material in the above examples is limited to single words, phrases, and patterns of limited range. One cannot study the behavioral compulsiveness of such material without suspecting a much more far-reaching compulsion from large-scale patterning of grammatical categories, such as plurality, gender and similar classifications (animate, inanimate, etc.), tenses, voices, and other verb forms, classifications of the type of "parts of speech," and the matter of whether a given experience is denoted by a unit morpheme, an inflected word, or a syntactical combination. A category such as number (singular vs. plural) is an attempted interpretation of a whole large order of experience, virtually of the world or of nature; it attempts to say how experience is to be segmented, what experience is to be called "one" and what "several." But the difficulty of appraising such a far-reaching influence is great because of its background character, because of the difficulty of standing aside from our own language, which is habit and a cultural *non est disputandum,* and scrutinizing it objectively. And if we take a very dissimilar language, this language becomes a part of nature, and we even do to it what we have already done to nature. We tend to think in our own language in order to examine the exotic language. Or we find the task of unraveling the purely morphological intricacies so gigantic that it seems to absorb all else. Yet the problem, though difficult, is feasible, and the best approach is through an exotic language, for in its study we are at long last pushed willy-nilly out of our ruts. Then we find that the exotic language is a mirror held up to our own.

In my study of the Hopi language, what I now see as an opportunity to work on this problem was first thrust upon me before I was clearly aware of the problem. The seemingly endless task of describing the morphology did finally end. Yet it was evident, especially in the light of Sapir's lectures on Navaho, that the description of the *language* was far from complete. I knew for example the morphological formation of plurals, but not how to use plurals. It was evident that the category of plural in Hopi was not the same thing as in English, French, or German. Certain things that were plural in these languages were singular in Hopi. The phase of investigation which now began consumed nearly two more years.

The work began to assume the character of a comparison between Hopi and western European languages. It also became evident that even the grammar of Hopi bore a relation to Hopi culture, and the grammar of European tongues to our own "Western" or "European" culture. And it appeared that the interrelation brought in those large subsummations of experience by language, such as our own terms "time," "space," "substance," and "matter." Since, with respect to the traits compared, there is little difference between English, French, German, or other European languages with the *possible* (but doubtful) exception of Balto-Slavic and non-Indo-European, I have lumped these languages into one group called SAE, or "Standard Average European."

That portion of the whole investigation here to be reported may be summed up in two questions: (1) Are our own concepts of "time," "space," and "matter" given in substantially the same form by experience to all men, or are they in part conditioned by the structure of particular languages? (2) Are there traceable affinities between (a) cultural and behavioral norms and (b) large-scale linguistic patterns? (I should be the last to pretend that there is anything so definite as "a correlation" between culture and language, and especially between ethnological rubrics such as "agricultural, hunting," etc., and linguistic ones like "inflected," "synthetic," or "isolating."[1] When I began the study, the problem was by no means so clearly formulated, and I had little notion that the answers would turn out as they did.)


## PLURALITY AND NUMERATION IN SAE AND HOPI

In our language, that is, SAE, plurality and cardinal numbers are applied in two ways: to real plurals and imaginary plurals. Or more exactly if less tersely: perceptible spatial aggregates and metaphorical aggregates. We say "ten men" and also "ten days." Ten men either are or could be objectively perceived as ten, ten in one group perception[2]—ten men on a street corner, for instance. But "ten days" cannot be objectively experienced. We experience only one day, today; the other nine (or even all ten) are something conjured up from memory or imagination. If "ten days" be regarded as a group it must be as an "imaginary," mentally constructed group. Whence comes this mental pattern? Just as in the case of the fire-causing errors, from the fact that our language confuses the two different situations, has but one pattern for both. When we speak of "ten steps forward, ten strokes on a bell," or any similarly described cyclic sequence, "times" of any sort, we are doing the same thing as with "days." *Cyclicity* brings the response of imaginary plurals. But a likeness of cyclicity to aggregates is not unmistakably given by experience prior to language, or it would be found in all languages, and it is not.

Our *awareness* of time and cyclicity does contain something immediate and subjective—the basic sense of "becoming later and later." But, in the habitual thought of us SAE people, this is covered under something quite different, which though mental should not be called subjective. I call it *objectified,* or imaginary, because it is patterned on the *outer* world. It is this that reflects our linguistic usage. Our tongue makes no distinction between numbers counted on discrete entities and numbers that are simply "counting itself." Habitual thought then assumes that in the latter the numbers are just as much counted on "something" as in the former. This is objectification. Concepts of time lose contact with the subjective experience of "becoming later" and are objectified as counted *quantities,* especially as lengths, made up of units as a length can be visibly marked off into inches. A "length of time" is envisioned as a row of similar units, like a row of bottles.

---

1 We have plenty of evidence that this is not the case. Consider only the Hopi and the Ute, with languages that on the overt morphological and lexical level are as similar as, say, English and German. The idea of "correlation" between language and culture, in the generally accepted sense of correlation, is certainly a mistaken one.

2 As we say, "ten at the *same time,*" showing that in our language and thought we restate the fact of group perception in terms of a concept "time," the large linguistic component of which will appear in the course of this paper.

In Hopi there is a different linguistic situation. Plurals and cardinals are used only for entities that form or can form an objective group. There are no imaginary plurals, but instead ordinals used with singulars. Such an expression as "ten days" is not used. The equivalent statement is an operational one that reaches one day by a suitable count. "They stayed ten days" becomes "they stayed until the eleventh day" or "they left after the tenth day." "Ten days is greater than nine days" becomes "the tenth day is later than the ninth." Our "length of time" is not regarded as a length but as a relation between two events in lateness. Instead of our linguistically promoted objectification of that datum of consciousness we call "time," the Hopi language has not laid down any pattern that would cloak the subjective "becoming later" that is the essence of time.

## NOUNS OF PHYSICAL QUANTITY IN SAE AND HOPI

We have two kinds of nouns denoting physical things: individual nouns, and mass nouns, e.g., "water, milk, wood, granite, sand, flour, meat." Individual nouns denote bodies with definite outlines: "a tree, a stick, a man, a hill." Mass nouns denote homogeneous continua without implied boundaries. The distinction is marked by linguistic form; e.g., mass nouns lack plurals,[3] in English drop articles, and in French take the partitive article *du, de la, des*. The distinction is more widespread in language than in the observable appearance of things. Rather few natural occurrences present themselves as unbounded extents; "air" of course, and often "water, rain, snow, sand, rock, dirt, grass." We do not encounter "butter, meat, cloth, iron, glass," or most "materials" in such kind of manifestation, but in bodies small or large with definite outlines. The distinction is somewhat forced upon our description of events by an unavoidable pattern in language. It is so inconvenient in a great many cases that we need some way of individualizing the mass noun by further linguistic devices. This is partly done by names of body-types: "stick of wood, piece of cloth, pane of glass, cake of soap"; also, and even more, by introducing names of containers though their contents be the real issue: "glass of water, cup of coffee, dish of food, bag of flour, bottle of beer." These very common container formulas, in which "of" has an obvious, visually perceptible meaning ("contents"), influence our feeling about the less obvious type-body formulas: "stick of wood, lump of dough," etc. The formulas are very similar; individual noun plus a similar relator (English "of"). In the obvious case this relator denotes contents. In the inobvious one it "suggests" contents. Hence the "lumps, chunks,

---

3 It is no exception to this rule of lacking a plural that a mass noun may sometimes coincide in lexeme with an individual noun that of course has a plural; e.g., "stone" (no pl.) with "a stone" (pl. "stones"). The plural form denoting varieties, e.g., "wines" is of course a different sort of thing from the true plural; it is a curious outgrowth from the SAE mass nouns, leading to still another sort of imaginary aggregates, which will have to be omitted from this paper.

blocks, pieces," etc., seem to contain something, a "stuff," "substance," or "matter" that answers to the "water," "coffee," or "flour" in the container formulas. So with SAE people the philosophic "substance" and "matter" are also the naive idea; they are instantly acceptable, "common sense." It is so through linguistic habit. Our language patterns often require us to name a physical thing by a binomial that splits the reference into a formless item plus a form.

Hopi is again different. It has a formally distinguished class of nouns. But this class contains no formal subclass of mass nouns. All nouns have an individual sense and both singular and plural forms. Nouns translating most nearly our mass nouns still refer to vague bodies or vaguely bounded extents. They imply indefiniteness, but not lack, of outline and size. In specific statements, "water" means one certain mass or quantity of water, not what we call "the substance water." Generality of statement is conveyed through the verb or predicator, not the noun. Since nouns are individual already, they are not individualized by either type-bodies or names of containers, if there is no special need to emphasize shape or container. The noun itself implies a suitable type-body or container. One says, not "a glass of water" but *kə·yi* "a water," not "a pool of water" but *pa·hə*, [4] not "a dish of cornflour" but *ŋəmni* "a (quantity of) cornflour," not "a piece of meat" but *sikʷi* "a meat." The language has neither need for nor analogies on which to build the concept of existence as duality of formless item and form. It deals with formlessness through other symbols than nouns.

## PHASES OF CYCLES IN SAE AND HOPI

Such terms as "summer, winter, September, morning, noon, sunset" are with us nouns, and have little formal linguistic difference from other nouns. They can be subjects or objects, and we say "at sunset" or "in winter" just as we say "at a corner" or "in an orchard." [5] They are pluralized and numerated like nouns of physical objects, as we have seen. Our thought about the referents of such words hence becomes objectified. Without objectification, it would be a subjective experience of real time, i.e., of the consciousness of "becoming later and later"—simply a cyclic phase similar to an earlier phase in that ever-later-becoming duration. Only by imagination can such a cyclic phase be set beside another and another in the manner of a spatial (i.e., visually perceived) configuration. But such is the power of linguistic analogy that we do so objectify cyclic phasing. We do it even by saying "a phase" and "phases" instead of,

---

[4] Hopi has two words for water quantities; *kə·yi* and *pa·hə*. The difference is something like that between "stone" and "rock" in English, *pa·hə* implying greater size and "wildness"; flowing water, whether or not outdoors or in nature, is *pa·hə*; so is "moisture." But, unlike "stone" and "rock," the difference is essential, not pertaining to a connotative margin, and the two can hardly ever be interchanged.

[5] To be sure, there are a few minor differences from other nouns, in English for instance in the use of the articles.

e.g., "phasing." And the pattern of individual and mass nouns, with the result-ing binomial formula of formless item plus form, is so general that it is implicit for all nouns, and hence our very generalized formless items like "substance, matter," by which we can fill out the binomial for an enormously wide range of nouns. But even these are not quite generalized enough to take in our phase nouns. So for the phase nouns we have made a formless item, "time." We have made it by using "a time," i.e., an occasion or a phase, in the pattern of a mass noun, just as from "a summer" we make "summer" in the pattern of a mass noun. Thus with our binomial formula we can say and think "a moment of time, a second of time, a year of time." Let me again point out that the pattern is simply that of "a bottle of milk" or "a piece of cheese." Thus we are assisted to imagine that "a summer" actually contains or consists of such-and-such a quantity of "time."

In Hopi, however, all phase terms, like "summer, morning," etc., are not nouns but a kind of adverb, to use the nearest SAE analogy. They are a formal part of speech by themselves, distinct from nouns, verbs, and even other Hopi "adverbs." Such a word is not a case form or a locative pattern, like "des Abends" or "in the morning." It contains no morpheme like one of "in the house" or "at the tree."[6] It means "when it is morning" or "while morning-phase is occurring." These "temporals" are not used as subjects or objects, or at all like nouns. One does not say "it's a hot summer" or "summer is hot"; summer is not hot, summer is only WHEN conditions are hot, WHEN heat occurs. One does not say "THIS summer," but "summer now" or "summer recently." There is no objectification, as a region, an extent, a quantity, of the subjective duration-feeling. Nothing is suggested about time except the per-petual "getting later" of it. And so there is no basis here for a formless item answering to our "time."


## TEMPORAL FORMS OF VERBS IN SAE AND HOPI

The three-tense system of SAE verbs colors all our thinking about time. This system is amalgamated with that larger scheme of objectification of the subjec-tive experience of duration already noted in other patterns—in the binomial formula applicable to nouns in general, in temporal nouns, in plurality and numeration. This objectification enables us in imagination to "stand time units in a row." Imagination of time as like a row harmonizes with a system of THREE tenses; whereas a system of TWO, an earlier and a later, would seem to correspond better to the feeling of duration as it is experienced. For if we inspect consciousness we find no past, present, future, but a unity embracing complexity. EVERYTHING is in consciousness, and everything in conscious-

---

6 "Year" and certain combinations of "year" with name of season names alone, can occur with a locative morpheme "at" but this is exceptional. It appears like historical detritus of an earlier different patterning, or the effect of English analogy, or both.

ness IS, and is together. There is in it a sensuous and a nonsensuous. We may call the sensuous—what we are seeing, hearing, touching—the "present" while in the nonsensuous the vast image-world of memory is being labeled "the past," and another realm of belief, intuition, and uncertainty "the future"; yet sensation, memory, foresight, all are in consciousness together—one is not "yet to be" nor another "once but no more." Where real time comes in is that all this in consciousness is "getting later," changing certain relations in an irreversible manner. In this "latering" or "durating" there seems to me to be a paramount contrast between the newest, latest instant at the focus of attention and the rest—the earlier. Languages by the score get along well with two tenselike forms answering to this paramount relation of "later" to "earlier." We can of course CONSTRUCT AND CONTEMPLATE IN THOUGHT a system of past, present, future, in the objectified configuration of points on a line. This is what our general objectification tendency leads us to do and our tense system confirms.

In English the present tense seems the one least in harmony with the paramount temporal relation. It is as if pressed into various and not wholly congruous duties. One duty is to stand as objectified middle term between objectified past and objectified future, in narration, discussion, argument, logic, philosophy. Another is to denote inclusion in the sensuous field: "I SEE him." Another is for nomic, i.e., customarily or generally valid, statements: "We SEE with our eyes." These varied uses introduce confusions of thought, of which for the most part we are unaware.

Hopi, as we might expect, is different here too. Verbs have no "tenses" like ours, but have validity-forms ("assertions"), aspects, and clause-linkage forms (modes), that yield even greater precision of speech. The validity-forms denote that the speaker (not the subject) reports the situation (answering to our past and present) or that he expects it (answering to our future)[7] or that he makes a nomic statement (answering to our nomic present). The aspects denote different degrees of duration and different kinds of tendency "during duration." As yet we have noted nothing to indicate whether an event is sooner or later than another when both are REPORTED. But need for this does not arise until we have two verbs: i.e., two clauses. In that case the "modes" denote relations between the clauses, including relations of later to earlier and of simultaneity. Then there are many detached words that express similar relations, supplementing the modes and aspects. The duties of our three-tense system and its tripartite linear objectified "time" are distributed among various verb cate-

---

[7] The expective and reportive assertions contrast according to the "paramount relation." The expective expresses anticipation existing EARLIER than objective fact, and coinciding with objective fact LATER than the status quo of the speaker, this status quo, including all the subsummation of the past therein, being expressed by the reportive. Our notion "future" seems to represent at once the earlier (anticipation) and the later (afterwards, what will be), as Hopi shows. This paradox may hint of how elusive the mystery of real time is, and how artificially it is expressed by a linear relation of past-present-future.

gories, all different from our tenses; and there is no more basis for an objectified time in Hopi verbs than in other Hopi patterns; although this does not in the least hinder the verb forms and other patterns from being closely adjusted to the pertinent realities of actual situations.

## DURATION, INTENSITY, AND TENDENCY IN SAE AND HOPI

To fit discourse to manifold actual situations, all languages need to express durations, intensities, and tendencies. It is characteristic of SAE and perhaps of many other language types to express them metaphorically. The metaphors are those of spatial extension, i.e., of size, number (plurality), position, shape, and motion. We express duration by "long, short, great, much, quick, slow," etc.; intensity by "large, great, much, heavy, light, high, low, sharp, faint," etc; tendency by "more, increase, grow, turn, get, approach, go, come, rise, fall, stop, smooth, even, rapid, slow"; and so on through an almost inexhaustible list of metaphors that we hardly recognize as such, since they are virtually the only linguistic media available. The nonmetaphorical terms in this field, like "early, late, soon, lasting, intense, very, tending," are a mere handful, quite inadequate to the needs.

It is clear how this condition "fits in." It is part of our whole scheme of OBJECTIFYING—imaginatively spatializing qualities and potentials that are quite nonspatial (so far as any spatially perceptive senses can tell us). Noun-meaning (with us) proceeds from physical bodies to referents of far other sort. Since physical bodies and their outlines in PERCEIVED SPACE are denoted by size and shape terms and reckoned by cardinal numbers and plurals, these patterns of denotation and reckoning extend to the symbols of nonspatial meanings, and so suggest an IMAGINARY SPACE. Physical shapes "move, stop, rise, sink, approach," etc., in perceived space; why not these other referents in their imaginary space? This has gone so far that we can hardly refer to the simplest nonspatial situation without constant resort to physical metaphors. I "grasp" the "thread" of another's arguments, but if its "level" is "over my head" my attention may "wander" and "lose touch" with the "drift" of it, so that when he "comes" to his "point" we differ "widely," our "views" being indeed so "far apart" that the "things" he says "appear" "much" too arbitrary, or even "a lot" of nonsense!

The absence of such metaphor from Hopi speech is striking. Use of space terms when there is no space involved is NOT THERE—as if on it had been laid the taboo teetotal! The reason is clear when we know that Hopi has abundant conjugational and lexical means of expressing duration, intensity, and tendency directly as such, and that major grammatical patterns do not, as with us, provide analogies for an imaginary space. The many verb "aspects" express duration and tendency of manifestations, while some of the "voices" express intensity, tendency, and duration of causes or forces producing manifestations. Then a special part of speech, the "tensors," a huge class of words, denotes only intensity, tendency, duration, and sequence. The function of the tensors is to express intensities, "strengths," and how they continue or vary, their rate of change; so that the broad concept of intensity, when considered as necessarily always varying and/or continuing, includes also tendency and duration. Tensors convey distinctions of degree, rate, constancy, repetition, increase and decrease of intensity, immediate sequence, interruption or sequence after an interval, etc., also QUALITIES OF strengths, such as we should express metaphorically as smooth, even, hard, rough. A striking feature is their lack of resemblance to the terms of real space and movement that to us "mean the same." There is not even more than a trace of apparent derivation from space terms.[8] So, while Hopi in its nouns seems highly concrete, here in the tensors it becomes abstract almost beyond our power to follow.

## HABITUAL THOUGHT IN SAE AND HOPI

The comparison now to be made between the habitual thought worlds of SAE and Hopi speakers is of course incomplete. It is possible only to touch upon certain dominant contrasts that appear to stem from the linguistic differences already noted. By "habitual thought" and "thought world" I mean more than simply language, i.e., than the linguistic patterns themselves. I include all the analogical and suggestive value of the patterns (e.g., our "imaginary space" and its distant implications), and all the give-and-take between language and the culture as a whole, wherein is a vast amount that is not linguistic but yet shows the shaping influence of language. In brief, this "thought world" is the microcosm that each man carries about within himself, by which he measures and understands what he can of the macrocosm.

The SAE microcosm has analyzed reality largely in terms of what it calls "things" (bodies and quasibodies) plus modes of extensional but formless existence that it calls "substances" or "matter." It tends to see existence through a binomial formula that expresses any existent as a spatial form plus a spatial formless continuum related to the form, as contents is related to the outlines of its container. Nonspatial existents are imaginatively spatialized and charged with similar implications of form and continuum.

The Hopi microcosm seems to have analyzed reality largely in terms of

---

8 One such trace is that the tensor "long in duration," while quite different from the adjective "long" of space, seems to contain the same root as the adjective "large" of space. Another is that "somewhere" of space used with certain tensors means "at some indefinite time." Possibly however this is not the case and it is only the tensor that gives the time element, so that "somewhere" still refers to space and that under these conditions indefinite space means simply general applicability, regardless of either time or space. Another trace is that in the temporal (cycle word) "afternoon" the element meaning "after" is derived from the verb "to separate." There are other such traces, but they are few and exceptional, and obviously not like our own spatial metaphorizing.

EVENTS (or better "eventing"), referred to in two ways, objective and subjective. Objectively, and only if perceptible physical experience, events are expressed mainly as outlines, colors, movements, and other perceptive reports. Subjectively, for both the physical and nonphysical, events are considered the expression of invisible intensity factors, on which depend their stability and persistence, or their fugitiveness and proclivities. It implies that existents do not "become later and later" all in the same way; but some do so by growing like plants, some by diffusing and vanishing, some by a procession of metamorphoses, some by enduring in one shape till affected by violent forces. In the nature of each existent able to manifest as a definite whole is the power of its own mode of duration: its growth, decline, stability, cyclicity, or creativeness. Everything is thus already "prepared" for the way it now manifests by earlier phases, and what it will be later, partly has been, and partly is in act of being so "prepared." An emphasis and importance rests on this preparing or being prepared aspect of the world that may to the Hopi correspond to that "quality of reality" that "matter" or "stuff" has for us.

## HABITUAL BEHAVIOR FEATURES OF HOPI CULTURE

Our behavior, and that of Hopi, can be seen to be coordinated in many ways to the linguistically conditioned microcosm. As in my fire casebook, people act about situations in ways which are like the ways they talk about them. A characteristic of Hopi behavior is the emphasis on preparation. This includes announcing and getting ready for events well beforehand, elaborate precautions to insure persistence of desired conditions, and stress on good will as the preparer of right results. Consider the analogies of the day-counting pattern alone. Time is mainly reckoned "by day" (ta-k, -tala) or "by night" (tok), which words are not nouns but tensors, the first formed on a root "light, day," the second on a root "sleep." The count is by ORDINALS. This is not the pattern of counting a number of different men or things, even though they appear successively, for, even then, they COULD gather into an assemblage. It is the pattern of counting successive reappearances of the SAME man or thing, incapable of forming an assemblage. The analogy is not to behave about day-cyclicity as to several men ("several days"), which is what WE tend to do, but to behave as to the successive visits of the SAME MAN. One does not alter several men by working upon just one, but one can prepare and so alter the later visits of the same man by working to affect the visit he is making now. This is the way the Hopi deal with the future—by working within a present situation which is expected to carry impresses, both obvious and occult, forward into the future event of interest. One might say that Hopi society understands our proverb "Well begun is half done," but not our "Tomorrow is another day." This may explain much in Hopi character.

This Hopi preparing behavior may be roughly divided into announcing; outer preparing, inner preparing, covert participation, and persistence. Announcing, or preparative publicity, is an important function in the hands of a special official, the Crier Chief. Outer preparing is preparation involving much visible activity, not all necessarily directly useful within our understanding. It includes ordinary practicing, rehearsing, getting ready, introductory formalities, preparing of special food, etc. (all of these to a degree that may seem over-elaborate to us), intensive sustained muscular activity like running, racing, dancing, which is thought to increase the intensity of development of events (such as growth of crops), mimetic and other magic, preparations based on esoteric theory involving perhaps occult instruments like prayer sticks, prayer feathers, and prayer meal, and finally the great cyclic ceremonies and dances, which have the significance of preparing rain and crops. From one of the verbs meaning "prepare" is derived the noun for "harvest" or "crop": *na' twani* "the prepared" or the "in preparation."[9]

Inner preparing is use of prayer and meditation, and at lesser intensity good wishes and good will, to further desired results. Hopi attitudes stress the power of desire and thought. With their "microcosm" it is utterly natural that they should. Desire and thought are the earliest, and therefore the most important, most critical and crucial, stage of preparing. Moreover, to the Hopi, one's desires and thoughts influence not only his actions, but all nature as well. This too is wholly natural. Consciousness itself is aware of work, of the feel of effort and energy, in desire and thinking. Experience more basic than language tells us that, if energy is expended, effects are produced. WE tend to believe that our bodies can stop up this energy, prevent it from affecting other things until we will our BODIES to overt action. But this may be so only because we have our own linguistic basis for a theory that formless items like "matter" are things in themselves, malleable only by similar things, by more matter, and hence insulated from the powers of life and thought. It is no more unnatural to think that thought contacts everything and pervades the universe than to think, as we all do, that light kindled outdoors does this. And it is not unna-tural to suppose that thought, like any other force, leaves everywhere traces of effect. Now, WE think of a certain actual rosebush, we do not suppose that our thought goes to that actual bush, and engages with it, like searchlight turned upon it. What then do we suppose our consciousness is dealing with when we are thinking of that rosebush? Probably we think it is dealing with a "mental image" which is not the rosebush but a mental surrogate of it. But why should it be NATURAL to think that our thought deals with a surrogate and not with the real rosebush? Quite possibly because we are dimly aware that we carry about with us a whole imaginary space, full of mental surrogates. To us, mental surrogates are old familiar fare. Along with the images of imaginary space, which we perhaps secretly know to be only imaginary, we tuck the thought of actually existing rosebush, which may be quite another story, perhaps just

---

[9] The Hopi verbs of preparing naturally do not correspond neatly to our "prepare"; so that *na'twani* could also be rendered "the practiced-upon, the tried-for," and otherwise.

because we have that very convenient "place" for it. The Hopi thought-world has no imaginary space. The corollary to this is that it may not locate thought dealing with real space anywhere but in real space, nor insulate real space from the effects of thought. A Hopi would naturally suppose that his thought (or he himself) traffics with the actual rosebush—or more likely, corn plant—that he is thinking about. The thought then should leave some trace of itself with the plant in the field. If it is a good thought, one about health and growth, it is good for the plant; if a bad thought, the reverse.

The Hopi emphasize the intensity-factor of thought. Thought to be most effective should be vivid in consciousness, definite, steady, sustained, charged with strongly felt good intentions. They render the idea in English as "concentrating, holding it in your heart, putting your mind on it, earnestly hoping." Thought power is the force behind ceremonies, prayer sticks, ritual smoking, etc. The prayer pipe is regarded as an aid to "concentrating" (so said my informant). Its name, na'twanpi, means "instrument of preparing."

Covert participation is mental collaboration from people who do not take part in the actual affair, be it a job of work, hunt, race, or ceremony, but direct their thought and good will toward the affair's success. Announcements often seek to enlist the support of such mental helpers as well as of overt participants, and contain exhortations to the people to aid with their active good will.[10] A similarity to our concepts of a sympathetic audience or the cheering section at a football game should not obscure the fact that it is primarily the power of directed thought, and not merely sympathy or encouragement, that is expected of covert participants. In fact these latter get in their deadliest work before, not during, the game! A corollary to the power of thought is the power of wrong thought for evil; hence one purpose of covert participation is to obtain the mass force of many good wishers to offset the harmful thought of ill wishers. Such attitudes greatly favor cooperation and community spirit. Not that the Hopi community is not full of rivalries and colliding interests. Against the tendency to social disintegration in such a small, isolated group, the theory of "preparing" by the power of thought, logically leading to the great power of the combined, intensified, and harmonized thought of the whole community, must help vastly toward the rather remarkable degree of cooperation that, in spite of much private bickering, the Hopi village displays in all the important cultural activities.

Hopi "preparing" activities again show a result of their linguistic thought background in an emphasis on persistence and constant insistent repetition. A sense of the cumulative value of innumerable small momenta is dulled by an

---

10 See, e.g., Ernest Beaglehole, *Notes on Hopi economic life* (Yale University Publications in Anthropology, no. 15, 1937), especially the reference to the announcement of a rabbit hunt, and on p. 30, description of the activities in connection with the cleaning of Toreva Spring—announcing, various preparing activities, and finally, preparing the continuity of the good results already obtained and the continued flow of the spring.

objectified, spatialized view of time like ours, enhanced by a way of thinking close to the subjective awareness of duration, of the ceaseless "latering" of events. To us, for whom time is a motion on a space, unvarying repetition seems to scatter its force along a row of units of that space, and be wasted. To the Hopi, for whom time is not a motion but a "getting later" of everything that has ever been done, unvarying repetition is not wasted but accumulated. It is storing up an invisible change that holds over into later events.[11] As we have seen, it is as if the return of the day were felt as the return of the same person, a little older but with all the impresses of yesterday, not as "another day," i.e., like an entirely different person. This principle joined with that of thought-power and with traits of general Pueblo culture is expressed in the theory of the Hopi ceremonial dance for furthering rain and crops, as well as in its short, piston-like tread, repeated thousands of times, hour after hour.

## SOME IMPRESSES OF LINGUISTIC HABIT IN WESTERN CIVILIZATION

It is harder to do justice in few words to the linguistically conditioned features of our own culture than in the case of the Hopi, because of both vast scope and difficulty of objectivity—because of our deeply ingrained familiarity with the attitudes to be analyzed. I wish merely to sketch certain characteristics adjusted to our linguistic binomialism of form plus formless item or "substance," to our metaphoricalness, our imaginary space, and our objectified time. These, as we have seen, are linguistic.

From the form-plus-substance dichotomy the philosophical views most traditionally characteristic of the "Western world" have derived huge support. Here belong materialism, psychophysical parallelism, physics—at least in its traditional Newtonian form—and dualistic views of the universe in general. Indeed here belongs almost everything that is "hard, practical common sense." Monistic, holistic, and relativistic views of reality appeal to philosophers and some scientists, but they are badly handicapped in appealing to the "common sense" of the Western average man—not because nature herself refutes them (if she did, philosophers could have discovered this much), but because they must be talked about in what amounts to a new language. "Common sense," as its name

---

11 This notion of storing up power, which seems implied by much Hopi behavior, has an analog in physics: acceleration. It might be said that the linguistic background of Hopi thought equips it to recognize naturally that force manifests not as motion or velocity, but as cumulation or acceleration. Our linguistic background tends to hinder in us this same recognition, for having legitimately conceived force to be that which produces change, we then think of change by our linguistic metaphorical analog, motion, instead of by a pure motionless changingness concept, i.e., accumulation or acceleration. Hence it comes to our naive feeling as a shock to find from physical experiments that it is not possible to define force by motion, that motion and speed, as also "being at rest," are wholly relative, and that force can be measured only by acceleration.

shows, and "practicality" as its name does not show, are largely matters of talking so that one is readily understood. It is sometimes stated that Newtonian space, time, and matter are sensed by everyone intuitively, whereupon relativity is cited as showing how mathematical analysis can prove intuition wrong. This, besides being unfair to intuition, is an attempt to answer offhand question (1) put at the outset of this paper, to answer which this research was undertaken. Presentation of the findings now nears its end, and I think the answer is clear. The offhand answer, laying the blame upon intuition for our slowness in discovering mysteries of the Cosmos, such as relativity, is the wrong one. The right answer is: Newtonian space, time, and matter are not intuitions. They are precepts from culture and language. That is where Newton got them.

Our objectified view of time is, however, favorable to historicity and to everything connected with the keeping of records, while the Hopi view is unfavorable thereto. The latter is too subtle, complex, and everdeveloping, supplying no ready-made answer to the question of when "one" event ends and "another" begins. When it is implicit that everything that ever happened still is, but is in a necessarily different form from what memory or record reports, there is less incentive to study the past. As for the present, the incentive would be not to record it but to treat it as "preparing." But OUR objectified time puts before imagination something like a ribbon or scroll marked off into equal blank spaces, suggesting that each be filled with an entry. Writing has no doubt helped toward our linguistic treatment of time, even as the linguistic treatment has guided the uses of writing. Through this give-and-take between language and the whole culture we get, for instance:

1. Records, diaries, bookkeeping, accounting, mathematics stimulated by accounting.
2. Interest in exact sequence, dating, calendars, chronology, clocks, time wages, time graphs, time as used in physics.
3. Annals, histories, the historical attitude, interest in the past, archaeology, attitudes of introjection toward past periods, e.g., classicism, romanticism.

Just as we conceive our objectified time as extending in the future in the same way that it extends in the past, so we set down our estimates of the future in the same shape as our records of the past, producing programs, schedules, budgets. The formal equality of the spacelike units by which we measure and conceive time leads us to consider the "formless item" or "substance" of time to be homogeneous and in ratio to the number of units. Hence our prorata allocation of value to time, lending itself to the building up of a commercial structure based on time-prorata values: time wages (time work constantly supersedes piece work), rent, credit, interest, depreciation charges, and insurance premiums. No doubt this vast system, once built, would continue to run under any sort of linguistic treatment of time; but that it should have been built at all, reaching the magnitude and particular form it has in the Western world, is a fact decidedly in consonance with the patterns of the SAE languages. Whether such a civilization as ours would be possible with widely different linguistic handling of time is a large question—in our civilization, our linguistic patterns and the fitting of our behavior to the temporal order are what they are, and they are in accord. We are of course stimulated to use calendars, clocks, and watches, and to try to measure time ever more precisely; this aids science, and science in turn, following these well-worn cultural grooves, gives back to culture an ever-growing store of applications, habits, and values, with which culture again directs science. But what lies outside this spiral? Science is beginning to find that there is something in the Cosmos that is not in accord with the concepts we have formed in mounting the spiral. It is trying to frame a NEW LANGUAGE by which to adjust itself to a wider universe.

It is clear how the emphasis on "saving time" which goes with all the above and is very obvious objectification of time, leads to a high valuation of "speed," which shows itself a great deal in our behavior.

Still another behavioral effect is that the character of monotony and regularity possessed by our image of time as an evenly scaled limitless tape measure persuades us to behave as if that monotony were more true of events than it really is. That is, it helps to routinize us. We tend to select and favor whatever bears out this view, to "play up to" the routine aspects of existence. One phase of this is behavior evincing a false sense of security or an assumption that all will always go smoothly, and a lack in foreseeing and protecting ourselves against hazards. Our technique of harnessing energy does well in routine performance, and it is along routine lines that we chiefly strive to improve it—we are, for example, relatively uninterested in stopping the energy from causing accidents, fires, and explosions, which it is doing constantly and on a wide scale. Such indifference to the unexpectedness of life would be disastrous to a society as small, isolated, and precariously poised as the Hopi society is, or rather once was.

Thus our linguistically determined thought world not only collaborates with our cultural idols and ideals, but engages even our unconscious personal reactions in its patterns and gives them certain typical characters. One such character, as we have seen, is CARELESSNESS, as in reckless driving or throwing cigarette stubs into waste paper. Another of different sort is GESTURING when we talk. Very many of the gestures made by English-speaking people at least, and probably by all SAE speakers, serve to illustrate, by a movement in space, not a real spatial reference but one of the nonspatial references that our language handles by metaphors of imaginary space. That is, we are more apt to make a grasping gesture when we speak of grasping an elusive idea than when we speak of grasping a doorknob. The gesture seeks to make a metaphorical and hence somewhat unclear reference more clear. But, if a language refers to nonspatials without implying a spatial analogy the reference is not made any clearer by gesture. The Hopi gesture very little, perhaps not at all in the sense we understand as gesture.

It would seem as if kinesthesia, or the sensing of muscular movement, though arising before language, should be made more highly conscious by linguistic use of imaginary space and metaphorical images of motion. Kinesthesia is marked in two facets of European culture: art and sport. European sculpture, an art in which Europe excels, is strongly kinesthetic, conveying great sense of the body's motions; European painting likewise. The dance in our culture expresses delight in motion rather than symbolism or ceremonial, and our music is greatly influenced by our dance forms. Our sports are strongly imbued with this element of the "poetry of motion." Hopi races and games seem to emphasize rather the virtues of endurance and sustained intensity. Hopi dancing is highly symbolic and is performed with great intensity and earnestness, but has not much movement or swing.

Synesthesia, or suggestion by certain sense receptions of characters belonging to another sense, as of light and color by sounds and vice versa, should be made more conscious by a linguistic metaphorical system that refers to nonspatial experiences by terms for spatial ones, though undoubtedly it arises from a deeper source. Probably in the first instance metaphor arises from synesthesia and not the reverse; yet metaphor need not become firmly rooted in linguistic pattern, as Hopi shows. Nonspatial experience has one well-organized sense, HEARING—smell and taste are but little organized. Nonspatial consciousness is a realm chiefly of thought, feeling, and SOUND. Spatial consciousness is a realm of light, color, sight, and touch, and presents shapes and dimensions. Our metaphorical system, by naming nonspatial experiences after spatial ones, imputes to sounds, smells, tastes, emotions, and thoughts qualities like the colors, luminosities, shapes, angles, textures, and motions of spatial experience. And to some extent the reverse transference occurs; for, after much talking about tones as high, low, sharp, dull, heavy, brilliant, slow, the talker finds it easy to think of some factors in spatial experience as like factors of tone. Thus we speak of "tones" of color, a gray "monotone," a "loud" necktie, a "taste" in dress: all spatial metaphor in reverse. Now European art is distinctive in the way it seeks deliberately to play with synesthesia. Music tries to suggest scenes, color, movement, geometric design; painting and sculpture are often consciously guided by the analogies of music's rhythm; colors are conjoined with feeling for the analogy to concords and discords. The European theater and opera seek a synthesis of many arts. It may be that in this way our metaphorical language that is in some sense a confusion of thought is producing, through art, a result of far-reaching value—a deeper esthetic sense leading toward a more direct apprehension of underlying unity behind the phenomena so variously reported by our sense channels.

## HISTORICAL IMPLICATIONS

How does such a network of language, culture, and behavior come about historically? Which was first: the language patterns or the cultural norms? In main they have grown up together, constantly influencing each other. But in this partnership the nature of the language is the factor that limits free plasticity and rigidifies channels of development in the more autocratic way. This is so because a language is a system, not just an assemblage of norms. Large systematic outlines can change to something really new only very slowly, while many other cultural innovations are made with comparative quickness. Language thus represents the mass mind; it is affected by inventions and innovations, but affected little and slowly, whereas TO inventors and innovators it legislates with the decree immediate.

The growth of the SAE language-culture complex dates from ancient times. Much of its metaphorical reference to the nonspatial by the spatial was already fixed in the ancient tongues, and more especially in Latin. It is indeed a marked trait of Latin. If we compare, say Hebrew, we find that, while Hebrew has some allusion to not-space as space, Latin has more. Latin terms for nonspatials, like *educo, religio, principia, comprehendo,* are usually metaphorized physical references: lead out, tying back, etc. This is not true of all languages—it is quite untrue of Hopi. The fact that in Latin the direction of development happened to be from spatial to nonspatial (partly because of secondary stimulation to abstract thinking when the intellectually crude Romans encountered Greek culture) and that later tongues were strongly stimulated to mimic Latin, seems a likely reason for a belief, which still lingers on among linguists, that this is the natural direction of semantic change in all languages, and for the persistent notion in Western learned circles (in strong contrast to Eastern ones) that objective experience is prior to subjective. Philosophies make out a weighty case for the reverse, and certainly the direction of development is sometimes the reverse. Thus the Hopi word for "heart" can be shown to be a late formation within Hopi from a root meaning think or remember. Or consider what has happened to the word "radio" in such a sentence as "he bought a new radio," as compared to its prior meaning "science of wireless telephony."

In the Middle Ages the patterns already formed in Latin began to interweave with the increased mechanical invention, industry, trade, and scholastic and scientific thought. The need for measurement in industry and trade, the stores and bulks of "stuffs" in various containers, the type of bodies in which various goods were handled, standardizing of measure and weight units, invention of clocks and measurement of "time," keeping of records, accounts, chronicles, histories, growth of mathematics and the partnership of mathematics and science, all cooperated to bring our thought and language world into its present form.

In Hopi history, could we read it, we should find a different type of language and a different set of cultural and environmental influences working together. A peaceful agricultural society isolated by geographic features and nomad enemies in a land of scanty rainfall, arid agriculture that could be made successful only by the utmost perseverance (hence the value of persistence and repetition), necessity for collaboration (hence emphasis on the psychology of teamwork and on mental factors in general), corn and rain as primary criteria of value, need of extensive PREPARATIONS and precautions to assure crops in the poor soil and precarious climate, keen realization of dependence upon nature favoring prayer and a religious attitude toward the forces of nature, especially prayer and religion directed toward the ever-needed blessing, rain— these things interacted with Hopi linguistic patterns to mold them, to be molded again by them, and so little by little to shape the Hopi world-outlook.

To sum up the matter, our first question asked in the beginning is answered thus: Concepts of "time" and "matter" are not given in substantially the same form by experience to all men but depend upon the nature of the language or languages through the use of which they have been developed. They do not depend so much upon ANY ONE SYSTEM (e.g., tense, or nouns) within the grammar as upon the ways of analyzing and reporting experience which have become fixed in the language as integrated "fashions of speaking" and which cut across the typical grammatical classifications, so that such a "fashion" may include lexical, morphological, syntactic, and otherwise systemically diverse means coordinated in a certain frame of consistency. Our own "time" differs markedly from Hopi "duration." It is conceived as like a space of strictly limited dimensions, or sometimes as like a motion upon such a space, and employed as an intellectual tool accordingly. Hopi "duration" seems to be inconceivable in terms of space or motion, being the mode in which life differs from form, and consciousness *in toto* from the spatial elements of consciousness. Certain ideas born of our own time-concept, such as that of absolute simul- taneity, would be either very difficult to express or impossible and devoid of meaning under the Hopi conception, and would be replaced by operational concepts. Our "matter" is the physical subtype of "substance" or "stuff," which is conceived as the formless extensional item that must be joined with form before there can be real existence. In Hopi there seems to be nothing corresponding to it; there are no formless extensional items; existence may or may not have form, but what it also has, with or without form, is intensity and duration, these being nonextensional and at bottom the same.

But what about our concept of "space," which was also included in our first question? There is no such striking difference between Hopi and SAE about space as about time, and probably the apprehension of space is given in substantially the same form by experience irrespective of language. The experi- ments of the Gestalt psychologists with visual perception appear to establish this as a fact. But the CONCEPT OF SPACE will vary somewhat with lan- guage because, as an intellectual tool,[12] it is so closely linked with the concomi- tant employment of other intellectual tools, of the order of "time" and "matter," which are linguistically conditioned. We see things with our eyes in the same space forms as the Hopi, but our idea of space has also the property of acting as a surrogate of nonspatial relationships like time, intensity, tendency, and as a void to be filled with imagined formless items, one of which may even be called "space." Space as sensed by the Hopi would not be connected mentally with such surrogates, but would be comparatively "pure," unmixed with extra- neous notions.

---

[12] Here belong "Newtonian" and "Euclidean" space, etc.

As for our second question: There are connections but not correlations or diagnostic correspondences between cultural norms and linguistics patterns. Although it would be impossible to infer the existence of Crier Chiefs from the lack of tenses in Hopi, or vice versa, there is a relation between a language and the rest of the culture of the society which uses it. There are cases where the "fashions of speaking" are closely integrated with the whole general culture, whether or not this be universally true, and there are connections within this integration, between the kind of linguistic analyses employed and various behavioral reactions and also the shapes taken by various cultural developments. Thus the importance of Crier Chiefs does have a connection, not with tenselessness itself, but with a system of thought in which categories different from our tenses are natural. These connections are to be found not so much by focusing attention on the typical rubrics of linguistic, ethnographic, or sociological description as by examining the culture and the language (always and only when the two have been together historically for a considerable time) as a whole in which concatenations that run across these departmental lines may be expected to exist, and, if they do exist, eventually to be discoverable by study.

# The Problem of Society: How We Become Selves

George Herbert Mead

What I am trying to do is to connect this entire evolutionary process with social organization in its most complex expression, and as that within which arise the very individuals through whose life-process it works, giving birth to just such elements as are involved in the development of selves. And, as I have said, the life-process itself is brought to consciousness in the conduct of the individual form, in his so-called self-consciousness. He gets a much more effective control over his environment than the ox can get over its. The process is one in which, in a certain sense, control is within his own grasp. If you think of it, the human being as a social form actually has relatively complete control over his environment. The animal gets a certain slight kind of control over its environment; but the human form, in societies, can determine what vegetation shall grow, what animals shall exist besides itself; it can control its own climate, erect its own buildings. It has, in a biological sense, complete control over its own environment. That is, it has attained to a remarkable degree an end which is implied in the whole living process—the control by the form of the environment within which it lives. To a degree human society has reached that goal.

It has often been pointed out, of course, that evolution does not reach any goal. The concept means simply the adaptation of a form to a certain environment. But adaptation is not simply the fitting of the form into the environment; it carries with it some degree of control over that environment. And in the case of the human form, of human society, we have that adaptation expressing itself in a very high degree of control. Of course, we cannot change the chemical and physical structure of things, but we can make them over into those forms that we ourselves need and which are of value to us. That is possible for us; and, as I have said with reference to the question of food and to the question of climatic influences, we can in a very large degree determine that control. So there is, within limits, a development toward complete adaptation where that adaptation expresses itself in control over the environment. And in that sense I think we can fairly say that human organization, as a social organization, does exercise control and has reached a certain goal of development.

Well now, this social process I have been sketching in these broad strokes has become of increasing interest to reflective thought throughout this whole period. Of course, to some extent it has always been of essential interest to man in the social situation in which he lives. What I am referring to specifically is the character of the social organism—its organization, its history, and the conditions under which it can be controlled. The statement of the functions of the different parts of the social organism is that study which we have in a so-called "social science," and more particularly in sociology. This had its inception in the thought of Comte, and then was enriched by the idea of evolution as brought in by Spencer. From that time on, the attempt to understand human society as an organization has been of increasing interest to the Western world. Men have been trying to see the habits out of which society has arisen, to find out under what conditions it operates, and how problems that arise in it can be definitely controlled. This involves looking at human institutions from the standpoint I have suggested, that is, as social habits.

While during the century there has been this increased interest in the study of the social organization, there has been a corresponding interest in the experience of the individual. Part of this is due to our scientific attitude. As we have seen, it is the unique experience of the scientist that presents the problem, and it is in the mind of the scientist that the hypothesis arises. It is not only in the scientist as such that this uniqueness of the experience has been recognized as of importance. After all, the scientist is simply making a technique out of human intelligence. His method is the same as that of all intelligent beings, even though it involves a simple rendering in self-consciousness of the whole process of evolution. That in the experience of all individuals which is peculiar to the individual, that which is unique in his experience, is of importance, and what the last century increasingly recognized was the importance of these unique individual experiences.

The emotional side of these experiences, as we know, registers itself in the folk poetry, in the lyric expression of the self—a registration of values from the point of view of the individual. There have always been some neat ways of scientific observation, although accurate presentation of it belongs really to the Modern world, that world which has grown up since the period of the Renaissance. But what I am particularly calling attention to is the interest we have in that which is peculiar to the individual as it is revealed in our literature, in our journals, and in our newspapers. The curious thing about the newspaper is that it records happenings to individual persons; and it assumes that it is of interest to us to know that a certain individual at a certain time was run over by an automobile or that a certain person fell down, hurt himself in such and such a way, and that John or Jane has had such and such an experience in such a place. It is curious to note the interest that centers about individuals, and the assumption that the world at large will be interested in these happenings.

Well now, what I want to connect with this journalese interest in happenings to particular individuals is the character of our literature, not simply in its lyric poetry, where the emotion of the individual is presented so that it can be handed on to others, but particularly in our novels and the drama. In these we have this interest in the experience of the individual presented as it has been during the last century because it does answer some very profound interest on the part of all the individuals who take up their morning and evening papers, who read all sorts of stories and novels, go to movies, listen to the radio, get those experiences of other individuals which, as I say, have an interest for us which is rather astonishing when one just stands off and looks at the situation. They seem to be so unrelated. We seem to be interested in just a particular occurrence. We speak of it as sensational and perhaps are apt to regard it as an attitude not entirely helpful on our part when we are interested in this fashion.

What is the import of this interest? I wanted to bring this up in sharp contrast to what I am going to develop later, that is, that the human self arises through its ability to take the attitude of the group to which he belongs— because he can talk to himself in terms of the community to which he belongs and lay upon himself the responsibilities that belong to the community; because he can recognize his own duties as against others—that is what constitutes the self as such. And there you see what we have emphasized, as peculiar to others, that which is both individual and which is habitual. The structure of society lies in these social habits, and only insofar as we can take these social habits into ourselves can we become selves.

We speak of this interest on the emotional side as "sympathy"—passing into the attitude of the other, taking the role of the other, feeling the other's joys and sorrows. That is the effective side of it. What we call the "intellectual side," the "rational side," is the recognition of common stimuli, of common emotions which call out responses in every member of the group. And insofar as one indicates this common character to others, he indicates it to himself. In this way, of course, by taking the attitude of the others in the group in their co-operative, highly complex activity, the individual is able to enter into their experiences. The engineer is able to direct vast groups of individuals in a highly complex process. But in every direction he gives, he takes the attitude of the person whom he is directing. It has the same meaning to him that it has to others. We enter thus into the attitudes of others, and so make our very complex societies possible. This development of a form that is able so to communicate with others that it takes on attitudes of those in the group, that it talks to itself as it talks to others, that imports into its own life this conversation and sets up an inner forum in which it works out the process that it is going to carry on, and so brings it to public consideration, with the advantage of that previous rehearsing, is all important. Sometimes we find that we can best think out an argument by supposing that we are talking to somebody who takes one particular side. We have an argument to present, and we think how we will present it to that individual. And as soon as we present it, we know that he would reply in a certain way. Then we reply in a certain fashion to him. Sometimes it is easier to carry out such a conversation by picking out a particular protagonist we know. In that way in the night hours we are apt to go through distressing conversations we have to carry out the next day. That is the process of thought. It is taking the attitude of others, talking to other people, and then replying in their language. That is what constitutes thinking.

Of course, conditions are different in a human society from simpler situations. I was pointing out the difference between a human society and society of invertebrates. The principle of organization is not that of physiological plasticity, not that of holding the form itself physiologically to its particular function; it is rather the principle of organization as found in the form of human intercommunication and participation. It is what the human individual puts into the form of significant symbols through the use of gestures. He is then able to place himself in the attitude of others, particularly into just such attitudes as those I have spoken of as human institutions. If institutions are social habits, they represent certain definite attitudes that people assume under certain given social conditions. So that the individual, insofar as he does take the role of others, can take the habitual attitude of the community against such social situations as these.

As I have pointed out, he does this in the process of indicating to others the important elements in a situation, pointing out those elements which are of importance in the social process, in a situation that represents one of these social habits, such as the family situation—one that involves the rights of different individuals in the community, such as a political situation. What the individual does is to indicate what the important characters in a co-operative process are. He indicates this to other members of the community; but as we shall see, especially in the case of vocal gestures, he indicates it to himself as to others; and just insofar as he does indicate it to himself as to others, he tends to call out in himself the same attitude as in others. There is a common attitude, that is, one which all assume under certain habitual situations. Through the use of language, through the use of the significant symbol, then, the individual does take the attitude of others, especially these common attitudes, so that he finds himself taking the same attitude toward himself that the community takes. This is what gives the principle of social control, not simply the social control that results from blind habit, but a social control that comes from the individual assuming the same attitude toward himself that the community assumes toward him. In a habitual situation everyone takes a certain attitude insofar as the habit is one which all have taken, that is, insofar as you have "institutions." If, now, the individual calls out this attitude in others by a gesture, by a word which affects himself just as it affects others, then he will call out the same attitude in himself that he calls out in others. In this way he will be acting toward himself as others act toward him. He will admonish himself as others would. That is, he will recognize what are his duties as well as what are his rights. He takes the attitude of the community toward himself. This gives the principal method of organization which, as I have said, we can study from the standpoint of a behavioristic psychology, a method which belongs to human society and distinguishes it from social organizations which one finds among ants and bees and termites. There one finds societies that run up into the millions; and we find these as finely organized as human societies are, and so organized that individuals' lives are largely determined by the life-process of the whole. We get far more complex and intricate organization, of course, in human society than among the invertebrates. This principle to which I have referred—organization through communication and participation—makes an almost indefinite organization possible. Now the study of the way in which this organization takes place, the history of it, the evolution of it, is what has been opened up to the human mind in the last century. We now see the way in which out of a primitive group there can gradually arise the very highly organized societies of the present day. We can study that process in the evolution of institutions, and we can see how that process is modified or may be modified in the presence of problematic situations.

This evolution also takes place in human society, but here it takes place not through physiological plasticity, not through the development of peculiar physiological function on the part of the separate individuals. It takes place through the development of what has been referred to on the logical side as a universe of discourse. That is, it takes place through communication and participation on the part of the different individuals in common activities. It takes place through the development of significant symbols. It is accomplished almost entirely through the development of vocal gestures, through the capacity of the individual to indicate by means of his own gestures to other forms and also to himself, those elements which are of importance in co-operative activity. So far as we can see, the stimuli that keep the invertebrates occupied are those of odor and contact. But we find no evidence of any language among them. It is through physiological development and plasticity that their very complex communities operate. But the human form, subject to no such development as this, can be interwoven into a community activity through its ability to respond to the gestures of other forms that indicate to it the stimuli to which it is to respond. We point things out. This pointing-out process may be with the finger, by an attitude of body, by direction of head and eyes; but as a rule it is by means of the vocal gesture, that is, a certain vocal symbol that indicates something to another individual and to which he responds. Such indication as this sets up a certain definite process of pointing out to other individuals in the group what is of importance in this co-operative activity.

The peculiar importance of the vocal gesture is that it affects the individual who makes it just as much as it affects the individual to whom it is directed. We hear what we say; if we are talking with our fingers we see what we are saying; if with attitudes of the body, we feel what we are saying. The effect of the attitude which we produce in others comes back on ourselves. It is in this way that participation arises out of communication. When we indicate something to another form, we are calling out in that other individual a certain response. The very gesture we make calls out a certain sort of response in him. If that gesture affects us as it affects him, it has a tendency to call out some response in ourselves. The gesture that affects another, when it is a vocal gesture, is one which may have the tendency to influence the speaker as it influences others. The common expression of this is that a man knows what he is saying when the meaning of what he is saying comes to him as really as it goes to another. He is affected just as the other is. If the meaning of what he says affects the other, it affects himself in the same way. The result of this is that the individual who speaks in some sense takes the attitude of the other whom he addresses. We are familiar with this in giving directions to another person to do something. We find ourselves affected by the same direction. We are ready to do the thing and perhaps become irritated by the awkwardness of the other and insist on doing it ourselves. We have called out in ourselves the same response we have asked for in another person. We are taking his attitude. It is through this sort of participation, this taking the attitudes of other individuals, that the peculiar character of human intelligence is constituted. We say something that means something to a certain group. But it not only means that to the group, it also means that to us. It has the same meaning for both.

There is a certain, what we would call, "unconscious direction" that takes place in lower vertebrate forms. A group of animals is said to set up a sentinel. Some one form is more sensitive than others to stimuli of danger. Now the action on the part of this one which is more sensitive than the rest, the action of running from danger, for example, does cause the other forms to run also. But the first one is not giving a signal in the human sense. It is not aware of giving such directions. Its mere running is a stimulus to the other forms to run in the same direction. It works in the same way as if the form knew what its business was, to catch the first evidence of the enemy and give the evidence to the whole group, thus setting them all going. But in the experience of the animal there is no such procedure, no such intent. The animal does not influence himself as he influences others. He does not tell himself of the danger as he tells it to others. He merely runs away.

The outstanding characteristic in human communication is that one is making a declaration, pointing out something that is common in meaning to the whole group and to the individual, so that the individual is taking the attitude of the whole group, so far as there is any definite meaning given. When a man calls out "Fire!" he is not only exciting other people but himself in the same fashion. He knows what he is about. That, you see, constitutes biologically what we refer to as a "universe of discourse." It is a common meaning which is communicated to everyone and at the same time is communicated to the self. The individual is directing other people how to act, and he is taking the attitude of the other people whom he is directing. If in this attitude of the other person he makes an objection, he is doing what the other person would do, and he is also carrying on the process which we call "thought." That is, you indicate to somebody else that he is to do something, and he objects to it. Well now, the person might in his attitude of the other make the same objection himself. You reply to the other person, trying to point out his mistake or admitting your own. In the same way, if you make some objection you reply to your own objection or admit your mistake to yourself. Thinking is a process of conversation with one's self when the individual takes the attitude of the other, especially when he takes the common attitude of the whole group, when the symbol that he uses is a common symbol, so that it has a meaning common to the entire group, to everyone who is in it and anyone who might be in it. It is a process of communication with participation in the experience of other people.

The mechanism that we use for this process is words, vocal gestures. And we need, of course, only a very few of these as compared with those we need when talking to others. A single symbol is enough to call out necessary responses. But it is just as real a conversation in terms of the significant symbols of language as if the whole process were expressed. We sometimes do our thinking out loud, in fully organized sentences; and one's thought can always presumably be developed into a complete grammatical unit. That is what constitutes thinking.

Now, it is this inner thought, this inner flow of speech and what it means—words with their meanings—that call out intelligent response; it is this that constitutes the mind, insofar as that lies in the experience of the form. But this is only a part of the whole social process, for the self has arisen in that social process; it has its being there. Of course, you could carry such a self as that over to a Robinson Crusoe island and leave him by himself, and he could carry that social process on by himself and extend it to his pets. He carries that on by himself, but it is only because he has grown up in society, because he can take attitudes and roles of others, that he can accomplish this.

This mental process, then, is one which has evolved in the social process of which it is a part. And it belongs to the different organisms that lie inside of this larger social process. We can approach it from the standpoint of evolution; and we can approach it more particularly from the standpoint of behavioristic psychology, where we can get back to what expresses itself in the mind. We also can get somewhat underneath the experience that goes on in the self in what we term "pathological psychology," a psychology that enables us to get hold of the various processes that are not themselves evidenced in this stream of inner conversation to which I have referred. The term "pathological" simply means that this type of psychology has been pursued largely in dealing with pathological cases. It is a study, for example, of the way in which our special world arises in our experience through our distance senses and our contact experiences—through the collation of the elements which we reach through vision and with the elements which we reach through the tactual sense—the process by which we have built up an implemental world by the use of our hands; for example, the process by which, for purposes of food, we reach with the hand for a distant object. Man comes into that process and gives to the organism a physical thing which is not the food, not the consummation, whatever it may be, but a physical thing. Our world is made up out of physical things. We deal with things as if we could handle them. We think of things as being "pulverized," broken up into parts so we can get hold of them. A physical thing is a unit into which we break up our environment. The process by which we build our world of physical things is a process, too, of which we are not immediately conscious. The child, the infant that is uncertainly groping toward a ball, is gradually building up a world of such physical things; but the process takes place underneath the level of our own consciousness. We cannot get at it in its immediate inception, only indirectly by this type of psychology, a psychology that does enable us to get into the workings of the individual process as it lies inside of the whole social process to which it belongs.

And this is what constitutes the self as such. A self which is so evidently a social individual that it can exist only in a group of social individuals is as much a result of the process of evolution as other biological forms. A form that can co-operate with others through the use of significant symbols, set up attitudes of others and respond to them, is possible through the development of great tracts in the central nervous system that are connected with our processes of articulation, with the ear, and so with the various movements that can go on in the human form. But they are not circumscribed within the conduct of a single form. They belong to the group. And the process is just as much an evolution as is the queen bee or the fighter among the ants. In those instances we get a certain particular evolution that is taking place, belonging to a certain particular society, one which could exist only in such a society. The same is true of the self. That is, an individual who affects himself as he affects another; who takes the attitude of the other insofar as he is using what we term "intelligible speech"; who knows what he himself is saying, insofar as he is directing his indications by these significant symbols to theirs with the recognition that they have the same meaning for them as for him; such an individual is, of course, a phase of the development of the social form. This is a branch of what we term "behavioristic psychology," one in which we can see how the self as such has developed.

What I want to make evident is that the development, the evolution, of mind as well as of institutions is a social evolution. As I have just stated, society in its organization is a form, a species that has developed; and it has many forms developing within it. You see, for example, at the present time in reference to the question of food that the problem is one which is met by very intricate social organizations. Where the individual himself responds simply to the odor or sight of food, we recognize it as a biological process. When the whole community responds to the need of food by the organization of its industries, of agriculture, of milling, of transportation, of cooking and preparation, we have the same process, only now, not by separate individuals, but by a social organization; and that organization is just as really an evolution as the stomach of the ox. That stomach is very complicated. The evolution of the social mechanism by which grain is sowed and reaped in South America and North America, is carried to great milling establishments and there converted into flour, and then carried and distributed by dealers so that the individual groups can get it and prepare it in such fashion that it can be readily assimilated —that is just as much evolution as the development of bacteriological laboratories in the digestive tract of an ox. It is a process, however, which takes place much more rapidly than it is taking place in the case of the ox. There we have something that answers to a physiological plasticity in the case of invertebrates —the adjustment of different organs within the body to accomplish what we accomplish by mechanical means. It is this ability to control our environment that gives us what we term "mind."

What we attach to the term "mind" particularly is its privacy. It belongs to the individual. And what takes place there takes place, we say, in the experience of the individual. He may make it accessible to others by telling about it. He may talk out loud. He may publish. He may indicate even by his uncontrolled gesture what his frame of mind is. But there is that which goes on inside of a man's mind that never gets published, something that takes place within the experience of the individual. Part of it, of course, is that which answers to what is going on in the physiological mechanism there, the suffering that belongs to one's teeth, the pleasure one gets in the palate. These are experiences which he has for himself because they are taking place within his own organism. But, though they are taking place within his own organism, and no one else can experience the same thing, the organism does not experience it as its own—it does not realize that the experience is its own—until a self has arisen. We have no reason to assume, for example, that in lower animals there are such entities as selves; and if no such entities, then that which takes place within the organism cannot be identified with such a self. There is pain; there is pleasure; there are feelings which are not exactly painful or pleasurable, such as heat or cold. These various feelings belong to the organism, the tensions of the various muscles, the movements of the joints, so essential in our intelligent social conduct. These belong to the organism in a certain sense. But the individual animal does not associate them with a self because it has no self; it is not a self.

A self can arise only where there is a social process within which this self has had its initiation. It arises within that process. For that process, the communication and participation to which I have referred is essential. That is the way in which selves have arisen. That is where the individual is in a social process in which he is a part, where he does influence himself as he does others. There the self arises. And there he turns back upon himself, directs himself. He takes over those experiences which belong to his own organism. He identifies them with himself. What constitutes the particular structure of his experience is what we call his "thought." It is the conversation which goes on within the self. This is what constitutes his mind. For it is through this so-called "thought," of course, that he interprets his experiences. Now that thought, as I have already indicated, is only the importation of outer conversation, conversation of gestures with others, into the self in which the individual takes the role of others as well as his own role. He talks to himself. This talking is significant. He is indicating what is of importance in the situation. He is indicating those elements that call out the necessary responses. When there are conflicts, the problem gives rise to the hypotheses that form in his mind; he indicates them to himself and to others. It is this process of talking over a problematic situation with one's self, just as one might talk with another, that is exactly what we term "mental." And it goes on within the organism.

# Relation of Mind to Response and Environment

## George Herbert Mead

We have seen that mental processes have to do with the meanings of things, and that these meanings can be stated in terms of highly organized attitudes of the individual. These attitudes involve not only situations in which the elements are simultaneous, but also ones which involve other temporal relationships, that is, the adjustment of the present response to later responses which are in some sense already initiated. Such an organization of attitudes with reference to what we term objects is what constitutes for us the meanings of things. These meanings in logical terminology are considered as universals, and this universality, we have seen, attaches in a certain sense to a habitual response in contrast to the particular stimuli which elicit this response. The universality is reflected in behavioristic terms in the identity of the response, although the stimuli that call out this response are all different. We can throw this statement into a logical form and say that the response is universal while the stimuli are particulars which are brought under such a universal.

These relations of attitudes to each other throw light upon the relation of a "substance" to its attributes. We speak of a house as, in a certain sense, a substance to which the attribute of color can be applied. The color is an accident which inheres in a certain substance, as such. This relationship of the inherence of a certain character in a certain substance is a relationship of a specific response, such as that of ornamenting objects about us, to the group of actions involved in dwelling in a house. The house must protect us; it must provide for us when we are asleep and when we are awake; it must carry the requisites of a family life—these are essentials that stand for a set of responses in which one inevitably implies the other. There are other responses, however, that vary. We can satisfy, not simply our taste, but also our whims in the ornaments we use. Those are not essential. There are certain responses that vary, whereas there is a certain body of more or less standardized responses that remain unchanged. The organized sets of responses answer to the meanings of things, answer to them in their universality, that is, in the habitual response that is called out by a great variety of stimuli. They answer to things in their logical relationships.

I have referred just now to the relationship of the substance as reflected in the body of habits, to the varied responses answering to the attributes. In the relationship of cause and effect there is the relation of the responses to each other in the sense of dependence, involving the adjustment of the steps to be taken with reference to the thing to be carried out. The arrangement which can appear at one time in terms of means and end appears at another time in terms of cause and effect. We have here a relationship of dependence of one response on another, a necessary relation that lies inside of a larger system.[1] It depends upon what we are going to do whether we select this means or another one, one causal series or another. Our habits are so adjusted that if we decide to take a journey, for instance, we have a body of related habits that begin to operate—packing our bags, getting our railroad tickets, drawing out money for use, selecting books to read on the journey, and so on. There are a whole set of organized responses which at once start to go off in their proper relationship to each other when a person makes up his mind that he will take a journey. There must be such an organization in our habits in order that man may have the sort of intelligence which he in fact has.

We have, then, in the behavioristic statement, a place for that which is supposed to be the peculiar content of mind, that is, the meanings of things. I have referred to these factors as attitudes. There is, of course, that in the world which answers to the group of attitudes. We are here avoiding logical and metaphysical problems, just as modern psychology does. What this psychology is seeking to do is to get control; it is not seeking to settle metaphysical questions. Now, from the point of view of behavioristic psychology, we can state in terms of attitudes what we call the meanings of things; the organized attitude of the individual is that which the psychologist gets hold of in this situation. It is at least as legitimate for him to state meaning in terms of attitudes as it was for an earlier psychologist to state it in terms of a static concept that had its place in the mind.

What I have pointed out is that in the central nervous system one can find, or at least justifiably assume, just such complexities of responses, or the mechanism of just such complexities of response, as we have been discussing. If we speak of a person going through the steps to which I have referred, in preparing for a journey, we then have to assume that, not only are the nervous elements essential to the steps, but that the relation of those responses in the central nervous system is such that if the person carries out one response, then he is inevitably ready to find the stimulus which will set free another related response. There must be an organization in the central nervous system in the way of its elements, its neurons, for all the combinations which can possibly enter into a mind and for just such a relationship of responses which are interdependent upon each other. Some of these have been identified in the physiological study of the nervous system, while others have to be assumed on the basis of such study. As I have said before, it is not the specific physiological

---

[1] Representation involves relation of earlier to later acts. This relation of responses gives implication (1924).

process which is going on inside of the neurons that answers to meaning. Earlier physiological psychologists had spoken of a specific psychical process, but there is nothing in the mechanical, electrical, and physical activity that goes on in the nerve which answers to what we term an idea. What is going on in the nerve in a particular situation is the innervation of a certain response which means this, that, and the other thing, and here is where the specificity of a certain nervous organization is found. It is in the central nervous system that organization takes place. In a certain sense you can say that it is in the engineer's office that the organization of the concern is carried out. But what is found there in the blueprints and body of statistics is not the actual production that is going on in the factory, even though that office does organize and co-ordinate those various branches of the concern. In the same way the central nervous system co-ordinates all the various processes that the body carries out. If there is anything in the organism as a purely physiological mechanism which answers to what we call experience, when that is ordinarily termed conscious, it is the total organic process for which these nervous elements stand. These processes are, as we have seen, attitudes of response, adjustments of the organism to a complex environment, attitudes which sensitize the form to the stimuli which will set the response free.

The point I want to emphasize is the way that these attitudes determine the environment. There is an organized set of responses which first send certain telegrams, then select the means of transportation, then send us to the bank to get money, and then see to it that we get something to read on the train. As we advance from one set of responses to another we find ourselves picking out the environment which answers to this next set of responses. To finish one response is to put ourselves in a position where we see other things. The appearance of the retinal elements has given the world color; the development of the organs in the ear has given the world sound. We pick an organized environment in relationship to our response, so that these attitudes, as such, not only represent our organized responses, but they also represent what exists for us in the world; the particular phase of reality that is there for us is picked out for us by our response. We can recognize that it is the sensitizing of the organism to the stimuli which will set free its responses that is responsible for one's living in this sort of an environment rather than in another. We see things as distant from us not only spatially but temporally; when we do this, we can do that. Our world is definitely mapped out for us by the responses which are going to take place.[2]

It is a difficult matter to state just what we mean by dividing up a certain situation between the organism and its environment. Certain objects come to exist for us because of the character of the organism. Take the case of food.

---

2 The structure of the environment is a mapping out of organic responses to nature; any environment, whether social or individual, is a mapping out of the logical structure of the act to which it answers, an act seeking overt expression.

If an animal that can digest grass, such as an ox, comes into the world, then grass becomes food. That object did not exist before, that is, grass as food. The advent of the ox brings in a new object. In that sense, organisms are responsible for the appearance of whole sets of objects that did not exist before.[3] The distribution of meaning to the organism and the environment has its expression in the organism as well as in the thing, and that expression is not a matter of psychical or mental conditions. There is an expression of the reaction of the organism's organized response to the environment, and that reaction is not simply a determination of the organism by the environment, since the organism determines the environment as fully as the environment determines the organs. The organic reaction is responsible for the appearance of a whole set of objects which did not exist before.

There is a definite and necessary structure or *gestalt* of sensitivity within the organism which determines selectively and relatively the character of the external object it perceives. What we term consciousness needs to be brought inside just this relation between an organism and its environment. Our constructive selection of an environment—colors, emotional values, and the like—in terms of our physiological sensitivities, is essentially what we mean by consciousness. This consciousness we have tended historically to locate in the mind or in the brain. The eye and related processes endow objects with color in exactly the same sense that an ox endows grass with the character of food, that is, not in the sense of projecting sensations into objects, but rather of putting itself into a relation with the object which makes the appearance and existence of the color possible, as a quality of the object. Colors inhere in objects only by virtue of their relations to given percipient organisms. The physiological or sensory structure of the percipient organism determines the experienced content of the object.

The organism, then, is in a sense responsible for its environment. And since organism and environment determine each other and are mutually dependent for their existence, it follows that the life-process, to be adequately understood, must be considered in terms of their interrelations.

The social environment is endowed with meanings in terms of the process of social activity; it is an organization of objective relations which arises in relation to a group of organisms engaged in such activity, in processes of social experience and behavior. Certain characters of the external world are possessed by it only with reference to or in relation to an interacting social group of individual organisms; just as other characters of it are possessed by it only with reference to or in relation to individual organisms themselves. The relation of the social process of behavior—or the relation of the social organism—to the social environment is analogous to the relation of the processes of individual

---

[3] It is objectionable to speak of the food-process in the animal as constituting the food-object. They are certainly relative to each other (MS).

biological activity—or the relation of the individual organism—to the physical-biological environment.[4]

The parallelism I have been referring to is the parallelism of the set of the organism and the objects answering to it. In the ox there is hunger and also the sight and odor which bring in the food. The whole process is not found simply in the stomach, but in all the activities of grazing, chewing the cud, and so on. This process is one which is intimately related to the so-called food. The organism sets up a bacteriological laboratory, such as the ox carries around to take care of the grass. Within that parallelism what we term the meaning of the object is found, specifically, in the organized attitude of response on the part of the organism to the characters and the things. The meanings are there, and the mind is occupied with these meanings. The organized stimuli answer to the organized responses.

It is the organization of the different responses to each other in their relationship to the stimuli they are setting free that is the peculiar subject matter of psychology in dealing with what we term "mind." We generally confine the term "mental," and so "mind," to the human organism, because there we find that body of symbols that enables us to isolate these characters, these meanings. We try to distinguish the meaning of a house from the stone, the cement, the bricks that make it up as a physical object, and in doing so we are referring to the use of it. That is what makes the house a mental affair.[5] We are isolating, if you like, the building materials from the standpoint of the physicist and the architect. There are various standpoints from which one can look at a house. The burrow in which some animal lives is in one sense the house of the animal, but when the human being lives in a house the house takes on what we term a mental character for him which it presumably has not for the mole that lives in the burrow. The human individual has the ability to pick out the elements in a house which answer to his responses so that he can control them. He reads the advertisement of a new form of a boiler and can then have more warmth, have a more comfortable dressing room than before. Man is able to control the

---

4 A social organism—a social group of individual organisms—constitutes or creates its own special environment of objects just as, and in the same sense as, an individual organism constitutes or creates its own special environment of objects (which, however, is much more rudimentary than the environment constructed by a social organism).

5 Nature—the external world—is objectively there, in opposition to our experience of it or in opposition to the individual thinker himself. Although external objects are there, independent of the experiencing individual, nevertheless they possess certain characteristics by virtue of their relations to his experiencing or to his mind, which they would not possess otherwise or apart from those relations. These characteristics are their meanings for him, or in general, for us. The distinction between physical objects or physical reality and the mental or self-conscious experience of those objects or that reality—the distinction between external and internal experience—lies in the fact that the latter is concerned with or constituted by meanings. Experienced objects have definite meanings for the individuals thinking about them.

process from the standpoint of his own responses. He gets meanings and so controls his responses. His ability to pick those out is what makes the house a mental affair. The mole, too, has to find his food, meet his enemies, and avoid them, but we do not assume that the mole is able to indicate to himself the peculiar advantages of his burrow over another one. His house has no mental characteristics. Mentality resides in the ability of the organism to indicate those things in the environment which answer to his responses, so that he can control those responses in various ways. This ability, from the point of view of behavioristic psychology, is what mentality consists in. There are in the mole and other animals complex elements of behavior related to the environment, but the human animal is able to indicate to itself and to others what the characters are in the environment which call out these complex, highly organized responses and by such indication is able to control the responses. The human animal has the ability over and above the adjustment which belongs to the lower animal to pick out and isolate the stimulus. The biologist recognizes that food has certain values, and while the human animal responds to these values as other animals do, it can also indicate certain characters in the food which mean certain things in its digestive responses to these foods. Mentality consists in indicating these values to others and to one's self so that one can control one's responses.

Mentality on our approach simply comes in when the organism is able to point out meanings to others and to himself. This is the point at which mind appears, or if you like, emerges. What we need to recognize is that we are dealing with the relationship of the organism to the environment selected by its own sensitivity. The psychologist is interested in the mechanism which the human species has evolved to get control over these relationships. The relationships have been there before the indications are made, but the organism has not in its own conduct controlled that relationship. It originally has no mechanism by means of which it can control it. The human animal, however, has worked out a mechanism of language communication by means of which it can get this control. Now, it is evident that much of that mechanism does not lie in the central nervous system but in the relation of things to the organism. The ability to pick these meanings out and to indicate them to others and to the organism is an ability which gives peculiar power to the human individual. The control has been made possible by language. It is that mechanism of control over meaning in this sense which has, I say, constituted what we term "mind." The mental processes do not, however, lie in words any more than the intelligence of the organism lies in the elements of the central nervous system. Both are part of a process that is going on between organism and environment. The symbols serve their part in this process, and it is that which makes communication so important. Out of language emerges the field of mind.

It is absurd to look at the mind simply from the standpoint of the individual human organism; for, although it has its focus there, it is essentially a social phenomenon; even its biological functions are primarily social. The subjective experience of the individual must be brought into relation with the natural, socio-biological activities of the brain in order to render an acceptable account of mind possible at all; and this can be done only when the social nature of mind is recognized. The meagerness of individual experience in isolation from the processes of social experience—in isolation from its social environment— should, moreover, be apparent. We must regard mind, then, as arising and developing within the social process, within the empirical matrix of social interactions. We must, that is, get an inner individual experience from the standpoint of social acts which include the experiences of separate individuals in a social context wherein those individuals interact. The processes of experience which the human brain makes possible are made possible only for a group of interacting individuals—only for individual organisms which are members of a society, not for the individual organism in isolation from other individual organisms.

Mind arises in the social process only when that process as a whole enters into, or is present in, the experience of any one of the given individuals involved in that process. When this occurs the individual becomes self-conscious and has a mind; he becomes aware of his relations to that process as a whole, and to the other individuals participating in it with him; he becomes aware of that process as modified by the reactions and interactions of the individuals— including himself—who are carrying it on. The evolutionary appearance of mind or intelligence takes place when the whole social process of experience and behavior is brought within the experience of any one of the separate individuals implicated therein and when the individual's adjustment to the process is modified and refined by the awareness or consciousness which he thus has of it. It is by means of reflexiveness—the turning-back of the experience of the individual upon himself—that the whole social process is thus brought into the experience of the individuals involved in it; it is by such means, which enable the individual to take the attitude of the other toward himself, that the individual is able consciously to adjust himself to that process, and to modify the resultant of that process in any given social act in terms of his adjustment to it. Reflexiveness, then, is the essential condition, within the social process, for the development of mind.

# PART II

# PARADIGM DEVELOPMENT

## 1950s–1970s

# INTRODUCTION

The formative stage of language and culture studies, approximately the first half of the twentieth century, was dominated by two concerns in linguistic anthropology: (1) the description of Native American languages; and (2) the Sapir-Whorf hypothesis, as discussed in Part I. The period of paradigm development, approximately 1950–1980, witnessed a continuation, though diminished, of those interests. In fact, the deep-seated interest in Sapir's and Whorf's views on language and culture culminated, temporarily, in a conference in 1954, attended by the leading linguistic anthropologists of the time. The hypothesis was examined and discussed in considerable detail at the conference, and the proceedings were published in 1956. Harry Hoijer's contributed paper, a summary and analysis of the hypothesis, is included here as the lead article in Part II.

After the conference and publication, the Sapir-Whorf hypothesis ceased to assume center stage in language and culture, although it did not disappear altogether. The basic idea of the Sapir-Whorf hypothesis—that language patterns can reveal patterns of culture—was maintained and applied in new, innovative ways. The use of language as an interpretative model for culture assumed even greater importance. In the early 1960s, two developments in particular represented advances in our understanding of the relationship of language and culture. One was initially called "ethnoscience," and the other eventually led to a paradigm of inquiry termed "structural anthropology."

Ethnoscience grew out of a scholarly movement to improve ethnography, the description of a society's culture through direct experience in a field research setting. The model for the "new ethnography," another term for ethnoscience, was structural linguistics. The comparatively sharp and clear methods which field linguists used to describe languages were borrowed and applied to ethnography, as a way of making ethnography more precise, reliable, and, in general, scientific. The new ethnography required more in-depth and detailed investigation of specific domains, such as kinship and ethnobiology, at the expense of a broader but more superficial description of a society. The general idea in ethnoscience was to identify a domain, collect the set of names or terms for the objects included in the domain (all of the kinship terms, for example), and then subject the terms to a feature or component analysis. The organization of underlying features thus revealed was taken to be a reflection of the knowledge that native practitioners of the culture possessed in the particular domain.

The methods and aims of the new ethnography are further spelled out in Charles Frake's article, "The Ethnographic Study of Cognitive Systems," reprinted here. A number of other definitive, paradigm-setting articles can be found in Tyler (1969); later collections present further developments, to be found in Spradley (1972), Casson (1981), and Dougherty (1985).

The theme of the unconscious nature of linguistic structure and the potential of phenomenon for uncovering deeper realms of meaning can also be found in the early writings of the renowned French anthropologist, Claude Lévi-Strauss. As can be seen in his article reprinted here, "Language and the Analysis of Social Laws," he applies insights and methods from linguistics to the study of social behavior. His final aim, however, is somewhat different from that of the language and culture scholars. Lévi-Strauss' concern is with the fundamental activity and organization of the human intellect. Invariant properties of language, though useful devices for analyzing social life, are valuable first and foremost as manifestations of a more basic structure of the human mind. In his words, ". . . the question may be raised whether the different aspects of social life (including even art and religion) can not only be studied by the methods, and with the help of concepts similar to those employed in linguistics, but also whether they do not constitute phenomena whose inmost nature is the same as that of language" (1963:67). That suggestion is similar to Boas' earlier formulation, only it is broader in scope. Whereas Boas and his students proposed that language as part of culture provided an analytical window into culture, Lévi-Strauss proposed that the structure of the human mind was responsible for the underlying similarity of social behavior, language, and cognition (or in American terms, culture).

Lévi-Strauss' structural approach to social life, language, and mind, was applied constructively to the cross-societal study of kinship and social exchange (1949). Further theoretical views can be found in a collection of his works published in 1963, from which the article reprinted here was taken.

The continuation of ethnoscience in the late 1960s and into the 1970s produced long-lasting results in two areas of research, color terms and ethnobiology. Brent Berlin's classic article, "Speculations on the Growth of Ethnobotanical Nomenclature," is reprinted here. Berlin and other ethnobiologists had begun to accumulate information of the classification and naming of plants by individuals in traditional society substantial enough to detect systematic patterns. Based on the data available at the time, Berlin proposed that the ethnobiological vocabulary of all languages can be described by six ethnobiological categories: generic, life form, specific, intermediate, varietal, and unique beginner. The uniformity and consistency across diverse societies from different areas of the world were far greater than had been expected. Moreover, the order of appearance, evolutionarily, of those in the lexicon of a society's language tends to correspond with the general degree of sociocultural and technological development. The orderly appearance of categories and nomenclature strongly suggests a common human perception and appreciation of the natural world. Language, categories, and mind appear to be closely related in that arena of interaction.

The "speculations" on ethnobiological categories and nomenclature were in fact based on substantial lexical evidence from a number of societies. They were speculative primarily in the sense that information from a larger number of societies was essential for a full testing of the hypotheses. Since the publication of the original article in 1972, a number of other ethnobiological studies have been completed, expanding the data base and in general confirming the results of the 1972 study. A detailed review, discussion, and summary of ethnobiological classification and nomenclature can be found in Berlin (1992).

The final article in the section of Part II on "Language, Culture, and Thought" is Michael Silverstein's "Shifters, Linguistic Categories, and Cultural Description," which was published in 1976. It could have as easily served as the final article in the second section, "Language, Culture, and Society." Moreover, it could have also served as the introductory article for either of the two sections of Part III, which includes publications on recent developments deriving from the development of paradigms in the middle decades of this century. In other words, the article is pivotal in the study of language, culture, and society and of far-reaching significance. What the article accomplishes is an initial clarification of the actual ways in which language, culture, and society can be related, not just a discussion of the potential that the study of language has for understanding culture and social behavior. The article was indeed "paradigm development," in that it redefined the nature of the relational territory, thereby making possible a major advancement in the understanding of this highly complex area.

Silverstein's article must be read in full in order for one to appreciate the complexity of the argument, but a summary can be attempted here. The essential first step in understanding how language and culture are related was to recognize that the framework for interpretation could not be the classical linguistic one. The default framework in linguistics has been the function of reference. Lexical items, linguistic categories, and grammar are typically viewed and analyzed in terms of how they serve propositionally to point to, to designate, objects in the environment. Language cannot, however, be limited to that one function; by its very nature it is multifunctional. Although language as reference is one type of language-culture relationship, it is at once highly formulated and thus highly restricted, far more than is the case for most other types of relationships. Silverstein demonstrated those points by showing that some highly codified, grammaticalized parts of speech cannot be explained and understood solely in relation to reference. Verb tense is one example, where tense locates speech in relation to another time and place, that is, to another context. Past tense, for instance, places a proposition in relation to a preceding context; it *shifts* the proposition to the initial state or action in which it occurred. What Silverstein then does is to show that *shifters* are of a limited number and type and that they are highly fixed morphologically, similar to the argument that reference is highly fixed and formulaic judged in relation to other functions of language. Recognition that shifters are not reducible to simple reference and that they are merely a small sub-set of linguistic devices that link language with culture opens the door for a broad, massive set of interlinkages including the social parameters of social interaction and discourse. Perhaps the "tip of the iceberg" metaphor is not out of place here. Limiting the study of language and culture to only one highly constrained function, referentiality, was to limit oneself to the tip of the iceberg, whereas the bulk of the relationships, rich and complex ones, were to be found in regards to other functions, such as expressing the nature of social relationships between interlocutors.

The central argument presented in the 1976 article has been expanded and refined in a large number of publications by Silverstein and his students. Two especially important publications are the collections of papers edited by Mertz and Parmentier (1985) and by Hickman (1987).

The articles in Section A of Part II primarily address aspects of the relationship between language, culture, and the implications for thought. The articles in Section B of Part II primarily address aspects of the relationship between language and culture as information in society. The focus is on how language is used in society and how language itself is fundamentally social. The lead article by the late Erving Goffman, in fact, addresses first the nature of social interaction as constructive of the social self and thus of society. In the social psychological tradition of George Herbert Mead, Goffman's contributions are especially important for language and culture studies. Descriptions of the social use of language are dependent on an understanding of how social interaction proceeds, in all of its complexity. To take an example from "On Face Work," the speech behavior of a person whose face (an aspect of presentation of self) has been challenged can only be understood adequately if one has a knowledge of the possible alternative courses of action and the social consequences. The speech behavior must be fitted into the interaction structure, both in sequential (syntagmatic) and vertical (paradigmatic) dimensions. An elaboration of the socially organized choices of behavior, both in terms of what behavior can meaningfully follow what behavior (the syntagmatic dimension) and what the choices are at each sequential node (the paradigmatic dimension), provides a framework for comprehending the meaning of the behavioral units and the behavioral episode.

Further examples and elaboration of the social interactional base can be found in Goffman's numerous books. Particularly relevant ones are *Frame Analysis* (1974) and *Forms of Talk* (1981).

"The Ethnography of Speaking," by Dell Hymes, is another pivotal article in the history of language-culture-society studies. The article developed a new perspective on the topic, thereby creating an important new sub-field of inquiry. In the earlier, formative period of language-culture-society, research tended to focus either on language and culture or on language and society, and it also tended to be holistic in the sense that the units were one language and one culture or society. Although important insights into the nature of language and of culture were gained in that approach, the restriction of language to linguistic structure and its function to reference was unnecessarily and excessively limiting. In effect, the culture of a society was treated as a structural blueprint for reference. The much richer, more complex, and more interesting relationship of language to culture in its other functions was rarely considered. Hymes' article was a major first step to remedy that oversight.

Hymes asked two basic questions: (1) what are the speech resources that are available to speakers in a speech community, and (2) how do speakers employ those resources so as to obtain desired results? The objective was to describe, ethnographically, the place and use of language in a speech community, not just in terms of coordinate language and culture structure and referentiality, but in terms of social consequences, aesthetic effects, creative use, and so on. That objective opened up inquiry into language and culture dramatically, and it required traditional methods of research in anthropology, the ethnographic (empirical) description and identification of the types, varieties, and levels of relationships among language, culture, and society.

Especially relevant to our interests here is the importance that social interaction assumes in Hymes' theoretical schema. Efforts to cope with units and concepts such as speech community, speech events, speech acts, and their interrelationships required that social interaction be taken into account. The patterns of relationships that can be discerned among the various components of speech episodes are instantiated in actual social contexts, and accordingly any meaningful analysis must attend to the behavior in context. The interplay of language and culture can only be seen in social behavior embedded in context. Social factors are also of premier importance in another way in Hymes' perspective. Among the major features that structure the functions of speech, such as praise, poetry, persuasion, and so on, are the social characteristics of speakers. Who the speakers and recipients are in speech plays a significant role in what the speech means. If all else in a speech event or episode is held constant except that in one instance the speaker is male and in the other the speaker is female, the meaning of the communication can be fundamentally different. The ethnography of speaking requires that the basic social roles and relationships of speakers in the community be given careful, usually primary, consideration.

Students interested in additional information about Hymes' work in language and culture should consult his *Foundations in Sociolinguistics* (1974). An important collection of articles and essays on the subject, with important observations and overviews by Hymes, was published ten years earlier in 1964.

An illustration of the central place of social relationships and interaction can be seen in John Gumperz' "Linguistic and Social Interaction in Two Communities." In that article, Gumperz examined aspects of linguistic variation in two speech communities, an agricultural Indian village, Khalapur, and a small Norwegian town, Hemnesberget. He found in both cases that speakers' repertoires are compartmentalized and that the partitions follow articulation points in social interaction and the major dimensions of social relationships. The linguistic resources of the speech communities showed various degrees of grammatical overlap, that is, of different but equivalent grammatical structures. Those points of overlap served as the starting point for the allocation of social role, status, and relationship. The social information regarding those relationships, such as "insider" versus "outsider," was encoded in the linguistic form, and the choice of linguistic structure alone transmitted basic social information.

Further illustrations of Gumperz' contributions to sociolinguistics can be found in his book (1982) and in the co-edited work with Dell Hymes (1972).

Susan Ervin-Tripp, in her survey article, "Sociolinguistics," showed that in any speech activity, language structure and choice involve social considerations. She demonstrated that descriptive rules can be written to reflect the organization of language form and social function. Three kinds of rules, in fact, were identified: (1) alternation rules, whereby one linguistic form can be substituted for another (such as "Hi!" versus "Good morning"), with predictable social consequences; (2) sequencing rules, whereby the ordering (and reordering) of units in serial fashion conveys social information (such as ignoring versus answering a direct question); and (3) co-occurrence rules, whereby constraints on class membership are socially based and generated (such as using only informal speech with close friends), thus favoring certain linguistic combinations and preventing others. The variables upon which the rules operate are similar to those identified by Hymes in "The Ethnography of Speaking," namely, topic, message, channel, speech act, and their integration with specifiable linguistic units. Speakers utilize those variables, applying rules and switching codes according to personnel, situations, and speech functions.

Additional publications by Ervin-Tripp can be found in the collection of her publications (1973) and in the co-edited work with Claudia Mitchell-Kernan (1977).

The final paper in Section II, "Words, Utterance, and Activities," by Roy Turner, represents another lineage of research deriving from social philosophy and sociology. The originator of that lineage was John L. Austin, whose book, *How to do Things with Words* (1962), can be taken as the beginning point. Turner's article makes two major points, one borrowed from Austin and the other representative of a line of contemporary sociology. Speech act theory is taken from Austin and his successors (for example, Searle 1969). The central tenet is that languages have specific forms of speech that constitute distinctive acts—hence speech acts—such as promising, denying, greeting, bequeathing, and so on. Those performative verbs, as they are also called, are taken to be especially interesting in that the structure and the method of the act is strictly, and thus clearly, determined. To promise someone is to engage in a behavior that is culturally prescribed and known to all members of the speech community. Turner's proposal is that if an exhaustive list of performative verbs could be determined for a language and society, then a researcher would have a way of reading conversations and having a blueprint, or formula, where the name of the activity would be derivable from the performative verb. Researchers would thus have a formula, of sorts, that would assist in the identification of the structure of verbal interaction. Given the complexity of the relationship between what is spoken and what is available as background, any clarity is to be highly valued. Turner's prescription is designed for that end.

Additional reading on this lineage of inquiry, sometimes called ethnomethodology to emphasize that the interlocutors' methods of interaction is what is sought, can be found in Boden and Zimmerman (1991), Cicourel (1973), Garfinkel (1967), Goodwin (1981), Moerman (1988), Sacks (1992), Sudnow (1972), and Turner (1974). Also for additional reading, but on a much broader scale (spanning the period of paradigm development and reflecting much of the scope of language and culture studies), readers can consult the collections of articles by Bauman and Sherzer (1974), Blount and Sanches (1977), and Sanches and Blount (1975).

## REFERENCES

Austin, John L.
  1962    *How to do Things with Words*. Oxford: Clarendon Press.
Bauman, Richard and Joel Sherzer, eds.
  1974    *Explorations in the Ethnography of Speaking*. Cambridge: Cambridge University Press (second edition, 1992).
Berlin, Brent
  1992    *Ethnobiological Classification: Principles of Categorization of Plants and Animals in Traditional Societies*. Princeton: Princeton University Press.
Blount, Ben G. and Mary Sanches, eds.
  1977    *Sociocultural Dimensions of Language Change*. New York: Academic Press.
Boden, Deirdre and Don H. Zimmerman, eds.
  1991    *Talk and Social Structure: Studies in Ethnomethodology and Conversation Analysis*. Oxford: Polity Press.
Casson, Ronald W., ed.
  1981    *Language, Culture, and Cognition: Anthropological Perspectives*. New York: Macmillan.
Cicourel, Aaron
  1973    *Cognitive Sociology: Language and Meaning in Social Interaction*. Harmondsworth: Penguin.
Dougherty, Janet W. D., ed.
  1985    *Directions in Cognitive Anthropology*. Urbana: University of Illinois Press.

Ervin-Tripp, Susan
1973   *Language Acquisition and Communicative Choice.* Selected and Introduced by A. Dil. Stanford: Stanford University Press.
Ervin-Tripp, Susan and Claudia Mitchell-Kernan, eds.
1977   *Child Discourse.* New York: Academic Press.
Garfinkel, Harold
1967   *Studies in Ethnomethodology.* Englewood Cliffs, NJ: Prentice-Hall.
Goffman, Erving
1974   *Frame Analysis.* New York: Harper & Row.
1981   *Forms of Talk.* Philadelphia: University of Pennsylvania Press.
Goodwin, Charles
1981   *Conversational Organization.* New York: Academic Press.
Gumperz, John J.
1982   Discourse *Strategies.* Cambridge: Cambridge University Press.
Gumperz, John J. and Dell H. Hymes, eds.
1972   *Directions in Sociolinguistics: The Ethnography of Communication.* New York: Holt, Rinehart, & Winston.
Hickman, Maya, ed.
1987   *Social and Functional Approaches to Language and Thought.* Orlando: Academic Press.
Hoijer, Harry, ed.
1956   *Language in Culture: Conference on the Inter-relations of Language and Other Aspects of Culture.* Chicago: University of Chicago Press.
Hymes, Dell H.
1974   *Foundations in Sociolinguistics: An Ethnographic Approach.* Philadelphia: University of Pennsylvania Press.
Hymes, Dell H., ed.
1964   *Language, Culture, and Society: A Reader in Linguistics and Anthropology.* New York: Harper and Row.
Lévi-Strauss, Claude
1949   *Les Structures Elémentaires de la Parenté.* Paris.
1963   *Structural Anthropology.* New York: Basic Books.
Mertz, Elizabeth and Richard J. Parmentier, eds.
1985   *Semiotic Mediation: Sociocultural and Psychological Perspectives.* Orlando: Academic Press.
Moerman, Michael
1988   *Talking Culture: Ethnography and Conversational Analysis.* Philadelphia: University of Pennsylvania Press.
Sacks, Harvey
1992   *Lectures on Conversation.* Volumes I and II. Oxford/Cambridge: Blackwell Publishers.
Sanches, Mary and Ben G. Blount, eds.
1975   *Sociocultural Dimensions of Language Use.* New York: Academic Press.
Searle, John
1969   *Speech Acts: An essay in the Philosophy of Language.* Cambridge: Cambridge University Press.
Spradley, James P., ed.
1972   *Culture and Cognition: Rules, Maps, and Plans.* San Francisco: Chandler.

Sudnow, David, ed.
1972    *Studies in Social Interaction.* New York: Free Press.
Turner, Roy, ed.
1974    *Ethnomethodology.* Baltimore: Penguin.
Tyler, Stephen A., ed.
1969    *Cognitive Anthropology.* New York: Holt, Rinehart, Winston.

# The Sapir-Whorf Hypothesis

## Harry Hoijer

The Sapir-Whorf hypothesis appears to have had its initial formulation in the following two paragraphs, taken from an article of Sapir's, first published in 1929.

> Language is a guide to "social reality." Though language is not ordinarily thought of as of essential interest to the students of social science, it powerfully conditions all our thinking about social problems and processes. Human beings do not live in the objective world alone, nor alone in the world of social activity as ordinarily understood, but are very much at the mercy of the particular language which has become the medium of expression for their society. It is quite an illusion to imagine that one adjusts to reality essentially without the use of language and that language is merely an incidental means of solving specific problems of communication or reflection. The fact of the matter is that the "real world" is to a large extent unconsciously built up on the language habits of the group. No two languages are ever sufficiently similar to be considered as representing the same social reality. The worlds in which different societies live are distinct worlds, not merely the same world with different labels attached.
>
> The understanding of a simple poem, for instance, involves not merely an understanding of the single words in their average significance, but a full comprehension of the whole life of the community as it is mirrored in the words, or as it is suggested by their overtones. Even comparatively simple acts of perception are very much more at the mercy of the social patterns called words than we might suppose. If one draws some dozen lines, for instance, of different shapes, one perceives them as divisible into such categories as "straight," "crooked," "curved," "zigzag" because of the classificatory suggestiveness of the linguistic terms themselves. We see and hear and otherwise experience very largely as we do because the language habits of our community predispose certain choices of interpretation" (In Mandelbaum 1949: 162).

The notion of language as a "guide to social reality" is not entirely original with Sapir. Somewhat similar ideas, though far less adequately stated, may be found in Boas' writings, at least as early as 1911. Thus we find in Boas' introduction to the *Handbook of American Indian Languages* a number of provocative passages on this theme, to wit:

> It seems, however, that a theoretical study of Indian languages is not less important than a practical knowledge of them; that the purely linguistic inquiry is

**113**

part and parcel of a thorough investigation of the psychology of the peoples of the world (p. 63).

...language seems to be one of the most instructive fields of inquiry in an investigation of the formation of the fundamental ethnic ideas. The great advantage that linguistics offer in this respect is the fact that, on the whole, the categories which are formed always remain unconscious, and that for this reason the processes which lead to their formation can be followed without the misleading and disturbing factors of secondary explanation, which are so common in ethnology, so much so that they generally obscure the real history of the development of ideas entirely (pp. 70–71).

As Greenberg points out . . ., approaches somewhat similar to the Sapir-Whorf hypothesis may be found among European writers, and are "particularly strong in the German-speaking world," where they can be "traced back at least as far as Herder in the latter part of the eighteenth century" (p. xx). Alexander von Humboldt is mentioned as having a profound influence in this development, together with more modern scholars like Ernst Cassirer, Johann Leo Weisgerber, and Jost Trier. To these we should probably add Charles Bally, Marcel Granet, Claude Lévi-Strauss, Jean Piaget, Alf Sommerfelt, and L. Wittgenstein.

The Sapir-Whorf hypothesis, however, gains especial significance by virtue of the fact that both these scholars had a major interest in American Indian languages, idioms far removed from any in the Indo-European family and so ideally suited to contrastive studies. It is in the attempt properly to interpret the grammatical categories of an American Indian language, Hopi, that Whorf best illustrates his principle of linguistic relativity, the notion that "users of markedly different grammars are pointed by their grammars toward different types of observations and different evaluations of externally similar acts of observation, and hence are not equivalent as observers but must arrive at somewhat different views of the world" (1952:11).

The purpose of this paper is threefold: (1) to review and clarify the Sapir-Whorf hypothesis, (2) to illustrate and perhaps add to it by reference to my own work on the Navaho language, and (3) to propose a series of studies intended to test and further develop the hypothesis.

The central idea of the Sapir-Whorf hypothesis is that language functions, not simply as a device for reporting experience, but also, and more significantly, as a way of defining experience for its speakers. Sapir says (1931:578), for example:

Language is not merely a more or less systematic inventory of the various items of experience which seem relevant to the individual, as is so often naïvely assumed, but is also a self-contained, creative symbolic organization, which not only refers to experience largely acquired without its help but actually defines experience for us by reason of its formal completeness and because of our unconscious projection of its implicit expectations into the field of experience. In this respect language is very much like a mathematical system which, also, records experience in the truest sense of the word, only in its crudest beginnings, but, as time goes on, becomes elaborated into a self-contained conceptual system which previsages all possible experience in accordance with certain accepted formal limitations. . . . [Meanings are] not so much discovered in experience as imposed upon it, because of the tyrannical hold that linguistic form has upon our orientation in the world.

Whorf develops the same thesis when he says (1952:5):

. . . that the linguistic system (in other words, the grammar) of each language is not merely a reproducing instrument for voicing ideas but rather is itself the shaper of ideas, the program and guide for the individual's mental activity, for his analysis of impressions, for his synthesis of his mental stock in trade. . . . We dissect nature along lines laid down by our native languages. The categories and types that we isolate from the world of phenomena we do not find there because they stare every observer in the face; on the contrary, the world is presented in a kaleidoscopic flux of impressions which has to be organized by our minds— and this means largely by the linguistic systems in our minds.

It is evident from these statements, if they are valid, that language plays a large and significant role in the totality of culture. Far from being simply a technique of communication, it is itself a way of directing the perceptions of its speakers and it provides for them habitual modes of analyzing experience into significant categories. And to the extent that languages differ markedly from each other, so should we expect to find significant and formidable barriers to cross-cultural communication and understanding. These barriers take on even greater importance when it is realized that "the phenomena of a language are to its own speakers largely of a background character and so are outside the critical consciousness and control of the speaker" (Whorf 1952:4).

It is, however, easy to exaggerate linguistic differences of this nature and the consequent barriers to intercultural understanding. No culture is wholly isolated, self-contained, and unique. There are important resemblances between all known cultures—resemblances that stem in part from diffusion (itself an evidence of successful intercultural communication) and in part from the fact that all cultures are built around biological, psychological, and social characteristics common to all mankind. The languages of human beings do not so much determine the perceptual and other faculties of their speakers vis-à-vis experience as they influence and direct these faculties into prescribed channels. Intercultural communication, however wide the difference between cultures may be, is not impossible. It is simply more or less difficult, depending on the degree of difference between the cultures concerned.

Some measure of these difficulties is encountered in the process of translating from one language into another that is divergent and unrelated. Each language has its own peculiar and favorite devices, lexical and grammatical, which are employed in the reporting, analysis, and categorizing of experience. To translate from English into Navaho, or vice versa, frequently involves much circumlocution, since what is easy to express in one language, by virtue of its lexical and grammatical techniques, is often difficult to phrase in the other. A simple illustration is found when we try to translate the English phrases *his horse* and *his horses* into Navaho, which not only lacks a plural category for nouns (Navaho łį·ʔ translates equally English *horse* and *horses*) but lacks as well the English distinction between *his, her, its,* and *their* (Navaho bilį́·ʔ may be translated, according to context, *his horse* or *horses, her horse* or *horses, its horse* or *horses,* and *their horse* or *horses*). These Navaho forms łį·ʔ, bilį́·ʔ make difficulties in English also because Navaho makes a distinction between a third person (the bì- in bilį́·ʔ) psychologically close to the speaker (e.g., *his* [that is, a Navaho's] *horse*) as opposed to a third person (the hà- of hàlį́·ʔ) psychologically remote (e.g., *his* [that is, a non-Navaho's] *horse*).

Differences of this order, which reflect a people's habitual and favorite modes of reporting, analyzing, and categorizing experience, form the essential data of the Sapir-Whorf hypothesis. According to Whorf (1952:27), it is in these "constant ways of arranging data and its most ordinary every-day analysis of phenomena that we need to recognize the influence . . . [language] has on other activities, cultural and personal."

The Sapir-Whorf hypothesis, it is evident, includes in language both its structural and its semantic aspects. These are held to be inseparable, though it is obvious that we can and do study each more or less independently of the other. The structural aspect of language, which is that most easily analyzed and described, includes its phonology, morphology, and syntax, the numerous but limited frames into which utterances are cast. The semantic aspect consists of a self-contained system of meanings, inextricably bound to the structure but much more difficult to analyze and describe. Meanings, to reiterate, are not in actual fact separable from structure, nor are they, as some have maintained (notably Voegelin 1949:36), to be equated to the nonlinguistic culture. Our interest lies, not in questions such as "What does this form, or form class, mean?" but, instead, in the question, "In what manner does a language organize, through its structural semantic system, the world of experience in which its speakers live?" The advantage of this approach to the problem of meaning is clear. As Bloomfield long ago pointed out, it appears quite impossible, short of omniscience, to determine precisely the meaning of any single form or form class in a language. But it should be possible to determine the limits of any self-contained structural-semantic system and the ways in which it previsages the experiences of its users.

To illustrate this procedure in brief, let us turn again to Navaho and one of the ways in which it differs from English. The Navaho color vocabulary includes, among others, five terms: łigài, diłxił, łižin, łčį́·ʔ, and dò·łiž, to be taken as one way of categorizing certain color impressions. łigài is roughly equivalent to English *white,* diłxił and łižin to English *black,* łčį́·ʔ to English *red,* and dò·łiž to English *blue* or *green.* Clearly, then, the Navaho five-point system is not the same as English white-black-red-blue-green, which also has five categories. English *black* is divided into two categories in Navaho (diłxił and ɬižin), while Navaho has but one category (dò·ɬìž) for the English *blue* and *green*. We do not, it should be noted, claim either that English speakers cannot perceive the difference between the two "blacks" of Navaho, or that Navaho speakers are unable to differentiate "blue" and "green." The difference between the two systems lies simply in the color categories recognized in ordinary speech, that is, in the ordinary everyday ways in which speakers of English and Navaho analyze color phenomena.

Every language is made up of a large number of such structural-semantic patterns, some of which pertain to lexical sets, as in the case of the Navaho and English color terms, and others of which pertain to sets of grammatical categories, such as the distinction between the singular and plural noun in English. A monolingual speaker, if his reports are to be understood by others in his speech community, is bound to use this apparatus, with all its implications for the analysis and categorization of experience, though he may of course quite often select from a number of alternative expressions in making his report. To quote Sapir again (Mandelbaum 1949:10–11):

> ...as our scientific experience grows we must learn to fight the implications of language. "The grass waves in the wind" is shown by its linguistic form to be a member of the same relational class of experiences as "The man works in the house." As an interim solution of the problem of expressing the experience referred to in this sentence it is clear that the language has proved useful, for it has made significant use of certain symbols of conceptual relation, such as agency and location. If we feel the sentence to be poetic or metaphorical, it is largely because other more complex types of experience with their appropriate symbolisms of reference enable us to reinterpret the situation and to say, for instance, "The grass is waved by the wind" or "The wind causes the grass to wave." The point is that no matter how sophisticated our modes of interpretation become, we never really get beyond the projection and continuous transfer of relations suggested by the forms of our speech. ... Language is at one and the same time helping and retarding us in our exploration of experience, and the details of these processes of help and hindrance are deposited in the subtler meanings of different cultures.

It does not necessarily follow that all the structural-semantic patterns of a language are equally important to its speakers in their observation, analysis, and categorizing of experience. In describing a language, we seek to uncover all its structural-semantic patterns, even though many of these exist more as potentialities of the system than in actual usage. For ethnolinguistic analysis we need to know, not only that a particular linguistic pattern exists, but also how frequently it occurs in everyday speech. We also need to know something of the degree of complexity of the pattern of expression. There are numerous patterns of speech, particularly among peoples who have well-developed arts of oratory and writing, that are little used by any except specialists in these pursuits. The patterns of speech significant to ethnoliguistic research fall clearly into the category of habitual, frequently used, and relatively simple structural-semantic devices; those, in short, which are common to the adult speech community as a whole, and are used by its members with the greatest ease.

Not all the structural patterns of the common speech have the same degree of semantic importance. In English, for example, it is not difficult to ascertain the semantic correlates of the structural distinction between singular and plural nouns; in most cases this is simply a division into the categories "one" versus "more than one." Similarly, the gender distinction of the English third-person singular pronouns, as between "he," "she," and "it," correlates fairly frequently with the recognition of personality and sex.

In contrast to these, there are structural patterns like that which, in many Indo-European languages, divides nouns into three great classes: masculine, feminine, and neuter. This structural pattern has no discernible semantic correlate; we do not confuse the grammatical terms "masculine," "feminine," and "neuter" with the biological distinctions among male, female, and neuter. Whatever the semantic implications of this structural pattern may have been in origin, and this remains undetermined, it is now quite apparent that the pattern survives only as a grammatical device, important in that function but lacking in semantic value. And it is perhaps significant that the pattern is an old one, going back to the earliest history of the Indo-European languages and, moreover, that it has disappeared almost completely in some of the modern languages of this family, notably, of course, in English.

In ethnolinguistic research, then, it is necessary to concentrate on those structural patterns of a language which have definable semantic correlates, and to omit those, like the Indo-European gender system, which survive only in a purely grammatical function. The assumption behind this procedure is as follows: every language includes a number of active structural-semantic categories, lexical and grammatical, which by virtue of their active status serve a function in the everyday (nonscientific) analysis and categorizing of experience. It is the study of these categories, distinctive when taken as a whole for each language, that yields, or may yield, significant information concerning the thought world of the speakers of the language.

One further point requires emphasis. Neither Sapir nor Whorf attempted to draw inferences as to the thought world of a people simply from the fact of the presence or absence of specific grammatical categories (e.g., tense, gender, number) in a given language. To quote Whorf (1952:44) on this point: the concepts of time and matter which he reports for the Hopi

> do not depend so much upon any one system (e.g., tense, or nouns) within the grammar as upon the ways of analyzing and reporting experience which have become fixed in the language as integrated "fashions of speaking" and which cut across the typical grammatical classifications, so that such a "fashion" may include lexical, morphological, syntactic, and otherwise systematically diverse means coordinated in a certain frame of consistency.

To summarize, ethnolinguistic research requires the investigator to perform, it seems to me, the following steps:

1. To determine the structural patterns of a language (that is, its grammar) as completely as possible. Such determination should include not only a statement of the modes of utterance but as well a careful indication of the frequency of occurrence of these modes, lexical and grammatical, in the common speech.

2. To determine, as accurately as possible, the semantic patterns, if any, that attach to structural patterns. This is a task neglected by most structural linguists who, as is repeatedly mentioned in the discussions that follow, are frequently content simply to label rather than to define both lexical units and grammatical categories. In this connection it is important to emphasize that the analyst must not be taken in by his own labels; he is to discover, where possible, just how the form, or form class, or grammatical category functions in the utterances available to him.

3. To distinguish between structural categories that are active in the language, and therefore have definable semantic correlates, and those which are not. It goes without saying that such distinction requires a profound knowledge of the language, and possibly even the ability to speak and understand it well. Mark Twain's amusing translation of a German folktale into English, where he regularly translates the gender of German nouns by the English forms "he," "she," and "it," illustrates, though in caricature, the pitfalls of labeling the grammatical categories of one language (in this case, German gender) by terms belonging to an active structural-semantic pattern in another.

4. To examine and compare the active structural-semantic patterns of the language and draw from them the fashions of speaking there evidenced. As in Whorf's analysis of Hopi (1952:25–45), while clues to a fashion of speaking may be discovered in a particular grammatical category or set of lexical items, its validity and importance cannot be determined until its range and scope within the language as a whole is also known. Whorf's conclusions as to the nature of the concept of time among speakers of English rest not alone on the tense distinctions of the English verb (mixed as these are with many other and diverse distinctions of voice, mode, and aspect) but as well on techniques of numeration, the treatment of nouns denoting physical quantity and phases of cycles, and a host of other terms and locutions relating to time. He says (1952:33):

> The three-tense system of SAE verbs colors all our thinking about time. This system is amalgamated with that larger scheme of objectification of the subjective experience of duration already noted in other patterns—in the binomial formula applicable to nouns is general, in temporal nouns, in plurality and numeration.

5. Taken together, the fashions of speaking found in a language comprise a partial description of the thought world of its speakers. But by the term "thought world" Whorf means

> more than simply language, i.e., than the linguistic patterns themselves. [He includes]...all the analogical and suggestive value of the patterns...and all the

give-and-take between language and the culture as a whole, wherein is a vast amount that is not linguistic yet shows the shaping influence of language. In brief, this "thought world" is the microcosm that each man carries about within himself, by which he measures and understands what he can of the macrocosm [1952: 36].

It follows then that the thought world, as derived from ethnolinguistic studies, is found reflected as well, though perhaps not as fully, in other aspects of the culture. It is here that we may search for connections between language and the rest of culture. These connections are not direct; we see, instead, in certain patterns of nonlinguistic behavior the same meaningful fashions that are evidenced in the patterns of the language. Whorf summarizes this facet of his researches in a discussion of "Habitual Behavior Features of Hopi Culture and Some Impresses of Linguistic Habit in Western Civilization" (1952: 37–52).

It may be helpful to outline briefly some aspects of Navaho culture, including the language, as illustration of the Sapir-Whorf hypothesis. In particular, I shall describe first some of the basic postulates of Navaho religious behavior and attempt to show how these fit in a frame of consistency with certain fashions of speaking evidenced primarily in the morphological patterns of the Navaho verb.

A review of Navaho religious practices, as described by Washington Matthews, Father Berard Haile, and many others, reveals that the Navaho conceive of themselves as in a particular relationship with the environment— physical, social, and supernatural—in which they live. Navaho man lives in a universe of eternal and unchanging forces with which he attempts to maintain an equilibrium, a kind of balancing of powers. The mere fact of living is, however, likely to disturb this balance and throw it out of gear. Any such disturbance, which may result from failure to observe a set rule of behavior or ritual or from the accidental or deliberate committal of some other fault in ritual or the conduct of daily activities, will, the Navaho believe, be revealed in the illness or unexplained death of an individual, in some other personal misfortune or bad luck to an enterprise, or in some community disaster such as a food shortage or an epidemic. Whereupon, a diviner must be consulted, who determines by ritual means the cause of the disturbance and prescribes, in accordance with this knowledge, the appropriate counteracting religious ceremony or ritual.

The underlying purpose of the curing ceremony is to put the maladjusted individual or the community as a whole back into harmony with the universe. Significantly, this is done, not by the shaman or priest acting upon the individual and changing him, nor by any action, by shaman or priest, designed to alter the forces of the universe. It is done by re-enacting one of a complex series of religious dramas which represent, in highly abstract terms, the events, far back in Navaho history, whereby the culture heroes first established harmony between man and nature and so made the world fit for human occupation. By re-enacting these events, or some portion of them, the present disturbance, by a kind of sympathetic magic, is compensated and harmony between man and universe restored. The ill person then gets well, or the community disaster is alleviated, since these misfortunes were but symptoms of a disturbed relation to nature.

From these numerous and very important patterns of Navaho religious behavior, it seems to me we can abstract a dominant motif belonging to the Navaho thought world. The motif has been well put by Kluckhohn and Leighton, who also illustrate it in many other aspects of Navaho culture. They call it, "Nature is more powerful than man," and amplify this in part by the Navaho premise "that nature will take care of them if they behave as they should and do as she directs" (1946:227–28). In short, to the Navaho, the way to the good life lies not in modifying nature to man's needs or in changing man's nature but rather in discovering the proper relation of nature to man and in maintaining that relationship intact.

Turning now to the Navaho language, let us look at some aspects of the verb structure, illustrated in the following two forms:

nìńtį *you have lain down.*
nìšíńłtį *you have put, laid me down.*

Both these verbs are in the second person of the perfective mode (Hoijer 1946); the ń- marks this inflection. Both also have a prefix nì-, not the same but subtly different in meaning. The nì- of the first means [*movement*] *terminating in a position of rest,* that of the second [*movement*] *ending at a given point.* The second form has the causative prefix ł- and incorporates the first person object, expressed in this form by ši-. The stem -tį, common to both forms, is defined *one animate being moves.*

The theme of the first verb, composed of nì- . . . -tį, means *one animate being moves to a position of rest,* that is, *one animate being lies down.* In the second verb the meaning of the theme, nì- . . . -ł-tį, is *cause movement of one animate being to end at a given point* and so, by extension, *put an animate being down* or *lay an animate being down.*

Note now that the first theme includes in its meaning what in English we should call both the actor and the action; these are not, in Navaho, expressed by separate morphemes. The subject pronoun prefix ń- serves then simply to identify a particular being with the class of possible beings already delimited by the theme. It functions, in short, to individuate one belonging to the class *animate being in motion to a position of rest.* The theme of the second verb, by reason of the causative ł-, includes in its meaning what in English would be called action and goal. Again the pronoun ši-, as a consequence, simply identifies or individuates one of a class of possible beings defined already in the theme itself. It should be emphasized that the forms used here as illustration are in no sense unusual; this is the regular pattern of the Navaho verb, repeated over and over again in my data.

We are now ready to isolate, from this necessarily brief analysis, a possible fashion of speaking peculiar to Navaho. The Navaho speaks of "actors" and "goals" (the terms are inappropriate to Navaho), not as performers of actions or as ones upon whom actions are performed, as in English, but as entities linked to actions already defined in part as pertaining especially to classes of beings. The form which is glossed *you have lain down* is better understood *you [belong to, equal one of] à class of animate beings which has moved to rest.* Similarly the second form, glossed *you have put, laid me down* should read *you, as agent, have set a class of animate beings, to which I belong, in motion to a given point.*

This fashion of speaking, it seems to me, is wholly consistent with the dominant motif we saw in Navaho religious practices. Just as in his religious-curing activities the Navaho sees himself as adjusting to a universe that is given, so in his habits of speaking does he link individuals to actions and movements distinguished, not only as actions and movements, but as well in terms of the entities in action or movement. This division of nature into classes of entity in action or movement is the universe that is given; the behavior of human beings or of any being individuated from the mass is customarily reported by assignment to one or other of these given divisions.

Analyses such as this one, though admittedly incomplete, point up the potential value of the Sapir-Whorf hypothesis in cross-cultural understanding. Further work is obviously needed, on languages and cultures as diverse as can be found, to develop the hypothesis. To this end, I venture to suggest the following study, arising mainly from my own experience, and designed to examine the question: If the thought world implies, as we have said, the existence of significant connections between language and the rest of culture, how are we to account for the fact that peoples very similar in the rest of their culture speak languages that are wholly unrelated, and that closely related languages are frequently spoken by peoples very different in the rest of their culture?

The data for a project centering about this question are already in large part collected; they require only to be completed and analyzed in terms of the Sapir-Whorf hypothesis. The project involves researches on the following cultures, chosen for their similarities and differences in culture area and linguistic affiliations.

1. The Navaho, who share a number of nonlinguistic culture patterns with their Hopi neighbors, speak a language (of the Athapaskan stock) that is not in the least related to Hopi (of the Shoshonean stock). There is already a great deal of linguistic and other cultural data on both these groups, though much is as yet unpublished. A Navaho grammar is now in preparation, and studies of Navaho nonlinguistic culture, published and in preparation, are numerous and detailed. For Hopi there is perhaps less published linguistic material but a considerable amount of data on the rest of the culture. A beginning has also been made on the characterization of the Hopi thought world; Whorf's Hopi studies are the most complete of his works (see especially 1952: 25–45).

Preliminary comparisons indicate that the Hopi and Navaho thought worlds are very different, despite the similarities between the two groups in certain overt cultural patterns. It should be kept in mind, however, that the likeness of Navaho to Hopi culture has probably been exaggerated; most of the similarities that led Wissler and others to put them into the same culture area are indeed superficial.

2. The Hopi and the Hopi-Tewa (the pueblo of Hano) offer a far better contrast. Here we find two peoples who, already sharing a general Puebloan culture, have lived in close association on First Mesa since about 1700. Their languages, however, are very divergent; the language of Hano is of the Tewan family and has its closest affiliations to the Rio Grande pueblos farther east. Data on Hano nonlinguistic culture have recently been collected by E. P. Dozier, who is now preparing them for publication. Unfortunately, there is as yet little work on the Tewan languages, though a beginning has been made on the Santa Clara dialect. It is interesting that the differences between Santa Clara Tewa, spoken in the Rio Grande region, and the Tewa of Hano are minor.

A study of one or more of the Rio Grande Tewa-speaking pueblos should be included in this project. In this comparison between Hopi, Hano, and the Tewa speakers of the Rio Grande, there are unusual possibilities. Some of the questions that now appear important are: How wide are the differences between the Hopi culture of First Mesa, that of the Hano, and that of the Rio Grande Tewa? To what extent have the Hano been acculturated to the Hopi? Is there a greater similarity between the Hopi and the Hano thought worlds than between those of the Hano and the Rio Grande Tewa? Since the move of the Hano people to First Mesa can be dated with some precision, it is possible in this project to gain some indication of the extent to which a thought world may change relative to changes in the rest of the culture.

3. The Hupa should be studied and contrasted with the Navaho. Here is an instance where two languages are indubitably and closely related; both Hupa and Navaho are of the Athapaskan stock. The nonlinguistic cultures, however, are widely divergent. Hupa has a northern California culture, very different from that of the Southwestern Navaho. Field data on the Hupa language are complete; the material is now being prepared for publication. Much material on Hupa nonlinguistic culture is already published and, more is in preparation.

4. A final phase of this project might involve a contrast of the Hopi with the Southern Paiute. The languages are related (both belong to the Shoshonean stock), but the nonlinguistic cultures offer the same order of difference as exists between the Navaho and the Hupa. There is much useful data on the Southern Paiute language, published by Sapir some years ago, and some published material on their nonlinguistic culture. It is probable, however, that more data may be needed.

It may be useful, in conclusion, to speculate a bit on the possible results of the project outlined above. The following quotation (Hoijer 1953:567) is relevant.

If language and culture have been regarded by some as distinct variables. . . it is perhaps because (1) they define language too narrowly and (2) they limit culture (especially in establishing culture areas) to its more formal and explicit features, those which are most subject to borrowing and change.

It is quite possible that the features of a language (largely phonemic) by means of which we link it to others in a stock or family are among the least important when we seek to connect it to the rest of culture. The fashions of speaking that Whorf finds so important to habitual behavior and thought are, after all, derived from the lexical, morphological, and syntactic patterns of a language, and these, in turn, are arrangements of phonemic materials. Two or more languages, then, may well have their phonemic materials from the same historical source and yet develop, under the stimulus of diverse microcosms, quite different fashions of speech. In short, the fact that languages belong to a common stock does not prove that they have the same fashions of speaking; such proof, if it is forthcoming at all, must be demonstrated empirically.

The cultures included in the same culture areas, on the other hand, tend to resemble each other only in discrete cultural features, those which are easily diffused, and not necessarily in the ways in which these features are combined into fashions of behaving or in the basic premises to which such fashions of behaving may point.

## REFERENCES

Boas, Franz, ed. "Introduction," *Handbook of American Indian Languages,* Part 1. Washington, D.C.: Smithsonian Institution, 1911.

Hoijer, Harry. "The Apachean Verb, Part III: The Prefixes for Mode and Tense," *International Journal of American Linguistics* 12 (1946): 1–13.

————. "The Relation of Language to Culture." In *Anthropology Today,* ed. A. L. Kroeber et al., pp. 554–73. Chicago: University of Chicago Press, 1953.

Kluckhohn, Clyde and Dorothea Leighton. *The Navaho.* Cambridge: Harvard University Press, 1946.

Mandelbaum, David G., ed. *Selected Writings of Edward Sapir.* Berkeley and Los Angeles: University of California Press, 1949.

Sapir, Edward. "Conceptual Categories in Primitive Languages," *Science* 74 (1931): 578.

Voegelin, C. F. "Linguistics without Meaning and Culture without Words," *Word* 5 (1949): 36–42.

Whorf, Benjamin L. *Collected Papers on Metalinguistics.* Washington, D.C.: Department of State, Foreign Service Institute, 1952.

# The Ethnographic Study of Cognitive Systems[1]

Charles O. Frake

## WORDS FOR THINGS

A relatively simple task commonly performed by ethnographers is that of getting names for things. The ethnographer typically performs this task by pointing to or holding up the apparent constituent objects of an event he is describing, eliciting the native names for the objects, and then matching each native name with the investigator's own word for the object. The logic of the operation is: if the informant calls object X a *mbubu* and I call object X a *rock*, then *mbubu* means *rock*. In this way are compiled the ordinary ethnobotanical monographs with their lists of matched native and scientific names for plant specimens. This operation probably also accounts for a good share of the native names parenthetically inserted in so many monograph texts: "Among the grasses (*sigbet*) whose grains (*bunga nen*) are used for beads (*bitekel*) none is more highly prized than Job's tears (*glias*)." Unless the reader is a comparative linguist of the languages concerned, he may well ask what interest these parenthetical insertions contain other than demonstrating that the ethnographer has discharged a minimal obligation toward collecting linguistic data. This procedure for obtaining words for things, as well as the "so-what" response it so often evokes, assumes the objective identifiability of discrete "things" apart from a particular culture. It construes the name-getting task as one of simply matching verbal labels for "things" in two languages. Accordingly, the "problem-oriented" anthropologist, with a broad, cross-cultural perspective, may disclaim any interest in these labels; all that concerns him is the presence or absence of a particular "thing" in a given culture.

If, however, instead of "getting words for things," we redefine the task as one of finding the "things" that go with the words, the eliciting of terminologies acquires a more general interest. In actuality not even the most concrete, objectively apparent physical object can be identified apart from some culturally defined system of concepts (Boas 1911:24–25; Bruner et al. 1956; Goodenough 1957). An ethnographer should strive to define objects[2] according

---

[1] In preparing this paper I have especially benefited from suggestions by Harold C. Conklin, Thomas Gladwin, Volney Stefflre, and William C. Sturtevant.

[2] In this paper the term *object* designates anything construed as a member of a category (Bruner et al. 1956:231), whether perceptible or not.

125

to the conceptual system of the people he is studying. Let me suggest, then, that one look upon the task of getting names for things not as an exercise in linguistic recording, but as a way of finding out what are in fact the "things" in the environment of the people being studied. This paper consists of some suggestions toward the formulation of an operationally-explicit methodology for discerning how people construe their world of experience from the way they talk about it. Specifically these suggestions concern the analysis of terminological systems in a way which reveals the conceptual principles that generate them.

In a few fields, notably in kinship studies, anthropologists have already successfully pushed an interest in terminological systems beyond a matching of translation labels. Since Morgan's day no competent student of kinship has looked upon his task as one of simply finding a tribe's words for "uncle," "nephew," or "cousin." The recognition that the denotative range of kinship categories must be determined empirically in each case, that the categories form a system, and that the semantic contrasts underlying the system are amenable to formal analysis, has imparted to kinship studies a methodological rigor and theoretical productivity rare among ethnographic endeavors. Yet all peoples are vitally concerned with kinds of phenomena other than genealogical relations; consequently there is no reason why the study of a people's concepts of these other phenomena should not offer a theoretical interest comparable to that of kinship studies.

Even with reference to quite obvious kinds of material objects, it has long been noted that many people do not see "things" quite the way we do. However, anthropologists in spite of their now well-established psychological interests have notably ignored the cognition of their subjects. Consequently other investigators still rely on stock anecdotes of "primitive thinking" handed down by explorers, philologists, and psychologists since the nineteenth century (Brown 1958:256; Hill 1952; Jespersen 1934:429; Ullman 1957:95, 308). Commonly these anecdotes have been cited as examples of early stages in the evolution of human thought—which, depending on the anecdote selected, may be either from blindly concrete to profoundly abstract or from hopelessly vague to scientifically precise. A typical citation, purporting to illustrate the primitive's deficient abstractive ability, concerns a Brazilian Indian tribe which allegedly has no word for "parrot" but only words for "kinds of parrots" (Jespersen 1934:429 ff.). The people of such a tribe undoubtedly classify the birds of their environment in some fashion; certainly they do not bestow a unique personal name on each individual bird specimen they encounter. Classification means that individual bird specimens must be matched against the defining attributes of conceptual categories and thereby judged to be equivalent for certain purposes to some other specimens but different from still others. Since no two birds are alike in every discernable feature, any grouping into sets implies a selection of only a limited number of features as significant for contrasting kinds of bird. A person learns which features are significant from his fellows as part of his cultural equipment. He does not receive this information from the birds. Consequently there is no necessary reason that a Brazilian Indian should heed those particular attributes which, for the English-speaker, make equivalent all the diverse individual organisms he labels "parrots." Some of this Indian's categories may seem quite specific, and others quite general, when compared to our grouping of the same specimens. But learning that it takes the Indian many words to name the objects we happen to group together in one set is trivial information compared to knowing how the Indian himself groups these objects and which attributes he selects as dimensions to generate a taxonomy of avifauna. With the latter knowledge we learn what these people regard as significant about birds. If we can arrive at comparable knowledge about their concepts of land animals, plants, soils, weather, social relations, personalities, and supernaturals, we have at least a sketch map of the world in the image of the tribe.

The analysis of a culture's terminological systems will not, of course, exhaustively reveal the cognitive world of its members, but it will certainly tap a central portion of it. Culturally significant cognitive features must be communicable between persons in one of the standard symbolic systems of the culture. A major share of these features will undoubtedly be codable in a society's most flexible and productive communication device, its language. Evidence also seems to indicate that those cognitive features requiring most frequent communication will tend to have standard and relatively short linguistic labels (Brown 1958:235–241; Brown and Lenneberg 1954). Accordingly, a commonly distinguished category of trees is more likely to be called something like "elm" by almost all speakers rather than labelled with an ad hoc, non-standardized construction like, "You know, those tall trees with asymmetrical, serrated-edged leaves." To the extent that cognitive coding tends to be linguistic and tends to be efficient, the study of the referential use of standard, readily elicitable linguistic responses—or *terms*—should provide a fruitful beginning point for mapping a cognitive system. And with verbal behavior we know how to begin.

The beginning of an ethnographic task is the recording of what is seen and heard, the segmenting of the behavior stream in such a way that culturally significant noises and movements are coded while the irrelevant is discarded. Descriptive linguistics provides a methodology for segmenting the stream of speech into units relevant to the structure of the speaker's language. I assume that any verbal response which conforms to the phonology and grammar of a language is necessarily a culturally significant unit of behavior. Method-ologies for the structural description of non-verbal behavior are not cor-respondingly adequate in spite of important contributions in this direction by such persons as Pike and Barker and Wright (Barker and Wright 1955; Pike 1954; cf. Miller et al. 1960:14–15). By pushing forward the analysis of units we know to be culturally relevant, we can, I think, more satisfactorily arrive at procedures for isolating the significant constituents of analogous and interrelated structures. The basic methodological concept advocated here—

the determination of the set of contrasting responses appropriate to a given, culturally valid, eliciting context—should ultimately be applicable to the "semantic" analysis of any culturally meaningful behavior.

## SEGREGATES

A terminologically distinguished array of objects is a *segregate* (Conklin 1954, 1962; cf. Lounsbury 1956). Segregates are categories, but not all categories known or knowable to an individual are segregates by this definition. Operationally, this definition of a segregate leaves a problem: how do we recognize a "term" when we hear one? How do we segment the stream of speech into category-designating units?

The segmentation of speech into the grammatically functioning units revealed by linguistic analysis is a necessary, but not sufficient, condition for terminological analysis. Clearly no speech segment smaller than the minimal grammatical unit, the morpheme, need be considered. However, the task requires more than simply a search for the meanings of morphemes or other grammatical units. The items and arrangements of a structural description of the language code need not be isomorphic with the categories and propositions of the message. Linguistic forms, whether morphemes or larger constructions, are not each tied to unique chunks of semantic reference like baggage tags; rather it is the use of speech, the selection of one statement over another in a particular socio-linguistic context, that points to the category boundaries on a culture's cognitive map (Chomsky 1955; Haugen 1957; Hymes 1961; Joos 1958; Lounsbury 1956; Nida 1951).

Suppose we have been studying the verbal behavior accompanying the selection and ordering of items at an American lunch counter.[3] The following text might be typical of those overheard and recorded:

"What ya going to have, Mac? Something to eat?"

"Yeah. What kind of sandwiches ya got besides hamburgers and hot dogs?"

"How about a ham 'n cheese sandwich?"

"Nah . . . I guess I'll take a hamburger again."

\* \* \*

"Hey, that's no hamburger; that's a cheeseburger!"

The problem is to isolate and relate these speech forms according to their use in naming objects. Some, but apparently not all, orderable items at a lunch counter are distinguished by the term *something to eat*. A possibility within the range of 'something to eat' seems to be a set of objects labelled *sandwiches*.

---

[3] Because this is a short, orally presented paper, suggested procedures are illustrated with rather simple examples from a familiar language and culture. A serious analysis would require much larger quantities of speech data presented in phonemic transcription. For a more complex example, intended as an ethnographic statement, see Frake 1961.

The forms *hamburger, hot dog, ham 'n cheese sandwich,* and *cheeseburger* clearly designate alternative choices in lunch-counter contexts. A customer determined to have a 'sandwich' must select one of these alternatives when he orders, and upon receipt of the order, he must satisfy himself that the object thrust before him—which he has never seen before—meets the criteria for membership in the segregate he designated. The counterman must decide on actions that will produce an object acceptable to the customer as a member of the designated segregate. The terminological status of these forms can be confirmed by analysis of further speech situations, by eliciting utterances with question frames suggested to the investigator by the data, and by observing non-verbal features of the situation, especially correlations between terms used in ordering and objects received.

In isolating these terms no appeal has been made to analysis of their linguistic structure or their signification. *Sandwich* is a single morpheme. Some linguists, at any rate, would analyze *hot dog* and even *hamburger* as each containing two morphemes, but, since the meaning of the constructions cannot be predicted from a knowledge of the meaning of their morphological constituents, they are single "lexemes" (Goodenough 1956) or "idioms" (Hockett 1958:303–318). *Ham 'n cheese sandwich* would not, I think, qualify as a single lexeme; nevertheless it is a standard segregate label whose function in naming objects cannot be distinguished from that of forms like *hot dog.* Suppose further utterances from lunch-counter speech show that the lexically complex term *something to eat* distinguishes the same array of objects as do the single morphemes *food* and *chow.* In such a case, a choice among these three terms would perhaps say something about the social status of the lunch counter and its patrons, but it says nothing distinctive about the objects designated. As segregate labels, these three frequently-heard terms would be equivalent.

Although not operationally relevant at this point, the lexemic status of terms bears on later analysis of the productivity of a terminological system. In contrast, say, to our kinship terminology, American lunch-counter terminology is highly productive. The existence of productive, polylexemic models such as *ham 'n cheese sandwich* permits the generation and labelling of new segregates to accommodate the latest lunch-counter creations. However, the non-intuitive determination of the lexemic status of a term requires a thorough analysis of the distinctive features of meaning of the term and its constituents (Goodenough 1956; Lounsbury 1956). Such an analysis of the criteria for placing objects into categories can come only after the term, together with those contrasting terms relevant to its use, has been isolated as a segregate label.

## CONTRAST SETS

In a situation in which a person is making a public decision about the category membership of an object by giving the object a verbal label, he is selecting a term out of a set of alternatives, each with classificatory import. When he asserts "This is an $X$," he is also stating that it is *not* specific other things, these other things being not everything else conceivable, but only the alternatives among which a decision was made (Kelly 1955). In lunch-counter ordering, 'hamburger,' 'hot dog,' 'cheeseburger,' and 'ham and cheese sandwich' are such alternatives. Any object placed in one of these segregates cannot at the same time belong to another. Those culturally appropriate responses which are distinctive alternatives in the same kinds of situations—or, in linguistic parlance, which occur in the same "environment"—can be said to *contrast*. A series of terminologically contrasted segregates forms a *contrast set*.

Note that the cognitive relation of contrast is not equivalent to the relation of class exclusion in formal logic and set theory. The three categories 'hamburger,' 'hot dog,' and 'rainbow' are mutually exclusive in membership. But in writing rules for classifying hamburgers I must say something about hot dogs, whereas I can ignore rainbows. Two categories contrast only when the difference between them is significant for defining their use. The segregates 'hamburger' and 'rainbow,' even though they have no members in common, do not function as distinctive alternatives in any uncontrived classifying context familiar to me.

## TAXONOMIES

The notion of contrast cannot account for all the significant relations among these lunch-counter segregates. Although no object can be both a hamburger and a hot dog, an object can very well be both a hot dog and a sandwich or a hamburger and a sandwich. By recording complementary names applied to the same objects (and eliminating referential synonyms such as *something to eat* and *food*), the following series might result:

Object A is named: *something to eat, sandwich, hamburger*
Object B is named: *something to eat, sandwich, ham sandwich*
Object C is named: *something to eat, pie, apple pie*
Object D is named: *something to eat, pie, cherry pie*
Object E is named: *something to eat, ice-cram bar, Eskimo pie.*

Some segregates include a wider range of objects than others and are subpartitioned by a contrast set. The segregate 'pie' *includes* the contrast set 'apple pie,' 'cherry pie,' etc. For me, the segregate 'apple pie' is, in turn, subpartitioned by 'French apple pie' and 'plain (or 'ordinary') apple pie.' Figure 1 diagrams the sub-partitioning of the segregate 'something to eat' as revealed by naming responses to objects A-E.[4]

---

[4] This example is, of course, considerably over-simplified. If the reader does not relate these segregates in the same way as our hypothetical lunch-counter speakers, he is not alone. Shortly after I completed the manuscript of this paper, a small boy approached me in a park and, without any eliciting remark whatsoever on my part, announced: "Hamburgers are more gooder than sandwiches." One could not ask for better evidence of contrast.

Again it is the use of terms, not their linguistic structure, that provides evidence of inclusion. We cannot consider 'Eskimo pie' to be included in the category 'pie,' for we cannot discover a natural situation in which an object labelled *Eskimo pie* can be labelled simply *pie*. Thus the utterance, "That's not a sandwich; that's a pie," cannot refer to an Eskimo pie. Similar examples are common in English. The utterance, "Look at that oak," may refer to a 'white oak' but never to a 'poison oak.' A 'blackbird' is a kind of 'bird,' but a 'redcap' is not a kind of 'cap.' For many English speakers, the unqualified use of *American* invariably designates a resident or citizen of the United States; consequently, for such speakers, an 'American' is a kind of 'North American' rather than the converse. One cannot depend on a particular grammatical construction, such as one of the English phrasal compounds, to differentiate consistently a single cognitive relation, such as that of inclusion (cf. Hockett 1958:316–317). Because English is not unique in this respect (Frake 1961), the practice of arguing from morphological and syntactic analysis directly to cognitive relations must be considered methodologically unsound.

Segregates in different contrast sets, then, may be related by inclusion. A system of contrast sets so related is a *taxonomy* (Conklin 1962; Gregg 1954; Woodger 1952). This definition does not require a taxonomy to have a unique beginner, i.e., a segregate which includes all other segregates in the system. It requires only that the segregates at the most inclusive level form a demonstrable contrast set.

Taxonomies make possible a regulation of the amount of information communicated about an object in a given situation (compare: "Give me something to eat" with "Give me a French apple pie a la mode"), and they provide a hierarchal ordering of categories, allowing an efficient program for the identification, filing, and retrieving of significant information (Herdan 1960:210–211). The use of taxonomic systems is not confined to librarians and biologists; it is a fundamental principle of human thinking. The elaboration of taxonomies along vertical dimensions of generalization and horizontal dimensions of discrimination probably depends on factors such as the variety

| something to eat | | | | |
|---|---|---|---|---|
| sandwich | | pie | | ice-cream bar |
| ham-burger | ham sandwich | apple pie | cherry pie | Eskimo pie |
| A | B | C | D | E |

OBJECTS:

FIGURE 1  Sub-partitioning of the segregate 'something to eat' as revealed by naming responses to objects A—E

of cultural settings within which one talks about the objects being classified (Frake 1961: 121–122), the importance of the objects to the way of life of the classifiers (Brown 1958; Nida 1958), and general properties of human thinking with regard to the number of items that the mind can cope with at a given time (Miller 1956; Yngve 1960).[5] Determining the precise correlates of variations in taxonomic structure, both intraculturally and cross-culturally, is, of course, one of the objectives of this methodology.

In order to describe the use of taxonomic systems and to work out their behavioral correlates, evidence of complementary naming must be supplemented by observations on the socio-linguistic contexts that call for contrasts at particular levels. One could, for example, present a choice between objects whose segregates appear to contrast at different levels and ask an informant to complete the frame: "Pick up that _____." Suppose we have an apple pie on the counter next to a ham sandwich. The frame would probably be completed as "Pick up that pie." If, however, we substitute a cherry pie for the ham sandwich, we would expect to hear "Pick up that apple pie." Variations on this device of having informants contrast particular objects can be worked out depending on the kind of phenomena being classified. Some objects, such as pies and plants, are easier to bring together for visual comparison than others, such as diseases and deities.

Another device for eliciting taxonomic structures is simply to ask directly about relations of inclusion: "Is $X$ a kind of $Y$?" Since in many speech situations even a native fails to elicit a term at the level of specification he requires, most, if not all, languages probably provide explicit methods for moving up and down a taxonomic hierarchy:

"Give me some of that pie." "What kind of pie d'ya want, Mac?"

"What's this 'submarine' thing on the menu?" "That's a kind of sandwich."

Once a taxonomic partitioning has been worked out it can be tested systematically for terminological contrast with frames such as "Is that an $X$?" with an expectation of a negative reply. For example, we could point to an apple pie and ask a counterman:

1. "Is that something to drink?"
2. "Is that a sandwich?"
3. "Is that a cherry pie?"

We would expect the respective replies to reflect the taxonomy of lunch-counter foods:

1. "No, it's something to eat."
2. "No, it's a pie."
3. "No, it's an apple pie."

---

[5] At least in formal, highly partitioned taxonomic systems an ordering of superordinates according to the number of their subordinates appears to yield a stable statistical distribution (the Willis distribution) regardless of what is being classified or who is doing the classifying (Herdan 1960:211-225; Mandelbrot 1956).

(Admittedly it is easier to do this kind of questioning in a culture where one can assume the role of a naive learner.)

In employing these various operations for exploring taxonomic structures, the investigator must be prepared for cases when the same linguistic form designates segregates at different levels of contrast within the same system ('man' vs. 'animal,' 'man' vs. 'woman,' 'man' vs. 'boy') (Frake 1961:119); when a single unpartitioned segregate contrasts with two or more other segregates which are themselves at different levels of contrast ("That's not a coin; it's a token." "That's not a dime; it's a token."); and when incongruities occur in the results of the several operations (terminological contrasts may cut across sub-hierarchies revealed high complementary naming; explicit statements of inclusion may be less consistent than complementary naming).

## ATTRIBUTES

Our task up to this point has been to reveal the structure or the system from which a selection is made when categorizing an object. When you hand a Navajo a plant specimen, or an American a sandwich, what is the available range of culturally defined arrays into which this object can be categorized? Methodological notions of contrast and inclusion have enabled us to discern some structure in this domain of cognitive choices, but we still have not faced the problem of how a person decides which out of a set of alternative categorizations is the correct one in a given instance. How does one in fact distinguish a hamburger from a cheeseburger, a chair from a stool, a tree from a shrub, an uncle from a cousin, a jerk from a slob?

A mere list of known members of a category—however an investigator identifies these objects cross-culturally—does not answer this question. Categorization, in essence, is a device for treating new experience as though it were equivalent to something already familiar (Brown 1958; Bruner 1957; Bruner et al. 1956; Sapir 1949). The hamburger I get tomorrow may be a quite different object in terms of size, kind of bun, and lack of tomatoes from the hamburger I had today. But it will still be a hamburger—unless it has a slice of cheese in it! To define 'hamburger' one must know, not just what objects it includes, but with what it contrasts. In this way we learn that a slice of cheese makes a difference, whereas a slice of tomato does not. In the context of different cultures the task is to state what one must know in order to categorize objects correctly. A definition of a Navajo plant category is not given by a list of botanical species it contains but by a rule for distinguishing newly encountered specimens of that category from contrasting alternatives.

Ideally the criterial attributes which generate a contrast set fall along a limited number of dimensions of contrast, each with two or more contrasting values or "components." Each segregate can be defined as a distinctive bundle of components. For example, the plant taxonomy of the Eastern Subanun, a Phillipine people, has as its beginner a contrast set of three segregates which together include almost all of the more than 1,400 segregates at the most specific level of contrast within the taxonomy. This three member contrast set can be generated by binary contrasts along two dimensions pertaining to habit of stem growth (See Table 1). Applications of componential analysis to pronomial systems and kinship terminologies have made this method of definition familiar (Austerlitz 1959; Conklin 1962; Goodenough 1956; Lounsbury 1956; McKaughan 1959; Thomas 1955; Wallace and Atkins 1960). The problem remains of demonstrating the cognitive saliency of componential solutions—to what extent are they models of how a person decides which term to use?—and of relating terminological attributes to actual perceptual discriminations (Frake 1961; Wallace and Atkins 1960). As a case of the latter problem, suppose we learn that informants distinguish two contrasting plant segregates by calling the fruit of one 'red' and that of the other 'green.' We set up 'color' as a dimension of contrast with values of 'red' and 'green.' But the terminology of 'color' is itself a system of segregates whose contrastive structure must be analyzed before color terms can serve as useful defining attributes of other segregates. Ultimately one is faced with defining color categories by referring to the actual perceptual dimensions along which informants make differential categorizations. These dimensions must be determined empirically and not prescribed by the investigator using stimulus materials from his own culture. By careful observation one might discover that visual evaluation of an object's succulence, or other unexpected dimensions, as well as the traditional dimensions of hue, brightness, and saturation, are criterial to the use of "color" terms in a particular culture (Conklin 1955).

Whether aimed directly at perceptual qualities of phenomena or at informants' descriptions of pertinent attributes (Frake 1961:122–125), any method for determining the distinctive and probabilistic attributes of a segregate must depend, first, on knowing the contrast set within which the segregate is participating, and, second, on careful observations of verbal and non-verbal features of the cultural situations to which this contrast set provides an appropriate response.

This formulation has important implications for the role of eliciting in ethnography. The distinctive "situations," or "eliciting frames," or "stimuli," which evolve and define a set of contrasting responses are cultural data to

TABLE 1  Defining attributes of the contrast set of stem habit
in the Subanun plant taxonomy

| CONTRAST SET | DIMENSIONS OF CONTRAST | |
| --- | --- | --- |
| | Woodiness | Rigidity |
| gayu 'woody plants' | W | R |
| sigbet 'herbaceous plants' | W̄ | R |
| belagen 'vines' | | R̄ |

be discovered, not prescribed, by the ethnographer. This stricture does not limit the use of preconceived eliciting devices to prod an informant into action or speech without any intent of defining the response by what evoked it in this instance. But the formulation—prior to observation—of response-defining eliciting devices is ruled out by the logic of this methodology which insists that any eliciting conditions not themselves part of the cultural-ecological system being investigated cannot be used to define categories purporting to be those of the people under study. It is those elements of *our informants'* experience, which *they* heed in selecting appropriate actions and utterances, that this methodology seeks to discover.

## OBJECTIVES

The methodological suggestions proposed in this paper, as they stand, are clearly awkward and incomplete. They must be made more rigorous and expanded to include analyses of longer utterance sequences, to consider non-verbal behavior systematically, and to explore the other types of cognitive relations, such as sequential stage relations (Frake 1961) and part-whole relations, that may pertain between contrast sets. Focussing on the linguistic code, clearer operational procedures are needed for delimiting semantically exocentric units ("lexemes" or "idioms") (Goodenough 1956; Nida 1951), for discerning synonomy, homonymy, and polysemy (Ullman 1957:63), and for distinguishing between utterance grammaticalness (correctly constructed message) (Chomsky 1957; Joos 1958). In their present form, however, these suggestions have come out of efforts to describe behavior in the field, and their further development can come only from continuing efforts to apply and test them in ethnographic field situations.

The intended objective of these efforts is eventually to provide the ethnographer with public, non-intuitive procedures for ordering his presentation of observed and elicited events according to the principles of classification of the people he is studying. To order ethnographic observations solely according to an investigator's preconceived categories obscures the real content of culture: how people organize their experience conceptually so that it can be transmitted as knowledge from person to person and from generation to generation. As Goodenough advocates in a classic paper, culture "does not consist of things, people, behavior, or emotions," but the forms or organization of these things in the minds of people (Goodenough 1957). The principles by which people in a culture construe their world reveal how they segregate the pertinent from the insignificant, how they code and retrieve information, how they anticipate events (Kelly 1955), how they define alternative courses of action and make decisions among them. Consequently a strategy of ethnographic description that gives a central place to the cognitive processes of the actors involved will contribute reliable cultural data to problems of the relations between language, cognition, and behavior; it will point up critical dimensions for meaningful cross-cultural comparison; and, finally, it will give us productive descriptions of cultural behavior, descriptions which, like the linguists' grammar, succinctly state what one must know in order to generate culturally acceptable acts and utterances appropriate to a given socio-ecological context (Goodenough 1957).

# Comment

by *Harold C. Conklin*
Columbia University

Dr. Frake has provided a very clear statement of certain recent efforts to improve ethnographic techniques for analyzing cognitive systems. While it is evident that some of the notions discussed in his paper derive from linguistic theory, as well as from principles developed first in biology and psychology, the methodological suggestions in it are of significance primarily to the ethnographer. Two major points seem to be of particular importance:

1. The demonstration of the *necessity*, for accurate and productive ethnography, of going beyond the identification and mere cataloguing of linguistic forms to the point where crucial structural semantic relations can be described systematically; and

2. The demonstration of the *need* for nonintuitive, but intraculturally designed, and rigorously applied, procedures for defining the basic elements and essential relations in the cognitive map of a people studied ethnographically. Implicitly and explicitly, Frake has illustrated the pitfalls of (a) cross-linguistic semantic matching; (b) the use of prearranged, response-defining eliciting techniques; and (c) the assumption of environmental absolutes.

In working from overt public labels to the culturally significant "objects" in the environment, there are four specific points which I think deserve underscoring:

1. The importance in ethnographic investigations of treating the semantic relations among segregates in a manner separate from the analysis of the phonology and grammar of the language concerned.

2. The importance of distinguishing those conceptual principles which generate systems of obligatory categories—and upon which there is unanimous agreement—from those principles and resulting categories which are less obligatory, or *irrelevant*.

3. The importance of distinguishing informants' direct responses from informants' actual uses of terms as indicators of important cognitive categories.

4. The importance—in analyzing folk taxonomies—of distinguishing the implications of vertical, hierarchic relations of class inclusion from those of contrast and subcategory intersection among folk taxa at the same level in a particular subhierarchy.

Some of the problems now facing the student of such aspects of ethnoscience as Frake has discussed can be subsumed under the following headings:

1. Methods for more precise delineation and evaluation of significant categories in terms of *minimal lexical units*—taking into consideration various types of complexity (unitary lexemes, composite lexemes, etc.) and various types of synonymy, polysemy, and homonymy, under conditions of controlled contrast.

2. Methods for delimiting the boundaries of significant semantic domains.

3. Methods for evaluating the relevant distinctions of order, or rank, of subsets within significant cognitive domains.

4. Methods of determining the types of articulation among multiple and interlocking hierarchies. (A segregate may not be restricted to only one hierarchy.)

5. Methods of determining different types of *contrast* relations between segregates in the same lexical subset. (In addition to antonomy and to simple dyadic and triadic contrast, such relationships may entail continuous, repetitive, reticulating, or discontinuous but sequential arrangements. The paradigmatic relations of some lexical domains have been relatively well explored, but for many others, the analysis of sublexemic, multidimensional contrasts has not yet begun.)

6. Methods of analyzing those areas of folk classification in which 'part of' and 'stage of' relations replace those of inclusion (i.e., 'kind of' relations).

This last point is of considerable interest and complexity. There may be several types of part-to-whole relations in any cognitive system. To illustrate some of the distinctions involved, we can consider the segregate labels:

| A | B | C |
|---|---|---|
| *being* | *body* | *man$^1$* (person) |
| *animal* | *head* | *man$^2$* (male persons) |
| *mammal* | *face* | *bone* |
| *dog* | *eye* | *skull* |
| *bulldog* | *eyeball* | *tooth* |
| | *pupil* | *molar* |
| | | *cusp* |

In comparing lists *A* and *B*, note that any member of the segregate *bulldog* is also a member of each higher terminologically distinguished class in the partial, five-level hierarchy indicated in *A*, whereas such a statement regarding the relations obtaining among the listed categories in $B$ is impossible. In $C$, inclusion and part-whole relations alternate.

To illustrate some of these points, and to indicate the important difference between the analysis of semantic structure and the presentation of an arbitrary arrangement, we can take a very familiar set of segregate labels, namely the terms used to designate the means of monetary exchange which we carry with us in wallet, pocket or purse.

Excluding a large number of referential synonyms, and designations for high denomination currency and for two-dollar bills (all of which are of restricted, specialized, or very uncommon occurrence), the following nine common segregate labels would certainly be recorded by any careful ethnographer:

1. dime (d)
2. fifty-cent piece (f)
3. five (v)
4. nickel (n)
5. one (o)
6. penny (p)
7. quarter (q)
8. ten (t)
9. twenty (w)

It should be noted that no common object of monetary exchange is excluded from this set of mutually exclusive and unanimously-agreed-upon categories. The large number of easily-determined contrastive attributes displayed by this array of common objects suggests many possible arrangements of these segregates other than the meaningless alphabetical listing above. For purposes of simple identification, numerous procedures may be established, described, and diagrammed. A different arrangement may be required to indicate the folk taxonomic relations obtaining among these conventionally labeled categories. Consider the two sets of diagrams in Fig. 1 (where lower case letters correspond to the nine parenthesized symbols in the list above). Set I—where $A = money$ (i.e., cash), $B = bill(s)$, and $C = coin(s)$ consists of four alternative representations of 12 English monolexemic segregate labels in a folk taxonomic subhierarchy. Set II—where arabic numerals correspond to those in the square brackets below—consists of four alternative representations of eight "couplets" of opposed attributes (corresponding to the 1a-to-8b "leads" below) which may be used to "key out" or identify any relevant object (coin or bill) as a member of one or another of our nine terminal folk taxa:

1a Shape, rectangular [1]
   2a Engraved portrait frame, broken oval [3]......................o
   2b Engraved portrait frame, unbroken oval [4]
      3a Hair, black [7]........................................v
      3b Hair, white [8]
         4a Neckpiece, black [13]................................w

          4b Neckpiece, white [14] ...............................t
1b Shape, discoidal [2]
    5a Edge, smooth [5]
        6a Head, facing left [9] ....................................n
        6b Head, facing right [10] ...............................p
    5b Edge, ridged [6]
        7a Obverse, with bird [11]
            8a Wings, symmetrical [15]..............................q
            8b Wings, asymmetrical [16] ...........................f
        7b Obverse, with torch [12]................................d

Comparing this partial analysis of our folk classification of money with an arbitrary key to the same terminal segregates (Sets I and II, respectively) illustrates a number of important, but not always obvious, features. If we are concerned with the way in which a set of categories is cognitively interrelated

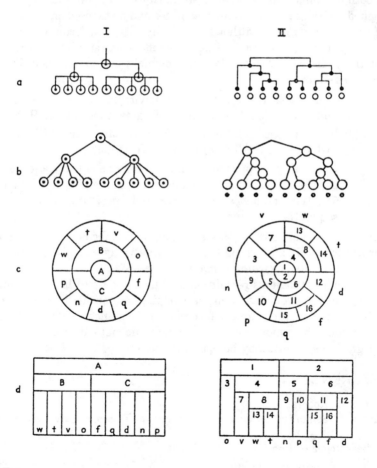

FIGURE 1

contrastively and hierarchically, detailed examination of physically observable differences in an array of objects cannot—by itself—provide decisive answers to questions of cognitive distinctiveness. That in Set II the opposition [1] : [2], but not [5] : [6] or [11] : [12], corresponds to an important cultural and cognitive distinction (B : C) can only be established by intracultural analysis as reflected in Set I. Furthermore, although I will not explore this aspect here, the exclusive relevance of color, size, and weight within contrast set C and of conspicuous arabic numerals and engraved human figures in contrast set B, is of considerable cognitive importance while most of the distinctions noted in Set II diagrams—however valid for identificational purposes—are arbitrarily selected and of no demonstrable cultural significance except to specialists in mintage and numismatics.

Looking at Fig. 1, one notes that the branching dendograms (a) and tree structures (b), as well as the circular and block diagrams (c), (d) are similar in both columns. This geometric similarity can be misleading, because the implied relations between connected nodes and juxtaposed enclosures are very different in the two sets, although vertically within each column the diagrams are completely transformable. These differences between Set I and Set II, which are those distinguishing a folk taxonomic *hierarchy* from a *key*, can be summarized as follows:

(1) Nodes or spaces in Set I necessarily represent culturally significant and conventionally-labeled segregates; those in Set II do not.

(2) Node or space relations in Set I necessarily imply hierarchic class inclusion vertically; those in Set II do not.

(3) Node or space placement in Set I is nonarbitrary and hence fixed positionally; node or space placement in Set II is based on arbitrary selection and hence such points can be permuted in their vertical or sequential ordering.

Despite the simplicity of this example, it does focus our attention on the importance of distinguishing between esthetically appealing and culturally valid statements regarding semantic structure.

While many problems remain, and while it may still be some time before a *complete* and adequate cognitive mapping is presented for any particular culture, Frake's preliminary formulation is a most welcome sign of the direction in which more rigorous ethnographic methods, including the study of cognitive systems, may be expected to develop.

## REFERENCES

Austerlitz, Robert
    1959    "Semantic components of pronoun systems: Gilyak." *Word* 15(1): 102–109.
Barker, Roger G. and Herbert F. Wright
    [1955]    *Midwest and its children, the psychological ecology of an American town.* Evanston, Row, Peterson.

Boas, Franz
1911 "Introduction." In *Handbook of American Indian Languages*, Bureau of American Ethnology Bulletin 40, Pt. 1, 1–83.
Brown, Roger
1958 *Words and things*. Glencoe, Free Press.
Brown, Roger and Eric H. Lenneberg
1954 "A study in language and cognition." *Journal of Abnormal and Social Psychology* 49(3):454–462.
Bruner, Jerome S.
1957 "Going beyond the information given." In Contemporary Approaches to Cognition; a Symposium Held at the University of Colorado. Cambridge, Harvard University Press, 41–70.
Bruner, Jerome S., J. J. Goodnow, and G. A. Austin
1956 *A study of thinking*. With an Appendix on Language by Roger W. Brown. New York, Wiley.
Chomsky, Noam
1955 "Semantic considerations in grammar." Georgetown University Monograph Series on Language and Linguistics, No. 8, 141–150.
1957 *Syntactic structures*. The Hague, Mouton.
Conklin. Harold C.
1954 "The relation of Hanunóo culture to the plant world." Unpublished Ph.D. dissertation. New Haven, Yale University.
1955 "Hanunóo color categories." *Southwestern Journal of Anthropology* 11(4): 339–344.
1962 "Lexicographical treatment of folk taxonomies." Work paper for Conference on Lexicography, Indiana University, Nov. 11–12, 1960. In "Problems in Lexicography." Fred W. Householder and Sol Saporta, eds. Supplement to *International Journal of American Linguistics*, vol. 28, no. 2—Indiana University Research Center in Anthropology, Folklore and Linguistics, Publication 21. Bloomington.
Frake, Charles O.
1961 "The diagnosis of disease among the Subanun of Mindanao." *American Anthropologist* 63(1): 113–132.
Goodenough, Ward H.
1956 "Componential analysis and the study of meaning." *Language* 32(1): 195–216.
1957 "Cultural anthropology and linguistics." Georgetown University Monograph Series on Language and Linguistics, No. 9, 167–173.
Gregg, John R.
1954 *The language of taxonomy, an application of symbolic logic to the study of classificatory systems*. New York, Columbia University Press.
Haugen, Einar
1957 "The semantics of Icelandic orientation." *Word* 13(3): 447–459.
Herdan, Gustav
1960 *Type-token mathematics, a textbook of mathematical linguistics*. The Hague, Mouton.
Hill, A. A.
1952 "A note on primitive languages." *International Journal of American Linguistics* 18(3): 172–177.

Hockett, Charles F.
1958    *A course in modern linguistics.* New York, Macmillan.
Hymes, Dell H.
1961    "On typology of cognitive styles in language" (with examples from Chinookan). *Anthropological Linguistics* 3(1): 22–54.
Jesperson, Otto
1934    *Language: its nature, development, and origin.* London, Allen & Unwin.
Joos, Martin
1958    "Semology: a linguistic theory of meaning." *Studies in Linguistics* 13(3): 53–70.
Kelly, George
1955    *The psychology of personal constructs.* New York, Norton.
Lounsbury, Floyd G.
1956    "A semantic analysis of the Pawnee kinship usage." *Language* 32(1): 158–194.
Mandelbrot, Benoit
1956    "On the language of taxonomy." In *Information Theory.* Colin Cherry, ed. New York, Academic Press, 135–145.
McKaughan, Howard
1959    "Semantic components of pronoun systems: Maranao." *Word* 15(1): 101–102.
Miller, George
1956    "Human memory and the storage of information." *IRE Transactions on Information Theory IT*, 2:129–137. New York, Institute of Radio Engineers.
Miller, George, Eugene Galanter and Karl Pribram
1960    *Plans and the structure of behavior.* New York, Holt-Dryden.
Nida, Eugene
1951    "A system for the description of semantic elements." *Word* 7(1): 1–14.
1958    "Analysis of meaning and dictionary making." *International Journal of American Linguistics* 24(4): 279–292.
Pike, Kenneth
1954    *Language in relation to a unified theory of the structure of human behavior.* Part 1. Glendale, Summer Institute of Linguistics.
Sapir, Edward
1949    "The psychological reality of phonemes." In *Selected Writings of Edward Sapir in Language, Culture, and Personality.* David G. Mandelbaum, ed. Berkeley and Los Angeles. University of California Press, 46–60.
Thomas, David
1955    "Three analyses of the Ilocano pronoun system." *Word* 11(2): 204–208.
Ullman, Stephen
1957    *The principles of semantics.* New York, Philosophical Library.
Wallace, Anthony and J. Atkins
1960    "The meaning of kinship terms." *American Anthropologist* 62(1): 58–80.
Woodger, J. H.
1952    *Biology and language, an introduction to the methodology of the biological sciences including medicine.* Cambridge, The University Press.
Yngve, Victor H.
1960    "A model and an hypothesis for language structure." *Proceedings of the American Philosophical Society* 104(5): 444–466.

# Language and the Analysis of Social Laws

## Claude Lévi-Strauss

In a recent work, whose importance from the point of view of the future of the social sciences can hardly be overestimated, Wiener poses, and resolves in the negative, the question of a possible extension to the social sciences of the mathematical methods of prediction which have made possible the construction of the great modern electronic machines. He justifies his position by two arguments (Wiener 1948:189–191).

In the first place, he maintains that the nature of the social sciences is such that it is inevitable that their very development must have repercussions on the object of their investigation. The coupling of the observer with the observed phenomenon is well known to contemporary scientific thought, and, in a sense, it illustrates a universal situation. But it is negligible in fields which are ripe for the most advanced mathematical investigation; as, for example, in astrophysics, where the object has such vast dimensions that the influence of the observer need not be taken into account, or in atomic physics, where the object is so small that we are only interested in average mass effects in which the effect of bias on the part of the observer plays no role. In the field of the social sciences, on the contrary, the object of study is necessarily affected by the intervention of the observer, and the resulting modifications are *on the same scale* as the phenomena that are studied.

In the second place, Wiener observes that the phenomena subjected to sociological or anthropological inquiry are defined within our own sphere of interests; they concern questions of the life, education, career, and death of individuals. Therefore the statistical runs available for the study of a given phenomenon are always far too short to lay the foundation of a valid induction. Mathematical analysis in the field of social sciences, he concludes, can bring results which should be of as little interest to the social scientist as those of the statistical study of a gas would be to an individual about the size of a molecule.

These objections seem difficult to refute when they are examined in terms of the investigations toward which their author has directed them, the data of research monographs and of applied anthropology. In such cases, we are dealing with a study of individual behavior, directed by an observer who is himself an individual; or with a study of a culture, a national character, or a pattern, by an observer who cannot dissociate himself completely from his culture, or from the culture out of which his working hypotheses and his methods of observation, which are themselves cultural patterns, are derived.

There is, however, at least one area of the social sciences where Wiener's objections do not seem to be applicable, where the conditions which he sets as a requirement for a valid mathematical study seem to find themselves rigorously met. This is the field of language, when studied in the light of structural linguistics, with particular reference to phonemics.

Language is a social phenomenon; and, of all social phenomena, it is the one which manifests to the greatest degree two fundamental characteristics which make it susceptible of scientific study. In the first place, much of linguistic behavior lies on the level of unconscious thought. When we speak, we are not conscious of the syntactic and morphological laws of our language. Moreover we are not ordinarily conscious of the phonemes that we employ to convey different meanings; and we are rarely, if ever, conscious of the phonological oppositions which reduce each phoneme to a bundle of differential features. This absence of consciousness, moreover, still holds when we do become aware of the grammar or the phonemics of our language. For, while this awareness is but the privilege of the scholar, language, as a matter of fact, lives and develops only as a collective construct; and even the scholar's linguistic knowledge always remains dissociated from his experience as a speaking agent, for his mode of speech is not affected by his ability to interpret his language on a higher level. We may say, then, that as concerns language, we need not fear the influence of the observer on the observed phenomenon, because the observer cannot modify the phenomenon merely by becoming conscious of it.

Furthermore, as regards Wiener's second point, we know that language appeared very early in human history. Therefore, even if we can study it scientifically only when written documents are available, writing itself goes back a considerable distance, and furnishes long enough runs to make language a valid subject for mathematical analysis. For example, the series we have at our disposal in studying Indo-European, Semitic or Sino-Thibetan languages is about four or five thousand years old. And, where a comparable temporal dimension is lacking, the multiplicity of coexistent forms furnishes, for several other linguistic families, a spatial dimension that is no less valuable.

We thus find in language a social phenomenon which manifests both independence of the object and long statistical runs; which would seem to indicate that language is a phenomenon fully qualified to satisfy the demands of mathematicians for the type of analysis Wiener suggests.

It is, in fact, difficult to see why certain linguistic problems could not be solved by modern calculating machines. With knowledge of the phonological structure of a language and the laws which govern the grouping of consonants and vowels, a student could easily use a machine to compute all the combinations of phonemes constituting the words of $n$ syllables existing in the vocabulary, or even the number of combinations compatible with the structure of the language under consideration, such as previously defined. With a machine into which would be "fed" the equations regulating the types of structures with which phonemics usually deals, the repertory of sound which human speech organs can emit, and the minimal differential values, determined by psychophysiological methods, which distinguish between the phonemes closest to one another, one would doubtless be able to obtain a computation of the totality of phonological structures for $n$ oppositions ($n$ being as high as one wished). One could thus construct a sort of periodic table of linguistic structures that would be comparable to the table of elements which Mendeleieff introduced into modern chemistry. It would then only remain for us to check the place of known languages in this table, to identify the positions and the relationships of the languages whose first-hand study is still too imperfect to give us a proper theoretical knowledge of them, and to discover the place of languages that have disappeared, are unknown, yet to come, or simply possible.

To add a last example: Jakobson has recently suggested that a language may possess several coexisting phonological structures, each of which may intervene in a different kind of grammatical operation (Jakobson 1948). Since there must obviously be a relationship between the different structural modalities of the same language, we arrive at the concept of a "metastructure" which would be something like the law of the group (*loi du groupe*) consisting of its modal structures. If all of these modalities could be analyzed by our machine, established mathematical methods would permit it to construct the "metastructure" of the language, which would in certain complex cases be so intricate as to make it difficult, if not impossible, to achieve on the basis of purely empirical investigation.

The problem under discussion here can, then, be defined as follows. Among all social phenomena, language alone has thus far been studied in a manner which permits it to serve as the object of truly scientific analysis, allowing us to understand its formative process and to predict its mode of change. This results from modern researches into the problems of phonemics, which have reached beyond the superficial conscious and historical expression of linguistic phenomena to attain fundamental and objective realities consisting of systems of relations which are the products of unconscious thought processes. The question which now arises is this: it is possible to effect a similar reduction in the analysis of other forms of social phenomena? If so, would this analysis lead to the same result? And if the answer to this last question is in the affirmative, can we conclude that all forms of social life are substantially of the same nature —that is, do they consist of systems of behavior that represent the projection, on the level of conscious and socialized thought, of universal laws which regulate the unconscious activities of the mind? Obviously, no attempt can be made here to do more than to sketch this problem by indicating certain points of reference and projecting the principal lines along which its orientation might be effective.

Some of the researches of Kroeber appear to be of the greatest importance in suggesting approaches to our problem, particularly his work on changes in the styles of women's dress (Kroeber and Richardson 1940). Fashion actually is, in the highest degree, a phenomenon which depends on the unconscious activity of the mind. We rarely take note of why a particular style pleases us, or falls into disuse. Kroeber has demonstrated that this seemingly arbitrary evolution follows definite laws. These laws cannot be reached by purely empirical observation, or by intuitive consideration of phenomena, but result from measuring some basic relationships between the various elements of costume. The relationship thus obtained can be expressed in terms of mathematical functions, whose values, calculated at a given moment, make prediction possible.

Kroeber has thus shown how even such a highly arbitrary aspect of social behavior is susceptible of scientific study. His method may be usefully compared not only with that of structural linguistics, but also with that of the natural sciences. There is a remarkable analogy between these researches and those of a contemporary biologist, G. Teissier, on the growth of the organs of certain crustaceans (Teissier 1936). Teissier has shown that, in order to formulate the laws of this growth, it has been necessary to consider the relative dimensions of the component parts of the claws, and not the exterior forms of these organs. There, relationships allow us to derive constants—termed parameters—out of which it is possible to derive the laws which govern the development of these organisms. The object of a scientific zoology, in these terms, is thus not ultimately concerned with the forms of animals and their organs as they are usually perceived, but is to establish certain abstract and measurable relationships, which constitute the basic nature of the phenomena under study.

An analogous method has been followed in studying certain features of social organization, particularly marriage rules and kinship systems (Lévi-Strauss 1949, passim). It has been shown that the complete set of marriage regulations operating in human societies, and usually classified under different headings such as incest prohibitions, preferential forms of marriage, and the like, can be interpreted as being so many different ways of insuring the circulation of women within the social group, or, of substituting the mechanism of a sociologically determined affinity for that of a biologically determined consanguinity. Proceeding from this hypothesis, it would only be necessary to make a mathematical study of every possible type of exchange between $n$ partners to enable one almost automatically to arrive at every type of marriage rule actually operating in living societies and, eventually, to discover others which are merely possible; one would also understand their function and the relationships between each type and the others.

This approach was fully validated by the demonstration, reached by pure deduction, that the mechanisms of reciprocity known to classical anthropology —namely, those based on dual organization and exchange-marriage between two partners or whose number is a multiple of two—are but a special instance of a wider kind of reciprocity between any number of partners. This fact has tended to remain unnoticed, because the partners in those matings, instead of giving and receiving from one another, do not give to those from whom they receive, and do not receive from those to whom they give. They give to and receive from different partners to whom they are bound by a relationship that operates only in one direction.

This type of organization, no less important than the moiety system, has thus far been observed and described only imperfectly and incidentally. Starting with the results of mathematical study, data had to be compiled; thus, the real extension of the system was shown and its first theoretical analysis offered (Ibid., pp. 278–380). At the same time, it became possible to explain the more general features of marriage rules such as preferential marriage between bilateral cross-cousins or with only one kind of cross-cousin, on the father's side (patrilateral), or on that of the mother (matrilateral). Thus, for example, though such customs had been unintelligible to anthropologists (Ibid., pp. 558–566), they were perfectly clear when regarded as illustrating different modalities of the laws of exchange. In turn, these were reduced to a still more basic relationship between the rules of residence and the rules of descent (Ibid., pp. 547–550).

Now, these results have only been achieved by treating marriage regulations and kinship systems as a kind of language, a set of processes permitting the establishment, between individuals and groups, of a certain type of communication. That the mediating factor, in this case, should be the *women of the group,* who are *circulated* between individuals, does not at all change the fact that the essential aspect of the phenomenon is identical in both cases.

We may now ask whether, in extending the concept of communication so as to make it include exogamy and the rules flowing from the prohibition of incest, we may not, reciprocally, achieve insight into a problem that is still very obscure, that of the origin of language. For marriage regulations, in relation to language, represent a complex much more rough and archaic than the latter. It is generally recognized that words are signs: but poets are practically the only ones who know that words have also been values. As against this, women are held by the social group to be values of the most essential kind, though we have difficulty in understanding how these values become integrated in systems endowed with a significant function. This ambiguity is clearly manifested in the reactions of persons who, on the basis of the analysis of social structures referred to (Ibid., p. 616), have laid against it the charge of "anti-feminism," because women are referred to as objects (Ibid., p. 45). Of course, it may be disturbing to some to have women conceived as mere parts of a meaningful system. However, one should keep in mind that the processes by which phonemes and words have lost—even though in an illusory manner—their character of value, to become reduced to pure signs, will never lead to the same results in matters concerning women. For words do not speak, while women do; as producers of signs, they can never be reduced to the status of symbols or tokens. But it is for this very reason that the position of women, as actually found in this system of communication between men that is made up of marriage regulations and kinship nomenclature, may afford us a workable image of the type of relationships that could have existed at a very early period in the development of language, between human beings and their words. As in the case of women, the original impulse which compelled men to exchange words must be sought for in that split-representation which pertains to the symbolic function. For, since certain terms are simultaneously perceived as having a value both for the speaker and the listener the only way to resolve this contradiction is in the exchange of complementary values, to which all social existence reduces itself.

These speculations may be judged utopian. Yet, granting that the assumptions made here are legitimate, a very important consequence follows that is susceptible of immediate verification. That is, the question may be raised whether the different aspects of social life (including even art and religion) can not only be studied by the methods, and with the help of concepts similar to those employed in linguistics, but also whether they do not constitute phenomena whose inmost nature is the same as that of language. That is, in the words of Voegelin, we may ask whether there are not only "operational" but also "substantial comparabilities" between language and culture (Voegelin 1949).

How can this hypothesis be verified? It will be necessary to develop the analysis of the different features of social life, either for a given society or for a complex of societies, so that a deep enough level can be reached to make it possible to cross from one to the other; or to express the specific structure of each in terms of a sort of general language, valid for each system separately and for all of them taken together. It would thus be possible to ascertain if one had reached their inner nature, and to determine if this pertained to the same kind of reality. In order to develop this point, an experiment can be attempted. It will consist, on the part of the anthropologist, in translating the basic features of the kinship systems from different parts of the world in terms general enough to be meaningful to the linguist, and thus be equally applicable by the latter to the description of the languages from the same regions. Both could thus ascertain whether or not different types of communication systems in the same societies—that is, kinship and language—are or are not caused by identical unconscious structures. Should this be the case, we would be assured of having reached a truly fundamental formulation.

If then, a substantial identity were assumed to exist between language structure and kinship systems, one should find, in the following regions of the world, languages whose structures would be of a type comparable to kinship systems in the following terms:

1. *Indo-European:* As concerns the *kinship systems,* we find that the marriage regulations of our contemporary civilization are entirely based on the principle that, a few negative prescriptions being granted, the density and fluidity of the population will achieve by itself the same results which other societies have sought in more complicated sets of rules; i.e., social cohesion obtained by marriage in degrees far removed or even impossible to trace. This statistical solution has its origin in a typical feature of most ancient Indo-European systems. These belong, in the author's terminology, to a simple formula of gener-

alized reciprocity (*formule simple de l'échange généralisé*) (Lévi-Strauss 1949). However, instead of prevailing between lineages, this formula operates between more complex units of the *brastsvo* type, which actually are clusters of lineages, each of which enjoys a certain freedom within the rigid framework of general reciprocity in effect at the level of the cluster. Therefore, it can be said that a characteristic feature of Indo-European kinship structure lies in the fact that a problem set in simple terms always admits of many solutions.

Should the linguistic structure be homologous with the kinship structure it would thus be possible to express the basic feature of Indo-European languages as follows: the languages have simple structures, utilizing numerous elements. The opposition between the simplicity of the structure and the multiplicity of elements is expressed in the fact that several elements compete to occupy the same positions in the structure.

2. *Sino-Thibetan kinship systems* exhibit quite a different type of complexity. They belong to or derive directly from the simplest form of general reciprocity, namely mother's brother's daughter marriage, so that, as has been shown (Ibid., 1949, pp. 291–380), while this type of marriage insures social cohesion in the simplest way, at the same time it permits this to be indefinitely extended so as to include any number of participants.

Translated into more general terms applicable to language that would correspond to the following linguistic pattern, we may say that the structure is complex, while the elements are few, a feature that may be related to the tonal structure of these languages.

3. The typical feature of *African kinship systems* is the extension of the bride-wealth system, coupled with a rather frequent prohibition on marriage with the wife's brother's wife. The joint result is a system of general reciprocity already more complex than the one with the mother's brother's daughter, while the types of unions resulting from the circulation of the marriage-price approaches, to some extent, the statistical mechanism operating in our own society.

Therefore one could say that African languages have several modalities corresponding in general to a position intermediate between 1) and 2).

4. The widely recognized features of *Oceanic kinship systems* seem to lead to the following formulation of the basic characteristics of the linguistic pattern: simple structure and few elements.

5. The originality of *American kinship systems* lies with the so-called Crow-Omaha type which should be carefully distinguished from other types showing the same disregard for generation levels (Murdock 1949). The important point with the Crow-Omaha type is not that two kinds of cross-cousins are classified in different generation levels, but rather that they are classified with consanguineous kin instead of with affinal kin as it occurs, for instance, in the Miwok system. But systems of the Miwok type belong equally to the Old and the New World; while when considering the differential systems just referred to as Crow-Omaha, one must admit that, apart from a few exceptions, these are only typical for the New World. It can be shown that this quite exceptional

feature of the Crow-Omaha system results from the simultaneous application of the two simple formulas of reciprocity, both special and general (*échange restreint* and *échange généralisé*), (Lévi-Strauss 1949, pp. 228–233), which elsewhere in the world were generally considered to be incompatible. It thus became possible to achieve marriage within remote degrees by using simultaneously two simple formulas, each of which independently applied could only have led to different kinds of cross-cousin marriages.

The linguistic pattern corresponding to that situation would be that certain of the American languages offer a relatively high number of elements, which succeed in becoming organized into relatively simple structures by compelling these to assume an asymmetrical form.

It must be kept in mind that in the above highly tentative experiment, the anthropologist proceeds from what is known to what is unknown to him: namely from kinship structures to linguistic structures. Whether or not the differential characteristics thus outlined have a meaning in so far as the respective languages are concerned, remains for the linguist to decide. The author, being a social anthropologist, and not a linguist, can only try to explain briefly to which specific features of kinship systems he is referring in this attempt toward a generalized formulation. Since the general lines of his interpretation have been fully developed elsewhere (Ibid.), short sketches were deemed sufficient for the purpose of this paper.

If the general characteristics of the kinship systems of given geographical areas, which we have tried to bring into juxtaposition with equally general characteristics of the linguistic structures of those areas, are recognized by linguists as an approach to equivalences of their own observations, then it will be apparent, in terms of our preceding discussion, that we are much closer to the understanding of the fundamental characteristics of social life than we have been accustomed to think.

The road will then be open for a comparative structural analysis of customs, institutions, and accepted patterns of behavior. We will be in a position to understand basic similarities between forms of social life, such as language, art, law, religion, that, on the surface, seem to differ greatly. At the same time, we will have the hope of overcoming the opposition between the collective nature of culture and its manifestations in the individual, since the so-called "collective consciousness" would, in the final analysis, be no more than the expression, on the plane of individual thought and behavior, of certain time and space modalities of these universal laws which make up the unconscious activity of the mind.

## BIBLIOGRAPHY

Jakobson, R. "The Phonemic and Grammatical Aspect of Language in their Interrelations." *Actes du 6ᵉ Congrès International des linguistes,* Paris, 1948.

Kroeber, A. L., and J. Richardson. "Three Centuries of Women's Dress Fashions." *Anthropological Records,* 1940, Berkeley.

Lévi-Strauss, C. *Les Structures Elémentaires de la Parenté*. Paris, 1949.

Murdock, G. P. *Social Structure*. New York, 1949.

Teissier, G. "La Description Mathématique des Faits Biologiques." *Revue de Métaphysique et de Morale*. Paris, January, 1936.

Wiener, N. *Cybernetics, or Control and Communication in the Animal and the Machine*. Paris, Cambridge, New York, 1948.

# Speculations on the Growth of Ethnobotanical Nomenclature

Brent Berlin

A general observation about the vocabularies of most languages is that they tend to increase in size over time. This pattern is more readily seen when one thinks in broad evolutionary terms, comparing the development of the rudimentary lexicon of early *Homo sapiens* to the complex vocabularies of modern man. We know almost nothing about the causal mechanisms involved in this lexical expansion but most anthropologists and linguists would not dispute that it most likely mirrors general cultural evolution.

That languages increase the size of their vocabularies through time is, of course, a trivial observation. The study of lexical growth becomes a topic of relevance only if it is possible to point out regularities that allow for useful generalizations and predictions about the broader problem of linguistic evolution.

In this essay, I hope to focus on the development of one area of vocabulary common to most, if not all, languages—names for categories of plants. I will assume that man's vocabulary for kinds of plants has developed over time, an assumption that allows one to ask at least the following questions: Can one observe regularities in the ethnobotanical lexicons of past and present day languages that allow one to make plausible inferences as to the major patterns of nomenclatural growth? If such patterns can be described, are they related to other aspects of man's sociocultural development? And, finally, do such regularities appear to have productive implications for the evolution of vocabulary generally?

I would like to propose in this openly speculative paper that one can recognize some rather general patterns in the development of ethnobotanical nomenclature that are not necessarily self evident. I cannot claim that the ideas presented here are based on well-documented empirical studies. Many of the examples I cite as evidence are drawn from incomplete descriptions. Nonetheless, as further information becomes available, I have become more strongly convinced that the nomenclatural principles sketched here have widespread applicability. I also believe that their recognition may serve as a useful starting point for research on the evolution of other lexical domains, specifically ethnozoological nomenclature, and, more broadly, on vocabulary generally.

# THE SIX UNIVERSAL CATEGORIES OF ETHNOBOTANICAL NOMENCLATURE

It now appears that the ethnobotanical lexicons of all languages can ultimately be described with the recognition of six major ethnobotanical categories. These six basic categories will be labeled as follows: (1) generic, (2) specific, (3) major life form, (4) varietal, (5) intermediate, (6) unique beginner.

The names of plant taxa occurring as members of these categories will be, accordingly, generic names, specific names, major life-form names, and so on.

It is furthermore suggested that in the life histories of individual languages, the encoding of each of these nomenclatural categories occurs in a relatively fixed order. *Generic* names are fundamental and will appear first. These will be followed in time by major *life-form* names and *specific* names. At yet a later period, *intermediate* taxa and *varietal* taxa will be labeled. Finally, the last category to be lexically designated in the development of any ethnobotanical lexicon will be the *unique beginner*. The suggested sequence can be seen diagrammatically as follows:

$$\text{generic} \rightarrow \left\{ \begin{array}{l} \text{life form} \\ \text{specific} \end{array} \right\} \rightarrow \left\{ \begin{array}{l} \text{intermediate} \\ \text{varietal} \end{array} \right\} \rightarrow \text{unique beginner}$$

Several clarifications of the above sequence should be noted. The first is to indicate that each of the nomenclatural categories, with the exception of the unique beginner, is theoretically an open class. Thus, given the appearance of the *generic* category a language may continue to encode generic taxa throughout its history. The same applies to the *specific* category. The major *life form*, *intermediate* and *varietal* categories are likely to be few membered classes when compared with the generic and specific. This observation is probably a reflection of the nature of the recognizable discontinuities of the plant world as will be seen in more detail in the following sections.

Secondly, it should also be observed that no temporal ordering is implied for some categories. Thus, no claim is made as to the priority, in time, of specific names over major life-form names. On the other hand, a claim is made that a language must have encoded *at least* one major life-form name and one specific name before the appearance of intermediate and varietal named taxa.

As well as noting a general progression in terms of an increase in the number of ethnobotanical nomenclatural categories in a particular language's history, one may also describe a regular sequence of lexical development for members *within each category*. Thus, given the appearance of the specific category, one may observe the further linguistic development of specific names from *lexically unmarked* to *lexically marked* expressions. The same observation holds for each category. This general feature suggests that languages may not only be rated in terms of the number of ethnobotanical nomenclatural categories encoded but can be ranked as well in terms of the extent to which members of particular categories have passed from an unmarked to a marked status.

## THE REALITY OF NATURAL GROUPINGS OF ORGANISMS

Man is by nature a classifying animal and nowhere is this fact exemplified more clearly than in his classification of the biological universe. But unlike the sometimes capricious and apparently arbitrary classification of certain social phenomena, all men appear to be constrained in their conceptualization of the world of plants and animals. It now seems clear that certain naturally occurring groupings of organisms are recognized as discrete classes in societies which maintain a direct and intimate contact with nature. While several ethnographers have long assumed this to be true (cf. especially Lévi-Strauss 1966), the recent work of Ralph Bulmer presents the most explicit statement to this effect. In a series of perceptive papers on the ethnoscience of the Karam of New Guinea (Bulmer 1967, 1968, 1970; Bulmer & Tyler 1968), Bulmer convincingly demonstrates the psychological reality of such natural groupings. Building on assumptions concerning the classification of the natural world which he attributes to Lévi-Strauss, Bulmer states that '. . . in any total classification of plants and animals there are important lower order categories which are seen as "objective" by the users of the classification and which are the smallest *logically* natural units defined by multiple criteria . . .' (Bulmer 1970:1072).

These minimal, naturally occurring units may or may not correspond in a one-to-one fashion to modern biologically defined taxa, although they generally do (Bulmer & Tyler 1968; Bulmer 1970; Berlin, Breedlove & Raven 1966; Diamond 1966). They are logically comparable, however, in that in numerous instances such groupings are formed on the basis of '. . . objective regularities and discontinuities in nature' (Bulmer 1970:1072).

The essence of Bulmer's generalizations are clearly in accord with recent research in Tzeltal botanical ethnography (Berlin, Breedlove & Raven, in preparation), as well as with the work of Conklin (1954), Lévi-Strauss (1966) and others who have worked closely with ethnobiological materials.

## THE PRIMACY OF GENERIC NAMES

In the ethnobiological lexicons of all languages, one is immediately struck by the structural uniformity of expressions which linguistically characterize man's recognition of the basic objective discontinuities of his biological world. These expressions are, for the most part, unique 'single-words' that can be said to be semantically unitary and linguistically distinct. Examples of such semantically unitary names in English folk biology would be *oak, pine* and *maple*. Primary terms of this sort appear to represent the most commonly designated concepts of the botanical world and can be referred to as *generic names*. There may or may not be expressions of greater generality (e.g. *tree, vine*) or specificity (e.g. *black oak, sugar maple*), a fact which later will be shown to have important evolutionary implications.

An explicit recognition of these psychologically based ethnobotanical generic terms can be traced ultimately to Theophrastus, the father of Western systematic botany (see Greene 1909). A more recent exploration of the subject has been provided by the ethnobotanist, Harley Harris Bartlett, in his important paper 'History of the generic concept in botany' (1940). Bartlett, a good field biologist with considerable ethnobotanical experience with several Malayan tribes, noted that a well-defined idea of genera could be found in all of these languages. For Bartlett, the '. . . concept of genus must be as old as folk science itself' (1940:341). He defined the concept as any class '. . . which is more or less consciously thought of as the *smallest* grouping requiring a *distinctive* name' (*ibid*: 356, emphasis added). While somewhat vague as a definition, Bartlett's idea concerning the fundamental nature of generic taxa and their corresponding distinctive labels is essentially correct. In fact, generic names can be seen to exhibit a readily identifiable linguistic structure which allows, in most cases, for their immediate recognition (Berlin 1969, Berlin, Breedlove & Raven n.d.; Conklin 1962: 122; Bulmer & Tyler 1968; Friedrich 1970).

The centrality of named generic taxa as 'semantic primitives' (Friedrich 1970: 156) in ethnobotanical classification is important for the growth of ethnobotanical nomenclature. The most obvious significance is that generic names are the first to become encoded in the ethnobotanical lexicons of all languages. Thus, one may postulate a stage in the development of the plant lexicon of any language whereby one finds a series of plant classes, each labeled by generic names, which partition a portion of a yet unlabeled taxon best glossed as 'plant.' (It will be shown that 'plant' is the last taxon to be uniquely labeled in any plant lexicon.)

It should be reiterated that the partition of the unlabeled category, 'plant,' is not exhaustive at such a stage and that numerous, potentially nameable classes remain unlabeled by generic forms and are linguistically ignored. I would also emphasize that folk generic taxa are likely to correspond to botanical genera *only* in those cases where the scientific classification reflects obvious morphological characteristics of plant groupings which are readily observable by simple visual inspection. Thus, some folk generics will match almost perfectly standard botanical genera, e.g. oaks, pines, etc., while others will be more inclusive, e.g. cacti, ferns, and so on.

## Horizontal Expansion of Generic Names

It is supposed, then, that at some point in the development of a language's ethnobotanical nomenclature one finds a single-leveled taxonomy comprised solely of generic taxa labeled by generic names. Over time, groupings of organisms earlier not recognized linguistically will be named. If one attempts to speculate on how this hypothetical early plant taxonomy expanded, the most plausible argument at the moment is that the direction was, at first, *horizontal*. By horizontal growth I mean the formation of new generic names. The linguistic process of *analogy*, i.e. when some new category is seen to be conceptually related to an already existing category and named accordingly, is an extremely common form of name formation in contemporary languages. One can assume it to have been productive at an earlier time as well. Heinz Werner has discussed this process from a psychological viewpoint and has referred to it as 'concrete transposition.' This process '. . . can frequently be observed in everyday speech. It occurs whenever one uses the expression "something like" or the suffix "-like" or "-ish',' for the description of an object. Concrete transposition is at the basis of many creations of words and changes of meanings . . .' (Werner 1954:204)

Concrete transposition forms an important part of the naming of behavior of the Tzeltal and Tzotzil Mayan Indians of Southern Mexico. When presented with a plant that is conceived to be 'related' to a known plant class *x*, the typical Tzeltal informant will respond *chyle pahaluk sok x*, i.e. 'it is likened to/related to *x*.' The same semantic information is indicated by the Tzotzil expression *k'os x* 'like *x*.' In both languages, the process is a very common one, allowing for the classification of the vast majority of all plants in the environment, inasmuch as most plants are seen to be related to *some* named class. An identical situation has been reported by Bright & Bright (5965) for the Tolowa-speaking Smith River Indians of California and by French (1960) for the Sahaptin Indians of Oregon.

The most thorough-going example of this kind of naming that I have found, however, is reported for a group of Arawak speakers of Surinam. Stahel (1944) notes that 'Arawak Indians in Surinam, when they are naming plants and animals, make liberal use of the suffix BALLI to reduce the number of primary or "generic" names of the hundreds maybe thousands of kinds they have to distinguish. For this purpose they have still two other words—DJAMARO and OJOTO. The first means the same as BALLI, the second "related to"' (1944: 268). As an example, one may note the following set of Arawak plant names, using Stahel's orthography.

| | |
|---|---|
| TÁTABU | *Diplotropis guianensis* Benth. |
| TÁTABUBALLI | *Coutarea hexandra* K. Schum. |
| TÁTABU DJAMARO | *Copaifera epunctata* Amsh. |
| TÁTABU OJOTO | *Ormosiopsis flava* Ducke. |

Stahel states that 'All four are high jungle trees. The first, "zwarte kabbes," is a well-known Surinam timber, the others are less important but all resemble TÁTABU" (*ibid*: 269).

There is some doubt that most linguistic anthropologists would treat the examples mentioned above as legitimate plant names. In a real sense, concrete transposition is a method of making new labels by the use of descriptive phrases. The principle, however, is a productive one and it may become so prevalent, in horizontal expansion of generic names, that descriptive phrases are eventually replaced by genuine lexical expressions.

Such an advance may be illustrated in certain of the Mayan languages whereby one notes the use of a *generic name* plus an *animal name* to refer to a plant class seen to be related to one indicated by the generic name alone. In Tzeltal one finds numerous sets like the following:

*č'omate²* 'chayote' (*Sechium edule* (Jacq.) Sw.)
*č'omate² č o* 'rat's chayote' (*Cyclanthera bourgeana* Naud. ex Char.)

*²išm* 'corn' (*Zea mays* L.)
*²išim ²ahaw* 'snake's corn' (*Anthurium* spp.)

*k'eweš* 'custard apple' (*Annona cherinola* Miller)
*k'eweš maš* 'monkey's custard apple' (*A. reticulata* L.).

In Yucatec Maya, the process is also typical, as can be seen in this example from Roys (1931: 223):

*Cat* 'tree cucumber' (*Paramentiera edulis* DC.)
*Cat-cuuc* 'squirrel's tree cucumber' (*P. aculeata* HBK.).

An identical process in naming generic classes which are seen to be related in some form or other is also found in Hanunóo (Conklin 1954) and Subanun (Frake, personal communication), both languages of the Philippines, and Nahuatl of Central Mexico (Paso y Trancoso 1886). In English one notes the pairs *cabbage:skunk cabbage*, *apple:horse apple*, and *oak:poison oak*. The usage of the English adjectives 'false' and 'mock' may lead to the formation of generic names in an analogous fashion, e.g. *lilac:false lilac*; *cypress:false cypress*; *orange:mock orange*, and so on.

It is important to note that names formed by analogy of the sort just described are *generic* forms and their designata *are not* conceptualized as subordinate taxa. Thus, *mock orange* is not a kind of orange, it is simply *like* orange in certain respects. This point is illustrated nicely by reference to the writings of Theophrastus as discussed by Edward Lee Greene in his little read *Landmarks of botanical history* (1909). Greene notes that about half of Theophrastus' generic names are complex expressions including a noun and an adjective. Several appear to be derived from generic names of a single constituent, e.g. *Calamos* 'reed grass' (*Arundo* spp.) and *Calamos Euosomos* 'sweet flag' (*Acornus calamus*). But Greene has no doubts about Theophrastus' classification of *Calamos* and *Calamos Euosomos* as distinct genera. He writes:

It is not imaginable that a botanist of Theophrastus' ripe experience and great attainments should think those large grass-plants and the sweet-flag to be of the same genus. Beyond doubt, however, the name Calamos Euosomos did originate in the notion that arundo and acornus are next of kin; for, however unlike they are as to size, foliage, and other particulars, there is a remarkably close similarity in their rootstocks, these being of almost the same size, form and color in the two. The gatherers of roots and herbs, as we know looked first of all to the 'roots' of things, and these were their first criteria of plant relationships. To these it should be perfectly natural to place the sweet-flag alongside arundo, the true

[Calamos] by its closely imitative 'root,' and then on account of the aromatic properties of the root to call the plant [Calamos Euosomos] (Greene 1909:123).

Finally, it should be observed that the conceptually central name in a pair consisting of a generic name and one formed by semantic analogy is *lexically unmarked*, i.e. it occurs in an unmodified form, while the noncentral and historically secondary expression is distinguished by a modifier of some sort. As will be seen a little further on, this process of lexical marking is a most productive form of name formation in the overall development of ethnobotanical nomenclature.

In summary, I have suggested that the original ethnobotanical vocabulary of any language (and, by implication, the vocabulary of early man) is at first comprised solely of semantically unitary linguistic expressions which mark the smallest conceptually relevant groupings of plants in man's environment. These expressions are known as *generic names*.

At the outset, the expansion of generic names is accomplished via the process of concrete transposition. It is expressed first in the form of descriptive or descriptive-like phrases or expressions which at a later period in the history of a language may be more formally codified by the formation of definite lexical forms. This form of expansion is to be joined by the processes of generalization and differentiation as nomenclature develops over time. Concrete transposition is to remain, however, as a potentially productive process throughout the history of a language's development.

## DIFFERENTIATION AND GENERALIZATION: THE APPEARANCE OF SPECIFIC AND MAJOR LIFE-FORM NAMES

I had at one time hoped to show that specific names become encoded in a language's ethnobotanical lexicon before the appearance of major life forms such as 'tree,' 'vine,' 'grass' and so on. The data that I have been able to gather at this time do not allow for a definitive answer as to which ethnobotanical category may be prior. I know of no language which lacks at least some specific plant names, although there may have been languages, such as that spoken by the Tasmanians, which lacked general life-form terms. The evidence on this point, however, is scant and probably unreliable.

Consequently, a weaker hypothesis is presented here which posits no temporal distinction as to the rise of specific and supra-generic categories, although further research may require a modification of this view.

## DIFFERENTIATION AND THE FORMATION OF SPECIFIC NAMES

In Bartlett's paper on the genus concept, he noted that: 'With enlarging experience, people make finer distinctions and need different names for newly distinguished entities which have previously been called by the same original name. The original name becomes generic in its application; variously qualified it provides the basis of specific names' (1940:349).

I would take issue only with Bartlett's phrase '. . . The original name becomes generic in its application . . .' It had *originally* been generic and, with enlarging experience, is merely partitioned into sub-classes.

There appears to be some psychological evidence to support such a position. Werner notes '. . . that the predominant developmental trend is in the direction of differentiation rather than of synthesis. [Likewise], the formation of general concepts from specific terms is of lesser importance in non-scientific communication though it is rather a characteristic of scientific endeavor. In other words, language in everyday life is directed toward the concrete and specific rather than toward the abstract and general. Because of this trend toward the concrete, semantic generalization develops slowly and by intermediate steps (Werner 1954:203).

If differentiation is to occur and be lexically encoded, there appears to be a fairly concise way in which one can imagine it happening. First, the division of a generic name is most probably binary, at least at the outset. This observation is borne out in fact in present day folk taxonomic systems which have been well studied. By far the greatest number of contrast sets comprised of specific taxa in folk biotaxonomies are comprised exactly of *two* specific names (Berlin, Breedlove & Raven in press; Conklin 1954:128).

## Type-specific Nomenclature

A highly regular labeling process can be described for the encoding of specific taxa, given the primarily binary partition of a generic taxon. In general, one specific category, because it is most widespread, larger, best known, or the like, will always be recognized as the typical species of the folk genus. This taxon can be referred to as the *type-specific*, the archetype, or the ideal type. 'Type-species' have long been recognized in systematic biology. The notion, codified by Linnaeus, can be seen to have its origin in folk biosystematics since earliest times and has been reported by many anthropologists working with societies intimately involved with nature. Dentan, who has worked extensively with the primitive Semai of Southeast Asia, notes: 'My impression is that the Semai think that some species are more "typical" of their categories than other species are. For example, *naga* (snakelike dragons) seem to represent the quintessence of "they beneath the earth." Giant monitors, in turn, are the prime representatives of "lizard," and regal python of "snake"' (Dentan 1968:35).

A strikingly general nomenclatural regularity can also be suggested as regards the relationship of the type specific, its contrasting non-typical specific, and the superordinate generic name. In the early stages of the division of a generic taxon into two specific categories, the *type-specific will invariably be polysemous with its superordinate generic in characteristic usage.* Stated in other terms, the type-specific taxon will be lexically *unmarked* in normal speech, being referred to by the identical linguistic expression as its superordinate generic. Such polysemous labeling of taxa at differing levels of generalization has been discussed by Hymes (1960), Frake (1962) and Conklin (1962) in reference to folk biosystematics and by Greenberg (1966) in reference to lexicon in general. Several examples will illustrate this nomenclatural principle. As Wyman and Harris have said in referring to Navaho ethnobotany, 'The situation is as if in our binomial system the generic name were used alone for the best known species of a genus, while binomial terms were used for all other members of the genus' (1941:120).

Washington Matthews (1886) was the first to recognize explicitly type-specific nomenclature in Navaho. In an especially careful piece of research for its time, Matthews notes that '. . . there are three species of juniper growing in the Zuni mountains; each has its own appropriate name, yet the generic name for juniper . . . appears in all' (1886:767). Diagrammatically:

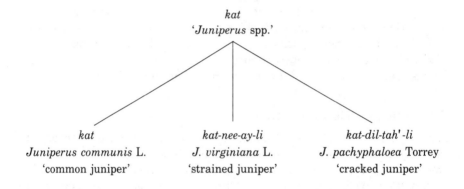

Several other examples found in Matthews show the same principle at work:

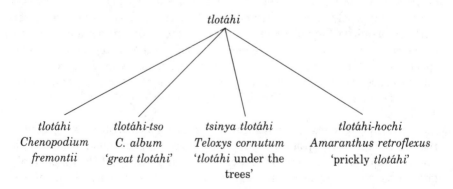

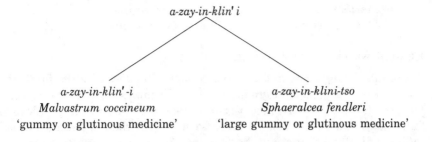

a-zay-in-klin' i

a-zay-in-klin' -i
*Malvastrum coccineum*
'gummy or glutinous medicine'

a-zay-in-klini-tso
*Sphaeralcea fendleri*
'large gummy or glutinous medicine'

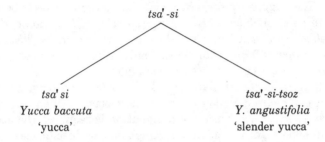

tsa' -si

tsa' si
*Yucca baccuta*
'yucca'

tsa' -si-tsoz
*Y. angustifolia*
'slender yucca'

Classical Nahuatl also exhibits this nomenclatural regularity in that the most common specific form included in a particular generic class is labeled polysemously by the generic name. Thus, one observes that in the Nahuatl classification of sedges, *tollin* included a '. . . type-species [sic] that carried simply the name *Tollin* and that [also] referred to the sedge family, various other related species of it having been grouped under the same name, each with a different determination' (Paso y Troncoso 1886:218).

A final example of polysemous generic and type-specific plant names can be seen again in the early work of Theophrastus, who, as a plant nomenclator, took great pains to preserve the essential structure of the names discovered to be in common usage in his day. As Greene says, Theophrastus '. . . left plant nomenclature as he found it' (1909:123). Greene captures the essence of the early botanist's view aptly: 'The Theophrastan nomenclature of plants is as simply natural as can be imagined. Not only are monotypic genera called by a single name; where the species are known to be several, the type-species of the genus—that is, that which is most historic—is without a specific name, at least very commonly, and only the others have each its specific adjective superadded to the generic appellation' (Greene 1909:120).

The following examples attest to this fact:

| [*Theophrastus' names*] | [*Modern equivalents*] |
|---|---|
| Peuce | *Pinus picea* |
| Peuce Idaia | *P. maritima* |
| Peuce conophoros | *P. pinea* |
| Peuce paralios | *P. halepensis* |

| Mespilos | Mespilos cotoneaster |
| Mespilos anthedon | Crataegus tominalis |

## Lexical Marking of Type-specific Names

While many languages find no need to mark linguistically the focal type-specific within a particular grouping of specific names, a circumstance which I suggest is characteristic of the process employed in the earliest specific name formation, situations of social intercourse may arise whereby one must be able to linguistically differentiate the type-specific category from its contrasting neighbor(s). The linguistic process by which this contrast comes to be indicated is also quite general. *Invariably, the type-specific will be modified with an attributive-like expression best glossed as 'genuine,' 'real,' or 'ideal-type.'*

Such a situation is found characteristically in many languages, of which Tzeltal and Hanunóo may be cited as examples.

In Tzeltal, *ʔič* is the generic name for 'chili pepper' (*Capsicum* spp.). In most contexts, *ʔič* can be used alone to refer to the most prominent specific class. However, when greater precision of designation is required, the attributive *bac'il* 'genuine' is readily applied to distinguish this specific class, *bac'il ʔič* 'genuine chili pepper' from its contrasting coordinate specific classes. Thus, one finds:

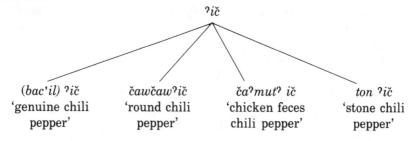

| *(bac'il) ʔič* | *čawčawʔič* | *čaʔmutʔ ič* | *ton ʔič* |
| 'genuine chili pepper' | 'round chili pepper' | 'chicken feces chili pepper' | 'stone chili pepper' |

An identical nomenclatural principle has been described for Hanunóo. Conklin, in an as yet unpublished ethnobotany of this people, notes that '. . . a shared term [i.e. a generic plant name partitioned by two or more specific names] when not followed by an attribute, may be read as that term plus *ʔurūŋan* "real." The resulting name is a preferred synonym, required where the designated plant name is distinguished from others in the same set' (Conklin 1954:259). An example can be seen in the classification of Job's tears.

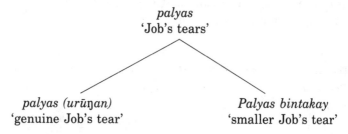

| *palyas (urūŋan)* | *Palyas bintakay* |
| 'genuine Job's tear' | 'smaller Job's tear' |

While the type-specific remains unmarked, or marked only in contexts where ambiguity might arise, the non-typical specific(s) will *obligatorily be marked.* The linguistic structure of such non-typical (or secondary) specifics appears to be of a specifiable form. *Such names will be comprised of the generic names* (in which they are included) *plus a modifying attributive-like expression. In all cases, such non-typical specific expressions will be binomial in structure.*

The feature(s) focused on by the modifying attributive-like expression is generally some obvious perceptual dimension such as color, size, growth habit, habitat, or the like. Such a situation may be diagrammatically indicated in the following hypothetical specific contrast sets.

GENERICS     *x*                *y*                *z*

SPECIFICS    (genuine) *x* red *x*    (genuine) *y* small *y*    (genuine) *z* water-place *z*

## Fossilization of the Type-specific Attributive

In some languages, for example, especially the Mayan language, Tzeltal, 'pattern pressure' appears to be working so as to make the presence of the type-specific attributive (i.e. 'genuine') obligatory or independent of context. As an example, the type-specific *bac il ?alčaš* 'genuine orange' is almost universally the preferred usage (vs. the simple unmarked *?alčaš*) in contexts where it contrasts with forms such as *pahal ?alčaš* 'sour orange' *?elemoneš ?alčaš* 'lemon orange,' etc. This tendency, I think, represents a later development which follows logically from the prior, unmarked usage.

An even further logical sequence can be seen at work in Tzeltal which may or may not have general validity as a subsequent development in all systems. In few membered contrast sets having two or three members one notes the tendency for the type-specific to assume a value on the semantic dimension indicated in the name(s) of its contrasting member(s). Thus, while a contrast set might have at one time included members labeled as:

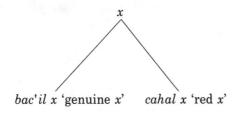

*bac'il x* 'genuine *x*'      *cahal x* 'red *x*'

where the semantic dimension of *color* appears indicated in the *marked non-typical* specific, it now becomes habitually labeled as:

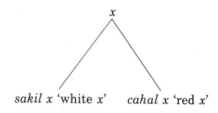

*sakil x* 'white *x*'   *cahal x* 'red *x*'

As concerns specific examples where the dimension of color is involved, I think it of no mean theoretical significance that the attributive replacing 'genuine' in the type-specific member is *sakil* 'white,' a rather 'typical color' in flower pigmentation (flower color being a major semantic dimension used to differentiate many closely related specifics) and almost neutral, as it were, in terms of its marking potential.

## The Development of Lexical Markings in Specific Nomenclature

I now want to summarize the theoretical developmental sequence for the lexical marking of specific plant names.

(a) First, the generic taxon is partitioned into a *type-specific* and one (or more) *non-typical specific(s)*. The type-specific is *lexically unmarked* and *polysemous* with its superordinate generic. The non-typical specific(s) is *lexically marked*, a feature leading to a binomial expression. Diagrammatically:

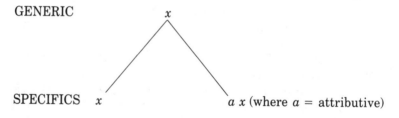

(b) Over time, the type-specific must be linguistically distinguished in certain contexts of semantic contrast from the non-typical specific(s). An optional 'type-marking' attributive is applied to the type-specific. Invariably it will best be glossed as 'genuine,' 'real,' or 'most typical.' Diagrammatically:

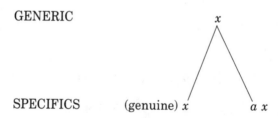

(c) In the penultimate stage, time, usage and binomial pattern-pressure of specific nomenclature will force the type-marking attributive, 'genuine,' to become obligatory. Once obligatory, its semantic marking function is radically reduced and ultimately it becomes completely neutralized. Diagrammatically:

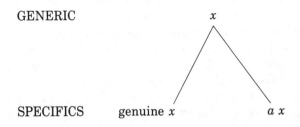

GENERIC                             $x$

SPECIFICS     genuine $x$          $a\ x$

(d) In the ultimate stage, pattern pressure will force the neutralized type-marking attributive to be replaced by an attributive from the same semantic dimension as the attributive indicated in the contrasting non-typical specific(s). Thus, a set of forms that were formally:

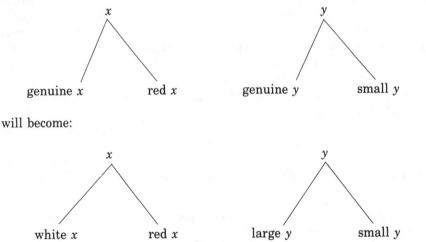

$x$                                 $y$

genuine $x$     red $x$         genuine $y$     small $y$

will become:

$x$                                 $y$

white $x$     red $x$        large $y$     small $y$

## THE RISE OF MAJOR LIFE-FORM NAMES

While generic and specific names account for the vast majority of names for plants in natural ethnobotanical vocabularies, a smaller number of forms occur which are of greater inclusiveness than generics and specifics. These expressions may be referred to as *life form* names. At some point in man's classification of the plant world, the concrete differences marked by generic names could be dispensed with in some contexts and higher order abstract names were developed which marked such major life forms as 'tree,' 'vine,' 'herb' and so on. This is not to say that such categories had not been *conceptually recognized* by man since earliest times. I find it difficult to conceive that such was not in fact the case. It is likely, however, that these higher order categories lacked simple, monolexemic designations. The development of life-form names is most certainly subsequent to the appearance of generic names in the evolution of ethnobotanical nomenclature.

While very little is known concerning the processes involved in the formation of life form names, it is clear that in many languages the labels for life form categories are drawn directly from the existing inventory of generic names. Furthermore, the labeling of major life form taxa can be seen to follow identical marking principles as those described for generic and specific names. Applying the principles which we have seen to be at work in the case of generics and specifics, one can make fairly good guesses as to which names get elevated to major class status: precisely those generic names which, because of their distribution and cultural importance, are most salient culturally. In many of these instances, the life form name and a subordinate generic are polysemous.

Buck's massive compilation of synonyms for the major Indo-European languages provides data on the rise of the major life form name "tree" that bears on this hypothesis: 'A widespread group of words for "tree," many of them meaning also "wood," go back to an IE word which probably denoted a particular kind of tree, namely the oak' (Buck 1949:48). And again: 'Noteworthy is the primacy of the oak, as shown in mythology and in the recurring use of "oak" as the tree par excellence, for "tree"' (*ibid.*: 528). Finally, Buck notes the reconstruction "Oak." I. IE* *derwo- dru-*, etc. in words for "oak," and for "tree," "wood," the former, specific use being probably the earlier' (*ibid.*).

The most recent and authoritative statement on the proto-Indo-European arboreal system is that of Paul Friedrich (1970). Friedrich rejects the generally accepted alternative hypothesis that *\*derwo* originally meant 'tree,' rather than 'oak.' His conclusions are especially interesting:

> . . . it seems probable that the primitive, arboreally oriented PIE distinguished several species of oak by distinct morphs, and that *\*ayg-*, *\*perkʷ-* and *\*dorw-* served in this way. As the oak and mixed-oak forests were reduced and contracted, and as the speakers of the PIE dialects migrated into their new homelands—two simultaneous processes during the third and second millennia—the denotations of the *\*dorw-* reflexes shifted to 'wood, tree, hardness,' and yet other referents; this would hold especially for the shift to 'fir, tar, pinewood' and the like in the Baltic and North Germanic dialects, since the speakers are thought to have migrated into northern coniferous zones during the centuries when the oaks were receding. It is also quite possible that even in PIE times the main name for the oak—a sort of *Urbaum*—was occasionally or dialectically applied to 'tree' in general. Within pre-Homeric Greek δρῦς and δρυός could denote either 'oak' or 'tree' with disambiguation through social or literary context. By Classical Greek times the meaning had narrowed to the original PIE 'tree.' In more recent centuries

the identical process has been documented in Germanic, where *eik* shifted from 'oak' to 'tree' in Icelandic—oaks being virtually absent in that country (Friedrich, 1970:146).

While the polysemous origins of life form names in nomenclaturally advanced languages have become obscure, their etymologies determinable only by historical reconstruction, such is not the case with numerous less advanced societies yet in the early stages of their nomenclatural life-histories. In fact, some data suggest that one is observing in some languages the actual accension of some supra-generic taxa, suggesting that such languages have only recently moved from the prior stage of ethnobotanical nomenclature of generic names only. Furthermore, it is not surprising to find polysemous generic and life form plant names in languages spoken by societies which are rather simple in their cultural-technological development.

The best reported cases now available to me are found in the Great Basin and the Southwestern areas of the United States, though there are doubtless other examples in other parts of the world. Trager (apparently unaware of an earlier paper by Albert Gatschet [1899] who reports the same data) noted that in several Southwestern Indian groups, the word for 'tree' was polysemous with the word for 'cottonwood,' the only deciduous tree which grows with abundance outside the major forests. For example, in Taos Pueblo '. . . the ordinary word for "tree" . . . *tûłǫ́nạ* is also the word for "cottonwood"' (Trager 1939:117). Furthermore, 'In Isleta and Sandia (southern Tiwa dialects not very different from the northern Taos and Picuris) the word *tûła* means "tree, cottonwood" . . .' (*ibid.*). Finally, in Hopi, '. . . we find the same word, *söhǫ́vi*, used for both' (*ibid.*).

A more recent study by Fowler and Leland on Northern Paiute ethnosystematics verifies Trager's observations for this Great Basin people. They state that '. . . the terms for cottonwood tree [*siŋábi*] can include the willow tree at one level and can also be used in popular speech for any deciduous tree' (Fowler & Leland 1967:387).

In a paper recently brought to my attention by Barbara Demory, Almstedt (1968) reports generic name-life form name polysemy for Diegueño, a Yuman-speaking group of Southern California. Here, however, the term for 'tree,' *isnyaaw*, is polysemous with another ecologically important tree, the California live oak, *Quercus agrifolia*. This species of oak has the widest distribution and is the most generally available source of edible acorns in the area inhabited by these people. For Almstedt, '. . . it seems logical that this name *isnyaaw* should be used for tree when the need arose' (1968:13).

Demory (in press) surveyed additional languages in the Hokan family and found numerous other examples of life form-generic polysemy. In each case, the generic of major cultural significance in that particular geographic area appears to have assumed life form status. Thus in Karok, *ʔípahA* 'juniper, tree'; Achumawi, *aswō* 'sugar pine, tree'; Atsugewi, *ajwi* 'kind of pine, tree'; Yana *baacul²i* 'broad leaf maple, tree'; Salinan, *hat'* 'oak, tree'; Chumash, *ku-wu* 'live oak, tree.'

Earlier work by Bright & Bright (1965:253–4) reports the term *tepo* as polysemously meaning both 'fir' and 'tree' and Gatschet notes Klamath *k'ōsh* as both 'pine' and 'tree' (1890: I, 546).

A final example of this nomenclatural regularity is found in Western Apache as described by Keith Basso. It is made even more important because Basso's data bear both on the rise of major life-form names as well as the formation of specific names. Basso writes:

> The situation among the Western Apaches is much the same as that you describe for the Great Basin and other portions of the Southwest. The term for cottonwood (*t'íís*) is also used for 'tree'; in addition, however—and this is what makes it interesting—*t'íís* may also designate a 'real cottonwood'— namely, those which are tall, heavily foliaged, and situated near the banks of flowing streams and creeks. A few cottonwoods, much more stunted and less green grow in dry washes and arroyos. These are called *t'íís da'iską́ą́* ('cottonwoods underfed'). *T'íís* in the sense of 'genuine cottonwood' is sometimes labeled *t'íís da'bííhii* 'cottonwood true'/'cottonwood correct' (Basso, personal communication).

Basso diagrams the taxonomic structure of these lexical items as follows:

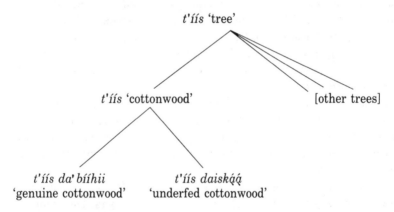

*t'íís* 'tree'

*t'íís* 'cottonwood'     [other trees]

*t'íís da'bííhii*          *t'íís daiską́ą́*
'genuine cottonwood'    'underfed cottonwood'

A linguistic expression does not become a major class form overnight, however. Presumably, the process is a relatively slow one. Data from Shoshone, another language of the Great Basin, may be relevant at this point. Wick Miller, who has been involved in an extensive study of the Shoshone, notes the common use of *sohopi* for tree, cottonwood, willow, aspen, stick and log, but is uncertain as to whether the term can be applied to *any* tree, e.g. 'What I do not know, and what would be of particular importance to you, is whether or not these terms [*sohopi*] can be used generically [i.e. inclusively] that is, can I say, for example, "an oak tree is a sohopi" ("cottonwood tree")?' (Miller, personal communication).

Fowler (personal communication), on further consideration, also questions the use of Northern Paiute *sivábi* for all deciduous trees, suggesting that the term might be restricted to aspen, cottonwood and willow. Ash, alder and mountain mahogany, potential candidates for *siŋábi*, grow outside the Northern Paiute range.

Miller's and Fowler's comments bring up an interesting point as concerns the assumption of supra-generic status by a particular generic taxon. We have no reason to assume that a recently elevated supra-generic should have, at the outset, an extension radically different from that of the generic from which it has arisen. Thus, a term which may eventually come to refer to all 'hard, single-stemmed, erect plants attaining a specified height' (i.e. 'trees'), might originally be restricted to a small sub-set of 'trees.' In the case of the Shoshone term *sohopi*, it might be restricted to 'cottonwood-like deciduous trees' (e.g. cottonwood, willow, aspen, etc.) and later come to refer to deciduous trees generally. An even later development might force the extension of the general term to include the obviously aberrant conifers, e.g. pines, firs, etc. This surely must have been the case with the general use of Indo-European *derwo* from 'oak' to 'tree' in general. A comparable situation is illustrated in Tzeltal where 'tree' is seen to include *only* truly woody stemmed organisms attaining a specified height, excluding such 'obvious' trees (from the folk western point of view) as *palms*, these latter forms being considered as unique generic classes.

The ultimate extension of the major class supra-generic 'tree' can perhaps best be illustrated in modern American English folk botany where any single-stemmed upright plant with leaves at the top is admitted to the class, allowing for the botanically unlikely assortment of such diverse organisms as oaks, pines, palms, banana (trees) and even certain tree-like bamboos.

## The Marking of 'Type Generics'

The examples I have thus far cited have all referred to languages where the culturally central generic term which gives rise to major life-form names remains unmarked, in common usage, being polysemous with its superordinate suprageneric. Reviewing examples of generic-specific polysemy, might one not also expect to find systems whereby the generic name becomes *marked*, at least in certain contexts? And might not these instances be seen as a subsequent development, just as was the case in generic-specific polysemy? In fact, such examples are found, though in the fossilized stage of development, in Tzeltal and Tzotzil, although there is also evidence of a similar situation in Kiowa Apache of Oklahoma.

The marking processes distinguishing what now might be called the 'type-generic' are identical to those described earlier for type-specifics. Thus, if modified, the polysemous form comes to be qualified linguistically with an expression best glossed as 'genuine.'

To illustrate, in Kiowa Apache, the term for 'tree' is *ʔádw* while that for 'cottonwood,' the most prominent deciduous form, is *a-hi*, a form literally translated as 'tree-real,' i.e. 'genuine tree' (see Trager 1939:118). For some speakers of Tzeltal, the term *bac'il ʔak* 'genuine vine' (<*ʔak* 'vine') occurs as a generic for the most important vine utilized in house construction binding, *Smilax subpubescens* A.DC. One also finds, for some speakers, the generic *bac'il ʔak* 'genuine grass' (<*ʔak* 'grass') for the most common and important grass employed as a major thatching in house roofing, *Muhlenbergia macroura* (HBK). Hitchc. Finally, in Zinacantan Tzotzil, the most important tree, both in house construction and as a firewood, is *bac i-teʔ* 'genuine tree' (<*teʔ* 'tree'), a form which refers to the prominent oak species of the area, *Quercus peduncularis* Née.

These terms in the Mayan languages just cited are not metaphorical or synonymous expressions for the informants who have them as terms in their respective nomenclatural systems, although synonymous expressions do exist. The fact that the attributive constituent *bac'il* 'genuine,' has become frozen in each case, its presence being obligatory, is quite analogous to the situations whereby the type-marking attributive fossilizes and becomes obligatory in specific names.

Finally, Gatschet (1899) reports a similar body of data from Nipissing, a dialect of Ojibwa. Here *andak* means 'evergreen tree' and *inin andak* 'real evergreen tree' or 'pine.' Likewise, *ātik* 'deciduous tree' includes the generic name *inin ātik* 'real deciduous tree,' i.e. 'maple.' One can see how a culturally central generic name in each case has become obligatorily marked linguistically by the form 'genuine.'

## Summary of the Development of Life-form Names

The theoretical development sequence for the appearance of major life form taxa may now be summarized as a series of at least four steps.

(a) At the outset, the newly encoded life form category is labeled polysemously with the most common generic form from which it was derived. Its extension is, at first: rather limited: perhaps only to those generics which are seen to be quite similar to the type-generic. Diagrammatically:

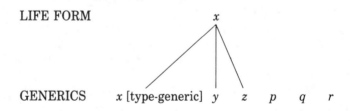

LIFE FORM        *x*

GENERICS    *x* [type-generic]   *y*   *z*   *p*   *q*   *r*

(b) Over time, the type-generic comes to be optionally marked, linguistically with the type-marking attributive, 'genuine.'

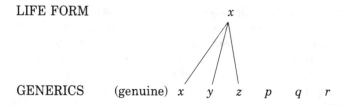

LIFE FORM                               *x*

GENERICS        (genuine)  *x*   *y*   *z*   *p*   *q*   *r*

(c) Further development leads to the fossilization (neutralization) of the type-marking attributive, 'genuine,' and it becomes obligatory. Meanwhile, the life form is expanding its referential extension, including taxa originally excluded.

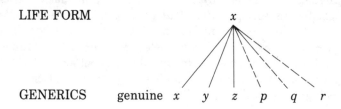

LIFE FORM                               *x*

GENERICS        genuine  *x*   *y*   *z*   *p*   *q*   *r*

(d) Final stages of growth are indicated when polysemy is totally obscured in the current forms, the original expressions having been replaced or otherwise changed.

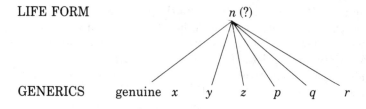

LIFE FORM                               *n* (?)

GENERICS        genuine  *x*   *y*   *z*   *p*   *q*   *r*

## THE APPEARANCE OF VARIETAL NAMES

It would appear that the naming of varietal taxa will, in general, *follow* the appearance of the major life-form taxa. This is not a contradiction, as it might at first seem, of the tendency for abstract terms to occur later in a language's history than highly specific ones. It is a reflection of the greater control over the processes of domestication that man has acquired only through long millennia of trial and error methods. All of the information available to me at the moment shows that legitimate varietal names occur almost exclusively in the classification of important cultivars. I would imagine that the same holds true for animals. The control over nature that is required in selecting and maintaining a particular race of corn, beans, rice, chili-pepper, squash or what have you, morphologically distinctive enough to merit habitual lexical designation, can be accomplished only by relatively advanced horticulturalists. Accordingly, one should not expect to find varietal ethnobotanical nomenclature except in the languages of societies which practice rather refined methods of cultivation. Even in these languages, varietal names will be restricted to highly important groups of cultivated plants.

Given the appearance of varietal taxa, however, it appears relatively simple to specify the linguistic structure of names used to refer to such taxa. In all cases, the specific name (logically of the form *attributive, generic*, order being irrelevant) will be formed by the *addition of another attributive*. And, as one might expect, the processes of lexical marking described earlier apply equally well in varietal name formation.

The general principles seen to be at work can be illustrated firstly in Tzeltal. In this language, the generic taxon *loʔbal* 'banana' includes at least twelve distinct specific classes, e.g. *bac'il loʔbal* 'genuine banana,' *sakil loʔbal* 'white banana,' *sera loʔbal* 'wax banana,' *cahal loʔbal* 'red banana,' etc. One of these specific forms includes two varietals labeled in the expected manner, i.e. the type-varietal occurring unmarked, in typical usage, but marked with the type-marking attributive, 'genuine,' if ambiguity occurs, and the non-typical varietal being obligatorily marked. Thus one notes the forms:

| | |
|---|---|
| *(bac'il) cahal loʔbal* | '(genuine) red banana' |
| *sakil cahal loʔbal* | 'white red banana' |

It is rare that varietal names include more than *two* modifying expressions, i.e. indicate classes of greater specificity than 'first-order' varietals. In Hanunóo, of the 1094 terminal taxa that are specific or varietal names, 961 are specific taxa and 97 are varietals. Of these 97 varietals, 87 are first-order forms, i.e. marked only by *two* attributives. Only two generic names include 'sub-varietals' comprised of more than *two* attributives and these occur in the highly important cultivars, corn and chili-peppers (Conklin 1954).

In actual speech, it is also rare that a varietal be referred to by its 'full name.' There is a strong tendency for such forms to participate in what Conklin has called 'abbreviation' (Conklin 1962:122), i.e. when a part of the name may be used to stand for the varietal class as a whole. In such cases, abbreviation will lead the primary, i.e. *specific*, attributive to function as a head of the expression, the resulting form in most cases being, then, binomial in form. As an example note the English varietals:

*butter lima(s) bean*
*baby lima(s) bean*

where *butter lima(s)* and *baby lima(s)* may occur as complete expressions. The same can be noted in Tzeltal, also for beans, where one notes the forms:

| | |
|---|---|
| *cahal šlumil čenek'* | 'red ground beans' |
| *ʔihk'al šlumil čenek* | 'black ground beans' |

where *cahal šlumil* 'red ground [ones]' and *ʔink'al šlumil* 'black ground [ones]' can occur alone.

## THE PROBLEM OF INTERMEDIATE TAXA

In examining the ethnobiological lexicon of numerous languages, I have noticed a strong tendency for the hierarchical depth of biotaxonomies to be uniformly shallow. Superordinate taxa of greater inclusiveness than the folk genus, the life form names, are invariably few in number and are inclusive of the majority of all named taxa. Subordinate taxa of lesser inclusiveness than folk genera, i.e. specific names, are likewise few in number and occur predominantly in those taxa with critical cultural importance (e.g. cultivated plants or domesticated animals). One may generalize and claim that *most folk biotaxonomies are comprised primarily of named generic, major life form, and specific taxa, with generic classes being by far the most numerous and psychologically significant.*

Covert 'mid-level' categories of greater inclusiveness than folk generic categories but not yet life-form categories may be seen to exist in many taxonomies and their recognition is of crucial importance to a full understanding of the complete classificatory structure (see Berlin, Breedlove & Raven 1968). However, the fact that these mid-level categories have not been labeled suggests that the need to distinguish such classes is as yet relatively unimportant in most cultural contexts.

Nonetheless, the question remains: Why are named intermediate taxa almost totally absent in natural ethnobiological taxonomies? The conclusion that I have tentatively come to is that such taxa are rare because they are basically unstable categories, a point which will be developed below.

How are named intermediate taxa likely to arise? At one point, it was suggested that the already present covert categories of this taxonomic rank would be the most probable candidates for labeling (see Berlin, Breedlove & Raven 1968:297). As research continues, this hypothesis appears not to be verified in fact. What has been discovered, however, is that named taxa of less inclusiveness than major life forms yet more inclusive than folk generics appear primarily as a response to situations whereby native polytypic generics must be distinguished from newly encountered generics (see now Berlin, Breedlove & Raven, n.d., for a detailed discussion).

Thus far, two distinct processes—or better said, paths—have been observed that account for the rise of named intermediate taxa. The first occurs in culture contact situations where certain introduced organisms must be incorporated into the native taxonomy. If the introduced plants are conceived to be similar—in the native view of the world—to a named polytypic native generic class and *yet not similar enough to be included as a specific of that generic*, a named higher order taxon will arise which includes both the native and introduced forms.

The second process, not as clearly understood as the first, occurs when some specific taxa become 'conceptually' distinct from their neighboring specific taxa. When this occurs, the conceptually distinctive taxon *will assume the status of a generic, will cease to be labeled by a binomial expression, and in so doing, will force the original generic to assume a superordinate taxonomic status.*

The first process can be illustrated with examples from Tzeltal. At the time of the Hispanic Conquest, the highland Mayan groups were introduced to two similar and yet quite distinct grain crops, wheat and sorghum. These grain-bearing crops were considered to be similar by the Tzeltal population to their own polytypic generic class of native corn, *ʔišim*. Logically enough, the two introduced classes were linguistically designated as *kašlan ʔišim* 'Castillian corn,' i.e. *'wheat'* and *móro ʔišim* 'Moor's corn,' i.e. *'sorghum.'* Their conceptual affiliation with corn is verified in that both names occur as responses to the query, *bitik sbil huhuten ʔišim* 'What are the names of each kind of corn?' Further questioning, however, clearly demonstrates that these two introduced plants are not kinds of *genuine* corn, or, as the Tzeltal would say, not *bac'il ʔišim*.

The new taxonomic structure, then, is seen as one where a superordinate class of greater inclusiveness than those which have been considered as generic groupings, has arisen. Diagrammatically:

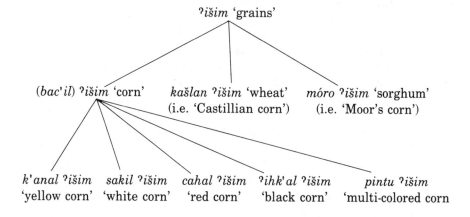

The newly formed superordinate taxon, *ʔišim*, may best be glossed as 'grains,' at least for the moment. And, in precise accord with the processes of lexical marking described earlier, the type-generic 'corn' is marked optionally by the attributive *bac'il* 'genuine' distinguishing it, in situations of ambiguity from 'wheat' and 'sorghum.' Otherwise, it is polysemous with the newly formed superordinate intermediate taxon, 'grain.'

Nomenclaturally, the recently introduced generic names are binomial in structure and in this respect do not conform to the otherwise linguistically unitary structure of other generic names. Time and usage, however, will tend to neutralize the marking properties of the attributive forms *kašlan* and *móro* and the expressions will come to be conceived of as single, semantic units. Geoghegan has aptly characterized the process as follows:

> Either because of frequency of perception, need to communicate or what-have-you, a single pattern can be established . . . i.e., rather than identification

proceeding from the use of two patterns, as in the first stage, a single unsegmented pattern recognition routine comes into use. At this point, the [complex] nature of the coding no longer has support (since only one feature rather than two is being used), and the complex term will have a tendency to decay, [becoming] a lexeme with a unitary cognitive representation (Geoghegan, personal communication).

A strikingly similar situation to that described for the Tzeltal data can be seen in the classificatory treatment of the introduced New World sweet potato (*Ipomea batatas*), among the primitive peoples residing in the vicinity of Mt Hagen in the Central New Guinea Highlands. The Mt Hagen material illustrates, furthermore, the interplay of lexical marking and cultural significance in an interesting and important way.

In Hagen ethnoscience, *oka* refers to the sweet potato, *I. batatas*. *Oka mapumb*, a contrasting generic, refers to the indigenous edible tuber, *Pueraria lobata*. A third name, *oka koeka*, refers to a wild, inedible tuberous vine and *oka kombkla* to a wild tuberless vine with leaves similar to *oka*.

Marilyn Strathern reports that all of the four above names are considered conceptually similar to one another in terms of a variety of characters. On the other hand, it is clear from Strathern's paper that each form refers to a distinctive generic class. Thus, *oka mapumb*, 'Pueraria' is *not* a kind of *oka*.

> *Oka mapumb* (Pueraria) may be contrasted with *oka ingk* (true [ingk] *oka*, i.e. sweet potato) or with *oka* alone, which, when unqualified, always refers to sweet potato [sic]. Only if modified by *mapumb*, *koeka*, etc., does *oka* mean something other than sweet potato. Conversely, Pueraria can only be referred to by employing a special suffix such as *mapumb*; it is never just *oka* (Strathern 1969:193).

Furthermore, additional evidence shows that *oka* is partitioned into various specific names, none of which include these forms *oka mapumb*, *oka kombkla*, etc.

In Strathern's words:

> *Oka* (sweet potato) may be divided into numerous secondary taxa. When collections of these names were made, only once did *mapumb* enter any list. In all the other cases the secondary taxa referred to divisions of *oka* = sweet potato, and excluded any mention of *oka mapumb*. *Mapumb* is thus not seen as a named type of sweet potato on a par with the other varieties (*konome*, *pora*, etc.) (Strathern 1969:193).

The linguistic and ethnographic evidence suggests that one may characterize the Hageners classification of the plants involved as follows:

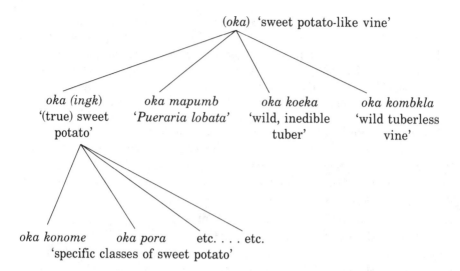

(*oka*) 'sweet potato-like vine'

| *oka (ingk)* | *oka mapumb* | *oka koeka* | *oka kombkla* |
| '(true) sweet potato' | '*Pueraria lobata*' | 'wild, inedible tuber' | 'wild tuberless vine' |

*oka konome*   *oka pora*   etc. . . . . etc.
'specific classes of sweet potato'

The Mt Hagen example, then, can be said to be strikingly parallel to the Tzeltal treatment of grains. Here one sees the possibly covert recognition of an intermediate taxon, *oka* 'sweet potato-like vines' that includes not only sweet potato but as well *Pueraria* and related vines. Unlike the Tzeltal case, however, the introduced generic, *oka*, has come to assume *unmarked status*, being optionally marked only in contexts of ambiguity. While the details of this development are unclear, one may make several inferences which are fairly well supported on linguistic grounds.

It is likely that at one point, before the introduction of the sweet potato, *oka*, referred, in its unmarked form, to *Pueraria lobata*. The terms *oka koeka* 'wild inedible tuber' and *oka kombkla* can be seen simply as examples of generic name extension formed on the basis of analogy as discussed above.

With the appearance of sweet potato, 'which is morphologically similar to *P. lobata*, one can surmise a period whereby the former class was linguistically referred to as *oka x*, where *x* must have represented some unknown qualifying expression.

Through time, the cultural importance of sweet potato increased dramatically, eventually exceeding that of *P. lobata*. At some point in this process, *oka* came to refer, in its unmarked form, to sweet potato and *P. lobata* became obligatorily indicated by the complex expression *oka mapumb*.

In fact, a process identical to the one just supposed can be documented with some accuracy for certain Tzeltal animal names.

The second process whereby superordinate intermediate taxa are named does not necessarily result from the introduction of new organisms. This situation occurs when a *native specific assumes the status of a generic category*. There may be a period in the process when the distinctive (conceptually) specific taxon is labeled by a unitary lexeme and not the standard binomial expression characteristic of most specific taxa.

The process can be illustrated by an example from Tzeltal and concerns the classification of oaks. For most informants, the generic *hihte⁊* 'oak' includes four specific taxa, *ca⁊pat hihte⁊* 'excrement barked oak,' *sahyok hihte⁊* 'white-footed oak,' *k'eweš hihte⁊* 'custard-apple oak,' and *čikinib hihte⁊* 'armadillo-eared oak.' This latter form may, for most informants, be cited in abbreviated form, i.e. simply *čikinib*. For some informants, the abbreviated form is, indeed, the preferred usage.

Some Tzeltal speakers, however, recognize only the first three classes of oaks as (*bac'il*) *hihte⁊* '(genuine) oaks' and treat *čikinib* as being a closely related but distinct and coordinate taxon. One Tzeltal Indian for whom the above classification of oaks holds, produced the following folk tree diagram:

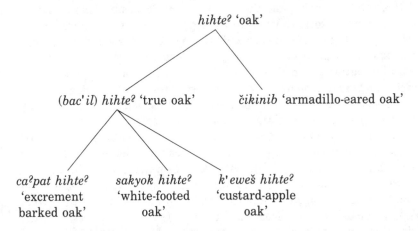

That such a situation could arise is partially explained by the fact that *čikinib* is by far the most divergent class of oaks referring to the native small-leafed oaks of the area (*Quercus acatenangenis, Q. sapotaefolia*). *čikinib* possesses scores of objective characters which readily distinguish it from the other three broad-leafed classes of '(true) oaks.'

I lack direct evidence that the higher order taxon *hihte⁊* is at the present time a fully stabilized taxon, and, as will be pointed out below, it may never become so.

In each of the examples just described it would appear that the intermediate taxa which have arisen are each unstable as the new generics continue to be used over time. In the case of the introduced grains, it was suggested that the new forms become conceptually 'a single unsegmented pattern,' to use Geoghegan's phrasing. In the case of *čikinib*, already a monolexemic form, the prior linguistic affiliation with *hihte⁊* is eventually lost (neutralized?) and the optional marking of the type generic (*bac'il*) *hihte⁊* will most likely be eliminated. One may predict that the same will occur with the type generic (*bac'il*) *⁊išim*. The final result will be the ultimate loss of the intermediate taxe, as *named* categories, although conceptually they will clearly continue to remain.

## Summary of the Development of Intermediate Names

One may summarize in tabular form the sequential steps that lead to the formation and final loss of named intermediate categories in Table I.

## THE LINGUISTIC RECOGNITION OF 'PLANT'

While man has no doubt tacitly recognized the world of plants as a conceptual category since earliest times, it does not appear to have been essential to provide the concept with a distinctive label until quite recently.

In contemporary languages of primitive peoples, a single, unique expression for 'plant' is notably lacking and there is no reason to assume that such was not the case in prehistoric times. Interestingly enough, when the notion of 'plant' is expressed, it is done via circumlocution or by the use of a form which is polysemous with some lower order major life-form term. We might surmise an identical situation in Theophrastus' time where it does not appear that a single common expression for the full category of the plant kingdom existed. The term Theophrastus chose for the domain as a whole, *phiton* was in everyday usage the word for cultivated plant, or 'herbaceous plant of cultivation,' with the sometimes restricted meaning of '(cultivated) tree' (Greene 1901:110).

In Kirwinian and Hanunóo, the term for 'tree' can be used in some contexts to refer to plants in general (Malinowski 1933; Conklin 1954). Likewise, in Ilongot, *ra²ek* is polysemously 'herbaceous plant' [i.e. not 'vine' or 'tree'] and 'plant' (M. Rosaldo, personal communication). Furthermore, in Spanish, *planta* appears polysemously as 'herbaceous plant, plant'; in Latin, note *herba* 'grass, plant,' and Russian *trava* 'grass, plant.' These data, while not conclusive, would seem to validate the suspicion that the label for the unique beginner in plant taxonomies is often drawn from one of the major class taxa, replicating a nomenclatural process which we have seen to be quite general in other areas of ethnobotanical nomenclature.

On the other hand, there is some evidence that the term for the plant might in some languages derive as a compound. In ancient Sumerian, the concept 'plant' was apparently designated by the conjunction of three lower-order terms which translated approximately as 'tree,' 'grass' and 'vegetable' (Robert McC. Adams, personal communication). This corresponds quite well with what we know of ancient Latin, where the expression of 'tree,' 'herb' (*arbor et herba*) was used to designate the more general concept. In this regard, Ullmann notes:

> There was in Latin no generic term for 'plant' in the modern sense: *arbor* and *herba* were the most comprehensive class-concepts in the botanical field. According to a recent enquiry, the modern meaning of 'plant' is first found in Albertus Magnus in the 13th century, whereas the French *plante* did not acquire this wider sense until 300 years later (Ullmann 1963:181).

Finally, while there is no commonly recognized term for 'plant' in Tzeltal, there are instances where something like the notion can be expressed by the

# TABLE 1 Hypothetical stages involved in the formation and subsequent loss of intermediate taxa

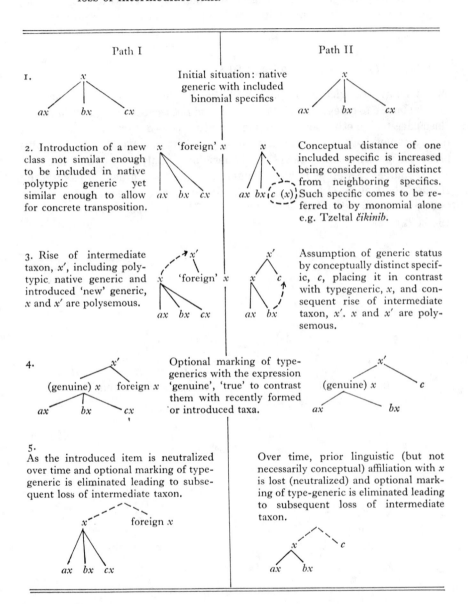

|  | Path I | | Path II |
|---|---|---|---|
| 1. | | Initial situation: native generic with included binomial specifics | |
| 2. | Introduction of a new class not similar enough to be included in native polytypic generic yet similar enough to allow for concrete transposition. | | Conceptual distance of one included specific is increased being considered more distinct from neighboring specifics. Such specific comes to be referred to by monomial alone e.g. Tzeltal *čikinib*. |
| 3. | Rise of intermediate taxon, *x'*, including polytypic native generic and introduced 'new' generic, *x* and *x'* are polysemous. | | Assumption of generic status by conceptually distinct specific, *c*, placing it in contrast with typegeneric, *x*, and consequent rise of intermediate taxon, *x'*. *x* and *x'* are polysemous. |
| 4. | | Optional marking of typegenerics with the expression 'genuine', 'true' to contrast them with recently formed or introduced taxa. | |
| 5. | As the introduced item is neutralized over time and optional marking of typegeneric is eliminated leading to subsequent loss of intermediate taxon. | | Over time, prior linguistic (but not necessarily conceptual) affiliation with *x* is lost (neutralized) and optional marking of type-generic is eliminated leading to subsequent loss of intermediate taxon. |

compound *te?-?ak?* , literally 'tree-vine.' It might be suggested that we see something like this going on in English folk biology, when we attempt to refer to the concept 'living things' often by the phrase 'plants-and-animals.'

## ETHNOZOOLOGICAL PARALLELS

While I have restricted my survey of the development of ethnobiological nomenclature to categories of plants, it should not be surprising to find rather close parallels in ethnozoological nomenclature. The data in this area are far from complete but those I have seen suggest that identical nomenclatural processes are at work. Type-specific-generic name polysemy can be found in animal names as well as in plant names. Thus, in the Chinese of Hong Kong Harbor, the Karam of New Guinea, and in Guarani of Argentina, one notes examples such as seen below (Anderson 1967:71; Dennler 1939:233; Bulmer 1968:622).

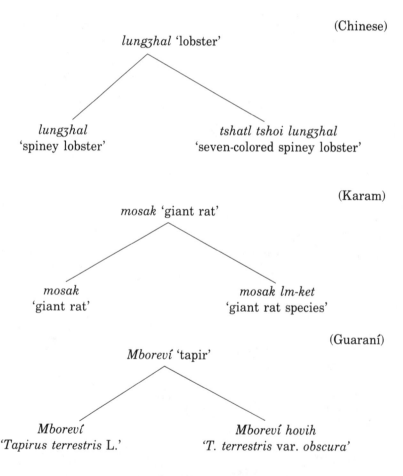

(Chinese)

*lungʒhal* 'lobster'

*lungʒhal*
'spiney lobster'

*tshatl tshoi lungʒhal*
'seven-colored spiney lobster'

(Karam)

*mosak* 'giant rat'

*mosak*
'giant rat'

*mosak lm-ket*
'giant rat species'

(Guaraní)

*Mboreví* 'tapir'

*Mboreví*
'*Tapirus terrestris* L.'

*Mboreví hovih*
'*T. terrestris* var. *obscura*'

Furthermore, the optional marking of the otherwise polysemous type-specific with an attributive glossed as 'genuine' is also found in animal nomenclature. Some selected examples are seen from Karam and Tonkawa (Bulmer 1968:624; Gatschet 1899:160):

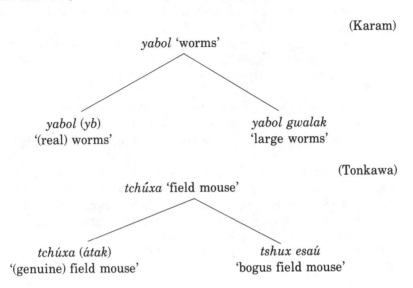

(Karam)

yabol 'worms'

yabol (yb)
'(real) worms'

yabol gwalak
'large worms'

(Tonkawa)

tchúxa 'field mouse'

tchúxa (átak)
'(genuine) field mouse'

tshux esaú
'bogus field mouse'

Apparently, generic name—life-form name polysemy is also a process observed in the development of ethnozoological nomenclature. Gatschet, in his large Klamath grammar notes that the Klamath '. . . often use . . . wíshink "garter snake" for "snake," the Modocs wámĕnigh (black snake) for the same order of reptiles, these species being the most frequent of their kind in their respective countries' (1890:II, 145). In Pomo, notes collected by the zoologist C. Hart Merriam (n.d.) show the form shah as meaning polysemously 'salmon' and 'fish' while in Shoshoni of the Snake River drainage we find ʔakai 'salmon, fish' (Wick Miller, personal communication). From Karam, Bulmer (1968) reports kmn as generically 'small edible mammals' but as well a life-form name indicating all 'game animals.'

As concerns evidence indicating type-generic lexical marking analogous to that found for plant names, Gatschet cites gúato 'bird' and guató-hi 'real bird, i.e. eagle'; likewise, sane is 'snake' while sanehi refers to 'rattlesnake, i.e. real snake' (Gatschet 1899:157).

I have only one example of life form—unique beginner polysemy in ethnozoological nomenclature. In Orok of Sakhalin Island, Austerlitz (1959:211) notes buju as meaning both 'bear' and 'animal.' It is not unlikely, however, that polysemy of this type will also be found widely as more information becomes available.

Finally, data from Tzeltal ethnozoology would seem to replicate in important ways some of the problems suggested in the discussion of the formation of intermediate taxa, especially as concerns the classificatory treatment of introduced organisms in the case of the New Guinea Mt Hagen materials.

At the conquest, the Spanish introduced to the Tzeltal three domestic animals which were to assume critical cultural importance: *chickens*, *sheep* and *pigs*. For each of these introduced organisms, there existed native classes for which the foreign animals could be seen as similar, namely, *birds*, *deer* and *wild pigs*.

On historical linguistic grounds, we know that the Pre-conquest Tzeltal terms for these native forms were *mut* 'bird,' *čih* 'deer' and *čitam* 'wild pig.' The situation at the present time is, however, as follows:

> *mut* 'chicken' vs. *te?tikil mut* 'bird' (lit. 'forest chicken')
> *čih* 'sheep' vs. *te?tikil čih* 'deer' (lit. 'forest sheep')
> *čitam* 'pig' vs. *wamal čitam* 'wild pig' (lit. 'brush pig')

In each case, the unmarked form has become restricted to the introduced animals, while the aboriginal organisms have become linguistically marked. Full information is lacking on the complete historical cycle leading to this outcome, but there are sufficient data to suggest that the situation is very close to that seen in the Mt Hagen treatment of *oka*.

One may note the following developmental sequence for one item of the set, *čih* 'deer.'

*Pre-conquest:*
čih 'deer'

Conquest:

| | | |
|---|---|---|
| čih 'deer' | *tunim čih* | 'sheep' [lit. 'cotton deer,' attested in some contemporary dialects of Tzeltal] |

*Early post conquest:*

| | | |
|---|---|---|
| (*te?-tikil*) čih | *tunim čih* | (Optional marking of native form) |
| 'forest deer' | 'cotton deer' | |

*Late post conquest:*

| | |
|---|---|
| *te?tekil čih* | (*tunim*) čih |
| (obligatory marking) | (optional marking) |

*Present:*

| | |
|---|---|
| *te?tikil čih* 'deer' | čih 'sheep' |
| | (optional marking of introduced form has become unnecessary) |

In both the Tzeltal and Mt Hagen data, it seems clear that a similar process has been followed, leading names for introduced organisms from a lexically marked to lexically unmarked status, and that this process is directly related to the high cultural significance of the organisms involved.

## AN ASIDE CONCERNING NOMENCLATURAL DEVOLUTION

At the beginning, I noted that vocabularies of languages tend to increase in size over time. This is, of course, generally true when total vocabulary is considered. Specific lexical domains, however, undergo not only growth but as well decay. As with lexical expansion, the likely underlying causal mechanisms must be ultimately related to cultural evolution. Wholesale vocabulary loss in some specific area must be due in part, at least, to the lessening of cultural importance associated with that particular area of human concern. Examples of such nomenclatural devolution can be found in almost any area of vocabulary, terms for agricultural implements or carriage lexicon being obvious examples in English.

As concerns ethnobotanical nomenclature particularly, it now seems likely that the direction of vocabulary loss will be from the particular to the general. To use the terminology of my colleagues Kay and Geoghegan, loss will occur 'from the bottom up.' With little introspection, speakers of English who have been reared in an urban setting will recognize at once that they know virtually no specific names for kinds of plants, that many generic names are recognizable linguistically only as 'names' of plants, the organisms referred to being totally unfamiliar. Nonetheless, abstract life-form names, such as 'tree' or 'grass' apparently remain as useful terms for referring to an ever-shrinking (both literally and figuratively) portion of one's natural environment.

The topic is an intriguing one deserving further study and English would be as good a language as any on which to begin research.


## CONCLUSIONS

Assuming a uniformitarian view for the growth of ethnobotanical vocabulary, I have attempted to outline a plausible sequence of development of nomenclatural categories characteristic of man's linguistic recognition of the plant world. I have argued for the primacy of generic taxa as the first ethnobiological categories to become encoded in a language's plant lexicon. Expansion appears to be horizontal at first, and with enlarging experience, develops both by differentiation and generalization. A similar argument has been made by Brown in reference to vocabulary as acquired by the child (Brown 1958) so one might suspect the process discussed here to have wider ontogenetic applicability as well.

Six major linguistic categories have been posited as sufficient for describing the names for classes of plants in all languages. It appears highly likely that these categories become encoded in the history of any language in the following order:

$$\text{generic} \rightarrow \left\{\begin{array}{l}\text{life form}\\\text{specific}\end{array}\right\} \rightarrow \left\{\begin{array}{l}\text{intermediate}\\\text{varietal}\end{array}\right\} \rightarrow \text{unique beginner}$$

An additional claim has been made which states that with the encoding of each category a specifiable process of lexical marking is operable, leading plant names from a *lexically unmarked* to a *lexically marked* status.

If the principles I have discussed prove to be general, they could allow for a plausible typological classification of the various types of ethnobotanical nomenclature seen in the languages of the world. It is also likely that a similar classification may be appropriate for ethnozoological nomenclature. I would speculate that the typological classification can best be interpreted as indicative of how plant nomenclature becomes encoded diachronically.

But a classification is not a theory. It is one thing to describe typological regularities and to suggest that their interpretation is best understood historically. It is quite a different task to outline the developmental processes involved in the change of one system into another.

On the other hand, one usually searches for causal explanations only after one has observed something that might be interesting to explain. Until recently, studies into the nature of the growth of vocabulary have been accorded little importance in linguistics and anthropology. I believe that as detailed descriptive reports reveal conclusively that aspects of man's lexicon develop in a regularly patterned fashion, efforts towards providing theoretical explanations of the processes involved will be increased. While I cannot predict what mechanisms will be finally suggested as causal explanations as future work proceeds, it seems likely that the details underlying the development of vocabulary must eventually be encompassed within some more general, technologically based theory of cultural evolution.

## REFERENCES

Almstedt, R. L. (1968). Diegueño tree: an ecological approach to a linguistic problem. *IJAL* **34**. 9–15.

Anderson, E. N. (1967). The ethnoichthyology of the Hong Kong boat people. (Unpublished Ph.D. dissertation in anthropology.) Berkeley: University of California.

Austerlitz, R. (1959). Gilyak religious terminology in the light of linguistic analysis. From the *Transactions of the Asiatic Society of Japan*. (Third series, vol. VII.) Tokyo.

Bartlett, H. H. (1940). History of the generic concept in botany. *Bull. Torrey Botanical Club* **67**. 349–62.

Berlin, B. (1969). Universal nomenclatural principles in folk science. Paper presented at the 1968 Annual Meeting of the American Anthropological Association, New Orleans.

Berlin, B., Breedlove, D. E. & Raven, P. H. (1966). Folk taxonomies and biological classification. *Science* **154**. 273–5. Reprinted in S. Tyler (ed.) (1968). *Cognitive anthropology*. New York: Holt, Rinehart and Winston.

_____ (1968). Covert categories and folk taxonomies. *AmA* **70**. 290–9.

_____ (in press) *Principles of Tzeltal plant classification*. New York: Seminar Press.

_____ (n.d.). Universal principles of nomenclature and classification in folk science.

Bright, W. & Bright, J. (1965). Semantic structures in Northwestern California and the Sapir-Whorf hypothesis. In E. A. Hammel (ed.), *Formal semantic analysis.* (*AmA* **67** (5) pt 2.) Washington, D.C.: American Anthropological Association.

Brown, R. (1958). How shall a thing be called? *Psychological Rev.* **65**. 14–21.

Buck, C. D. (1949). *A dictionary of selected synonyms in the principal Indo-European languages.* Chicago: University of Chicago Press.

Bulmer, R. (1967). Why is the cassowary not a bird? A problem of zoological taxonomy among the Karam of the New Guinea Highlands. *Man* **2**. 1–25.

———— (1968). Worms that croak and other mysteries of Karam natural science. *Mankind* **6**. 621–39.

———— (1970). Which came first, the chicken or the egghead? In J. Pouillon et P. Maranda (eds), *Échanges et communications. Mélanges offerts á Claude Lévi-Strauss á l'occasion de son 60eme anniversaire.* The Hague: Mouton and Co.

Bulmer, R. & Tyler, R. (1968). Karem classification of frogs. *Jnl Polynesian Soc.* **77**. 333–85.

Conklin, H. C. (1954). The relation of Hanunóo culture to the plant world. (Unpublished Ph.D. dissertation in anthropology.) New Haven: Yale University.

———— (1962). Lexicographic treatment of folk taxonomies. In F. W. Householder and S. Saporta (eds), *Problems in lexicography.* (Research Center in Anthropology, Folklore and Linguistics, Publication 21; (and) *IJAL* **28** (2) pt 4.) Bloomington: Indiana University.

Demory, B. (1971). The word for 'tree' in the Hokan language family. In *Informant.* Long Beach: California State College, Department of Anthropology.

Dennler, J. G. (1939). Los nombres indígenas en Guaraní de los mamíferso de la Argentina y países limíitrofes y su importancia para la systematica. *Physis* **16**. 225–44.

Dentan, R. K. (1968). The Semai: a nonviolent people of Malaya. In G. Spindler and L. Spindler (eds), *Case studies in cultural anthropology.* New York: Holt, Rinehart and Winston.

Diamond, J. M. (1966). Classification system of primitive people. *Science* **151**. 1102–4.

Fowler, C. S. & Leland, J. (1967). Some Northern Paiute native categories. *Ethnology* **6**. 381–404.

Frake, C. O. (1962). The ethnographic study of cognitive systems. In T. Gladwin and W. C. Sturtevant (eds), *Anthropology and human behavior.* Washington, D.C.: Anthropological Society of Washington.

French, D. (1960). Types of native taxonomic process. Paper presented at the Fifty-ninth Annual Meeting of the American Anthropological Association, Minneapolis.

Friedrich, P. (1970). *Proto-Indo-European trees.* Chicago: University of Chicago Press.

Gatschet, A. S. (1890). *The Klamath Indians of Southwestern Oregon.* (Contributions to North American Ethnology, vol. II.) Washington, D.C.: Department of Interior, U.S. Geographical and Geological Survey of the Rocky Mountain Region.

———— (1899). 'Real,' 'true,' or 'genuine' in Indian languages. In *AmA* I. 155–61. New York: G. P. Putnam's Sons.

Greenberg, J. H. (1966). Language universals. In T. A. Sebeok (ed.), *Current trends in linguistics, vol. 3, theoretical foundations.* The Hague: Mouton and Co. 61–112.

Greene, E. L. (1909). *Landmarks of botanical history*. (Smithsonian Miscellaneous Collections, vol. 54.) Washington, D.C.

Hymes, D. (1960). More on lexicostatistics. *CAnthr* I. 338–45.

Lévi-Strauss, C. (1966). *The savage mind*. Chicago: University of Chicago Press.

Malinowski, B. (1935). *Coral gardens and their magic*, vol. II. New York: American Book Company.

Mathews, W. (1886). Navajo names for plants. *Amer. Naturalist* **20**. 767–77.

Merriam, C. H. (n.d.). Field checklists, Pacific Coast Region. U.S. Department of Agriculture biological survey. (Notes in the library of the Archaeological Research Facility, Department of Anthropology, University of California, Berkeley.)

Paso y Trancoso, F. del (1886). La botanica entre los Nahuas. *Anales del Museo Nacional de México*. III. Mexico.

Roys, R. L. (1931). *The ethno-botany of the Maya*. (Middle American Research Series, no. 2.) New Orleans: Tulane University, Department of Middle American Research.

Stahel, G. (1944). Notes on the Arawak Indian names of plants in Surinam. *Jnl N.Y. Botanical Garden* **45**. 268–79.

Strathern, M. (1969). Why is the Pueraria a sweet potato? *Ethnology* **8**. 189–98.

Trager, G. (1939). 'Cottonwood' = 'tree': a Southwestern linguistic trait. *IJAL* **9**. 117–18.

Ullmann, S. (1963). Semantic universals. In J. H. Greenberg (ed.), *Universals of language* (2nd edition). Cambridge, Mass.: MIT Press. 217–62.

Werner, H. (1954). Change of meaning: a study of semantic processes through the experimental method. *Jnl General Psychology* **50**.181–208.

Wyman, L. C. & Harris, S. K. (1941). *Navajo Indian medical ethnobotany*. (Bulletin 366, Anthropological series 3.5.) Albuquerque: University of New Mexico.

# Shifters, Linguistic Categories and Cultural Description
## Michael Silverstein

This reading will try to develop consequences of the statement that speech is meaningful social behavior. In itself, this statement is one of those set phrases of pidgin science that are used to ensure minimal trade relations in the contact community of linguists and social anthropologists. It gives us no analytic or descriptive power. What I wish to do here is demonstrate that we do, in fact, already have a full, subtle "language" with which to describe the elaborate meaning structures of speech behavior. It is a language that speaks of the "function" of signs, their modes of signification, distinguishing from among the types of sign functions *shifters* or *indexes*. The meaning of this functional sign mode always involves some aspect of the context in which the sign occurs. In making the nature of this involvement clearer, I hope to demonstrate that this "pragmatic" analysis of speech behavior—in the tradition extending from Peirce to Jakobson—allows us to describe the real linkage of language to culture, and perhaps the most important aspect of the "meaning" of speech.

At one level, language has long served anthropologists as a kind of exemplar for the nature of things cultural. It seems to display these "cultural" properties with clarity in the tangible medium of articulate phonetic speech. Thus, and at another level, could the analytic lessons of linguistics be transferred analogically to other social behavior, giving a kind of structuralized anthropology, or, more remarkably, could the actual linguistic (especially lexicographic) structures of language be called culture. I will be developing the argument that this received point of view is essentially wrong. That aspect of language which has traditionally been analyzed by linguists, and has served as model, is just the part that is functionally unique among the phenomena of culture. Hence the structural characteristics of language in this traditional view cannot really serve as a model for other aspects of culture, nor can the method of analysis. Further, linguistic (or lexicographical) structures that emerge from the traditional grammatical analysis must of necessity bear a problematic, rather than isomorphic, relationship to the structure of culture.

## LINGUISTIC AND OTHER COMMUNICATION

To say of social behavior that it is meaningful implies necessarily that it is communicative, that is, that the behavior is a complex of signs (sign vehicles) that signal, or stand for, something in some respect. Such behavioral signs are significant to some persons, participants in a communicative event, and such behavior is purposive, that is, goal oriented in the sense of accomplishing (or in failing to accomplish) certain ends of communication, for example, indicating one's social rank, reporting an occurrence, effecting a cure for a disease, and so forth. In general, then, we can say that people are constituted as a society with a certain *culture* to the extent that they share the same means of social communication.

Language as a system of communication has the same characteristics as the rest of culture. So in order to distinguish analytic subparts of culture, such as language, we have traditionally distinguished among types of communicative events on the basis of the signaling medium. In the case of language, the signaling medium is articulate speech, and events can be isolated on this basis.

## Speech Events

By such analysis, a *speech event*, endowed with an overt goal in a socially shared system of such purposive functions, consists of some sequence of speech behaviors in which some speaker or speakers signal to some hearer or hearers by means of a system of phonetic sign vehicles called speech messages or utterances. The utterances are organized into a system for the participants by virtue of their knowledge of a linguistic code, or grammar. The speech event takes place with the participants in given positions, or loci, and over a certain span of time. The roles of speaker and hearer may be taken by different individuals during the course of such an event. Many other characteristics of such speech events must also be taken into consideration, among them the other sociological aspects of the individuals in the roles of speaker and hearer, which are frequently salient in defining the event, the prior speech events (if any), the gestural or kinesic communication that invariably accompanies spoken language, the distinction between roles of hearer and audience, and so forth. A description of the speech event must minimally take into account these fundamental defining variables.

Speech events so defined, moreover, are co-occurrent with events based on distinct signaling media, and these together make up large-scale cultural routines. Descriptively, the simplest speech events would be those which themselves constituted the entire goal-directed social behavior. It is doubtful that such events exist. In our own culture, reading a scholarly paper can come close to being a speech event pure and simple, the purpose of which is expressible in terms of informative discourse among social categories of scholars. The possibility of distinct forms of symbolism that can be involved in these events is not at issue. I am dealing here only with the purposive nature of the speech event in a system of social action. The more embedded speech events are those which are part of such large-scale cultural enterprises as complex rituals including speech, song, dance, dress, etc., where the meaning of the speech behavior in the speech events is usually integrally linked to the presence of these other signaling media. Analytically, the problem of trying to give the meanings of signals in such a situation is very complex.

## Referential Speech Events

But the ultimate justification for the segmentation of speech from other signaling media lies in one of the purposive uses that seems to distinguish speech behavior from all other communicative events, the function of *pure reference*, or, in terms more culturally bound than philosophical, the function of description or "telling about." The referential function of speech can be characterized as communication by propositions—predications descriptive of states of affairs—subject to verification in some cases of objects and events, taken as representations of truth in others. Reference so characterized is a communicative event, and the utterances of referential discourse are made up of sign units in grammatical arrangements, the meaning of the whole being a descriptive or referring proposition. It is this referential function of speech, and its characteristic sign mode, the semantico-referential sign, that has formed the basis for linguistic theory and linguistic analysis in the Western tradition.

## Referential Linguistic Categories

All *linguistic analysis* of the traditional sort proceeds on the basis of the contribution of elements of utterances to the referential or denotative value of the whole. And it is on this basis that the traditional segmentation, description, and definition of all linguistic categories is made. Our standard ideas about the significant segmentation of utterances all rest on sameness or difference of utterances in terms of referring or describing propositions, coded in speech. Plural vs. singular "number," for example, as a pure referential linguistic category, can be analyzed by the contribution of such markers to propositions describing more-than-one vs. not-more-than-one entity. In English, this is illustrated by *The boys run* vs. *The boy runs*, where noun suffixed with -s and unsuffixed verb signal the category of plural-number subject, and unsuffixed noun and verb suffixed with -s signal the category of singular-number subject. Thus we segment $-s]_N$ $-O]_v$: $-O]_N$ $-s]_v$. Durative or progressive vs. punctual "aspect" as a pure referential category contributes to propositions describing events as continuous or ongoing (where they are not necessarily so) vs. momentaneous or complete. In English, this is illustrated by *The boy was jumping* vs. *The boy jumped*, with segmentation $be\,(-ed)\ -ing]_v$: $O\,(-ed)]_v$, *be* + *ed* represented by *was*.

Any form of grammatical analysis in this referential mode, from Greco-Roman to transformational-generative, defines the signs, the categories, and their rules of combination and arrangement in this fashion. All of our analytic techniques and formal descriptive machinery have been designed for referential signs, which contribute to referential utterances in referential speech events.

(We shall see below that certain among the referential categories cause difficulties with this whole approach.) When we speak of linguistic categories, we mean categories of this referential kind; hence one of the principal reasons social functions of speech have not been built into our analyses of language: the sign modes of most of what goes on in the majority of speech events are not referential.

## Semantics and Linguistic Analysis

The study of the "meaning" of linguistic signs is usually called semantics. It is clear from the way I have characterized traditional linguistic investigation, however, that the actual object of study of semantics has been the referential meanings of utterances, of the words and categories and arrangements in terms of which we can analyze them. For the purposes of this reading, the term will be restricted in this way, so that semantics is the study of pure referential meaning, embodied in propositions coded by speech. This property of speech, abstract reference or description, can be called its *semanticity*.

From an operational point of view, all grammatical analysis of the traditional sort depends on this semanticity. To be able to analyze linguistic categories, we must be able to give evidence about the semantic relations of parts of sentences. We must ultimately be able to say, in other words, whether or not a certain stretch of language is semantically equivalent, within the grammar, to some other stretch of language. By determining such equivalence relations, we can build up a notion of defining, or *glossing*, certain grammatical stretches of a language in terms of others. But glossing is itself a referential speech event.

## Metasemantics

Glossing speech events take language itself, in particular the semantics of language, as the referent, or object of description. These events use language to describe the semantics of language, and are thus *metasemantic* referential speech events. Such metasemantic speech events are the basis of all grammatical analysis and description, and hence of all semantic description as well. They are the basic activity of the traditional linguistics, which may be seen as the discovery of the glosses of a language, of the class of all possible metasemantic speech events in the language. Leonard Bloomfield's (1933) "fundamental postulate" is essentially one about the semantic and formal equivalence of certain sentences that underlie utterances within a speech community. Similarly, such semantic equivalence at the level of phrases and sentences has become the stock-in-trade of the transformational grammarian, who postulates a common "underlying" structure for semantically equivalent "surface" syntactic arrangements.

But it is interesting that metasemantic speech events are a natural occurrence in everyday speech, a culturally learned speech function. In our society, parents are constantly glossing words for children by using grammatically complex but semantically equivalent expressions, expressions that make the same contribution to reference of utterances as the glossed items.

The metasemantic property of language, the property that makes semantic analysis (and hence semantically based grammar) possible, is the one that is unique to language, and upon which rests the speech function of pure reference. It is what makes language unique among all the cultural codes for social communication. Anthropologists have long analyzed ritual, myth, or other media of social behavior as making symbolic statements about categories of social structure. But of what medium other than referential speech can we say that the behavioral signs can describe the meanings of the signs themselves? There are no naturally occurring "metamythic" events in the same way that there are metalinguistic ones, nor "metaritualistic" events with the same functional possibilities. It is in other functional properties of language, which can be exploited in speech events, that the commonalty of language and many other cultural media lies.

## Simultaneous Nonreferential Functions

Speech events that do not have referential functions accomplish socially constituted ends comparable to those of nonspeech events. For example, it is frequently through speech that we set social boundaries on an interaction, rather than through the physical separation of participants. To characterize such behavior abstractly, we note that we can choose the language in which we speak so as to preclude comprehension on the part of some individuals present; we can use a language all understand, but with pronominal markers that make the intended boundaries of participation clear; we can use phraseology only some can understand; we can spell out the written representations of words in the presence of those illiterate in some written language; and so forth. This purposive privacy function of the speech behavior is simultaneous with, but analytically distinct from, whatever referential function there is in the event for speaker and intended hearer(s), for only they participate in those roles in the referential communication.

One of the most interesting aspects of speech behavior, in fact, is this multifunctionality of what appear to be utterances in sequence, the traditionally recognized referential nature of some parts of utterances seeming to have intercalated many other functional elements simultaneously. From the point of view of the traditional semantico-referential linguistics, these other functional modes of language use seem to be "riding on" descriptive propositions. But this is a rather limited point of view. For it takes considerable analysis of the use of such speech itself to characterize what is going on in such cases as those given above. The only behavioral data are the speech signals themselves. To say, for example, that the speaker is using a different "language," just in the semantico-referential sense, presupposes a grammatical description of each of the distinct referential media, and hence presupposes the isolation of the referential function of speech in two distinct systems of semantic signals. So the functional analysis of a given use of speech behavior requires that we can contrast signs, all other things remaining the same. From the point of view of functional analysis, then, we must make sophisticated hypotheses of *isofunctionality*, or comparability of function of the signaling media, before any structural description is justifiable.

## Reference and "Performative" Speech

Just like reference, however, other uses of speech get some socially constituted "work" done; they accomplish or "perform" something, whether achieving privacy, as in the example above, or marking the social status of the participants, or making a command for someone to do something, or effecting a permanent change in social status, for example, marrying two people or knighting someone.

Much recent analysis has been focused on this performative aspect of language use, in what I have here termed purposive or functional speech events. Following upon the work of Austin, some have distinguished between "performative" aspects of speech and the "semantic" content (the term not rigorously circumscribed as it is here). Others, particularly the philosopher Searle (1969), have distinguished "speech acts" represented by utterances as distinct from their propositional content. (It is somewhat unfortunate, by the way, that "speech act" has been used as a term for the level of purposive functional speech events, since I will be using it in another sense below.)

All these approaches, in other words, start with a basically semantico-referential linguistic analysis from which the linguistic categories, the grammatical arrangements, etc., emerge in the traditional way. They tack onto this analysis a description of how these semantico-referential categories can be "used" performatively. This approach entirely misses the point that referential speech events are, a fortiori, speech events, endowed with the same kind of purposefulness as other speech events. Reference is one kind of linguistic performance among many. The linguistic categories that emerge from analysis of speech in the semantico-referential modes are not necessarily the same as those that emerge from other functional modes, and it is presumptuous to speak of arrangements of a basically propositional nature being "used" in other ways.

The physical signals of distinct functional modes of speech may be partially alike, since they seem to be superimposed in the same formal utterances, but the meanings, in this larger sense of functional cultural meanings, are different, and hence we have distinct signs. The priority of reference in establishing linguistic categories and structure rests squarely on the manipulability of this mode by the metalinguistic property. But reference itself is just one, perhaps actually a minor one, among the "performative" or "speech act" functions of speech. We do not use basically "descriptive" linguistic structure to accomplish other communicative goals; description happens to be one of those goals, one that overlaps in formal structure of signals with other functional ends.

## Abbreviatory Extensions

In certain cases, of course, the extension of descriptive referential language to other performative uses is patent. One such class of events is conversational abbreviations used as requests. A statement to another person in a room with an open window such as "I'm cold" or "It's cold in here" could lead to a discussion until the interlocutor is asked to close the window and does so. Or, more naturally for sophisticated persons in our society, we can abbreviate, the statement itself leading to the accomplishment of the action.

Several subtypes of statements require such experience and deduction based on full forms of linguistic sequences. But such seemingly descriptive utterances used as abbreviatory request events are very circumscribed and constitute a level of delicacy of manipulatory signaling highly susceptible to failure. In general, the point holds that descriptive reference is one among the speech functions, not the basis for all others.

## Pragmatic Meanings of Linguistic Signs

The linguistic signs that underlie utterances, then, appear in speech that serves many socially constituted functions. The *meanings* of such signs, as they emerge from grammatical analysis, are traditionally described in terms of their contribution to referring propositional speech, of necessity a partial description. The problem set for us when we consider the actual broader uses of language is to describe the total meaning of constituent linguistic signs, only part of which is semantic in our narrowed terminology. We must begin with the facts of purposive utterances in speech events, and isolate their several functions. The linguistic signs have distinct kinds of meanings which depend on their contribution to the several kinds of functional speech events we can isolate.

We can see in this way that while some linguistic signs have semantic meanings, contributing to reference, others have nonsemantic meanings, contributing to other distinct speech functions. In general, we can call the study of the meanings of linguistic signs relative to their communicative functions *pragmatics*, and these more broadly conceived meanings are then *pragmatic meanings*. Semantic meaning is, of course, in one sense a special form of pragmatic meaning, the mode of signification of signs that contributes to pure referential function. This fits exactly with the discovery that grammatical analysis of the traditional sort is equivalent to discovering the class of all possible metalinguistic or glossing referential speech events.

## Pragmatic Categories

General pragmatic meaning of signs and more particular semantic meaning are largely superimposed in the formal signals of speech. In fact, there is a class of signs called *referential indexes,* to be characterized below, in which the two modes are linked in the same categories, segmentable and isolable simultaneously in at least two functional modes, one referential, one not. By examining only those categories that unite at least two functional modes in the same isolable speech fraction, for example an English deictic *this* or *that,* we might get the mistaken idea that the superimposition is always of discrete referential categories intercalated with otherwise functional ones. If speech consisted only of pure referential categories (which traditional linguistic theory postulates) and referential indexes, then all isolable segments would have semantic meanings, and some residual segments would have an additional pragmatic mode. This is false, as we shall see, since utterances include nonreferential and hence nonsemantic formal features.

It is thus possible to have entirely distinct analyses of the same overt speech material from different functional points of view. The linguistic signs that have various pragmatic meanings are only apparently represented at the "surface" of speech in continuous utterances. We may recall Victor Hugo's couplet, "Gal, amant de la Reine, alla (tour magnanime!) /Gallamment de l'arène à la Tour Magne à Nîmes." Analysis in general leads to this kind of superimposed structural heterogeneity, depending on the functional mode of the pragmatic meanings of utterances. Once we realize that distinct pragmatic meanings yield distinct analyses of utterances, we can sever our dependence on reference as the controlling functional mode of speech, dictating our traditional segmentations and recognition of categories. We can then concentrate on the manifold social pragmatics that are common to language and every other form of socially constituted communication in society.

## THE NATURE OF LINGUISTIC SIGNS

Having discussed the framework of function in terms of which all meaning is constituted, I shall turn now to an examination of the nature of the modes of signification of linguistic signs in utterances. By means of the analysis of propositional content in the referential mode, we will be able to see the limitations in principle of pure semantic grammatical approaches, and use the critical overlapping of functions in referring indexes to motivate a separation of three principal classes of sign modes. In particular, we can elaborate on the class of indexes, which appear to give the key to the pragmatic description of language.

### Utterance and Sentence, Message and Code

For purposes of semantico-referential description, all *utterances,* or *messages,* in speech events are analyzed as instances of *sentences.* Such sentences are constructed from a finite repertoire of elements according to rules of arrangement, and express referential propositions. These constituents and the rules together constitute a *code* or *grammar* for the language. We separate here, then, the several individual instances or *tokens* occurring in actual speech from the semantico-grammatical *types* or elements of sentences in a language, which these instances are said to represent in speech.

In a given speech event, an utterance or message occurs in context. The traditional grammatical analysis of such utterances, however, depends upon the hypotheses of sameness and difference of segments of underlying sentences in the code, other tokens of which are manipulable in glossing speech events by the metalinguistic property of the medium. In other words, semantico-grammatical analysis can function only if sign tokens preserve their reference in all the speech events in which they occur, including the crucial glossing event or its equivalent. We explain this sameness of reference by postulating the underlying sign type, with a semantico-referential meaning. We must always be able to distinguish sentence-bound, context-independent types from utterance-bound, contextualized tokens in this pure semantico-referential analysis of language. Where this property of speech signals is not found, the traditional form of grammatical analysis breaks down.

## Propositional Analysis

Using the traditional grammatical approach, we can analyze any sentence the signs of which are purely referential, that is, where tokens in metalinguistic usage can be said to represent precisely the same underlying type. We can analyze as distinct sentence elements a great number of the nouns of a language, such as English *table, chair, man* (in several "senses"); a great number of verbs, such as *stand, run, eat*; and a number of apparent grammatical categories, such as 'number' and 'aspect,' which I discussed above. So predications of timeless truths coded by sentences with such elements are readily analyzable as such, e.g., *Unicorns drink ambrosia.* (The verb here is "tenseless"; that is, does not refer to the present but to all time.)

This example has a plural noun-phrase subject and a transitive predicate with verb and mass object noun, and it codes the universal proposition that all unicorns drink ambrosia. We might represent this proposition, in a kind of rough-and-ready way, without logical quantification, as 'drink (unicorns, ambrosia),' showing that 'drink' is a "transitive" predicate of two places that makes a claim about an "agent" (represented by the subject in grammatical construction) and a "patient" (represented by the object). For each of the sign types that make up the constituents of the sentence, we can gloss another token of the form with a paraphrase—*A unicorn is . . . , Ambrosia is . . . , To drink is to . . .*—under hypotheses about the grammatical categories they represent. (It would require a treatise in grammatical analysis to give the heuristics of discovery. Language in the semantico-referential mode being a loose system, much of the analysis must be completed to justify a particular hypothesis.) For the residual grammatical categories, such as [mass] : [count] nouns, and subject-of-verb-representing-agent, object-of-verb-representing-patient, we can show the proportionality of meanings under transformational manipulation, as our (post-) Saussurean principles demand.

## Referential Indexes in Propositional Speech

However, the situation becomes more complex for propositional analysis of sentences that include referential indexes, such as signs for 'tense.' I specified above that the verb *drink* in the example was "tenseless." But consider on the other hand an utterance such as that represented by the common example *The boy hit the ball*. By a similar sort of grammatical analysis, we can say that a sentence of English is represented here with agent and patient and transitive verb. The noun phrases *the boy* and *the ball* are both "definite" (a term the analysis of which I do not wish to take up here). But when such an utterance is made with "past tense" verb token, how are we to give the meaning (and hence analyze) the underlying categorial types?

Clearly, the form *hit* is to be segmented as $hit]_v$ + Past (: $hit]_v$ + Present : : $walk]_v$ + Past : $walk]_v$ + Present). Under such an analysis, we can gloss the stem *hit* and give its "senses" as grammatically complex paraphrases. But what of the morphological segment Past that we wish to attribute to the sentence underlying the utterance? While it is perfectly feasible to segment such a category as a residual of the grammatical analysis, as we can see in the proportion just above, to give a semantico-referential meaning in terms of glossing is impossible; and yet there is clearly a contribution to reference not explicable by grammatical arrangement. The category of past tense, in other words, is not represented in utterances by pure referential sign tokens, and hence a strict semantico-referential analysis is powerless to describe this obvious category of language. (That this fact has not hindered the description of languages merely attests the truth that the natives' theories do not always tell us what the natives are really doing, nor do they prevent obvious solutions that are strictly out of theoretical bounds.)

## Indexical Presupposition of Reference

In order to describe the meaning of this kind of category, we have to make certain observations about the class of tokens of "tense" in utterances. These contribute to propositions by describing the time of an event; that is, the whole proposition makes some claim to be verifiable for a particular time. In this sense such sign tokens are referential. But more specifically, the past tense tokens refer to a time $t_r$, that is assertedly prior to the time $t_{sp}$ at which the utterance containing them is spoken. In other words, temporal categories, and past tense in particular, compare the time for which the proposition of a referential speech event is asserting something with the time of the referential speech event itself. So the referential meaning of any categorial type 'tense' to which we want to assign the several tokens depends upon a comparison of the time referred to with the time of utterance in each speech event incorporating the token.

The proper utterance or interpretation of each token of the past tense category, then, presupposes the knowledge of the time at which the speech event takes place. A tense category takes the time of the speech event as the fixed point of comparison in referring to another time, $t_r$. It assumes cognitive "existence" of $t_{sp}$, just as $t_{sp}$ demands cognitive "existence" only when such a tense category, or its equivalent occurs.

## Double-Mode Linguistic Categories

This kind of referential index has also been called a *shifter*, because the reference "shifts" regularly, depending on the factors of the speech situation. It is very interesting that these presupposing, referential indexes, or shifters, are what Jakobson (1957) calls "duplex signs," operating at the levels of code and message simultaneously. The segmentation of sentences in the semantico-referential mode leads to the recognition of this semantic residue, unanalyzable by the methods depending on the metalinguistic property, but constituting a distinct kind of superimposed linguistic type that fits tongue-in-groove with pure semantic categories. Such categories as tense unite in a single segmentable sign vehicle a referential or quasi-semantic meaning and an indexical or pragmatic one. The referential value of a shifter, moreover, depends on the presupposition of its pragmatic value.

All languages incorporate these duplex signs, referential indexes. They are pervasive categories, which anchor, as it were, the semantico-referential mode of signs, those which represent pure propositional capabilities of language, in the actual speech event of reference, by making the propositional reference dependent on the suitable indexing of the speech situation. Not only is tense such a duplex category, but also *status*, which, following Whorf, indicates the truth value for the speaker in a referential event of the proposition encoded by the semantico-grammatical elements; *deixis*, which indicates the spatio-temporal relations of some presupposed referent in the speech event to speaker, hearer, or other referent; and so forth. A very large part of the Whorfian oeuvre (1956), in fact, can now be seen as a first attempt to draw out the Boasian implications of how pure referential (semantic) categories and duplex (referential-indexical) ones combine differently from language to language to accomplish ultimately isofunctional referential speech events. What one language accomplishes in utterances with a single referential index (for example, tense), another accomplishes with a combination of semantic category plus referential index (for example, aspect + status). Whorf himself lacked the theoretical terminology with which to make this clear, and his writings have had the sad fate of being misrepresented in the "popular" anthropological literature for a generation, under the guise of some vague "relativity" taken literally, rather than as the metaphorical idiom of the then-beginning atomic age.

## Rules of Use

A consideration of such duplex signs brings up the question of how the indexical mode of such segmentable elements of utterances is to be described, that is, to be given a systematic account in terms of sign types and meanings. We have seen that the particularly indexical aspect of the meaning of such shifters involves a presupposition of the "existence" of, or cognitive focus on, some specific value in the domain of variables of the speech situation. On the one hand, the referential contribution of a shifter depends on the specific value of one or more of the variables being realized; on the other hand, the specific value being realized during some specific utterance permits the category to occur as a shifter of that specific sort.

We can summarize these converse properties of implication between contextual variable and indexical token by a general function we can call a *rule of use* or *rule of indexicality*. We can say that a rule of use is a general constraint on the class of actual shifter tokens occurring in the class of actual speech contexts. In this sense, the specifically indexical aspect of a shifter token can be said to represent some indexical type, that is, some underlying general sign that stands in the same relation to its tokens—permitting us to analyze them as "the same"—as the usual sort of general semantico-referential sign. It is clear that the senses in which we have sign types in these two modes are quite different, a fact not always easy to grasp, for the one depends on rules of use for definition of the type, the other on the metalinguistic operations of glossing speech events or the equivalent.

## Formal Description of Indexicality

A rule of use is a general function that describes the relationship between speech context, given as a set of variables, some of which must have specific values, and some portion of the utterance, some message fraction. Recalling the minimal description of the speech event given at the outset, we can say that speaker x speaks to hearer y about referent z, using message fraction $\theta_n$ (message itself $\theta$), analyzable in terms of semantico-referential grammar G, at time t, in spatial configuration $l_x, l_y, (l_z)$—the referent need not be present independent of its creation by the speech event itself—plus other factors. Some of the variables will be present in a description as such, while for others we will have to specify particular values in order to characterize the appropriate use of the shifter.

Thus, for English past 'tense,' where we refer in the speech event to a time before the time of the utterance, we can describe the indexical aspect of this shifter by the schema:

$$\text{sp}(x, y, t_r < t_{sp}, \{-ed\}, G_E, t_{sp}, 1, \ldots) \rightarrow \text{Past tense}$$

where $t_r$ is the specific value of the referent z, and $t_{sp}$ is the specific value of the time of utterance. For assertive 'status,' where the speaker asserts the truth of the proposition being uttered, in English we use a heavily stressed inflected verb, such as auxiliary or modal, in the general case. We can describe this by:

$$sp\,(x,y,T\,(f\,(z_1, \ldots, z_n)\,),[A\dot{u}\dot{x}],G_E,t,l, \ldots) \rightarrow \text{Assertive}$$

where the proposition $f(z_1, \ldots, z_n)$ may take several arguments and $T(f)$ is the truth-value indicator.

Such rules of use for shifters are necessary to describe their indexical mode of meaning, much as rules of a grammar G are necessary to describe their semantico-referential meaning. In these cases, where two modes are united in the same category, we have a fortunate illustrative case. But in both modes of a shifter, the description can proceed only by defining sign types for occurring tokens. In the referential mode, this is accomplished through traditional referentially based linguistic analysis, which leaves shifters as residuals. In the indexical mode, it is accomplished through the constitution of general rules of use.

## Peirce's Trichotomy of Signs

These two modes of signification combined in the classical shifter illustrate 2 of the 3 elementary sign types given by one semiotic analysis of C. S. Peirce (1932). Altogether, he presented three trichotomies of signs, each one classified on a distinct basis. The first was based on the nature of the sign vehicle, the second on the nature of the entity signaled, and the third, the most important, on the nature of the relationship between entity signaled and signaling entity, that is, on the nature of the meaning that is communicated. (Of the 27 logically possible sign types, only 10 occur, though I will not develop this Peircean deduction here.)

The three sign types, each characterized by its own type of meaning for the users, are icon, index, and symbol. *Icons* are those signs where the perceivable properties of the sign vehicle itself have isomorphism to (up to identity with) those of the entity signaled. That is, the entities are "likenesses" in some sense. *Indexes* are those signs where the occurrence of a sign vehicle token bears a connection of understood spatio-temporal contiguity to the occurrence of the entity signaled. That is, the presence of some entity is perceived to be signaled in the context of communication incorporating the sign vehicle. *Symbols* are the residual class of signs, where neither physical similarity nor contextual contiguity hold between sign vehicle and entity signaled. They form the class of "arbitrary" signs traditionally spoken of as the fundamental kind of linguistic entity. Sign vehicle and entity signaled are related through the bond of a semantico-referential meaning in the sense elaborated earlier.

Every linguistic sign token is an icon of the linguistic sign type, and in this sense every linguistic sign trivially incorporates an iconic mode. Further, every symbol token is an index of the symbol type, since its use in context depends upon cognitive "existence" of that part of the semantico-referential grammar which explains its referential value. In this sense, as Peirce noted, there is exemplified the progressive relationship of inclusion of the three sign modes.

## Icons

I do not deal here extensively with iconism in language, since, interesting though the subject be, it is largely peripheral to our concern with the cultural contextualization of language. At the formal level of single units, however, all languages are seen to contain *onomatopoeias*, which duplicate the thing signaled in the physical medium of sound. Thus, *bzzz*, to a speaker of English, is an onomatopoeia that means 'noise that sounds like the sign vehicle,' used particularly to describe bees' flight, high-speed saws cutting through wood, and so forth. It is usually assimilated as a lexical item to the phonemic pattern of the language. Since monosyllables in English require a vowel, it is written out as *buzz*, pronounced [bʌz(ː)] or [bəz:]. This assimilation is frequently found for onomatopoeias, giving a remarkable variety to those in different languages said to represent the same noise. But this should not obscure the fact that, to the users, the iconic mode of meaning is the one that gives the sign significance in speech.

There are many kinds of icons in languages, ranging from *replicas* and *images*, where the physical properties of signal and thing signaled are indistinguishable or totally alike, through *diagrams*, where the perceived parts are structurally isomorphic. Many diagrams are speech-internal. Universal laws of sequencing of morphemes, for example, are frequently direct or inverse diagrams of syntactic units, and so forth.

## Symbols

In the symbolic mode of sign mechanism, language is most "language-like" in the traditional sense. From the negative characterization of no necessary physical or contextual connection between sign vehicle token and entity signaled, the symbolic mode of communication depends entirely on an abstract connection, motivated through semantico-grammatical sign types and their rules of combination. This kind of pure reference forms the closed system of classical discussions of language semantics. The referential value of sign tokens in any given event depends only upon the general propositional contributions of the sign types in certain arrangements that underlie the tokens. This propositional value of the signs in terms of equivalence relations can be analyzed by metasemantic manipulation. Such symbols, then, are what we described in the section above on propositional analysis.

## Symbols vs. Shifters

It is to be observed that the symbolic mode of signs is one mechanism for achieving reference in actual referential speech events. The implementation of the symbols by tokens depends on—presupposes—the knowledge of the grammar G in a pure referential event. In contrast, the shifters, referential indexes, are a mechanism in which there is no abstract system of propositional equivalence relations, but only the rules of use which specify the relationship of actual referent of the sign token to the other variables of the context, among them the sign vehicle. The referential value of a shifter is constituted by the speech event itself; shifters may presuppose any variables of the speech event, including the semantically based grammar G (for example, anaphoric "switch reference"). So we must distinguish between semantically constituted symbols, the abstract propositional values of which are implemented in actual referential events, and the shifters, or referential indexes, the propositional values of which are linked to the unfolding of the speech event itself. These are two distinct types that merge in the apparent structure of utterances but are analytically separable.

## Indexes

We have seen indexical reference exemplified in shifters. But it remains to observe that *indexicality*, the property of sign vehicle signaling contextual "existence" of an entity, is itself a sign mode independent of the other two. In the duplex categories illustrated above, the referential value depended upon the indexical value. Of course, then, it is possible to conceive of indexical signs of language which do not overlap with referential categories, that is, do not contribute to achieving reference. Such *nonreferential indexes*, or "pure" indexes, are features of speech which, independent of any referential speech events that may be occurring, signal some particular value of one or more contextual variables.

From the point of view of pragmatic analysis, we have to recognize such nonreferential indexical contributions of speech behavior, regardless of the dominant speech event occurring. These various indexical elements of language go into constituting distinct speech events. They are functionally discrete, but behaviorally they potentially overlap with referential speech in multifunctional utterances, as we noted above. Pure indexical features of utterances are describable with rules of use, just as are referential indexes. But the rules of use do not specify a referent independent of those created by other elements of the utterance, for these indexes are not referential. The "meaning" of these indexes is purely pragmatic and does not intersect with semantico-referential meaning exemplified in symbols.

## Nonreferential Indexes

Such indexes as do not contribute to the referential speech event signal the structure of the speech context. Some of the most interesting of these indexes, certainly for the social anthropologist, are those that index features of the personae of the speech event. For example, *sex indexes* for some languages are formally systematic categories or other obvious features. In the Muskogean languages of the southeastern United States, such as Koasati (Haas 1944), there was a suffix -s (or its etymological equivalent) that appeared (with characteristic phonological alternations in shapes) on the inflected verb forms of every nonquotative utterance spoken by a socially female individual. In direct quotation, as we might expect, the sex of the original speaker is indexically preserved. It is important to see that the referential value of the utterance, and of the verb especially, is exactly the same, whether or not the form has the suffix. The suffix makes no referential contribution, but rather its presence or absence provides the categorial information about the sociological sex of the speaker. Not only "first person" forms of verbs, in utterances referring to speaker, but verb forms of all "persons" take this suffix, and the referential content of the speech in both suffix-bearing and suffixless forms is unaffected.

A more complex case is reported by Sapir (1929) for Yana, a language of California, in which there is one form of all major words in utterances spoken by sociological male to sociological male, and another form for all other combinations. The two forms are typically related by the operation of phonological changes in the one form and not in the other. And these pairs of related forms can function referentially in exactly the same way; the only difference in utterances containing them is in the pragmatic suitability for certain classes of speaker and hearer. These essentially morphological and phonological mechanisms of sex indexing must be functionally abstracted from utterances and described by rules of use, for example, Koasati sp $(\male(x),y,z,V]+s,G_K,t,l, \ldots)$; I will take up the characterization of the Yana case further below, in discussing rule mechanisms.

Exactly the same sort of nonreferential indexical mode is found in *deference indexes*, where speech signals inequalities of status, rank, age, sex, and the like. For example, we may take those of Javanese, reported by Geertz (1960) and more lucidly by Uhlenbeck (1970) and Horne (1967; 1973), where one of the modes of contrast is between a vocabulary set and certain grammatical restrictions (the variety called krɔmɔ) used basically by lower-to-higher or high-to-high on these scales, while other, "unmarked" vocabulary items and all constructions (ŋɔkɔ) are used in the opposite cases. It is interesting that most vocabulary items and virtually all constructions do not have these alternate forms, yet the power of the alternation was apparently very great in traditional Javanese society. Here again, the propositional content of the utterances with corresponding krɔmɔ/ŋɔkɔ vocabulary is just the same, while the deference they index between speaker and hearer differs. The rules of use based on the parameters for deference are always of the form sp (H(x),L(y), . . .), sp (L(x),H(y), . . .) and so on.

These deference indexes frequently and especially intersect with the referential indexes called "first and second person pronouns" in the standard literature, giving, as for example in Thai and Burmese (Cooke 1970), upwards of a score of sets of segmentable "pronouns" for use as referential personal index plus pure deference index combined into one apparent surface category. In many languages (see Brown and Gilman 1960), functionally analogous marking of social deference in pronominal indexes is accomplished by skewing otherwise referential categories of 'person' and 'number.' These special effects, *pragmatic metaphors* (to be dealt with below), are to be distinguished from a distinct indexical expression of social deference with unique formal signals.

A distinct nonreferential bifurcation of lexical items into complementary indexical sets was widespread in Australian Aboriginal speech communities. As described by Dixon (1971; 1972) for Dyirbal, a language of the Cairns Rain Forest in Northern Queensland, there is an "everyday" set of lexical items, and a "mother-in-law" set, which had to be used by a speaker only in the presence of his classificatory mother-in-law or equivalent affine. In other words, the mother-in-law vocabulary, totally distinct from the everyday one, indexes the specified affinal relation between speaker (x) and some "audience"—not the socially defined addressee (y)—in the speech situation. As such, the switch in vocabulary serves as an *affinal taboo index* in the speech situation, maintaining and creating sociological distance.

It is interesting that the grammatical structure in the traditional sense remains exactly the same in these two kinds of situations. What changes is the entire set of nongrammatical lexical items. Moreover, since the ratio of everyday to mother-in-law vocabulary is approximately 4:1, the strictly semantic content of propositions coded in everyday vocabulary will require more elaborate grammatical constructions and many more lexical items to code in mother-in-law vocabulary. Semantic content was apparently severely reduced in actual communication. Further, the glossing possibilities back and forth, under the same grammar, can be exploited, as was done by Dixon, to justify semantic description. But the principle of this being a pure indexical device, independent of the semantico-referential content, makes the general form of the rule of use sp ( ↗x] [Af(x,y′) ],y,z,{ $L_2$ }, . . .), where Af(x,y′) expresses the relationship between speaker and "audience" and $L_2$ (:$L_1$) represents the disjunct set of lexical items.

So there is a distinction between referential indexes, such as tense, and nonreferential ones, such as the disjunct sets of forms to code sociological relations of personae in the speech situation. Some phenomena, however, appear to be interesting borderline cases between shifters and pure indexes. In Javanese, where the basic distinction of vocabulary into krɔmɔ and ŋɔkɔ sets is a pure deference index, there is another, less pervasive distinction between a set of lexical forms (krɔmɔ iŋgyel) showing deference of speaker to some exalted human referent. This set of forms, coded in stems having to do with parts of the body, personal activities, and so forth, occurs in both krɔmɔ, and ŋɔkɔ styles. It constitutes an independent axis of lexical choice, but one which intersects with the speaker-hearer deference when the hearer is also the focused referent (that is, sp (x,y,y, . . .) ). Since the lexical alternants have the same basic propositional value in krɔmɔ iŋgyel or plain styles, under strict semantic analysis we should want to describe this speaker-referent deference switch as a pure indexical one. But especially in the case of speaking about the addressee, where the reference is perforce of an indexical sort, the two systems krɔmɔ : ŋɔkɔ, krɔmɔ iŋgyel : [plain] seem to merge. The actual facts of any given instance probably rest ultimately on the distinction between indexically presupposed and indexically created referent, another axis of classification.

## Indexical Presupposition

In all cases of indexes, we have constructed indexical sign types by rules of use. These rules of use state the relationship of mutually implied existence of sign vehicle token and certain aspects of the context of discourse. For all of the shifters we examined in the section on referential indexes, we could furthermore say that the aspect of the speech situation was *presupposed* by the sign token. That is, a given shifter token is uninterpretable referentially without the knowledge of some aspect of the situation.

A particularly clear case of such presupposition is the operation of deictics, in English, for example, *this* and *that* in the singular. When we use a token of the full noun phrase *this table* or *that table* (with stressed full vowel in both words), pointing out thereby some particular object, the referent of the token of *table* must be identifiable, must "exist" cognitively, for the deictic itself to be interpretable. The proper use of the token of the deictic presupposes the physical existence of an actual object which can properly be referred to by *table*, or it presupposes a prior segment of referential discourse which has specified such a referent. Otherwise the use of the deictic token is inappropriate; it is uninterpretable and confusing. (There is a related noun phrase incorporating reduced-vowel "deictic" form, with reduced stress and distinct intonation pattern, used for nondeictic definite reference, no presupposition of referent being involved, and no prior discourse necessary.) If we use the wrong deictic for the referent, or use the deictic with the wrong lexical noun (one that does not properly describe an object in correct position for the deictic), again confusion results, or correction by the interlocutor: "Oh, you mean that other table!" or "This is not a table, it's a chair!"

The use of the deictic, then, is maximally presupposing, in that the contextual conditions are required in some appropriate configuration for proper indexical reference with a deictic token. The general pattern of all the shifters is similar. Some aspect of the context spelled out in the rule of use is fixed and presupposed, in order for the referential contribution to be made. And in this sense, reference itself is once more seen to be an act of creation, of changing the contextual basis for further speech events. Recall that one of the ways in which the presupposition of the deictic can be satisfied is to have referred to the entity in question.

## Indexical Creativity

But there is a general *creative* or *performative* aspect to the use of pure indexical tokens of certain kinds, which can be said not so much to change the context, as to make explicit and overt the parameters of structure of the ongoing events. By the very use of an indexical token, which derives its indexical value from the rules of use setting up the indexical types, we have brought into sharp cognitive relief part of the context of speech. In some cases, the occurrence of the speech signal is the only overt sign of the contextual parameter, verifiable, perhaps, by other, co-occurring behaviors in other media, but nevertheless the most salient index of the specific value. Under these circumstances, the indexical token in speech performs its greatest apparent work, seeming to be the very medium through which the relevant aspect of the context is made to "exist." Certainly, the English indexical pronouns *I/we* and *you* (vs. *he/she/it/they*) perform this creative function in bounding off the personae of the speech event itself; in those languages, such as Chinook (Columbia River, North America) with 'inclusive' and 'exclusive' pronominal indexes, the boundary function becomes even more finely drawn. Social indexes such as deference vocabularies and constructions, mentioned above, are examples of maximally creative or performative devices, which, by their very use, make the social parameters of speaker and hearer explicit. Adherence to the norms specified by rules of use reinforces the perceived social relations of speaker and hearer; violations constitute a powerful rebuff or insult, or go into the creation of irony and humor.

## Classification of Index Types/Tokens

Indexical tokens range on a sliding scale of creativity or performative value from the extreme of presupposition displayed by deictics to the extreme of creativity displayed by subtle social indexes. The particular placement of any given indexical token depends to a great extent on the factors of the individual context of its use: how many events are simultaneously occurring; how many independent media are signaling the factors of the context; what prior events have taken place; how many co-occurrent indexes of a given functional sort are occurring in speech. As we have seen, the different kinds of indexical types have inherent ranges on the functional scale of presupposition. Underlying all these specific usages, however, are the rules of use, *norms* as it were, for the relationship of mutual existence between contextual variables and speech signals.

The referential vs. nonreferential nature of indexes, a measure of the independence of indexes from the semantico-referential mode of communication, is one axis of classification, of indexical types. The presuppositional vs. creative nature of indexes, a measure of the independence of indexes from every other signaling medium and mode in speech events, is another axis of classification, of indexical tokens. Because the two classifications interact, borderline cases exist. The speaker-referent deference vocabulary of Javanese, for example, seems to be used referentially or nonreferentially in a way that depends upon the presuppositional or performative nature of the given token in context. This discourse reference, the actual unfolding referential speech event, is once more seen to be distinct from abstract (semantic) propositional reference, implemented in discourse. The former type, characteristic of referential indexes and described with rules of use, responds to such indexical properties as presupposition/performance, while the latter, based on semantico-grammatical analysis, does not.

A kind of four-cell array is thus generated by these *functional characteristics* of indexes, in which we can place the examples discussed, and provide for further examples (see table 1).

TABLE 1

Functional Characteristics of Indexes

|  | presupposing | creative (performative) |
|---|---|---|
| referential | locative deictics, tense<br>first person pronominals | second person pronominals |
| nonreferential | Dyirbal "mo-in-law" lexicon<br>social sex markers | deference indexes of speaker-hearer relations |

Referential, presupposing indexes contribute to propositional description in discourse, but only by taking as a starting point the value of some contextual variable, as for the computation of time reference in tense categories. Nonreferential presupposing indexes reflect in speech the existence of some specific values of contextual variables, such as the presence of affine audience in mother-in-law lexical items. Referential, relatively performative indexes contribute to propositional description in discourse, and in addition function as the signal for the existence of speech-event features, as in the choice of pronominals, which assign the event roles of speaker, hearer, audience, and referent to certain individuals in the maximal case. Finally, nonreferential, relatively performative indexes serve as independent speech signals establishing the parameters of the interaction themselves, as in deference forms, which in effect establish overtly the social relations of the individuals in the roles of speaker and hearer, speaker and audience, or speaker and referent.

## Functional Aggregation in Indexical Forms

The Thai example cited above in which social deference indexes are united with pronominal referential indexes points up the fact that even indexical categories can be pragmatically multifunctional. On the one hand, the pronominals have discourse-referential values that contribute to description, and on the other hand, they have nonreferential values that structure the factors of the speech situation. The first indexical aspect contributes to the propositional mode of speech, while the second constitutes part of the social mode of marking equality or inequality. By analysis of the surface categories of speech, we might segment the pronominals as semantico-grammatical residuals, and then attempt to specify the pragmatic meaning of the forms. But inasmuch as two modes are united here in one surface category, it would take considerably more analysis to see that two distinct rules of use are involved, based on two distinct functions of the forms. At a functional level, then, there are *two* indexes which happen to be represented by the same surface indexical category, one a shifter, one not. This functional and hence analytic distinctness of the two modes must always be the starting point for the isolation of the pragmatic categories in language, and must rest ultimately on a sensitive analysis of the speech-event function of utterances, a task which is essentially social anthropological.

## Referential Analogy in Discourse

The situation is even more interesting in the case of pragmatic metaphors connected with pronominal shifters referring to the hearer (sp (x,y,y, . . .) )), a phenomenon found in many languages. Instead of distinct forms indexing the quality of speaker-hearer social relations, the "second person" pronouns incorporate skewing of otherwise semantic categories (see Benveniste 1950; 1956). To analyze these data, we have to distinguish two kinds of extension or analogy of referential categories in discourse.

The so-called pronouns frequently seem to incorporate categories of 'person' and 'number,' so that we tend to speak of "first and second person singular and plural" for pronominal forms. "Third person" pronouns can be true substitutes, *anaphoric devices* that obviate the need for repetition of a full, lexically complex referring noun phrase (thus, *The man sat down. He . . .*). In the referential mode, they act as *negative indexes* in never indexing speaker or hearer participants in speech events. But "first and second person" forms are referential indexes, the contribution to discourse reference of which comes about by functionally distinct rules of use; such forms have no anaphoric properties.

When we use a "third person" pronoun, the singular or plural number is derived by the rules of anaphora from the semantic 'number' specification of the noun phrase it replaces. In this pure semantic mode, plural 'number' signals more-than-one of whatever entity is referred to by the lexical stems of the noun in question. But some occurrences of plural number category derive secondarily only at the level of discourse reference by a kind of summing up of individual semantically established entities (thus, English, *Jack and Jill went up a hill. They . . .*). It is at this second level of reference that the first and second person pronominal indexes get their apparent "singular" and "plural" forms. For English 'we' ≠ 'I' + 'I'; the form *we* is an index that refers to and presupposes a speaker and at least one other individual in the referential speech event, sp (x,y,x&w,*we*, $G_E$,t,l, . . .). Similarly, second person plural refers to and indexes hearer and at least one other persona, for example, Russian sp (x,y,y&v,*vy*,$G_R$,t,l, . . .). Only by the summation of the individual referents in discourse, which are referentially indexed by such pronominals, does their 'singular' or 'plural' referential value emerge.

With this analysis of the distinction between anaphoric and nonanaphoric pronominal indexes ("person"), and of semantically based (cardinal "number") vs. discourse-based (summed "number") reference to quantity, it is possible to see the nature of the skewings in so-called "honorific second person pronouns."

## Pragmatic Metaphors of Grammatical Categories

For some languages, Russian for example, or French, we can index the same kind of speaker-hearer deference that is indicated elsewhere by vocabulary switch (see Friedrich 1966; Ervin-Tripp 1971), when addressing a single addressee, by using the "second person plural" (*vy, vous*) rather than the "singular" (*ty, tu*). In other words, the semantic cardinal number category, in its summed discourse use, either refers to plural addressees or refers to a single addressee, concomitantly indexing the deference of speaker to hearer. In some languages, for example Italian, the deferential second person index uses what is otherwise the "third singular (feminine)" pronominal form for combined referential indexing and social indexing. In other words, third singular feminine anaphoric, or nonpersonal pronoun, either replaces a third singular feminine semantic noun or refers to and indexes a singular addressee while indexing deference of speaker to hearer. Some languages, such as German and Worora (Northern Kimberley, Western Australia), switch both person (2→3) and number (sg. →pl.) to express this deference. In those languages with a 'dual' number category, more highly marked than 'plural,' deference is indicated along the axis of number by switch to dual-number addressee index. This occurs, for example, in Yokuts of south central California (Newman 1944) and Nyangumata of northern West Australia (O'Grady 1964). (Curiously, in both these languages, the deference must be accorded to a genealogically specified persona, mother-in-law and equivalent in the first, mother's brother and equivalent in the second.)

What unites all of these seemingly isofunctional usages is the unidirectionality, in every case, of switch from "second person pronoun" to "third," from expected "singular number" to "plural" (or "dual"), or both concomitantly. There is a kind of metaphor based on the discourse-referential value of the categories, it would seem. In the one case, it is shift out of the realm of second person address, where an individual is indexed in the speech situation face-to-face, to the realm of anaphora, where an already established entity is understood as the referent of the substitute. This makes the addressee larger than life by taking away the individual personhood implied by the face-to-face address. In the second case, it is a shift out of the realm of the singular, where an individual is referred to, and into the realm of nonsingular, where, as it were, the summed number of individuals referred to is greater than one. This makes the addressee count for more than one social individual; to his persona accrues the social weight of many, as compared with the speaker. (The "royal 'we'" does the inverse, we should note.)

Such universals in expression, examples of isofunctional indexing with seeming metaphorical plays upon semantic categories, are an important demonstration of the interplay between the semantic mode of language and the pragmatic constitution of social categories through speech. The semantically based analysis of categories, even with "fudges" to permit incorporation of the analytic residue of shifters, does not capture these generalizations. The perspective must be one that frees us from dependence on semantic categories, or even referential ones, as the defining segmentation of speech requiring analysis.

## Functional and Formal Analogues

In each of these cases, I have been claiming a kind of functional comparability of the parallel formations. Rules of use are norms between the contextual variables and some formal feature of the message. To be *functionally analogous*, then, indexes must be described by rules of use that specify analogous contexts under analogous speech events. (Obviously, the utterance fractions in different languages can hardly be expected to be alike.) When indexes seem to be accomplishing analogous socially constituted tasks, we can speak of cross-linguistic comparability. So the claim of functional analogy from a heuristic point of view makes hypotheses about the social parameters of speech events. From a theoretical point of view it depends upon the results of social anthropology for a framework of description of social categories, for the structural significance of the pattern of indexical speech norms in the given society. Universals of functional signification thus are the necessary means for creating a real science of language pragmatics—that is, for establishing the ethnography of speech—just as within the semantic mode, universal hypotheses about phonetics and reference are the necessary empirical correlates of semantico-grammatical analysis.

On the other hand, *formally analogous* indexicals depend upon cross-systemic specification of equivalence of message fractions. In the case of the pragmatic metaphors illustrated above, there is formal comparability in the expression of deference through the pronominal categories themselves, which can be isolated in the referential mode in every one of the languages in question. (Note how the formal analysis in one mode depends on isofunctionality in others, as was mentioned above.) The languages all use formally similar categorial substitutions, definable in the semantico-referential mode, to index deferential address. From a formal point of view, then, we seek some way of characterizing as structurally analogous the message fractions serving as indexes. But any such structural specification depends upon analysis of forms, which itself rests on finding some isofunctional basis for comparison. Ultimately, then, cross-linguistic formal analogy and functional analogy are, like phonetic and referential frameworks in the semantic mode, linked as hypotheses that serve to justify a particular analysis.

## Formal Distinctions Signaling Functional Ones

The parallel formal-functional analogy of all the pragmatic metaphors for speaker-hearer deference is an exceptional case. Ordinarily, given some social parameters constituted on nonspeech grounds and indexed in some language, we might want to ask whether or not these are indexed in some other language and, if so, how. The sex indexes of several American Indian languages mentioned above are somewhat diverse functionally, but all formally overlap in apparent phonological changes at the ends of words, in particular of inflected verbs. The Thai pronominal system for first and second persons—independent words that index in complex ways the various inequalities resulting in deference—includes among the grounds of deference distinction of sociological sex. So the several American Indian systems seem to isolate the social variable of sex, indexing it with a unique formal set of changes. (The ethnographic record establishes the great salience of the distinction, at least in the societies speaking Muskogean languages, but its cultural position has not been established.) The Thai (and other Southeast Asian) systems assimilate the social variable of sex to the functional characterization of inequality more generally, making a pointed ethnographic statement on equivalences of stratification. It is always necessary, as this example demonstrates, to take the functional perspective in terms of rules of use to be able to see in what way such pragmatic items fit into systematic sociological patterns, of which linguistic ones are a major part.

## Formal Characterization of Indexes

From the formal point of view, the sign vehicles that function in an indexical mode are extremely varied. As we noted when dealing with the privacy function of language, switch of semantico-referential grammar can itself serve as an index. We have seen vocabulary, affixes, phonological rules, and syncretistic pronominal categories serving indexical functions within utterances. Indexical devices such as anaphoric pronouns, mentioned above, which maintain discourse reference in certain surface structural configurations, are formally defined only over at least two noun phrases, frequently found in distinct semantico-referential sentences. Intonation patterns and stress shifts are further kinds of features that are characteristically indexes, though I have not dealt with them directly by example. And syntactic constructions, such as the distinction between "active" and "passive" forms of utterances, or the English "performative" construction *I* [V] *you* [X], are virtually always pragmatic units, formally isolable on functional grounds. In other words, the range of possible formal elements that can serve as speech indexes, according to our traditional semantico-grammatical understanding, includes the entire range of language-level indexing, discourse-sequence level, sentence level, word and affix level, and phonological alternations that can be characterized by rules, including intonation and other nonsegmental gradient devices.

The description of all these occurring pragmatic formal features of speech presents a vast problem for our traditional ideas of what a grammar (G) is. From the point of view of a semantico-referential grammar, it would appear that every pragmatic index is a kind of "structural idiom," where the constructions cannot be analyzed according to semantico-referential combinatory regularities. This would make by far the greater bulk of a description of speech into a list of such "idioms." The undesirability of such an alternative is manifest, given the kinds of regularities of pragmatic function exemplified above.

So some attempt to patch up traditional grammar cannot serve as a principled description of the pragmatics of language—a fact that most contemporary linguistic theorists have not yet appreciated. For the characterization of pragmatics as dependent on semantico-referential analysis—the "performative" approach discussed above—becomes totally hopeless once we consider that only a portion of the indexicals in speech are shifters, with connection to the semantically based grammar in the speech function of reference. The remainder of the indexes are just functionally independent of reference as such.

The question, then, becomes one of how to represent speech as the apparently continuous formal medium it is, while at the same time preserving the pragmatic distinction among (1) the pure referential function or semantic aspect of meaning, from which semantico-referential systems derive their analyzability, and on which one facet of referential speech acts rests; (2) the shifter function, or indexical-referential aspect of meaning, constituted by rules of use at the level of discourse reference; and (3) the pure indexical functions, serving other functional modes independent of reference, for which nonreferential rules of use are constituted. In (2) we have a point of overlap between (1) and (3)—hence their duplex nature. But a formal descriptive "pragmatic grammar" must integrate semantics, valid as a specialized mode, into an inclusive system.

# PRAGMATICS AND CULTURAL DESCRIPTION

I have analytically separated functional modes of speech behavior, further showing the modes of meaning so constituted in linguistic signs. I want now to characterize briefly the integration of these modes in a systematic pragmatics of language, indicating how this purports to be a more adequate descriptive paradigm for speech and other communicative behavior. This will lead naturally to a consideration of the relationship of such pragmatic description to broader ethnographic or "cultural" description.

## Functional Alternatives in Rules of Use

Rules of use for both shifters and other, nonreferential indexes show the existential relationship of contextual variables to some overt utterance fraction. The rules of use for shifters specify the referent (z) as well, consonant with the fact that such categories contribute to referential speech events. It would seem that formally, the third variable (corresponding to z) in nonreferential rules of use should be the functionally determined kind of entity which is being indexed, for example some sociological domain, such as kinship, sex, rank; some spatial configuration, such as the "proxemic" configuration of persons in the speech event; and so forth. In other words, not only referential speech events, but all other types as well have rules of use that specify the functional domain over which the particular pragmatic mode of meaning is being realized. So not only do we specify rules of use for sp $(x,y,z^r, \ldots)$ where $z^r$ is "referent," but also sp $(x,y,z^f, \ldots)$ where $z^f$ is a variable of functions more generally, defined by the range of speech events.

Under such a generalization, the "rules of use" we specify for shifters, the "duplex" categories, must be further analyzed into what are indeed two elementary functional modes. One such functional mode is referential, with variable $z^r$ specified; another functional mode is nonreferential, with some variable $z^f$ to be specified, such as $z^t$ "temporal parameter," $z^p$ "privacy-boundary," and so forth. In shifters, an elementary referential function and a distinct elementary indexical function are united in the same surface speech category, but if we examine them carefully, we can see that the referent $z^r$ is frequently of a different domain from the indexed $z^f$. Deictics, as we saw, presuppose the referent from previous discourse, for example, as well as the speaker or hearer location, and refer to the locus of the presupposed referent relative to that of speaker or hearer.

## The Constitution of Speech Acts

We can call each one of these elementary functionally specific rules of use a *speech act*. We can note that such norms for pragmatic meaning relations depend upon the functional specification of speech at the level of speech events, for it is at this higher level of analysis that one can recognize various pragmatic modes, the socially constituted "tasks" which speech behavior accomplishes or "performs." Reference is one such pragmatic mode, and referential speech acts are of two kinds, which explain the nature of the referring utterance fraction. On the one hand, the shifters motivate elementary referential rules of use, where referent is specified with respect to some speech-event variable(s). On the other hand, the semantico-referential entities motivate rules of use which merely specify *variable* $z^r$ and presuppose (index) the grammar G; that is, the referential value is determined by the semantico-grammatical rules implemented in a functionally referential speech event, no further specification being required. Other pragmatic modes define distinct kinds of speech acts, many of which, as we have seen, overlap in precisely the same, multifunctional surface indexes. For example Thai "pronouns" represent in utterances a bimodal shifter of personal referent, as well as a social index of deference. The widespread pragmatic metaphors for deference use otherwise referential categories in multiple functions expressing equality/inequality.

Speech acts are the elementary indexical formulae for specifying the pragmatic meaning or *function$_2$* of speech signs. They operate within the framework of *purposive function$_1$* of socially constituted behavior already discussed above. We can speak of the "referential function$_2$" of actual signs in the sense of the contribution they make to achieving a valid instance of function$_1$ of describing. Similarly, we can speak of the "socially seriating function$_2$" of actual signs in the sense of the contribution they make to the function$_1$ of defining hierarchies within social categories. Speech is multifunctional$_1$ in the sense that it can simultaneously be used to constitute distinct kinds of events. Speech is multifunctional$_2$ in the sense that apparent elements of surface form actually incorporate meanings of several distinct indexical types. This accords with our traditional notions of *grammatical function*, an instance of function$_2$, always ultimately specified in terms of the contribution of elements to the semantico-referential system.

The analysis of speech acts is thus a generalization of the analysis of semantico-referential systems, providing for meaning relations and language uses distinct from those of the traditionally analyzed sort. In a mathematical analogy, it is the more general structure of which the previously explored type turns out to be a special case. More particularly, the speech acts for semantico-referential signs function$_1$ exclusively in referential speech events—abbreviatory extensions and such aside—and are vacuously specified, with the exception of presupposing the grammar G.

## The "Grammar" of Speech Acts

Such a characterization permits us to see at least the nature of a more inclusive kind of "grammar," which includes the traditional sort as a component. If grammar G, as in our present understanding, is a finite, recursive set of rules which relate semantico-referential representations to utterance types (or "sentences" in "surface form"), we can recall from the first part of this paper that the meanings within G are defined in terms of the function$_1$ of pure reference, and the sentences are segmentable into constituents on this basis. In pure referential sentences, the surface elements so functioning$_1$ form a continuous sequence.

To construct a *grammar* (G$'$) *of speech acts*, the analogous generalization is a set of rules which relate pragmatic meanings—functions$_2$ specified by functionally$_1$ indexed variables—to the "surface form" of utterances. Utterances are, we have several times remarked, continuous in nature. The great bulk of such utterances, moreover, give the appearance of formal integration in terms of phrase, word, and affix structure, especially for referential segments, the shifters and semantic elements. This would seem to indicate that the traditional grammatical rules (G) must be incorporated into pragmatics (G$'$), that is, that at least some speech acts consist of rules showing the contextual dependence of traditional grammatical rules for generating surface forms.

This is further confirmed by two pragmatic examples I have already mentioned. One is the switch of semantico-referential language, which can serve as an index. Here the whole set of rules of the traditional sort is a function of—indexes—the grammatical competence of speaker, hearer, and audience. So obviously our pragmatic description should show the selection of rules G$^L$, not just an infinite set of messages $\{ \theta^L_i \}$, as a function of contextual variables. The second case is the Yana male vs. female indexing. Here phonological rules, which show the regularities of shape in pairs of forms for the majority of words in the language, characterize the context-sensitive indexing, rather than any affixation or other segmental material. We would want to characterize the indexing here as the dependence of the implementation of certain phonological rules upon the variables of speaker-hearer sociological sex. Any phonological indexes of this sort, such as those marking geographical *dialect* of the speaker, or class-affiliated *variety*, must be similarly treated.

So a grammar of speech acts G$'$ consists of rules of use that map the variables of speech events into rules generating utterances. With this characterization, we have moved from the heuristic device of directly relating contextual variables to "surface" utterance fractions—detailing, in other words, the definition of an index—to constructing a pragmatic system that explains the relation between apparent structural continuity of surface form and its multifunctional$_{1,2}$ nature. For any given utterance fraction, there may be many speech acts which motivate its presence in a speech event, that is, any utterance fraction may be a constituent of pragmatic structures in several modes, or a constituent in some mode and not a constituent in others. Reference, in particular, the function$_1$ which has heretofore motivated all our ideas about utterance constituency, motivates only one such pragmatic structure, at the core of which are essentially rules of use selecting G. The shifters require distinct functional$_2$ rules of G$'$, though they function$_1$ also in referential events.

## Multifunctionality and Pragmatic Strategy

There is a structure to a pragmatic grammar so constituted, the details of which are now only partially clear. Speech acts are ordered, for example, a reflection of *pragmatic markedness relations* among functional$_2$ meanings of utterance fractions. For example, there is a hierarchical relation among all the kinds of sociological variables leading to deference indexes, which can be formally described by intrinsic ordering of the speech acts characterizing their use (see Ervin-Tripp 1971 for flow-chart characterization). And further, there are markedness relations of speech-event function$_1$ of utterance fractions, so that features of utterances contribute normally to some functional$_1$ mode, less appropriately, though possibly, to others. Pragmatic metaphors mentioned above are a case in point, basically semantic categories being extended, as it were, filling out "holes" in the pragmatic structure.

The multifunctionality of apparent utterances means that there is a kind of pragmatic indeterminacy of utterances taken out of context, and the possibility for strategic uses of language in the context of speech events. Out of context, we can only have recourse to the referential mode in determining the meaning of utterances, which, with certain exceptions for shifters, is essentially "context-free." Additionally, and especially in context where indexes are relatively creative or performative, there can be pragmatic indeterminacy in utterances that can be manipulated by the individuals in an interaction. This leads to such phenomena as *pragmatic contradiction*, or "double-bind" behaviors, which play upon two or more communicative media signaling contradictory indexical meanings to the receiver of the concurrent messages, or upon contradictory highly presupposing indexes within the same medium. Similarly, there is *residual semanticity*, the semantico-referential meaning which a speaker can claim after the fact for potentially highly pragmatically charged speech. Thus the characteristic speaker's denial of speech offensive to the hearer takes the form of "All I said was . . ." with a semantico-referential paraphrase or repetition of the referential content of the original utterance. A speaker can create a social persona for himself, playing upon the hearer's perspective of *imputed indexicality*, where the speaker has characteristics attributed to him on the basis of the rules of use for certain utterance fractions. Thus the phenomenon underlying the plot of *My Fair Lady*. Finally, *diplomatic nonindexicality*, on the analogy of diplomatic nonrecognition in foreign policy, allows the hearer to respond to speech as though it constituted a semantico-referential event, all the while understanding completely the distinct function$_2$ of the indexes which overlap in surface form.

Pragmatic contradiction and imputed indexicality are alike in depending on the unavoidably high functional$_2$ potential of utterances. Residual semanticity and diplomatic nonindexicality are alike in depending on the universal metasemantic awareness of people, whereby the semantico-referential function$_1$ of speech is the officially or overtly recognized one, the one to which actors may retreat with full social approval. (This point was made several times by Sapir.) But all of these *pragmatic strategies*, manipulation of pragmatic function$_2$ in actual behavior, depend in the last analysis upon the shared understanding of norms for indexical elements in speech acts. Obviously, some individuals are better at these pragmatic strategies than others, just as some individuals have a more explicit and accurate conception of the pragmatics of their own language. I wonder whether the two skills are related.

## Metapragmatics

If strategy requires purposive manipulation of pragmatic rules, then it may also require an overt conceptualization of speech events and constituent speech acts. Such characterization of the pragmatic structure of language is *metapragmatics*, much as the characterization of semantico-grammatical structure is metasemantics. The distinction between these two realms is vast, however. While language as a pure referential medium serves as its own metalanguage in metasemantic referential speech events, there can be no metapragmatic speech events in which use of speech in a given functional mode explicates the pragmatic structure of that very functional mode. The metapragmatic characterization of speech must constitute a referential event, in which pragmatic norms are the objects of description. So obviously the extent to which a language has semantic lexical items which accurately refer to the indexed variables, to the constituents of speech, and to purposive function is one measure of the limits of metapragmatic discussion by a speaker of that language.

## Limits to Metapragmatic Awareness

But more importantly, it would appear that the nature of the indexical elements themselves, along formal-functional$_1$ dimensions, limits metapragmatic awareness of language users. Indexes were characterized as segmental vs. nonsegmental, that is affix, word, phrase vs. some other feature of utterances; as referential vs. nonreferential, that is, shifter vs. nonshifter index; and as relatively presupposing vs. relatively creative or performative. It is very easy to obtain accurate pragmatic information in the form of metapragmatic referential speech for segmental, referential, relatively presupposing indexes. It is extremely difficult, if not impossible, to make a native speaker aware of nonsegmental, nonreferential, relatively creative formal features, which have no metapragmatic reality for him. Indexes of the first type, which are susceptible of accurate conscious characterization, are, of course, closest in their formal-functional$_1$ properties to semantico-referential segments, for which metasemantic manipulation is possible. Notice once again that metasemantic speech events (see above) are thus a special, equational sort of metapragmatic event. The extent to which signs have properties akin to those of strictly segmental, semantico-referential ones, in fact, is obviously a measure of the ease with which we can get accurate metapragmatic characterizations of them from native speakers. Investigation of the triply distinct formal-functional$_1$ elements of speech, on the other hand, requires interpretative observation in a functional$_1$ framework.

I think that every fieldworker has had such experiences, where a careful sorting out of kinds of pragmatic effects ultimately just cannot rely on the metapragmatic testimony of native participants. (That so-called generative semanticists insist on the validity of their own "intuitions" about pragmatics in *Gedankenforschungen* simply attests to the unfortunate naïveté and narrowness of most contemporary linguists on matters of speech observation and of systematic pragmatic theory.) In the course of investigating Wasco-Wishram (Chinookan), for example, I attempted to systematize with informants the diminutive-augmentative consonantisms which are ubiquitous in speech acts of endearment/repulsion felt by speakers toward referent, without referential contribution. They form a pragmatic metaphor on the more "physical" speaker estimation of size relative to a standard—the classic syncategorematic problem of small elephants and the like. These effects are entirely phonological, most consonants participating in pairs (or $n$-tuples) which alternate by phonological rules regardless of their position in lexical items. A lexical item thus appears in overt form with two or more sets of consonants, for example, the nominal adjectives for size, the paradigm elaborated example, *i- -qbai*λ (super-augmentative), *i- -g$^{(w)}$ai*λ (augmentative), *i- -k $^w$aic* (quasi-diminutive), *i- -k'$^w$aic'* (diminutive), *i- -k'$^w$εit'θ* (super-diminutive). Upon request for repetition of a lexical item with such effects that had occurred in discourse, informants invariably gave a lexically normal form—the pragmatically "unmarked" form. So requesting a repetition of *i-ǰa-muqbal* 'her belly [which I think is huge and repulsive, by the way],' one gets *i-ča-muqʷal*. "But you just said '-*muqbal*' didn't you; that means great big one, no?" "No, it's *ičamuqʷal*." . . . "Well, how do you say 'her great big belly'?" "*Iagai*λ *ičamuqʷal* ['It's large, her belly']." Notice that the last question is interpreted as a request for an interlinguistic metasemantic equation, the pragmatic marker of rules for augmentative consonantism being beyond studied manipulation.

## Metapragmatic Lexical Items

A certain amount of reference to pragmatics at the level of speech events (purposive function$_1$) is accomplished in every language of which I am aware by quotation framing verbs, the equivalents of English phrases such as *he said (to him), he told (it) to him, he asked (of him), he ordered him,* and so forth. It is remarkable how many languages have only constructions expressing the first few of these, which serve to name the entire, undifferentiated set of speech events. Framed by such verbs, which describe certain speech events, and the inflections of which describe the participants, we find reported speech, the messages purportedly used. There is a whole range of devices for reporting speech events, from exact quotation through indirect quotation through pseudoquotation, paraphrase, and descriptive reference, the subtleties of which I cannot explore here.

Additionally, languages incorporate lexical items which in certain constructions refer to, that is, name, the speech event of which a token forms an utterance fraction. I have already adumbrated their description above (see *Reference and "Performative Speech,"* pp. 192–193 above). In English, for example, these items fit into the schema *I/we* [V] *you* [X], where the verb V is inflected for present, nonprogressive (punctual) tense-aspect. They actually name the socially constituted speech event of which they form an utterance fraction: *christen, dub, sentence,* and so forth, particularly socially salient routines which are primarily linguistic events behaviorally. They are referential, creative (or performative) indexes which are most important to ethnographic description, since they individualize certain ongoing functions$_1$ of speech as they are happening. They constitute a message about the function$_1$ of the medium, functionally$_2$ a pragmatic act. The cross-cultural investigation of these *metapragmatic shifters* is a very urgent and important anthropological desideratum.

## Lexical Items in General

The metapragmatic content of certain lexical items brings up the complementary question of the pragmatic content of lexical items. As I have discussed above, metasemantic events that equate meanings of segmental, semantico-referential forms of language are the basis for grammatical analysis, and vice versa. Obviously, in the semantico-referential mode alone, the ideal language would consist of elementary referring grammatical categories and their rules of hierarchical combination. But, as many linguists, particularly Bloomfield (1933) and Chafe more recently (e.g., 1970) have seen, lexical items—the elements that enter into metasemantic equations—form a kind of irreducible set of "idioms" or "basic irregularities," the existence of which is really inexplicable on the basis of semantico-grammatical theory. True lexical items have that unpredictable quality of specialization or extension or multiple senses in their referential functions$_1$ which makes them what they are, referential primes of some sort.

But it is precisely at the level of pragmatics that the coding of seemingly arbitrary chunks of referential "reality" becomes clear. For *lexical items are abbreviations for semantic complexes* made up of semantico-referential primes in grammatical constructions (Weinreich 1966; Silverstein 1972 and refs. there), *together with* all of the *indexical modalities* of meaning that make the functional$_1$ result unexpected. In other words, traditional semantico-grammatical analysis can never hope to specify meanings for lexical items finer than the grammatical structure of implicit referential categories allows, for every lexical item includes a pragmatic residue—an indexical component motivated only at the level of speech acts, actual discourse reference being only one such mode. (Certain kinds of lexical content in the discourse-reference mode have been characterized by linguists as ad hoc "selectional" restrictions on the co-ccurrence of lexical items.)

So such lexical items as so-called kinship terms or personal names in any society can hardly be characterized by a "semantic" analysis. It is the pragmatic component that makes them lexical items to begin with; it is the pragmatic functions$_2$ that make them anthropologically important, as Schneider, among others, have never ceased pointing out (see Schneider 1965; 1968). Further, so-called folk taxonomies of nominal lexical items, again "semantically" analyzed by a procedure of ostensive reference, essentially ripped from the context of speech, give us no cultural insight. For the whole pragmatic problem of why these lexical abbreviations form a cultural domain, rather than some other collection, why these lexical items occur at all, rather than some other semantic combinations, remains entirely to be explored. The so-called ethnoscientific structure of these vocabulary items turns out to be, from the point of view of a functional linguistics, a restatement of the fact that these semantico-referential abbreviations, rather than others, in fact occur.

## Pragmatic Structure and Cultural Function

The linkage between the pragmatic grammar subsuming the traditional sort and the rest of "culture" is through the two types of function of speech. On the one hand, the cultural function$_1$ of speech comes from its goal-directed nature, which is to accomplish some kind of communicational work. Frequently, as we have seen, there are explicit lexical items which are shifters referring to such functions$_1$ in overtly recognized speech events. But these labels are not necessary for certain social functions$_1$ to be recognized. On the other hand, the cultural function$_2$ is the whole meaning structure described by the speech acts of a pragmatic grammar. As I have mentioned, all but a part of this function$_2$ is not susceptible, in general, to consciousness and accurate testimony by native participants, much as rules of semantico-grammatical systems are not. But these speech elements, which represent recurrences of behavior, have such indexical modes of meaning as presuppose and create the very categories of society which form the parameters of the speech event.

It is unreasonable, then, to take naïve native participant testimony, metabehavioral interpretation, as anything more than an *ethnosociology* which partially (and problematically) overlaps with a true *functional$_{1,2}$ sociology* in terms of a pragmatic grammar based on indexical meaning. For the investigation of the latter must proceed with all the difficulties of interpretative hypotheses that are at once descriptive and comparative (see *Functional and Formal Analogues*, above pp. 209–210, and Goodenough 1970). And the interesting result is to see the ways in which societies use specifically linguistic means to constitute and maintain certain social categories, one society merging some of those given by comparative perspective, another society keeping them distinct. With a strictly linguistic focus, the pragmatic structures of speech give insight into the use of the same apparent "surface" material in distinct functional modes. And we can study the universal constraints on this rich patterning. From a broader anthropological perspective, the pragmatic system of speech *is* part of culture—in fact, perhaps the most significant part of culture—and a part the structure and function[1,2] of which is probably the real model for the rest of culture, when the term is a construct for the meaning system of socialized behavior.

## Cultural Meaning

*Language* is the systematic construct to explain the meaningfulness of speech behavior. We have seen that iconic, indexical, and uniquely symbolic modes of meaningfulness accrue to speech behavior. Thus any notion of language has to be inclusive enough to comprise these distinct modes, in particular, as I have stressed and elaborated, the indexical modes that link speech to the wider system of social life. The investigation here has claimed for language the uniqueness of a real symbolic mode, as that term can be justifiably used for pure semantic signs. I have linked this property to the possibility of the traditional semantico-grammatical analysis in terms of metasemantics, and have found the other linguistic modes to be categorically distinct. The pragmatic aspect of language, for example, that which is constituted by its indexical mode, can similarly depend upon metapragmatic uses of speech itself in only very limited areas. Otherwise it depends upon sensitive observation and comparative illumination of functional[1,2] speech acts and speech events for the indexical mode to be understood.

If language is unique in having a true symbolic mode, then obviously other cultural media must be more akin to the combined iconic and indexical modes of meaningfulness. In general, then, we can conclude that "cultural meaning" of behavior is so limited, except for speech, and see a *cultural description* as a massive, multiply pragmatic description of how the social categories of groups of people are constituted in a criss-crossing, frequently contradictory, ambiguous, and confusing set of pragmatic meanings of many kinds of behavior.

If there can be such apparent vagueness about pragmatic meaning, then one might be tempted to see in actual behavior the only level of integration, of orderliness, in culture. But for the social anthropologist, as for the linguist, regularities of pragmatic form and function[2] will ultimately define the orderliness and integration of such meaning systems. We need invoke "symbolism" for a certain modality of speech alone; the vast residue of language is culture, and culture is pragmatic.

## Shake Well Before Using (*L'envoi*)

We must be careful how we use terms like "sign," "symbol," "semantic," "meaning," "function," and other lexical items referring to entities of semiotic theory. I have tried to be consistent in usage in this reading, which necessitated, for example, using subscripts on certain terms. This intended careful semantico-referential function$_1$ of usage must be the sole criterion of judgment of the argument here that culture is, with the exception of a small part of language, but a congeries of iconic-indexical systems of meaningfulness of behavior.

Usage of the same terms by others should be similarly scrutinized for actual referential content, which may differ considerably in terms of the underlying theory. We must not be carried away by the rhetorical—that is, pragmatic— force of scientific argumentation, wherein, contradictorily enough, lies its sole power as natural communication, this reading, alas, being another token of the type.

# On Face-Work: An Analysis of Ritual Elements in Social Interaction

## Erving Goffman

Every person lives in a world of social encounters, involving him either in face-to-face or mediated contact with other participants. In each of these contacts, he tends to act out what is sometimes called a *line*—that is, a pattern of verbal and nonverbal acts by which he expresses his view of the situation and through this his evaluation of the participants, especially himself. Regardless of whether a person intends to take a line, he will find that he has done so in effect. The other participants will assume that he has more or less willfully taken a stand, so that if he is to deal with their response to him he must take into consideration the impression they have possibly formed of him.

The term *face* may be defined as the positive social value a person effectively claims for himself by the line others assume he has taken during a particular contact. Face is an image of self delineated in terms of approved social attributes —albeit an image that others may share, as when a person makes a good showing for his profession or religion by making a good showing for himself.[1]

A person tends to experience an immediate emotional response to the face which a contact with others allows him; he cathects his face; his "feelings" become attached to it. If the encounter sustains an image of him that he has long taken for granted, he probably will have few feelings about the matter. If events establish a face for him that is better than he might have expected, he is likely to "feel good"; if his ordinary expectations are not fulfilled, one expects that he will "feel bad" or "feel hurt." In general, a person's attachment to a particular face, coupled with the ease with which disconfirming information can be conveyed by himself and others, provides one reason why he finds that participation in any contact with others is a commitment. A person will also have feelings about the face sustained for the other participants, and while these feelings may differ in quantity and direction from those he has for his own face, they constitute an involvement in the face of others that is as immediate and

---

1 For discussions of the Chinese conception of face, see the following: Hsien Chin Hu 1944; Yang 1945; Macgowan 1912; Smith 1894. For a comment on the American Indian conception of face, see Mauss 1954.

spontaneous as the involvement he has in his own face. One's own face and the face of others are constructs of the same order; it is the rules of the group and the definition of the situation which determine how much feeling one is to have for face and how this feeling is to be distributed among the faces involved.

A person may be said to *have,* or *be in,* or *maintain* face when the line he effectively takes presents an image of him that is internally consistent, that is supported by judgments and evidence conveyed by other participants, and that is confirmed by evidence conveyed through impersonal agencies in the situation. At such times the person's face clearly is something that is not lodged in or on his body, but rather something that is diffusely located in the flow of events in the encounter and becomes manifest only when these events are read and interpreted for the appraisals expressed in them.

The line maintained by and for a person during contact with others tends to be of a legitimate institutionalized kind. During a contact of a particular type, an interactant of known or visible attributes can expect to be sustained in a particular face and can feel that it is morally proper that this should be so. Given his attributes and the conventionalized nature of the encounter, he will find a small choice of lines will be open to him and a small choice of faces will be waiting for him. Further, on the basis of a few known attributes, he is given the responsibility of possessing a vast number of others. His coparticipants are not likely to be conscious of the character of many of these attributes until he acts perceptibly in such a way as to discredit his possession of them; then everyone becomes conscious of these attributes and assumes that he willfully gave a false impression of possessing them.

Thus while concern for face focuses the attention of the person on the current activity, he must, to maintain face in this activity, take into consideration his place in the social world beyond it. A person who can maintain face in the current situation is someone who abstained from certain actions in the past that would have been difficult to face up to later. In addition, he fears loss of face now partly because the others may take this as a sign that consideration for his feelings need not be shown in the future. There is nevertheless a limitation to this interdependence between the current situation and the wider social world; an encounter with people whom he will not have dealings with again leaves him free to take a high line that the future will discredit, or free to suffer humiliations that would make future dealings with them an embarrassing thing to have to face.

A person may be said to *be in wrong face* when information is brought forth in some way about his social worth which cannot be integrated, even with effort, into the line that is being sustained for him. A person may be said to *be out of face* when he participates in a contact with others without having ready a line of the kind participants in such situations are expected to take. The intent of many pranks is to lead a person into showing a wrong face or no face, but there will also be serious occasions, of course, when he will find himself expressively out of touch with the situation.

When a person senses that he is in face, he typically responds with feelings of confidence and assurance. Firm in the line he is taking, he feels that he can hold his head up and openly present himself to others. He feels some security and some relief—as he also can when the others feel he is in wrong face but successfully hide these feelings from him.

When a person is in wrong face or out of face expressive events are being contributed to the encounter which cannot be readily woven into the expressive fabric of the occasion. Should he sense that he is in wrong face or out of face, he is likely to feel ashamed and inferior because of what has happened to the activity on his account and because of what may happen to his reputation as a participant. Further, he may feel bad because he had relied upon the encounter to support an image of self to which he has become emotionally attached and which he now finds threatened. Felt lack of judgmental support from the encounter may take him aback, confuse him, and momentarily incapacitate him as an interactant. His manner and bearing may falter, collapse, and crumble. He may become embarrassed and chagrined; he may become shamefaced. The feeling, whether warranted or not, that he is perceived in a flustered state by others, and that he is presenting no usable line, may add further injuries to his feelings, just as his change from being in wrong face or out of face to being shamefaced can add further disorder to the expressive organization of the situation. Following common usage, I shall employ the term *poise* to refer to the capacity to suppress and conceal any tendency to become shamefaced during encounters with others.

In our Anglo-American society, as in some others, the phrase "to lose face" seems to mean to be in wrong face, to be out of face or to be shamefaced. The phrase "to save one's face" appears to refer to the process by which the person sustains an impression for others that he has not lost face. Following Chinese usage, one can say that "to give face" is to arrange for another to take a better line than he might otherwise have been able to take,[2] the other thereby gets face given him, this being one way in which he can gain face.

As an aspect of the social code of any social circle, one may expect to find an understanding as to how far a person should go to save his face. Once he takes on a self-image expressed through face he will be expected to live up to it. In different ways in different societies he will be required to show self-respect, abjuring certain actions because they are above or beneath him, while forcing himself to perform others even though they cost him dearly. By entering a situation in which he is given a face to maintain, a person takes on the responsibility of standing guard over the flow of events as they pass before him. He must ensure that a particular *expressive order* is sustained—an order that regulates the flow of events, large or small, so that anything that appears to be expressed by them will be consistent with his face. When a person manifests these compunctions primarily from duty to himself, one speaks in our society of pride; when he does so because of duty to wider social units, and receives support from these units in doing so, one speaks of honor. When these compunctions have to do with postural things, with expressive events derived from the way in which

---

2 See, for example, Smith, footnote 1.

the person handles his body, his emotions, and the things with which he has physical contact, one speaks of dignity, this being an aspect of expressive control that is always praised and never studied. In any case, while his social face can be his most personal possession and the center of his security and pleasure, it is only on loan to him from society; it will be withdrawn unless he conducts himself in a way that is worthy of it. Approved attributes and their relation to face make of every man his own jailer; this is a fundamental social constraint even though each man may like his cell.

Just as the member of any group is expected to have self-respect so also he is expected to sustain a standard of considerateness; he is expected to go to certain lengths to save the feelings and the face of others present, and he is expected to do this willingly and spontaneously because of emotional identification with the others and with their feelings.[3] In consequence, he is disinclined to witness the defacement of others.[4] The person who can witness another's humiliation and unfeelingly retain a cool countenance himself is said in our society to be "heartless," just as he who can unfeelingly participate in his own defacement is thought to be "shameless."

The combined effect of the rule of self-respect and the rule of considerateness is that the person tends to conduct himself during an encounter so as to maintain both his own face and the face of the other participants. This means that the line taken by each participant is usually allowed to prevail, and each participant is allowed to carry off the role he appears to have chosen for himself. A state where everyone temporarily accepts everyone else's line is established.[5] This

---

3 Of course, the more power and prestige the others have, the more a person is likely to show consideration for their feelings, as H. E. Dale 1941 suggests. "The doctrine of 'feelings' was expounded to me many years ago by a very eminent civil servant with a pretty taste in cynicism. He explained that the importance of feelings varies in close correspondence with the importance of the person who feels. If the public interest requires that a junior clerk should be removed from his post, no regard need be paid to his feelings; if it is a case of an Assistant Secretary, they must be carefully considered, within reason; if it is a Permanent Secretary, his feelings are a principal element in the situation, and only imperative public interest can override their requirements."

4 Salesmen, especially street "stemmers," know that if they take a line that will be discredited unless the reluctant customer buys, the customer may be trapped by considerateness and buy in order to save the face of the salesman and prevent what would ordinarily result in a scene.

5 Surface agreement in the assessment of social worth does not, of course, imply equality; the evaluation consensually sustained of one participant may be quite different from the one consensually sustained of another. Such agreement is also compatible with expression of disagreement so that it will convey an evaluation of the other that the other will be willing to convey about himself. Extreme cases are provided by wars, duels, and barroom fights, when these are of a gentlemanly kind, for they can be conducted under consensual auspices, with each protagonist guiding his action according to the rules of the game, thereby making it possible for his action to be interpreted as an expression of a fair player openly in combat with a fair opponent. In fact, the rules and etiquette of any game can be analyzed as a means by which the image of a fair player can be expressed, just as the image of a fair player can be analyzed as a means by which the rules and etiquette of a game are sustained.

---

*On Face-Work: An Analysis of Ritual Elements in Social Interaction*   **225**

kind of mutual acceptance seems to be a basic structural feature of interaction, especially the interaction of face-to-face talk. It is typically a "working" acceptance, not a "real" one, since it tends to be based not on agreement of candidly expressed heart-felt evaluations, but upon a willingness to give temporary lip service to judgments with which the participants do not really agree.

The mutual acceptance of lines has an important conservative effect upon encounters. Once the person initially presents a line, he and the others tend to build their later responses upon it, and in a sense become stuck with it. Should the person radically alter his line, or should it become discredited, then confusion results, for the participants will have prepared and committed themselves for actions that are now unsuitable.

Ordinarily, maintenance of face is a condition of interaction, not its objective. Usual objectives, such as gaining face for oneself, giving free expression to one's true beliefs, introducing depreciating information about the others, or solving problems and performing tasks, are typically pursued in such a way as to be consistent with the maintenance of face. To study face-saving is to study the traffic rules of social interaction; one learns about the code the person adheres to in his movement across the paths and designs of others, but not where he is going, or why he wants to get there. One does not even learn why he is ready to follow the code, for a large number of different motives can equally lead him to do so. He may want to save his own face because of his emotional attachment to the image of self which it expresses, because of his pride or honor, because of the power his presumed status allows him to exert over the other participants, and so on. He may want to save the others' face because of this emotional attachment to an image of them, or because he feels that his coparticipants have a moral right to this protection, or because he wants to avoid the hostility that may be directed toward him if they lose their face. He may feel that an assumption has been made that he is the sort of person who shows compassion and sympathy toward others, so that to retain his own face, he may feel obliged to be considerate of the line taken by the other participants.

By *face-work* I mean to designate the actions taken by a person to make whatever he is doing consistent with face. Face-work serves to counteract "incidents"—that is, events whose effective symbolic implications threaten face. Thus poise is one important type of face-work, for through poise the person controls his embarrassment and hence the embarrassment that he and others might have over his embarrassment. Whether or not the full consequences of face-saving actions are known to the person who employs them, they often become habitual and standardized practices; they are like traditional plays in a game or traditional steps in a dance. Each person, subculture, and society seems to have its own characteristic repertoire of face-saving practices. It is to this repertoire that people partly refer when they ask what a person or culture is "really" like. And yet the particular set of practices stressed by particular persons or groups seems to be drawn from a single logically coherent framework of possible practices. It is as if face, by its very nature, can be saved only in a certain number of ways, and as if each social grouping must make its selections from this single matrix of possibilities.

The members of every social circle may be expected to have some knowledge of face-work and some experience in its use. In our society, this kind of capacity is sometimes called tact, *savoir-faire,* diplomacy, or social skill. Variation in social skill pertains more to the efficacy of face-work than to the frequency of its application, for almost all acts involving others are modified, prescriptively or proscriptively, by considerations of face.

If a person is to employ his repertoire of face-saving practices, obviously he must first become aware of the interpretations that others may have placed upon his acts and the interpretations that he ought perhaps to place upon theirs. In other words, he must exercise perceptiveness.[6] But even if he is properly alive to symbolically conveyed judgments and is socially skilled, he must yet be willing to exercise his perceptiveness and his skill; he must, in short, be prideful and considerate. Admittedly, of course, the possession of perceptiveness and social skill so often leads to their application that in our society terms such as politeness or tact fail to distinguish between the inclination to exercise such capacities and the capacities themselves.

I have already said that the person will have two points of view—a defensive orientation toward saving his own face and a protective orientation toward saving the others' face. Some practices will be primarily defensive and others primarily protective, although in general one may expect these two perspectives to be taken at the same time. In trying to save the face of others, the person must choose a tack that will not lead to loss of his own; in trying to save his own face, he must consider the loss of face that his action may entail for others.

In many societies there is a tendency to distinguish three levels of responsibility that a person may have for a threat to face that his actions have created. First, he may appear to have acted innocently; his offense seems to be unintended and unwitting, and those who perceive his act can feel that he would have attempted to avoid it had he foreseen its offensive consequences. In our society one calls such threats to face *faux pas, gaffes,* boners, or bricks. Secondly, the offending person may appear to have acted maliciously and spitefully, with the intention of causing open insult. Thirdly, there are incidental offenses; these arise as an unplanned but sometimes anticipated by-product of action—action the offender performs in spite of its offensive consequences, although not out of spite. From the point of view of a particular participant, these three types of threat can be introduced by the participant himself against his own face, by himself against the face of others, by the others against their own face, or by

---

6 Presumably social skill and perceptiveness will be high in groups whose members frequently act as representatives of wider social units such as lineages or nations, for the player here is gambling with a face to which the feelings of many persons are attached. Similarly, one might expect social skill to be well developed among those of high station and those with whom they have dealings, for the more face an interactant has, the greater the number of events that may be inconsistent with it, and hence the greater the need for social skill to forestall or counteract these inconsistencies.

the others against himself. Thus the person may find himself in many different relations to a threat to face. If he is to handle himself and others well in all contingencies, he will have to have a repertoire of face-saving practices for each of these possible relations to threat.

## THE BASIC KINDS OF FACE-WORK

*The avoidance process.* The surest way for a person to prevent threats to his face is to avoid contacts in which these threats are likely to occur. In all societies one can observe this in the avoidance relationship[7] and in the tendency for certain delicate transactions to be conducted by go-betweens.[8] Similarly, in many societies, members know the value of voluntarily making a gracious withdrawal before an anticipated threat to face has had a chance to occur.[9]

Once the person does chance an encounter, other kinds of avoidance practices come into play. As defensive measures, he keeps off topics and away from activities that would lead to the expression of information that is inconsistent with the line he is maintaining. At opportune moments he will change the topic of conversation or the direction of activity. He will often present initially a front of diffidence and composure, suppressing any show of feeling until he has found out what kind of line the others will be ready to support for him. Any claims regarding self may be made with belittling modesty, with strong qualifications, or with a note of unseriousness; by hedging in these ways he will have prepared a self for himself that will not be discredited by exposure, personal failure, or the unanticipated acts of others. And if he does not hedge his claims about self, he will at least attempt to be realistic about them, knowing that otherwise events may discredit him and make him lose face.

Certain protective maneuvers are as common as these defensive ones. The person shows respect and politeness, making sure to extend to others any ceremonial treatment that might be their due. He employs discretion; he leaves unstated facts that might implicitly or explicitly contradict and embarrass the positive claims made by others.[10] He employs circumlocutions and deceptions,

---

[7] In our own society an illustration of avoidance is found in the middle- and upper-class Negro who avoids certain face-to-face contacts with whites in order to protect the self-evaluation projected by his clothes and manner. See, for example, Johnson 1943. The function of avoidance in maintaining the kinship system in small preliterate societies might be taken as a particular illustration of the same general theme.

[8] An illustration is given by Latourette 1942. "A neighbor or a group of neighbors may tender their good offices in adjusting a quarrel in which each antagonist would be sacrificing his face by taking the first step in approaching the other. The wise intermediary can effect the reconciliation while preserving the dignity of both."

[9] In an unpublished paper Harold Garfinkel has suggested that when the person finds that he has lost face in a conversational encounter, he may feel a desire to disappear or "drop through the floor," and that this may involve a wish not only to conceal loss of face but also to return magically to a point in time when it would have been possible to save face by avoiding the encounter.

[10] When the person knows the others well, he will know what issues ought not to be raised and what situations the others ought not to be placed in, and he will be free to

phrasing his replies with careful ambiguity so that the others' face is preserved even if their welfare is not.[11] He employs courtesies, making slight modifications of his demands on or appraisals of the others so that they will be able to define the situation as one in which their self-respect is not threatened. In making a belittling demand upon the others, or in imputing uncomplimentary attributes to them, he may employ a joking manner, allowing them to take the line that they are good sports, able to relax from their ordinary standards of pride and honor. And before engaging in a potentially offensive act, he may provide explanations as to why the others ought not to be affronted by it. For example, if he knows that it will be necessary to withdraw from the encounter before it has terminated, he may tell the others in advance that it is necessary for him to leave, so that they will have faces that are prepared for it. But neutralizing the potentially offensive act need not be done verbally; he may wait for a propitious moment or natural break—for example, in conversation, a momentary lull when no one speaker can be affronted—and then leave, in this way using the context instead of his words as a guarantee of inoffensiveness.

When a person fails to prevent an incident, he can still attempt to maintain the fiction that no threat to face has occurred. The most blatant example of this is found where the person acts as if an event that contains a threatening expression has not occurred at all. He may apply this studied nonobservance to his own acts—as when he does not by any outward sign admit that his stomach is rumbling—or to the acts of others, as when he does not "see" that another has stumbled.[12] Social life in mental hospitals owes much to this process; patients employ it in regard to their own peculiarities, and visitors employ it, often with tenuous desperation, in regard to patients. In general, tactful blindness of this kind is applied only to events that, if perceived at all, could be perceived and interpreted only as threats to face.

A more important, less spectacular kind of tactful overlooking is practiced when a person openly acknowledges an incident as an event that has occurred,

---

introduce matters at will in all other areas. When the others are strangers to him, he will often reverse the formula, restricting himself to specific areas he knows are safe. On these occasions, as Simmel suggests, ". . . discretion consists by no means only in the respect for the secret of the other, for his specific will to conceal this or that from us, but in staying away from the knowledge of all that the other does not expressly reveal to us." 1950.

11 The Western traveler used to complain that the Chinese could never be trusted to say what they meant but always said what they felt their Western listener wanted to hear. The Chinese used to complain that the Westerner was brusque, boorish, and unmannered. In terms of Chinese standards, presumably, the conduct of a Westerner is so gauche that he creates an emergency, forcing the Asian to forgo any kind of direct reply in order to rush in with a remark that might rescue the Westerner from the compromising position in which he had placed himself. (See Smith 1894). This is an instance of the important group of misunderstandings which arise during interaction between persons who come from groups with different ritual standards.

12 A pretty example of this is found in parade-ground etiquette which may oblige those in a parade to treat anyone who faints as if he were not present at all.

---

*On Face-Work: An Analysis of Ritual Elements in Social Interaction*  **229**

but not as an event that contains a threatening expression. If he is not the one who is responsible for the incident, then his blindness will have to be supported by his forbearance; if he is the doer of the threatening deed, then his blindness will have to be supported by his willingness to seek a way of dealing with the matter, which leaves him dangerously dependent upon the cooperative forbearance of the others.

Another kind of avoidance occurs when a person loses control of his expressions during an encounter. At such times he may try not so much to overlook the incident as to hide or conceal his activity in some way, thus making it possible for the others to avoid some of the difficulties created by a participant who has not maintained face. Correspondingly, when a person is caught out of face because he had not expected to be thrust into interaction, or because strong feelings have disrupted his expressive mask, the others may protectively turn away from him or his activity for a moment, to given him time to assemble himself.

*The corrective process.* When the participants in an undertaking or encounter fail to prevent the occurrence of an event that is expressively incompatible with the judgments of social worth that are being maintained, and when the event is of the kind that is difficult to overlook, then the participants are likely to give it accredited status as an incident—to ratify it as a threat that deserves direct official attention—and to proceed to try to correct for its effects. At this point one or more participants find themselves in an established state of ritual disequilibrium or disgrace, and an attempt must be made to re-establish a satisfactory ritual state for them. I use the term *ritual* because I am dealing with acts through whose symbolic component the actor shows how worthy he is of respect or how worthy he feels others are of it. The imagery of equilibrium is apt here because the length and intensity of the corrective effort is nicely adapted to the persistence and intensity of the threat.[13] One's face, then, is a sacred thing, and the expressive order required to sustain it is therefore a ritual one.

The sequence of acts set in motion by an acknowledged threat to face, and terminating in the re-establishment of ritual equilibrium, I shall call an *interchange*.[14] Defining a message or move as everything conveyed by an actor during a turn at taking action, one can say that an interchange will involve two or more moves and two or more participants. Obvious examples in our society may be found in the sequence of "Excuse me" and "Certainly," and in the exchange of presents or visits. The interchange seems to be a basic concrete unit of social activity and provides one natural empirical way to study interaction of

---

[13] This kind of imagery is one that social anthropologists seem to find naturally fitting. Note, for example, the implications of the following statement by Margaret Mead (1934), "If a husband beats his wife, custom demands that she leave him and go to her brother, real or officiating, and remain a length of time commensurate with the degree of her offended dignity."

[14] The notion of interchange is drawn in part from Chapple 1940 and from Horsfall and Arensberg 1949. For further material on the interchange as a unit see Goffman 1953.

all kinds. Face-saving practices can be usefully classified according to their position in the natural sequence of moves that comprise this unit. Aside from the event which introduces the need for a corrective interchange, four classic moves seem to be involved.

There is, first, the challenge, by which participants take on the responsibility of calling attention to the misconduct; by implication they suggest that the threatened claims are to stand firm and that the threatening event itself will have to be brought back into line.

The second move consists of the offering, whereby a participant, typically the offender, is given a chance to correct for the offense and re-establish the expressive order. Some classic ways of making this move are available. On the one hand, an attempt can be made to show that what admittedly appeared to be a threatening expression is really a meaningless event, or an unintentional act, or a joke not meant to be taken seriously, or an unavoidable, "understandable" product of extenuating circumstances. On the other hand, the meaning of the event may be granted and effort concentrated on the creator of it. Information may be provided to show that the creator was under the influence of something and not himself, or that he was under the command of somebody else and not acting for himself. When a person claims that an act was meant in jest, he may go on and claim that the self that seemed to lie behind the act was also projected as a joke. When a person suddenly finds that he has demonstrably failed in capacities that the others assumed him to have and to claim for himself—such as the capacity to spell, to perform minor tasks, to talk without malapropisms, and so on—he may quickly add, in a serious or unserious way, that he claims the incapacities as part of his self. The meaning of the threatening incident thus stands, but it can now be incorporated smoothly into the flow of expressive events.

As a supplement to or substitute for the strategy of redefining the offensive act or himself, the offender can follow two other procedures: he can provide compensations to the injured—when it is not his own face that he has threatened; or he can provide punishment, penance, and expiation for himself. These are important moves or phases in the ritual interchange. Even though the offender may fail to prove his innocence, he can suggest through these means that he is now a renewed person, a person who has paid for his sin against the expressive order and is once more to be trusted in the judgmental scene. Further, he can show that he does not treat the feelings of the others lightly, and that if their feelings have been injured by him, however innocently, he is prepared to pay a price for his action. Thus he assures the others that they can accept his explanations without this acceptance constituting a sign of weakness and a lack of pride on their part. Also, by his treatment of himself, by his self-castigation, he shows that he is clearly aware of the kind of crime he would have committed had the incident been what it first appeared to be, and that he knows the kind of punishment that ought to be accorded one who would commit such a crime. The suspected person thus shows that he is thoroughly capable of taking the role of the others toward his own activity, that he can still be used as a responsible participant in the ritual process, and the rules of conduct which he appears to have broken are still sacred, real, and unweakened. An offensive act may arouse anxiety about the ritual code; the offender allays this anxiety by showing that both the code and he as an upholder of it are still in working order.

After the challenge and the offering have been made, the third move can occur: the persons to whom the offering is made can accept it as a satisfactory means of re-establishing the expressive order and the faces supported by this order. Only then can the offender cease the major part of his ritual offering.

In the terminal move of the interchange, the forgiven person conveys a sign of gratitude to those who have given him the indulgence of forgiveness.

The phases of the corrective process—challenge, offering, acceptance, and thanks—provide a model for interpersonal ritual behavior, but a model that may be departed from in significant ways. For example, the offended parties may give the offender a chance to initiate the offering on his own before a challenge is made and before they ratify the offense as an incident. This is a common courtesy, extended on the assumption that the recipient will introduce a self-challenge. Further, when the offended persons accept the corrective offering, the offender may suspect that this has been grudgingly done from tact, and so he may volunteer additional corrective offerings, not allowing the matter to rest until he has received a second or third acceptance of his repeated apology. Or the offended persons may tactfully take over the role of the offender and volunteer excuses for him that will, perforce, be acceptable to the offended persons.

An important departure from the standard corrective cycle occurs when a challenged offender patently refuses to heed the warning and continues with his offending behavior, instead of setting the activity to rights. This move shifts the play back to the challengers. If they countenance the refusal to meet their demands, then it will be plain that their challenge was a bluff and that the bluff has been called. This is an untenable position; a face for themselves cannot be derived from it, and they are left to bluster. To avoid this fate, some classic moves are open to them. For instance, they can resort to tactless, violent retaliation, destroying either themselves or the person who had refused to heed their warning. Or they can withdraw from the undertaking in a visible huff—righteously indignant, outraged, but confident of ultimate vindication. Both tacks provide a way of denying the offender his status as an interactant, and hence denying the reality of the offensive judgment he has made. Both strategies are ways of salvaging face, but for all concerned the costs are usually high. It is partly to forestall such scenes that an offender is usually quick to offer apologies; he does not want the affronted persons to trap themselves into the obligation to resort to desperate measures.

It is plain that emotions play a part in these cycles of response, as when anguish is expressed because of what one has done to another's face, or anger because of what has been done to one's own. I want to stress that these emotions function as moves, and fit so precisely into the logic of the ritual game that it would seem difficult to understand them without it.[15] In fact, spontaneously expressed feelings are likely to fit into the formal pattern of the ritual interchange more elegantly than consciously designed ones.

## MAKING POINTS: THE AGGRESSIVE USE OF FACE-WORK

Every face-saving practice which is allowed to neutralize a particular threat opens up the possibility that the threat will be willfully introduced for what can be safely gained by it. If a person knows that his modesty will be answered by others' praise of him, he can fish for compliments. If his own appraisals of self will be checked against incidental events, then he can arrange for favorable incidental events to appear. If others are prepared to overlook an affront to them and act forbearantly, or to accept apologies, then he can rely on this as a basis for safely offending them. He can attempt by sudden withdrawal to force the others into a ritually unsatisfactory state, leaving them to flounder in an interchange that cannot readily be completed. Finally, at some expense to himself, he can arrange for the other to hurt his feelings, thus forcing them to feel guilt, remorse, and sustained ritual disequilibrium.[16]

When a person treats face-work not as something he need be prepared to perform, but rather as something that others can be counted on to perform or to accept, then an encounter or an undertaking becomes less a scene of mutual considerateness than an arena in which a contest or match is held. The purpose of the game is to preserve everyone's line from an inexcusable contradiction, while scoring as many points as possible against one's adversaries and making as many gains as possible for oneself. An audience to the struggle is almost a necessity. The general method is for the person to introduce favorable facts about himself and unfavorable facts about the others in such a way that the only reply the others will be able to think up will be one that terminates the interchange in a grumble, a meager excuse, a face-saving I-can-take-a-joke laugh, or an empty stereotyped comeback of the "Oh yeah?" or "That's what you think" variety. The losers in such cases will have to cut their losses, tacitly grant the loss of a point, and attempt to do better in the next interchange. Points made by allusion to social class status are sometimes called snubs; those made by allusions to moral respectability are sometimes called digs; in either case one deals with a capacity at what is sometimes called "bitchiness."

---

15 Even when a child demands something and is refused, he is likely to cry and sulk not as an irrational expression of frustration but as a ritual move, conveying that he already has a face to lose and that its loss is not to be permitted lightly. Sympathetic parents may even allow for such display, seeing in these crude strategies the beginnings of a social self.

16 The strategy of maneuvering another into a position where he cannot right the harm he has done is very commonly employed but nowhere with such devotion to the ritual model of conduct as in revengeful suicide. See, for example Jeffreys 1952.

In aggressive interchanges the winner not only succeeds in introducing information favorable to himself and unfavorable to the others, but also demonstrates that as interactant he can handle himself better than his adversaries. Evidence of this capacity is often more important than all the other information the person conveys in the interchange, so that the introduction of a "crack" in verbal interaction tends to imply that the initiator is better at footwork than those who must suffer his remarks. However, if they succeed in making a successful parry of the thrust and then a successful riposte, the instigator of the play must not only face the disparagement with which the others have answered him but also accept the fact that his assumption of superiority in footwork has proven false. He is made to look foolish, he loses face. Hence it is always a gamble to "make a remark." The table can be turned and the aggressor can lose more than he could have gained had his move won the point. Successful ripostes or comebacks in our society are sometimes called squelches or toppers; theoretically it would be possible for a squelch to be squelched, a topper to be topped, and a riposte to be parried with a counter-riposte, but except in staged interchanges this third level of successful action seems rare.[17]

## THE CHOICE OF APPROPRIATE FACE-WORK

When an incident occurs, the person whose face is threatened may attempt to reinstate the ritual order by means of one kind of strategy, while the other participants may desire or expect a practice of a different type to be employed. When, for example, a minor mishap occurs, momentarily revealing a person in wrong face or out of face, the others are often more willing and able to act blind to the discrepancy than is the threatened person himself. Often they would prefer him to exercise poise,[18] while he feels that he cannot afford to overlook what has happened to his face and so becomes apologetic and shame-

---

[17] In board and card games the player regularly takes into consideration the possible responses of his adversaries to a play that he is about to make, and even considers the possibility that his adversaries will know that he is taking such precautions. Conversational play is by comparison surprisingly impulsive; people regularly make remarks about others present without carefully designing their remarks to prevent a successful comeback. Similarly, while feinting and sandbagging are theoretical possibilities during talk, they seem to be little exploited.

[18] Folklore imputes a great deal of poise to the upper classes. If there is truth in this belief it may lie in the fact that the upper-class person tends to find himself in encounters in which he outranks the other participants in ways additional to class. The ranking participant is often somewhat independent of the good opinion of the others and finds it practical to be arrogant, sticking to a face regardless of whether the encounter supports it. On the other hand, those who are in the power of a fellow-participant tend to be very much concerned with the valuation he makes of them or witnesses being made of them, and so finds it difficult to maintain a slightly wrong face without becoming embarrassed and apologetic. It may be added that people who lack awareness of the symbolism in minor events may keep cool in difficult situations, showing poise that they do not really possess.

faced, if he is the creator of the incident, or destructively assertive, if the others are responsible for it.[19] Yet on the other hand, a person may manifest poise when the others feel that he ought to have broken down into embarrassed apology—that he is taking undue advantage of their helpfulness by his attempts to brazen it out. Sometimes a person may himself be undecided as to which practice to employ, leaving the others in the embarrassing position of not knowing which tack they are going to have to follow. Thus when a person makes a slight gaffe, he and the others may become embarrassed not because of inability to handle such difficulties, but because for a moment no one knows whether the offender is going to act blind to the incident, or give it joking recognition, or employ some other face-saving practice.

## COOPERATION IN FACE-WORK

When a face has been threatened, face-work must be done, but whether this is initiated and primarily carried through by the person whose face is threatened, or by the offender, or by a mere witness,[20] is often of secondary importance. Lack of effort on the part of one person induces compensative effort from others; a contribution by one person relieves the others of the task. In fact, there are many minor incidents in which the offender and the offended simultaneously attempt to initiate an apology.[21] Resolution of the situation to everyone's apparent satisfaction is the first requirement; correct apportionment of blame is typically a secondary consideration. Hence terms such as tact and *savoir-faire* fail to distinguish whether it is the person's own face that his diplomacy saves or the face of the others. Similarly, terms such as *gaffe* and *faux pas* fail to specify whether it is the actor's own face he has threatened or the face of other participants. And it is understandable that if one person finds he is powerless to save his own face, the others seem especially bound to protect him. For example,

---

19 Thus, in our society, when a person feels that others expect him to measure up to approved standards of cleanliness, tidiness, fairness, hospitality, generosity, affluence, and so on, or when he sees himself as someone who ought to maintain such standards, he may burden an encounter with extended apologies for his failings, while all along the other participants do not care about the standard, or do not believe the person is really lacking in it, or are convinced that he is lacking in it and see the apology itself as a vain effort at self-elevation.

20 Thus one function of seconds in actual duels, as well as in figurative ones, is to provide an excuse for not fighting that both contestants can afford to accept.

21 See, for instance, Jackson Toby 1952, "With adults there is less likelihood for essentially trivial issues to produce conflict. The automatic apology of two strangers who accidentally collide on a busy street illustrates the integrative function of etiquette. In effect, each of the parties to the collision says, 'I don't know whether I am responsible for this situation, but *if* I am, you have a right to be angry with me, a right that I pray you will not exercise.' By defining the situation as one in which both parties must abase themselves, society enables each to keep his self-respect. Each may feel in his heart of hearts, 'Why can't that stupid ass watch where he's going?' But overtly *each plays the role of the guilty party* whether he feels he has been miscast or not."

in polite society, a handshake that perhaps should not have been extended becomes one that cannot be declined. Thus one accounts for the *noblesse oblige* through which those of high status are expected to curb their power of embarrassing their lessers,[22] as well as the fact that the handicapped often accept courtesies that they can manage better without.

Since each participant in an undertaking is concerned, albeit for differing reasons, with saving his own face and the face of the others, then tacit cooperation will naturally arise so that the participants together can attain their shared but differently motivated objectives.

One common type of tacit cooperation in face-saving is the tact exerted in regard to face-work itself. The person not only defends his own face and protects the face of the others, but also acts so as to make it possible and even easy for the others to employ face-work for themselves and him. He helps them to help themselves and him. Social etiquette, for example, warns men against asking for New Year's Eve dates too early in the season, lest the girl find it difficult to provide a gentle excuse for refusing. This second-order tact can be further illustrated by the wide-spread practice of negative-attribute etiquette. The person who has an unapparent negatively valued attribute often finds it expedient to begin an encounter with an unobtrusive admission of his failing, especially with persons who are uninformed about him. The others are thus warned in advance against making disparaging remarks about his kind of person and are saved from the contradiction of acting in a friendly fashion to a person toward whom they are unwittingly being hostile. This strategy also prevents the others from automatically making assumptions about him which place him in a false position and saves him from painful forbearance or embarrassing remonstrances.

Tact in regard to face-work often relies for its operation on a tacit agreement to do business through the language of hint—the language of innuendo, ambi-

---

[22] Regardless of the person's relative social position, in one sense he has power over the other participants, and they must rely upon his considerateness. When the others act toward him in some way, they presume upon a social relationship to him, since one of the things expressed by interaction is the relationship of the interactants. Thus they compromise themselves, for they place him in a position to discredit the claims they express as to his attitude toward them. Hence in response to claimed social relationships every person, of high estate or low, will be expected to exercise *noblesse oblige* and refrain from exploiting the compromised position of the others.

Since social relationships are defined partly in terms of voluntary mutual aid, refusal of a request for assistance becomes a delicate matter, potentially destructive of the asker's face. Chester Holcombe 1895 provides a Chinese instance: "Much of the falsehood to which the Chinese as a nation are said to be addicted is a result of the demands of etiquette. A plain, frank 'no' is the height of discourtesy. Refusal or denial of any sort must be softened and toned down into an expression of regretted inability. Unwillingness to grant a favor is never shown. In place of it there is seen a chastened feeling of sorrow that unavoidable but quite imaginary circumstances render it wholly impossible. Centuries of practice in this form of evasion have made the Chinese matchlessly fertile in the invention and development of excuses. It is rare, indeed, that one is caught at a loss for a bit of artfully embroidered fiction with which to hide an unwelcome truth."

guities, well-placed pauses, carefully worded jokes, and so on.[23] The rule regarding this unofficial kind of communication is that the sender ought not to act as if he had officially conveyed the message he has hinted at, while the recipients have the right and the obligation to act as if they have not officially received the message contained in the hint. Hinted communication, then, is deniable communication; it need not be faced up to. It provides a means by which the person can be warned that his current line or the current situation is leading to loss 'of face, without this warning itself becoming an incident.

Another form of tacit cooperation, and one that seems to be much used in many societies, is reciprocal self-denial. Often the person does not have a clear idea of what would be a just or acceptable apportionment of judgments during the occasion, and so he voluntarily deprives or depreciates himself while indulging and complimenting the others, in both cases carrying the judgments safely past what is likely to be just. The favorable judgments about himself he allows to come from the others; the unfavorable judgments of himself are his own contributions. This "after you, Alphonse" technique works, of course, because in depriving himself he can reliably anticipate that the others will compliment or indulge him. Whatever allocation of favors is eventually established, all participants are first given a chance to show that they are not bound or constrained by their own desires and expectations, that they have a properly modest view of themselves, and that they can be counted upon to support the ritual code. Negative bargaining, through which each participant tries to make the terms of trade more favorable to the other side, is another instance; as a form of exchange perhaps it is more widespread than the economist's kind.

A person's performance of face-work, extended by his tacit agreement to help others perform theirs, represents his willingness to abide by the ground rules of social interaction. Here is the hallmark of his socialization as an interactant. If he and the others were not socialized in this way, interaction in most societies and most situations would be a much more hazardous thing for feelings and faces. The person would find it impractical to be oriented to symbolically conveyed appraisals of social worth, or to be possessed of feelings—that is, it would be impractical for him to be a ritually delicate object. And as I shall suggest, if the person were not a ritually delicate object, occasions of talk could not be organized in the way they usually are. It is no wonder that trouble is caused by a person who cannot be relied upon to play the face-saving game.

## THE RITUAL ROLES OF THE SELF

So far I have implicitly been using a double definition of self: the self as an image pieced together from the expressive implications of the full flow of events in an undertaking; and the self as a kind of player in a ritual game who copes honorably or dishonorably, diplomatically or undiplomatically, with the judg-

---

23 Useful comments on some of the structural roles played by unofficial communication can be found in a discussion of irony and banter in Tom Burns 1953.

mental contingencies of the situation. A double mandate is involved. As sacred objects, men are subject to slights and profanation; hence as players of the ritual game they have had to lead themselves into duels, and wait for a round of shots to go wide of the mark before embracing their opponents. Here is an echo of the distinction between the value of a hand drawn at cards and the capacity of the person who plays it. This distinction must be kept in mind, even though it appears that once a person has gotten a reputation for good or bad play this reputation may become part of the face he must later play at maintaining.

Once the two roles of the self have been separated, one can look to the ritual code implicit in face-work to learn how the two roles are related. When a person is responsible for introducing a threat to another's face, he apparently has a right, within limits, to wriggle out of the difficulty by means of self-abasement. When performed voluntarily these indignities do not seem to profane his own image. It is as if he had the right of insulation and could castigate himself qua actor without injuring himself qua object of ultimate worth. By token of the same insulation he can belittle himself and modestly underplay his positive qualities, with the understanding that no one will take his statements as a fair representation of his sacred self. On the other hand, if he is forced against his will to treat himself in these ways, his face, his pride, and his honor will be seriously threatened. Thus, in terms of the ritual code, the person seems to have a special license to accept mistreatment at his own hands that he does not have the right to accept from others. Perhaps this is a safe arrangement because he is not likely to carry this license too far, whereas the others, were they given this privilege, might be more likely to abuse it.

Further, within limits the person has a right to forgive other participants for affronts to his sacred image. He can forbearantly overlook minor slurs upon his face, and in regard to somewhat greater injuries he is the one person who is in a position to accept apologies on behalf of his sacred self. This is a relatively safe prerogative for the person to have in regard to himself, for it is one that is exercised in the interests of the others or of the undertaking. Interestingly enough, when the person commits a gaffe against himself, it is not he who has the license to forgive the event; only the others have that prerogative, and it is a safe prerogative for them to have because they can exercise it only in his interests or in the interests of the undertaking. One finds, then, a system of checks and balances by which each participant tends to be given the right to handle only those matters which he will have little motivation for mishandling. In short, the rights and obligations of an interactant are designed to prevent him from abusing his role as an object of sacred value.

## SPOKEN INTERACTION

Most of what has been said so far applies to encounters of both an immediate and mediated kind, although in the latter the interaction is likely to be more attenuated, with each participant's line being gleaned from such things as written statements and work records. During direct personal contacts, however, unique informational conditions prevail and the significance of face becomes especially clear. The human tendency to use signs and symbols means that evidence of social worth and of mutual evaluations will be conveyed by very minor things, and these things will be witnessed, as will the fact that they have been witnessed. An unguarded glance, a momentary change in tone of voice, an ecological position taken or not taken, can drench a talk with judgmental significance. Therefore, just as there is no occasion of talk in which improper impressions could not intentionally or unintentionally arise, so there is no occasion of talk so trivial as not to require each participant to show serious concern with the way in which he handles himself and the others present. Ritual factors which are present in mediated contacts are here present in an extreme form.

In any society, whenever the physical possibility of spoken interaction arises, it seems that a system of practices, conventions, and procedural rules comes into play which functions as a means of guiding and organizing the flow of messages. An understanding will prevail as to when and where it will be permissible to initiate talk, among whom, and by means of what topics of conversation. A set of significant gestures is employed to initiate a spate of communication and as a means for the persons concerned to accredit each other as legitimate participants.[24] When this process of reciprocal ratification occurs, the persons so ratified are in what might be called a *state of talk*—that is, they have declared themselves officially open to one another for purposes of spoken communication and guarantee together to maintain a flow of words. A set of significant gestures is also employed by which one or more new participants can officially join the talk, by which one or more accredited participants can officially withdraw, and by which the state of talk can be terminated.

A single focus of thought and visual attention, and a single flow of talk, tends to be maintained and to be legitimated as officially representative of the encounter. The concerted and official visual attention of the participants tends to be transferred smoothly by means of formal or informal clearance cues, by which the current speaker signals that he is about to relinquish the floor and the prospective speaker signals a desire to be given the floor. An understanding will

---

24 The meaning of this status can be appreciated by looking at the kinds of unlegitimated or unratified participation that can occur in spoken interaction. A person may overhear others unbeknownst to them; he can overhear them when they know this to be the case and when they choose either to act as if he were not overhearing them or to signal to him informally that they know he is overhearing them. In all of these cases, the outsider is officially held at bay as someone who is not formally participating in the occasion. Ritual codes, of course, require a ratified participant to be treated quite differently from an unratified one. Thus, for example, only a certain amount of insult from a ratified participant can be ignored without his avoidance practice causing loss of face to the insulted person; after a point they must challenge the offender and demand redress. However, in many societies, apparently, many kinds of verbal abuse from unratified participants can be ignored, without this failure to challenge constituting a loss of face.

*On Face-Work: An Analysis of Ritual Elements in Social Interaction* **239**

prevail as to how long and how frequently each participant is to hold the floor. The recipients convey to the speaker, by appropriate gestures, that they are according him their attention. Participants restrict their involvement in matters external to the encounter and observe a limit to involvement in any one message of the encounter, in this way ensuring that they will be able to follow along whatever direction the topic of conversation takes them. Interruptions and lulls are regulated so as not to disrupt the flow of messages. Messages that are not part of the officially accredited flow are modulated so as not to interfere seriously with the accredited messages. Nearby persons who are not participants visibly desist in some way from exploiting their communication position and also modify their own communication, if any, so as not to provide difficult interference. A particular ethos or emotional atmosphere is allowed to prevail. A polite accord is typically maintained, and participants who may be in real disagreement with one another give temporary lip service to views that bring them into agreement on matters of fact and principle. Rules are followed for smoothing out the transition, if any, from one topic of conversation to another.[25]

These rules of talk pertain not to spoken interaction considered as an ongoing process, but to *an* occasion of talk or episode of interaction as a naturally bounded unit. This unit consists of the total activity that occurs during the time that a given set of participants have accredited one another for talk and maintain a single moving focus of attention.[26]

The conventions regarding the structure of occasions of talk represent an effective solution to the problem of organizing a flow of spoken messages. In attempting to discover how it is that these conventions are maintained in force as guides to action, one finds evidence to suggest a functional relationship between the structure of the self and the structure of spoken interaction.

The socialized interactant comes to handle spoken interaction as he would any other kind, as something that must be pursued with ritual care. By automatically appealing to face, he knows how to conduct himself in regard to talk. By repeatedly and automatically asking himself the question, "If I do or do not act in this way, will I or others lose face?" he decides at each moment, consciously or unconsciously, how to behave. For example, entrance into an occasion of spoken interaction may be taken as a symbol of intimacy or legitimate purpose, and so the person must, to save his face, desist from entering into talk with a given set of others unless his circumstances justify what is expressed about him by his entrance. Once approached for talk, he must accede to the others in order to save their face. Once engaged in conversation, he must demand only the amount of attention that is an appropriate expression of his

---

[25] For a further treatment of the structure of spoken interaction see Goffman, footnote 14.

[26] I mean to include formal talks where rules of procedure are explicitly prescribed and officially enforced, and where only certain categories of participants may be allowed to hold the floor—as well as chats and sociable talks where rules are not explicit and the role of speaker passes back and forth among the participants.

relative social worth. Undue lulls come to be potential signs of having nothing in common, or of being insufficiently self-possessed to create something to say, and hence must be avoided. Similarly, interruptions and inattentiveness may convey disrespect and must be avoided unless the implied disrespect is an accepted part of the relationship. A surface of agreement must be maintained by means of discretion and white lies, so that the assumption of mutual approval will not be discredited. Withdrawal must be handled so that it will not convey an improper evaluation.[27] The person must restrain his emotional involvement so as not to present an image of someone with no self-control or dignity who does not rise above his feelings.

The relation between the self and spoken interaction is further displayed when one examines the ritual interchange. In a conversational encounter, interaction tends to proceed in spurts, an interchange at a time, and the flow of information and business is parcelled out into these relatively closed ritual units.[28] The lull between interchanges tends to be greater than the lull between turns at talking in an interchange, and there tends to be a less meaningful relationship between two sequential interchanges than between two sequential speeches in an interchange.

This structural aspect of talk arises from the fact that when a person volunteers a statement or message, however trivial or commonplace, he commits himself and those he addresses, and in a sense places everyone present in jeopardy. By saying something, the speaker opens himself up to the possibility that the intended recipients will affront him by not listening or will think him forward, foolish, or offensive in what he has said. And should he meet with such a reception, he will find himself committed to the necessity of taking face-saving action against them. Furthermore, by saying something the speaker opens his intended recipients up to the possibility that the message will be self-approving, presumptuous, demanding, insulting, and generally an affront to them or to their conception of him, so that they will find themselves obliged to take action against him in defense of the ritual code. And should the speaker praise the recipients, they will be obliged to make suitable denials, showing that they do not hold too favorable an opinion of themselves and are not so eager to secure indulgences as to endanger their reliability and flexibility as interactants.

Thus when one person volunteers a message, thereby contributing what might

---

27 Among people who have had some experience in interacting with one another, conversational encounters are often terminated in such a way as to give the appearance that all participants have independently hit upon the same moment to withdraw. The disbandment is general, and no one may be conscious of the exchange of cues that has been required to make such a happy simultaneity of action possible. Each participant is thus saved from the compromising position of showing readiness to spend further time with someone who is not as ready to spend time with him.

28 The empirical discreteness of the interchange unit is sometimes obscured when the same person who provides the terminating turn at talking on one interchange initiates the first turn at talking in the next. However, the analytical utility of the interchange as a unit remains.

easily be a threat to the ritual equilibrium, someone else present is obliged to show that the message has been received and that its content is acceptable to all concerned or can be acceptably countered. This acknowledging reply, of course, may contain a tactful rejection of the original communication, along with a request for modification. In such cases, several exchanges of messages may be required before the interchange is terminated on the basis of modified lines. The interchange comes to a close when it is possible to allow it so do so— that is, when everyone present has signified that he has been ritually appeased to a degree satisfactory to him.[29] A momentary lull between interchanges is possible, for it comes at a time when it will not be taken as a sign of something untoward.

In general, then, a person determines how he ought to conduct himself during an occasion of talk by testing the potentially symbolic meaning of his acts against the self-images that are being sustained. In doing this, however, he incidentally subjects his behavior to the expressive order that prevails and contributes to the orderly flow of messages. His aim is to save face; his effect is to save the situation. From the point of view of saving face, then, it is a good thing that spoken interaction has the conventional organization given it; from the point of view of sustaining an orderly flow of spoken messages, it is a good thing that the self has the ritual structure given it.

I do not mean, however, to claim that another kind of person related to another kind of message organization would not do as well. More important, I do not claim that the present system is without weaknesses or drawbacks; these must be expected, for everywhere in social life a mechanism or functional relation which solves one set of problems necessarily creates a set of potential difficulties and abuses all its own. For example, a characteristic problem in the ritual organization of personal contacts is that while a person can save his face by quarreling or by indignantly withdrawing from the encounter, he does this at the cost of the interaction. Furthermore, the person's attachment to face gives others something to aim at; they can not only make an effort to wound him unofficially, but may even make an official attempt utterly to destroy his face. Also, fear over possible loss of his face often prevents the person from initiating contacts in which important information can be transmitted and important relationships re-established; he may be led to seek the safety of solitude rather than the danger of social encounters. He may do this even though others feel that he is motivated by "false pride"—a pride which suggests that the ritual code is getting the better of those whose conduct is regulated by it. Further, the "after you, Alphonse" complex can make the termination of an interchange difficult. So, too, where each participant feels that he must sacrifice a little more

---

29 The occurrence of the interchange unit is an empirical fact. In addition to the ritual explanation for it, others may be suggested. For example, when the person makes a statement and receives a reply at once, this provides him with a way of learning that his statement has been received and correctly received. Such "metacommunication" would be necessary on functional grounds even were it unnecessary on ritual ones.

than has been sacrificed for him, a kind of vicious indulgence cycle may occur—much like the hostility cycle that can lead to open quarrels—with each person receiving things he does not want and giving in return things he would rather keep. Again, when people are on formal terms, much energy may be spent in ensuring that events do not occur which might effectively carry an improper expression. And on the other hand, when a set of persons are on familiar terms and feel that they need not stand on ceremony with one another, then inattentiveness and interruptions are likely to become rife, and talk may degenerate into a happy babble of disorganized sound.

The ritual code itself requires a delicate balance, and can be easily upset by anyone who upholds it too eagerly or not eagerly enough, in terms of the standards and expectations of his group. Too little perceptiveness, too little savoir-faire, too little pride and considerateness, and the person ceases to be someone who can be trusted to take a hint about himself or give a hint that will save others embarrassment. Such a person comes to be a real threat to society; there is nothing much that can be done with him, and often he gets his way. Too much perceptiveness or too much pride, and the person becomes someone who is thin-skinned, who must be treated with kid gloves, requiring more care on the part of others than he may be worth to them. Too much savoir-faire or too much considerateness, and he becomes someone who is too socialized, who leaves the others with the feeling that they do not know how they really stand with him, or what they should do to make an effective long-term adjustment to him.

In spite of these inherent "pathologies" in the organization of talk, the functional fitness between the socialized person and spoken interaction is a viable and practical one. The person's orientation to face, especially his own, is the point of leverage that the ritual order has in regard to him; yet a promise to take ritual care of his face is built into the very structure of talk.

## FACE AND SOCIAL RELATIONSHIPS

When a person begins a mediated or immediate encounter, he already stands in some kind of social relationship to the others concerned, and expects to stand in a given relationship to them after the particular encounter ends. This, of course, is one of the ways in which social contacts are geared into the wider society. Much of the activity occurring during an encounter can be understood as an effort on everyone's part to get through the occasion and all the unanticipated and unintentional events that can cast participants in an undesirable light, without disrupting the relationships of the participants. And if relationships are in the process of change, the object will be to bring the encounter to a satisfactory close without altering the expected course of development. This perspective nicely accounts, for example, for the little ceremonies of greeting and farewell which occur when people begin a conversational encounter or depart from one. Greetings provide a way of showing that a relationship is still what it was at the termination of the previous coparticipation, and, typically, that this relationship involves sufficient suppression of hostility for the participants temporarily to drop their guards and talk. Farewells sum up the effect of the encounter upon the relationship and show what the participants may expect of one another when they next meet. The enthusiasm of greetings compensates for the weakening of the relationship caused by the absence just terminated, while the enthusiasm of farewells compensates the relationship for the harm that is about to be done to it by separation.[30]

It seems to be a characteristic obligation of many social relationships that each of the members guarantees to support a given face for the other members in given situations. To prevent disruption of these relationships, it is therefore necessary for each member to avoid destroying the others' face. At the same time, it is often the person's social relationship with others that leads him to participate in certain encounters with them, where incidentally he will be dependent upon them for supporting his face. Furthermore, in many relationships, the members come to share a face, so that in the presence of third parties an improper act on the part of one member becomes a source of acute embarrassment to the other members. A social relationship, then, can be seen as a way in which the person is more than ordinarily forced to trust his self-image and face to the tact and good conduct of others.


## THE NATURE OF THE RITUAL ORDER

The ritual order seems to be organized basically on accommodative lines, so that the imagery used in thinking about other types of social order is not quite suitable for it. For the other types of social order a kind of schoolboy model seems to be employed; if a person wishes to sustain a particular image of himself and trust his feelings to it, he must work hard for the credits that will buy this self-enhancement for him; should he try to obtain ends by improper means, by cheating or theft, he will be punished, disqualified from the race, or at least made to start all over again from the beginning. This is the imagery of a hard, dull game. In fact, society and the individual join in one that is easier on both of them, yet one that has dangers of its own.

Whatever his position in society, the person insulates himself by blindnesses,

---

[30] Greetings, of course, serve to clarify and fix the roles that the participants will take during the occasion of talk and to commit participants to these roles, while farewells provide a way of unambiguously terminating the encounter. Greetings and farewells may also be used to state, and apologize for, extenuating circumstances—in the case of greetings for circumstances that have kept the participants from interacting until now, and in the case of farewells for circumstances that prevent the participants from continuing their display of solidarity. These apologies allow the impression to be maintained that the participants are more warmly related socially than may be the case. This positive stress, in turn, assures that they will act more ready to enter into contacts than they perhaps really feel inclined to do, thus guaranteeing that diffuse channels for potential communication will be kept open in the society.

half-truths, illusions, and rationalizations. He makes an "adjustment" by convincing himself, with the tactful support of his intimate circle, that he is what he wants to be and that he would not do to gain his ends what the others have done to gain theirs. And as for society, if the person is willing to be subject to informal social control—if he is willing to find out from hints and glances and tactful cues what his place is, and keep it—then there will be no objection to his furnishing this place at his own discretion, with all the comfort, elegance, and nobility that his wit can muster for him. To protect this shelter he does not have to work hard, or join a group, or compete with anybody; he need only be careful about the expressed judgments he places himself in a position to witness. Some situations and acts and persons will have to be avoided; others, less threatening, must not be pressed too far. Social life is an uncluttered, orderly thing because the person voluntarily stays away from the places and topics and times where he is not wanted and where he might be disparaged for going. He cooperates to save his face, finding that there is much to be gained from venturing nothing.

Facts are of the schoolboy's world—they can be altered by diligent effort but they cannot be avoided. But what the person protects and defends and invests his feelings in is an idea about himself, and ideas are vulnerable not to facts and things but to communications. Communications belong to a less punitive scheme than do facts, for communications can be by-passed, withdrawn from, disbelieved, conveniently misunderstood, and tactfully conveyed. And even should the person misbehave and break the truce he has made with society, punishment need not be the consequence. If the offense is one that the offended persons can let go by without losing too much face, then they are likely to act forbearantly, telling themselves that they will get even with the offender in another way at another time, even though such an occasion may never arise and might not be exploited if it did. If the offense is great, the offended persons may withdraw from the encounter, or from future similar ones, allowing their withdrawal to be reinforced by the awe they may feel toward someone who breaks the ritual code. Or they may have the offender withdrawn, so that no further communication can occur. But since the offender can salvage a good deal of face from such operations, withdrawal is often not so much an informal punishment for an offense as it is merely a means of terminating it. Perhaps the main principle of the ritual order is not justice but face, and what any offender receives is not what he deserves but what will sustain for the moment the line to which he has committed himself, and through this the line to which he has committed the interaction.

Throughout this paper it has been implied that underneath their differences in culture, people everywhere are the same. If persons have a universal human nature, they themselves are not to be looked to for an explanation of it. One must look rather to the fact that societies everywhere, if they are to be societies, must mobilize their members as self-regulating participants in social encounters. One way of mobilizing the individual for this purpose is through ritual; he is taught to be perceptive, to have feelings attached to self and a self expressed through face, to have pride, honor, and dignity, to have considerateness, to have tact and a certain amount of poise. These are some of the elements of behavior which must be built into the person if practical use is to be made of him as an interactant, and it is these elements that are referred to in part when one speaks of universal human nature.

Universal human nature is not a very human thing. By acquiring it, the person becomes a kind of construct, built up not from inner psychic propensities but from moral rules that are impressed upon him from without. These rules, when followed, determine the evaluation he will make of himself and of his fellow-participants in the encounter, the distribution of his feelings, and the kinds of practices he will employ to maintain a specified and obligatory kind of ritual equilibrium. The general capacity to be bound by moral rules may well belong to the individual, but the particular set of rules which transforms him into a human being derives from requirements established in the ritual organization of social encounters. And if a particular person or group or society seems to have a unique character all its own, it is because its standard set of human-nature elements is pitched and combined in a particular way. Instead of much pride, there may be little. Instead of abiding by the rules, there may be much effort to break them safely. But if an encounter or undertaking is to be sustained as a viable system of interaction organized on ritual principles, then these variations must be held within certain bounds and nicely counterbalanced by corresponding modifications in some of the other rules and understandings. Similarly, the human nature of a particular set of persons may be specially designed for the special kind of undertakings in which they participate, but still each of these persons must have within him something of the balance of characteristics required of usable participants in any ritually organized system of social activity.

## BIBLIOGRAPHY

Burns, Tom. "Friends, enemies and the polite fiction." *American Sociological Review* 18 (1953): 654–62.

Chapple, Eliot D. "Measuring human relations." *Genetic Psychological Monographs* 22 (1940): 3–147, especially pp. 26–30.

Dale, H. E. *The Higher Civil Service of Great Britain.* New York: Oxford University Press, 1941, p. 126 n.

Garfinkel, Harold. Manuscript, n.d.

Goffman, E. "Communication conduct in an island community." Unpublished Ph.D. dissertation, Dept. of Sociology, University of Chicago, especially chs. 12 and 13, pp. 165–95, 1953.

Holcombe, Chester. *The Real Chinaman.* New York: Dodd, Mead, 1895, pp. 274–75.

Horsfall, A. B. and C. A. Arensberg "Teamwork and productivity in a shoe factory." *Human Organization* 8 (1949): 13–25, especially p. 19.

Hu, Hsien Chin. "The Chinese concept of 'Face.'" *American Anthropologist* 46 (1944): 45–64.

Jeffreys, M. D. W. "Samsonic suicide, or suicide of revenge among Africans." *African Studies* 11 (1952): 118–22.

Johnson, Charles. *Patterns of Negro Segregation*. New York: Harper & Row, 1943, ch. 13.

Latourette, K. S. *The Chinese: Their History and Culture*, Vol. 2. New York: Macmillan, 1942, p. 211.

Macgowan, J. *Men, and Manners of Modern China*. London: Unwin, 1912, pp. 301–12.

Mauss, Marcel. *The Gift*, tr. Ian Cunnison. London: Cohen and West, 1954, p. 38.

Mead, Margaret. "Kinship in the Admiralty Islands." *Anthropological Papers of the American Museum of Natural History* 34 (1934): 183–358.

Smith, Arthur H. *Chinese Characteristics*. New York: Felming H. Revell Co., 1894, pp. 16–18.

Toby, Jackson. "Some variables in role conflict analysis." *Social Forces* 30 (1952): 323–37.

Wolff, Kurt H., ed. *The Sociology of Georg Simmel*. Glencoe, Ill.: Free Press, 1950, pp. 320–21.

Yang, Martin C. *A Chinese Village*. New York: Columbia University Press, 1945, pp. 167–72.

# The Ethnography of Speaking
## Dell H. Hymes

## INTRODUCTION

The role of speech in human behavior has always been honored in anthropological principle, if sometimes slighted in practice. The importance of its study has been declaimed (as by Malinowski [1935]), surveyed with insightful detail (as in Sapir [1933]), and accepted as a principle of field work (see citations in Hymes 1959).

That the study of speech might be crucial to a science of man has been a recurrent anthropological theme. Boas (1911) came to see language as one in kind with ethnological phenomena generally (he interpreted ethnology as the science of mental phenomena), but revealing more of basic processes because more out of awareness, less subject to overlay by rationalization. Some anthropologists have seen language, and hence linguistics, as basic to a science of man because it provides a link between the biological and sociocultural levels. Some have seen in modern linguistic methodology a model or harbinger of a general methodology for studying the structure of human behavior.

American anthropology has played an important part in the progress of linguistics in this country, through the careers of Boas, Sapir, Bloomfield, and their students, and through the opportunities offered by American Indian languages. It has contributed to the development of particular techniques and concepts, and has used linguistics as a tool for other lines of research. In both respects, anthropology's involvement with linguistics has come to be shared now by psychology. Having assimilated modern advances in linguistics, many psychologists have contributed studies of considerable relevance and value in recent years. One need cite only the work of Charles Osgood, George Miller, and Roger Brown. Hybridization between linguistic concepts, and the technologies of the computers and experimental psychology, is producing perhaps the most rapidly growing sector in the study of speech, one with which anthropology must keep informed liaison.

Indeed, diffusion of the tools of modern linguistics may be a hallmark of the second half of this century. In the course of such diffusion, presumably three things will hold true: 1. the discipline of linguistics will continue to contribute studies of the history, structure, and use of languages; 2. in other disciplines, linguistic concepts and practices will be qualified, reinterpreted, subsumed, and perhaps sometimes re-diffused in changed form into linguistics; 3. linguistics

**248**

will remain the discipline responsible for coordinating knowledge about verbal behavior from the viewpoint of language itself.

In any event, the joint share of linguistics and psychology in the burgeoning study of verbal behavior seems vigorous and assured. Has anthropology a share apart from some of its practitioners becoming linguists and psychologists, and apart from its traditional role as an intellectual holding company under the aegis of culture? Is the role of prime collaborator of linguistics among the sciences now to pass to psychology? Sheer weight of numbers may determine. It would be of no importance were it not for the value to linguistics and anthropology of a strengthening, not a relaxing, of mutual concern.

In one regard, there is no danger of lapse. Modern linguistics is diffusing widely in anthropology itself among younger scholars, producing work of competence that ranges from historical and descriptive studies to problems of semantic and social variation. Most such work is on well-defined linguistic problems; its theoretical basis is established, its methodology well grounded, and its results important, especially for areas in which languages rapidly dwindle in number. There is no need to detail the contribution which such work makes to anthropological studies, nor to argue its permanent value to linguistics proper. If anything, the traditional bonds between linguistics and anthropology in the United States are more firmly rooted now than a decade ago.

What may lapse is an opportunity to develop *new* bonds, through contributions to the study of verbal behavior that collaboration between anthropology and linguistics can perhaps alone provide. This is more than a matter of putting linguistics to work in the study of other scientific problems, such as cognitive behavior or expressive behavior. The role of speech in both is important, and has engaged anthropological attention: the cognitive problem in association with the name of Whorf, the expressive problem more recently under the heading of "paralinguistics." But to pursue these problems, and to try to give them firm anthropological footing, is to broach the study of a new problem area, one of which little account is taken.

There are indeed several underdeveloped intellectual areas involving speech to which anthropology can contribute. All are alike in that they need fresh theoretical thought, methodological invention, and empirical work, and have roots in anthropology's vocation as a comparative discipline. Among these areas are the revitalization of dialectology (perhaps under the heading of "sociolinguistics"); the place of language in an evolutionary theory of culture; the semantic typology of languages; and the truly comparative study of verbal art.[1] Fortunately, all those mentioned have begun to attract attention. For the anthropological study of behavior there is another area of importance, one that

---

[1] Towards the first of these, see Gumperz (1961); towards the other three, see respectively, Hymes (1961c, 1961a, and 1960a [for the typology at the close of the latter]). Such developments will require rapprochement with established philological disciplines, which control much of the essential data.

seems general, central, and neglected. It can be called the *ethnography of speaking*.

In one sense this area fills the gap between what is usually described in grammars, and what is usually described in ethnographies. Both use speech as evidence of other patterns; neither brings it into focus in terms of its own patterns. In another sense, this is a question of what a child internalizes about speaking, beyond rules of grammar and dictionary, while becoming a full-fledged member of its speech community. Or, it is a question of what a foreigner must learn about a group's verbal behavior in order to participate appropriately and effectively in its activities. The ethnography of speaking is concerned with the situations and uses, the patterns and functions, of speaking as an activity in its own right.

What the content of this area may be in detail, what a description of it as a system might be like—these things are hard to state, although I shall attempt it in this paper. Field studies devoted to the topic hardly exist, nor has there been much attention to what the theory and method of such studies would be. Occasional information can be gleaned, enough to show that the patterns and functions of speaking can be very different from one group to another—how speech enters into socialization and education, for example, may differ strikingly. But the evidence is not enough to itemize all variables, or to show a system. Hence the orientation of what follows must be toward the field work that is necessary.

Why undertake such field work? The reasons are several: because the phenomena are there, ready to be brought into order; so that systematic descriptions can give rise to a comparative study of the cross-cultural variations in a major mode of human behavior (a "comparative speaking" beside comparative religion, comparative law, and the like), and give it its place in theory; for the contribution to other kinds of concern, such as studies of the formation of personality in early years.

I shall attempt to bring out the nature and problems of this area by indicating first that study of speech as a factor in cognitive and expressive behavior leads to concern with the ethnographic patterning of the uses of speech in a community. Then I shall sketch a descriptive framework for getting at such a patterning. A "notes-and-queries" survey of the role of speech in socialization will bring much of the content and method in the frame of one problem. Finally, I shall sketch the changes in theoretical perspective that underlie the whole.

## SPEECH IN COGNITIVE AND EXPRESSIVE BEHAVIOR

The role of speech in cognitive behavior is an old concern of anthropology. In recent years discussion has most often had reference to Whorf's views. There is not space here to evaluate the ideas and studies that are pertinent, and I can only refer to two other papers (Hymes 1961*a*, *b*). It can be briefly said that there is no question but that speech habits are among the determinants of non-linguistic behavior, and conversely. The question is that of the modes and amounts of reciprocal influence.

If our concern is the role of phonological habits in the perception and interpretation of sounds, there exists an abundance of theory, technique, and experimental work. If our concern is the role of semantic habits in perception and interpretation of experience, there is no such abundance. Some experimental testing has been done (see comment in Hymes 1961b), but we cannot adequately investigate the role of semantic habits in ordinary behavior without knowledge of the semantic habits that are available to play a role, and such knowledge can be gained only by description in relation to native contexts of use. In other words, we need a semantic analysis that is a part of ethnography.

The need for such an ethnographic semantics has been pointed out before, and it is the theme of Malinowski's *Coral Gardens and Their Magic* Part II. How to implement an ethnographic semantics, however, how to devise its methodology, largely remains. Malinowski saw clearly the need to analyze meaning in contexts of use, but his method amounted in practice to massive narrative. An ethnographic semantics may be bulky, but it need not be on principle interminable, nor endlessly ad hoc. It should be more than a narrative reflection of reality. It should be a structural analysis, achieving the economies of the rules of a grammar in relation to a series of analyses of texts.

In the past generation Jakobson and his associates have done most to develop such a structural semantics. In recent years a fresh wave of American interest has appeared in significant papers by linguists such as Haugen (1957) and Joos (1958), and by ethnographers such as Conklin (1955, 1962), Goodenough (1956a, 1957), and Lounsbury (1956). Here as in other studies there are two general approaches, as Jakobson has so brilliantly set forth; on the one hand to trace an item through all the various contexts in which it can occur, characterizing it in terms of its ability to co-occur with other items, and on the other to place an item within a set which can occur in particular contexts, characterizing it in terms of its substitutability for other items of that set. The two approaches have various names, such as the syntagmatic and paradigmatic axes (see Jakobson and Halle 1956). The first approach is essentially that of a concordance; the second approach can be termed that of a contrast within a frame, or better, contrast within a relevant (or valid) frame. Here I want to side with those who consider the latter the more fundamental of the two, since it validates the structural relevance of the items whose distribution is studied by the first approach, and adds information of its own; and assert that use of this fundamental "contrast within a frame" approach must lead linguistics into ethnography, and ethnography into analysis of patterns of speaking.

Here I can only outline the argument. The paradigmatic approach requires discovering a relevant frame or context, identifying the items which contrast within it, and determining the dimensions of contrast for the items within the set so defined. The approach has been successful for phonology and grammar, but only partly so for lexicon. Indeed, it is much disputed that a structural approach can be applied to the whole of a language, when the whole of vocabulary is considered. Yet it would be remarkable, and should be a source of embarrassment, if the paradigmatic principle fundamental to the core of language should fail us here. Recognizing this, linguists associated with the glossematic school have proposed modes of analysis of "content-structure" and defended the possibility of extending them to all of lexicon on principle. These modes may prove fruitful, despite theoretical criticisms, although some seem to smack too much of the ad hoc and arbitrary at present. In any case these approaches tend to stay within received bodies of linguistic data rather than to move outward into the exploration of speech behavior and use. Such exploration is essential, whether one is concerned with semantics delimited as dealing with designation and intension, or whether one is concerned also with what one might then term "pragmatic meaning," as the ethnography of speaking must be. (Cf. Firth's inclusion in his conception of "semantics" of this pragmatic dimension of meaning, which he places beyond lexicography in the province of "sociological linguistics" [1935:27].)

The need for such exploration is easy to see. One source of the present impasse in structural analysis of content is precisely the limitations of the contexts available in the usual linguistic materials. The usual corpus provides sufficient contexts for phonological and grammatical analysis, but for semantic analysis of only a few limited sets of frequently recurring elements, such as case-endings and prepositions. That is one reason Wells writes, regarding the possibility of structural analysis of items such as the Latin stem *tabul-*, "the only reliable method now available depends upon treating it as a member of some C[ontent]-paradigm. This we do not see how to do" (Wells 1957).

Scholars sometimes have been willing also to posit dimensions of contrast for a few other domains, apparently universal or "given," such as kinship terms, numerals, pronouns. But in fact even the seemingly most obvious domains cannot be taken for granted. It may sometimes be assumed that, although languages segment experience differently, what they segment is the same, as if it were a matter of different jigsaw puzzles fashioned from the same painting. But recent work shows that structural analysis of meaning must first demonstrate that a domain *is* a domain for speakers of the language in question. What the domain includes, what it excludes, what features define it and its elements, cannot be prescribed in advance, even for kinship (cf. Conant 1961) or color terms (Conklin 1955). (The principle is generally true for cultural phenomena; cf. on residence rules, Goodenough [1956b], and on the structure of the family, Adams [1960].)

The exploration of native contexts of use to validate domains is the basis of the success of Conklin and Frake, and it points the way for the structural analysis of all of speech. All utterances occur contrastively in contexts, but for much of lexicon and most larger units of speech, the contextual frames must be sought not in the usual linguistic corpus, but in behavioral situations. One must reciprocally establish the modes and settings of behavior relevant to speech, and the sets of verbal items that occur within them; dimensions of contrast and rules of use, whether purely semantic (designative) or concerned with other imports and functions, can then be found. (The sets would often not be perceived from a formal linguistic point of view, being formally diverse, e.g., a set of greetings may range from "Hi" to "it's a damned good thing you got here when you did, Jack.")

The approach of course requires the structural analysis of the community in relation to speech that would constitute an ethnography of speaking. This approach is an answer to the problem posed by Hjelmslev (1957:283): "Une description structurale ne pourra s'effectuer qu'à condition de pouvoir réduire les classes ouvertes à des classes fermées."

For understanding and predicting behavior, contexts have a cognitive significance that can be summarized in this way. The use of a linguistic form identifies a range of meanings. A context can support a range of meanings. When a form is used in a context, it eliminates the meanings possible to that context other than those that form can signal; the context eliminates from consideration the meanings possible to the form other than those that context can support. The effective meaning depends upon the interaction of the two. (Recently stated by Joos [1958], this principle has also been formulated by Buhler [1934:183] and Firth [1935:32].)

Important also is the point that the cognitive role of speech is no all-or-nothing, but a matter of what, where, and when. Speech is cognitively more important in some activities than others, some times more than others, for some persons more than others, for some societies more than others. The amount and kind of influence may change as between the child and the adult, and there are the obvious problems of the relative importance of their languages for multilinguals.

Such concern with speech in contexts of behavior leads toward analysis of individual patterns in particular native situations. If, from a grammar, we can not read off the role that speech habits play in present-day behavior, neither can we do so from an experimental situation novel to the culture. Nor can the assessment be made from compartmentalized accounts of speech habits and of other habits, compared point-for-point in some millennial future. The analysis must be made on the ground. We must know what patterns are available in what contexts, and how, where, and when they come into play. The maxim that "meaning is use" has new force when we seriously study the role of semantic habits in behavior.

In sum, description of semantic habits depends upon contexts of use to define relevant frames, sets of items, and dimensions of contrast. Moreover, persons and groups may differ in the behavior that is mediated by speech. Thus analysis of the role of speech in cognitive behavior leads into analysis of the ethnographic context of speech.

The same holds true for the role of speech in expressive behavior. Of course there is a cognitive aspect to expressive behavior, insofar as it presupposes the sharing of a code, so that semantic habits do not exhaust the cognitive role of speech. Likewise, there is an expressive aspect to the cognitive style of an individual or group, and in general, all speech phenomena can be interpreted by a hearer as expressive of a speaker. But expressive studies tend to emphasize speech as an aspect of personality, and to throw into prominence features of speech, such as tone of voice and hesitation pauses, that lie outside lexicon and grammar —phenomena which have recently been systematized in a preliminary way under the heading of "paralinguistics." (For a general survey of both cognitive and expressive aspects of personality, linguistically viewed, see Hymes [1961b].) The principal study to result so far from the work in paralinguistics, that of Pittenger, Hockett and Ranehy (1960) is based on the heuristic, if somewhat intuitive, use of the principle of contrast within a frame, applied to the unfolding of a psychiatric interview. Indeed, the main task confronting paralinguistics is to determine the import of the phenomena it has isolated by further study of their contrastive use in situations. In general, advances in analysis of the expressive role of speech also lead into analysis of the ethnographic context.[2]

Among other anthropological concerns which lead into such analysis, there is the aspect of culture change involving programs of fundamental education, concerned with literacy and multilingualism. In introducing new uses for indigenous forms of speech, and in extending foreign forms of speech into local contexts, the patterns and functions of speaking on both sides need to be analyzed, so as to anticipate points of congruence and conflict (cf. Weinreich 1953 and Hymes 1961c).

Now it is time to consider how the analysis of the ethnographic context of speech may be carried out. There are a number of lines of research whose goals overlap those of an ethnography of speaking, and whose results and methods must contribute. Since these lines of research have so far not fused or had the particular focus and scope that is of concern here, it is worthwhile, perhaps necessary, to take this opportunity to broach the descriptive problem, and to outline a method of approach. My way of getting at it is of course without

---

[2] Mahl (1959) has discussed an "instrumental aspect of language" as constituting a gap in psychology. He argues that "The instrumental model is the more general and valid one for purposes of inferring emotional states from language behavior" (p.40) and that the instrumental model is more closely linked to behavior than the representational (cognitive, or lexicon-and-grammar focused) model. But a cognitive approach may be concerned with the effect of a speech-derived symbolic map on problem-solving, planning, and the like, and hence can also be called "instrumental," since it also deals with speech as tool-using behavior. In exploring the signalling of emotional states, Mahl deals with what will here be termed expressive function, and in pointing to the effect of this signalling of the behavior of others, he deals with what will here be termed directive function. His use of "instrumental" subsumes the two. I particularly value Mahl's analysis because he insists on "including the situational and/or the nonlexical contexts of messages" (p. 105) and in effect demands the equivalent of an ethnography of speaking in relation to the analysis of speech events for certain psychological purposes.

prejudice to ways that prove rewarding to others. Approaches to ethnographic analysis devised under linguistic influence, although they may diverge, are likely to show strong resemblance at many points.[3]

## DESCRIPTIVE ANALYSIS OF SPEAKING

The descriptive focus is the speech economy of a community. The scope is all behavior relevant to a structural ("emic," in Pike's terminology) analysis of this. The approach is not to consider behavioral reality a pie and the speech economy a unique slice. It is a question of an organizing perspective on a social reality that is the same for differing analytical frameworks. I believe that structural analysis in this particular framework will be of value in its own right and will feed back into analyses from other perspectives.

By structural analysis is meant more than the placing of data in an articulated set of categories. Such placing is a necessary starting point, and also a desired outcome, when systems that have been individually analyzed are studied comparatively. But for the individual system, structural analysis means a scientific and moral commitment to the inductive discovery of units, criteria, and patternings that are valid in terms of the system itself. An illustration is the interrelation between phonetics as a starting point, the phonemic analysis of a given language, and the use of the results of that analysis in general linguistics, e.g., in phonemic typology; or, ethnological categories as a starting point, the ethnographic analysis of, say, the residence rules of a community, and the use of the results of that analysis in a comparative study. The categories presented here for an ethnography of speaking must be taken as ways of getting at individual systems, as analogous to a phonetics and perhaps part of a practical phonemics. The intent is heuristic, not *a priori*.

The point seems obvious, but experience shows it to be easily mistaken. Let me put it another way. What would be an appropriate improvement, or correction, of what follows? Not an argument that there *really are* 3, or 8, or 76, factors or functions of speech—in general. That would be equivalent to arguing how many phonemes there *really are*—in general. The problem, of course, is how many phonemes, or factors and functions, there are in some one determi-

---

3 E. T. Hall, *The Silent Language,* is especially worthwhile. Details apart, my only reservation is that the 10 primary message systems, the 3 levels of culture, the 3 components of messages, the 3 principal types of patterns, and the 100-category map of culture should be taken more frankly as heuristic devices. In particular the 10 primary message systems seem but one convenient breakdown, rather than rooted in biology, and the components (set, isolate, pattern) and pattern types (order, selection, congruence) seem a valid but partial extrapolation of a linguistic model. Several such extrapolations, particularly those of Hall and Trager, of Jakobson, of Pike (1954, 1955, 1960), and of Uldall, have each their contribution to perspective, but none has yet carried the day. The Hall and Trager framework of components (set, isolate, pattern) converges in a noteworthy way with the trimodal framework (manifestation, feature, distribution modes) of Pike.

nate system. What the range in number of factors and functions may be, what invariants of universal scope there may be—answers to these questions may perhaps be glimpsed now, but must wait for demonstration on the structural analyses of many systems. An appropriate improvement or correction, then, is one that contributes to that job, that makes of this paper a better practical phonetics and phonemics.

It can be asked: to what extent is analysis from the perspective of speaking itself valid structurally to a given case? Activity defined as speaking by one group may be defined as something else by another. But differences of this sort are themselves of interest. Some behavior will be organized and defined in terms of speaking in every group, and the import of this behavior may be missed if not investigated as such. Only a focus on speaking answers the structural question, and provides data for comparative study of the differential involvement of speaking in the structure of behavior in different groups. In one sense, a comparative ethnography of speaking is but one kind of comparative study of the utilization of cultural resources.

Note that the delimitation of the speech economy of a group is in relation to a population or community, however defined, and not in relation to the homogeneity or boundaries of a linguistic code. If several dialects or languages are in use, all are considered together as part of the speech activity of the group. This approach breaks at the outset with a one language-one culture image. Indeed, for much of the world the primary object of attention will not coincide with the units defined as individual languages. The patterning of a linguistic code will count as one among several analytical abstractions from verbal behavior. In cultural terms, it will count as one among several sets of speech habits. The specialization of particular languages or varieties to particular situations or functions, and the implications of each for personality, status, and thinking, will be a normal part of a description. Standard analysis of each code will of course be necessary, but the broader framework seems more "natural," indeed, more properly anthropological. The structure of this argument also applies if the focus of attention is not a population but an individual personality.[4]

A necessary step is to place speaking within a hierarchy of inclusiveness: not all behavior is communicative, from the viewpoint of the participants; not all communication is linguistic; and linguistic means include more than speech. One can ask of an activity or situation: is there a communicative act (to oneself or another) or not? If there is, is the means linguistic or non-linguistic (gesture, body-movement) or both? In a given case, one of the alternatives may be necessary, or optional, or proscribed. The allocation of communication

---

4 Aberle (1960) argues that language has been an inadequate model for culture-and-personality studies, having only two terms, the individual and the sacred cultural pattern, whereas a third term, the cultural system in which persons participate but do not share, is necessary. In Aberle's terms, I am saying here that the two-term model is inadequate for linguistics studies as well. "Ethnography of speaking" involves a speech equivalent of "cultural system".

among behavior settings differs from group to group: what, for example, is the distribution of required silence in a society—as opposed to occasions in which silence, being optional, can serve as a message? (To say that everything is communication is to make the term a metaphor of no use. If necessary, the wording could be changed to: not all behavior is message-sending...not all message-sending is linguistic...etc.) The allocation of communicative means may also differ. For any group, some situations must be speech situations, some may be, some cannot be. Which situations require writing, derivative codes of singing, whistling, drumming, non-linguistic uses of the voice or instruments, or gesture? Are certain messages specialized to each means?

The distribution of acts and means of communication in the round of behavior is one level of description. Patterns of occurrence and frequency are one kind of comparison between groups. Much more complex is the analysis of the communicative event itself. (In discussing it, I shall refer to speech and speaking, but these terms are surrogates for all modes of communication, and a descriptive account should be generalized to comprise all.) Let me emphasize again that what I present is not a system to be imposed, but a series of questions to be asked. Hopefully, the questions will get at the ingredients, and from the ingredients to the structure of speaking in a group.

There seem to be three aspects of speech economy which it is useful to consider separately: *speech events,* as such; the *constituent factors* of speech events; and the *functions of speech.* With each aspect, it is a question of focus, and a full description of one is partly in terms of the rest.

## Speech Events

For each aspect, three kinds of questions are useful. Taking first the speech events within a group, what are instances of speech events? What classes of speech events are recognized or can be inferred? What are the dimensions of contrast, the distinctive features, which differentiate them? (This will include reference to how factors are represented and functions served.) What is their pattern of occurrence, their distribution vis-à-vis each other, and externally (in terms of total behavior or some selected aspect)?

One good ethnographic technique for getting at speech events, as at other categories, is through words which name them. Some classes of speech events in our culture are well known: Sunday morning sermon, inaugural address, pledge of allegiance. Other classes are suggested by colloquial expressions such as: heart-to-heart-talk, salestalk, talk man-to-man, woman's talk, bull session, chat, polite conversation, chatter (of a team), chew him out, give him the lowdown, get it off his chest, griping, etc. I know no structural analysis. Clearly the material cannot be culled from a dictionary alone: instances and classes of speech events may be labelled by quite diverse means, not only by nouns, but also by verbs, phrases, and sentences. In response to the question, "Nice talk?", a situation may be titled by the response "Couldn't get a word in edgewise."

Insofar as participants in a society conceive their verbal interaction in terms of such categories, the critical attributes and the distribution of these are worth discovering.

Take "cussing out," a Wishram Chinook's English label for a class of aboriginal speech events. A set of verb stems differentiates varieties of "cussing out." What alternative events (linguistic or non-linguistic) are possible in the same situation, such as dismissal or beating? With regard to factors, who cusses out whom, when and where, in what style or code, about what? With regard to function, is there an aesthetic element, are speakers rated as to ability, what does "cussing out" do for speakers, what effect is expected or follows for hearers? What is the role of "cussing out" in maintenance of social system, cultural values, personality systems? (The analysis of Hausa *roka* (praise singing) by Smith [1957] is an interesting work along these lines, as is Conklin [1959].)

An interesting question about speech events concerns what can serve to close them, or to close a sequence within one.

## Factors in Speech Events

Any speech event can be seen as comprising several components, and the analysis of these is a major aspect of an ethnography of speaking. Seven types of component or factor can be discerned. Every speech event involves 1. a Sender (Addresser) ; 2. a Receiver (Addressee) ; 3. a Message Form; 4. a Channel; 5. a Code; 6. a Topic; and 7. Setting (Scene, Situation).[5]

*The set of seven types of factor is an initial ("etic") framework.* For any group, the indigenous categories will vary in number and kind, and their instances and classes must be empirically identified. For example, Sender and Addresser, or Receiver and Addressee, need not be the same. Among the eastern Chinookan groups, a formal occasion is partly defined by the fact that the words of a chief or sponsor of a ceremony are repeated by a special functionary to the assembled people. In general, the categories of these two factors must be investigated in terms of the role system of the group studied. Moreover, depending upon beliefs and practices, the categories of Senders and Receivers variously overlap the membership of the human group. The coming of a flock of ravens brought warning for the Kwakiutl, and, indeed, there was a corresponding category of Receiver: an individual whose afterbirth had been eaten by ravens could, as an adult, perceive raven cries as one or another of a limited set of Kwakiutl utterances. A stone is one type of potential Sender among the Fox. Infants may or may not be counted as a class of potential Addressees and talked to; they were so counted among the Mohave and Tlingit, who thought infants

---

5 In what follows I am most immediately indebted to Roman Jakobson's presentation of factors and functions in his concluding remarks to the Conference on Style held at Indiana University, April 1958, sponsored by the Social Science Research Council. The published statement identifies six factors and corresponding functions (Jakobson 1960). Jakobson's rich discussion should be carefully read. I have also pervasive debts to Kenneth Burke, Kenneth L. Pike, Sinclair (1951) and Barker and Wright (1955).

capable of understanding speech. (The practice with infants and pets varies in our own society.) The form of a Message, or the typical form of a class of Messages, is a descriptive fact that becomes significant especially as an aesthetic and stylistic matter, whether in relation to the resources of a code (Newman [1940] has shown that Yokuts and English stand in sharp contrast), to a particular context (Riffaterre [1959] takes this relation as fundamental to analysis of style), or to a particular referential content (as when some linguists find that the modifier "Trager-Smith" fits their sentence rhythms better as "Smith-Trager").

Cross-cultural differences in Channels are well known, not only the presence of writing, but also the elaboration of instrumental channels among West African peoples such as the Jabo, the whistling of tones among some of the Mazatecs of Mexico, etc.

It has already been noted that the Code factor is a variable, given a focus on the speech habits of a population. The range is from communities with different levels of a single dialect to communities in which many individuals command several different languages. The presence of argots, jargons, forms of speech disguise, and the like enters here. Terms such as "dialect," "variety," "vernacular," "level," are much in discussion now (see Ferguson and Gumperz 1960, Hill 1958, Kenyon 1948). It is clear the status of a form of speech as a dialect, or language, or level, cannot be determined from linguistic features alone, nor can the categories be so defined. There is a sociocultural dimension (see Wolff 1959, on the non-coincidence of objective linguistic difference and communicative boundary), and the indigenous categories must be discovered, together with their defining attributes and the import of using one or another in a situation. Depending on attitude, the presence of a very few features can stamp a form of speech as a different style or dialect.[6]

The Topic factor points to study of the lexical hierarchy of the languages spoken by a group, including idioms and the content of any conventionalized utterances, for evidence and knowledge of what can be said. To a large extent this means simply that semantic study is necessary to any study of speaking. An ethnography of speaking does also call special attention to indigenous categories for topics. One needs to know the categories in terms of which people will answer the question, "What are they talking about?", and the attributes and

---

6 The phenomena which Voegelin treats as "casual" vs. "noncasual" belong here. Voegelin (1960) sees the need for an empirical, general approach to all forms of speech in a community, discussing their variation in number and kind between communities, and the situational restrictions on their use. His discussion takes "casual" as a residual, unmarked category, whereas the need is to assume that all speech manifests some positively marked level or style, and to discover the identifying traits. He generalizes that neither formal training nor specialized interest contributes to proficiency in casual speech, and that judgments of proficiency are not made, but evaluations of proficiency among the Menominee (Bloomfield 1927) and the Crow (Lowie 1935) show that his implication of "casual" is misleading. Indeed, for some groups, most utterances might have to be classed in Voegelin's terms as "noncasual," for training in proper speaking is intensive and proficiency stressed (e.g., the Ngoni of Nyasaland and many groups in Ghana).

patterns of occurrence for these categories. The old rhetorical category of *topoi* might go here as well.

The Setting factor is fundamental and difficult. It underlies much of the rest and yet its constituency is not easily determined. We accept as meaningful such terms as "context of situation" and "definition of the situation" but seldom ask ethnographically what the criteria for being a "situation" might be, what kinds of situations there are, how many, and the like. Native terms are one guide, as is the work of Barker and Wright (1955) to determine *behavior settings* and to segment the continuum of behavior.[7]

Some of the import of these types of factors will be brought out with regard to the functions of speech. With regard to the factors themselves, let us note again that native lexical categories are an important lead, and that contrast within a frame is a basic technique for identifying both instances and classes, and for discovering their dimensions of contrast.

Given the relevant instances and classes for a group, the patterning of their distribution can be studied. One way is to focus on a single instance or class, hold it constant, and vary the other components. As a sort of concordance technique, this results in an inventory, a description of an element in terms of the combinability of other elements with it. As a general distributional technique, this can discover the relations which obtain among various elements: whether co-occurrence is obligatory, or optional, or structurally excluded. Sometimes the relation will hold for only two elements (as when a certain category of Receiver may be addressed only by a certain category of Sender), sometimes for several. The relation may characterize a class of speech events.

---

[7] Jakobson treats the last two factors (his Context and Referent). together as one factor. To stress my descriptive concern with factors, I eschew the theoretically laden term "Context" for a factor here, retaining "Setting" (cf. Barker and Wright 1955) with "Scene" (Burke 1945) and "Situation" (Firth 1935, following Malinowski) as alternatives. As factors, I distinguish Setting and Topic because the same statement may have quite different import, as between, say, a rehearsal and a performance. In one sense, it is simply a question of what one has to inventory in describing the speech economy of a group. Settings and Topics seem to me to involve two obviously different lists, and lists on the same level as Addressers, Addressees, Channels, etc. Put otherwise, "Who said it? Who'd he say it to? What words did he use? Did he phone or write? Was it in English? What'd he talk about? Where'd he say it?" seem to me all questions of the same order. With functions I cannot avoid using "Context." I agree with Jakobson that referential function involves context (as an earlier section makes plain), but find this no difficulty if a function may be defined in relation to more than one factor. I also agree with Jakobson that all aspects of a speech event are aspects of context from one point of view, but I have argued that all aspects may be viewed in terms of any one factor; and the level at which all are aspects of context merges all, not just context and reference, while the level at which the others are distinct seems to me to distinguish context and reference as well, as I hope the illustrations, especially the literary ones, show. Certainly if reference is less than the total import of a sentence, then shifting the line "And seal the hushéd casket of my soul" from early in the sonnet "To Sleep" to its close (as manuscripts show Keats did), enhanced the effect of the line and its contribution to the poem, without changing its reference.

In this way we can discover the rules of appropriateness for a person or group. (And indications that such rules have been violated are of special help in discovering them.) From a linguistic (Code) point of view, such rules may account for variance in the speech material on which a description is based, explaining why some grammatically possible utterances do not occur (e.g., to illustrate each type of factor: because the informant is not an appropriate Sender, the linguist not an appropriate Receiver, a different choice of words or order is preferred, the sequence is sung, and cannot be dictated apart from that mode of channel, the sequence indicates a speech variety or level which the informant avoids or must not use, the topic is tabued, the situation which would elicit the utterance has never occurred or been imagined, such a thing is said only in a context to which the linguist has no access). From an ethnographic point of view, the discovery of such rules of appropriateness is of practical importance for participant observation, and it is central to the conception of speaking as a system. *One way that patterns of speaking constitute a system is in virtue of restrictions on the co-occurrence of elements.*

Relevant data have been noted by ethnographers, especially as incident to lexical items of interest, such as kin terms. Linguists have taken account of such data when intrusive into the formal code, as when different morphemic shapes or different paradigms are used according to the sex of the speaker and hearer. (Haas 1944 is the best treatment.) The participants in speech may then be admitted as environments for use of the principle of complementary distribution, and the different forms treated as lexically or grammatically equivalent; but such data are likely to be regarded as a frayed edge of grammar rather than as an opening into the broader system of speaking. (Such facts have sometimes served as casements for vision of different men's and women's "languages," but serious characterization of speech differences between men and women in a society hardly exists.)

A descriptive analysis of patterns of speaking in terms of indigenous instances of the constructive factors of speech events is worthwhile in its own right, and it feeds back into prediction and inference about behavior. Given a speech event in the limited sense of a concrete message, frequently the main interest is in what can be told about one or more of its constituent elements. What can be told about the Sender, either as to identity (age, sex, social class, and the like) or as to motive, attitude, personality?; what can be told about the Receiver, including his or her likely response?; about the Context (including antecedent circumstances, verbal or non-verbal)?; and so on. (For the fieldworker or learning child, the question may be what can be told about the Code; for the communications engineer, what can be told about the Channel.) We may consider relations between elements, or consider all as evidence about a certain one.

The saliency of this focus is of course that it is what we often have to work with, namely, text of one sort or another. Inquiry of this sort is common in and out of science. But in our own society the success of such inquiry presupposes a knowledge of the relations—diagnostic, probabilistic—that obtain among the constitutive elements of speech events. We share in the patterns of speaking behind the text or message, and can to some extent ask ourselves, what would be different if the Sender were different?; if the Sender's motives were different?; and so on. In another society this contrast-within-a-frame technique must appeal to an explicit analysis of patterns of speaking.

## Functions in Speech Events

The third aspect of speech events is that of function. Within anthropology the functions of speech (or language) have usually been discussed in terms of universal functions. While it is important to know the ways in which the functions of speaking are the same in every group and for every personality, our concern here is with the ways in which they differ. One way to approach this is to reverse the usual question, "what does a language contribute to the maintenance of personality, society, and culture?" and to ask instead, "what does a personality, society, or culture contribute to the maintenance of a language?" Especially if we ask the question in situations of culture change, we can see the various functional involvements of speech and of given languages.

Some students of standard languages have defined for them functions and correlative attitudes. These in fact apply to all languages, and serve to contrast their roles. To illustrate: among the Hopi-Tewa the language serves prestige, unifying, and separatist functions, and there is great language pride as well as language loyalty. Among the Eastern Cherokee the hierarchy of functions seems just the reverse; the retention of the language serves mainly a separatist function, and there is an attitude of loyalty, but hardly of pride. Perhaps we think too much in terms of nineteenth-century European linguistic nationalism to notice that some languages do not enjoy the status of a symbol crucial to group identity. The Fulnío of Brazil have preserved group identity over three centuries by giving up their territory to maintain their language and major ceremony, but the Guayqueries of Venezuela have preserved group identity by maintaining a set of property relations. Of indigenous language and religion there has been no trace for generations. One suspects that the Guayqueries' involvement with their language differed from that of the Fulnío.

When only a few speakers of a language are left in a community, the survival of the language becomes almost entirely dependent on its manifest and latent functions for the personalities concerned. Thus Swanton rescued an important and independent Siouan language, Ofo, partly by luck; he happened to be in the unsuspected presence of the last speaker, and followed up a chance remark. But it was partly due to the personality of the woman, who could be an informant because she had practiced the language frequently to herself in the years since all other speakers had died.

These examples of the broad functional involvements of speech, and of languages, raise questions that can be answered only within general ethnography or social anthropology. While the same holds for an ethnography of speaking at other points, insofar as it is a special focus and not a separate subject-matter, it looms large here because the necessary conceptual framework exists almost entirely outside linguistics. There are still points and progress to be made, however, by concentrating on the linguistic discussions of the function of speech in terms of the constructive factors of the speech event.

Within the tradition of linguistics, functions of speech have commonly been an interpretation of factors of the speech event in terms of motive or purpose, obtaining a set of functions one for each factor discriminated. Sometimes a particular feature, a linguistic category, or literary genre is associated with a function. For example, the 1st person pronoun, interjections, and the lyric poem have been associated with expressive function (focus on the Sender within the speech event) ; the 2nd person pronoun, imperatives, and rhetoric or dramatic poetry with the directive function; and the 3rd person pronoun, and epic poetry, with the referential function.[8]

Some conception of speech functions must figure in any theory of behavior, if it is to give any account of speaking. The same holds for an account of language in a theory of culture. Indeed, rival views on many issues involving speech can best be interpreted as involving differing assumptions about the importance or existence of various functions. For an ethnography of speaking, then, the question is not, should it have a conception of speech functions, but, what should that conception be?

There can be only a preliminary outline at present, and, as a guide for field work, its concern should be for scope and flexibility. It should not conceive the functions of speech too narrowly, as to number or domain, and it should not impose a fixed set of functions. While some general classes of function are undoubtedly universal, one should seek to establish the particulars of the given case, and should be prepared to discover that a function identifiable in one group is absent in another.

One can point to seven broad types of function, corresponding to the seven types of factor already enumerated. (Each type can be variously named, and the most appropriate name may vary with circumstances; alternatives are given in parentheses.) The seven are: 1. Expressive (Emotive) ; 2. Directive (Conative, Pragmatic, Rhetorical, Persuasive) ; 3. Poetic; 4. Contact; 5. Metalinguistic; 6. Referential; 7. Contextual (Situational).

In the simplest case, each of the types of function can be taken as focusing upon a corresponding type of factor, and one can single out questions and comments, and units as well, that primarily are associated with each.

"You say it with such feeling" points to expressive function, and a language may have units which are conventionally expressive, such as French [h] ("Je te

---

8 Snell (1952) attempts to subsume all linguistic features, including parts of speech and grammatical categories, under Bühler's classification of three types of linguistic function ("Auslosung," "Kundgabe," "Darstellung," equivalent to Snell's "Wirkungs-, Ausdrucks- und Darstellungsfunktion," and corresponding to directive, expressive, and referential function here). This might be valuable to the coding of personality expression in speech. But Snell's linguistic base is narrowly within Indo-European, the application is *a priori*, and three functions are not enough. His work has been reviewed as interesting, but not convincing (Winter 1953).

H'aime") and English vowel length ("What a fiiiiiiine boy"), used to convey strong feeling. (A feature can be conventionally an expressive device only where it is not referential, i.e., for phonic features, not functioning phonemically to differentiate lexical items.) "Do as I say, not do as I do" points to directive function, and imperatives have been cited as primarily directive units. "What oft was thought, but ne'er so well expressed" points to poetic function, focused on message form, as does "The sound must seem an echo to the sense." Feet, lines, and metrical units generally are primarily poetic in function. "If only I could talk it instead of having to write it" and "Can you hear me?" point to contact function; breath groups may be channel units, in the case of speaking, as are pages in the case of print. "Go look it up in the dictionary" points to metalinguistic function, to concern with the code underlying communication; words such as "word," and technical linguistic terms, which make talk about the code possible, serve primarily metalinguistic function. Quotation marks have metalinguistic function when they signal that a form is being cited or glossed, but channel function when enclosing quoted or imagined speech. "What are you going to talk about?", "What did he have to say?" focus on topic and point to referential function. Most lexical and grammatical units are primarily referential, and are analyzed by descriptive linguistics in terms of that function. "When will you tell him?", "As mentioned above," "You can't talk like that here!!", "If you're going to use that scene at all, you'll have to put it later in the play," are primarily contextual in function as are a sign flashing "On the Air" and the statement of scene at the beginning of an act of a play "(Elsinore. A platform before the castle)".

All features of the speech event, including all features of the linguistic code, may participate in all of the functions. This point must be made, because certain features are often treated exclusively in terms of a single function. But, as Kenneth Burke has pointed out, any utterance, for example, even an interjection, may secondarily serve as a title for contexts to which it is appropriate, and hence have a referential aspect. Some interpret the linguistic code as a series of levels entirely in terms of referential function, and see other functions, such as the expressive, as pertaining only to the level of the entire utterance and beyond. Of course all functions (including the referential) come into play only at the level of the entire utterance; no utterance, no functions. But when analytical matters are in question, all functions have to be discussed with regard to all levels. Not only are there conventional expressive units corresponding to each level of the code, but a wide range of functions can be illustrated with regard to a unit such as the phoneme. Although the initial task of descriptive analysis is to treat phonemes in their contribution to referential function (identifying and differentiating utterances), this does not exhaust their functional involvement. To take /p/ as an example: expressively, Burke has noted "two kinds of p," the heavily aspirated one conveying distaste and rejection (1957, p. 12ff.). Patterning of /p/s can participate in poetic function, organizing the middle line of a stanza by Wallace Stevens, "The romantic intoning, the declaimed clairvoyance / Are parts of apotheosis, appropriate / And of its nature, the idiom thereof!" The functional load of /p/ in a community cannot be analyzed apart from the nature and use of various channels, as when among the Pima the functional load of /p/ differs between singing and recitation, or as when among the Jabo of Liberia a drum does not differentiate /p/ from other consonants, but signals only the occurrence of the type. Conventional names for phonemes, permitting them to be discussed in the abstract, have to do with metalinguistic function, and even a quite simple society may have a term that names a distinctive feature such as nasalization (Halkomelem Salish s'amqs n (-qs n "nose"); see description of the circumstances in Elmendorf and Suttles (1960), p.7). As abbreviation, "P" may mediate reference, as when on an athletic uniform it signifies the school, or when large vs. small "p" distinguishes the winner of letters in major vs. minor sports. If uniforms worn in games bear the letter, and practice jerseys do not, the element (such as "P") has contextual function. In such cases the phonological structure of the language conditions what occurs.

These illustrations are minor, but if features conceived as most internal to the code, most removed from external involvement, participate in a variety of functions, the argument serves for features generally. To restrict linguistic description or psychological study to speech habits conceived only in terms of referential function is to restrict understanding, especially of aspects of speech important to behavior and the formation of personality. If the meaning of a linguistic form is defined as the total disposition to use it, then several functions play a part in meaning, since all contribute to the total disposition. Analysis in terms of referential function comes first, so that other functions may be set aside for an interval; but this can not be a permanent strategy.

These illustrations are simply pointers to broad areas. In a given case and with regard to, say, expressive function, one would want to discover the inventory of units which could conventionally serve expressive function, as well as the kinds of inference about expressiveness made by participants in speech events in the group, and the evidence underlying such inferences. One would expect groups to differ in number of conventional expressive units and in the frequency of their use, as well as in kinds of inference made as to expressiveness, and the features (of whatever sort) used as evidence. One would seek to identify the kinds of expressive function recognized or implicit in the behavior of the group. A Sender can not help but express attitudes towards each of the other factors in a speech event, his audience, the style of his message, the code he is using, the channel he is using, his topic, the scene of his communication. An external observer can of course interpret a speech event as expressive in terms of all of these, by attending to each in turn. But the primary ethnographic problem is to determine which kinds of expressive function, any or all, are present as intended or perceived by the participants of the speech event. Which are, so to speak, being "encoded" and "decoded"? Similarly, one could investigate a speech event entirely with regard to directive function, or, with regard to metalinguistic function, one could attend exclusively to evidence of shared signal systems, not only to the grammar and dictionary which serve referential function, but the degree to which there are codes for expressive and other functions.

One would seek, as with other aspects of speech events, to discover the dimensions of contrast among functions, and the patterns of their occurrence in the behavior of the group.

To study the distribution of speech functions in the round of behavior raises several difficult problems. The first problem is that of the relation of particular functions to particular instances or classes of speech event. The same speech event can be viewed in terms of all seven types of function, and variously so. (A given utterance of "Once more unto the breach, dear friends, once more," might be taken as expressive of Shakespeare, Henry V, or Laurence Olivier; as directive and determinant of the subsequent action of soldiers or actors; as exemplifying iambic pentameter blank verse and as worse or better than an alternative such as "Once more, once more into the breach, dear friends"; as more effective when heard than when read; as evidence for the phonemic system of author or actor; as telling something about the progress of the siege of Harfleur; as signalling, should someone enter at that point, that it is Shakespeare's play and/or just past the prologue of Act III.) Even narrowing the perspective to that of a single participant in the situation, more than one function is usually present in a given speech event. Jakobson's way of handling this is to consider that all types of functions are always compresent, and to see a given speech event as characterized by a particular hierarchy of functions. There are clear cases of the validity of this approach, as when expressive function (signalled perhaps by intonation) dominates referential function, and there are interesting cases of its manipulation, as when a teen-age daughter protests, "But all I said was...", editing out the intonation that had been perceived as insult. She is claiming the privileged status generally ascribed to the referential function in our culture. Our cultural view is the opposite of the fact, however, if the Dutch linguist de Groot (1949) is right in his "Law of the Two Strata," which asserts that whenever the referential and expressive import of a message conflict, the expressive import is overriding. Such conflict had been noted by Sapir (1931), and it underlies Bateson's concept of the "double bind" of many children who become schizophrenic. Conflict, however, raises doubt that all messages can be analyzed in terms of a hierarchy of functions such that one function is dominant. The defining characteristic of some speech events may be a balance, harmonious or conflicting, between more than one function. If so, the interpretation of a speech event is far from a matter of assigning it to one of seven types of function.

This brings us to a second problem, that of the relation of particular functions to the constituent factors of speech events. Although types of function have been presented in a preliminary way as correlates of types of factor, the relationships between the two are more complex. Indeed, it would be a great mistake to analyze an actual situation as if each type of factor simply determined a single type of function.

Here is where an ethnographic approach diverges perhaps from that sketched by Jakobson. Jakobson's work represents a decisive advance or anthropology and linguistics. It inspires concern with speech functions, which have had only sporadic attention in recent years; it breaks with the confinement of most schemes to two or three functions (referential: expressive: conative),[9] and it recognizes that all features of a message may participate in all functions. But regarding the relation of functions to factors, Jakobson states:

"Each of these six factors determines a different function of language. Although we distinguish six basic aspects of language, we could, however, hardly find verbal messages that would fulfill only one function. The diversity lies not in monopoly of some one of these several functions, but in a different hierarchical order of functions. The verbal structure of a message depends primarily on the predominant function." (Jakobson 1960:353).

The divergence may be only verbal, however, since Jakobson has subsequently said that "determine" is not the right word, and that rather each type of function is focused upon, centered upon a given factor. Such a view does not exclude participation of more than one. Certainly it is doubtful that particular functions of a concrete case can ever be defined in terms of factors singly. The definition seems always to involve two or more factors (or instances or classes within a type of factor).

Thus, the expressive function of features must be defined in relation to referential function. The function which Malinowski called "phatic communion" can be taken as a kind of alternating or reciprocal expressive function of speech, as when housewives exchange stories about their children or anthropologists about their field work. Now, having designated a factor of "CONTACT, a physical channel and psychological connection between the addresser and the addressee, enabling both of them to enter and stay in communication" (p. 353), Jakobson correlates with it "messages primarily serving to establish, to prolong, or to discontinue communication to check whether the channel works ("Hello, do you hear me?"), to attract the attention of the interlocutor or to confirm his continued attention and places "phatic communion" here ("This set for CONTACT, or in Malinowski's terms PHATIC function" [p. 355].) The psychological connection between participants in communication seems to me significantly independent of the nature and state of the channel, and referrable primarily to them rather than to it. Messages to establish, prolong or discontinue communication may neither intend nor evoke a sense of communion; there may be a clear channel and no rapport. The resolution is probably to take the reference to "a physical channel" and "psychological connection" as indicating two main subtypes of contact function. (Thomas Sebeok has pointed out the im-

---

9 When earlier work distinguishes more than two or three functions, it usually is elaborating within one of these. Ogden and Richards list five functions in *The Meaning of Meaning*, but their focus is on the Sender's intention, and the elaboration falls within the expressive type.

portance of the factor of noise also in relation to analysis of channel and contact.) In any case, if phatic communion is a function of speech in the behavior of a group, it must be identified empirically and particulars given as to participants and situations. Even if universal, phatic communion differs greatly in its occasions and importance from group to group, and ethnographically cannot be read off as the equivalent of one factor.

More striking is the case of the factor of Message Form. This cannot be associated directly or univocally with Poetic function. The relation between a printed message and a Receiver (not Addressee) acting as proof-reader is a pure and obvious case of a function associated with message-form. And the more the proof-reader can divorce his response to the message-form from concern with any other aspect, especially reference, the better. Moreover, any sustained concern with the poetic aspect of message-form must take it in relation with other factors. Use of phonic substance is interpretable only in relation to reference: the phonemes in "The murmuring of innumerable bees" suggest bee-sound only in connection with the topic announced by the meaning of the words. (Pope's passage on "The sound must seem an echo to the sense" illustrates this.) Recent work on criteria for stylistic analysis has taken as fundamental that the stylistic value of a feature depends upon its perception in relation to a delimited verbal context (Riffaterre 1959). (Jackobson has subsequently explained that the label "poetic" should not be misleading; in his view "poetic" function need not concern poetry, but concerns any case of *einstellung* on the message, so that the message becomes from a certain point of view self-sufficient. Poetry as such would thus be but a principal subtype, proof-reading perhaps a minor one.)

In general, a message or feature has a particular function in behavior only for specified classes of participants in the speech event. An act of speech may have directive, yet no referential value, for someone who knows nothing of the language involved. Many misunderstandings arise from situations in which the referential value of a message is understood, but not the expressive or directive import, because the Receiver does not share the Sender's conventional understandings, or code, for these. In short, speech functions must be defined in contexts of use.

The distribution of speech functions brings out one of the ways in which speaking constitutes a system. If the speech economy of a group is stated in terms of the interdependence of various factors, this constitutes a simple system. The statement that combinations of factors are not at all possible, are not chance, but governed by rules, is an example. To constitute a functional system, the speech economy would have to be not only analyzable into structure of parts, but also be such that the condition of some of these parts determines whether a certain property G will occur in the system; the parts are subject to variation such that if nothing compensates for the variation, G will no longer occur; if one (or some) of these parts vary within certain limits, the other of these parts will vary so as to compensate for the "initial variation" and G will be maintained; if one (or some) of these parts vary beyond certain limits, compensation will be impossible and G will no longer occur. When these conditions are met, the parts of the system can be called "functional" with respect to G. (Nagel 1953, 1956. I am indebted to Francesca Wendel Cancian at this point.)

It is easy to see how phonemes constitute a functional system, as when variation in one is compensated for by variation in another to maintain phonemic distinction. Such interpretation is well known in linguistics, and indeed, phonemic theory such as that of André Martinet (1955) should be better known as an example of a structural-functional theory of change. Interpretation of speaking in such terms is a challenge that has not generally been met. For any one speech function in the behavior of a group, the various factors (Sender, Receiver, etc.) can be taken as state-coordinates whose values vary within certain limits to maintain it. Communication can be taken as a cover-term for most of the specific functions, or as a very general function in its own right. If it is taken as a property being maintained, we can see that it in fact may depend upon the values of other functions. This might be in terms of a whole community, as in the analysis of the maintenance or loss of intelligibility between dialects. Let us consider single speech events. The members of a group have conceptions and expectations as to the distribution of speech functions among situations, and insofar as several functions are compresent, it is a matter of expectations as to the distribution of speech functions among situations, and insofar as several functions are compresent, it is a matter of expectations as to relative hierarchy. These expectations may be anything from formal cultural norms to the projection of individual needs. If two persons meet, and perceive the situation in terms of conflicting hierarchies of speech function, communication will be broken off or the other person silently judged unfavorable, unless adjustment is made.

Let us take the relation of expressive and referential functions, broadly conceived. A group of wives may be chatting about personal experiences with children. If another woman insists on exact information, she is failing to perceive dominance of expressive or phatic function in the situation. Polite inquiry is appropriate, but not persistent challenge as to fact. Or a group of wives may be discussing children in behavioral science terms. If another woman interposes purely associative and biographical comments about her own children, she is failing to perceive the dominance of a referential function. Evidence is appropriate, but not anecdotes irrelevant to the views and theory being exchanged. In either case, the offender may be excluded from communication, or avoided under similar circumstances later. A good deal of interpersonal behavior can be examined in similar terms. In general, instances of the breaking off of communication, or uneasiness in it, are good evidence of the presence of a rule or expectation about speaking, including differences in functional hierarchy.

Three aspects of speech economy have been outlined now, the speech events, their constitutive factors, and various types of functions. Each is one perspective on the whole of verbal behavior, and full description of each must be partly in terms of the others. An approach in these terms should be useful whether one's interest is a comparative study of human behavior, or the behavior typical of a group, or the varying behavior of individuals within a group.

## SPEECH IN SOCIALIZATION

I now want to survey the role of speaking in socialization. In one sense this role is one part of the kind of descriptive analysis that has been proposed. In another sense, it is a question of the induction of new recruits into the ongoing adult system. Whichever perspective is chosen, and we often shift back and forth in ordinary thinking, it is worthwhile to single out speech in socialization because, from a comparative viewpoint, it has been entirely neglected; there is far too little attention to it in the study of individual groups; and it presumably underlies much of the variation in individual adult behavior.

Studies of the child's acquisition of speech have concentrated on mastery of the code for referential function. Far too few such studies have been informed by modern linguistics as to the structural nature of what it is the child learns, but the number is increasing. Adequate studies of the child's acquisition of the other functions of speech have been more or less unknown to American linguistics and anthropology, but recently the work of Russian psychologists on the directive function has gained recognition (Luria 1959; Luria and Yurovich 1959). The Russian scholars consider the child's acquisition of speech ("the secondary signalling system") in interaction with adults as fundamental to the child's development of control over its own behavior and of its picture of the world. Their experimental work has shown that the development of capacity to understand an utterance (referential function) does not have as automatic consequence the capacity to respond adequately, to have behavior directed by it. The capacity for the directive functioning of speech develops independently and by stages in the first years of life. Thus before the age of 1½ years a child responds to a verbal request for a toy fish by getting and handing the object, but is not able to do so if another toy (say a cat) is closer, and between it and the fish. It will orient toward the object named, but maintain the directive function of the word only until the external situation (the toy cat) conflicts, then grasp and offer the intervening toy. At 3 to 3½ years, if a child is to perform a certain task of pressing a ball, it will not achieve the necessary control over its responses if simply given preliminary verbal instructions, but if it gives itself the appropriate verbal commands, it will succeed. At this age, however, the success is only for positive commands. If the child gives itself the command "Don't press," it not only fails to stop pressing, but presses even harder. Only at the age of 4 to 4½ years does the verbal command "Don't press" actually acquire inhibitory effect, according to these studies.

Thus the directive function of speech depends partly upon maturation, and is partly independent of the dependence upon maturation of control of referential function. As for another salient function, the expressive, observations indicate that it begins to be acquired quite early. Expressive use of intonation and other features may precede referential control. In short, the three most prominent types of function (referential, expressive, directive) appear to develop in childhood in partial independence of each other and in varying relation to the process of maturation.

It also appears that mastery of these functions varies in education and adult life. The basic patterns of the referential function, of grammar and lexicon, are shared as prerequisites to the maintenance of communication at all. There are of course differences at some levels of control of resources for reference. And there seems to be a quite looser rein as to the other functions and greater individual variability. Individuals differ greatly, for example, in control of intonation patterns in our society; some never learn the right intonation for announcing a joke, and some, having learned a certain intonation as students, as part of a pattern of quick repartee, carry it in later life into situations in which it acts to cut off every conversational sequence. And if we extend our horizon from the usual scope of linguistic descriptions to the full repertoire of conventional linguistic habits, to the recurrent linguistic routines and situational idioms of daily verbal behavior, variation in individual mastery is even more apparent. The consequences range from social discomfort to exclusion from or failure in significant areas of activity, because ignorant or maladroit; or, on the other hand, recruitment for and success in certain areas, because adept. There may be a consequence for the possibility of psychotherapy. Such differences may characterize whole subcultures that in basic patterns share the same language.[10]

Concern with differences in individual verbal behavior leads to concern with differences in the role of speech in socialization, and through that, to differences which obtain between groups, whether subcultures or whole societies. Russian psychologists emphasize that the vital functions of speech are acquired in interaction with adults, but seem not to consider the consequences for their experimental norms of different cultural patterns of interaction. This lack they share with most writers, who, if they point out the socialization importance of language, do so in a generic way.[11]

The role of speech in socialization, the context of its acquisition, may vary in every aspect of the patterning of speech events, factors, and functions. Some kinds of variation can be highlighted in a notes-and-queries way with respect to the speech materials and resources available, the processes often stressed in study of personality formation, social structure and organization, and cultural values and beliefs.

What are the cognitive and expressive resources of the linguistic codes of the

---

10 Cf. the work now being done by Basil Bernstein (1958, 1959, 1960a, 1960b, 1961). He contrasts two modes of speech, *formal* and *public,* associated with the English middle-class and lower-class, respectively. Bernstein finds that the two modes arise because two social strata place different emphases on language potential, that once this emphasis is placed, the resulting modes of speech progressively orient speakers to different types of relationships to objects and persons, and that this is reflected in differences of verbal intelligence test scores, of verbal elaboration of subjective intent, and otherwise.

11 George Herbert Mead is one example. Another is A. Irving Hallowell, whose inventory article on "Culture, Personality, and Society" states: "A necessary condition for socialization in man is the learning and use of a language. But different languages are functionally equivalent in this respect, and one language is comparable with another because human speech has certain common denominators" (Hallowell 1953, p. 612).

community? What portion of these are available to children, to what extent and in what sequence? Among the Nupe there are few terms of sexual matters and most knowledge about them is acquired by observation and experience. If there is more than one linguistic code, which is learned first, if either is? (Among the Chontal of Oaxaca, children learn a "second language," Spanish, first, in the home, and Chontal and some other aspects of native culture only in adolescence.) Is there a specialized baby-talk? If so, what is its content (referential, expressive, directive)? Are there verbal games, perhaps metalinguistic in that they draw attention to features of the code as such? (Since much significance has been attached to the child's acquisition of personal pronouns, and means of self-reference, these should be singled out.) What are the *linguistic routines* which the child is taught or can acquire?

A linguistic routine is a recurrent sequence of verbal behavior, whether conventional or idiosyncratic. Its pattern may be obvious and concrete, as in single sequences such as the numerals 1 to 10, the days of the week, the ABC's, or as in antiphonal sequences such as in many children's games, as well as dult games and ceremonies. Or the pattern may not be obvious because it is not concrete, but consists of some regular sequence of emotion or topic. Instruction may be couched as "Then he says...and then you say...", but often it is not a matter of the exact words. (In magic and instruction from supernatural helpers, of course often it is.) Or it may be a formal pattern such as a limerick. Feedback may be involved, and the patterning of the routine resemble a branching tree diagram. (A good "line" or salesman's pitch has alternative ways of reaching the same goal.) A vast portion of verbal behavior in fact consists of recurrent patterns, of linguistic routines. Description has tended to be limited to those with a manifest structure, and has not often probed for those with an implicit pattern. Analysis of routines includes identification of idiomatic units, not only greeting formulas and the like, but the full range of utterances which acquire conventional significance, for an individual, group, or whole culture. Description is usually limited to idioms of phrase length which, because their reference is not predictable from their parts, must be independently listed in a dictionary as lexical units (e.g., "kick the bucket"). Even for clear referential categories such as those of place and personal names, a carefully considered description of the status and formation of idioms is rare (see Hoijer 1948, pp. 182–3 for a fine example), and conventionalization in terms of other functions is important in behavior and personality formation. There are utterances conventionalized in metalinguistic and contextual function, but especially interesting here are those with directive or expressive function. A child's play in imitation of adult roles, as a girl with her dolls, may reveal many of the conventionalized sequences of her family—sequences which have recurred in situations until in some sense they "name," "stand for" the situation and carry a significance, expressive or directive, not predictable from their constituent parts. A mother may find herself using expressions to her child that her own mother had used to her, and with horror, having sworn as a child never to do so.

The number and range of such idioms varies between individuals, families, groups. These and linguistic routines play a great part in the verbal aspect of what Lantis (1960) points to as "vernacular culture," the handling of day-to-day situations, and they are essential in verbal art, in the oral performance of myths, sung epics, many speeches and lectures. The text of these is not identical from one performance to the next, but the general sequence is more or less constant, and most of the verbal content is drawn from a standard repertoire. They fill the slots of a speech, as words fill the slots of a sentence. (Their presence can sometimes be detected when a performer finds himself not communicating. Sequences which he had drawn on as ready coin may prove to have no conventional value for a new audience, which struggles for an interpretation of something intended merely as formulas or labels). The acquisition of conventional sequences, both idioms and routines, is a continuous process in life, and herein resides some of the theoretical interest, for to a great extent these sequences exist in the cambium between idiosyncrasy and culture. They exhibit persisting effort toward the patterning and predictability of behavior. Some sequences become idiomatic for a person or group because of a memorable novelty (see Hockett 1958, 304ff.), but more because sensed as appropriate or as needed. Most do not achieve generality or persistence, but some would lose value if they did, being intended or enjoyed as distinctive, or private to a few.

Turning to the formation of personality, how does speaking figure in the economy of punishment and reward, as alternative to physical acts (spanking, hugging) and to deprivation or giving of things such as candy? At what stage in psycho-sexual development is pressure about speech applied, if any is? How intensive is it? Autobiographical materials from Ghanaian students reveal great childhood anxiety about speech. When is socialization pressure about weaning, toilet-training, self-feeding and the like applied in relation to the child's verbal development? In some groups it is after the demands can be verbally explained, in some not. What is the incidence of stuttering and other speech defects, if any? There is evidence that this depends upon socialization pressures, being absent in some groups, and perhaps among the Pilagá characteristic of girls rather than, as among us, of boys. If there is bilingualism, do speech defects appear in both or but one language? How much does speech figure in the transmission of skills and roles? Among some groups, such as the Kaska (Canada) it figures very little. Does a baby talk facilitate or retard acquisition of adult speech patterns? Is speaking a source of pleasure, or oral, perhaps erotic gratification? That some languages are extremely rich in vocabulary showing sound symbolism, some quite poor, suggests differential enjoyment of the phonic substance of language.

From the viewpoint of the social system of the group, how does speaking enter into definition of the roles acquired or observed by children? In what way does this determine or reflect how speaking is acquired? How relatively significant is speaking in aggressive roles, such as that of warrior? of shaman or priest? (Perhaps the role of speaking in interaction with parents will correspond to the role of speaking in interaction with enemies or the supernatural.) How do residence rules, marriage rules, and the like affect the composition of the household in which the child learns to speak? In affecting the number and relative ages of children, these things affect the rate of mastery of adult patterns; there is evidence that singletons master speech more rapidly, children near the same age less rapidly, twins most slowly. Twins and children near the same age may develop and rely on their own verbal code vis-à-vis each other. If there is multilingualism, are the roles and settings of the languages kept distinct? If so, the child probably will acquire the languages without confusion, but if not, there may be personality difficulties. Are there situations and roles in which it is necessary to translate between two languages? If not, the child may very well master each without acquiring ability to do so. Such external factors have much to do with the effect of multilingualism on personality, including cognitive structure. In what settings are children required to speak, forbidden, permitted? What proportion of total behavior settings for the group permit the presence and speaking of children? A Russian visitor to France was astonished when the children of his host kept silent at the table: Russian children would have been reprimanded for *not* joining in the conversation with a guest.

The values and beliefs of the group of course pervade all this. What are the beliefs regarding children as participants in speech? Some believe neonates capable of understanding speech. The Ottawa believed the cries of infants to be meaningful, and had specialists in their interpretation. The Tlingit believed the talk of women to be the source of conflict among men, and an amulet was placed in a baby girl's mouth to make her taciturn. Are skill and interest in speech demanded, rewarded, ignored, or perhaps repressed? The Ngoni of Nyasaland value skill in speech, believing it part of what constitutes a true Ngoni, and so take pains to instill it in children and maintain it in adults. The remarkable polyglot abilities of Ghanaian students in Europe perhaps reflect similar values in their own cultures. What values are held and transmitted with regard to the language or languages spoken? We have noted presence and absence of pride as between the Hopi-Tewa and Eastern Cherokee. The problem of bilingualism among immigrant children in the United States has been noted as one of the sense of inferiority associated with the non-English language. Concern for excellence of speech seems universal, but the degree and manifestation vary. Some groups tolerate sloppy pronunciation, some do not. If baby talk is present, is it believed easier for children? In sounds and forms it may in fact be as hard as the adult equivalents, and have the latent function of delaying the child's acquisition of these. What evidential status is accorded the statements of children? What degree and kind of intellectual awareness of speaking is present? What folk conceptions of a metalinguistic sort, as reflected in words for linguistic features or the abstraction of these for use in games and speech surrogates? Neighboring dialects may differ, as when one group of Mazatec abstract the tones of their language for a whistled code, while the Soyaltepec Mazatec do not. Bloomfield (1927) has ascribed the erroneous and sometimes injurious folk conceptions about language in our own culture to mistaken generalization from learning of writing, a later and conscious matter, relative to the largely unconscious learning of speech. Values and beliefs regarding speaking, or a language, may be interwoven with major institutions, and much elaborated, or peripheral and sketchy.

## CONCLUSION

Speech cannot be omitted from a theory of human behavior, or a special theory for the behavior of a particular group. But whether we focus on the cognitive or expressive or directive role of verbal behavior, or on the role of speech in socialization, we find a paucity of descriptive analysis of "ethological" studies of speaking in context. There are to be sure many studies that are in one way or another linguistic. But either speaking is taken for granted, or used as means to other ends, or only special kinds of speaking (or writing) are valued and considered. Of speaking as an activity among other activities, of the analysis of its patterns and functions in their own right, there is little. There are bits of data and anecdotes, and a variety of conceptual schemes which impinge, but there are no well focused field studies or systematic theories. The angle of vision has not been such as to bring speaking into focus.

Herein lies the responsibility for the degree of sterility that has dogged a good deal of anthropological discussion of language and culture. The relation between language and culture seems a problem, it crops up whenever a thoughtful anthropologist tries to construct an integrated view of culture or behavior, yet discussion usually trails off irresolutely. We may set language and culture side by side, and try to assess similarities and differences; or we may try to see if something, a method or a model, that has worked for language will work for culture; or we may look to a future of point-for-point comparisons, once all partial cultural systems have been neatly analyzed; or we may redefine or subdivide the problem. We do not want to usher language out of culture; a suggestion to that effect some years ago was quickly suppressed. But having kept language within culture, many seem not very sure what to do about it (except perhaps to recall that some of our brightest friends are linguists, and a credit to the profession).

I do not want to seem to reject efforts such as those characterized above. In particular, there is much to be gained from a determination of the properties of language which are generically cultural and those which are not. The search for formal analogues between linguistics and other systems can be revealing, and some extensions of linguistic-like methodology to other areas of culture seem quite important. Indeed, I would see linguistics in this case as an avenue for the introduction into anthropology of qualitative mathematics. But successes along these lines will not put an end to the language-and-culture problem. It will remain uneasily with us because of the terms in which it is posed, terms which preclude an ultimate solution, if we think of such a solution as being a general theory of culture or of behavior that will integrate the phenomena we consider linguistic with the rest. The difficulty is that we have tried to relate language, described largely as a formal isolate, to culture, described largely without reference to speaking. We have tried to relate one selective abstraction to another, forgetting that much that is pertinent to the place of speech in behavior and culture has not been taken up into either analytic frame. The angle of vision has been in effect a bifurcated one, considering speech primarily as evidence either of formal linguistic code or of the rest of culture.

Why has this been so? Neglect of speaking seems tolerable, I think, because of several working assumptions. Speech as such has been assumed to be without system; its functions have been assumed to be universally the same; the object of linguistic description has been assumed to be more or less homogeneous; and there has been an implicit equation of one language = one culture.

To put these working assumptions in qualified form:

a. The relation of language to speech has been conceived as that of figure to ground. Structure and pattern have been treated in effect as pretty much the exclusive property of language (*la langue: la parole*). For speech as a physical phenomenon, there is a truth to this view. The qualitatively discrete units of the linguistic code stand over against continuous variation in the stream of speech. For speech as a social phenomenon, the case is different. Speaking, like language, is patterned, functions as a system, is describable by rules.[12]

b. The functions of speech have been of concern only with regard to properties judged (correctly or not) to be universal. Or, if differences have been of concern, these have been differences in the content of the code, along Whorfian lines, not differences in speaking itself. Speaking as a variable in the study of socialization has been largely ignored. (Speaking is not even mentioned in the section on "Oral Behavior" of the article, "Socialization," in the *Handbook of Social Psychology* [Child 1954].)

c. Descriptive method has been concerned with a single language or dialect, isolable as such and largely homogeneous. There has been much concern for neatness and elegance of result, and often a readiness to narrow the object of attention so as to achieve this. This object may be defined as one or a few idiolects, the habit of one or a few individuals (and in their roles as speakers, not as receivers); awkward data have often been excluded, if they could be identified as loanwords or a difference of style. The homogeneously conceived object has been a standpoint from which to view speech phenomena in general. Looking out from it, many speech phenomena appear as variation in or of it, due perhaps to personality, social level, or situation. Recently the support for

---

12 Because the distinction *la langue: la parole* usually implies that only the former has structure, Pike has rejected it (1960:52). I follow him in assuming that *la parole* has structure also, but believe that the distinction can be usefully retained. Within Pike's system, it can perhaps be treated as a difference in focus.

a broader conception of the object of linguistic attention has increased, through concern with bilingual description, a unified structure of several dialects, the relations between standard and colloquial varieties of languages, and the like. But most such work remains tied to the conception of a single language as primary and the locus of structure. Gleason has shown concern for "generalizations about linguistic variation as a characteristic feature of language. Here is the basis for a second type of linguistic science" (1955, 285ff.). But this second type of linguistic science is seen as thoroughly statistical, in contrast to the qualitative nature of descriptive linguistics. The possibility for a second type of linguistic science that is structural is not conceived.

d. Multilingualism of course has never been denied, but the use of linguistic units in ethnological classification, a prevailing cultural rather than societal focus, an individuating outlook, all have favored thinking of one language = one culture.

The sources of these working assumptions cannot be traced here, except to suggest that they are an understandable part of the ideology of linguistics and anthropology during their development in the past two generations. One need has been to refute fallacies about primitive languages, to establish the quality of all languages *sub specie scientia,* and this has been in accord with the relativistic message of cultural anthropology. To pursue differences in function among languages might seem to give aid and comfort to the ethnocentric. Another need has been to secure the autonomy of the formal linguistic code as an object of study apart from race, culture, history, psychology, and to develop the appropriate methods for such study. The complexity and fascination of this task turns attention away from speech, and concentrates it on the regularities of the code. Not all variables can be handled at once. Part of the anthropological background has been noted in d. above. We should add that where the one language = one culture equation has been conceptually dissolved, it has been in terms of historical independence, rather than in terms of complex social *inter*dependence between, say, several languages in a single culture.

Now it is desirable to change these assumptions, and to take as a working framework: 1. the speech of a group constitutes a system; 2. speech and language vary cross-culturally in function; 3. the speech activity of a community is the primary object of attention. A descriptive grammar deals with this speech activity in one frame of reference, an ethnography of speaking in another. So (what amounts to a corollary, 3b), the latter must in fact include the former. The number of linguistic codes comprised in the ethnography of speaking of a group must be determined empirically.

Nothing said here should be taken to belittle linguistics and philology in their current practice. Malinowski, who advocated an ethnography of speech similar in spirit, if different in form, claimed a debt to the standard linguistic disciplines, yet treated them as grey dust against the fresh green of the field. For any work involving speech, however, these disciplines are indispensable (and Malinowski's efforts failed partly for lack of modern linguistics). Anthropology needs them and should foster them. What I am advocating is that anthropology recognize interests and needs of its own, and cultivate them; making use of linguistics, it should formulate its own ethnographic questions about speech and seek to answer them.[13]

We may be entering a period in which the pioneering studies of speech will be distributed among many disciplines. The new impetus in psychology is a case in point. A special opportunity, and responsibility, of anthropology is for comparative study of the patterning and functions of speech. This is a fundamental empirical problem for a science of behavior, one for which I propose the name "ethnography of speaking."

## REFERENCES

Aberle, David F. "The influence of linguistics on early culture and personality theory," in Essays in the Science of Culture in Honor of Leslie A. White, Gertrude E. Dole and Robert L. Carneiro, eds. New York: Crowell, 1960, pp. 1–29.

Barker, Roger G., and Louise Shedd. "Behavior units for the comparative study of cultures," in Studying Personality Cross-culturally. Bert Kaplan, ed. New York: Harper & Row, 1961, pp. 457–476.

Barker, Roger G., and Herbert F. Wright. Midwest and its Children, the Psychological Ecology of an American Town. New York: Harper & Row, 1955.

Bernstein, Basil. "Some sociological determinants of perception. An inquiry into subcultural differences." The British Journal of Sociology 9, no. 2 (1958): 159–174.

———. "A public language: some sociological implications of a linguistic form." The British Journal of Sociology 10, no. 4 (1959): 311–326.

———. "Language and social class (research note)." The British Journal of Sociology 11, no. 3 (1960): 271–276. (a)

———. "Sozio-Kulturelle Determinanten des Lernens. Mit besonderer Berucksichtigung der Rolle der Sprache." Kolner Zeitschrift fur Soziologie und Sozialpsychologie, Sonderheft 4 (1960): 52–79. (b)

———. "Aspects of language and learning in the genesis of the social process." Journal of Child Psychology and Psychiatry 1 (1961): 313–324.

Bloomfield, Leonard. "Literate and illiterate speech." American Speech 2 (1927): 432–439.

---

[13] Jakobson suggests the well known term "sociology of language" and insists that these concerns cannot be eliminated from linguistics. Linguistics and sociology should indeed develop this area, but so should anthropology, and for comparative perspective its contribution is essential. I am writing here chiefly to persuade that contribution. Moreover, I look for much of that contribution to come from those younger anthropologists who are reviving ethnography as a proud intellectual discipline, and for whom "ethnography," "ethnoscience," "ethnotheory" are significant and prestigeful terms. Hence the "ethnography" of my slogan. As for the "speaking," it reflects a theoretical bias that I hope shortly to be able to develop in more detail, relating it to a variety of other ideas, including some of Talcott Parsons'. I am especially sorry not to say more about Firth's work here. Only when the paper was long overdue at the printer did I discover that Firth had clearly posed the general problem of factors and functions of speech more than a generation ago (1935). In large part I have only come upon a concern already there in his writings, unfortunately unread, although I differ from his conceptualization at several points (Cf. Firth 1935, 1950, and Bursill-Hall 1960).

Boas, Franz. "Introduction," in *Handbook of American Indian Languages*. F. Boas, ed. (*Bureau of American Ethnology Bulletin* 40, pt. 1): 1–83, 1911.

Bühler, Karl. *Sprachtheorie* (Jena), 1934.

Burke, Kenneth. *A Grammar of Motives*. New York: Prentice-Hall, 1945.

———. *A Rhetoric of Motives*. New York: Prentice-Hall, 1951.

———. "Freedom and authority in the realm of the poetic imagination," in *Freedom and Authority in Our Time*. Lyman Bryson, Louis Finkelstein, R. M. MacIver, Richard McKeon, eds. Conference of Science, Philosophy and Religion. New York: Harper & Row, 1953, pp. 365–375.

———. "Linguistic approach to problems of education," in *Modern Philosphies and Education* (*Fifty-fourth yearbook of the National Society for the Study of Education*, Part I), Chicago, 1955, pp. 259–303.

———. *The Philosophy of Literary Form. Studies in Symbolic Action*. Rev. ed., abridged by the author. New York: Vintage Books, 1957.

———. "The poetic motive," *The Hudson Review* 11 (1958): 54–63.

Bursill-Hall, G. L. "Levels analysis: J. R. Firth's theories of linguistic analysis I." *The Journal of the Canadian Linguistic Association* 6, no. 2 (1960): 124–135.

Child, Irvin L. "Socialization," in *Handbook of Social Psychology*, Gardner Lindzey, ed. Cambridge: Addison-Wesley, 1954, pp. 655–692.

Conant, Francis P. "Jarawa kin systems of reference and address: a componential comparison." *Anthropological Linguistics* 3, no. 2 (1961): 19–33.

Conklin, Harold C. "Hanunóo color categories." *Southwestern Journal of Anthropology* 11, no. 4 (1955): 339–344.

———. "Linguistic play in its cultural setting." *Language* 35, no. 4 (1959): 631–636.

———. "Lexicographical treatment of folk taxonomies. Workpaper for Conference on Lexicography, Indiana University, Nov. 11–12, 1960," in *Problems in Lexicography*, Fred W. Householder and Sol Saporta, eds. (*Supplement of International Journal of American Linguistics*, vol. 28, no. 2—*Indiana University Research Center in Anthropology, Folklore and Linguistics, Publication 21*). Bloomington, 1962.

De Groot, A. "Structural linguistics and syntactic laws." *Words* 5 (1949): 1–12.

Elmendorf, William W., and Wayne Suttles. "Pattern and change in Halkomelem Salish dialects." *Anthropological Linguistics* 2, no. 7 (1960): 1–32.

Ferguson, Charles, and John J. Gumperz, eds. *Linguistic diversity in South Asia: Studies in Regional, Social, and Functional Variation* (*Indiana University Research Center in Anthropology, Folklore, and Linguistics, Publication 13*). Bloomington, 1960.

Firth, J. R. "The technique of semantics." *Transactions of the Philological Society*, 1935, pp. 7–33. Reprinted in his *Papers in Linguistics 1934–1951*. London: Oxford University Press, 1957.

———. "Personality and language in society." *Sociological Review* 42 (II): 8–14, 1950. Ledbury, England. Reprinted in his *Papers in Linguistics 1934–1951*. London: Oxford University Press, 1957, pp. 177–189.

Frake, Charles O. "The diagnosis of disease among the Subanun of Mindanao." *American Anthropologist* 63, no. 1 (1961): 113–132.

Gleason, H. A., Jr. *An Introduction to Descriptive Linguistics*. New York: Holt, Rinehart and Winston, 1955.

Goodenough, Ward H. "Componential analysis and the study of meaning." *Language* 32, no. 1 (1956): 195–216. (*a*)

Goodenough, Ward H. "Residence rules." *Southwestern Journal of Anthropology* 12 (1956): 22–37. (*b*)

———. "Cultural anthropology and linguistics," in *Report of the Seventh Annual Round Table Meeting on Linguistics and Language Study,* Paul L. Garvin, ed. (*Georgetown University Monograph Series on Language and Linguistics,* no. 9). Washington D.C., 1957, 167–173.

Gumperz, John J. "Speech variation and the study of Indian civilization." *American Anthropologist* 63, no. 5 (1961): 976–988.

Haas, Mary. "Men's and women's speech in Koasati." *Language* 20 (1944): 142–149.

———. "Interlingual word taboos." *American Anthropologist* 53 (1951): 338–344.

Hall, Edward T. *The Silent Language.* New York: Doubleday, 1959.

Hallowell, A. Irving. "Culture, personality, and society," in *Anthropology Today, an Encyclopedic Inventory.* Prepared under the chairmanship of A. L. Kroeber. Chicago: University of Chicago Press, 1953, pp. 597–620.

Haugen, Einar. "The semantics of Icelandic orientation." *Word* 13, no. 3 (1957): 447–459.

Hill, Trevor. "Institutional linguistics." *Orbis* 7 (1958): 441–455 (Louvain).

Hjelmslev, Louis. "Dans quelle mesure les significations des mots peuvent-elles être considérées comme formant une structure?" *Reports for the Eighth International Congress of Linguists* 2, 268–286 (Oslo), 1957.

Hockett, Charles F. *A Course in Modern Linguistics.* New York: Macmillan, 1958.

Hoijer, Harry. "The structure of the noun in the Apachean languages." *Actes du XXVIIIe Congrès International des Américanistes (Paris 1947).* Paris: Société des Américanistes, 1948, pp. 173–184.

Hymes, Dell H. "Field work in linguistics and anthropology" (Annotated bibliography), *Studies in Linguistics* 14 (1959): 82–91.

———. "Ob-Ugric metrics." *Anthropos* 55 (1960): 574–576. (*a*)

———. "Phonological aspects of style: some English sonnets," in *Style in Language.* T. A. Sebeok, ed. Cambridge: The Technology Press; New York: Wiley, 1960, pp. 109–131. (*b*)

———. "On typology of cognitive styles in language (with examples from Chinookan)." *Anthropological Linguistics* 3, no. 1 (1961): 22–54. (*a*)

———. "Linguistic aspects of cross-cultural personality study," in *Studying Personality Cross-culturally.* Bert Kaplan, ed. New York: Harper & Row, 1961, pp. 313–359. (*b*)

———. "Functions of speech: an evolutionary approach," in *Anthropology and Education,* Fred Gruber, ed. Philadelphia, University of Pennsylvania Press, 1961. (*c*)

———. "Abstract of Vachek (1959)." *International Journal of American Linguistics* 27 (1961): 166–167. (*d*)

Jacobs, Melville. *Kalapuya texts (University of Washington Publications in Anthropology,* 11). Seattle, 1945.

Jakobson, Roman. "Concluding statement: linguistics and poetics," in *Style in Language.* T. A. Sebeok, ed. Cambridge: The Technology Press; New York: Wiley, 1960, pp. 350–373.

Jakobson, Roman, and Morris Halle. *Fundamentals of Language.* The Hague: Mouton, 1956.

Joos, Martin. "Semology: a linguistic theory of meaning." *Studies in Linguistics* 13, no. 3 (1958): 53–70.

Kenyon, John S. "Cultural levels and functional varieties of English." *College English* 10 (1948): 31–36. Reprinted in *Readings in Applied English Linguistics,* H. B. Allen, ed. New York: Appleton-Century-Crofts, pp. 215–222.

Lantis, Margaret. "Vernacular culture." *American Anthropologist* 62 (1960): 202–216.

Lévi-Strauss, Claude. *Anthropologie Structurale.* Paris: Librairie Plon, 1958.

Lounsbury, Floyd G. "A semantic analysis of the Pawnee kinship usage." *Language* 32, no. 1 (1956): 168–194.

Lowie, Robert H. *The Crow Indians.* New York: Holt, Rinehart and Winston, 1935.

Luria, A. R. "The directive function of speech I, II." *Word* 15 (1959): 341–352, 453–464.

Luria, A. R., and F. Ia. Yurovich. *Speech and the Development of Mental Processes in the Child.* J. Simon, trans. London: Staples Press, 1959.

Mahl, G. F. "Exploring emotional states by content analysis," in *Trends in Content Analysis,* I. Pool, ed. Urbana: University of Illinois Press, 1959, pp. 83–130.

Malinowski, Bronislaw. *Coral gardens and their magic II: The language of magic and gardening.* London, 1935.

Martinet, André. *Economie des changements phonétiques (Bibliotheca Romanica, series prima, Manualia et Commentationes,* X) Berne, Editions A. Francke, 1955.

Nagel, Ernst. "Teleological explanation and teleological systems," in *Vision and action,* Sidney Ratner, ed. New Brunswick: Rutgers University Press, 1953.

———. "A formalization of functionalism," in his *Logic Without Metaphysics, and Other Essays in the Philosophy of Science.* Glencoe: Free Press, 1956.

Newman, Stanley S. "Linguistic aspects of Yokuts style," in *Yokuts and Western Mono Myths,* Ann Gayton and S. S. Newman, eds. *University of California Publications, Anthropological Records,* 5), 1940, 4–8.

Ogden, C. K., and I. A. Richards. *The Meaning of Meaning.* London, 1923.

Pike, Kenneth L. *Language in Relation to a Unified Theory of the Structure of Human Behavior,* I, II, III Preliminary edition. Glendale: Summer Institute of Linguistics, 1954, 1955, 1960.

Pittenger, Robert, Charles F. Hockett, and J. S. Danehy. *The First Five Minutes.* Ithaca: Paul Martineau, 1960.

Riffaterre, Michael. "Criteria for style analysis." *Word* 15 (1959): 154–174.

Robins, R. H. "Linguistics and anthropology." *Man* 59 (1959): 175–178.

Sapir, Edward. "Communication." *Encyclopedia of the Social Sciences* 4 (1931): 78–81).

———. "Language." *Encyclopedia of the Social Sciences* 9 (1933): 155–169.

Sinclair, Angus. *The Conditions of Knowing.* London: Routledge and Kegan Paul, 1951.

Slama-Cazacu, Tatiana. *Langage et contexte.* The Hague: Mouton, 1961.

Smith, M. G. "The social functions and meaning of Hausa praise singing." *Africa* 27 (1957): 27–44.

Snell, Bruno. *Der Aufbau der Sprache.* Hamburg: Claassen Verlag, 1952.

Uldall, Hans. *Outline of Glossematics, I (Travaux du Cercle Linguistique de Copenhague,* X). Nordisk Sprog Kulturforlag, 1957.

Vachek, Josef. "The London group of linguists." *Sborník Prací Filosofické Fakulty Brenské University, Rocnik* 8 (Rada Jazykovidná, A7), 106–133, 1959.

Voegelin, C. F. "Casual and noncasual utterances within unified structure," in *Style in Language,* T. A. Sebeok, ed. Cambridge: The Technology Press; New York: Wiley, 1960, pp. 57–68.

Weinreich, Uriel. *Languages in Contact.* Linguistic Circle of New York, 1953.

Wells, Rulon. "Is a structural treatment of meaning possible?" *Reports for the Eighth International Congress of Linguists* 1 (1957): 197–209 (Oslo).

Winter, Werner. "Review of Bruno Snell." *Der Aufbau der Sprache,* in *Language* 29 (1953): 193–195.

Wolff, Hans. "Intelligibility and inter-ethnic attitudes." *Anthropological Linguistics* 1, no. 3 (1959): 34–41.

# Linguistic and Social Interaction in Two Communities

## John J. Gumperz

### THE UNIVERSE OF SOCIOLINGUISTIC ANALYSIS

Sociolinguistics has been described as the study of verbal behavior in terms of the social characteristics of speakers, their cultural background, and the ecological properties of the environment in which they interact (Hymes 1962; Ervin-Tripp 1964). In this paper we will explore some of the formal aspects of this relationship. We will examine the language usage of specific groups and attempt to relate it to linguistically distinct dialects and styles on the one hand and variables employed in the study of social interaction on the other.

The raw material for our study is the distribution of linguistic forms in everyday speech. As is usual in descriptive analysis, these forms are first described in terms of their own internal patterning at the various strata (phonemic, morphemic, etc.) of linguistic structure (Lamb 1964; Gleason 1964). Ultimately, however, the results of this analysis will have to be related to social categories. This condition imposes some important restrictions on the way in which data are gathered. Since social interaction always takes place within particular groups, linguistic source data will have to be made commensurable with such groups. We therefore choose as our universe of analysis a speech community: any human aggregate characterized by regular and frequent interaction over a significant span of time and set off from other such aggregates by differences in the frequency of interaction. Within this socially defined universe forms are selected for study primarily in terms of who uses them and when, regardless of purely grammatical similarities and differences. If two grammatically distinct alternatives are employed within the same population, both will have to be included. On the other hand, in those cases where socially significant differences in behavior are signaled by grammatically minor lexical or phonemic correlates, the latter cannot be omitted from consideration.

### Verbal Repertoires

Procedures such as these enable us to isolate the verbal repertoire, the totality of linguistic forms regularly employed in the course of socially significant interaction. Since spoken communication of all kinds is describable by a finite set of

**283**

rules which underlie the formation of all possible sentences, verbal repertoires must have structure. The structure of verbal repertoires, however, differs from ordinary descriptive grammars. It includes a much greater number of alternants, reflecting contextual and social differences in speech. Linguistic interaction, as Bernstein (1964) has pointed out, can be most fruitfully viewed as a process of decision making, in which speakers select from a range of possible expressions. The verbal repertoire then contains all the accepted ways of formulating messages. It provides the weapons of everyday communication. Speakers choose among this arsenal in accordance with the meanings they wish to convey.

## Grammatical and Social Restraints on Language Choice

Ultimately it is the individual who makes the decision, but his freedom to select is always subject both to grammatical and social restraints. Grammatical restraints relate to the intelligibility of sentences; social restraints relate to their acceptability. In expressing his opinion about the weather, Smith might say, "It looks as if it isn't going to rain today," or "It looks like it ain't gonna rain today." Both messages have similar referents and, in comparison to ungrammatical sentences like "Its look it like gonna ain't rain today," are equally likely to be understood. Since linguistic analysis deals with grammatical restraints on language choice, alternations such as the above are not considered part of the linguistic structure. If they are listed at all they are relegated to the realm of free variation. What then can be the reason for their persistence and what is their function in the overall communication process?

If the choice among them were completely a matter of individual freedom, the connotations of his message would be idiosyncratic to the speaker and this would result in misunderstanding. The power of selection is therefore limited by commonly agreed-on conventions which serve to categorize speech forms as informal, technical, vulgar, literary, humorous, etc. To be sure, such conventions are subject to considerably greater variations than grammatical restraints, but wherever they are well established, the style of a message also gives advance information about its content. When we hear, "Mr. President, Ladies and Gentlemen," we suspect that we are in for something like a formal address or a political speech. We can turn on the radio and recognize a news broadcast without actually understanding the words that are being spoken. In listening to someone talking on the telephone, we can make a good guess as to whether he is talking to a friend or taking care of routine business. The more we know about a particular society, the more efficiently we can communicate in it. Speech styles provide advance information about the nature of messages and speed up communication in somewhat the same way that titles and tables of contents help in reading a book. The social etiquette of language choice is learned along with grammatical rules and once internalized it becomes a part of our linguistic equipment. Conversely, stylistic choice becomes a problem when we are away from our accustomed social surroundings. Expressions which are customary in our own group might quite easily offend our interlocutor and jeopardize our mutual relationship by mislabeling messages.

When regarded from this point of view, social restraints on language choice are an important component of the relationship between signs and their meanings. Every message must conform to the grammatical restraints of the verbal repertoire but it is always interpreted in accordance with social restraints. As Bernstein (1964) says, "Between language and speech there is social structure." This connection must be statable in terms of regular rules allocating particular sets of forms to particular kinds of interaction. These rules should allow us to predict which of the several possible alternative realizations of messages is most likely to be employed in any instance.

## Social Relationships and Social Occasions

Our discussion of social interaction will employ the term social relationship to refer to regular patterns or types of interaction. Every society has a finite number of such relationships. They are abstracted from everyday behavior in somewhat the same way that linguistic forms are derived from language texts. Some common examples are: The father-son relationship, salesman-customer relationship, husband-wife relationship, etc. All such types of interaction are carried on by individuals, but in analyzing social relationships we think of participants not as persons but as occupants of statuses defined in terms of rights and obligations. An individual occupies a number of such statuses. He may be a father, an employer, a passenger on a public conveyance, a member of a club, etc. Each is associated with fairly well-defined norms of behavior. Any one social relationship focuses on one of these while others remain suspended.

As Goffman (1963) has shown, social acts always form part of broader social settings—more or less closely defined behavioral routines which are regarded as separate in a society. Our usual round of activities is segmented into a number of such routines: we eat breakfast, travel to the office, participate in meetings, go out on dates, etc. Social occasions limit the participants and more importantly limit the kinds of social relationships that may be brought into play. They are in turn divisible into subroutines, encounters, or speech events (Goffman 1964, Hymes 1961). On our way to work we may first turn to our neighbor and then strike up a conversation with a stranger. During a meeting we may step aside with one or two participants to talk about a side issue. While generally related to broader social settings, encounters more narrowly restrict the selection of social relationships and thus bear a somewhat closer relation to modes of acting and speaking.

Let us now examine some common variants such as "dine—eat," "house—mansion," "talk—lecture," or even "going—goin'." All such sets refer to broadly similar classes of objects and activities. They share some attributes, but differ in other more specific features. Dining and eating both indicate consumption of food, but the former tends to imply more elaborate menus and more rigidly defined etiquette than the latter. Similarly mansions are more spacious and better furnished than houses. Beyond this, however, the difference in referents also carries some important implications about the social positions of the actors concerned. Not everyone can "dine." Certainly not two laborers during a dinner break, no matter how well prepared the food they consume and how good their table manners. To use dine in their case might be appropriate in jest, but not in normal conversation.

Alternation of this type may thus be viewed from two perspectives. In the realm of semantics it selects among subclasses of referents. In the sphere of social interaction it reflects the positions actors wish to assume relative to each other, i.e., the quality of their relationship. Whenever a set of linguistic forms is interchangeable within the same frame without significant change in meaning, it is this second aspect which becomes most important. In the course of any one encounter mutual relationships are constantly defined and redefined in accordance with the speaker's ultimate aim. But each encounter sets bounds to this type of variation. Social restraints of language choice express the norm defining such bounds. If he violates these, an actor risks misunderstanding.

## Co-occurrence Restrictions

Aside from their purely social aspects, restraints on language choice have one other important set of characteristics. This concerns the linguistic relationship among the constituents of a statement. An alternant once chosen sets limits to what can follow within the same utterance. In the example of alternation given above, the form "ain't" must be followed by "gonna"; similarly, "as if" in the first example requires a following "isn't going to."

Speech events differ in the rigidity with which such co-occurrence restrictions apply. In some cases (e.g., public ceremonies, religious rituals, etc.) modes of speaking are narrowly prescribed; in others (e.g., conversations among personal friends, party chitchat, etc.) there may be scope for a wide range of alternate sequences. Regardless of particular instances, however, discourse of all types always shows some form of co-occurrence restrictions. From the point of view of linguistic structure, it is important to note that co-occurrence restrictions apply, not to any particular segment within an utterance, but always to the utterance as a whole. The informal ending "-in" in items such as "going" could hardly appear with learned verbs like "purchase." Substitution of a learned alternant for a colloquial word also requires elimination of colloquial pronunciations. Co-occurrence rules affect all linguistic strata (Joos 1960). They simultaneously condition the morphological and phonological realizations of messages. This property enables us to segment verbal repertoires into distinct speech varieties. A verbal repertoire then is not simply composed of linguistic forms. It is always a set of varieties, each with its own internal grammatical structure.

A survey of the literature on bilingualism and dialectal variation from the point of view of language choice shows that linguistic interaction in all communities involves alternation among distinct varieties. But this is not to say that the same or similar connotational meanings are realized through grammatically equivalent choices in all cases. In an American community, the substitution of "goin' " for "going" may signal a switch from formality to informality (Fischer 1958) : in France, on the other hand, like ends may be accomplished by selecting *tu* rather than *vous* (Brown and Gilman 1960). In Java, the rules of linguistic etiquette may require alternate use of High Javanese, Low Javanese, and local dialect forms (Geertz 1961). Whenever several languages or dialects appear regularly as weapons of language choice, they form a behavioral whole, regardless of grammatical distinctness, and must be considered constituent varieties of the same verbal repertoire.

## Compartmentalized and Fluid Repertoires

The concept of the verbal repertoire allows us to deal with speech communities of all types. Monolingual and multilingual repertoires can be analysed within the same general framework. They differ in internal grammatical diversity and more importantly in the co-occurrence rules. In multilingual repertoires, co-occurrence rules tend to be more rigid. Verbal behavior seems to be neatly divided among a series of compartments: choice of an initial form commits the speaker to a particular line of approach. The monolingual repertoires, on the other hand, show a greater degree of flexibility. Different types of verbal behavior seem to shade off into one another.

Allocation of speech varieties to social relationships, co-occurrence rules, and internal language distance provide the structural criteria for the analysis of speech behavior. As indices, these are independent of particular languages and cultures. They form a general framework for the study of speech communities of all types in terms which are commensurable with the anthropologist's social structure.

## SOCIAL ORGANIZATION IN KHALAPUR[1]

The data for our analysis are drawn from Khalapur, an agricultural village about 80 miles north of Delhi, India, in the Gangetic *doab* (the plain between the Ganges and Jumna rivers), and Hemnesberget (Hemnes), a small commercial settlement in the Rana fjord of Northern Norway just south of the Arctic circle.

The Gangetic *doab* is one of the most fertile and densely settled regions of northwestern India. Since the turn of the century, it has developed into a major sugar producing region. With its population of about 3,000, Khalapur is somewhat larger than most neighboring villages, but its economy and social organization are typically rural. The main Delhi railroad and a major highway pass within three miles of Kalapur; and two industrial sugar mills six miles away employing several hundred persons consume most of the village cane crop. Until

---

1 For more detailed ethnographic data on Khalapur, see Hitchcock and Minturn 1963.

recently, the village remained quite separate from the interurban communication network. There are many signs that this isolation is beginning to break down. Community development is showing its effect and a recently established Intercollege (Junior College) provides instruction up to the college sophomore level to students from many surrounding localities. Paved roads have recently been constructed, and a regular *tonga* service (horse-drawn taxi) now connects with the railroad.

Khalapur inhabitants are divided by profound differences in ritual status, wealth, political power, occupation, and education, affecting every aspect of daily interaction. In the ritual sphere, 31 distinct castes or extended kin groups are recognized. Ninety percent of these are Hindu, and ten percent are Muslim. Each is set off from its neighbors by differences in marriage patterns and ritual practices. Castes may be ranked along the usual ritual prestige scale with Brahmans, Rajputs (Warrior-landholders), and merchants at the top, and untouchable Chamars (landless laborers) and Sweepers at the bottom.

Distribution of wealth and political power shows only partial agreement with this ranking. Rajputs are the dominant caste. They constitute more than 40% of the population and own 90% of the land. All others, including Brahmans, are dependent on them for their subsistence. But Rajputs are in turn sectioned off by residence patterns into seven neighborhoods. Political and economic control in each neighborhood is held by a few wealthy families. As a result of their wealth, political power, and education, these families have become an aristocracy set off from their poorer Rajput neighbors, whose holdings are small compared to theirs. These latter are often tenants and may be economically no better off than the bulk of the lower caste population. Wealthy families often maintain friendlier relations with powerful merchants or artisans and with other landholding castes from neighboring villages than with their poorer caste brothers.

The new intercollege and the resulting increase in educational opportunities have added another dimension to the ritual and socio-economic distinctions. Education is now within the reach of all groups. The majority of students still come from the Rajputs and upper castes, but now both the poor and the wealthy have access to schooling. Many lower caste persons have obtained government or commercial employment and have become the equals of the influential Rajput families in education and general sophistication.

Although the recent changes in technology and education have begun to loosen the rigidity of intergroup separation, social stratification is still an integral part of the village value system and is symbolized in a variety of ways in dress, posture, and everyday demeanor. Untouchable women are readily recognizable by their *lahnga* (skirts) and their silver jewelry. Educated men tend to wear Western type shirts and pajamas or khaki trousers, while the ordinary farmer wears the traditional kurta and dhoti, which may be made of mill cloth or of material grown and woven within the village. Others oriented towards Congress Party politics are beginning to replace their locally made cloth with the homespun material produced in the Gandhi centers and sold through the local Congress organization stores.

Whenever two or more people sit together on the cots which serve for most seating, rigid seating rules are observed. If all are members of one caste, the oldest person sits at the head of the cot (which has a special name); others sit next in order of prestige ranking. If a Brahman is present he will be offered the head seat. Lower caste persons and sometimes also poor Rajputs will sit on the floor and untouchables at a slight distance from the group. Wealthy merchants or artisans or other distinguished visitors however may find a seat on a special cot. Similar patterns apply also to seating at a feast where the upper castes tend to sit together in an order determined partly by ritual status and partly by wealth whereas the poorer lower castes sit aside in their own separate place. Only caste brothers may smoke from the same hookah (water-pipe) and they do so in order of rank. Special pipes may be kept for respected guests from other castes.

In speaking, each caste is designated by a special caste title and each person by a term of reference which usually reflects his caste affiliation or his occupation. Relatively strict rules of deference seem to apply to interaction with everyone except one's closest friends and one's family members. Since the term "friend" may be synonymous with "relative," the two groups tend to overlap. So great is the guardedness which governs interaction that even an age mate from an adjoining neighborhood is accorded respect behavior and is addressed by his title rather than by his family name.


## KHALAPUR VERBAL REPERTOIRE[2]

### Local Speech and Standard Language

Intra-village communication in Khalapur is carried on primarily in the local dialect (Grierson 1916). The official standard language, however, is Hindi and villagers list themselves as speakers of Hindi for census purposes. The standard is learned either in elementary school, through residence in cities or through outside contacts. Educated persons, village leaders, businessmen, and all those who deal regularly with urbanites speak it. In village interaction Hindi symbolizes the new status relationships created by the increasing involvement of villagers in state politics, modern commerce, village development, and state education. Norms call for the use of Hindi in contacts with representatives of the post-independence elite, as well as in the classroom and on the lecture platform. Those individuals who do not speak Hindi modify their speech with appropriate loan words when the social occasion demands. Purely local relationships, on the other hand, always require the dialect and everyone, including

---

2 A detailed analysis of Khalapur phonology is given in Gumperz 1958b. Our phonetic transcription here differs slightly from the above. The vowels ə, i, and u are short; vowels ī, ū, e, o, æ, ɔ, and a are long. For discussion of the various subvarieties of Hindi in the Hindi language area, see Gumperz 1960.

highly educated villagers, uses it to symbolize participation in these relationships. The dialect and standard Hindi define the linguistic bounds of the verbal repertoire. A portion of the grammatical characteristics of this repertoire are common to all speech varieties. There is, for example, a common core of phonemes which are realized by the same pronunciations regardless of which style is spoken. Similarly the basic grammatical categories of noun and verb inflection are shared. But we also find a significant number of differences and these constitute the inventory of structural variants from which speakers select in accordance with situational and co-occurrence restraints. Some examples of these are given below.

On the level of phonology, the dialect shows a special set of contrasts between retroflex and nonretroflex /n/ and /ṇ/ and /l/ and /ḷ/ and between retroflex flap /ṛ/ and retroflex stop /ḍ/., as well as a special set of diphthongs consisting of vowels followed by a short up glide: /ūi/ /āi/ /ōi/. The Hindi distinction between alveolar /s/ and palatal /š/ is lacking. Another dialect feature is the frequency of medial double consonants in words such as dialect (K) *loṭṭa* 'jug' *vs.* Hindi (H) *loṭa*. Word pairs resulting from this difference in phonemic distribution are frequently mentioned in popular stereotypes of dialect speech. Morphological differences are most frequent in the phonological realization of shared morphemic categories, i.e., in inflectional endings. The dialect lacks a feminine plural suffix, e.g., (K) *bhæs* 'female buffaloes,' (H) *bhæsē*. The plural oblique case suffix is (K) o and (H) õ, e.g., (K) *bhæso-ka* 'of the female buffaloes' (H) *bhæsō-ka*. Dialect verbs have the infinitive suffix -*n* and the past participle ending -*ya* in place of Hindi ending -*na* and past participle -*a*, e.g., (K) *bolan,* 'to speak' (H) *bolna*, (K) *bolya* 'spoke' (H) *bola*. There are syntactical differences in the use of inflected subjunctive forms, e.g., (K) *bolœ* 'he speaks' when Hindi calls for a complex construction of present participle plus auxiliary, e.g., (H) *bolta hœ* 'he speaks.' Striking differences occur in the system of function words, i.e., grammatically important pronouns, adverbs of place and manner, conjunctions, post-positions (corresponding to prepositions in English), e.g.:

| Dialect | Hindi | English |
| --- | --- | --- |
| o | wo or wah | he |
| wa | wo or wah | she |
| mhara | həmara | our |
| -lo | -tak | until |
| -tæ | -se | from |
| ib | əb | now |
| inghæ | yəhā | here |
| təlæ | nīce | below |
| kyukkər | kæsa | how |
| kətek | kitna | how much |

## Additional Speech Varieties

The Khalapur repertoire is subdivided into several additional speech varieties with somewhat more limited occurrence. In a previous study, several minority subdialects were described which reflect the social isolation of the three local untouchable groups (Gumperz 1958). These groups are segregated residentially, wear special clothing and ornaments, and are in many ways culturally distinct. Here we will deal with superposed variants (i.e., variants occurring within a single population) in the speech of the majority of Rajputs and touchable castes. Members of these groups distinguish between two forms of the vernacular: *moṭī bolī* and *saf bolī*. The former is used primarily within the family circle, with children and with close relatives as well as with animals and untouchable servants. It symbolizes the informality that attends these relationships. *Saf bolī*, on the other hand, reflects the guardedness of the relationships outside the immediate friendship group and the respect towards elders. *Moṭī bolī* contains the greatest number of purely local features. Among its phonetic characteristics are: a special high allophone [ɨ] of the phoneme /ə/ occurring before /i/ in the next syllable; a pronounced pitch glide on the vowel preceding the medial voiced aspirate in words such as *pīdha* 'steel'; a very pronounced up glide in the phonetic realization of diphthongs /ūi/ /ai/ /oi/. Morphologically this style shows greater frequency of deviant function words of the type listed in the dialect column above. In *saf bolī*, on the other hand, the above phonetic features are closer to standard Hindi and dialect function words such as *kətek* and *kyukkər* tend to be replaced by their Hindi equivalents.

Yet another speech variety characterizes interaction of villagers with merchants in the lócal bazaar, wandering performers, and priests—the traditional hinge groups of rural India. This regional speech variety is grammatically intermediate between the local vernacular and Hindi. In pronunciation it shows no diphthongs of the type /ui/ but retains the retroflex/nonretroflex nasal and lateral distinction. In grammar the Hindi-like present tense construction is employed and Hindi function words prevail. There are furthermore three varieties of what is ordinarily called Hindi. Before independence Urdu served as a medium of instruction and some of the elder village residents still employ Urdu forms (Gumperz 1960) in interaction with strangers. Such usages have a distinctly old-fashioned flavor. Village Hindi itself has a conversational and an oratorical style. The latter is characterized by a large number of Sanskrit loan words which affect both the lexicon and the system of functors (e.g., conversational *aur* 'and,' oratorical *tətha* 'and'), and by initial and final consonant clusters in words such as *kriṣṇa* 'name of the God,' *gram* 'village' (conversational *gāw*). In phonology this style shows many special initial and final consonant clusters. The oratorical style, as its name implies, serves as the norm for public lectures and for some classroom lectures. It is used on such social occasions even though the audience often does not understand the Sanskrit expressions. Intelligibility is achieved by interspersing such lectures with explanatory passages in conversational Hindi or in the regional dialect.

## SOCIAL ORGANIZATION IN HEMNESBERGET[3]

Hemnesberget (or Hemnes), is a commercial settlement of about 1,300 inhabitants in the Rana Fjord of Northern Norway. Until the 19th century, the Rana area, located in one of the most sparsely settled regions in Europe, was directly controlled by a small aristocracy of merchants, landowners, and government officials who controlled the land and monopolized the trading rights. Vast differences in wealth and education separated them from the majority of the population, who were their tenants, fishermen, and estate laborers. In the late 19th century, trade monopolies were abolished and land turned over to settlers. The region is now one of small farmers, who earn their livelihood through dairying, lumbering, fishing, and boatbuilding.

Government-sponsored economic development during the last three decades has turned the Rana area into an important iron and steel producing center. The area of Mo-i-Rana at the head of the fjord has grown from about 1,000 inhabitants in the 1920's to almost 20,000 in 1960, largely through immigration from southern Norway and Trondheim. The city reflects this growth in its several department stores, hotels, restaurants, and cinemas. A railroad from Trondheim to Mo-i-Rana and on to Bodø was recently completed and the road system is steadily improving. But Hemnes remains relatively unaffected by these developments. Although regular once-a-day boat service to Mo and two daily buses to the nearby railroad station are available, and a few people commute to Mo by private auto or motorcycle, for the bulk of local residents, life centers in and around Hemnes. They form their friendships primarily with other local inhabitants. Our interviews showed that events in Mo-i-Rana or even in neighboring small towns are only of marginal interest to them.

With the disappearance of the earlier aristocratic upper classes, the bulk of the inhabitants now stem from similar social backgrounds. The social system shows a fluidity of class structure quite similar to that described by Barnes for Southern Norway (1954). Extremes of poverty and wealth are absent. Occupationally the residents fall into four groups: artisans and workers, small shopkeepers and farmers, large merchants, and officials. These differences in occupation carry with them some real distinctions in authority. Yet for all but a few individuals who tend to identify with the older aristocratic classes, the local value system

---

3 Ethnographic data cited is based largely on the work of Jan-Petter Blom (1964), although the author takes full responsibility for the interpretation presented here. In local usage the term Hemnes refers to both the town and the entire region, while Hemnesberget is the name of the town proper. In the present paper the two terms are sometimes used interchangeably.

tends to minimize such distinctions, the usual way of expressing this sentiment being, "we are all equal here in Hemnes."

## Hemnesberget Verbal Repertoire

The internal social homogeneity of Hemnes is reflected in the somewhat lessened compartmentalization of the verbal repertoire. Inhabitants speak both a local dialect, Ranamàl (R), and a standard. The former is the native tongue and the chief medium of intravillage communication. But whereas the Khalapur vernacular is divided into several linguistically distinct subdialects and superposed speech varieties, the Hemnes variety shows only minor distinctions relating to residence patterns and generational discrepancies rather than rigid social cleavages.

The Hemnes standard is Bokmàl (B) (or Riksmàl as it used to be called), one of the two officially recognized literary languages in Norway (Haugen 1959). Bokmàl is universally accepted throughout Northern Norway, while the other literary language, Nynorsk (formerly Landsmàl), is more current in central and western coastal districts. Children learn the standard in school and in church and through regular exposure to radio broadcasts. Since education is universal and Hemnes residents are highly literate, Bokmal can be said to be somewhat more firmly established in Hemnes than Hindi in Khalapur.

In spite of their familiarity with Bokmàl, villagers take considerable pride in the dialect as a vehicle for spoken discourse. Unlike its Khalapur equivalent, Ranamal is not simply an in-group tongue, regarded as out of place in urban contexts and not worthy of serious scholarly attention. Hemnes residents consider their local speech suitable for oral interaction both in their home surroundings and outside. Although they may often employ Bokmàl in their dealings in the city they insist on their right to use the dialect, to show, as they put it "that we are not ashamed of our origin." Local norms thus confine Bokmàl to a very limited number of social relationships, relating to literature, church, and some types of interaction with nonlocals.

## Grammatical Differences

Some of the more important grammatical distinctions between Bokmàl (B) and Ranamàl (R) are listed below. The dialect has a series of alveolar palatalized consonants /tj dj nj lj/ which contrast with their nonpalatalized counterparts. Some differences in the distribution of vowel phonemes are frequent correspondences between (B) /i/ and (R) /e/ and (B) /e/ and (R) /æ/, e.g., *men/mœn* 'but' and *til/tel* 'to, towards.' As in Khalapur, broader grammatical categories are shared and distinctions occur primarily in the phonological realizations of particular allomorphs. Thus the plural suffix with nouns like *hœst* 'horse' is (B) -er and (R) -a. The present tense for the verb 'to come' is (R) *œm* and (B) *komer*. Other important differences affect commonly employed function words:

| Bokmål | Ranamål | English |
|---|---|---|
| dere | dɔk | you (plural) |
| han | hanj | he |
| vem | kem | who |
| wa | ke | what |
| vordan | ke . . . lesn | how |
| til | tel | towards |
| fra | ifrɔ | from |
| mellom | imelja | in between |

## LINGUISTIC CHARACTERISTICS OF KHALAPUR AND HEMNES REPERTOIRES

Comparison of our two verbal repertoires with respect to the internal linguistic distinctions among constituent varieties brings out some interesting points of similarity. Ultimately verbal repertoires are socially defined concepts, but it would seem from our study and from other work along similar lines (Gumperz 1964) that they also have certain linguistic characteristics which set them off from verbal repertoires in other societies. These characteristics stem from the fact that internal differences tend to be localized in specific strata of structure. We have already suggested that there is considerable overlap in our two verbal repertoires. In terms of the stratificational model of language structure proposed by Lamb (1964), this overlap tends to be greatest in the sememic (semantic categories) and lexemic (grammatical categories) strata and in phonetics. Major form classes and inflectional categories as well as word order rules seem almost identical within our two repertoires. In the realm of phonology, the totality of distinct segments can be divided into two sets: a common core, i.e., a set of obligatory distinctions which everyone in the community makes, and a set of optional distinctions. The phonetic realizations of alternants in constituent varieties vary only with respect to the optional distinctions and not with respect to the obligatory distinctions. Thus in (K) *katek* and (H) *kitna*, 'how much,' the allophones of /k/ and /t/ are the same in each case, and (K) /ə/ is phonetically the same as (H) /ə/ in *həmara* 'our.' In Hemnes also, (B) *til* and (R) *tel* 'to' share the same realizations of initial /t/ and the /e/ of *tel* is the same as the /e/ in (B) *vem* 'who.' Similar instances of phonetic overlap were also noted by Ferguson (1959).

Aside from optional distinctions in phonology, linguistic differences among constituent varieties seem to be concentrated largely in what Lamb (1964) calls the morphemic stratum (the phonological realizations of lexemic categories). It would seem that wherever alternation among linguistic variants by the same populations creates grammatical overlap, this overlap provides the structural basis for the isolation of verbal repertoires.

## SPEECH VARIATION AND SOCIAL RELATIONSHIPS
## IN KHALAPUR AND HEMNES

The fact that verbal repertoires in both communities are compartmentalized has some important social implications. From the point of view of local populations it means that many of the activities that individuals might be called on to engage in require considerable linguistic as well as technical skill. To talk to a government official, or to deal with a local merchant, a Khalapur villager must control distinct rules of linguistic etiquette. He must be able to manipulate not one, but several grammatical systems. In all societies there are certain specialized activities which require special vocabularies. Scientific and legal discourse as well as communication among artisans would be difficult without carefully defined technical vocabularies. Furthermore, oral and written communications require different types of syntax. But phonemic and morphophonemic differences of the type found in our study are hardly related to the nature of the activities they symbolize. They constitute culture restraints imposed upon interaction above and beyond what can be justified on purely technical grounds and are thus ritual in the sense in which this word is used by Leach (1954:10).

Ritual barriers to interaction affect different spheres of activity in our two communities. In Hemnes they apply only to a limited number of scholarly, literary, administrative, and religious relationships, while the bulk of intravillage communication reflects the lack of rigidly defined stratification within the community. In Khalapur, on the other hand, ritual barriers affect every aspect of community life. They are part of the elaborate rules of etiquette which are also evident in dress, seating, and smoking, and seem to mirror the guardedness which attends the bulk of interpersonal relations. In contrast to Hemnes, Khalapur village life is not a single whole, but rather a broad grouping of sets of distinct relationships signaled by differences in linguistic and other modes of behavior. The details of this grouping are in themselves of interest, since they provide interesting insights into social structure. Thus servants as well as junior kin may be addressed in *moṭī bolī*. The two statuses seems to share some common characteristics. Similarly religious, political, and educational activities all require the oratorical style and are thus regarded as related. The difference between Hindi and the regional dialect suggests a status distinction between two types of nonlocals: traditional merchants and itinerants and modern businessmen and government officials. More detailed analysis of this type should furnish fruitful insights into native status definitions.

## LINGUISTIC INTERACTION IN KHALAPUR AND HEMNES

Our discussion of verbal repertoires so far has dealt only with normative aspects of language choice. We have described the constituent speech varieties in terms of the social relationships they normally symbolize. Behavior in actual encounters, however, is not always predictable on the basis of these associations alone. Just as individual words may be used in meanings which are different from their primary referents, so also speech styles need not always signal the exact social relationships with which they are associated. Thus speakers may employ the word 'fox' either in its primary meaning to designate an animal or to refer to a human being to whom they wish to assign some of the connotations of 'foxiness.' Similarly some aspects of formal lecture style can be introduced into informal discussions to convey some of the connotations of formality for the sake of emphasis.

This use of superposed variation constitutes a different dimension of linguistic behavior. We account for it by distinguishing two types of interaction: transaction and personal. Transactional interaction centers about limited socially defined goals, i.e., a religious service, a petition, a job interview, etc. Participants in such interaction in a sense suspend their individuality in order to act out the rights and obligations of relevant statuses.

In personal interaction, on the other hand, participants act as individuals, rather than for the sake of specific social tasks. This behavior predominates in periods of relaxation among friends, and within peer groups. It is also common in scholarly discussions where the subject is more important than the social characteristics of participants. It gives scope to all facets of experiences, and individuals may resort to changes in speech style in order to underscore particular meanings. Personal switching is associated with differences in emphasis and in topic, and thus contrasts with transactional switching, which correlates with such alterations in the formal characteristics of encounters as changes in participants or in their relative statuses.

The linguistic effect of personal switching is a loosening of co-occurrence restrictions. Forms which would not appear together in transactional encounters may now co-occur. Some social restraints on language choice of course always remain. Strictures on obscenity and other types of taboos are rarely violated no matter how free the dialogue. Baby talk is not appropriate in most discussion among adults.

It is important to note that personal switching achieves its effect in non-transactional encounters because there exists a regular association between choice of linguistic form and social relationships in transactional encounters. It is this latter association which gives rise to relevant differences in connotation. Stylistic alternation which remains confined to transactional encounters need not necessarily lead to linguistic change, since the differences between variants are reinforced by nonlinguistic correlates. When switching occurs in personal encounters, on the other hand, situational reinforcement is lacking and hence there is a greater likelihood of change. Both types of linguistic alternation must be taken into account in sociolinguistic study.

The balance of personal and interactional switching varies both from community to community and from subgroup to subgroup within the same population. An individual's expertise in manipulating speech varieties is a function of his position within the social system. In Khalapur, poorer Rajputs and members of the lower castes who spend their days in physical labor and interact primarily within the immediate kin group tend to use *moṭī bolī*. They sound ill at ease when required to switch to *saf bolī* when they become agitated. Their knowledge of the regional speech and of standard Hindi furthermore is limited to a few stereotyped phrases which they tend to intersperse with *moṭī bolī* forms. Wealthier Rajputs, merchants and artisans, those who held clerical positions, and especially political leaders, show the greatest skill in switching. Intergroup differences in linguistic expertise are somewhat smaller in Hemnes but there are nevertheless many farmers and local artisans who show less skill in spoken Norwegian than those who are called upon to use it regularly.

In Khalapur only *moṭī bolī* and *saf bolī* alternate in personal switching. Hindi and regional speech occur exclusively in transactional interaction. Our field observations furthermore show personal switching primarily in gatherings of politically more active Rajputs who are not necessarily close kin. Here *saf bolī* is the usual form of speech while *moṭī bolī* is used in joking and in quarreling. Although there seems to be some correlation between linguistic expertise and personal switching in Khalapur, the connection is probabilistic rather than causal, since not all speakers who are highly adept at stylistic manipulation engage in the latter.

Personal switching was the object of a special study in Hemnesberget, reported in greater detail elsewhere (Gumperz 1964; Blom 1964). Linguistic data were collected through tape recorded informal discussions with groups of two types: members of purely local "closed" friendship networks (Barnes 1954) and members of "open" networks. The former included individuals whose significant social relationships were confined to Hemnes. The latter were made up of university students, a clerk in a local office, and others who maintained relationships both with Hemnes residents and with the urban elite.

All groups were exposed to topical stimuli ranging from local issues such as fishing, personal relationships in Hemnes, etc., to superlocal issues such as city life, government investment, national politics, etc. It was found that local groups tended not to switch from the dialect to standard Norwegian except in transactional encounters (i.e., when talking to the anthropologist observers). Internal discussion within the group was carried on entirely in the dialect regardless of topic. Open network groups on the other hand engaged both in transactional and in personal switching. They tended to use a high proportion of standard Norwegian forms both when talking to the observers and in their own internal discussion dealing with supralocal topics.

In our field interviews we were unable to determine any differences in attitude toward language use among these groups. Members of both groups adhered to the prevalent norms which call for dialect forms in all types of oral interaction. In fact, when tapes of open network group discussions were played back to one participant, she expressed surprise and stated she had not realized that she had been using Bokmål forms.

Our data seem to indicate that intergroup distinctions in linguistic behavior are attributable to the different ways in which participants of open and closed network groups in Hemnes society define their mutual relationships. All members of open network groups share in a much broader range of experiences than those who belong to closed networks. They regard each other as students, literati, or part of the politically conscious national elite as well as friends and fellow Hemnes residents. Hence they feel compelled to symbolize these additional relationships through stylistic shifts when the discussion demands it.

In assessing the effect of personal switching for linguistic change we take into account both the specific varieties which are affected as well as the position of the group within the local social system. In the case of Khalapur we might predict that *moṭī bolī* is on its way out since the behavior of upper class Rajputs who use it in personal switching is being increasingly imitated by others. The prevalence of personal switching among open network groups in Hemnes however, is not necessarily an indication that the local dialect is about to be replaced by standard Norwegian. Open network groups such as we studied are relatively marginal in the community as a whole. Their members will probably find employment elsewhere and pass out of the community. Any radical shift in the verbal repertoire such as changeover from a compartmentalized to a fluid structure (which the loss of the local dialect would imply) should, if our analysis is correct, also require a restructuring of social relationships within the majority group.


## CONCLUSION

Our comparison of verbal behavior in Khalapur and Hemnes is intended to be suggestive rather than definitive. Nevertheless we hope that the information we present demonstrates the fruitfulness of the verbal repertoire as a sociolinguistic concept. We have stated that a verbal repertoire is definable both in linguistic and social terms. As a linguistic entity it bridges the gap between grammatical systems and human groups. The common view that language stands apart from social phenomena, which is held by anthropologists of many persuasions (Sapir 1921:228; Radcliffe-Brown 1957:143; Nadel 1951:89), would seem to be valid only if we confine our analysis to single homogeneous systems abstracted from the totality of communicative behavior. If, however, we follow the procedure suggested in this paper and consider the linguistic resources of human groups to be divisible into a series of analytically distinct speech varieties, showing various degrees of grammatical overlap and allocated to different social relationships, then the connection between linguistic and social facts is readily established. It is the language distance between these varieties rather than the internal phonological or morphological structure of specific varieties which most readily reflects the social environment. Since language distances can be studied through contrastive linguistic analysis independently of extralinguistic phenomena, their measurement provides a valuable index for the study of society.

Social restraints on language choice, on the other hand, are also a part of social structure. They are thus susceptible to analysis in terms of generalized relational variables which apply to interaction in all human groups. The study of particular sets of grammatical systems and cultural norms in terms of these variables enables us to treat linguistic behavior as a form of social behavior, and linguistic change as a special case of social change.

## REFERENCES

Bernstein, Basil. "Elaborated and restricted codes: their social origins and some consequences." *American Anthropologist* 66, no. 6 (1964): 59–69.

Blom, Jan-Petter. "Friendship networks in Hemnes." Unpublished, 1964.

Brown, R. W. and A. Gilman. "The pronouns of power and solidarity." In *Style in Language,* Thomas Sebeok, ed. Cambridge: Technology Press of Massachusetts Institute of Technology, 1960.

Ervin-Tripp, Susan. "An analysis of the interaction of language, topic, and listener." *American Anthropologist* 66, no. 6 (1964): 86–102.

Ferguson, Charles A. "Diglossia." *Word* 15 (1959): 325–340.

Fischer, John L. "Social influences in the choice of a linguistic variant." *Word* 14 (1958): 47–56.

Geertz, Hildred. *The Javanese Family.* Glencoe: Free Press, 1963.

Gleason, H. A. "The organization of language." *Georgetown University Monographs in Linguistics and Language Teaching.* Washington: Georgetown University Press, 1964.

Goffman, Erving. *Behavior in Public Places.* Glencoe: Free Press, 1963.

Gumperz, John J. "Dialect differences and social stratification in a North Indian village." *American Anthropologist* 60 (1958): 668–681. (*a*)

――――. "Phonological differences in three Hindi village dialects." *Language* 34 (1958): 212–224. (*b*)

――――. "Formal and informal standards in the Hindi regional language area" (with C. M. Naim). In *Linguistic Diversity in South Asia,* C. A. Ferguson and J. J. Gumperz, eds. Bloomington, Indiana: Indiana University Research Center, 1960.

――――. "On the ethnology of linguistic change." In *Sociolinguistics,* William O. Bright, ed. The Hague: Mouton, 1966.

Hitchcock, John T. and Leigh Minturn. "The Rajputs of Khalapur." In *Six Cultures: Studies in Child Rearing,* Beatrice B. Whiting, ed. New York: John Wiley, 1963.

Hymes, Dell. "The ethnography of speaking." In *Anthropology and Human Behavior,* T. Gladwin and W. D. Sturtevant, eds. Washington, D.C.: Anthropological Society of Washington, 1962, pp. 15–53.

Joos, Martin. "The isolation of styles." *Report of the 10th Annual Round Table Meeting on Linguistics and Language Studies,* R. S. Harrell, ed. Georgetown University, 1960.

Lamb, Sidney M. "The sememic approach to structural semantics." *American Anthropologist* 66, no. 3, part 2, (1964): 57–78.

Leach, E. R. *Political Systems of Highland Burma.* Cambridge, Mass.: Harvard University Press, 1954.

Nadel, S. F. "The foundations of social anthropology." Glencoe: Free Press, 1951.

Radcliffe-Brown, A. R. *A Natural Science of Society.* Glencoe: Free Press, 1957.

Sapir, Edward. *Language.* New York: Harcourt Brace Jovanovich, 1921.

# Sociolinguistics
## Susan M. Ervin-Tripp

## I. INTRODUCTION

> Group therapy session:
> Joe: Ken face it, you're a poor little rich kid.
> Ken: Yes, Mommy. Thank you.
>
> Class notes No. 11 of Harvey Sacks
>
> Classroom scene:
> Mrs. Tripp: Miss Hayashijima?
> Student: Yes, sir.

The possibility of insult and of humor based on linguistic choices means that members agree on the underlying rules of speech and on the social meaning of linguistic features. Linguistic selection is deeply enmeshed in the structure of society; members can readily recognize and interpret socially codified deviations from the norms.

During the past few years, the systematic study of the relation of linguistic forms and social meaning has greatly accelerated. The formal recognition of a field of sociolinguistics has been marked in the United States by courses, programs, seminars, and textbooks (Bright 1966; Fishman 1968; Hymes 1964b; Gumperz and Hymes 1964, in press; Lieberson 1966). In two respects, the recent history of the field seems different from that of psycholinguistics. Psychologists were largely consumers in the interaction between the fields of psychology and linguistics. Out of concerns that arose from theoretical questions indigenous to psychology, they found that linguistic methods and concepts could provide entirely new ways of accounting for phenomena they had already observed and raise new questions of great interest to them as psychologists. In contrast, many of the central figures in the development of sociolinguistics are regarded as linguists and have developed their sociolinguistic concepts because they found social features continually central to linguistic descriptions. A second difference lies in the disciplinary diversity of social scientists; it is not clear just what the "socio-" implies in the new field. It will be obvious in this article that anthropologists, sociologists, social psychologists, and psychotherapists all have trodden on the terrain we shall define as sociolinguistic, without being much aware of each other.

This article is confined to micro-sociolinguistics, though some references to larger social phenomena are unavoidable. Sociolinguistics in this context will include studies of the components of face-to-face interaction as they bear on, or are affected by, the formal structure of speech. These components may include the personnel, the situation, the function of the interaction, the topic and message, and the channel. As Fishman has pointed out, sociolinguistics is thus distinct from "communication." "It is concerned with *characteristics of the code* and their relationship to characteristics of the communicators or the communication situation, rather than with message or communication functions and processes alone" 1967, p. 590.

During the past decade, psycholinguistics has been profoundly affected by the impact of structural linguistics. Psychologists have come to recognize that verbal output and comprehension are guided by "rules,"[1] so that unique sentences can be produced and understood by speakers in the same speech community. Currently, performance models are beginning to be developed which can account for speech, imitation, comprehension, and other forms of performance, and studies are being made of the development of these abilities in children and of the interpretation of deviant utterances (Chapman 1967; Ervin-Tripp and Slobin 1966; Slobin and Welsh 1967).

In this article, evidence will be assembled to show that the rules of verbal output and comprehension must be organized to specify social features. We can assume that the next step will be the development of sociolinguistic performance models, studies of socialization and the development of sociolinguistic competence (Slama-Cazacu 1960; Slobin 1967), and research on the interpretation of sociolinguistically deviant behavior.

This article has three main sections. The first will provide some detailed examples of what kinds of sociolinguistic rules we can expect to find, the second will define specific features which may be the components of sociolinguistic rules, and the third will examine examples of research on differences in rules between different speech communities.

## II. SOCIOLINGUISTIC RULES

## A. Alternation Rules

### 1. American Rules of Address

A scene on a public street in contemporary U.S.:
"What's your name, boy?" the policeman asked. . .
"Dr. Poussaint. I'm a physician. . . ."
"What's your first name, boy? . . ."
"Alvin."

—Poussaint (1967, p. 53)

---

1 "Rules" in this article are not prescriptive but descriptive. They may not be in conscious awareness. Unlike habits, they may include complex structures inferred from the occurrence of interpretable and appropriate novel behavior.

Anybody familiar with American address rules (see footnote 1) can tell us the feelings reported by Dr. Poussaint: "As my heart palpitated, I muttered in profound humiliation . . . . For the moment, my manhood had been ripped from me . . . . No amount of self-love could have salvaged my pride or preserved my integrity . . .[I felt] self-hate." It is possible to specify quite precisely the rule employed by the policeman. Dr. Poussaint's overt, though coerced, acquiescence in a public insult through widely recognized rules of address is the source of his extreme emotion.

Brown and Ford (Hymes, 1964*b*) have done pioneering and ingenious research on forms of address in American English, using as corpora American plays, observed usage in a Boston business firm, and reported usage of business executives. They found primarily first name (FN) reciprocation or title plus last name (TLN) reciprocation. However, asymmetrical exchanges were found where there was age difference or occupational rank difference. Intimacy was related to the use of multiple names.

Expanding their analysis from my own rules of address, I have found the structure expressed in the diagram in Fig. 1. The advantage of formal diagraming is that it offers precision greater than that of discursive description (Hymes 1967). The type of diagram presented here, following Geoghegan (in press), is to be read like a computer flow chart. The entrance point is on the left, and from left to right there is a series of selectors, usually binary. Each path through the diagram leads to a possible outcome, that is, one of the possible alternative forms of address.

Note that the set of paths, or the rule, is like a formal grammar in that it is a way of representing a logical model. The diagram is not intended as a model of a process of the actual decision sequence by which a speaker chooses a form of address or a listener interprets one. The two structures may or may not correspond. In any case, the task of determining the structure implicit in people's knowledge of what forms of address are possible and appropriate is clearly distinct from the task of studying how people, in real situations and in real time, make choices. The criteria and methods of the two kinds of study are quite different. Just as two individuals who share the same grammar might not share the same performance rules, so two individuals might have different decision or interpretation procedures for sociolinguistic alternatives, but still might have an identical logical structure to their behavior.

The person whose knowledge of address is represented in Fig. 1 is assumed to be a competent adult member of a western American academic community. The address forms which are the "outcomes" to be accounted for might fit in frames like "Look, – – – –, it's time to leave." The outcomes themselves are formal sets, with alternative realizations. For example, first names may alternate with nicknames, as will be indicated in a later section. One possible outcome is no-naming, indicated in Fig. 1 by the linguistic symbol for zero [Ø].

The diamonds indicate selectors. They are points where the social categories allow different paths. At first glance, some selectors look like simple external features, but the social determinants vary according to the system, and the

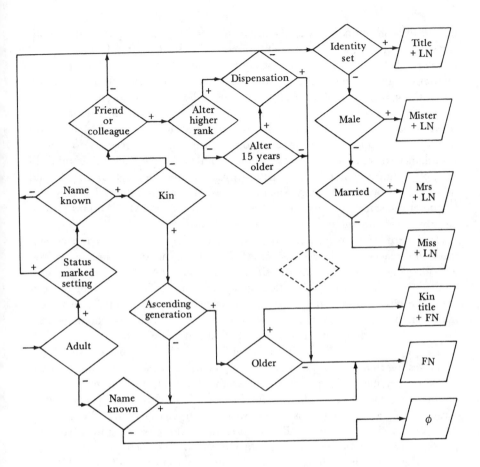

FIGURE 1
An American Address System

specific nature of the categories must be discovered by ethnographic means. For example, "older" implies knowledge of the range of age defined as contemporary. In some southeast Asian systems, even one day makes a person socially older.

The first selector checks whether the addressee is a child or not. In face-to-face address, if the addressee is a child, all of the other distinctions can be ignored. What is the dividing line between adult and child? In my own system, it seems to be school-leaving age, at around age 18. An employed 16-year-old might be classified as an adult.

*Status-marked situations* are settings such as the courtroom, the large faculty meeting, or Congress, where status is clearly specified, speech style is rigidly prescribed, and the form of address of each person is derived from his social identity, for example, "Your honor," "Mr. Chairman." The test for establishing the list of such settings is whether personal friendships are apparent in the address forms or whether they are neutralized (or masked) by the formal requirements of the setting. There are, of course, other channels by which personal relations might be revealed, but here we are concerned only with address alternations, not with tone of voice, connotations of lexicon, and so on.

Among nonkin, the dominant selector of first-naming is whether alter is classified as having the status of a colleague or social acquaintance. When introducing social acquaintances or new work colleagues, it is necessary to employ first names so that the new acquaintances can first-name each other immediately. Familiarity is not a factor within dyads of the same age and rank, and there are no options. For an American assistant professor to call a new colleague of the same rank and age "Professor Watkins" or "Mr. Watkins" would be considered strange, at least on the West Coast.

*Rank* here refers to a hierarchy within a working group, or to ranked statuses like teacher–pupil. In the American system, no distinction in address is made to equals or subordinates since both receive FN. The distinction may be made elsewhere in the linguistic system, for example, in the style of requests used. We have found that subordinates outside the family receive direct commands in the form of imperatives more often than equals, to whom requests are phrased in other ways at least in some settings (see below).

A senior alter has the option of dispensing the speaker from offering TLN by suggesting that he use a first name or by tacitly accepting first name. Brown and Ford (Hymes 1964a) have discussed the ambiguity that arises because it is not clear whether the superior, for instance, a professor addressing a doctoral candidate or younger instructor, wishes to receive back the FN he gives. This problem is mentioned by Emily Post: "It is also effrontery for a younger person to call an older by her or his first name, without being asked to do so. Only a very underbred, thick-skinned person would attempt it" (Post 1922, p. 54). In the American system described in Fig. 1, age difference is not significant until it is nearly the size of a generation, which suggests its origin in the family. The presence of options, or dispensation, creates a locus for the expression of individual and situational nuances. The form of address can reveal dispensation, and therefore be a matter for display or concealment of third parties. No-naming or $\emptyset$ is an outcome of uncertainty among these options.[2]

The *identity* set refers to a list of occupational titles or courtesy titles accorded people in certain statuses. Examples are Judge, Doctor, and Professor. A priest, physician, dentist, or judge may be addressed by title alone, but a plain citizen or an academic person may not. In the latter cases, if the name

---

2 In the system in Fig. 1, it is possible to create asymmetrical address by using FN to a familiar addressee who cannot reciprocate because of rank or age difference, and his unwillingness or lack of dispensation, e.g., a domestic servant. E. Hughes has noted a shift from TLN to FN by physicians whose patients move from private fees to Medicare. This usage does not fit into the rule in Fig. 1.

is unknown, there is no address form (or zero, $\emptyset$) available and we simply no-name the addressee. The parentheses below refer to optional elements, the bracketed elements to social selectional categories.

|  |  |
|---|---|
| [Cardinal]: | Your excellency |
| [U.S. President]: | Mr. President |
| [Priest]: | Father( + LN) |
| [Nun]: | Sister( + religious name) |
| [Physician]: | Doctor( + LN) |
| [Ph.D., Ed.D.], etc.: | (Doctor + LN) |
| [Professor]: | (Professor + LN) |
| [Adult], etc.: | (Mister + LN) |
|  | (Mrs. + LN) |
|  | (Miss + LN) |

Wherever the parenthetical items cannot be fully realized, as when last name (LN) is unknown, and there is no lone title, the addressee is no-named by a set of rules of the form as follows: Father $+\emptyset\rightarrow$ Father, Professor $+\emptyset\rightarrow\emptyset$, Mister $+\emptyset\rightarrow\emptyset$, etc. An older male addressee may be called "sir" if deference is intended, as an optional extra marking.

These are my rules, and seem to apply fairly narrowly within the academic circle I know. Nonacademic university personnel can be heard saying "Professor" or "Doctor" without LN, as can school teachers. These delicate differences in sociolinguistic rules are sensitive indicators of the communication net.

The zero forms imply that often no address form is available to follow routines like "yes," "no," "pardon me," and "thank you." Speakers of languages or dialects where all such routines must contain an address form are likely in English either to use full name or to adopt forms like "sir" and "ma'am," which are either not used or used only to elderly addressees in this system.

One might expect to be able to collapse the rule system by treating kin terms as a form of title, but it appears that the selectors are not identical for kin and nonkin. A rule which specifies that *ascending generation* only receives title implies that a first cousin would not be called "cousin" but merely FN, whereas an aunt of the same age would receive a kin title, as would a parent's cousin. If a title is normally used in direct address and there are several members of the kin category, a first name may also be given (e.g., Aunt Louise). Frequently there are additional features marked within a given family such as patrilineal vs. matrilineal, and near vs. distant. Whenever the address forms for an individual person's relatives are studied, this proves to be the case, in my experience.

Presumably, the individual set of rules or the regional dialect of a reader of this article may differ in some details from that reported in Fig. 1. Perhaps sociolinguists will begin to use a favorite frame of linguists: "In my dialect we say . . ." to illustrate such differences in sociolinguistic rules. For example, I have been told that in some American communities there may be a specific status of familiarity beyond first-naming, where a variant of the middle name is optional among intimates. This form then becomes the normal or unmarked address form to the addressee.

"What's your name, boy?"
"Dr. Poussaint. I'm a physician."
"What's your first name, boy?"
"Alvin."

The policeman insulted Dr. Poussaint three times. First, he employed a social selector for race in addressing him as "boy," which neutralizes identity set, rank, and even adult status. If addressed to a white, "boy" presumably would be used only for a child, youth, or menial regarded as a nonperson.

Dr. Poussaint's reply supplied only TLN and its justification. He made clear that he wanted the officer to suppress the race selector, yielding a rule like that in Fig. 1. This is clearly a nondeferential reply, since it does not contain the FN required by the policeman's address rule. The officer next treated TLN as failure to answer his demand, as a non-name, and demanded FN; third, he repeated the term "boy" which would be appropriate to unknown addressees.

According to Fig. 1, under no circumstances should a stranger address a physician by his first name. Indeed, the prestige of physicians even exempts them from first-naming (but not from "Doc") by used-car salesmen, and physicians' wives can be heard so identifying themselves in public in order to claim more deference than "Mrs." brings. Thus the policeman's message is quite precise: "Blacks are wrong to claim adult status or occupational rank. You are children." Dr. Poussaint was stripped of all deference due his age and rank.

Communication has been perfect in this interchange. Both were familiar with an address system which contained a selector for race available to both black and white for insult, condescension, or deference, as needed. Only because they shared these norms could the policeman's act have its unequivocal impact.

## 2. Comparative Rule Studies

The formulation of rules in this fashion can allow us to contrast one sociolinguistic system with another in a systematic way. A shared language does not necessarily mean a shared set of sociolinguistic rules. For instance, rules in educated circles in England vary. In upper class boarding schools, boys and some girls address each other by LN instead of FN. In some universities and other milieux affected by the public school usage, solidary address between male acquaintances and colleagues is LN rather than FN. To women it may be Mrs. or Miss + LN by men (not title + LN) or FN. Women usually do not use LN. Thus sex of both speaker and addressee is important.

In other university circles, the difference from the American rule is less; prior to dispensation by seniors with whom one is acquainted, one may use Mister or Mrs. rather than occupational title as an acceptably solidary but deferential form. Note that this is the solidary usage to women by some male addressees in the other system. The two English systems contrast with the American one in allowing basically three, rather than two classes of alternatives for nonkin: occupational title + LN, M + LN, and FN/LN. The intermediate class is used for the familiar person who must be deferred to or treated with courtesy.

Two Asian systems of address have been described recently. The pioneering work of William Geohegan (in press) described the naming system of a speaker of Bisayan, a Philippine language. Geohegan's formal presentation of the system in a talk some years ago was the model for the rules in the figures in this article. As in most systems, children routinely receive the familiar address form. The Bisayan system, like the American and English, chooses on the basis of relative rank, relative age, and friendship. But there are important differences. In the United States, all adult strangers are treated with deference; in the Bisayan system, social inferiors do not receive titled address. In the American system for nonkin, added age, like higher rank, merely increases distance or delays familiar address; in the Bisayan system, inferiors or friends who are older receive a special term of address uniting informality and deference.

The Korean system is even less like the American (Howell 1967). In Korea, relative rank must first be assessed. If rank is equal, relative age within two years is assessed, and if that is equal, solidarity (e.g., classmates) will differentiate familiar from polite speech. This system differs both in its components and its order from the American and Bisayan rules. Both inferiors and superiors are addressed differently from equals. Many kinds of dyads differ in authority— husband-wife, customer-tradesman, teacher-pupil, employer-employee—and in each case, asymmetrical address is used. Addressees more than two years older or younger than the speaker are differentially addressed, so that close friendship is rigidly age-graded. Solidary relations arise from status, just as they do between equal colleagues in the American system, regardless of personal ties. There are more familiar address forms yet to signal intimacy within solidary dyads. If the English system has three levels, there are even more in the Korean system. Since the criteria were multiple in the Howell study, instead of a single frame, the comparison is not quite exact.

As Howell pointed out, the Korean system illustrates that the dimension of approach that Brown and Gilman (1960) called solidarity may in fact have several forms in one society. In the Korean system intimacy is separable from solidarity. This separation may also exist in the American system but in a different way. One is required to first-name colleagues even though they are disliked. On the other hand, as Brown and Ford (Hymes 1964b) showed, nicknames may indicate friendship more intimate than the solidarity requiring FN. They found that various criteria of intimacy, such as self-disclosure, were related to the *number* of FN alternates, such as nicknames and sometimes LN, which were used to an addressee, and they suggested that intimacy creates more complex and varied dyadic relations which speakers may signal by address variants. Thus, in the American system two points of major option for speakers exist: the ambiguous address relation between solidary speakers of unequal age or status and intimacy. Systems can be expected to vary in the points where address is prescribed or where options exist; Brown and Ford suggested a universal feature, on the other hand, in saying that in all systems frequent and intimate interaction should be related to address variation.[3] This, they suggest is related to a semantic principle of greater differentiation of important domains.

## 3. Two-Choice Systems

The brilliant work of Brown and Gilman (1960) which initiated the recent wave of studies of address systems was based on a study of T and V, the second person verbs and pronouns in European languages. In English, the same alternation existed before "thou" was lost.

One might expect two-choice systems to be somewhat simpler than a system

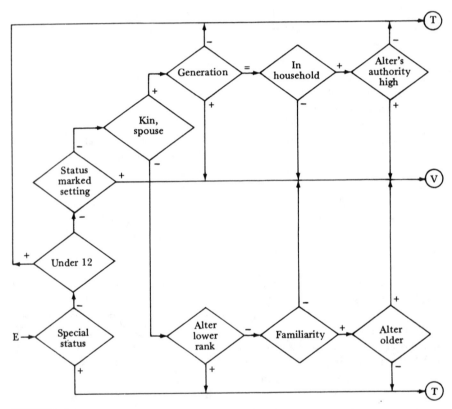

FIGURE 2
Nineteenth Century Russian Address

---

3 William Geohegan has privately suggested that in his Philippine studies the extremely high intimacy in families resulted in use of paralinguistic rather than lexical alternatives for "address variation" of the type Brown and Ford discuss.

like Bisayan, which in Geohegan's description gives 19 output categories. But the number of outcomes can be few although the number of selectors is many or the kinds of rules relating them complex. Figure 2 gives a description of the nineteenth century rules of the Russian gentry, as I derive them from the excellent analysis by Friedrich (1966), which gives sufficiently full detail to permit resolution of priorities. *Special statuses* refers to the tsar and God, who seem not to fit on any status continuum. *Status marked settings* mentioned by Friedrich were the court, parliament, public occasions, duels, and examinations. *Rank* inferiors might be lower in social class, army rank, or ethnic group, or be servants. *Familiarity* applied to classmates, fellow students, fellow revolutionaries, lovers, and intimate friends. There does not seem to be the prescription in the Korean and American solidary relation. A feature of the system which Friedrich's literary examples illustrate vividly is its sensitivity to situational features. Thus T means "the right to use Ty," but not the obligation to do so. Within the kin group, household is of considerable importance because of the large households separated by distance in traditional Russia.

A slightly later Eastern European system described by Slobin (1963) is given in Fig. 3. The Yiddish system is somewhat more like the American than like the Russian system in that deference is always given adult strangers regardless of rank. However, an older person receives deference, despite familiarity, unless he is a member of the kin group. In the American system, familiarity can neutralize age.

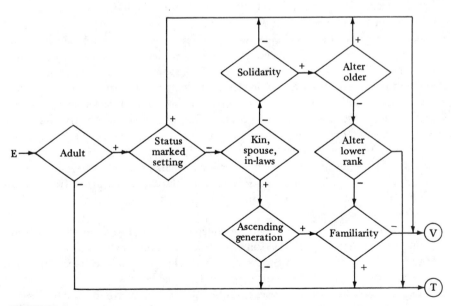

FIGURE 3
Yiddish Address System

How have these systems changed? We have some evidence from the Soviet Union. The Russian revolutionaries, unlike the French, decreed V, implying that they wanted respect more than solidarity. The current system is identical to the old with one exception: Within the family, asymmetry has given way to reciprocal T, as it has in most of western Europe, at least in urbanized groups. For nonkin in ranked systems like factories, superiors receive Vy and give Ty:

> When a new employee is addressed as Ty, she says: "Why do I call you *'vy'* while you call me *'ty'*?"
> Kormilitzyn gleefully shoots back a ready answer: "If I were to call everyone *'vy'* I'd never get my plan fulfilled. You don't fulfill plans by using *'vy'* (Kantorovich, 1966, p. 30).

Evidently the upperclass habit of using *"vy"* until familiarity was established (a system reflecting the fact that the T/V contrast itself came in from above as a borrowing from French) has seeped downward. "A half-century ago even upon first meeting two workers of the same generation would immediately use *'ty'*. Today things are different. Middle-aged workers maintain *'vy'* for a long time, or else adopt the intermediate form which is very widespread among people within a given profession: *'ty'* combined with first name and patronymic" (Kantorovich 1966, p. 81).

Kantorovich, true to the 1917 decree, complains about three features of the current system: *ty* to inferiors regardless of age, *ty* to older kin, and first names alone among young acquaintances. Thus he favors the more deferential alternative in each case. Social change in Russia has been relatively slow in sociolinguistic rules, has affected family life more than public life, and has spread the practices of the gentry among the workers.

The Puerto Rican two-choice system in Fig. 4 is quite simple since it is a system of children. The data were generously supplied by Wallace Lambert and his collaborators from a large-scale study of comparative address systems in several cultures. Elementary and high school students filled in questionnaires about the forms of address given and received. In this chart, interlocale and inter-subject differences have been suppressed. The striking feature of this system is that it requires only three discriminations. It is likely, of course, that adult informants would elaborate further details. Intimacy, in this system, refers to close ties of friendship, which can occur with others of widely varying age, e.g., with godparents, and is quite distinct from solidarity, which arises from status alone. Adolescent girls, for example, do not give "tu" to a classmate unless she is a friend.

Lambert and his collaborators have collected slightly less detailed data from samples of schoolchildren in Montreal, from a small town in Quebec, from Mayenne, France, and from St. Pierre et Michelon, an island colony with close ties to France, much closer than to nearby Canada.

The system of kin address varies considerably. In both Mayenne and St. Pierre, all kin and godparents receive "tu." In Quebec, the urban middle class is moving in this direction, but the lower class and the rural regions from which it

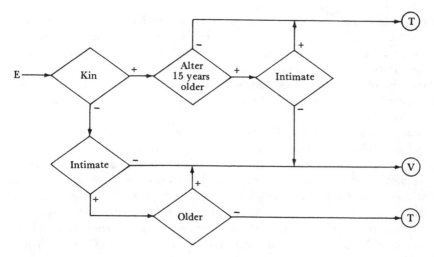

FIGURE 4
Puerto Rican Address System (Children)

derives retain an address system like Puerto Rico's in which distance (including age) within the family is important. In some families, even older siblings receive "vous." If changes in kin address arise during social change, one would expect between-family differences to be greater than in nonkin address, since sanctions are intrafamily. Generally, "intimate" means parents, then aunts, uncles, and godparents, then grandparents. Some interfamily differences might be accounted for by finding which family members live in the household, which nearby, and which far away.

Lambert and Tucker (in press) have referred to a study of the social connotations of this changing system for urban school children in Montreal. Children were asked to judge taped family interaction varying in "tu" or "vous" to parents, and in the outcome of the interaction—giving or not giving the child a requested bicycle. In addition to the class differences (*tu* users richer, more educated families), the judges drew from the pronoun usage a set of expectations about family values, resulting in favorable judgments when the interaction outcome was congruent. For instance, *tu*-using families sound modern and tolerant, the mothers more active, the fathers more tolerant than *vous*-using families, if they prove child-centered. However, it is *vous*-using families that sound religious, with a good family spirit, an active mother and tolerant father when the decision goes against the child.

Sex of addressee appears to be a feature of adult systems, or may influence the probabilities of intimacy where there is a selector. In Quebec, adults generally give "tu" to children and young men, regardless of familiarity. In St. Pierre, except to upper class girls, who are less likely to receive "tu" under any conditions, acquaintance legitimizes "tu" and is necessary even in addressing children. In Mayenne, middle class little boys said they received "tu" from everyone (and reported often reciprocating to strangers), but otherwise familiarity seems to be required, as in Puerto Rico, in the Mayenne system. Boys generally receive T from employers, and in the country and the urban lower class they receive T from service personnel. It should be noted that the analysis from the children's standpoint of what they think they receive is an interesting reflection of the fact that people know what they should say themselves, and they also expect some standard form from others. In analyzing the adult rule systems, however, the children's data are not the best; the adults of rural or lower class background may have different rules (e.g., service personnel, perhaps) than others.

The compressed presentation here of Lambert's work has indicated several directions for research on social criteria of address selection. Lambert has shown that these rules are sensitive indicators of differences between social groups and of social change. One must look beyond the address system for independent social features correlated with address systems of a defined type. In order to do such studies, a clear-cut formal system for typing properties of address systems (like language typologies) is necessary.

Lambert (1967b) has discussed the development of address rules with age. There are several interesting problems in the learning of these systems, one being the visibility of the various social selectors. One can assume that rank graduations in an adult system might be learned late (at least in terms of generalizability to new addressees), as would generation differentiations not highly related to age. A second problem emphasized by Lambert is the system of alternation itself. Children in most language communities learn fairly early to employ the asymmetry of first and second person (for a case study see McNeill, 1963). Thus if they always received T and gave V, there might be less difficulty; however, they see others exchanging reciprocal V and T as well as asymmetrical address, and they give T to some alters. These problems could be studied in natural language communities where the language structure provides different category systems and social selectors (Slobin 1967).

## 4. Socialization

Adults entering a new system because of geographical or occupational mobility may have to learn new sociolinguistic rules. A contrastive analysis of formal rules, in combination with a theory of social learning, would allow specification of what will happen.

First, we can predict what the speaker will do. We can expect, on the basis of research on bilinguals (Ervin-Tripp, in press; Haugen 1956), that the linguistic alternatives will at first be assimilated to familiar forms, to "diamorphs." Thus a Frenchman in the United States might start out by assuming that Monsieur = Mister, Madame = Mrs., and so on.

However, the rules for occurrence of these forms are different in France. In the polite discourse of many speakers, routines like "merci," "au revoir," "bonjour," "pardon" do not occur without an address form in France, although they may in the United States. One always says "Au revoir, Madame" or some alternative address form. "Madame" differs from "Mrs." in at least two ways.

Unknown female addressees of a certain age are normally called "Madame" regardless of marital status. Further, Mrs. $+ \emptyset = \emptyset$; Madame $+ \emptyset =$ Madame. As a matter of fact, the rule requiring address with routines implies that when LN is not known, there cannot be a "zero alternate"—some form of address must be used anyway, like the English "sir." As a result of these differences in rules, we can expect to hear elderly spinsters addressed as "Pardon me, Mrs."

How do listeners account for errors? I suggested earlier that shifting at certain points in sociolinguistic rules is regularly available as an option. Normally, it is interpreted as changing the listener's perceived identity or his relation to the speaker. The result may be complimentary, as "sir" to an unknown working class male, or insulting, as "Mommy" to an adolescent male. If the learner of a sociolinguistic system makes an error that falls within this range of interpretable shifts, he may constantly convey predictably faulty social meanings. Suppose the speaker, but not the listener, has a system in which familiarity, not merely solidarity, is required for use of a first name. He will use TLN in the United States to his new colleagues and be regarded as aloof or excessively formal. He will feel that first-name usage from his colleagues is brash and intrusive. In the same way, encounters across social groups may lead to misunderstandings within the United States. Suppose a used-car salesman regards his relation to his customers as solidary, or a physician so regards his relation to old patients. The American using the rule in Fig. 1 might regard such speakers as intrusive, having made a false claim to a solidary status. In this way, one can pinpoint abrasive features of interaction across groups.

Another possible outcome is that the alternative selected is completely outside the system. This would be the case with "Excuse me, Mrs." which cannot be used under any circumstances by rule 1. This behavior is then interpreted with the help of any additional cues available, such as the face, dress, or accent of a foreigner. In such cases, if sociolinguistic rules are imperfectly learned, there may be social utility in retaining an accent wherever the attitude toward the group of foreigners is sufficiently benign; it is better to be designated a foreigner than to risk insulting or offending addressees.

## 5. Integrated Sociolinguistic Rules

The rules given above are fractional. They are selective regarding the linguistic alternations accounted for. They define only specific linguistic entries as the universe of outcomes to be predicted. If one starts from social variables, a different set of rules might emerge. This is the outlook of William Geohegan (in press) and Ward Goodenough (1965), as well as Dell Hymes (1964a), who suggested taking "a specific or universal function, such as the distinguishing of the status or role of man and woman, derogation, respect, or the like, and... investigating the diverse means so organized within the language habits of the community,... [rather than] looking for function as a correlative of structure already established" (p. 44).

Using such an approach, Goodenough examined behavior toward a range of statuses, and found that it was possible to rank both the statuses and the forms of behavior into Guttman scales and equivalent classes, grouped at the same scale point (1965). In this way, various kinds of verbal and nonverbal behavior can be shown to be outcomes of the same social selectors.

Deference, the feature studied by Goodenough, may be indicated by pronoun alternations, names or titles, tone of voice, grammatical forms, vocabulary, and so on (Capell 1966, pp. 104ff; Martin, in Hymes 1964b). Deferential behavior in some systems may be realized only in special situations such as in introductions or in making requests. If one compares an isolated segment of two sociolinguistic systems, he cannot legitimately conclude that a given social variable is more important in one system than in the other. It may simply be realized through a different form of behavior.

It is not clear how the different realizations of social selectors might be important. Address, pronominal selection, or consistent verb suffixing (as in Japanese) can be consciously controlled more readily, perhaps, than intonation contours or syntactic complexity. Frenchmen report "trying to use 'tu'" with friends. Such forms can be taught by rule specification to children or newcomers. Forms which allow specific exceptions, or which have options so that too great or too little frequency might be conspicuous, cannot be taught so easily. Such rules can be acquired by newcomers only by long and intense exposure rather than by formal teaching.

Some alternations are common and required, others can be avoided. Howell reported that in Knoxville, Tennessee, Negroes uncertain of whether or not to reciprocate FN simply avoided address forms to colleagues (Howell 1967, pp. 81–83), an approach that Brown and Ford also observed in the academic rank system. In a pronominal rank system like French or Russian such avoidance is impossible. Among bilinguals, language switching may be employed to avoid rank signaling (Howell 1967; Tanner 1967). The avoidable selector can be considered a special case of the presence of options in the system. Tyler (1965) has noticed that morphological deference features (like the Japanese) are more common in societies of particular kinship types, such as lineage organization.

This description was primarily drawn from the standpoint of predicting a speaker's choice of alternatives in some frame. It is also possible to examine these rules from the standpoint of comprehension or interpretation, as have Blom and Gumperz (in press) in their discussion of *social meaning*. Just as one can comprehend a language without speaking it, as actors we can interpret the social meaning of the acts of others without necessarily using rules identical to our own. The relation between production and comprehension rules remains to be studied.

## B. Sequencing Rules

### 1. Leave-Taking

After an introduction, when you have talked for some time to a stranger whom you have found agreeable, and you then take leave, you say, "Good-by, I am

very glad to have met you," or "Good-by, I hope I shall see you again soon"—
or 'some time." The other person answers, "Thank you," or perhaps adds, "I
hope so, too."

Emily Post (1922, p. 9)

The sequential events mentioned in this description are Introduction + Conversation + Leave-taking. Leaving aside the components of the first two, elsewhere specified, leave-taking (LT) has two parts, for the two actors.

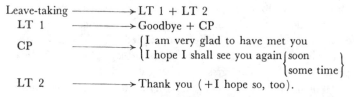

Leave-taking ⟶ LT 1 + LT 2
LT 1 ⟶ Goodbye + CP
CP ⟶ { I am very glad to have met you
       I hope I shall see you again { soon
                                     { some time }
LT 2 ⟶ Thank you ( + I hope so, too).

This is a notation, borrowed from grammars, illustrating a phrase structure rule. The plus marks indicate sequential events, the arrows expansions or replacements in the "derivation tree" to be read as "rewrite leave-taking as LT 1 + LT 2," the braces alternatives, and the parentheses optional elements. The more general rule states that introduction always precedes the other two events. Presumably the rules will indicate that while introduction and leave-taking are relatively fixed routines, conversation can be expanded to hours. We can regard these routines as transition markers between speech events.

## 2. Summons Sequence

A phone rings in Jim's home:
Jim:     Hello.
George:  Hi, how are you?
Jim:     O.K., but listen, I'm in a phone booth and this is my last dime.
         Barbara's phone is busy and I won't be able to meet her at seven. Could
         you keep trying to get her for me and tell her?
George:  What the hell are you talking about?

Adapted from Schegloff (in press)

Jim was a sociology student who was trying to violate rules of telephone conversation. The rules derived by Schegloff from a large sample of phone conversations can be characterized as follows:

Summons Sequence ⟶ Summons + Answer + Continuation + Response
Summons ⟶ { Courtesy Phrase [to stranger]
          { Attention-call [nonstranger]
          { Telephone bell. . .
Answer [phone] ⟶ Greeting 1 ( + Identification [office])
Continuation ⟶ (Greeting 2) + (Identification) + Message
Response ⟶ (Deferral + ) Reply to message

Following every summons, there are three phases to complete the cycle. The omission of any part, if a second party is present, is unusual and must be accounted for. The summons can be realized in a variety of ways, depending on whether alter is physically present, known, and so on. To a stranger one might say "pardon me!" or "hey!" Attention-calls include "waiter!" "Dr. Conant!" "Joe!" Their selection rules would be close to Fig. 1.

Alter must answer a summons. Lecturers may find it hard to ignore waving hands in the audience. If there is nonresponse, the summons is repeated. On the phone: "Hello...Hello...Hello?...Hello!" There are definite limits (longer for children) for such repetitions of summonses.

The next major step is that following the limited routines of exchanging greetings, the caller gives a message, explaining his reason for calling. In the example, Jim tried to play the role of caller rather than called. He did this by giving George a chance to give a message and by giving a message itself semantically deviant and appropriate only to George's status as caller.

If the caller did not intend a summons, or if his need has vanished, he fills the continuation position with an account: "Never mind." "I was just saying hello." "I was just checking the phone." If he states a request, alter must respond.

We have not stated the rule in its full detail. The realizations of Greeting 1 vary, according to circumstance. Thus the alternatives might be "Yes," on an intercom, "Good morning, Macy's," for a receptionist on an institutional telephone, "Hello," on other outside phones. Greeting 2 has different alternation sets than Greeting 1, for example "Hi," to a friend, "How are you," to a friend, "Hello," to others. Thus the realizations of particular units in the sequencing rules may involve alternations which are dependent on social features. Also, some of the optional positions may be selected or omitted by social criteria.

The selection of certain alternates may entail an expansion at that position in the sequence. For example, if "How are you?" occurs as the Greeting 2 realization, the addressee must reply. The result may be an embedded interchange about his health. The called person at this point, like anyone asked this question, has two options. He can either give a routine response to nonintimate alters, such as "Okay," or "Fine," or, if the alter is a friend, he has the option of describing the real state of his health. Indeed, he may be obligated to do so since a close friend might be insulted at not being informed of his broken leg at the time of the conversation rather than later. Sacks has described the routine response as an obligation to lie, but formally it is a neutralization of the semantic selection feature—simply a briefer route.

If Greeting 2 establishes that the caller is a friend, the addressee has the option of providing a new greeting which is for a friend, as Greeting 1 was not:

"Hello."

"Hi, Joe. How are you?"

"Oh, hi. I'm okay..."

Note that by this system, "hi" is more intimate than "hello." Not so in 1922, when Emily Post said that "hello" is "never used except between intimate friends who call each other by the first name" (1922, p. 19).

In the conversation just cited, *identification* is through the channel of voice recognition. Between strangers, identification is required, according to Sacks' evidence (in press). Sacks has pointed out that self-identifications, introductions, and third-party categorizations are important social devices. Since everyone has many statuses, the selection in each case where a status (other than a proper name) is given follows certain fixed rules, among them consistency with other choices. In a series of such events in the same situation, the categories tend to be members of the same contrast set, e.g., occupations.

### 3. Invitation Sets

Slots in sequences such as the summons sequence are not necessarily recognized by the speakers or labeled by them. Sacks, for example, has cited in lectures the observation that many encounters include an optional sequence at a time when a newcomer enters a group or a dyad begins conversation. These he called "pre-invitation," "pre-invitation/rejection," "invitation," and "rejection."

*a. Pre-invitation.*
"Hello? Hello. What are you doing?"
"Nothing."

The person called interprets the question as a preliminary to an invitation. If the reply is "nothing" the caller might suggest coming over, might launch into a long conversation, and so on. The person called does not talk about the things he is doing that are irrelevant to the supposed invitation.

*b. Pre-invitation/rejection.*
"Can I see you for a moment?"
"What do you want?"

The question is designed to gather information suitable for deciding about offering an invitation or a rejection. So too, according to Sacks' analysis, the sequence in Pittenger, Hockett, and Danehy's *The First Five Minutes:*

Therapist: What brings you here...?
Patient: I don't feel like talking.

Sacks observes that the patient knows that her acceptability for therapy depends on her answer, also that she must reveal her private concerns to someone who is not yet defined as her regular physician, appropriate to such disclosures. Here the open-ended question underlines the ambiguity of the new relationship.

*c. Rejection.* When a wife greets her husband by announcing that her visiting friends are discussing nursery schools or the sewing circle, she implies his absence would be welcome. In this act, the wife asserts that the activity of the group is bound to a category of which he is not a member.

*d. Invitation.* Sacks cited the late arrival of a member to a group therapy session:

"Hi. We were having an automobile discussion."
"...discussing the psychological motives for..."
"drag racing in the streets."

Here the latecomer was invited into the conversation by three members in one sentence.

Emily Post referred to such practices as "including someone in conversation," and suggested that it can be done without an introduction, for example, by saying to a friend who arrives during a conversation with a gardener, "[Hello, Gladys,] Mr. Smith is suggesting that I dig up these cannas and put in delphiniums." This is evidently a semi-introduction, since it allows the superior to address the inferior, but without the implication of equality lying in a full introduction.

These four slots are not recognized by speakers as such. They enter into complex sequencing rules which have not yet been analyzed sufficiently; it is clear, for example, that the first two occupy different positions, one being uttered by the summoner, the other by the respondent. Rejection/invitation are alternatives in the same rule. The function of and sequence rules for these speech acts can be checked not only from natural conversations but by experimental omission or alteration of the temporal location in the sequence of acts.

## 4. Narratives

Labov and Waletzky (1967) recently presented a framework for the analysis of informal narratives or oral versions of personal experience. Narratives, whether formal or casual, involve problems of sequencing *par excellence,* since it is inherent in the problem of narration that the hearer must understand the sequence in the *referent* events. The article defined a series of clause types in terms of their permutation properties. The preservation of causal relations implied by narrative sequence is evident as early as age 6, according to Brent and Katz, in very simple tasks (1967). A basic contrast in the analysis of Labov and Waletzky is between free clauses, which could occur anywhere in the narration (e.g., descriptions of character of hero), and clauses which must occur before, after, or between certain others, which define their displacement range.

By utilizing the units of this formal analysis to characterize the whole narrative sequence, Labov and Waletzky were able to identify five portions in the maximally expanded narrative, which they call orientation, complication, evaluation, resolution, and coda. The minimum possible narrative has only complication. While they noted that the amount of narrative structure used beyond the minimum was related to the verbal skill of the speaker, it was also apparent that differences of group styles, age, and so on could be profitably examined through such formal means.

## 5. Tying Rules

In his class lectures, Sacks has discussed many details of sequencing within conversations. One problem has to do with the sequence of speakers. In a dyadic conversation, he has found that the rule is alternation of adequate complete utterances between the two speakers. But in larger groups, more complex patterns obtain. The next speaker may be indicated by asking a question. Then the addressee has the right to the floor whenever he chooses to talk, and the asker has the right after the responder. The rule is such that other material can intervene between question and response. "When I've asked a question, then the pause between my talk and yours is your silence," according to Sacks. Thus a question is a "first speaker form," since it implies that a second speaker is called on. So, in the groups he has studied, is an insult.

Second speaker forms include pronouns tying back to earlier utterances, and pro-verbs. Some forms are even more complex, such as "I still say, though..." which implies a third activity of which some prior one was done by the same person.

The result of using the sequence features Sacks has discussed is that a great deal of information can be obtained from single utterances. In the example, "Ken face it, you're a poor little rich kid," he points out that we know that Ken is the addressee, that Ken now has the right to speak, that he has the right to give an insult to the speaker, and that some categorization device (e.g., Mommy) in a contrast set with "kid" is likely.

## 6. Speech Event Analysis

Sequence rules are appropriate for the description of what may be called "speech events," which, in turn, may be parts of or coterminous with *focused interaction* (Goffman 1963). Traditionally, anthropologists were aware of such organized units only in the case of ceremonies and tales, where preservation of the same thematic sequences, or even the same wording, was highly valued. These repeated routines were, of course, obvious even to the most casual observer. *The Book of Common Prayer,* for example, clearly labels each speech event, its components, and the alternatives at each point.

Even so simple a sequence as a short telephone conversation, as Schegloff has shown, has underlying structural rules. These rules refer to abstract categories not evident on the surface of behavior. Since multiparty interactions must be even more complex, we can assume that the rules for such encounters will not be simple. At least, one cannot expect that the rules of speech events are any simpler than the grammar of sentences.

Frake (1964) identified segments of the speech event as *discourse stages.* Components of the stages or coterminous with them are *exchanges,* which Frake defined as "sets of utterances with a common topic focus," probably similar to Watson and Potter's (1962) *episodes. Speech acts* are utterances or utterance sets with an interpretable function. Examples might be the routines that can mark the boundaries of episodes such as "That reminds me..." promises, jokes, apologies, greetings, requests, or insults. Speech acts, unlike functions, are cultural units, and must be discovered by ethnological methods.

Some of the features of order between these units have been considered in the context of narration by Labov and Waletzky (1967) and others. The displacement sets and other categories they have defined for clauses can also apply to other units such as speech acts. Where displacement occurs, of self-identification, for instance, it may be marked by special routines, "By the way, my name is — — — —" which would not be used except for the deviation.

The categories which Schegloff and Sacks discussed are sufficiently general in many cases so that one can expect them to be found universally. The summons sequence is a good candidate. Schegloff showed, with respect to telephone conversations, that the basic rules he gave, with called answering first, caller providing initial topic, and so on, are required by the distribution of information at the start. On the other hand, the specific selections available within each formal category in this case are likely to be highly culture- or group-specific. The strategy for the discovery of alternations and of sequencing rules is similar. In the latter case, one tests the response of members to omissions or permutations, rather than to substitutions.

## C. Co-occurrence Rules

### 1. Types of Rules

"How's it going, Your Eminence? Centrifuging okay? Also, have you been analyzin' whatch'unnertook t'achieve?"

The bizarreness of this hypothetical episode arises from the oscillations between different varieties of speech. It violates the co-occurrence rules that we assume English to have.

In the preceding section, we were concerned with the selection of lexical items, pronouns, or inflectional alternatives. We conceived of each instance as involving social selectors. Once a selection has been made, however, later occurrences within the same utterance, conversation, or even between the same dyad may be predictable. Whenever there is predictability between two linguistic forms, we can speak of co-occurrence rules.

Co-occurrence rules could be of two kinds. Predictability through time might be called horizontal, since it specifies relations between items sequentially in the discourse. Another type might be called vertical, specifying the realization of an item at each of the levels of structure of a language. For instance, given a syntactical form, only certain lexicon may normally be employed, and a particular set of phonetic values may realize the lexicon. If one learned political terms in New York and gardening terms in Virginia, the phonetic coloring of the lexicon might reflect their provenance in the individual's history. The most striking case lies in the well-practiced bilingual who uses French syntax and pronunciation for French vocabulary and English syntax and pronunciation for English vocabulary.

In the example, the following are violations of vertical co-occurrence:

1. "How's it going" is a phrase from casual speech, but the suffix "-ing" is used, rather than "-in" which is normal for casual speech.
2. An elliptical construction is used in the second utterance, which contains only a participle, but the formal "-ing" appears again.
3. A technical word, "centrifuge" is used in the elliptical construction.
4. The "-in" suffix is used with the formal "analyze."
5. Rapid informal articulation is used for the pedantic phrase "undertook to achieve."

Horizontal co-occurrence rules refer to the same level of structure, and might be lexical or structural. The vocabulary in the example oscillates between slang and technical terms, the syntax between ellipsis and parallel nonellipsis. In bilingual speech, one may find structural predictability independent of lexicon, as in an example of Pennsylvania German:

Di kau ist over di fens jumpt.

Here the syntax and grammatical morphemes are German, the lexicon English. Horizontal co-occurrence rules governing selection of morphemes are common with lexical switching and phrase switching allowed. Diebold (1963) also gave examples in which Greek-Americans who can speak both languages with "perfect" co-occurrence rules, if they employ English loanwords in the Greek discourse, realize them in the Greek phonological system. This would suggest that for these speakers, horizontal phonological rules override vertical realization rules.

One of the startling aberrations in the example is the use of slang to a cardinal. We would expect to find that deferential address forms would be co-occurrent with formal style. One pictures a cardinal in a microbiology laboratory addressed by a janitor who knows technical terms but cannot fully control formal syntax and phonology. Like ungrammatical sentences, sociolinguistically deviant utterances become normal if one can define setting and personnel to locate them. This is of course the point. Wherever there are regular co-occurrences, deviant behavior is marked and may carry social meaning.

The most extreme forms of co-occurrence restrictions are likely to be found in ritualized religious speech in traditional societies. Here it would be blasphemous to utter the wrong speech. Indeed, Gumperz has suggested that linguistics first began with the Sanskrit scholars' efforts to identify the formal features of religious texts and transmit them unchanged. It is co-occurrence restrictions which allow the recognition of language in multilingual societies.

At the opposite extreme are the conditions in American college lecturing, where technical terms, slang, and informal and formal syntax may alternate to some extent. Friedrich also gives examples (1966) of delicate communication of changing relationships by shifts within conversations.

## 2. Style

*a. Formal style.* Style is the term normally used to refer to the co-occurrent changes at various levels of linguistic structure within one language. Hymes (1964) has commented that probably every society has at least three style levels: formal or polite, colloquial, and slang or vulgar.

If Hymes is right about a polite style which contrasts with the unmarked (or "normal") colloquial, it might be proposed that this is the style preferred in public, serious, ceremonial occasions. Co-occurrence restrictions are particularly likely because of the seriousness of such situations. The style becomes a formal marker for occasions of societal importance where the personal relationship is minimized. We would expect that the distant or superior form of address and pronoun is universally employed in public high style. In Figs. 1 and 2 "status-marked situations" which call for titles and V may also call for polite style. Thus speakers who exchange colloquial style normally might change to this style in certain public occasions such as funerals or graduation ceremonies.

It might generally be the case in English that in otherwise identical situations, an alter addressed with TLN receives polite style more than one addressed with FN. Howell (1967, p. 99) reported such correlations in Korean. Formal lexicon and "-ing" should be related. Fischer (Hymes 1964b) found that "criticizing, visiting, interesting, reading, correcting" and "flubbin, punchin, swimmin, chewin, hittin" occurred in a single speaker's usage. It is not clear here whether it is lexical style or topic that is at issue, since there were no examples of denotative synonyms with different vocabulary. Examples of the sort given in Newman (Hymes 1964b), and found plentifully in English lexicon for body functions (e.g., urinate vs. weewee), provide clearer evidence for co-occurrence restrictions between lexicon and structure.

Labov (1966) did include "-ing" vs. "-in" in his study of style contrasts in different social strata, and he found that it worked precisely as the phonological variables did. Polite style in a speaker might require a certain higher frequency of [r], of [ ð ] rather than [d] in, e.g., "this," and of "-ing" (see Figs. 5 and 6). While the variables differentiating polite form casual style tended to be the same in different classes, the precise frequency reached for each variable varied (Labov, 1966). Thus his evidence suggests co-occurrence rules for grammatical morphemes and phonology. Labov (1966) and Klima

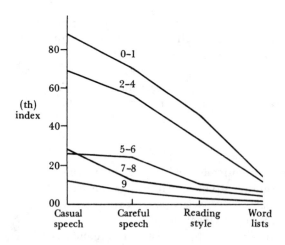

FIGURE 5

Class and style stratification of [th] in thing, three, etc., for adult native New York City speakers (Labov, 1966)

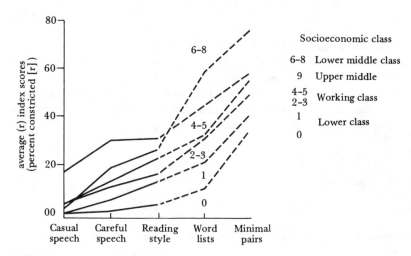

FIGURE 6

Class stratification of [r] in guard, car, beer, beard, etc., for native New York City adults (Labov 1966)

(1964) considered the formal description of phonological and syntactic style features, respectively.

*b. Informal style.* In trying to sample different styles while interviewing, Labov made the assumption that speakers would use a more formal style during the interview questioning than at other times. He used several devices for locating such shifts contextually: speech outside the interview situation; speech to others, usually in the family; rambling asides; role-playing (specifically, getting adults to recite childhood rhymes); and answers to a question about a dangerous experience. He found that when "channel cues" (changes in tempo, pitch range, volume, or rate of breathing) indicated a change to casual or spontaneous speech within a speech episode, the phonological features changed. In the examples illustrating the shifts, lexicon and syntax changed too.

It is commonly the case that as one moves from the least deferent speech to the most, from the informal to the ceremonial, there is more elaboration and less abbreviation. Probably this difference is a universal, for two reasons. One is that elaboration is a cost, and is therefore most likely to occur in culturally valued situations or relationships (Homans 1958). The other is that a high degree of abbreviation is only possible in in-group communication. While ceremonials may be confined to a sacred few, wherever they have a public function and must communicate content, we can assume that this principle of elaboration holds. Elaboration could be defined with respect to a surface structure, or to the complexity of embedded forms in the syntax, or some such criteria. A very brief poem might be, in fact, more complex in terms of rules and "effort" of compression more complex than a discursive report of the "same" content. Some forms are unambiguous: suffixed vs. unsuffixed forms, as in Japanese honorifics or polite verb suffixes, titles vs. nontitles, and so on.

From a formal grammatical standpoint, ellipsis is more complex than non-ellipsis, since the grammar must contain an additional rule. It is not clear how ellipsis might be handled in a performance model. However, ellipsis in the syntactical sense is clearly more common in informal speech. Some examples can be given from questions and answers:

"Do (you(want(more cake?"
"I would like more cake."
"I'd like more cake."
"I would."
"Me."

From Soskin and John's text of (1963) of a married couple; we find the following:

Bet you didn't learn it there....
Your name? (from attendant)...
Want me to take it...
Wanna take your shoes off?...
Getting seasick, dear?...
Think I can catch up with them?...
Not that way!...
Directly into it....

The formal rules for sentence contractions and ellipsis are readily written.

Another form of ellipsis is that used in conversational episodes in second-speaker forms or to complete one's own earlier utterances. From Soskin and John (1963):

That fish, Honey....
But I have a handicap....
Like this?...
Which? This? Down here?...
You should be able to....
Undulating!...
Yeah, if you want to....
Rowed!...
With both of them!...
Well, you wanted to....
You sure are....
Well, I could....

These forms of ellipsis are learned. Brent and Katz (1967) found that pronominalization is rare in young children; it is obligatory in second speaker rules. Bellugi (1967) found also that contractions occur later than uncontracted forms in the speech of children.

Semantic compression is also available in casual speech among intimates as will be evident later.

Phonetically, a form which occurs in casual speech more than in polite styles is rapid speech, which entails horizontal restrictions.

"What are you doing?"
"Whaddya doin?"
"Whach doon?"

There are regular phonetic alternations related to rate, e.g.:

1. Retention of syllable of major stress and peak pitch.
2. As degree of speeding increases, loss of segments with weakest stress.
3. Loss or assimilation of semivowels.
   [r] in postvocalic position lost.
   [d] + [y] → [j], e.g., "Whadja do?"
   [t] + [y] → [č], e.g., "Whacha doin?"[4]
4. Marginal phonological distinctions like /hw/ vs. /w/ may be lost, perhaps part of of casual speech style.
5. Unstressed vowels centralized.

There is a *reverse* set of rules available to speakers used to the above alternations. The extra-slow may be employed in sounding-out for a dictionary or over the telephone. Thus normal "school" may become slow [sɨkuwɨl].

## 3. Registers and Occupational Argots

Husband: Whaddya say you just *quit*...
  Wife: I can't simply *quit* the airlines because *notice must* be *given,* but I'll certainly take what you *say* into *consideration,* and *report* it to my *superiors*...
Husband: I don't *know* you. I don't feel *close* to you.
  Wife: Well, I'm *awfully sorry.* There's *nothing* I can do right now because I *am* preparing a *meal,* but *if* you'll *wait* until *after* I've made the *beverage,* perhaps—
Husband: I can't *stand* it. I want *out,* I want a *divorce!*
  Wife: Well, all I can *say* is, it's been nice having you *aboard*—
                                                    Nichols and May (1959)

The register of airlines or tourist businesses is revealed here in lexical choices like meal, beverage, and aboard, and "preparing a meal" rather than "getting breakfast." Register is reflected primarily in lexicon, since different topics are required in different milieux. However, in this case the paralinguistic features

---

4 Alert readers will note these "rules" will not account for non-voicing of [č] in ellipsis of underlying "what are" but not of "what did," suggesting the rules cannot use merely surface phonetic segments.

also change, including stress on words like "must," "am," "if," "after," "do," "about," "will," "back," which would usually not be stressed. In the register of psychologists are both professional lexicon like "interaction" and syntactic structures like the passive "It was felt that."

*Slang* is similar to register variation in that the alternates are primarily lexical. As Newman (Hymes 1964*b*) has pointed out, the actual forms used are not necessarily different, but in sacred or slang contexts they take on a different meaning, so that in speaking of slang vocabulary one must include both form and semantic features. Since slang is highly transitory by definition, it will be understood in a given sense only within the group or network where it developed or to which it has moved at a given time. Thus one might predict that the selection rules for slang should restrict it to addressees to whom one claims a solidary relation. By this interpretation, a college lecture laced with slang is a claim on the identification of the audience. The nature of co-occurrence restrictions with slang needs investigation.

### 4. Linguistic Repertoire

Co-occurrence restrictions refer to the selection of alternates within the repertoire of a speaker in terms of previous or concomitant selections. The range of alternates should be known in a study of restriction. In an American monolingual, the range is likely to include informal style, slang, perhaps an occupational register, and some formal style. Labov (1964) has pointed out, however, that it is rare to control a very wide stylistic range unless one is a speech specialist, and that upwardly mobile persons usually lose the "ability to switch 'downwards' to their original vernacular" (p. 92).

In many parts of the world, a code that is relatively distinct from the casual vernacular is used in formal situations. This condition, called "diglossia" in Ferguson's (Hymes 1964*b*) classic article, may, because of the greater code difference, be accompanied by more co-occurrence restriction than is style shifting, where the common features of the styles may outweigh their differences. Examples where the codes are related are Greece, German Switzerland, Haiti, and Arab countries. Standard languages coexisting with local dialects are somewhat less distinguished, and historically the dialect does not usually maintain itself except phonetically, though there may be ideological resistance to borrowing from the standard (Blom and Gumperz, in press).

Where diglossia takes the form of bilingualism (Fishman 1967), one might at first assume that the co-occurrence restrictions would primarily govern the high form. Such a condition exists in many American bilingual communities with English as the high form. However, these are not usually pure cases, since English is the vernacular if there are casual contacts outside the immigrant community. Under these conditions, there can be considerable interpenetration (Gumperz 1967; Ervin-Tripp, in press).

Co-occurrence restrictions in common-sense terms refer to "language-mixing." Some bilingual communities have strong attitudinal opposition to switching (usually they mean lexical co-occurrence). Blom and Gumperz (in press) found that in a Norwegian village, speakers were unconscious of the use of standard forms and were very upset to hear tapes showing lack of co-occurrence restrictions in behavior. In practice, the maintenance of coordinate or segregated systems depends upon social factors. Coordinate bilingualism is possible if there is a complete range of equivalent lexicon in both systems, and social support for the bilingualism. If this is not the case, some topics cannot be discussed, some emotions cannot be conveyed, and borrowing, perhaps surrounded by a routine disclaimer frame, will occur. The other social conditions permitting such segregation in diglossia are the closed network circumstances reported by Blom and Gumperz (in press), where certain topics and transactional types simply would not occur in casual discourse. Thus American researchers can find rich grounds for the study of behavioral support or loss of co-occurrence rules, in either English style, registers, or multilingualism.

## III. SWITCHING

If a given speaker is observed during his daily round, all the features of his speech may show some systematic changes. The total repertoire of some speakers is far greater than others. Some are bilinguals, and some are community leaders with a wide range of styles reflecting their varying relationships and activities. In this section, we shall bring together evidence on some of the major classes of variables affecting variation within individual speakers.

### A. Personnel

In any act of communication, there is a "sender" and one or more "receivers" who together may be called "interlocutors" (Hymes 1962). In addition, there may be present an audience which is not the primary addressee of the message. The distribution of these roles has been discussed elsewhere (Ervin-Tripp 1964). The role of sender, or speaker, is rarely distributed in equal time to all participants. There appear to be four factors which affect the amount of talking each participant may do. One factor is the situation. In informal small-group conversation, the roles of sender and receiver may alternate. In a sermon, the sender role is available to only one participant; in choral responses in a ritual, or in a question period following a lecture, the role of sender is allocated at specific times. The allocation of the role of sender is specified by sequencing rules for each type of speech event, and a sender may select his successor by a question or a gaze. A second, related, determinant of the amount of talking is the role the participant has in the group and his social and physical centrality. He may be a therapy patient, chairman, teacher, or switch board operator, so that his formal status requires communication with great frequency; he may informally select such a role, as in the case of a raconteur or expert on the topic at hand. Third there is a personal constant carried from group to group. The net effect of the second and third factors is that the sending frequency of participants in a group is almost always unequal, and it has been shown to have regular mathematical properties in ad hoc discussion groups (Stephan and Mishler 1952; Bales and Borgatta 1955). Because relative frequency of speaking is steeply graded, not evenly distributed, in a large group the least frequent speaker may get almost no chance to speak. Knutson (1960) was able to produce radical alterations in participation rates by forming homogeneous groups on the basis of participation frequency. He found that talkative persons were generally regarded as better contributors, so there was great surprise when the homogeneously quiet group produced better work, by objective outside ratings.

The receiver role is also unequally distributed, even in face-to-face groups, being allocated in work talk to the most central, the most powerful, those with highest status, the most frequent speakers, and in highly valued groups, to the most deviant. In social conversation, proximity may be important (Hare 1962, p. 289; Schachter 1951).

In addition to their roles within the interaction situation, the personnel bring with them other statuses. These are, according to Goodenough (1965), "rights, duties, privileges, powers, liabilities, and immunities." I have mentioned that one of the functions of identity marking in speech is to indicate precisely what is required in the relationship. In any particular interaction, of course, not all the statuses of all participants are relevant. Obviously, the specific relations tying participants are most salient, e.g., a husband and his wife or an employer and his employee.

In addition to determining the forms that interaction might take, the identity of alter, and his relation to ego, will establish whether interaction is possible or obligatory. For example, following a death in the family, there is a specific sequence of persons who must be informed (Sacks' example).

Personnel include the audience as well as the receiver. The presence of others can, wherever there are options, weigh the selectors differently, according to whether one wants to conceal or display them to others. Thus, in a medical laboratory, technicians employ more formal and deferential speech to doctors when the supervisor or patients are present. In public the relation doctor-technician takes precedence over familiarity, so that, "Hey, Len, shoot the chart to me, will ya?" becomes, "Do you want the chart, Doctor?" Note the co-occurrence of formal structure and formal address.

I indicated in Section II that there are formal constraints on address. The rules for reference to third parties are more complex, for they are related both to the third party and to the addressee. In the American system, where the adult personnel present exchange FN they may regularly omit T in reference to third parties whom they normally address with TFN or TLN. If an addressee is lower in age or rank, e.g., a child or employee, and uses T to the referent, then T is used by both parties in reference. Thus "Daddy" might be used in addressing a child. Emily Post recommended that women refer to their husbands as TLN to inferiors in rank or age, "my husband" to strangers, and FN to friends "on the dinner list" (1922, p. 54). The friend, however, could not necessarily address the husband by FN (presumably some familiarity criterion was in use). "It is bad form to go about saying 'Edith Worldly' or 'Ethel Norman' to those who do not call them Edith or Ethel, and to speak thus familiarly of one whom you do not call by her first name, is unforgivable."

When the addressee is equal or slightly superior in rank, and thus eligible for receiving confidences (Slobin et al., in press), when they share statuses which exclude the referent party, emotion toward the referent may be revealed. These constraints apply in particular to pejorative or affectionate nicknames toward persons addressed with TLN.

To the extent that the referent and addressee are alike, there is an implication of deference to the addressee in the form of reference selected. In the Japanese system of honorifics and "stylemes" (Martin, in Hymes 1964b) both the terms for the referent and the verb suffixes are altered by deference, i.e., by selectors of relative rank, age, sex, and solidarity. In the most polite style, dialect forms are absent and the suffixes are employed. Children of ages 8 or 9 first learn control over reference, but still employ dialect forms freely and do not differentiate age of addressees by the "stylemes" (i.e., linguistic markers) of polite speech (Horikawa et al., 1956). Possibly there is in Japanese, as in English, a rule by which reference employs honorifics when a child is addressed; thus it becomes the normal name for the referent.

*Deference* is undoubtedly a social feature present in all sociolinguistic systems to some degree. The most elaborate structural forms are evidently those found in the Far East. Geertz' description of the Javanese system is of general importance; he contrasted "stylemes," including affixes and function morphemes governed by co-occurrence restrictions, as in our formal style, with honorific vocabulary which is more sporadic. It seems, like the American "sir," to be governed by a rule of frequency (Martin, in Hymes 1964b), rather than required presence or absence (Geertz 1960).

Language choice itself, rather than stylistic alternatives, may be governed by addressee features of rank, age, and solidarity. Rubin's (1962) characterization of the alternation between Spanish and Guarani in Paraguay, according to addressee, nearly matches Fig. 2, with V = Spanish, and T = Guarani.

*Familiarity* entered into several of the address rules in Section II. Familiarity increases the probability that an addressee will be talked to, and for this reason familiar interaction is likely to be marked by many forms of ellipsis at all levels, unless some setting or deference constraints interfere. Omissions of subject and modal follow this pattern in English, as a form of syntactic ellipsis. In-group slang frequently is situationally selected by familiarity of addressee.

When a friend is addressed in the Two Person Communication game, in which separated parties communicate solely by verbal messages, the selections among nonsense forms or colors are coded more efficiently, even though there is no feedback. In studies of sorority girls, comparison of speech to friend and nonfriend addressees repeatedly revealed a contrast in the *time* to describe objects when the speaker saw one and the hearer an array. The friends were both more succinct and more successful. Only in part was this difference because of reference to obviously private experience; e.g., "It's the color of Jan's new sweater." Most conspicuous was the contrast between technical descriptions to nonfriends and metaphorical description to friends; e.g., "It's an elephant doing the push-ups." The striking feature of these metaphorical descriptions is that they are very successful even when a nonfriend encounters them; thus, the question arises, Why not use metaphor to strangers? Two explanations need testing: possibly the use of metaphor seems self-revealing; our formal educational system clearly downgrades metaphorical forms of description. The contrast between Brent and Katz' (1967) college students and Job Corps Negroes illustrates the latter fact; given geometrical forms, descriptions much like college students' familiar speech were given by the less educated subjects.

How does the similarity of speech between friends arise? It is a common feature of interaction between two persons that if the parameters of speech· are different they become more similar during the interaction. Thus, a given person's speech may vary depending on the speech features of the addressee. This phenomenon has been noted in the production features of rate, durations, and silence (e.g., Matarazzo *et al.* 1965), and is clearly the case for such features as lexical selection and syntax in addressing children. Ramanujan has commented that Brahmins adopt stereotyped non-Brahmin speech when addressing non-Brahmins; thᵊ same comparison needs to be made across social classes in this country. Address to children, i.e., baby talk, is also likely to be stereotyped. If in fact the similarity is an effect of the speech of alter, it should increase during the course of a long interaction; if it arises purely from stereotypes, it may remain unchanged.

In multilingual communities there must be some regularities in the control over the code to be used if both are to speak in the same code (Barker 1947; Herman 1961). Perhaps the more powerful controls the code choice, if setting and topic permit an option. Deference might be realized either by the adaptation of the lower ranked person to the preference of the higher, or by respectful avoidance of imitation—"keeping one's place." Cross-cultural research is needed to locate systematic features of social systems which may predict which party in a dyad changes more, and in which linguistic features. Further speculations are given in Grimshaw's survey paper (in press).

The most dramatic example of language shift affected by addressee is baby talk. This is a speech style occurring in many societies (Ferguson 1964) for address to infants, and often to pets and lovers. In English, baby talk affects all levels of structure.

Most speakers are likely to be conscious of baby-talk lexicon, as they often are of the lexical features of styles. Baby-talk lexicon includes words like "potty," "weewee," "bunny," "night-night," "mommy," and "daddy." Many other words in adult speech become appropriate for speaking to infants when the suffix "-ie" is added. Work in progress by Kerry Drach and Ben Kobashigawa suggests that speech to children may be dramatically different in syntax, being simpler, and containing fewer errors, fewer subordinate clauses, more repetitions, and more imperatives and questions requiring feedback.

Phonological effects and paralinguistic features are especially conspicuous.

Samples of talk to infants show certain general phonetic changes such as palatalization. Most striking is the use of a higher pitch and a sing-song, wide-ranging intonation. The younger the infant, the higher the pitch. Observations of the social distribution of this style show it to be more common in addressing other people's children than one's own. For instance, nurses use the paralinguistic features, at least, in persuading children, and in cooperative nurseries comparison of own-child and other-child addressees shows a distinct shift to more age attribution to own child.

Children themselves use many of the features of adult baby talk very early. In addressing younger siblings they may adopt lexical and paralinguistic features of the adult baby talk as early as age 2. In role-play, they use phrases and address terms from baby talk, e.g.; "Goo-goo, little baby," and freely employ the sing-song intonation in addressing "babies." In other respects, their role play is stereotyped rather than strictly imitative, for example, in the frequent use of role-names. It may be that the intonational and lexical features of baby talk may function simply as role markers in their play.

## B. Situation

A situation refers to any constellation of statuses and setting which constrains the interaction that should or may occur—what Barker and Wright (1954) called the "standing behavior patterns." A situation, like a status, is a cultural unit, so that ethnological study is necessary to determine classes of situations.

At the university, a class is a situation. From the standpoint of the authorities, the criteria include the presence of an authorized instructor, students, and an approved time and place. From the standpoint of the instructor and students, there are strong constraints on function and on topical relevance.

Recently a student and faculty strike at the University of California brought these criteria to light. Instructors varied in which features of the definition they suspended in their effort to meet their obligations to the students but not to the university administration. Some met at a different time, others at a different place. Some used the same setting but discussed strike issues or public affairs. When the administration threatened to fire instructors who "failed to meet their obligations," it was not at all clear whether they used a minimal or maximal set of criteria.

Situation is most clearly defined when there are jointly dependent statuses and locales: church and priest, school and teacher, store and salesgirl, bus and driver, restaurant and waitress, plane and stewardess, clinic and physician. If the same personnel encounter each other elsewhere, for instance, at a baseball game, address terms (as distinct from attention-getting terms) may remain the same, but everything else about the interaction is likely to change.

If we examine these clear cases, we see that there are constraints on expected activities, rights, and obligations, and that there are, in several cases, clearly defined speech events such as the church service, the classroom lecture, the order to the waitress, the welcome, oxygen lecture of the stewardess, and the medical history in the clinic. Both the activities and the speech events are likely to be specific to the locale, though we might conceive of asking some information questions of the teacher or physician when he is off duty.

Because the activities and speech events have sequencing rules, they may be demarcated into discourse stages. The boundaries may be marked by routines or by code changes. After a church service, priest and parishioner may exchange personal greetings as friends, the priest using a radically different style than in his sermon. After a formal lecture, the opening of the floor to questions in cases of diglossia is signaled by a switch to the "lower" code, e.g. colloquial Arabic or Guarani (Ferguson, in Hymes 1964b; Rubin, in press). These are predictable discourse stages, and in this respect they differ from shifts which are at the option of the participants. Blom and Gumperz (in press) mentioned that local residents of Hemnesberget might use standard Norwegian when enacting their roles as buyer and seller, but if one wished to initiate a private conversation on personal matters, he would shift to the local dialect.

Analogous style switches occur here between colloquial speech and occupational argots, according to personnel present or situation. In some academic communities, it is considered a breach of etiquette to use occupational argot or discuss occupational topics at a dinner party or other "social situation"; others define these rules solely by personnel. Thus, the topic and register may change when wives are listening or when there is occupational diversity among the participants.

One strategy in identifying situations is to look for folk terminology for them, such as church service, party, interview, picnic, lunch break, conversation, chat, class, and discussion. The status-oriented interaction between customers and sales personnel or waitresses has no name, and the interaction arising from statuses in work organizations has no folk name in English. If there is some independent and reliable way of identifying situational categories, then the difference between the named and the unnamed is important, for it suggests that the named situations enter into members' accounts.

*Restricted languages* illustrate situational constraints vividly. In hamburger stands and short-order cafes in the United States, abbreviated forms of speech appear. In these settings, there is a premium on speed in transmission of orders from the waitress to the cook. The number of alternatives is semantically limited, with certain high probabilities. In the ordering, one can see evidence that the code has been reduced almost to the minimum required for efficiency, within the structure of English syntax, by radical ellipsis. In studies by Brian Stross (1964) and by Marion Williams (1964), corpora were collected in a range of local settings:

| | |
|---|---|
| one | one hamburger |
| two sweets | two sweet rolls |
| barbeef | barbecued beef sandwich |
| boil five | 5-minute boiled egg |
| burger without | one hamburger without onions |

| | |
|---|---|
| beeny up | bacon and eggs, sunny side up |
| bacon and | bacon and eggs (differs with locale) |
| one M. O. | one hamburger, mustard only |
| L. T. plain | lettuce and tomato salad |
| ham and over rye | ham and eggs over, on rye |
| five squirt three | five coffees, three with cream |

Stross pointed out that the underlying rule for all of these instances, except the last, is (number) + (name) + (describer). This kind of syntax appears in normal English in phrases like "five hamburgers without onions." The odd appearance of the restricted syntax arises from the optional omission of *any* of these elements, and from the appearance in the describer class of items like "and" and "without" which normally do not appear alone. It is hard to think of any way of omitting the function word rather than the noun in "without onions," but in the case of "ham and eggs" it seems possible that the form could be "ham eggs." This would violate the general rule that the last item be a describer and obviously subordinate. Note that when there is an adjective-noun phrase in the gloss, the two can be compressed into one word by making the adjective a prefix, as in "barbeef."

The abbreviation devices summarized by Stross include loss of segments (burger), use of initials (especially to replace conjoined nouns), loss of name (of most probable item), container for contents (cup for spaghetti), and preparation unique to an item (boil for egg).

The last item on the list does not follow the structural rule. It comes from a trucker's cafe, in which the corpus was kitchen talk rather than waitress ordering. This corpus was distinguished by a lot of colorful slang, much of it from vintage army usage and pejorative in tone. The efficiency pressure did not take priority here, and the structural rules were therefore different. Single word examples are "wop" for spaghetti, "pig" for hot dogs, "rabbit" for salad, and "grease" for fries. Longer units of the slang type are "burn a cow" for two well-done hamburgers, "bowl a slop" for a bowl of the soup of the day, "cap'ns galley" for pancakes topped by egg. That abbreviation did not dominate is suggested in cases which the other rule would reduce: "one order grease," "one wop with balls." In the last case humor wins out over brevity, which would yield "one wop with" or even "wop with." "One green bitch with T.I." for green goddess salad with thousand island dressing could have reduced to "green T.I." or "bitch T.I."

Restaurants in Switzerland and London were observed, and similar forms of restricted language were found only in London's "Wimpy bars." Here the forms are so similar to American hamburger stands that one can guess that some of the language traveled with the product. In the interchanges in other restaurants, no evidence of radical ellipsis was found. One reason may be that observations were made within kitchens and, as we have seen in regard to the trucker's cafe, kitchen talk evidently is not constrained by the same brevity pressures as orders to the kitchen.

The mere cataloging of cultural units is not likely to bear much fruit unless the features of the situations which effect sociolinguistic rules can be identified. Moscovici (1967) has cleverly manipulated situational features in the Two Person Communication game. It is common to speak of "formal" situations, but it is not clear what makes a situation formal. Labov has suggested that degree of self-monitoring constitutes a dimension permitting alignment of situations on a continuum. Work- or status-oriented situations vs. person-oriented situations provides another contrast. In the first case, there is likely to be some criterion of achievement in an activity; in the second, the focus of attention can be turned to selves and to expressions of personal emotions. Watson (1958) distinguished work, family, and sociable interaction. But these differences are essentially differences in function.

## C. Speech Acts, Topic, and Message

"What are you talking about?" "We were just saying hello." "We were telling jokes." "I was introducing Joe." Subordinate to organized exchanges like parties and work situations are classes we have called "speech acts." In the above examples, their identity is suggested by the folk classification. Here the informants can label segments of interaction.

There also must be unlabeled interaction. "Hello. Where is the post office?" addressed to a passerby, or, "My name is George Landers. What time is it?" to a stranger, violate, according to Labov, sequencing rules. If this is the case, the conjoined segments must have identifiable properties by which the rules can be characterized abstractly. In bilingual interaction, the segments may entail language shift.

There is no reason to assume that speech acts are the same everywhere. Certain special forms of discourse like poetry and speech-making may have components known only to specialists. Whether and why there are labels used in the teaching of these performances is itself a sociolinguistic problem.

Speech acts in English include greetings, self-identification, invitations, rejections, apologies, and so on. The ones identified so far tend to be routines, but we can expect to find other more abstract units as research proceeds.

When conversations have an explicit message with informational content, they can be said to have a *topic*. "What are you talking about?" "Nothing." "Gossip." "Shop talk." "The weather." "The war." "We were having an automobile discussion about the psychological motives for drag-racing in the streets." In everyday discourse, the question of topic is most likely to occur in invitations or rejections so that the answers serve either to exclude a new arrival or to give him enough information to participate. Besides selecting personnel for participation, topics may be governed by a continuity rule. In a formal lecture in a university, there is a constraint on continuity and relevance, just as there is in technical writing, where editing can enforce the constraint. Evidences of constraint are apologies for deviation: "That reminds me..." "Oh, by the way..." "To get back to the question..." "To change the subject..." Cultural rules regarding speech events may include constraints as to the grounds for relevance.

Kjolseth (1967) has found in analysis of some group interaction that topical episodes are key factors in speakers' tactics:

> A performer's tactic may be to direct his episode as a probe into the preceding episode. In contrast, in another situation his tactic may be to extend and elaborate some antecedent episode. On still another occasion his tactic may be to close off and limit a previous episode.... These tactical types are based on, or defined in terms of, two qualities abstracted from the performances: a) the episodic locus of relevances drawn from the existent conversation resource, and b) the purpose of the episode with respect to surrounding episodes."

Lennard and Bernstein (in press) have examined topical continuity in therapeutic sessions, and found the amount of continuity to be related to satisfaction. The three examples given by Kjolseth would involve topical continuation, recycling, or change, respectively. These general features of speech events require that members be able to identify relevance but not necessarily label topics.

There is yet a third form of evidence that topic may be a cultural unit. Bilinguals can frequently give reliable accounts of topical code-switching, and their behavior often corresponds, in general, to their accounts (Ervin-Tripp 1964).

We can thus argue that *topic* must be a basic variable in interaction, on the grounds that speakers can identify topical change as generating code-shift, that speakers can sometimes report what they are talking about, and that topical continuity, recycling, and change may be normative features of speech events, or at least relevant to values regarding good conversations.

The analysis of *messages* refers to two-term relationships, whereas *topic* is a single term allowing for simple taxonomies. Here I intend to refer only to the manifest or explicit message. The reason for the distinction is that latent content categories typically refer to intent (e.g., Dollard and Auld 1959; Katz 1966; Leary 1957; Marsden 1965). My position here is that intent or function is part of the constellation of social features out of which interaction is generated. It can be realized in a variety of ways, of which verbal interaction is only one. We seek regular rules by which one can relate underlying categories with their formal realizations or the formal features of interaction with their social meanings. Failure to discover such rules has led to considerable discouragement with the evident arbitrariness of content classifications in studies of natural discourse.

The manifest message, on the other hand, is the product of the social features of the situation as well as of intent, and is therefore inseparable from the interaction product. All the selections made in realization of the functions of communication can carry some kind of information, whether about the speaker, the situation, the hearer, or the topic. In detail, given alternations cannot do all at once, though they may be ambiguous as to which is intended. In this case, the *message* is intended to refer only to what is said or implied about the topic. There have been numerous summaries of ways of classifying messages (e.g., Pool 1959). A recent innovation is logical analysis (Véron *et al.* 1965). The underlying structure of logical linkages between terms in utterances is analyzed, and semantic relations are then described in terms of logical relations between pairs of units (e.g., equivalence, inference, conjunction, specification of conditions, sequential relations, explanation, and opposition, causes). A Markov semantic analysis revealed very large and consistent differences between subject groups, which were, in the study reported, clinical categories.

The same speaker information potentially can be realized through different means, for example, through explicit message content and through paralinguistic features. The conflict between these messages creates an interesting question about which is dominant. According to Mehrabian and Wiener (1967), who used controlled stimulus materials, regardless of the instructions to the listeners, the tone of voice is the dominant signal for judging affect. What is called the "double bind" must be a consequence of more than conflicting messages; for instance, it could be a requirement of overt response to the overt message on one occasion and to the paralinguistic cue on another, with no signal as to which is required.

The definition of appropriate units for analysis is important in comparing results of different studies. Watson and Potter (1962) discussed a macro-unit, the episode, which is defined by the stability of component features: the role system of the participants, the major participants, the focus of attention, and the relationship toward the focus of attention. The unit thus may be less than an utterance in length or may include the contributions of many speakers. In Lennard's research, one might say that satisfaction is related to the length of episodes. Watson and Potter chose the term "focus of attention" in order to differentiate cases where the topic is a person's experience, an on-going activity, or an abstract referential category as in a "discussion."

In thematic analyses, it is common to use either episodic (Katz 1966) or sentence units (Auld and White 1956). However, the sentence is not, strictly speaking, a unit in oral discourse. One can see texts in which long sequences of clauses linked by "and then..." occur. Are these separate sentences or one sentence? There have been four criteria used separately with different results: message criteria, structural or linguistic units (e.g., any segment containing a verb or naming phrases in isolation; John and Berney 1967); pauses, and intonational contours (Dittman and Llewellyn 1967).

## D. Functions of Interaction

### 1. Criteria

Firth (Hymes 1964*b*) was one among many who sought to identify the functions of speech. He included phatic communion (solidarity); pragmatic efficiency (accompanying work); planning and guidance; address; greetings, farewells, adjustment of relations, and so on; and speech as a commitment (courts, promises). Primarily, his view of function was the social value of the act.

To a psychologist, function is likely to be viewed from the standpoint of the interacting parties, either the sender or the receiver. Soskin has played tapes to listeners and asked them to report what they would *say* and what they would *think*. This method assumes that function is effect. It is close to Blom and Gumperz' (in press) criterion of social meaning.

A second method is to analyze actual instances of acts and to infer whether the receiver's response satisfied the speaker, either from his overt behavior or by questioning him. This method includes action, response, and reaction. It is derived from Skinner's (1957) theory that speech is operant behavior which affects the speaker through the mediation of a hearer. Feedback and audience consistency presumably "shape" effective speech in the normal person. In this method, function is identified by classes of satisfactory listener responses.

If intent, conscious or unconscious, is imputed to a speaker on the basis of some features of the content or form of his speech, a third form of functional analysis appears. This, of course, is the method of latent content analysis (e.g., Katz 1966; Watson 1958).

A set of function categories was devised to account for the initiation of dyadic interaction on the basis of a corpus of instances of action, response, and reaction (Ervin-Tripp 1964): The list includes explicit requests for goods, services, and information; implicit requests for social responses; offering of information or interpretations; expressive monologues; routines; and speech to avoid alternative activities.

Soskin and John (1963) devised a category system based on a combination of structural and semantic features. We can use their system to subclassify each of the above functional categories. For example, the following might all be requests for the loan of a coat:

"It's cold today." (structone)
"Lend me your coat." (regnone)
"I'm cold." (signone)
"That looks like a warm coat you have." (metrone)
"Br-r-r." (expressive)
"I wonder if I brought a coat." (excogitative)

One simple way to examine requests is to compare regnones, in which the request function is explicit, with all other categories, in terms of social distribution. In a term paper, Bessie Dikeman and Patricia Parker (1964) found that within families indirect request forms dominated between equals, almost half were regnones when seniors addressed juniors, and from juniors, regnones dominated. Examples from their paper are these:

"Where's the coffee, Dremsel?" (it is visible).
(to wife) [gloss: bring me the coffee]
"Is that enough bacon for you and Thelma?" (to husband)
[gloss: save some for Thelma]
"It's 7:15" (to daughter)
[gloss: hurry up]
"Mother, you know I don't have a robe. Well, we're

having a slumber party tomorrow night."
"Oh, dear I wish I were taller." (to adult brother)
[gloss: get down the dishes]

In factory settings, by contrast, requests to subordinates were more often regnones and often direct imperatives.

In a sample of requests offered during 80 hours of observation in a university office, Carol Pfuderer (1968) found that the major selector was familiarity and rank.

1. Whatever their status, familiar peers used direct imperatives.
2. When the peer was farther away, the imperative was followed by tag questions, "please," address forms, with rising pitch, e.g., "ask Marcy, why don't you?"'
3. Requests within the addressee's territory were deferential, even to familiar peers.
4. Requests to addressees of either higher or lower rank took the form of modal questions ("Would you get me some coffee, Jeanie?"), pragmatic neutralizations, or displacement of addressee. Neutralization refers to cases where two different functions could be realized by identical speech acts, which are therefore ambiguous, in intent.
5. Pragmatic neutralizations included information questions ("Has anyone gone to Accounting this week?" "Whose turn is it to make coffee this week, Ruby?") and structones ("It's stuffy in here"; "Someone has to see Dean Smith").
6. Where there was a large rank difference upward, the request might be displaced to an addressee nearer in rank. For example, a request for a stapler by a seated secretary was given not to the senior professor standing next to it but to a peer standing equidistant from it, and the deferential form was used: "Joan, would you please get the stapler for me?"

Request and persuasion require action on the part of alter so that the obligations and privileges inherent in the social relations of the personnel are likely to be realized in differences in linguistic expression. We might expect pragmatic neutralization when the requestor is deferent or reluctant to ask at all, or in situations where requests are highly frequent and familiarity produces high mutual nurturance and assurance of interpretability. In the restaurant studies, "please" was used for requested acts extraneous to the addressee's duties, perhaps a version of the territoriality feature in Miss Pfuderer's findings.

We can expect that where variant address forms exist, they might alternate in request situations. Milla Ayoub (1962), in a discussion of bipolar kin terms in Arabic, pointed out that in addition to proper names, a mother could call her son by either of two terms that can also mean "my mother." When a parent wishes to cajole or placate a child, but not command him, he uses these bipolar terms. This is particularly the case with sons. These terms are never heard in direct commands.

In discussing current address practices in the Soviet Union, Kantorovich (1966) mentioned that friends might switch from "$ty$" to "$vy$" with first name and patronymic when help was asked.

## 2. Approval-Seeking

In human communication, as among lower primates (Diebold 1967), many of the signals for what we have called "requests for social responses" are gestural or paralinguistic. Rosenfeld (1966) found that among American males, liking was related to the following factors in the speaker's behavior: long sentences, few self-words, and high reinforcement of the speech of alter through head nods and verbal routines; among women, frequent initiation of utterances, many sentences per speech, many speech disturbances and false starts, many questions and many words referring to alter, and reinforcement by nods produced greater liking by strangers. Rosenfeld also found which of these features were subject to conscious manipulation under instructions and role-playing: volubility, frequency of speaking and length of sentences, and more speech disturbances, as well as verbal reinforcing routines. The major omission is the semantic component (the kind Dale Carnegie discusses) of orienting the *content* of the interaction to alter rather than self. Probably address forms change also, among friends, when affiliative functions are primary. Tyler (1965), for example, suggested that certain address alternatives in the Koya kin system are employed when cross-cousins engage in the joking relationship which is their privilege. It was noted earlier that such alternates might even be used in deferential address with familiar addressees, for example, "Dr. S." rather than "Dr. Smith" from technician to physician when outsiders were absent.

There may prove to be classes of functionally equivalent responses by alter, such as head nods and brief verbal routines both occurring as options in response to the same stimuli. The identification of these response classes in turn can provide a criterion for recognizing the speech variables which elicit them from alter, and thus provide grounds for classifying "approval-seeking behavior," more objective than the intuition of judges. Of course whether or not there is any empirical value in these categories depends on whether or not they enter into speech rules consistently.

## 3. Effects of Function Shifts

Functions can enter into rules for the selection of settings by participants, the selection of addressees, and formal changes within the interaction.

"Oh my back, it's killing me today. I can hardly move."

"Yeah, it must be the weather. My leg's been aching all day."

"I was supposed to get a shot of cortisone today, but my husband couldn't take me to the doctor's."

"I hurt my leg in the army . . ." (long description).

"Oh. Well, I must get back to work."

Something went wrong in this interaction. The woman did not, in effect, respond to the man's story of woe and terminated the conversation.

The collection of large corpora of natural sequences might not yield enough such instances for analysis by classification; a role-playing method might be one approximation. We might find that responses to statements of physical distress take the form of inquiries of cause, routine sympathy expressions, or offers of help. In this case, none of these happened. Instead, the addressee himself made a statement of physical distress and preempted the floor. Watson and Potter (1962) stated that when the focus of attention of conversation is tied to self, "interaction is governed by rules of tact." Presumably these include certain obligations of response and limitations on inquiry topics. Only a method which allows gathering data on appropriate responses and testing the consequences of inappropriate responses can identify what these rules might be.

In the course of any given discourse segment, we can expect to find changes in the functions, which, in turn, affect form. These episodes arise from:

1. Sequencing rules within the speech event.
2. Changes in the activity, if any, accompanying the interaction (e.g., a ball game, dinner preparation).
3. Disruptive events such as the arrival of new personnel, accidents like bumps, sneezes, and phone calls, which require routines to correct the situation.
4. Shifts arising from unexpected responses of alter, leading to changes in tactics or a change in function.
5. Function satiation. Functions presumably oscillate in patterned ways in stable groups.
6. Topic-evoked shifts in functions. Under the impact of instructions or of associative dynamics, the topic may change in the course of the conversation. These changes can alter the available resources for the participants and thereby change their intent. If the topic shifts from childrearing to economics, for example, a bachelor may find he has greater resources for displaying knowledge and receiving recognition. He may speak more and use more technical vocabulary, perhaps even to the point that listeners do not understand. Many such instances have been observed in the speech of bilinguals when topic and language were controlled by instructions (Ervin 1964; Ervin-Tripp 1964, 1967).

Blom and Gumperz (in press) found that among university-trained villagers, many features of standard Norwegian appeared when topics shifted from local to nonlocal. But they found that the change depended on the message. In the offering of information, speakers with a large repertoire of speech alternatives can maximize credibility by adopting the most suitable role. Thus, discussion of university structure might elicit use of more standard Norwegian forms than would gossip about instructors, where student speech features would be adopted, especially those shared with addressees.

Gumperz has noted that among Puerto Ricans in Jersey City, in situations where Spanish is spoken, English is an attention getter. In Trukese and Ponapean (Fischer 1965), a phonotactic feature of the other language is a marker for function shifting of specific kinds that fit the stereotypes of the groups, just as a dialect feature might be here.

As functions change, address too may change through a conversation. David Day has described changes when an argument occurred in a class regarding an instructor's views of the student's beliefs. Address progressed from FN to Dr.

LN to Professor LN. In comments with other students as addressee, LN was used in reference to the instructor in front of him. Concurrently, slang decreased.

When there is agreement about the normal, unmarked address form to alters of specified statuses, then any shift is a message. Friedrich (Hymes 1964*b*) gave convincing cases of momentary shifts at times of personal crises. He pointed out that in a public setting, friends would mask their intimacy with V; in talking of personal topics they could invoke their friendship with "ty" and remove it for impersonal topics with "vy."

Kantorovich (1966, p. 43) gave similar examples in current practice: "I say '*ty*' to my subordinates, but I certainly don't do this in order to belittle them. I know that they'll answer me with '*vy*,' but this isn't grovelling—it's a mark of respect. . . . Somebody I call '*ty*' is somehow closer to me than someone I have to call '*vy*'. . . . If I get mad at one of my workers, and he needs a bawling out, I frequently switch to '*vy*'. . . ."

". . . When cursing, many people who customarily use '*ty*' suddenly switch to '*vy*,' and many who are on a mutual '*vy*' basis switch to '*ty*'" (Kostomarov, 1967).

In systems with age or rank asymmetries of address, the use of the more deferential form to an equal or subordinate can mean either that they are receiving respect or are being put off at a distance. Brown and Gilman (1960) found that conservatives use V more than radicals. To account fully for the interpretation of such actions by the receivers, we need to know the other signals, such as tone of voice and other address features, and the available ambiguities of the relationship. In the case of courtship, for example, the important dimension is closeness or distance, and address changes would be so interpreted.

## E. Rules for Switching

I have emphasized throughout this article that linguistic interaction is a system of behavior in which underlying functions are realized through an organized set of output rules within a social situation. If the function requires conveying an explicit message with informational content, some semantic information is presented in the alternatives selected. Other alternatives require the representation of social information.

In addressee-dominated rules like those in Section II, the effects of function switching can be represented as transformations upon the outputs of the addressee rules. They may take the form of simple replacements, e.g., if familiarity exists, different names may be employed as a direct representation of varied functions. Thus a mode or selector for familiarity and for function is added to the branching rules. Similarly, Tyler (1966) has formal rules for selection of kin reference according to situation, after other semantic selectors.

Blom and Gumperz (in press) have suggested that metaphorical switching simply consists of treating the addressee as though his social features were different. In this case, the rule acts upon the selection points. In the case of Dr. Poussaint, hostile intent was represented in the selection of Adult − rather than Adult + at the first selection point. Presumably this possibility suggested itself by the existence of a traditional southern system of address to Negroes in which all but the very old (aunty) were addressed as children. When Sacks asked his students to play the role of boarders with their families during vacation, their silence, politeness of address and request, and withdrawal from gossip and semantic ellipsis in conversation were interpreted by their families as evidence of sickness or hostility.

The Russian example implies that a simple transformation upon the output forms can express hostility; on the other hand, the inversion may be a consequence of transformation of selection features, making the friend a nonfriend and the formal associate an inferior. Such general rules are a necessity if familiarity is absent, since they permit the interpretation of new instances on the basis of the hearer's general knowledge of the system of sociolinguistic rules.

"Rules" could refer to structures for generating or interpreting speech, to reports of beliefs about practices, or to standards of correctness. We have given examples of all three kinds of rules, not always clearly distinguishing them. Labov's Index of Linguistic Insecurity (1966) compared the last two.

Behavioral rules and reports about behavior are likely to be systematically different. If the norms contain a probability or frequency factor, a speaker's beliefs are, instead, categorical (Labov 1966). Beliefs about the social selectors in sociolinguistic rules are more likely to include features of personnel (since categorization devices realize these features) than to note functional variation. Syntactical variables are not remembered (Sachs 1967) beyond the time needed for decoding, unless they are markers that help us classify the speaker.

In multilingual communities, phonological, syntactic, and semantic shifting is not observed (Gumperz 1964, 1967). Even borrowed vocabulary is unnoticed by members if values oppose borowing (Blom and Gumperz, in press). Some speakers cannot remember the language in which they just spoke, let alone report it to an interviewer. These phenomena are not merely grounds for distrusting members' reports. Just as reference to a relative (Tyler 1966) is affected by more than the semantic dimensions of reference, so the act of describing even to one's self, is a product which could realize a variety of functions. Members' reports are likely to be as sensitive to social variation as any speech act mentioned in this article, and therefore prove as amenable to study.


## IV. LINGUISTIC DIVERSITY

### A. The Fundamentals of Communication

The fundamental fact about language is its obvious diversity. Moving from country to country, region to region, class to class, and caste to caste, we find changes in language. Linguistic diversity apparently is related to social interaction.

Linguistic similarity must be explained, for it is clear that separated sets of speakers will develop different languages. Two quite different bases for similarity can be examined: the fundamental requirement of mutual intelligibility among people who belong to the same social community, and the consequences of variability in overt behavior in terms of social values.

A test for mutual intelligibility might be the Two Person Communication game. First used by Carroll (1958) several decades ago, it has recently been revived (Maclay 1962; Krauss and Weinheimer 1964; Brent and Katz 1967). A hearer out of sight of a speaker selects, constructs, or in some way responds to instructions from a speaker regarding a set of materials. Feedback may or may not be allowed. The advantage of this method is that one can examine the relation between success in the objective task and various speech features, and that the social relation of speaker and hearer can be controlled. For our question about the degree of similarity required for intelligibility, we shall assume optimal social attitudes (Wolff, in Hymes 1964b) and simply concern ourselves with features of linguistic structure. No feedback is allowed, and we shall ask what the bare minimum of linguistic similarity might be that would allow successful transmission of messages about referents.

1. There must be shared categories of meaning so that speakers will attend to the same features of the referent materials.

2. There must be shared lexicon identifying the significant referents, attributes, relationships, and actions, and shared central meanings for this lexicon. Languages which are related and have many cognates are instances.

3. The shared lexicon must be recognizable. Thus its morphophonemic realizations must be similar, and the phonological and phonetic systems must be sufficiently alike to allow recognition of the similar items. Precisely what these limitations entail is not clear. Wurm and Laycock (1961) have shown that both phonetic and phonemic differences can lead to asymmetrical intelligibility of cognates among related dialects. They have found instances where A understood B but not vice versa. They suggested use of a phonetic hierarchy of rank to account for such cases. For instance, they found that the speaker using a stop could understand a speaker using a homologous fricative, but not the reverse. This suggestion is important and needs further testing. I would have predicted the reverse, on the grounds that a speaker's repertoire in comprehension includes child variants, which tend to be of "higher rank" phonetically than their adult models.

A second point they make is that the phonological system relationships, i.e., those found in contrastive analysis, may allow predictions. We can suppose that one-to-one high frequency substitutions might be easy to recognize where the phonetic realization, but not the phonological system, is affected. Comprehension of foreign accents is easiest in such cases. O'Neil (in press) found that Faroese could understand Icelanders, but not vice versa, because of many-to-one conversion rules.

Further, there must be some similarities in phonotactic rules so that the lexical forms can be related. In instances of children's renditions of adult words, we often find that adults cannot comprehend because of the radical alteration in the word formation. Thus [mana] and [ŋən] are unlikely to be recognized as "banana" and "gun," and [me] and [ni] in another child are even less likely to recognized as "blanket" and "candy," although each arises from regular replacement rules (Ervin-Tripp 1966). In each case, the initial consonant is nasal if a nasal occurs anyplace in the adult word, and it is homologous with the initial consonant of the model word. Other word length and syllable-forming canons differ for two children.

4. There must be shared order rules for the basic grammatical relations. By basic relations (McNeill 1966), we mean subject-verb, verb-object, and modifier-head. Unless these minimal structures can be identified, the communication of messages is not possible, although topics or labels could be listed. Of course, these order constraints do not apply where the lexical items could only express one of these relations, as often is the case.

There has been, to my knowledge, no research raising precisely the above structural questions and using the Two Person Communication game. Esper (1966) studied the transmission of linguistic forms through a series of speakers experimentally, employing referents and artificial languages, but in a different procedure. He found surprisingly rapid morphological regularization, which suggests that this is the "natural" tendency historically, within socially isolated groups.

Stewart (1967) has commented on two natural instances of cross-language communication where precisely these factors might impair intelligibility. He cited two examples in which the dialect might impair intelligibility: "Ah 'own know wey 'ey lib," he argued, contains sufficient changes in phonetic realizations, word-formation rules, and so on, to seriously impair recognition of "I don't know where they live." "Dey ain't like dat" is likely to be misunderstood as "They aren't like that" rather than "They didn't like that." The dialect translation of the first would be "Dey not like dat" or "Dey don't be like dat," depending on a semantic contrast, not realized in standard English, between momentary and repeated conditions. This second example indicates that the basic grammatical relations may be the same, but misunderstanding still remains possible. Of course, Stewart was not discussing the highly restricted referential situation of our experiment.

The fascinating permutations on this experimental procedure would permit testing many analogs of natural language change and language contact. We have predicted that when speaker A addresses listener B, under optimal social conditions, the success of the initial communication depends on structural relations between languages *a* and *b*. If B has had earlier experience with other speakers of *a*, we might expect him to have learned to translate features of *a* into *b*, to some extent. It must take some frequency of instances to recognize structural similarities. We already know that A will provide better instructions, even without any feedback, with time (if he is old enough) (Krauss and Weinheimer 1964). Where exchange is always unidirectional, B learns to understand language *a* to some degree, and becomes a "passive bilingual." Note that

B is not just listening but is required by the task to perform actions; thus, he is not like a television watcher.

If give-and-take can occur, it is conceivable that a third language, *c,* might develop, with shared properties drawn from *a* and *b.* Such a development would be like the growth of a pidgin between two monolinguals under the press of trade or other limited encounters (Reinecke, in Hymes 1964*b*). One test of the degree to which *c* is actually intermediate between the other two, or a composite, is to test whether when *c* is the code, A can communicate more successfully with B than he first did with B. That is, we assume that if *c* is closer to *b* than was *a,* it should be a more efficient means of communication, even to a neophyte listener.

The encounter of speakers from different language communities has had a variety of outcomes in natural conditions, including mutual bilingualism, the evolution of a pidgin, and one-way bilingualism (Reinecke, in Hymes 1964*b*; Weinreich 1953). It might be possible to explore the social conditions yielding these varied results by controlled manipulation of conditions.

An important feature of this procedure is that it can allow separate assessment of *comprehension* and *speech similarity.* If system *a* is understood or perhaps translated into *b* by the listener, there is no implication that B necessarily can speak language *a.* It is quite a separate issue whether features of *a* enter into the speech of B; under some social conditions, features could perhaps be transmitted without comprehension.

Several recent studies of intergroup "comprehension" make the issue of objective measurement of intelligibility important. Peisach (1965) has studied replacement of omitted items (the Cloze procedure) in passages of children's speech. She found that middle class children do better than lower class children in replacing every *n*th word verbatim in the middle class samples of speech, and on the lower class speech they do as well as the lower class children. When similarity of grammatical category alone is considered, she found Negro speech replaceable equally by all, but white speech easier for the middle class children (and for white children). The Cloze procedure requires actual omission of the appropriate response. It can be considered a form of comprehension test only if one believes in the "analysis-by-synthesis" theory of comprehension; it is not, on its face, a comprehension measure. Another way of stating the results is that middle class children can predict and imitate lower class and Negro speech, but lower class and Negro children are unwilling (or unable) to produce middle class and white speech by the fifth grade. Harms (1961) found the opposite among adults, who "understood" speakers of high social rank best, or of their own level when using Cloze.

Labov and Cohen (1967) have some striking evidence suggesting that many Negro children, also in New York, can comprehend but not produce standard English. Many of the children highly motivated to imitate sentences gave back "I asked Alvin if he knows how to play basketball" as "I aks Alvin do he know how to play basketball." These translations are regarded by the children as accurate imitations. Likewise "Nobody ever saw that game" would become

"Nobody never saw that game." For the deep grammatical differences not arising by deletion rules out of the standard grammar, the children frequently *understood* but were not able to produce the standard forms. Nor did they notice the difference, going directly to the meaning (Jacqueline Sacks 1967).

Two groups can communicate extremely well, indeed perfectly, though they speak different languages. Multilingual conversations are an everyday occurrence in many social milieux. There may be interspersed lexical borrowings in both languages, but if there is a common semantic core, mutual communication can survive very different realization rules.

If it is the case that the social life of a community could be carried on without speech similarity, then we cannot explain language similarity solely by the demands of basic communication. A more profound account is needed.

## B. Communicative Frequency

A common explanation for the evidence of linguistic similarity and its distribution is the frequency of communication between speakers. The most obvious determinants of frequency are proximity, work, power, and liking. If one undertakes to write a rule predicting who will speak to whom, with a given intent, proximity always enters into the rule. Thus in housing projects, people at positions near high-traffic points are talked with more; in classrooms, neighbors become acquainted; and in small groups, seating controls interchange frequency (Hare and Bales 1963).

Some selection factors may make proximity secondary, except as a cost component, so that we find people commuting hours to a place of work or flying six thousand miles to a conference. In small groups, resources or status, assigned or assumed, may increase frequency of interchange (Bales *et al.* 1951). Considerable research suggests that people select "similar" addressees for social interaction, which, in turn, increases their liking. Homans, in fact, pointed out that the interaction arising from sheer proximity could create "sentiments" (1950) and thereby increase liking. All of these features which measurably increase interaction in studies of face-to-face groups have cumulative effects that are visible sociologically.

These features of face-to-face interaction compounded over many individuals should be evident in the geographical distribution of linguistic features. One of the oldest forms of sociolinguistics is dialect geography. The distribution of particular speech features is mapped, the boundaries being isoglosses. Normally these are not identical for different speech features. Extensive studies have been made of such distributions in Europe and in the United States—for instance, of bag vs. sack, grea/s/y vs. grea/z/y. In general, linguistic features reveal the patterns of migration, intermarriage, and transportation routes. If there are natural barriers or social barriers to marriage or friendship, isoglosses may appear. Thus, McDavid (1951) noted that the rise of the large northern ghettoes in the past 40 years has led to an increase in the linguistic distance between northern whites and Negroes. Individual lexical items may follow the salesman: "tonic" is used in the Boston marketing area for soft drinks, and "chester-field" for couch or sofa in the San Francisco wholesale region.

The political boundaries between communities are sharp but may not seriously affect interaction frequency over time. This we can infer from the fact that isoglosses do not match political boundaries. Isoglosses often do not even correspond with each other; that is, individual features may not diffuse at the same time or in the same way. Changes, as one would expect on a frequency model, are gradual. Gumperz (1958), in a study of phonemic isoglosses, found that changes were gradual even within the isoglosses. The functional load or practical importance of the contrast gradually decreased until it disappeared, and the phonetic distinctiveness also decreased.

The most extreme test of the argument that frequency of communication reduces speech diversity occurs in bilingual contacts. Gumperz (1967) located a border region between Indo-Aryan and Dravidian speaking sectors of India in which speakers were bilingual, using Marathi and Kannada in different settings. These border dialects have become increasingly similar in centuries of bilingualism. They have the same semantic features, syntax, and phonology, and differ only in the phonemic shape of morphemes, what we might call the vocabulary and function words. Each dialect is essentially a morpheme-by-morpheme translation of the other. However, other speakers of Kannada still identify this dialect as a form of Kannada because they recognize its morphemes—it is simply a deviant form, as Jamaican Creole is a deviant form of English.

This example illustrates both convergence of speech with high interaction frequency, and the maintenance of contrast. The convergence occurs at those levels of language we believe are least conscious and least criterial for the identification of the language. Speakers tend to identify languages by the shape of the morphemes, by the vocabulary, but even more by its function words and inflectional and derivational morphemes. The Kannada-Marathi example demonstrates that in spite of high contact frequency, speakers may insist on maintaining linguistic diversity, and that they may, in fact, believe it to be greater than it is.

There are many instances, to be discussed later, where frequency is high but speech distinctiveness is maintained. Castes in India interact with high frequency; Negro servants in the United States interact with employers; lower class pupils interact with teachers; and monolingual Spanish-speaking grandmothers interact with monolingual English-speaking grandsons—yet diversity persists.

High frequency of communication is a necessary but not a sufficient condition for increased linguistic similarity. High frequency of communication must result, at a minimum, in passive bilingualism of both parties, active bilingualism of one party, or a lingua franca. The only necessity is that each understand the speech of the other.

We do not yet know what the consequences of passive control of two systems must be. Active control typically leads to convergence at certain levels, starting with semantic boundaries and frequency of syntactic options, (Earle 1967; Ervin 1961; McNeill 1966; Ervin-Tripp, in press). We have argued that there are cognitive reasons for such fusions and that they tend to take place when social conditions, such as contact with monolinguals, reading, and strong values about co-occurrence restrictions, do not provide strong support for system separation. Presumably, passive control of a second language has less impact.

Only one study has directly related the communication frequency of individual persons who all communicate to speech similarity. Hammer *et al.* (1965) measured the observed centrality of individuals, and also the person-to-person frequency for every pair in a New York coffee shop with a regular clientele. They obtained speech samples and used the Cloze procedure. Central persons were most predictable, and each person most successfully predicted the omitted items from the speech of persons with whom he interacted most.

It is not quite clear what is measured in Cloze. All phonological features are missing. What is included are semantic factors that influence collocations, vocabulary, and perhaps some aspects of grammar. This study at first seems to support frequency as a critical variable in similarity, but it may not actually meet the critical limitations. The study was done in a social setting, interaction was social, and the members were parts of friendship networks. That is, some third variables may have determined both interaction frequency and similarity on Cloze. The hidden variable seems to be cohesiveness.

## C. Cohesiveness and Linguistic Diversity

It seems that people talk like those with whom they have the closest social ties. We do not know precisely why this is the case; it may be that the features of social relationships which bring about this result are not the same for all types of speech similarity. In social networks and groups, there is a high frequency of interaction. The high attraction of others in the group or network means that they not only serve as models but can also act as reinforcing agents in their responses to speech, affecting attitudes toward features in the community repertoire. In addition, there might be secondary reinforcement in sounding like a valued person.

All levels of speech appear to be affected. With respect to the phonetic realization of phonemes, age may constrain changes in the system. Even under optimal conditions, many persons over 12 years old seem to have difficulty changing their phonetic realization rules except under careful monitoring.

Labov (1966) has argued that the everyday vernacular is stabilized by puberty on the basis of the peer model. Cultures where peer ties are weaker (if any exist) would provide a valuable comparison.

The *functions* of communication in cohesive networks necessarily include a high frequency of requests for social reinforcement, and of expressive speech. The social group may or may not be concerned with information and opinion exchange for its own sake. Davis (1961), in a study of the maintenance or dissolution of "great books" discussion groups, found that if there were many members of a social network in such a group, its durability was enhanced for college-educated members and decreased for noncollege-educated. He suggested that for the latter there might be a conflict between interaction practices in the network and the constraints of the discussion group. Bossard (1945) commented on large differences between families in the extent of information-exchange in dinner table conversation.

The most ingenious work on interfamily differences in communication has been conducted by Basil Bernstein. He has pointed out (in press *a, b*) that communicative patterns and socialization methods within families are related to occupational roles and to the character of a family's social network. Empirical support was found in mothers' reports of use of appeals to children, emphasis on different functions of language, and encouragement of interaction. In turn, London five-year-olds differed by social class (and by mothers' reports) in the variety of nouns and adjectives, use of relative clauses, use of pronouns with extraverbal referents, and in ability to switch style with task. That some of these differences may reflect performance customs rather than capacity is suggested by the report of Cowan (1967) that American working class children, though less successful than middle class children on the Two Person Communication game, learned fast when paired with middle class partners.

Hess and Shipman (1965), who observed actual mother–child interaction in Negro preschool families, found considerable social class variation and between-family variation in the extent to which mothers used the situation to elicit labeling and informational communication from the children. The measures correlated two years later with oral comprehension. Schatzman and Strauss (1955) found social class differences in oral narratives that may be related to Bernstein's distinction. See also Lawton (1964).

There has been too little study of natural interaction *within* social groups to extricate what the important differences are—whether they lie in the amount of interaction of children with adults vs. peers and siblings, whether there are differences in encounters with strangers and training of children in competence with outsiders, or whether there are differences in emphasis in intragroup speech functions.

Because evidence about the verbal skills of lower class Negroes came from formal testing situations and classrooms, there have been widespread misconceptions about "verbal deprivation" in American society, with expensive educational consequences. Recent investigators such as Labov and Cohen (1967) in Harlem and Eddington and Claudia Mitchell in San Francisco and Oakland have recorded natural interaction. All have found that Negro lower class speakers are highly verbal in terms of speech frequency. Both adolescents and children engage with great skill in verbal games for which they have complex traditions. "Controlled situations" may, in fact, obscure the very skills which have been most developed within a particular group.

"General verbal deprivation" could conceivably exist. It most probably would be found in unusual social isolation, or in cases of social marginality, particularly where a language has been lost but there has not been full access to a range of functions in a second language. For further detailed discussion of research on this point and some new data, see Cazden (1966, 1967).

*Topics* of discourse are likely to be different in cohesive networks as a result of differing values and interests. This produces considerable impact on the semantic structure and lexicon.

One way of studying differences in messages arising from communication is to examine content shifts, under acculturation, where there may be radical changes in social allegiances. A study of this phenomenon in Japanese women married to Americans showed that there was considerable difference between women who gave messages typical of their age-mates in Tokyo and those who were more like American women, even when speaking Japanese (Ervin-Tripp 1967). Word associations, sentence completions, TATs, story completions, and semantic differentials were all used in both languages. In general, the women who remained more Japanese in response content would rather be Japanese than American, preserve more Japanese customs, and keep up strong ties to Japan. The chief characteristics of the women who shifted to American responses were that they identified with American women, had close American friends, read American magazines, and met somewhat less opposition to their marriage from Japanese friends and family. The last point implies that in Japan they may have been less conservative. Though both sets of women would seem, on the surface, to have had a cohesive tie to an American partner, the interviews revealed striking differences. Marriages in Japan involve far more social separation of husband and wife than here; for example, there is little joint socializing with nonkin. Many of the Japanese women in this country do not regard their husbands as confidants in trouble, and may, indeed, seldom see them. When either the husband or an American friend was regarded as a close confidant, the messages were more American. It is, in fact, not easy to give "typically American" responses on many of these tests, so their ability to do so represents a considerable degree of subtle learning.

*Semantic* innovation is one of the striking features of cohesive groups. There may be new activities requiring new names; there may be finer discriminations required along continua; and there may be new conceptual categories. These are realized by lexical innovations which spread within the network. Examples are "she's in high drag" in the homosexual network, referring to a male homosexual in women's clothing (Cory 1952); "prat," "breech," "insider," "tail pit," and "fob," pickpocket jargon for pockets (Conwell 1937); "cooling the mark out" by the confidence man (Goffman 1952); and "trivial," "motivated," and "reflexive," terms used among transformationalists and ethnomethodologists, respectively, with special meanings. Many examples can be found in Mauer (1962).

A glimpse of the workings of this process can be seen in the Two Person Communication game.

Krauss and Weinheimer (1964) found that reference phrases became abbreviated with practice. Given the limitation on necessary referential distinctions, abbreviated coding is efficient. The result is not merely a change in the external shape of the form but a semantic shift, since the simplest term comes to have the specific meaning of the highly qualified phrase. The authors mention analogies like "hypo" among photographers and "comps" among graduate students.

Brent and Katz (1967) made comparisons of types of coding of drawings by middle class whites and by Negro Job Corps teen-agers. Unfortunately, they used geometric shapes, which gives a distinct advantage to subjects who are formally educated. They found that the Negro subjects were relatively successful although they used nontechnical names like "sharp-pointed piece," "a square wiggling," and "the funny looking piece." It would be an advantage to use materials equally strange or equally familiar to both groups and to control network features of the speaker and listener. We have strong evidence that members of the same social group prefer nontechnical communication. Where materials are neutral (e.g., nonsense forms), nontechnical, highly metaphorical communication is most efficient in terms of both brevity and success in a non-feedback condition.

Even though the semantic distinctions made are not new, group *jargon* or new morphophonemic realizations for lexical categories are common in cohesive groups. Occasionally, such terminology arises to allow secrecy before outsiders (though Conwell and Mauer commented that secrecy is better served by semantic shift employing conventional morphemes). New morphemes are the most apparent mark of an in-group, whether or not they realize novel semantic distinctions. In fact, the best test for the symbolic value of the marker is whether it has referential meaning and, if so, whether it is translatable. Conwell (1937) pointed out that the pickpocket's terminology is not used before outsiders, but it is used to test the trustworthiness of a member of the network and to find how much he knows. In simple terms, the use of such terms can symbolize membership if the group is large or boundary maintenance is important; if the group is small, like a family, and its members known, the terms are used to indicate solidarity. Bossard (1945) cited examples of family words; many baby words or nicknames survive with such social meanings.

Where the incidence of social or regional dialect difference coincides with density of friendship network, the *structural* dialect features, including syntax and phonology, may come to be markers of cohesiveness. Blom and Gumperz (in press) found that the local dialect of Hemnesberget, Norway, had this significance to its residents.

Labov (1963) observed that the rate of dialect change was different in Martha's Vineyard among young men, depending upon their social loyalties. There was a change in progress very markedly differentiating young men from their grandparents. The men who went along in this direction were those who had the strongest local ties and did not want to move off-island. It is not clear whether or not interaction frequencies were also affected by the different values. The effect showed up in articulation.

Strong social ties affect all aspects of linguistic systems; our evidence suggests that the most quickly affected are the semantic system and lexicon—in short, the vocabulary. The structural morphemes evidently are not as sensitive to the forces of cohesion as are other morphemes.

## D. Identity Marking

Every society is differentiated by age and sex; in addition, rank, occupational identities, and other categories will be found. Since the rights and duties of its members are a function of these identities, it is of great social importance to establish high visibility for them. Sometimes this has been done by legislation controlling permissible clothing, house type, and so on. Everywhere it seems to be the case that information about social identity is contained in speech variables. In urban societies, the social function of such marking is greater, since it may be the only information available; on the other hand, the social sanctions for violation may be reduced. McCormack (1960) has noted the spread of upper caste dialect features in urban lower caste speakers in India.

In some cases, there may be more frequent communication within, rather than between, categories. Clearly, this is not always the case; within the western family, communication occurs with high frequency across both sex and age categories. Therefore, something other than frequency of communication or group cohesion must account for the preservation of speech diversity which marks social identity.

It is not precisely clear what features of speech mark *sex* in the United States. In some languages (Haas, in Hymes 1964*b*; Martin, in Hymes 1964*b*) lexicon, function words, and phonological rules are different for males and females. The study of the training of boys by women in such societies would be enlightening. There are clearly topical differences arising from occupational and family status and, therefore, possibly semantic differences and differences in lexical repertoire. Masculinity–femininity tests have leaned heavily on differences in lexicon, particularly in the meanings realized, or in collocations. Sociolinguistic rules are probably not the same; e.g., speech etiquette concerning taboo words. Men and women do not use terms of address in quite the same way, and young women, at least, use more deferential request forms than young men. In fact, it is commonly the case in many languages that women employ more deferential speech, but one can expect that such differences are related to other indicators of relative rank. For example, in jury deliberations (Strodtbeck *et al.* 1957), women are several steps lower in social class, in terms of their speech frequency and evaluation by fellow jurors. Labov (1966) and Levine and Crockett (1966) found more situational style shifting by women; Fischer (Hymes 1964*b*) recorded the formal "-ing" suffix relatively more often from girls than boys.

*Age* differences in speech arise both through language change and age-grading. Though grandparent and grandchild may communicate, they are unlikely to have the same system. Labov (1963, 1966) related several such changes to current distributions. For instance, he points out the spread of "r" in New York City. In the top social class, in casual speech, "r" was used by only 43%

of the respondents over 40 years old but by twice as many of the younger respondents. Changes like ice box-refrigerator (for the latter object), and victrola-phonograph-record player-stereo are apparent to all of us.

In addition, certain lexicon or structures may be considered inappropriate at a particular age. Newman (Hymes 1964*b*) remarked that slang is for the young Zunis. Children over a certain age are expected to stop using nursery terms like "bunny," "piggy," "potty," and "horsie," except in addressing infants. Pig Latin and other playful transforms (Conklin, in Hymes 1964*b*) may be age-restricted. Stewart has claimed that a form he calls "basilect" is learned among Washington, D.C. Negroes from their peers in early childhood and begins to disappear, under negative sanctions, around age 7 or 8. Adolescents studied in New York (Labov and Cohen 1967) had forms similar to the adolescent speech of some Washington D.C. speakers, including two features absent in standard English: a completive or intensive-perfective "I done seen it" or "I done forgot it" (semantically contrasted with the simple past or perfect); and a distinction with *be* analogous to the distinction between habitual use and momentary or ongoing action (a distinction made in the standard language only for other action verbs): "He be with us all the time," vs. "He with us right now" (He walks every day vs. He's walking right now).

Many statuses entail the learning of specialized languages or superposed varieties. The Brahmin, for example, is likely to have studied English and to have many more borrowings in his speech than the non-Brahmin. Brahmins can sometimes be identified by such borrowed forms or by literary vocabulary (McCormack 1960), just as psychologists' occupational register can identify them. In addition, the functions and topics imposed by occupations can alter the speech of parents in the home, and in "anticipatory socialization" the children from different occupational milieux may be affected.

One way to differentiate similarity arising from cohesion from difference arising from identity marking is the presence of negative sanctions. Ramanujan pointed out (1967) that Brahmin parents specifically reject non-Brahmin items or use them with pejorative connotations. The Brahmins show, in several respects, that they value the preservation of markers of their identity. They consciously borrow more foreign forms and preserve their phonological deviance so that their phonological repertoire is very large. They have maintained more morphological irregularities (like our strong verbs) in their development of various inflectional paradigms, even though the evidence suggests that the earlier language (now written) was more regular. The evidence from the Esper experiment (1966) and the evolution of the non-Brahmin dialects is that regularization is the more normal destiny unless some factor interferes. In cases of phonological difference from the non-Brahmin dialects, in the realization of cognates, they have, in morphemes where the realizations fall together in the two dialects and would thus be indistinguishable, innovated a distinction. The semantic space is far more differentiated, as is the lexicon. The learning of a language full of irregularities is obviously more difficult—every child spontaneously regularizes. Like the Mandarin learning Chinese characters, the Brahmin puts additional effort into the maintenance of an elite dialect because the reward is its distinctive marking of his identity.

One might assume that lower castes would adopt prestige speech, and there is, as cited earlier, some evidence of such tendencies in urban milieux. One way of preventing such spread is the use of a non-Brahmin style when addressing non-Brahmins which, of course, reduces frequency of exposure. In addition, there are sanctions against such emulation.

American Negro speech may provide an example of identity marking although the evidence is ambiguous. Stewart has argued (1967) that Negro speech is based on creoles used in the early slave period, and that this history accounts for some of the basic semantic and syntactical differences Labov and Cohen (1967) have recently cited, which appear in various black communities all over the country. Labov has suggested that working class casual speech features connote solidarity, reducing the impact of standard English heard in school on casual style.

Certainly the clearest evidence of the identity-marking function of language is language maintenance during contact. Fishman (1967) has extensively discussed various features of language maintenance programs. Although the dominant groups in the United States have strongly favored language shift by immigrants, to the point of legislating against vernacular education, some groups continued to resist the loss of their language. Those who succeeded best, according to Kloss (in Fishman, 1967), did so either by total isolation (like the Canadian Dukhobors) or by living in sufficiently dense concentrations to allow a high frequency of ingroup communication and the use of their language for the widest range of social functions. In particular, many maintained their own educational facilities, e.g., Chinese, Japanese, and Russians, promoting in-group cohesion among the children. A critical turning point lies in the speech practices of teen-agers. Where they are forced to mix with outsiders in large urban schools or consolidated rural school districts, the group language tends to disappear.

In parts of the world where there is a stabilized condition of great language diversity, as in Africa and Asia, it is quite normal to retain the group vernacular as a home language but to be bilingual for wider communication. Probably the degree of language distance in these cases is relatively small, as Gumperz has pointed out (1967). In these instances, the shape of morphemes is an important identity marker; shifting between co-occurrent sets of morphemes by such bilinguals is merely a more extreme instance of the small group vocabulary of the family, stabilized through time by endogamy and by the high value placed on group identity markers.

An extreme case in the opposite direction occurs in initial invention of pidgins. Here values of identity may be unimportant, and the practical need to communicate dominates. In fact, pidgins tend to develop when the norms which sustain co-occurrence rules are missing. Thus they appear in the transitory encounters of traders away from home, in the fortuitous combination of diverse speakers in the setting of work—in plantations, mines, and harbor cities.

In this respect, African urbanization and slavery shared a feature, and we may guess that earlier circumstances of urbanization in Europe also gave rise to pidgins. Pidgins are characterized structurally by morphological simplification and regularization, and by use of material from more than one language. At first, they are spoken with the phonetic features of the respective mother tongues. Of course, with time the pidgin can come to symbolize the subordinate-employer relation. Temporary communication systems much like pidgins occur widely in contact conditions in the United States. These situations have never been given the serious study they deserve.

When a pidgin becomes the mother tongue of its speakers (and thereby technically a creole), it may acquire all the values of group identity of other vernaculars. Meredith (1964) quoted a speaker of Hawaiian Pidgin (a creole language) who was subjected to a university requirement of mastery of standard English: "Why you try change me? I no want to speak like damn haole!" Meredith reported "hostility, disinterest, and resistance to change" in the remedial class.

## E. Attitudes Toward Speech Diversity

In studying phonological diversity in New York City speech, Labov (1966) identified three different categories of social phenomena arising from diversity. These he called "indicators," "markers," and "stereotypes."

*Indicators* are features which are noted only by the trained observer. For example, few people are aware that "cot" and "caught" are distinguished in some areas and not in others. Indicators are features which are functions of social indices like class or region but neither vary with style in a given speaker nor enter into beliefs about language.

*Markers,* in Labov's system, vary with both group memberships and style of the speaker, and can be used in role-switching. In the New York City system, he found that "r," "oh," and "eh" were very powerful markers, in that they changed radically according to the self-monitoring of the speaker. In Fig. 5, the use of less [t] and more [th] with increased self-monitoring is shown by the slopes. A speaker who in rapid excited speech might say, "It wasn't a good day but a bid one," or "Ian saw tree cahs goin by," might in reading say "bad," and "Ann saw three cars going by."

*Stereotypes,* like their social counterparts, may or may not conform to social reality, and tend to be categorical. Thus, although a working class man might use [t] or [d] only 40% to 50% of the time, he will be heard as always saying "dis," "dat," and "ting." Evidence suggests that children as young as 2 or 3 years old may notice and remember differences like "bath" vs. "baf," and "window" vs. "winda," though they may ignore simple phonetic shifts.

*Hypercorrection* involves the spread of a speech feature from a higher prestige group to another, with overgeneralization of the feature based on a categorical stereotype. In Fig. 6, the upper middle class used "r" considerably less in self-conscious speech than did the lower middle class, who believed it to be characteristic of the best speech. A more common example can be seen in the contrast between standard English "He and I came" and nonstandard "Him and me came." Hypercorrect versions can be found which yield "She wrote to him and I" or "She wrote to he and I." Lexical examples were given by Ian Ross (1956) and even by Emily Post (1922); usually these are instances of the extension of formal, literary, or commercial vocabulary into casual speech. Labov (1966) has shown that hypercorrection is greatest among speakers who score high on a Linguistic Insecurity Index, derived from comparison of what they report they say and what they select as correct in pairs which, in fact, are not markers. Levine and Crockett (1966) also found that the second highest group shifted most with style.

Blau (1956) has observed a very similar phenomenon among upwardly mobile persons in quite different measures of insecurity: these people report more nervousness, are more likely to discriminate against Negro neighbors than any other types, and in these respects the members of high and low social classes are more alike than the intermediate people, provided they are mobile.

Labov (1966) has suggested that there may be "unconscious" stereotypes which account for borrowings which are not from prestige groups. He suggested that the masculinity connotation of working class casual speech might be such an instance. His measure of subjective reaction to speech samples required subjects to rank the speaker occupationally, thus, clearly asking for social class indicators rather than features implying some other social meaning.

The richest variety of work along this line is that of Lambert (1963, 1967) and his collaborators, who have had the same speaker use "guises" to produce samples. These then are rated for a great range of features like personality, intelligence, and physical traits. French Canadians, he found, rated a "French guise" as less intelligent and less a leader than the English-Canadian guise. In a study in Israel (Lambert et al. 1965), on the other hand, it was found that Arabic-speaking and Hebrew-speaking subjects had mutually hostile stereotypes when judging the guises. Tucker and Lambert (in press) found that evaluation by northern white and southern Negro college students differed in that Mississippi Negro college speech was least favored by the whites, and southern educated white speech least favored by the Negroes. Top-valued forms were the same for both groups.

Harms (1961) recorded speech from different social classes and found that 10–15 second samples could be differentiated by listeners. Regardless of their own class, they rated high-ranked speakers as more credible. This method, like that of Lambert's, does not allow isolation of the critical linguistic features. Lambert, on the other hand, has been able to identify a far wider range of social meanings in the speech variations than did the single scales of Labov and of Harms.

Triandis et al. (1966) tried to balance various sources of judgment by counterbalancing race, messages (on discrimination legislation), and standard vs. nonstandard grammar. Slides were shown while a tape was played. College students who were uninfluenced by race as "liberals" were still much influenced by grammar, even more than by the message, in their judgment of the man's character, ideas, value, and social acceptability. Three-fourths of the variance on admiration and evaluation is carried by the linguistic contrast. A new test for liberals might be this: "Would you want your daughter to marry a man who says ain't?"

Some consequences of these stereotypes about language can be seen in Rosenthal and Jackson's (1965) finding that IQ rose 15 points when teachers were told arbitrary children were "fast gainers." Linguistic variables may convey the same message.

## F. Rules for Diversity

William Labov has begun to use his large collection of material on speech of different New York City groups to discover rules accounting both for stylistic and intergroup diversity quantitatively. He has been able to use quantitative functions because he has been measuring articulation ranges and frequencies of occurrence as speech variables, as well as using quantitative measures of social variables. Thus the rules he can find are not categorical in structure like those in Section II.

Figure 5 shows that a phonetic feature is a linear function both of social class and of style. Because of the apparently regular change with style, Labov hypothesized that there is a single dimension he called "self-monitoring" underlying the style differences. Obviously, the relationship can be expressed by a linear equation in which the phonetic variable $= a(\text{class}) + b(\text{style}) + c$.

In the case of hypercorrection of the kind shown in Fig. 6, the measure of linguistic insecurity can be used as a function of style, increasing its slope. For such phonetic variables, the function is $a(\text{class}) + b(\text{style})$ (Linguistic Insecurity Index) $+ c$. Some adjustments are made for age as well, since there is an interaction of age, class, and norms.

These rules are important innovations. They treat linguistic phenomena as continuous variables. Whether the use of continuous measures is possible except at the phonetic and semantic edge of linguistics is not clear; frequencies certainly are quantifiable for discrete categories too. The rules, like those in Section II, introduce social features as integral components. Normally, social features are mentioned in linguistic descriptions as a last resort, such as in a few style variations like those in Japanese where morphological rules must consider addressee. Finally, they include, in a single formal description, the differences *between* speakers and the differences *within* speakers. The fact that this is possible is impressive evidence of the existence of an over-all sociolinguistic system larger than the cognitive structure of members individually. As Labov has pointed out, a single member sees the system only along the coordinates of his own position in it; he only witnesses the full style variation of his own social peers. In fact, the possibility of writing rules which transcend class suggests a new criterion for a speech community.

What do sociolinguistic rules, the major emphasis of this article, imply for the social psychologist? Most narrowly, they provide him with new and far more sensitive indices of class or group identification, socialization, and role-shifting than interviewing alone can supply. The great precision with which linguistic features can be specified makes them technically ripe both for measurement and for deeper and richer study of the process of interaction. Linguistic interaction is deeply embedded in nearly all our social processes, in socialization in the family, into new occupations, and into a new community. Sociolinguistic rules are central to, even if they do not totally compose the organized structure which generates our social acts and through which we interpret others. Just as the study of linguistic structure is seen by many as a penetrating route to cognitive structure in the individual, so may sociolinguistic rules lead to rules for social action.

## APPENDIX. TAPE RECORDING

Several social psychologists have had severe disappointments when they found that the taped material they had made at great expense was useless because of poor recording method or storage. For details of method see Samarin (1967) and Slobin (1967).

### 1. Equipment

First, make sure that the recording machine itself has a wide enough frequency range for good voice recordings by testing *at the speed needed*. If a battery machine is required, the Nagra, the Sony, or the Uher are available, with new products appearing monthly. Videotapes may require better quality sound receiving equipment as a supplement.

An additional investment in microphones and earphones other than those supplied with the machine usually is worthwhile. Lavalier (neck) microphones are desirable if a separate channel is available for each person, and if scraping of clothing or handling of the microphone can be avoided. In groups, stereo arrangements can both provide a wider range of close recording and give binaural cues for identifying speakers while minimizing background noise. Wireless microphones for children's groups, or figure-eight microphones for lined-up speakers and the filtering out of noise at the sides may be appropriate. If several microphones are used simultaneously, it is necessary to provide occasional synchronizing cues by voice or other device except on stereo.

### 2. Tape

Tape print-through can create blurred recordings by the transfer of magnetic patterns from one layer of tape to another. It can be minimized by the use of "low print-through" tape. Reducing the recording level will also decrease print-through, which is usually not serious if the original recording is very clear.

At the time of purchase, leaders should be spliced to tapes lacking them. A leader spliced at both ends of a tape allows one to label it *before* it is used, minimizing accidental erasures. Box labeling or reel labeling is untrustworthy. Tape labeling is related to a log or index file.

### 3. Recording Techniques

Reverberation and other background noise is the chief enemy. If there is one wall, face the microphone away from it to deaden its input. If there is more than one, or metal cabinet, or floor reverberations, use curtains, coats, or any means of deadening the sound reflection. Open the windows if the outside is quiet. The microphone should be removed from the noisy machine, and placed equidistant from speakers—if possible, about a foot from them. Point the tail of the microphone at noise sources or too noisy personnel, to deaden their input.

*Take the time to learn to record well,* to train field workers under realistic conditions, and to test with as much care as one checks a team of coders. Good recordings should allow discrimination of Ruth and roof, boot and boots, mutts and much, sin and sing.

### 4. Storage

If recordings are made in a hot climate, mail them out and have them copied on a high-quality machine immediately for storage on low print-through tape. While Mylar tapes last relatively well, temperatures should be constant around 60°–70°C, and humidity kept low, if necessary with silica gel. Store on edge, far from sources of magnetism such as electric outlets and appliances. Language laboratories in large universities often have suitable storage room. Rewind tapes annually to reduce print-through and warping.

## REFERENCES

Auld, F., Jr., and Alice M. White. "Rules for dividing interviews into sentences." *Journal of Psychology* 42(1956): 273–281.

Ayoub, Milla. "Bi-polarity in Arabic kinship terms." In *Proceedings of the Ninth International Congress of Linguists,* H. G. Lunt, ed. The Hague: Mouton, 1962, pp. 1100–1106.

Bales, R. F., and E. F. Borgatta. "Size of groups as a factor in the interaction profile." In *Small Groups,* A. Hare, E. F. Borgatta, and R. F. Bales, eds. New York: Wiley, 1955, pp. 396–413.

Bales, R. F., F. Strodtbeck, T. Mills, and Mary E. Roseborough. "Channels of communication in small groups." *American Sociological Review* 6(1951): 461–468.

Barker, G. C. "Social functions of language in a Mexican-American community." *Acta Americana* 5(1947): 185–202.

Barker, R., and H. F. Wright. *Midwest and its Children.* Evanston, Illinois: Row, Peterson, 1954.

Bellugi, Ursula. "The acquisition of negation." Ph. D. dissertation, Harvard Graduate School of Education, 1967.

Bernstein, B., ed. *Language, Primary Socialisation and Education.* London: Routledge and Kegan Paul, in press. (a)

Bernstein, B. "A socio-linguistic approach to socialisation: with some references to educability." In *Directions in Sociolinguistics,* J. J. Gumperz and D. Hymes, eds. New York: Holt, Rinehart and Winston, 1972.

Blau, P. "Social mobility and interpersonal relations." *American Sociological Review* 21(1956): 290–295.

Blom, J. P., and J. J. Gumperz. "Some social determinants of verbal behavior." In *Directions in Sociolinguistics,* J. J. Gumperz and D. H. Hymes eds. New York: Holt, Rinehart, and Winston, 1972.

Boomer, D. S., and A. T. Dittman, "Hesitation pauses and juncture pauses in speech." *Language and Speech* 8(1965): 215–220.

Bossard, J. H. S. "Family modes of expression." *American Sociological Review* 10 (1945): 226–237.

Brent, S. B., and Evelyn W. Katz. "A study of language deviations and cognitive processes." OEO-Job Corps Project 1209, Progress Report No. 3, Wayne State University, 1967.

Bright, W., ed. *Sociolinguistics.* The Hague: Mouton, 1966.

Brown, R. W., and A. Gilman. "The pronouns of power and solidarity." In *Style in Language,* T. Sebeok, ed. Cambridge, Massachusetts: M. I. T. Press, 1960, pp. 253–276.

Capell, A. *Studies in Socio-linguistics.* The Hague: Mouton, 1966.

Carroll, J. B. "Process and content in psycholinguistics." In *Current Trends in the Description and Analysis of Behavior,* R. Glaser, ed. Pittsburgh, Pennsylvania: University of Pittsburgh Press, 1958, pp. 175–200.

Cazden, Courtney B. "Subcultural differences in child language: An inter-disciplinary review." *Merrill-Palmer Quarterly* 12 (1966): 185–219.

Cazden, Courtney B. "On individual differences in language competence and performance." *Journal of Special Education* 1(1967): 135–150.

Chapman, Robin S. "The interpretation of deviant sentences." Ph.D. Dissertation, University of California, Berkeley, 1967.

Conwell, C. *The Professional Thief.* Chicago, Illinois: University of Chicago Press, 1937.

Cory, D. W. *The Homosexual in America.* New York: Greenberg, 1952.

Cowan, P. "The link between cognitive structure and social structure in two-child verbal interaction." Symposium presented at the Society for Research on Child Development meeting, 1967.

Davis, J. A. "Compositional effects, systems, and the survival of small discussion groups." *Public Opinion Quarterly* 25 (1961): 574–584.

Diebold, A. R. "Code-switching in Greek-English bilingual speech." *Georgetown University Monograph* 15, 1963.

Diebold, A. R. "Anthropology and the comparative psychology of communicative behavior." In *Animal Communication: Techniques of Study and Results of Research,* T. Sebeok, ed. Bloomington, Indiana: Indiana University Press, 1967.

Dikeman, Bessie and Patricia Parker. "Request forms." Term paper for Speech 160B, University of California, Berkeley, 1964.

Dittman, A., and Lynn G. Llewellyn. "The phonemic clause as a unit of speech decoding." *Journal of Personality and Social Psychology* 6 (1967): 341–348.

Dollard, J., and F. Auld, Jr. *Scoring Human Motives: A Manual.* New Haven, Connecticut: Yale University Press, 1959.

Drach, K., B. Kobashigawa, C. Pfuderer, and D. Slobin. "The structure of linguistic input to children." Language Behavior Research Laboratory Working Paper No. 14, Berkeley, California, 1968.

Earle, Margaret J. "Bilingual semantic merging and an aspect of acculturation." *Journal of Personality and Social Psychology* 6 (1967): 304–312.

Ervin, Susan M. "Semantic shift in bilingualism." *American Journal of Psychology* 74 (1961): 233–241.

Ervin, Susan M. "Language and TAT content in bilinguals." *Journal of Abnormal and Social Psychology* 68 (1964): 500–507.

Ervin-Tripp, Susan M. "An analysis of the interaction of language, topic, and listener." *American Anthropologist* 66, no. 6, part 2 (1964): 86–102.

Ervin-Tripp, Susan M. "Language development." In *Review of Child Development Research*, Lois and Martin Hoffman, eds. Vol. 2, New York: Russell Sage Foundation, 1966, pp. 55–106.

Ervin-Tripp, Susan M. "An Issei learns English." *Journal of Social Issues* 23, no. 2 (1967): 78–90.

Ervin-Tripp, Susan M. "Becoming a bilingual." In "Proceedings of the 1967 UNESCO Conference on the Description and Measurement of Bilingualism," in press.

Ervin-Tripp, Susan M., and D. I. Slobin. "Psycholinguistics." *Annual Review of Psychology* 18 (1966): 435–474.

Esper, E. A. "Social transmission of an artificial language." *Language* 42 (1966): 575–580.

Ferguson, D. A. "Baby talk in six languages." *American Anthropologist* 66, no. 6, Part 2 (1964): 103–114.

Fischer, J. L. "The stylistic significance of consonantal sandhi in Trukese and Ponapean." *American Anthropologist* 67 (1965): 1495–1502.

Fishman, J. A. *Language Loyalty in the United States.* The Hague: Mouton, 1966.

Fishman, J. A. "Bilingualism with and without diglossia; diglossia with and without bilingualism." *Journal of Social Issues* 23, no. 2 (1967): 29–38.

Fishman, J. A. "Review of J. Hertzler: A sociology of language." *Language* 43 (1967): 586–604.

Fishman, J. A. *Readings in the Sociology of Language.* The Hague: Mouton, 1968.

Frake, C. O. "How to ask for a drink in Subanun." *American Anthropologist* 66, no. 6, part 2 (1964): 127–132.

Friedrich, P. "Structural implications of Russian pronominal usage." In *Sociolinguistics*, W. Bright, ed. The Hague: Mouton 1966, pp. 214–253.

Geertz, C. *The Religion of Java.* Glencoe, Illinois: Free Press, 1960.

Geohegan, W. "Information processing systems in culture." In *Explorations in Mathematical Anthropology*, P. Kay, ed. Cambridge, Massachusetts: M.I.T. Press, 1971.

Goffman, E. "Cooling the mark out." *Psychiatry* 15 (1952): 451–463.

Goffman, E. "Alienation from interaction." *Human Relations* 10 (1957): 47–60.

Goffman, E. *Behavior in Public Places.* Glencoe, Illinois: Free Press, 1963.

Goodenough, W. H. "Rethinking 'status' and 'role': toward a general model of the cultural organization of social relationships." In *The Relevance of Models for Social Anthropology*, M. Banton, ed. London: Tavistock, 1965, pp. 1–24.

Grimshaw, A. D. "Sociolinguistics." In *Handbook of Communication* N. Maccoby, ed. in press.

Gumperz, J. J. "Phonological differences in three Hindi dialects." *Language* 34 (1958): 212–224.

Gumperz, J. J. "Hindi-Punjabi code-switching in Delhi." In *Proceedings of the Ninth International Congress of Linguists*, H. G. Lunt, ed. The Hague: Mouton, 1964, pp. 1115–1124.

Gumperz, J. J. "On the linguistic markers of bilingual communication." *Journal of Social Issues* 23, no. 2 (1967): 48–57.

Gumperz, J. J., and D. Hymes, eds. *The Ethnography of Communication*. *American Anthropologist* 66, no. 6 (1964).

Gumperz, J. J. and D. Hymes, eds. *Directions in Sociolinguistics*. New York: Holt, Rinehart, and Winston, 1972.

Hammel, E. A., ed. *Formal Semantic Analysis*. *American Anthropologist* 67, no. 5, pt. 2 (1965).

Hammer, Muriel, Sylvia Polgar, and K. Salzinger. "Comparison of data-sources in a sociolinguistic study." Paper presented at American Anthropological Association meeting, Denver, Colorado, 1965.

Hare, A. P. *Handbook of Small Group Research*. Glencoe, Illinois: Free Press, 1962.

Hare, A. P., and R. F. Bales. "Seating position and small group interaction." *Sociometry* 26 (1963): 480–486.

Harms, L. S. "Listener comprehension of speakers of three status groups." *Language and Speech* 4 (1961): 109–112.

Haugen, E. "Bilingualism in the Americas: A bibliography and research guide." *American Dialect Society* 26 (1956).

Herman, S. "Explorations in the social psychology of language choice." *Human Relations* 14 (1961): 149–164.

Hess, R. D., and Virginia Shipman. "Early experience and the socialization of cognitive modes in children." *Child Development* 36 (1965): 869–886.

Homans, G. C. *The Human Group*. New York: Harcourt Brace Jovanovich, 1950.

Homans, G. C. "Social behavior as exchange." *American Journal of Sociology* 62 (1958): 597–606.

Horikawa, K., Y. Ohwaki, and T. Watanabe. "Variation of verbal activity through different psychological situations." *Tohoku Psychologica Folia* 15 (1956): 69–90.

Howell, R. W. "Linguistic choice as an index to social change." Ph.D. dissertation, University of California, Berkeley, 1957.

Hymes, D. "The ethnography of speaking." In *Anthropology and Human Behavior*, T. Gladwin and W. C. Sturtevant, eds. Washington, D. C.: Anthropological Soc. Washington, 1962, pp. 13–53.

Hymes, D. "Directions in (ethno-) linguistic theory." *American Anthropologist* 66, no. 3, pt. 2 (1964): 6–56. (*a*)

Hymes, D. *Language in Culture and Society*. New York: Harper and Row, 1964. (*b*)

Hymes, D. "Toward ethnographies of communication." *American Anthropologist* 66, no. 6, pt. 2 (1964): 1–34. (*c*)

Hymes, D. "Models of the interaction of language and social setting." *Journal of Social Issues* 23, no. 2 (1967): 8–28.

Jakobson, R. "Linguistics and poetics." In *Style in Language*, J. Sebeok ed. Cambridge, Massachusetts: M.I.T. Press, 1960, pp. 350–377.

John, Vera and Tomi D. Berney. "Analysis of story retelling as a measure of the effects of ethnic content in stories." OEO Project No. 577, Yeshiva University, New York. 1967.

Joos, M. "The five clocks." *International Journal of American Linguistics* 28, pt. 5 (1962).

Kantorovich, V. *Ty i vy: Zametki pisatelya* (*Ty* and *vy*: a writer's notes). Moscow: Izd-vo pol. lit., 1966.

Katz, Evelyn. "A content-analytic method for studying themes of interpersonal behavior." *Psychological Bulletin* 66 (1966): 419–422.

Kjolseth, J. R. "Structure and process in conversation." Paper at American Sociological Society meetings, San Francisco, 1967.

Klima, E. S. "Relatedness between grammatical systems." *Language* 40 (1964): 1–20.

Knutson, A. L. "Quiet and vocal groups." *Sociometry* 23 (1960): 36–49.

Kostomarov, V. G. "Russkiy rechevoy stiket (Russian speech etiquette)." *Russkiy yazyk za rubezhom* 1 (1967): 56–62.

Krauss, R. M., and S. Weinheimer. "Changes in reference phrases as a function of frequency of usage in social interaction; a preliminary study." *Psychonomic Science* 1 (1964): 113–114.

Labov, W. "The social motivation of a sound change." *Word* 19 (1963): 273–309.

Labov, W. "Phonological correlates of social stratification." *American Anthropologist* 66, no. 6 (1964): 164–176.

Labov, W. *The Social Stratification of English in New York City.* Washington, D.C.: Center for Applied Linguistics, 1966.

Labov, W., and P. Cohen. "Systematic relations of standard and nonstandard rules in the grammars of Negro speakers." *Project Literacy Reports,* 1967, No. 8, Cornell University, Ithaca, New York.

Labov, W., and J. Waletzky. "Narrative analysis: Oral versions of personal experience." In *Essays on the Verbal and Visual Arts,* June Helm, ed. Seattle: University of Washington Press, 1967, pp. 12–44.

Lambert, W. E. "Psychological approaches to the study of language. II. On second-language learning and bilingualism." *Modern Language Journal* 47 (1963): 114–121.

Lambert, W. E. "A social psychology of bilingualism." *Journal of Social Issues* 23, no. 2 (1967): 91–109. (*a*)

Lambert, W. E. "The use of *Tu* and *Vous* as forms of address in French Canada: A pilot study." *Journal of Verbal Learning and Verbal Behavior* 6 (1967): 614–617. (*b*)

Lambert, W. E., M. Anisfeld, and Grace Yeni-Komshian. "Evaluational reactions of Jewish and Arab adolescents to dialect and language variations." *Journal of Personality and Social Psychology* 2 (1965): 84–90.

Lambert, W. E., and G. R. Tucker. "A social-psychological study of interpersonal modes of address: I." A French-Canadian illustration, in press.

Lawton, D. "Social class language differences in group discussions." *Language and Speech* 7 (1964): 183–204.

Leary, T. *Interpersonal Diagnosis of Personality.* New York: Ronald Press, 1957.

Lennard, H. L., and A. Bernstein. *Patterns in Human Interaction.* San Francisco: Jossey-Bass Press, 1969.

Levine, L., and H. J. Crockett, Jr. "Speech variation in a Piedmont community: Postvocalic." *Sociological Inquiry* 36, no. 2 (1966): 204–226.

Lieberson, S., ed. "Explorations in sociolinguistics." *Sociological Inquiry* 36, no. 2 (1966).

McCormack, W. "Social dialects in Dharwar Kannada." *International Journal of American Linguistics* 26, no. 3 (1960): 79–91.

McDavid, R. I. "Dialect differences and inter-group tensions." *Studies in Linguistics* 9 (1951): 27–33.

Maclay, H., and S. Newman. "Two variables affecting the message in communication.

In *Decisions, Values, and Groups,* Dorothy K. Wilner, ed. New York: Pergamon Press, 1960, pp. 218–219.

McNeill, D. "The psychology of *you* and *I*: A case history of a small language system." Paper presented at American Psychological Association meeting, 1963.

McNeill, D. "Developmental psycholinguistics." In *The Genesis of Language,* F. Smith and G. A. Miller, eds. Cambridge, Massachusetts: M. I. T. Press, 1966, pp. 15–84.

Markel, N. N. "The reliability of coding paralanguage: pitch, loudness, and tempo." *Journal of Verbal Learning and Verbal Behavior* 4 (1965): 306–308.

Marsden, G. "Content-analysis studies of therapeutic interviews: 1954–1964." *Psychological Bulletin* 63 (1965): 298–321.

Matarazzo, J. D., A. N. Wiens, and G. Saslow. "Studies in interview speech behavior." In *Research in Behavior Modification: New Developments and their Clinical Implications,* L. Krasner and P. Ullman, eds. New York: Holt, Rinehart, and Winston, 1965, pp. 179–210.

Mauer, D. W. *The Big Con.* New York: New American Library, 1962.

Mehrabian, A., and M. Wiener. "Decoding of inconsistent communications." *Journal of Personality and Social Psychology* 6 (1967): 109–114.

Meredith, G. M. "Personality correlates of pidgin English usage among Japanese-American college students in Hawaii." *Japanese Psychological Research* 6 (1964): 176–183.

Moscovici, S. "Communication processes and the properties of language." In *Advances in Experimental Social Psychology,* Vol. 3, L. Berkowitz, ed. New York: Academic Press, 1967, pp. 226–271.

Nichols, M., and Elaine May. "Conversation at breakfast." *Echo Magazine* 1, no. 1 (1959).

O'Neil, W. A. "Transformational dialectology." *Proceedings of the Second International Congress of Dialectologists,* Marburg. (in press).

Peisach, Estelle C. "Children's comprehension of teacher and peer speech." *Child Development* 36 (1965): 467–480.

Pfuderer, Carol. "A scale of politeness of request forms in English." Term paper for Speech 164A, University of California, Berkeley, 1968.

Piaget, J., and B. Inhelder. *The Child's Conception of Space.* London: Routledge and Kegan Paul, 1956.

Pittenger, R. E., C. F. Hockett, and J. J. Danehy. *The First Five Minutes.* Ithaca, New York: Martineau, 1960.

Pool, I. *Trends in Content Analysis.* Urbana, Illinois: University of Illionis Press, 1959.

Post, Emily. *Etiquette.* New York: Funk and Wagnalls, 1922.

Poussaint, A. F. "A Negro psychiatrist explains the Negro psyche." *New York Times Magazine,* August 20, 1967, 52 ff.

Ramanujan, A. K. "The structure of variation: A study in caste dialects." In *Social Structure and Social Change in India,* B. Cohn and M. Singer, eds. New York: Aldine, 1967, pp. 461–474.

Romney, A. K., and F. G. D'Andrade, eds. "Transcultural Studies in Cognition." *American Anthropologist* 66, no. 3, pt. 2 (1964).

Rosenfeld, H. M. "Approval seeking and approval-inducing functions of verbal and nonverbal responses in the dyad." *Journal of Abnormal and Social Psychology* 4 (1966): 597–605.

Rosenthal, R., and Lenore Jackson. "Teacher's expectancies: Determinants of pupil's I.Q. gains." *Psychological Reports* 19 (1966): 115–118.

Ross, I. "U and non-U: An essay in sociological linguistics." In *Noblesse Oblige,* Nancy Mitford, ed. New York: Harpers, 1956, pp. 55–92.

Rubin, Joan. "Bilingualism in Paraguay." *Anthropological Linguistics* 4 (1962): 52–58.

Rubin, Joan. *National Bilingualism in Paraguay.* The Hague: Mouton, 1968.

Sachs, Jacqueline S. "Recognition memory for syntactic and semantic aspects of connected discourse." *Perception and Psychophysics* 2 (1967): 437–442.

Sacks, H. "On some features of a method used in selecting identifications: An exercise in the formal study of natural social activities." ms. in press.

Samarin, W. J. *Field Linguistics: A Guide to Linguistic Field Work.* New York: Holt, Rinehart and Winston, 1967.

Schachter, S. "Deviation, rejection, and communication." *Journal of Abnormal and Social Psychology* 46 (1951): 190–207.

Schatzman, L., and A. Strauss. "Social class and modes of communication." *American Journal of Sociology* 6 (1955): 329–338.

Schegloff, E. "Sequencing in conversational openings." In *Directions in Sociolinguistics,* J. J. Gumperz and D. Hymes, eds. New York: Holt, Rinehart and Winston, 1972.

Skinner, B. F. *Verbal Behavior.* New York: Appleton-Century-Crofts, 1957.

Slama-Cazacu, Tatiana. "Some features of the dialogue of small children." *Problems of Psychology* 4 (1960): 377–387.

Slobin, D. I. "Some aspects of the use of pronouns of address in Yiddish." *Word* 19 (1963): 193–202.

Slobin, D. I., ed. *A Field Manual for Cross-cultural Study of the Acquisition of Communicative Competence.* University of California, Berkeley, A.S.U.C. Bookstore, 1967.

Slobin, D. I., S. H. Miller, and L. W. Porter. "Forms of address and social relations in business organization." *Journal of Personality and Social Psychology* 8 (1968): 289–293.

Slobin, D. I., and C. A. Welsh. "Elicited imitation as a research tool in developmental psycholinguistics." Language Behavior Research Laboratory Working Paper No. 10, Berkeley, California, 1967.

Soskin, W. F., and Vera John. "The study of spontaneous talk." In *The Stream of Behavior,* R. G. Barker, ed. New York: Appleton-Century-Crofts, 1963.

Stephan, F. F., and E. G. Mishler. "The distribution of participation in small groups: An exponential approximation." *American Sociological Review* 22 (1952): 713–719.

Stewart, W. A. "Urban Negro speech: sociolinguistic factors affecting English teaching." In *Social Dialects and Language Learning,* R. Shuy, ed. Champaign, Illinois: Nat'l Council of Teachers of English, 1964, pp. 10–18.

Stewart, W. A. "Sociolinguistic factors in the history of American Negro dialects." *The Florida FL Reporter* 5, no. 2 (1967): 1–4.

Strodtbeck, F. L., Rita James, and C. Hawkins. "Social status and jury deliberations." *American Sociological Review* 22 (1957): 713–719.

Stross, B. "Waiter-to-cook speech in restaurants." Term paper, Speech 160B, University of California, Berkeley, 1964.

Tanner, Nancy. "Speech and society among the Indonesian elite: A case study of a multilingual community." *Anthropological Linguistics* 9, pt. 3 (1967): 15–40.

Triandis, H. C., W. D. Loh, and Leslie Levin. "Race, status, quality of spoken English, and opinions about civil rights as determinants of interpersonal attitudes." *Journal of Personality and Social Psychology* 3 (1966): 468–472.

Tucker, G. R., and W. Lambert. "White and Negro listeners' reactions to various

American-English dialects," paper presented at Eastern Psychological Association meeting, 1967.

Tyler, S. "Koya language morphology and patterns of kinship behavior." *American Anthropologist* 67 (1965): 1428–1440.

Tyler, S. "Context and variation in Koya kinship terminology." *American Anthropologist* 68 (1966): 693–707.

Véron, E., C. E. Sluzki, F. Korn, A. Kornblit, and R. Malfe. *Communication and Neurosis.* University of Buenos Aires Inst. Sociologia. (mimeo.), 1965.

Watson, Jeanne. "A formal analysis of sociable interaction." *Sociometry* 21 (1958): 269–281.

Watson, Jeanne, and R. J. Potter. "An analytic unit for the study of interaction." *Human Relations* 15 (1962): 245–263.

Weinreich, U. *Languages in Contact.* Linguistic Circle of New York, 1953.

Williams, Marion. "Restaurant syntax." Term paper, Speech 160B, University of California, Berkeley, 1964.

Wurm, S. A., and D. C. Laycock. "The question of language and dialect in New Guinea." *Oceania* 32 (1961): 128–143.

# Words, Utterance, and Activities

## Roy Turner

It is increasingly recognized as an issue for sociology that the equipment that enables the "ordinary" member of society to make his daily way through the world is the equipment available for those who would wish to do a "science" of that world.[1] This might be formulated as the sociologist's "dilemma," but only so long as a notion of science is employed that fails to recognize the socially organized character of *any* enterprise, including the enterprise of doing science. A science of society that fails to treat speech as both topic and resource is doomed to failure. And yet, although speech informs the daily world and is the sociologists's basic resource, its properties continue to go almost unexamined. Linguistic models have had some recent influence on the development of sociolinguistics, but it is still not at all clear that any specifically linguistic properties of talk can be related to central sociological concerns. If we take sociology to be, in effect, "a natural history of the social world," then sociologists are committed to a study of the *activities* such a world provides for and of the methodical achievement of those activities by socialized members.

In 1955, the British linguistic philosopher J. L. Austin set foot on sociological territory when he claimed a concern with the "business" of any utterance considered as a piece of talk. In the course of beginning to map out the configurations, Austin identified an important class of utterances which he termed *performatives*.[2] A crucial test an utterance must meet to gain membership in that class is described as follows: "If a person makes an utterance of this sort we should say that he is *doing* something rather than merely *saying* something." Austin (1961:222) gives the following examples of what would count as performative utterances.

---

[1] Some particularly relevant discussions of this issue are to be located in Cicourel (1964), Garfinkel (1967), Garfinkel and Sacks, "On Formal Structures of Practical Actions," in McKinney and Tiryakian (forthcoming), Blum, "The Sociology of Mental Illness," and Moerman, "Analyzing Lue Conversation: Providing Accounts, Finding Breaches, and Taking Sides," and in Sudnow (1969).

[2] Austin's work on performatives is treated at great length in Austin (1965) and more briefly in "Performative Utterances" in Austin (1961). This is the place to acknowledge my great indebtedness to Austin's writings. In developing a critique of his concept of performative utterances here, I am biting the hand that has fed me for several years. I would like to make it quite clear that my perfunctory treatment of Austin's concept, in the service of elaborating some tools useful for conventional analysis, does no justice to the power and richness of *How To Do Things with Words*. The book is a sociological gold mine, waiting for prospectors.

**367**

Suppose for example, that in the course of a marriage ceremony I say, as people will, "I do"—(sc. take this woman to be my lawful wedded wife). Or again, suppose that I tread on your toe and say, "I apologize." Or again, suppose that I have the bottle of champagne in my hand and say, "I name this ship the *Queen Elizabeth*." Or suppose I said, "I bet you sixpence it will rain tomorrow."

This sounds like a promising beginning, in that it sets out to provide some rigorous connection between talk (utterances) on the one hand, and activities (doing) on the other. More than that, it suggests that at least some talk can be analyzed *as* the doing of activities, thus taking us at once beyond the naive view that perhaps at best talk merely "reports" activities. If Austin substantiates his claims, then, the links thus established between the utterances and activities are very much the business of sociology. In this reading I shall consider Austin's treatment of performative utterances in some detail, although I shall not do so in the spirit of providing an exposition or critique of Austin's work as an end in itself. My concern, rather, is with the elaboration of arguments that may underpin some actual procedures—primitive though they may be—for "taking apart" stretches of talk in the examination of its constituent activities. Later in the reading I shall provide some transcribed talk as data and attempt a brief demonstration of how such materials may be analyzed in a sociologically relevant way so as to elucidate commonplace and recurrent activities. Indeed, very briefly I shall try to indicate how "substantive findings" may be derived from such an analysis, but let me emphasize that the point of the reading is not so much to present a set of findings as to demonstrate and discuss possible procedures for "analyzing utterances into activities."[3]

Before looking further into Austin's treatment of performatives, let me suggest what might be their potential importance for sociological analysis in purely formal terms. Suppose for a moment that an exhaustive list of performative "verbs" could be constructed, and that a formula could be provided to identify a performative utterance constructed out of an appropriate verb form; for example, if "to bequeath" were an item in the list of performative verbs, then a corresponding utterance might be constructed along the following lines:

I bequeath + [object name] to [person, kin or organization term]
yielding, for example,
I bequeath [my watch] to [Jehovah's Witnesses].

If such a list and such a set of formulas could be provided, we should have achieved the following: *we should be in a position to scan transcripts of talk and formally identify items as instances of activities, where the name of the activity would be derivable from the performative verb* (for example, the activity of bequeathing). I assume this would be a significant sociological achievement

---

[3] I borrow the phrase from the unpublished lectures of Harvey Sacks. Although I have tried to keep the record of specific borrowings straight, I have taken too much from Sacks to hope that a few footnotes will be an adequate measure of his writings as a resource.

in that it would provide the analyst with a tool with which he could system-atically analyze transcribed conversations into at least one class of their constituent activities and identify mechanically some of the things persons *accomplish* through "talk." Indeed, presumably such a resource would provide the ultimate in contemporary sociological validation of methods, in that it could be fairly readily computerized.

Unfortunately, Austin's own elaboration of performatives provides at least two grounds on which such a procedure must fail. An examination of those grounds will, I believe, enable us to grasp both the fundamental usefulness of the notion of performatives and the ultimate failure of Austin's treatment to come to terms with social-organizational parameters of activities. I shall discuss briefly each of these grounds in turn.

## THE EXISTENCE OF "IMPLICIT" AND "PRIMITIVE" PERFORMATIVES

The development of a mechanical procedure for the extraction of performative utterances from a transcript, and hence the mechanical identification of a set of activities, depends upon both the "listable" character of performative verbs (which would therefore need to be finite in number) and the ability to generate an unambiguously identifiable formula from any item in the list. Leaving aside the problem of constructing such a list, this requirement fails on the grounds that the formulaic appearance of a suitable verb form is not a necessary condition for the identification of a performative utterance. Thus Austin (1965: 32–33) notes:

> It is both obvious and important that we can on occasion use the utterance 'go' to achieve practically the same as we achieve by the utterance 'I order you to go': and we should say cheerfully in either case, *describing subsequently what someone did*, [emphasis added] that he ordered me to go. It may, however, be uncertain in fact, and so far as the mere utterance is concerned, is always left uncertain when we use so inexplicit a formula as the mere imperative 'go,' whether the utterer is ordering (or is purporting to order) me to go or merely advising, entreating or what not me to go. Similarly, 'There is a bull in the field.' may or may not be a warning, for I *might* just be describing the scenery and 'I shall be there,' may or may not be a promise. Here we have primitive as distinct from explicit performatives; and there may be nothing in the circumstances by which we can decide whether or not the utterance is performative at all. Anyway, in a given situation, it can be open to me to take it as *either* one or the other. It was a performative formula—*perhaps*—but the procedure in question was not sufficiently explicitly invoked. Perhaps I did not *take it as* an order or was not anyway *bound* to take it as an order. The person did not *take it as* a promise: i.e. in the particular circumstance he did not accept the procedure, on the ground that the ritual was incompletely carried out by the original speaker.

So much, then, for the mechanical recognition of performative utterances. But there is more to be learned from this discussion than the mere fact that no mechanical recognition procedure can be derived from Austin's analysis. Consider, for instance, the precise form of the initial condition for admission of an utterance to the class of performatives, as quoted earlier in the reading: "If a person makes an utterance of this sort *we should say* [emphasis added] that he is *doing* something rather than merely *saying* something." The situation invoked here is not that of the doer of the activity but of the potential reporter of the activity and what he "should" say in giving such a report. Similarly, in elaborating the problems of implicit and primitive performatives, Austin again, as a test of the character of the original utterance, appeals to the situation of "describing subsequently what someone did." In terms more familiar to sociologists, it appears that Austin is preoccupied with the giving of *warranted accounts* of events. Thus, I take it that the following hypothetical example is in the spirit of Austin's analysis.

A, returning from church, where he has just heard B utter the words "I do" at the appropriate moment in a wedding ceremony, meets C, an old friend of both A and B. A tells C he has just seen B, and C asks, "Oh, what was he doing?" Now, according to Austin, it would be "odd" for A to reply, "He was just saying a few words," *under the condition that it could be said*, "He just got married." I assume that it is indeed a basic fact of daily life that "reports" or "descriptions" are so constrained, and that behavioral or technical descriptions of events would frequently be treated as bizarre, humorous, in bad taste, or in some way incompetent. Nevertheless, there is a deeper issue here that I must briefly explore. In order to do this I want to make some changes in my hypothetical example.

A reads in the newspaper that B has recently married. He meets C (who has been out of town) on the street and says, "Say, B just got married." Now given that A was not present at the wedding—and indeed may never have been present at any wedding, being quite vague as to the structure of such an occasion—he certainly cannot be *reporting* on an utterance he did not hear. In this case we might be inclined (to use Austin's own criterion) to say that A was "bringing C up-to-date," "announcing" that B had got married, or whatever. Announcing, after all, is surely plausible business for an utterance to do.

Austin himself, in a classic paper, has provided for the possibility of an utterance's constituting an act of "excusing" or "justifying," where one condition of the utterance's doing that work is that *it occurs in the context of the following upon an "accusation."* Thus:

> You dropped the tea-tray: Certainly but an emotional storm was about to break out: or, Yes, but there was a wasp (1961:124).

Suppose, then, that in the face of an accusation a person answers, "He ordered me to do it." Austinian logic would require us to treat such an utterance as *doing* the activity, "excusing" or "justifying." What then of his treatment of utterances like "He ordered me to do it" as derived from, dependent upon, and reporting on an earlier employment of a performative? In looking at some piece of talk as the "later" report which serves as evidence for the "earlier" existence of a performative utterance, Austin appears to claim that utterances can be treated as reports or descriptions *without reference to the interactional location of the utterance in question.*

Consider, then, the following difficulty which seems to be entailed by Austin's treatment of performatives.

We should find it "odd" to say that Jones had "uttered a few words" in the circumstances that what Jones did could be seen as "getting married." Should we not also find it odd to say that *A* was "describing" some earlier talk of *B*'s as a performative, in the circumstance that what *A* was doing was "providing an excuse"?

In short, Austin's treatment of "explicit" performatives as model forms to which other (related) utterances are to be assimilated as "implicit" or "primitive" varieties leads him to overlook the "business" (the character *as an activity*) of utterances that he is inclined to treat as reports or descriptions of other utterances. "Context" and "convention," which are invoked to characterize the work of explicit performatives and as criterial for seeing other utterances as "weaker" forms of performatives, cannot be permitted to go off duty when we seek to analyze other classes of utterances. Indeed, Austin himself is finally led to take explicit notice of describing as an activity, itself to be seen as a *located phenomenon*, when he argues that

> The total speech act in the total speech situation is the *only actual* phenomenon which, in the last resort, we are engaged in elucidating (1965: 147).

It may be, of course (as I shall discuss in some detail in the data sections of the reading), that *this* kind of recognition severs—or at least greatly weakens—the link between formulas for *doing* activities and the procedure whereby we decide *what* activity has been done: remember that at some point Austin's solution to the problem is simply to participalize the performative verb to locate a "name" for the activity achieved by the performative utterance (for example, "I apologize" is doing "apologizing").

At this point I shall turn to the second ground (provided by Austin's own analysis) for undercutting the possibility of a "mechanical" procedure for identifying instances of performative utterances.

## THE CONVENTIONAL SUPPORTS OF PERFORMATIVES

Recall that the issue is the possibility of locating members of a class of performative utterances (and hence activities) on the basis of developing some formula providing for their recognition. Even if the first objection to such a possibility (the existence of "implicit" and "primitive" performatives) did not exist, such an approach would still fail. For, as Austin notes, the successful employment (indeed, the existence) of utterances having a performative force depends upon two conditions, which we might refer to as social-organizational supports. The two conditions, as Austin states them are

There must exist an accepted conventional procedure having a certain conventional effect, the procedure to include the uttering of certain words by certain persons in certain circumstances. (1965:26).

The particular persons and circumstances in a given case must be appropriate for the invocation of the particular procedure invoked. (1965:34).

This seems reasonable enough, in that it argues that it is not the mere stringing together of words into utterances that automatically produces activities but that utterances are to be examined as being situated. Thus, I may say as many times as I wish, "I bequeath the Crown Jewels to my son," but I have bequeathed nothing, and therefore have not performed an act of bequeathing, since the Crown Jewels are not mine to dispose of. Austin is fond of pointing out that utterances embedded in jokes or state plays do not carry their normal performative force: an actor and actress do not "in fact" become man and wife by nightly going through a representation of a wedding ceremony.

It is a sufficient objection to locating instances of performative utterances by formula, then, to note that two appearances of the "same" utterance may not count as two instances of the "same" activity (if one is spoken within the framework of a stage play, for example). But again, there is surely more to say about utterances and their settings than can be generated by considering how performatives may "fail" for want of some proper "fit" between situational elements. Thus, to mention a possibility without pursuing it in any detail, "doing a joke" may be achieved precisely by virtue of the fit between utterance and setting; the utterance "I promise" may come off as a successful joke, where it would be perverse to see it as merely an instance of a spoiled "promise."

For the sociologist, further, Austin's two conditions can be faulted on the grounds that they simply take for granted matters that persons in the society may have to decide, negotiate, or assert as premises for bringing off activities. Thus, granted that the events of a stage play do not have the force of the activities they merely depict, *that it is a stage play* must itself be made demonstrable as a framework for viewing. The "brute fact" of being a stage play is not in itself a guarantee that at least some represented activities may not be fully consequential. Thus, to take a gross instance, if you and I decide to rehearse a scene from a script on the sidewalk downtown, wherein I press a gun in your ribs and say, "This is a stick-up," the "brute fact" that it is, after all, a play, will not necessarily prevent my being cut down by a passing armed policeman. Even "happenings" and other advanced forms of "spontaneous" theater take place at announced times in announced places. Pirandellian tricks depend for their effect upon their being viewed as theatrical devices; a literal "confusion" between depicted and "for real" events is no part of the theater that trades upon realism and spontaneity.

I shall now provide some transcribed pieces of talk and employ them for a discussion of some elementary procedures for analyzing activities. Although I still plan to travel a little further with Austin, I think the journey will be more eventful if it leads us to confront the concrete problems of dealing with actual bits of interaction.

Here, then, is a piece of talk pulled out of a transcript made from a tape-recorded occasion. I shall deliberately withhold any description of the occasion or the setting for the moment, since issues concerning their relevance are part of what we have to discuss.

BERT: Yeah, yeah, that's correct. I uh uh really did know im and uh he was with me in the Alexander Psychiatric Institute in in Alexander, Western Province. I I don't remember his name but we uh we always buddied around together when uh we were at the hospital and we always (( )) French. And uh I saw him out at Western City about three weeks ago, and I said to 'm, "Hello, howarya doing?" He said "I don't know you—who are you?" "Well, lookit," I said, "You *must* know me." He says, "No, I don't know you." Now he was with another fellow there too— waal he didn't want to admit that he was in a mental hospital uh in a hospital—he didn't want to admit it to the other fellow that was with him. So he just walked off and that was it. He wouldn't say hello to me. He wouldn't say nothin!

ROB: What was your view there? Do you have your own views on that? A touchy point.

BERT: Uh.

?: (( ))

JAKE: Perhaps he didn't like the idea of being in that place. Maybe he didn't want/

BERT: Well no he had to say it—there was another fellow with him you see/

JAKE: Well he didn't want to admit/

BERT: Who hadn't been in a mental hospital probably, and he *was* in the hospital. He didn't want *him* to know.

ART: You mean he

?: This other guy

COUNS: But he

BERT: Oh, oh never been in a hospital

BERT: He didn't want to know his friends.[4]

Now, given such materials as these, the practical issue is: How might they be taken apart in a sociologically relevant way—that is to say, as a demonstration of their orderliness? An initial paradox seems to be that as societal members we find that such materials are often terribly obvious, if not trite (and I imagine that the reader was able to find sense in the talk on the basis of a very rapid reading, despite the fact that he has no personal knowledge of Bert and the other speakers); while as sociologists, confronted with the task of obtaining some leverage in providing an analytical description, the very same set of utterances become forbiddingly opaque. It becomes opaque, I

---

[4] This transcript was supplied to me by Anthony Crowle.

believe, under the condition that as sociologists we suppose that we must locate instances (or indicators) of concepts posited by an explicit theory; and yet we obviously have no such theory to guide us in analyzing talk in any detail. Thus an elementary problem might be formulated as: What are we to attend to as units—words, sentences, utterances?

Let us assume that we are agreed for the moment that we want to locate and look at instances of activities. The problem still remains. I take it that Austin did not doubt that we can *recognize* activities; indeed, his method of operation seems to require, first, the collection of a number of performative utterances, treated as non-problematic in itself, after it has been explained what shall count as a performative utterance, and, then, the search for formal criteria that distinguish the class of performatives from other classes of utterances. Of course, if we isolated the formal criteria, we should then have no problem in scanning further candidates of performatives to decide their membership status; but that scarcely solves the problem of how we assemble our first collection of utterances on the basis of which the formal criteria are to be derived.

As a solution to the vexed problem of the relation between the shared cultural knowledge (members' knowledge) that the sociologist possesses and the analytical apparatus that it is his responsibility to produce, I propose the following:

*The sociologist inevitably trades on his members' knowledge* in recognizing the activities that participants to interaction are engaged in; for example, it is by virtue of my status as a competent member that I can recurrently locate in my transcripts instances of "the same" activity. This is not to claim that members are infallible or that there is perfect agreement in recognizing any and every instances; it is only to claim that no resolution of problematic cases can be effected by resorting to procedures that are supposedly uncontaminated by members' knowledge. (Arbitrary resolutions, made for the sake of easing the problems of "coding," are of course no resolution at all for the present enterprise.)

The sociologist, having made his first-level decision on the basis of members' knowledge, must then *pose as problematic* how utterances come off as recognizable unit activities. This requires the sociologist to *explicate the resources* he shares with the participants in making sense of utterances in a stretch of talk. At every step of the way, inevitably, the sociologist will continue to employ his socialized competence, while continuing to make explicit *what* these resources are and *how* he employs them. I see no alternative to these procedures, except to pay no explicit attention to one's socialized knowledge while continuing to use it as an indispensable aid. In short, sociological discoveries are ineluctably discoveries *from within the society.*

Now leaving the programmatics aside, let me cite once again Austin's admonition that "the total speech act in the total speech situation is the *only actual* phenomenon which, in the last resort, we are engaged in elucidating." Supposing we decide to take this seriously, how do we bring it to bear on the data presented above? What, for example, is "the total speech situation" of the talk recorded and transcribed?

Consider the possibility that more than one technically correct description of the occasion of the talk might be provided. Thus I could propose that a tape recording was made of Bert and a few acquaintances sitting around having an evening's chat. Another possible description of the occasion is as follows: A number of former mental patients voluntarily attended an evening group discussion sponsored by a mental health association; the discussion was in the charge of a counselor whose instructions were to help members of the group discuss their problems. As between these two possible descriptions I offer the latter as the more useful, employing the following criterion: the latter description characterizes the occasion as that occasion was organized, announced, and made available to the participants; an act of self-identification as a "former mental patient" was any member's entitlement to attend, and his entitlement to see that his fellow participants (apart from the "counselor") were likewise "former mental patients."

Why does this matter? It matters, I argue, in that it provides participants with an orientation and a set of criteria for contributing and recognizing activities. Whatever one says during the course of the evening may be treated as "something said by a former mental patient," not on the "technical" grounds that after all one *is* such a person but on the grounds that that identification is occasioned and thereby warranted as relevant.

Presumably this does not end a characterization of the "total speech situation" of any unit of speech smaller than the whole conversation. Thus consider Bert's remark, "So he just walked off and that was it." I assume that in order to see the sense of this remark it is necessary to notice its ties to at least the earlier parts of the utterance from which it is extracted. Notice, for instance, that given its position in the utterance, the "he" in the remark "So he just walked off and that was it" can be given a determinate reading by hearers (and now readers). Put crudely, then, one task of an analysis such as this is to make explicit just what features of the occasion and the talk are appealed to as providing for the force of an utterance or the character of an activity.

I hear Bert's remarks in this portion of the talk as constituting a "complaint," or "doing complaining." In so identifying it, I am unable to locate any obvious syntactic properties that might be seen as structural correlates of complaints, nor do I have any operational means for identifying its boundaries. I take it that Bert may have begun his complaint in an utterance previous to the first utterance given here; and I further assume that Bert's last utterance given here (but not the end of the talk), "He didn't want to know his friends," is in some sense "part of" the complaint. I know of no a priori reason an activity should be expected to require so many words or so many utterances; in any piece of data being considered it will be an issue to note the boundedness of an activity.

I now want to look at the production of a recognizable complaint in some detail, to look at the resources and components of Bert's complaint. I use the term resources carefully, since I take it that there is an issue of bringing off an activity in such a way that one's hearers can bring to the talk the necessary equipment and materials to make out its intended character.

Commonsensically there is no difficulty in saying that the basis of Bert's complaint is a "snub." More specifically, I take it that Bert's account is of "a former mental patient being snubbed," and thus is produced as an instance of "the kind of thing that can happen to a former mental patient."

Let us assume for the moment that a snub or slight, in the form of a refusal of recognition, can happen to "anyone." For the person to whom it has happened, such an event can presumably constitute a puzzle—that is to say, it is an event requiring an explanation. If I walk down the corridor and meet a colleague I encounter in such circumstances daily, and if we exchange greetings, then an interactional routine will have been achieved that—*for members*—is nonproblematic. Thus, if you are accompanying me at the time and you ask, "Why did that guy smile at you?" I assume that an answer such as "He's a colleague of mine" will be sufficient, that is, that it would be "odd" for you to persist, "I know that, but why did he smile at you?" A snub becomes a puzzle, presumably, just because such a nonproblematic routine is breached.

Now if after being snubbed one makes that event the basis of an anecdote for others, one thing they may do, it seems, is to offer possible "explanations" or queries directed to uncovering "what happened." One readily available explanation has the consequence of inviting you to reconsider the event, to see that it wasn't a snub after all, perhaps that "there was some mistake"—that it wasn't who you thought it was. He looked remarkably like an old friend, but you caught only a glimpse, and it was probably a stranger. I mention this routine treatment because if we look carefully at Bert's first utterance we can see that Bert orients to the possibility of this being forthcoming from his hearers, and forestalls it: "I uh uh really did know im." The reader should notice here the interplay between common-sense knowledge offered as how I make out what is going on, and sociological concern, in that I take it as an analytical responsibility to account for the remark "I uh uh really did know im," while having recourse to members' knowledge in providing the substance of my account.

Now if we look at Bert's first utterance as a unit, it seems that it (a) recounts the occurrence of the snub, and (b) provides an explanation for it. Nevertheless, at the same time it is via the character of the explanation that I see that Bert is constructing a complaint. In effect, this leads us to consider the "mechanics" of doing an activity. If Bert is to bring off a successful instance of a complaint, he must build it out of components that will provide for its recognition by hearers who are presumed to be—like Bert, and like readers—"experts" in constructing and recognizing a repertoire of activities. In looking at the talk in detail, then, we are discovering how the materials at hand are made to serve the requirements of certain invariant properties of activities. The following considerations lead me to argue that the explanation provides for Bert to be seen as "complaining."

Recall Austin's requirement for the successful achievement of a performative utterance, that "the particular persons and circumstances in a given case must be appropriate for the invocation of the particular procedure involved." How is that relevant to the present issue? In the first place, since we are not analyzing as data the talk that took place between Bert and his acquaintance upon the occasion of the snub, we are hardly in a position to characterize that "total speech situation" in a way that a transcript of the occasion might permit. What we have, rather, is Bert's characterization of the occasion, developed as a resource for constructing a complaint. In effect, then, we are dealing with the societal member's concern with providing for the "appropriateness" of the "particular persons and circumstances" as features that will properly orient hearers to the sense of the occasion—that is, orient them to a sense of the occasion that will enable them to recognize what Bert is *now* doing. This permits us to ask: *How* does Bert provide such an orientation?

Notice first, then, that Bert does not simply tell his listeners that he was snubbed by "an acquaintance," "an old friend" or "a guy I knew," although presumably any of these would have been a sufficient and proper identification of the party to allow for what happened to be seen as a snub. Bert identified the snubber as a man who "was with me in the Alexander Psychiatric Institute." Now I take it that this identification is not warranted simply by its literal correctness, since a range of possible "correct" identifications is always available (in this case, for example, "a fellow I used to know in Western Province") and it is not a matter of indifference which item of a set of possible items is selected. One thing we can note about the identification selected, then, is a relevance provided by the occasion, by the presence of this collection of hearers, in that the party mentioned is mentioned now as "one of us." Beyond that, the identification of the snubber as "he was with me in the Alexander Psychiatric Institute" provides that Bert himself could be seen by the other party as a "released mental patient."

Bert tells his listeners that on recognizing the other party he said to him, "Hello, howarya doing?" Now given that he has already indicated *that* (and *how*) they were acquainted, a greeting is seen to be in order and to require a greeting in return, since an exchange of greetings is a procedure permitted among acquainted persons; and upon one party's offering a greeting the other is taken to be under obligation to return it. In short, I take it that Bert is invoking what I have just stated in the form of a "norm," and that it is by reference to such a procedure that it becomes "obvious" to his listeners that "something was wrong" when instead of the greeting the greeted party returned with "I don't know you—who are you?" That this is the case is further provided for by Bert's remark, "He wouldn't say hello to me. He wouldn't say nothin!" As I understand Bert's remark, assumption of shared knowledge that a greeted acquaintance has an *obligation* to respond with a greeting is both a requirement and a resource for seeing how Bert is entitled to say "He *wouldn't* say hello to me," in that he is thus enabling his listeners to find the "absence of a greeting" as a motivated act.[5]

So far, then, all we have seen is an account of a breached norm, the norm that requires acquainted persons to acknowledge one another upon meeting face-to-face. This component of the account constitutes the occurrence of a "trouble," in this case, a snub.

If we look further at the utterance we find that Bert claims to see *why* he was offered a slight by an acquaintance who owed him at least the return of a greeting. Thus, Bert remarks: "Now he was with another fellow there too— waal he didn't want to admit that he was in a mental hospital uh in a hospital—he didn't want to admit it to the other fellow that was with him. So he just walked off and that was it."

Now the interesting question to ask is: *How does this come off as an explanation?* To set it up with heuristic naïveté, what could Bert be talking about in saying of the other party, "He didn't want to admit . . . that he was in a mental hospital?" How does the question of making an admission arise? To put the question in somewhat different form, we may ask: Are there any resources that Bert's listeners (as well as ourselves) might bring to bear on this remark to see in it the sense it is presumably intended to have (as grounds for the refusal to return a greeting)? How might it be seen that a returned greeting would be, or would lead to, an "admission to the other fellow" that he had been in a mental hospital? To put it differently, and in common-sense terms, it might be argued that it would have been entirely inconsequential for Bert's former fellow-patient to have responded, for example, "Pretty good, thanks. How's yourself?"

I take it that Bert is able to trade upon an "obvious" feature of "chance encounters," namely, their informational value. The paradigm case is suggested by the following hypothetical conversation.

> *A*: Who was that guy who waved from across the street?
> *B*: Oh, just a fellow I knew in the Marines.
> *A*: Really? I didn't know you were in the Marines! When was that?

Bert's friend, then, could be depicted as motivated to refuse an acknowledgment of the acquaintance on the grounds that it might have opened him up to "explaining" to his companion "who" Bert was—where the relevant sense of "who" would require a reference to the basis of their being acquainted. But beyond that, there are other norms relating to the situation of renewing acquaintance that are possibly being invoked here.

An issue in the orderly conduct of conversation may be termed "the distribution of speaker's rights."[6] Thus Sacks has pointed out with respect

---

[5] On the notion of "relevant absences," see Sacks, unpublished lectures and research notebooks. Compare Schegloff's discussion of "conditional relevance" in Schegloff (1968).

[6] See Sacks, "On Formal Structures of Practical Actions," in McKinney and Tiryakian (forthcoming); see also Speier (1968).

to questions and answers as paired units that a potentially infinite chain of utterances may be produced under the auspices of the following rule: *The questioner has a right to talk again when an answer is returned*, that is, when the answerer finishes his turn at talking the right to speak passes back to the questioner, *and the questioner has a right to ask another question* (thus providing for another answer and a further question; and so the cycle may be repeated, as court transcripts nicely indicate). Similarly, Schegloff (1968) has indicated that within the structure of a telephone call the caller may select the first topic for talk. With respect to face-to-face social contacts among the acquainted it appears to be the case that a simple exchange of greetings— "hello," "hello"—may constitute an adequate "conversation," and the parties may separate without breach of the relationship. However, it further appears to be the case that the initial greeter has the right to talk again when a greeting is returned, and that he thus becomes a "first speaker" with respect to rights of topic selection. If this is the case, then (as I take it Bert and his listeners could see), to acknowledge a greeting by returning a greeting is to open oneself up to the initial greeter's developing a conversation and to his initiating a topic. In the cited incident, Bert would have had the right to so talk, providing that his acquaintance did not attach the opening of topical talk to the utterance returning a greeting.

If we shift our attention for the moment from the initiation of talk to the issue of the *management of relationships*, conversations can be seen as having sequential properties; that is, when related parties meet, the conversational possibilities may be constrained by "what happened last time" or by events that have intervened. Thus, persons employ opening slots in conversations to "bring one another up-to-date," or—when the passage of time has been considerable, or "circumstances" have changed—to talk over "when we last saw each other," or, as in reunions, to "talk over old times." Notice again that I am suggesting this not as an analysis independent of members' knowledge and members' concerns but as integral to them, and I take it that it is a commonplace experience to "look forward to" or "avoid" persons with whom such conversations are to be expected.

In this connection[7] it is relevant to note that Bert's development of the

---

[7] Stan Persky pointed out to me the importance, for the account, of the encounter being seen as "the first since the hospital." An instance of the fulfillment of such a threat is contained in the following account given me by a former mental patient, in response to my asking if he would greet "fellow former patients" he might meet on the street:

Al: Yes I do. I stop and say hello to them and one case I came across was . . . we used to buy our groceries from the New Market Store and he was the manager—of the New Market Store. Well, he went out to State Hospital. I met him out there and I said hello to him out there and talked to him for a while. A year later I met him downtown in Western City. He was with his wife and I said, "Oh, hello, Mr Robbins. Remember me out at State Hospital? And his wife looked at me and said, "He's never been out in State Hospital." But there was no mistaking it. It was him. (laughs) I thought that was quite funny. Data taken from Turner (1968).

situation permits his hearers to see that indeed "bringing up-to-date" might have been in order, in that this was apparently a first meeting since the hospital days, and in a city more than a thousand miles from the hospital. In short, the locational and temporal features of the occasion are not simply descriptive but are *explanatory:* a "reunion" would have "normally" been in order, and a reunion could be seen as precisely what a former mental patient who is "passing" could anticipate as a threat. Returning a greeting, then, is not without cost.[8] For Bert's acquaintance, the return of a greeting, carrying with it an acknowledgment of their relationship, would have entitled Bert to develop talk about what each had done "since the hospital," etc. Thus potential conversational partners may avoid eye contacts, give signs of "being in a hurry," or balk at the first interchange, where the "danger" is seen to be located at some later (and unspecifiable) spot in the conversation that mutual acknowledgment may generate.

To recapitulate, I have suggested that the visible breach of a norm requiring acquainted persons to acknowledge one another, or at least return a proffered greeting, has constituted a trouble for Bert—he has been snubbed. Bert saw and made available to his hearers an explanation of the snub; it was by no means a case of mistaken identity but rather a matter of "deliberate" (motivated) refusal to "know a friend" on the part of one who might find that the cost of an acknowledgment would be disclosure to a companion that he had been a "mental patient."

But—and this I suppose to be crucial—it isn't the mere fact that the snubber had been a "mental patient" that constitutes *Bert's* embarrassment or chagrin: for Bert the complaint-worthy item is presumably *that he sees that he himself had been identified as a "former mental patient";* the snubber's own problems stemmed from *Bert's* former-patient status.

This I take to be the feature of the account that constitutes it as a complaint, where the complaint could be formulated, for example, as "He wouldn't talk to me because I've been a mental patient." The complaint, then, is directed to the recurrent kinds of "troubles" that persons can find themselves inheriting along with an unwanted categorical identification—in this case the identification that constitutes the tie between participants to the group talk and that is taken by them to generate the occasion in the first place. The complaint thus becomes a *category-generated activity*, providing for any members of the category (such as Bert's hearers) to see that "what happened to him" could happen to "us."

Earlier in the reading I mentioned briefly that the analysis of talk into activities here presented could be seen to provide for at least a suggestion of "substantive findings." What I have in mind is that the preceding discussion permits some comments on the traditional sociological literature on former

---

[8] Compare the anecdote cited by Schegloff to make the point "that conversational oaks may out of conversational acorns grow," in Schegloff (1968:1094).

mental patients and their "problems," a literature which, with few exceptions beyond the writings of Erving Goffman, establishes as its framework of inquiry a set of psychiatric assumptions concerning the character of such "problems."[9] On the basis of the analysis presented here I believe I am warranted in suggesting that the categorical identification "former mental patient" (as used by former mental patients themselves and by others) does the work of organizing and structuring accounts of persons' behavior and difficulties. That is to say, under the conditions that a person can be categorized *as* a former mental patient, such an identification can and will be used by members as explanatory and predictive of what such persons "do."

For persons in the rehabilitative professions, such an identification provides the auspices for searching out (and finding), for example, residual illness, bizarre behavior, having a relapse, etc. "Former mental patients" themselves, on the other hand, make use of their membership in the category to both locate and explain a set of interactional "difficulties" that they provide accounts of as recurrent events in transactions with friends, family, neighbors, etc. Notice that although I have constantly appealed to membership in the category "former mental patient" to elucidate what I took it participants to the talk were orienting themselves to, I have not *as part of my own analytical apparatus* attributed any special properties to such category incumbents, on the grounds (hopefully clear by now) that the invocation of the category as part of the "total speech situation" is the only relevant feature for my purposes.

What I want to note, then, is that a plausible view of at least one class of "problems" of "former mental patients" is that such problems are generated out of the same raw materials that provide for "normal" interactional routines, in particular, the invocation of norms governing such matters as meeting an old friend. It is in finding that such norms may be breached systematically, and the breach accounted for by the identification "former mental patient," that Bert is able to propose that "what happened" constituted a complaint-worthy event. Further, not only is it the case that such persons may find their "problems" cut from the same cloth that allows "normals" to manage relationships in a satisfactory way, it also seems to be the case that "former mental patients" employ the same standard methodical procedures for "giving accounts," "constructing complaints," etc., as are available to "anyone." Even persons who claim that their lives have been "ruined" as a consequence of time spent in the mental hospital may still retain intact their grasp on "how to do things with words"—*their* claims, in effect, validating *my* claim.

---

[9] I am thinking particularly of *Stigma*, (Goffman, 1963b), but the structure of interactionally generated problems is a theme in all of Goffman's writings. It is interesting to note by contrast that when Freeman and Simmons (1963:233), in a book-length study of the "problems" of former mental patients, turn their attention to the issue of "stigma" it is to note the embarrassment created for "the family" by having a former mental patient in their midst.

A few concluding remarks about words, utterances, and activities. A traditional sociological approach treats speech either as a source of "hidden" realities—such as values, attitudes and beliefs—waiting for the sociologist to uncover them, or as the reporting of members' "perceptions" of social facts, to be verified or falsified by "scientific" procedures. The initial value of Austin's work is that it at least brings our attention back to the fact that, as persons go about their business, some of that business is done (and not merely reported upon) *in* and *through* talk. It also helps us to see that an inventory of "norms" or "role expectations" fails to come to terms with the fact that members may (and do) assert, argue, hint at, deny, undercut, etc., the "relevant" situational features of accountable actions, *upon the occasion of giving accounts.* Some recent sociological writings do stress the "negotiated" or "emergent" character of interaction but usually fail to demonstrate how the structure of any given piece of talk can be displayed as an interlocking set of activities. Without linked demonstrations, of course, such programmatic statements must resemble "advice" given at a level of generality, which leaves the researcher still facing the crucial problem of how to analyze the tapes or transcripts that constitute his data. Too often such theories of interaction become the rugs under which the data are conveniently swept. The reader who wishes to utilize such "theoretical" writings is typically left to ask, "Now what do I do?" It is in the hope of avoiding another such exhortation that I have attempted to spell out in some detail what an analysis of talk into its constituent activities might look like.[10]

In building upon and departing from Austin's work I have argued:

- That all and any exchanges of utterances—defining an utterance for the moment as one speaker's turn at talking—can in principle be regarded as "doing things with words";

---

[10] A few sociologists have recently tried to develop models based on premises derived from transformational grammar. Despite the intrinsic interest of such work, and the cogency of the arguments, such writings differ from the work of linguists proper in one crucial respect; they fail to tie their theoretical arguments to the analysis of particular instances of data. Thus, whatever insensitivity to social structure the sociologist may find in some linguistic treatments of the deep structure of sentences, at least the linguist typically spells out in detail the steps whereby he arrives at his analysis, thus permitting his colleagues to pinpoint their criticisms and requiring them to demonstrate the basis of alternative treatments of the same data. It is for this reason that I have taken the space to spell out rather literally how I "hear" talk in the transcript presented above. Readers are free to perform their own analyses of the data in alternative to mine. In this connection I cannot resist quoting Gilbert Ryle's comment (in Chappel, 1964:26) on his problems in arguing the "stock use" of an "ordinary" expression with his colleagues: "One's fellow-philosophers are at such pains to pretend that they cannot think what its stock use is—a difficulty which, of course, they forget about when they are teaching children or foreigners how to use it, and when they are consulting dictionaries." The point, I take it, is that our concern in treating interaction is not to see how ingenious we can be in torturing alternative senses out of utterances, but that our task is to characterize their employment as it is located in the talk—such as we may (and do) find ourselves engaged in. Wittgenstein (1958:18) might almost have had traditional sociology in mind when he spoke of "the contemptuous attitude towards the particular case."

- That there is no a priori reason to suppose that syntactical or lexical correspondences exist between units of speech and activities:
- That in constructing their talk, members provide for the recognition of "what they are doing" by invoking culturally provided resources;
- That "total speech situations" are to be elucidated as the features oriented to by members in doing and recognizing activities, and assessing their appropriateness;
- That in undertaking such elucidations, sociologists *must* (and do) employ their own expertise in employing and recognizing methodical procedures for accomplishing activities;
- That the task of the sociologist in analyzing naturally occurring scenes is not to deny his competence in making sense of activities but to *explicate* it;
- That such explication provides for a cumulative enterprise, in that the uncovering of members' *procedures* for doing activities permits us both to replicate our original data and to generate new instances that fellow members will find recognizable.

I would particularly like to emphasize this last claim that the sociological apparatus that emerges from the detailed study of interaction is a set of descriptions of *methods and procedures* (for accomplishing and locating activities). Work that is currently proceeding along these lines suggests that the logic of the "programming" whereby socialized members "produce" social structure will result in a more viable central core for a "scientific" sociology than the existing common-sense division of the discipline into "substantive fields."[11] The building of this core as an empirical enterprise depends upon the sociologist's recognition that he has no choice but to reflect upon and analyze the social order to which he himself subscribes.

## REFERENCES

Austin, J. L.
  1961   *Philosophical Papers.* J. G. Urmson and G. L. Warnock, eds. New York: Oxford University Press.
  1965   *How to Do Things with Words.* J. O. Urmson, ed. New York: Oxford University Press.

---

[11] I am thinking of work such as Sacks, "The Search for Help," in Sudnow (1969), Garfinkel (1967), Blum, "The Sociology of Mental Illness," in Sudnow (1969), Speier (1968a, 1968b), Cicourel (1968), Turner, "Some Formal Properties of Therapy Talk," in Sudnow (1969), Bittner (1967a, 1967b), Schegloff (1968), Smith (1969), Moerman, "Being Lue: Uses and Abuses of Ethnic Identifications," in American Ethnological Society (1967:153–169), and Moerman, "Analyzing Lue Conversation," in Sudnow (1969). In this last work Moerman makes a similar argument with respect to the "resource" character of what the sociologist may state as formal "norms."

Bittner, Egon
1967a   Police Discretion in Emergency Apprehension of Mentally Ill Patients. *Social Problems* 14:278–292.
1967b   The Police on Skid-Row: A Study of Peace Keeping. *American Sociological Review* 32:699–715.
Blum, Alan
1969    The Sociology of Mental Illness, in *Studies in Social Interaction*, David Sudnow, ed. New York: Free Press.
Chappel, V. C., ed.
1964    *Ordinary Language*. Englewood Cliffs, NJ: Prentice-Hall.
Cicourel, Aaron V.
1964    *Method and Measurement in Sociology*. New York: Free Press.
1968    *The Social Organization of Juvenile Justice*. New York: Wiley.
Freeman, Howard D. and Ozzie G. Simmons
1963    *The Mental Patient Comes Home*. New York: Wiley.
Garfinkel, Harold
1967    *Studies in Ethnomethodology*. Englewood Cliffs, NJ: Prentice-Hall.
Garfinkel, Harold, and Harvey Sacks
1970    On Formal Structures of Practical Actions, in *Theoretical Sociology: Perspectives and Developments*, John C. McKinney and Edward Tiryakian, eds. New York: Appleton, Century, Crofts.
Goffman, Erving
1963    *Stigma: Notes and Management of Spoiled Identity*. Englewood Cliffs, NJ: Prentice-Hall.
Moerman, Michael
1967    Being Lue: Uses and Abuses of Ethnic Identifications. *American Ethnologist* 153–169.
1969    Analysing Lue Conversation: Providing Accounts, Finding Breaches, and Taking Sides, in *Studies in Social Interaction*, David Sudnow, ed. New York: Free Press.
Sacks, Harvey
1969    The Search for Help, in *Studies in Social Interaction*, David Sudnow, ed. New York: Free Press.
Schegloff, Emanuel A.
1968    Sequencing in Conversational Openings. *American Anthropologist* 70 (December): 1075–1095.
Speier, Matthew
1968a   Procedures for Speaking and Hearing. Unpublished mimeographed paper.
1968b   Some Conversational Sequencing Problems for Interactional Analysis: Findings on the Child's Methods for Opening and Carrying On Conversational Interaction. Unpublished mimeographed paper.
Smith, Dorothy E.
1969    A Sub-version of Mental Illness. Unpublished mimeographed paper.
Turner, Roy
1958    Talk and Troubles: Contact Problems of Former Mental Patients. Ph.D. diss. Department of Sociology, University of California at Berkeley.
1969    Some Formal Properties of Therapy Talk, in *Studies in Social Interaction*, David Sudnow, ed. New York: Free Press.

Wittgenstein, Ludwig
  1958   *The Blue and the Brown Books.* New York: Harper and Row.
Zimmerman, Don H., and Melvin Power
  1970   The Everyday World as a Phenomenon, in *Understanding Everyday Life*,
         Jack Douglas, ed. Chicago: Aldine.

# PART III

# DIRECTIONS

## 1980s-1990s

# INTRODUCTION

The articles in Part III have all been published since 1980. They represent a number of new lines of inquiry; but several persistent themes, such as the Sapir-Whorf hypothesis and the presentation of self through choice of language form, are also present, representing continuity in language, culture, and society research.

Jane Hill's article, "The Grammar of Consciousness and the Consciousness of Grammar," addresses a classic issue in the field of language and culture, dating back to Boas. As documented in articles in Part I and Part II, language structure and patterns of use are to a large extent out of the awareness of individual speakers. That phenomenon makes the structure and pattern stable, since individuals cannot easily access and alter them, thereby enhancing their value as research devices. Hill capitalizes on those features by demonstrating that speakers can become aware of linguistic phenomena of which they were previously unaware and use them to their advantage. She shows that in Mexico speakers of Mexicano (also called Aztec or Nahuatl) and Spanish have developed an interesting form of bilingualism. Spanish has been appropriated as a second language and given sharply symbolic different symbolic value from Mexicano. Spanish is the language of matters external to the local community, especially of the the larger polity and economy. Spanish can therefore be used not only for and with outsiders but to designate one's own separation and distance from one's own community, much as in the situation described for Hemnesberget by Gumperz (in Part II). However, elements of Spanish have been "refunctionalized" into Mexicano as markers or indicators of power. The power that Spanish represents, derived from its larger national political and economic base, has been appropriated and internalized into the community via borrowing from Spanish of lexicon and grammatical units into Mexicano. The effect is to create and mark power and status of men in the community who appropriate the Spanish linguistic items. The recognition of the symbolic role of Spanish in one arena of usage allowed speakers to import, or refunctionalize, that symbolic value into their own native language and culture system.

The refunctionalization of features from one language into another constitutes a culturally creative use of language toward social goals or ends. It is similar to what Gumperz described for the speech communities of Khalapur and Hemnesberget, and it has been reported for numerous other speech communities (see Gal 1979; Heller 1988). Individuals specifically interested in additional sources on Mexicano can consult Hill and Hill (1986).

John Lucy's article, "Whorf's View on the Linguistic Mediation of Thought," goes far to clarify the morass of confusion and errors that surround Whorf's work. Lucy identifies the major problems that have hampered understanding of Whorf's writings and contributions. The most common misconception was that Whorf claimed that language determines thought and thus world view. What Whorf actually claimed was that the way that speakers habitually think, the assumptions about the world that they commonly and routinely make, lead them to categorize and classify the world in predictable and patterned ways. What an investigator has to learn is what the basic, fundamental assumptions are. Whorf sought to demonstrate for speakers of a given language what some of the assumptions were and how they were codified in the language. That would allow him to illustrate what the consequences were for the way speakers used the language to construct reality. Lucy focuses on three of the particular problems that Whorf addressed, number (singular and plural), count-mass nouns (lakes versus water, for example), and time, explaining clearly in each case what Whorf attempted in his comparison between English and the Hopi language of the American Southwest. English and Hopi differ, for example, in the kinds of phenomena that cardinal numbers can quantify. Whereas speakers of English can say "ten men" and "ten days," Hopi speakers can say the Hopi equivalent of "ten men," but not "ten days," since days are not quantifiable in the same way that singular objects like men are.

References for additional reading on this long-standing issue of language and culture can be found in the References Cited for Parts I and II. Lucy's ideas on Whorf and linguistic relativity are further expanded in his two books published in 1992.

As an example of the old and the new in language and culture, Eugene Hunn retraces some of the central ideas and issues in cognitive anthropology that informed the work on language, classification,and thought and shows how they can contribute to and become part of a new area on interest—human ecology. His "Ethnoecology: The Relevance of Cognitive Anthropology for Human Ecology" is a ground-breaking article that deserves more attention than it has received. Hunn's point of departure for his synthesis of cognitive-semiotic anthropology with ecological anthropology is that culture is an ideational system that is also adaptational. Culture allows individuals not merely to have knowledge about the world but to adapt to social and ecological environments. Hunn shows that the equation CULTURE:BEHAVIOR::LANGUAGE:SPEECH is only partly correct, for it omits content of culture and of language that is ecologically effective. A more inclusive view of culture, Hunn argues, would be that culture is what one must know to act effectively in one's environment.

The broader framework in which Hunn works is evolution, biological and cultural. Individuals are subject to constraints from both biological and cultural systems, and their effective behavior, including survival, must be in relation to those systems. Hunn is thus able to propose that a better equation is CULTURE:BEHAVIOR::GENOTYPE:PHENOTYPE, drawing the second part of the equation from evolutionary theory. The basics of that theory are that an individual inherits genetic material, a genotype, that sets limits on morphology and behavior, but that the end results of morphology and behavior are a consequence of interaction with the environment. Hunn's proposal, then, is that culture sets limits—defines possibilities—for behavior, which is a consequence of the interplay of those limits and the environments in which they are actualized. Language enters the picture in the nomenclatural and classificational systems that individuals have of their environment and ecological relations within it, hence "ethnoecology" as in "ethnoscience," "ethnobiology," and "ethnomethodology." Language is an expression of the core of the ideational system, and it thus names and highlights the critical environmental and ecological information that allows adaptation.

Additional reading on cultural evolution can be found in Boyd and Richerson (1985) and Durham (1991), and information on the ecosystem concept can be found in Moran (1984).

Recent developments in language, culture, and thought can also be seen in the article by Paul Kay, Brent Berlin, and William Merrifield, "Biocultural Implications of Systems of Color Naming." Along with ethnobiology, color terminology has been one of the central pursuits in nomenclatural and classificational systems, and there is a large body of literature on the subject. The article reprinted here is a state-of-the-art summary of research on color naming systems. The authors show that across societies and cultures the naming of colors, as in plants and animals, is far from arbitrary. Semantic universals exist, based on the limitations posed by the physiology of color perception and on levels of technological development of the societies in question. An implicational scale exists, in which basic color terms are present in a more or less stable order. Some variation in the sequence, however, is present, as the authors document; and interestingly, the causes of the variation are not fully understood. Especially intriguing is the pivotal role that the basic color yellow seems to play in the variant evolutionary sequences that have documented in the 111 languages in the World Color Survey. Kay, Berlin, and Merrifield show very clearly that cultural vocabularies of color terms are constrained by biology but that cultural factors also come into play.

Among the large number of publications on color terms, the seminal work of Berlin and Kay (1969; second edition, 1992) is the logical place to begin further reading.

Through the influence of developmental psychology, anthropologists have long been interested in the socialization of children. Language and culture contributed to that area only marginally until the 1960s, when an outline of research possibilities were provided by Dell Hymes (see his article in Part II). Hymes presented a case for the study of the acquisition of communicative competence, cogently arguing that children who acquired only the vocabulary and grammar of their language would not be able to communicate effectively with other members of their social groups. The children would also have to learn the cultural rules of language use in order to be able to communicate competently. At approximately the same time as Hymes called for a language and culture approach to socialization, linguists and psychologists began to develop a research interest in the emergence of language in children. Together, those two new research agendas acted as a catalyst to stimulate anthropological research that borrowed from all three disciplines (anthropology, psychology, and linguistics). The sub-discipline has typically been referred to as language acquisition and socialization, while the specific research focus has been mostly on the use of language for the socialization of children, including their socialization in the use of language according to the cultural rules and canons of their society.

The article by Elinor Ochs and Bambi Schieffelin provides a summary overview of the types of research carried out on children's communicative development. They identify the major lines and types of research that have been attempted, pointing out that the focal point of much of the research has been on the relative contributions of biology as opposed to social influences to the socialization process. The nature-nurture position has at times been polarized, primarily with linguists arguing for an innatist source of language, whereas anthropologists have argued for an environmental position as contributory to the emergence and certainly to the social use of language. Ochs and Schieffelin make their position clear, specifically that the process of becoming a competent member of society deeply influences the process of acquiring language and that becoming a competent member is realized to a large degree through language. They present evidence for their perspective from three societies with which they have firsthand research experience—Anglo-American while middle class, Kaluli (New Guinea), and Samoan. Much of the force of their argument is to show that several of the fundamental assumptions of the innatist position are contradicted by the evidence, namely, that the speech that is addressed to children and that what they hear is not fragmentary, ill-formed, and "degenerate." To the contrary, it is highly culturally organized and patterned, to the extent that basic grammatical distinctions are clearly influenced by social contexts and the cultural rules which constrain them. The discovery and documentation of those contexts and rules necessitate ethnographic research, which is a constant feature of language and culture research.

A large body of literature on child language acqusition and socialization has been produced during the past three decades. Publications that are specifically anthropological or that have substantial anthropological content include Goodwin (1990), Heath (1983), Ochs (1988), Ochs and Schieffelin (1979, 1986), Schieffelin (1990), and Snow and Ferguson (1977).

Another area of language and culture studies that began to emerge fully in the 1980s was language and gender. A burgeoning literature exists, and the topic will undoubtedly grow in interest and importance. Michael Silverstein's

"Language and the Culture of Gender: At the Intersection of Structure, Usage, and Ideology" provides an in-depth analysis of the issues central to that area. As the subtitle indicates, his perspective is synthetic and holistic. The central argument is that although linguistic structure, patterns of usage, and ideology about language and gender appear to be independent realms, their interrelationship is sufficiently complex that independent analyses will fail to capture what is truly systematic about language, culture, and gender. Especially problematic is the tendency in ideological analyses to oversimplify or skew toward only one linguistic function, reference, and generalizations about reference, thereby minimizing the actual patterns of usage.

Silverstein's analysis shows that there is a triple intersection of the structural (gender marked forms such as he/she), the pragmatic (actual uses of marked forms to index gender), and the ideological (purposive awareness and correctness in regard to structure and use). In contemporary Modern English, the structural is marked in a class of noun phrases, the pragmatic emerges from social power asymmetries, and the ideological can be characterized as a power struggle. Silverstein's point about the triple intersection is that the components are in a constant dialectic, with action taken on any one feature influencing both of the others. Conflation of he/she to a genderless pronoun, for example, changes the way that indexing of social status is accomplished, reinforcing the ideological base that led to the conflation in the first instance. If that pattern persists to bring about change, not all of the structural marking, however, will be affected, since gender is not simply marked by third person pronouns. The relationships among structure, pragmatics, and ideology are multiple, complex, and mutually reinforcing.

Among the numerous publications on language and gender, anthropologically oriented ones that readers may want to consult include Cameron (1990), Coates and Cameron (1988), Perry, Turner, and Sterk (1992), Philips, Steele, and Tanz (1987), Shibamoto (1985), and Tannen (1990).

The article by the editor, "Parental Speech and Language Acquisition: An Anthropological Perspective," addresses the importance of culture in the language socialization of very young children. A focal point of the debate about nature and nurture, mentioned above, has centered on the characteristics of the emergence of language in infants and toddlers. The issue is not simply whether language emerges solely as a consequence of biological maturation, due to some language acquistion module of the brain, but of the extent to which the characteristics of the language that emerge in children is due to inherently biological capacity and the extent to which it is shaped by culturally constrained learning. Whatever the specifics, brain maturation clearly must be involved centrally in the language acqusition process, but equally clearly, cultural features must also be present, else children would all end up speaking more or less the same language in more or less the same way. As a way of trying to clarify the role of culture in the language socialization process, some anthropological research has looked at what the socializers actually do in social interaction with language-acquiring children.

A comparatively small body of information has been accumulated (see Blount, 1972, 1984; Ochs 1988; Pye 1986; and Schieffelin 1990).

The first point to be made about research findings is that in all cases language socialization is culturally patterned. In no society are children left to their own devices to learn language and appropriate behavior however they can. The adjustment of speech to the language-learning child takes many different forms, but two features in particular stand out. One is that the socialization is predicated on what the social status of children is in the society in question. In Samoa, children tend to be oriented toward the speech of adults, consistent with the status accorded to adults and to the different levels among them, whereas in American English-speaking families, children are talked to more on the level of conversational peers. A second generalization is that parental speech to children who have only barely begun to acquire any language at all tends to be laced with special linguistic features, such as high pitch, whisper, vowel lengthening, and consonant cluster reduction. Those features appear to serve to attract and maintain the attention of young children, which is one of the salient problems of verbal interaction with them. In effect, competent members of the speech community, as socializers, appear to model behavior for children, including whether to vocalize and how to use vocalizations interactively.

Among the large number of publications on language socialization, interested readers may wish to consult Blount (1988), Kaye (1982), Field, Sostek, Vietze, and Liederman (1981), Forman, Minick, and Stone (1993), and Rogoff (1990).

The final article in Part III, "Genre, Intertextuality, and Social Power," by Charles Briggs and Richard Bauman, traces the history of the concept of genre in language and culture studies. In a sense, then, the article retraces the core issues raised in the introductions to the three parts of the reader. The authors begin with a discussion of the way Franz Boas and his followers used genre as a classificational tool in regard to texts in Native American languages. Boas collected numerous folktales and myths, especially of native populations of the Northwest Coast, and the concept of genre was used to classify them into types. The classification was essentially taken as categorical, in much the same way that linguistic structure was taken as fixed, invariant; and thus the study of texts, by genre, would reveal fixed patterns reflective of culture. The Whorfian notion of unexamined assumptions, fixed prototypes (cryptotypes in his terminology), was similar, although culturally more deep-seated than Boasian genres.

Turning to the next major period in the history of languge and culture, Briggs and Bauman note that in the ethnography of speaking, genre has a different position. Although Hymes was not principally concerned with the concept, at least not initially, his views of speech events and linguistic routines prefigured genres. The authors note that in Hymes' writings, the concept of genre is expanded into interactional realms. Just as Hymes expanded the notion of relativity of language structure to the much richer relativity of language use, genre was expanded from a category or type to a nexus, or point of articulation, among components of speech events to a perspective on ways of speaking within and across communities. Genre was not seen simply as a device for segregating types of speech production into classes, which could then be compared as static categories; rather, genre was a device which offered speakers ways of crafting their messages in culturally constructive ways. In other words, genre was a culturally creative device.

Briggs and Bauman show how Hymes' views on genre have been used and extended by a number of other anthropologists working within the theoretical perspectives, first of the ethnography of communication and then in the analysis of texts produced by ethnography and ethnographers. They show how the creation and manipulation of texts is embedded in social action and is accompanied by social effects. Again, the social self and its intertwining with language use as envisioned by Mead, Goffman, Gumperz, and Ervin-Tripp, as outlined in the introductions and explicated in the articles, parallels the development of the discussion on genres. The socially constructive employment of categories or patterns is, in fact, a theme in many of the articles in the reader, as in Hill's account of the importation of status with the use of Spanish into Mexicano-speaking communities in Mexico; in Hunn's conceptualization of effective individual adaptation to the environment; in Ochs and Schieffelin's depiction of child socialization in the three societies they describe; in Silverstein's triplex of structure, pragmatics, and ideology of gender expression in language; and in Blount's perspectives on the social bases and consequences of parental speech.

Finally, the Briggs and Bauman article concludes with an in-depth discussion of how linguistic anthropology and cultural anthropology have similar interests, despite divergent concerns and methodologies. Extending their ideas, the similarities are deep and profound, not merely disparate and overlying points of contact. While language is a fundamental, indissoluble part of culture, it is not the whole of culture; and the history of language and culture studies begins and ends with the perspective that the part can be revealing of the whole. Language and culture studies have progressed from the somewhat simplistic but accurate observation by Boas that the unconscious nature of linguistic structure can be a window in the unconscious nature of culture to the complicated interrelations among linguistic structure, language use, and language ideology expressed in the work of later theorists, especialy Hymes and Silverstein. This reader is designed to show some of the pathways and high points of the progression.

A number of recent works on aspects of language and culture may be of interest to students who want to pursue additional reading. A sampling of those works include Bauman (1986), Briggs (1986), Duranti and Goodwin (1992), Gossen (1974), Hanks (1992), Kuipers (1990), Myers-Scotton (1993), Sherzer (1983, 1991), and Urban (1992).

# REFERENCES

Bauman, Richard
1986    *Story, Performance, and Event: Contextual Studies of Oral Narrative.*
        Cambridge: Cambridge University Press.
Berlin, Brent and Paul Kay
1969    *Basic Color Terms: Their Universality and Evolution.* Berkeley and Los
        Angeles: University of California Press (second edition, 1992).
Blount, Ben G.
1972    Aspects of Luo Socialization. *Language in Society* 1:236–248.
1984    Mother-Infant Interaction: Features and Functions of Parental Speech
        in English and Spanish, *In* The Development of Oral and Written
        Language in Social Contexts, A. Pellegrini and T. Yawkey, eds. Norwood,
        NJ: Ablex.
Blount, Ben G., ed.
1988    *Current Topics in Child Language Acquisition.* Special Issue of *Language
        Sciences*, Volume 10, Number 1.
Boyd, Robert and Peter J. Richerson
1985    *Culture and the Evolutionary Process.* Chicago: University of Chicago
        Press.
Briggs, Charles L.
1986    *Learning How to Ask: A Sociolinguistic Appraisal of the Role on the
        Interview in Social Science Research.* Cambridge: Cambridge University
        Press.
Cameron, Deborah, ed.
1990    *The Feminist Critique of Language: A Reader.* London: Routledge.
Coates, Jennifer and Deborah Cameron, eds.
1988    *Women in Their Speech Communities.* London: Longman.
Duranti, Alessandro and Charles Goodwin, eds.
1992    *Rethinking Context: Language as an Interactive Phenomenon.* Studies in
        the Social and Cultural Foundations of Language 11. Cambridge:
        Cambridge University Press.
Durham, William H.
1991    *Coevolution: Genes, Culture, and Human Diversity.* Stanford: Stanford
        University Press.
Field, Tiffany, A. M. Sostek, P. Vietze, and P. H. Liederman, eds.
1981    *Culture and Early Interactions.* Hillsdale, NJ: Lawrence Erlbaum.
Gal, Susan
1979    *Language shift: Social Determinants of Linguistic Change in Bilingual
        Austria.* New York: Academic Press.
Goodwin, Marjorie H.
1990    *He-Said-She-Said: Talk as Social Organization among Black Children.*
        Bloomington: Indiana University Press.
Gossen, Gary H.
1974    *Chamulas in the World of the Sun: Time and Space in a Maya Oral
        Tradition.* Cambridge: Harvard University Press.
Hanks, William F.
1990    *Referential Practive: Language and Lived Space among the Maya.*
        Chicago: University of Chicago Press.

Heath, Shirley B.
1983    *Ways with Words: Language, Life, and Work in Communities and Classroom.* Cambridge: Cambridge University Press.

Heller, Monica
1988    *Codeswitchnig: Anthropological and Sociolinguistic Perspectives.* Contributions to the Sociology of Language, 48. New York: Mouton de Gruyter.

Hill, Jane H. and Kenneth C. Hill
1986    *Speaking Mexicano: Dynamics of Syncretic Language in Central Mexico.* Tucson: University of Arizona Press.

Kaye, Kenneth
1982    *The Mental and Social Life of Babies: How Parents Create Persons.* Chicago: University of Chicago Press.

Kuipers, Joel C.
1990    *Power in Performance: The Creation of Textual Authority in Weyewa Ritual Speech.* Philadelphia: University of Pennsylvania Press.

Lucy, John A.
1992    *Language, Diversity, and Thought: A Reformulation of the Linguistic Relativity Hypothesis.* New York: Cambridge University Press.
1992    *Grammatical Categories and Cognition: A Case Study of the Linguistic Relativity Hypothesis.* New York: Cambridge University Press.

Moran, Emilio, ed.
1984    *The Ecosystem Concept in Anthropology.* Boulder: Westview Press.

Myers-Scotton, Carol
1993    *Social Motivations for Codeswitching: Evidence from Africa.* Oxford: Clarendon Press.

Ochs, Elinor
1988    *Culture and Language Development: Language Acquisition and Language Socialization in a Samoan Village.* Cambridge: Cambridge University Press.

Ochs, Elinor and Bambi B. Schieffelin, eds.
1979    *Developmental Pragmatics.* New York: Academic Press.
1986    *Language Socialization across Cultures.* Cambridge: Cambridge University Press.

Perry, Linda A. M., Lynn H. Turner and Helen M. Sterk, eds.
1992    *Constructing and Reconstructing Gender: The Links among Communication, Language, and Gender.* Albany: State University of New York Press.

Philips, Susan U., Susan Steele and Christine Tanz, eds.
1987    *Language, Gender, and Sex in Comparative Perspective.* Cambridge: Cambridge University Press.

Pye, Clifton
1986    Quiche Mayan Speech to Children. *Journal of Child Language* 13:85–100.

Rogoff, Barbara
1990    *Apprenticeship in Thinking: Cognitive Development in Social Context.* New York/London: Oxford University Press.

Schieffelin, Bambi B.
1990    *The Give and Talk of Everyday Life: Language Socialization of Kaluli Children.* Cambridge: Cambridge University Press.

Sherzer, Joel
  1983    *Kuna Ways of Speaking.* Austin: University of Texas Press.
  1991    *Verbal Art in San Blas: Kuna Culture through Its Discourse.* Cambridge: Cambridge University Press.
Shibamoto, Janet S.
  1985    *Japanese Women's Language.* New York: Academic Press.
Snow, Catherine and Charles A. Ferguson, eds.
  1977    *Talking to Children: Language Input and Acquisition.* Cambridge: Cambridge University Press.
Tannen, Deborah
  1990    *You Just Don't Understand: Women and Men in Conversation.* New York: William Morrow and Company.
Urban, Greg
  1991    *A Discourse-Centered Appraoch to Culture: Native South American Myths and Rituals.* Austin: University of Texas Press.

# The Grammar of Consciousness and the Consciousness of Grammar

Jane H. Hill

Sociolinguistics should be a tool for the exploration of the role of human linguistic capacities in the dynamic of the world system. However, while both the political economic study of the world system and the structuralist study of language have made important advances in recent years, there has seemed to be little possibility of uniting them. In the present paper I propose one avenue toward such a union, using tools for the investigation of the practice of speaking developed by Mikhail Bakhtin and V. I. Voloshinov.[1] Their work suggests the shape of a theory of the linguistic foundations of consciousness, that lens that, in Marxist political economic thought, focuses the material and symbolic historical dynamic within the acting subject. I will illustrate this possibility through a brief study of the Mexicano (Nahuatl or Aztec are other names for this language) usage found in peasant communities in the Malinche Volcano region of Tlaxcala and Puebla in central Mexico.

The Malinche Volcano is a Mexicano-speaking (or, more properly, a bilingual) island in a Spanish sea. The maintenance of the Mexicano language there among people who have been in intimate contact with Spanish speakers for nearly 500 years would seem to be a textbook example of the symbolic dimension of peasant conservatism. However, as I hope to show in this paper, we find, in fact, that Mexicano usage on the Malinche is not single-mindedly conservative. Instead, its speakers have drawn upon the resources of Spanish in complex ways. Their usage today constitutes an ongoing negotiation with the symbolic power of Spanish; the form of their practice in this negotiation is closely related to the structural position of individuals in the material sector.

---

[1] It has become customary to include a discussion of whether Voloshinov's *Marxism and the Philosophy of Language* (1973 [1930]), with its great article on reported speech, was really written by Bakhtin. My own view is that until the question is definitively settled (and currently I believe it is not), we should give credit to both scholars. In the present paper I have neglected the terminological categories of Voloshinov's work in favor of those developed by Bakhtin in *Problems of Dostoevsky's Poetics*, (1973 [1929]), but the two treatments of the interactions of the word are closely related. The theoretical foundations of the treatment in Marxism are detailed in the Voloshinov work; in Bakhtin's treatment, they are not (scholars like Todorov have emphasized Bakhtin's eclecticism).

In terms of human geography, the Malinche Volcano region has been identified by Nutini and Isaac (1974) as an area of sloped-terrace rainfall maize agriculture which is surrounded by irrigated cash-crop agriculture in the Valley of Puebla-Tlaxcala. Members of the Malinche towns (which range in population from a few hundred people to as many as 20,000) hold their lands privately; communal land, whether held by the towns or held under the Mexican government's *ejido* or collective farm system, constitutes only a small proportion of the area under cultivation. Lastra and Horcasitas (1979) in their linguistic survey of the state of Tlaxcala have confirmed that the Malinche region can also be defined by a uniquely high proportion of Mexicano speakers. The people of the Malinche constitute themselves as a region; this self-definition is symbolically warranted in myths like that of the Pillo, who brought water to the towns and, with the help of the ants, entered the earth and turned into a powerful being who was able to defeat the evil "government of Puebla" (the largest city of the region). At his death, the Pillo ordered that his body should be divided into pieces, and each piece wrapped in its own shroud and buried in a principal town of the Malinche:

1. . . . *ic San Pablo del Monte, La Resurrección, ic San Luis Teolocholco,*
   In San Pablo del Monte, La Resurreccion, in San Luis Teolocholco,

   *ic Huamantla, nochi in nonqueh pueblohtin que in tōcazqueh in īnacayō*
   in Huamantla, in all of those towns that they would bury his flesh

   *cada in īpedazo de īnacayō ye mortaja.*
   each piece of his flesh already in its shroud.

The work of struggle against the "city"—the Spanish-speaking world with its market economy—begun in mythic times by the Pillo continued. Throughout the 19th century the Malinche was the locus of ongoing peasant banditry, which was shaped during the early years of the Mexican Revolution into an effective guerrilla force. This force was not, however, fortunate in its alliance with other peasant groups. Its most important leader, General Domingo Arenas, was assassinated by elements of the Zapatista army (to this day Malinche people believe that the murder took place on Emiliano Zapata's order, and they remember his army as a band of vicious thieves).

The people of the Malinche region define themselves as cultivators—*campesinos*. It is important to note at the outset, however, that a substantial proportion of the adult male population of the region is involved in regular wage labor, largely in small independent factories. While there is a good deal of controversy in the political economic literature about the structural position of populations like that of the Malinche, my own view is that the facts are best handled within the framework developed by the Mexican anthropologist Arturo Warman, who treats a similar population in the state of Morelos as a "peasantry" (Warman 1980) which has maintained relative autonomy from the capitalist sector. Warman argues that such populations live within a separate "peasant mode of production," and have bargained, albeit on increasingly unfavorable terms, with the capitalist sector (and particularly with the state) to retain their autonomy. They return to the capitalist sector that *sine qua non* of peasant status, a fund of rent, which includes a complex sum of low wages in the capitalist sector, wages largely expended within that sector, and also includes support within the communities of a labor force upon which that sector can draw. This support includes not only the provision of subsistence, but also provision to the capitalist sector of physical access to the labor force, including education (schools are built by cooperative labor), transportation (roads are also built cooperatively, and bus systems are local private enterprises), and the provision (also through cooperative work) of the plumbing and electrical systems that make it possible for women to run households with little help from men, and that bring in the acculturating forces of national and regional mass media. Warman believes that this contribution of the peasant mode of production to the development of the Mexican capitalist sector is a fundamental one; Mexican industrialization, he argues, is "made of corn" (Warman 1980:176).

One result of the very unfavorable balance of negotiating power between the peasant sector and the national capitalist sector has been an extraordinarily complex involution of social and economic systems within the peasant communities. These systems are characterized by emphasis on maize, a semi-sacred subsistence crop, the cultivation of which is so uneconomic in modern Mexico that it has been largely abandoned by other sectors. Economic exchange within the community is dominated by systems of reciprocity and redistribution; recent studies, such as that of Olivera on Tlaxcalancingo (1967), show that three-fifths of community income goes into this "ritual" sector. This sector includes the system of *compadrazgo*, or ritual kinship, which, along with blood kinship, structures reciprocity and is extraordinarily elaborated in the Malinche region (Nutini and Bell 1980; Nutini 1984). Redistributive exchange is structured through the system of *mayordomías*, graded ranks of stewardships of holy images. Both *compadrazgo* and *mayordomía* are seen within the towns as "sacred" duties, but they can be easily seen to have an economic function. It is certainly not, however, one that yields a net profit to the participants, and in the Malinche region a man usually ends his ritual career, as Eric Wolf put it, "old and poor." But this ritual sector, in spite of the fact that it drains resources from the towns into the capitalist sector through ritually required expenditure, is fundamental in structuring access to subsistence resources of the communities.

In order to sustain the involuted system of maize cultivation and ritually regulated exchange, Warman has shown that the peasant sector must borrow tools from the capitalist sector. Warman was particularly interested in use by peasants of commercial credit, which in Mexico is available through state banks for investment in cash-crop cultivation. In Morelos, peasants use the profits from such capitalized cash cropping to prop up the money-losing maize cultivation system. On the Malinche, probably the most important material borrowing from the capitalist sector is that of wages. Rothstein (1974) has shown that in the Malinche town of San Cosme Mazãtecochco, most surplus from wages is turned to the buttressing of a man's position as a cultivator—toward investment in land, in fertilizers, in herbicides, and in cash-crop ventures, the profits of which can be turned toward continuing maize cultivation.

In the symbolic sector, the principal instrument that the peasant sector has appropriated and turned toward the maintenance of its involuted autonomy is the Spanish language. Mexicano and Spanish have been given sharply differentiated symbolic significance. Spanish is the language of money and the market, of the city, of evil personages in myths, and of social distance. To speak Spanish to a fellow townsman can be an aggressive denial of intimacy; the use of Spanish to outsiders to the region, regardless of their ethnicity, registers social distance in that context as well. Spanish is also the language of obscenity and of "nonsensical" drunken speech. But, in line with Brown and Gilman's (1960) proposal that expressions of social distance will also be expressions of power, Spanish elements have been refunctionalized within the Mexicano language as markers of the "power code," the register of Mexicano through which important men mark their identity, and through which even men who are not *principales* (men of high rank in the ritual hierarchy) mark their discourses as profound and authoritative. (I use the term "men" on purpose; women hardly use the hispanicized Mexicano power code.)

In contrast to the symbolic position of the Spanish language and elements borrowed from it into Mexicano, which mark power and distance, Mexicano is par excellence the language of intimacy, solidarity, mutual respect, and identity as a *campesino*. Mexicano is required at major community rituals such as the sealing of the vows between new *compadres*, or the blessing of newlyweds. Obscene "inverted greetings" in Mexicano are used by young men to test the ethnicity of strangers encountered on the roads; the return of the correct Mexicano comeback is a password allowing entrée into the town. Mexicano is the language of eating and drinking together, and even when guests at a party are speaking Spanish, they will often call loudly for more food and drink, or offer toasts, in Mexicano. The discourses of cultivation are considered particularly characteristic of Mexicano, and are often used by informants to illustrate the essential nature of the language.

The reader can immediately see that this functional balance between Spanish and Mexicano is potentially fraught with contradictions. A speaker manifesting hispanicization in the "power code" is always vulnerable to being seen as expressing social distance and "outsiderness" to his town, or as expressing the arrogance and lack of respect thought to be characteristic of Spanish speakers. Within Mexicano usage, Spanish, essential to expressing the status of men and the seriousness of their discourses, can be seen also as a source of pollution from the capitalist sector. Even in the speech of cultivators who are fully committed to the community and its complex organizations, one can observe a struggle against this ambivalence of Spanish forms. In the usage of factory workers, who are perhaps of all inhabitants of the Malinche those who are most exposed to the structural contradictions of the regional situation, one can see the escalation of this ongoing struggle into a ferocious purism that threatens the validity of the Mexicano power code; indeed, purism is precisely tuned to the struggle for power between factory workers, who are beginning to show signs of becoming a classical *evolué* sector, and the *principales*, who adhere to what is thought to be the "traditional" way of life of the towns, with cultivation and selfless community service the way to a respected old age. Bartra (1978) has suggested that in the negotiation for peasant autonomy the balance has now tipped in favor of the capitalist sector, which has refunctionalized the community support of factory workers from a fund of rent into a wage supplement, such that these workers must be considered not a peasantry, but a rural proletariat that does not control a means of production. On the symbolic side, we might suggest that the Spanish-speaking capitalist sector has succeeded in refunctionalizing Mexicano purism, latent in Mexicano communities for hundreds of years (cf. Karttunen and Lockhart 1976), into a weapon through which the symbolic bulwark of peasant autonomy, the Mexicano language, can be attacked. The attack may succeed, for the lexical resources to satisfy purist demands for a *legítimo mexicano*—a pure Mexicano, without Spanish influence—no longer exist, and are precisely most lacking among the most purist group, young and middle-aged factory workers, who spend much of their lives in a Spanish-speaking environment.[2]

The concept of "consciousness" in Marxist thought would seem to provide an analytical locus at which the material and the symbolic sides of human adaptation could be linked. However, the classical work on consciousness, such as that of Lukács (1968), gives little attention to what people actually say and do and often even denigrates such attention as "empiricism." The form of consciousness is derived on a priori theoretical grounds, and the ideal "vanguard leaders" of the proletariat function as "practitioners" much as Chomsky's "ideal native speakers" function as the bearers of linguistic competence—they are theoretical abstractions, far from the behavior of real human beings. The program for the study of language suggested by Bakhtin and Voloshinov, which, particularly in the work of Voloshinov, is grounded in a Marxist structural analysis of human interaction, offers the possibility of an alternative—a rigorously empirical investigation of the "practice" of language, which will be a window on consciousness, whether peasant, bourgeois, or

---

[2] This is not the only refunctionalization of Mexicano symbolic values by the Spanish-speaking sector. The Mexican state has "folklorized" (Jaulin 1979) Mexicano speech, turning it into a source of handy lexical vehicles for indigenist patriotism. It is interesting to note that one of the main expressions of this, the giving of Mexicano personal names such as *Xochitl* (Flower) and *Cuauhtemoc* (Eagle Descended) (the name of the last ruler of the Mexica Aztec) to children, has penetrated the Malinche, being currently popular among the best-educated young couples. Many local priests strongly oppose such names, and I know of at least one case where a couple took advantage of the town priest's brief absence at a conference to have a more liberal-minded visitor baptize their child. Mexicano surnames such as *Xaxalpa* (Sandy Place) and *Tecxis* (Land Snail) are common on the Malinche.

proletarian. This program admits the systemic aspects of language, as well as the study of usage.

For Bakhtin and Voloshinov, the central structural element of a new kind of language study (which their translators usually call "translinguistics" (cf. Todorov 1981; Bakhtin 1980 [1935]) is the "voice," and the theoretical possibilities for the juxtaposition of "voices" is the central problem of translinguistic study. A single utterance can combine a variety of voices in an intertextual polyphony or dialogue, in which both ideology and the language system function as constraints on combination. It is important to emphasize that the study of the language system remains fundamental to translinguistics. The language system of linguistics is the context-free, relatively permanent, "centripetal" side of language, the domain of "monologue," which can exploit the language system in order to constrain the possibilities for discourse. This monologic voice is somewhat similar to the "ideal native speaker," the locus of competence, but it is an active voice, using the systemic side of language as a resource for the practice of dominance. Added to this "linguistics" is the central translinguistic domain, the context-bound, shifting, responsive, intertextual, "centrifugal" production of meaning in language, which is found prototypically in the negotiations of a dialogue on equal terms, and not in monologic dominance. In dialogue as well, both conflicting ideologies and the systemic constraints of grammar are resources for the combination of voices.

In Bakhtin's analyses, the systemic unit is the context-bound utterance of the voice, the "word." In his study of the poetics of Dostoevsky, Bakhtin classifies this "word" into three major types. The first, the direct word, is "aimed directly at its object," and constitutes a claim of "semantic authority" by the speaker over that object (Bakhtin 1973 [1929]:164). A speaker whose usage is dominated by the direct word, a word to which he attributes only referential and propositional value, constructs a monologue that is ideologically consistent within itself and permits no challenge. This "direct word" of translinguistics is perhaps closest to the "word" of linguistics. The structuralist claim that language systems "admit of no positive terms" (as Saussure put it), but contain units that gain their meaning or positivity exclusively by their structural relations within the system, is a linguistic account of the ideological consistency of the monologue.

The second type of translinguistic word is the objectivized word. Instead of treating an object directly, the objectivized word makes an object of the word of another voice, through typifying it or through assigning it to a particular "character," according to a scheme proposed by an author. Most instances of represented and reported speech that have the function of "sketching character" are assigned by Bakhtin to the category of objectivized words. They are still a part of monologue, not of dialogue, since to objectify or typify another's word requires a dominant authorial voice, which makes these objects and types serve its own ideology.

The third type of translinguistic word is the "double-voiced" word. This is oriented toward another person's word, but without objectification or typification, just as in egalitarian dialogue speakers engage each other's voices. Bakhtin divides the double-voiced word into three subtypes. The first two are "passive." These include stories where the author speaks through the voice of some character; such speech often becomes an example of the monologic direct word. The second "passive" subtype includes parody and irony, which also tend to become part of an ideologically controlling, monologic voice, if the words that are parodied are allowed no independence or resistance against the author.

The last subtype is the "active" word. Here, the word of the other "exerts influence from within" (Bakhtin 1973 [1929]:164). Examples of this type include genuinely dialogic relationships between voices, in "hidden dialogue" and in polemic, in which words exhibit what Bakhtin calls a "sidelong glance" at the words of others. Here, the word of the other can resist and interrupt the authorial voice, and their relationship can be a struggle for dominance, with the embedded voice having a good chance at victory.

While Bakhtin and Voloshinov took as their principal research site the study of reported speech in the novel, Bakhtin notes specifically that multilingual communities would be appropriate sites for translinguistic investigation.

> Dialogical relationships are possible among linguistic styles, social dialects, etc., if those phenomena are perceived as semantic positions, as a sort of linguistic Weltanschauung, i.e., if they are perceived outside the realm of linguistic investigation [Bakhtin 1973 (1929):152].

Bakhtin himself treated this research possibility only briefly, as in his discussion of the influence of the heteroglossic 16th-century marketplace on the poetic technique of Rabelais (Bakhtin 1968 [1940]), or in his brief discussion of the moment of choice faced by Russian peasants between the multiple languages (each representing an ideological stance) in their environment, mentioned in "Discourse of the Novel" (Bakhtin 1980 [1935]). But it seems clear that the perception among speakers that a symbolic code is also a "position" must be shaped by the material forces of power; what can be done with this perception will then be shaped by the systemic forces of ideology and of grammatical practice.

Let us begin our analysis of the practice of speaking in Malinche Mexicano, using Bakhtin's system, with a passage uttered at the beginning of a traditional story by a 40-year-old cultivator from San Miguel Canoa. The speaker is already beginning his rise in the religious hierarchy of his town, and has had an important *mayordomía* that took enormous amounts of time and money. Don Otilio cultivates just over a hectare of land, and supplements this subsistence base with wage work as a construction worker in the city of Puebla during the agricultural off seasons. He cultivates only maize, and sells maize about twice a year to raise a bit of cash, in spite of the loss sustained thereby. The passage cited in example 2 below is the beginning of the story of the Pillo and is filled with symbols of militant peasant autonomy. Yet, because it is a serious story, it is appropriate for Don Otilio to load its introduction with Spanish loan words, even though, in general, traditional stories of this type display a low frequency of Spanish loans (about half that seen in "power code" registers). Spanish loans are in bold type.

2. *Nicmolhuilīz cē* **cuento** *de in nēc* **antepasado** *ōcmihtahuiliāyah in*
   I will tell a story of that ancestor (that) they used to tell

   *tocohcoltzitzīhuān nēca* **tiempo** *ōmo***vivir***huiliaya īpan Malīntzīn cē,*
   our grandfathers (about) that time when there lived on the Malinche A,

   *cē persona ītōca ōc***nombrar***ohqueh Pillo.*
   a person his name they named him Pillo.

In this example the Mexicano morphological and syntactic system is intact and dominates the Spanish loans. While loan nouns can receive Mexicano inflectional and derivational affixation, here, since there is no occasion for use of possessives, diminutives, and the like on the loan nouns they appear without any affixes, but with Mexicano determiners and demonstratives such as *cē* (one) and *nēc(a)* (that). Spanish loan nouns never receive Mexicano absolute suffixes (most Mexicano nouns include, in the nonpossessed form, a root and an "absolutive suffix" *-tl, -tli,* or *-li,* for example, *tempāmi-tl* [wall—absolutive], *tōch-tli* [rabbit—absolutive]). This is a loan-incorporation strategy that is quite common in the languages of the world, which Markey (1983) has called "marking reversal." The "marked" loan nouns are rendered "unmarked" by being assigned to a "marked" noun class, the small class of nouns in Mexicano, such as *chichi* (dog), which do not appear with absolutive suffixes. The verbs *vivir* (to live) and *nombrar* (to name) are here fully incorporated into Mexicano, being affixed with theme formatives and person and aspect markers precisely as if they were Mexicano words. Complex sentence elements, such as *nēca tiempo ōmovivirhuiliaya* (that time [when] there used to live), are formed by adjunction rather than exhibiting the Spanish complementation and relativization markers such as *que,* which appear in some Malinche usage (as in example 6 below). The use of Spanish loans of this type occurs even in the speech of Mexicano "monolinguals" (more properly "incipient bilinguals," [cf. Diebold 1961]); the speaker in example 2 speaks Spanish haltingly, with a good deal of interference from Mexicano, as will be illustrated below in example 7.

In Bakhtin's terms, the Spanish loan words in the passage above are examples of the "direct word." They have two values, a referential one and a "semantic position," that of representing seriousness and power, which is wholly determined within the Mexicano system; the same words would certainly not be particularly potent within a Spanish discourse. That is, they are fully dominated by a "Mexicano" voice, and turned to its purpose. However, we can see in other passages uttered by this same speaker moments in which the latent ambivalence of such usage is brought to the surface, and the Mexicano voice is forced to address directly the problem of its dominance. This can be seen in the passage in example 3. Here, the speaker is a little drunk, and he has been reflecting on his poverty and the "sacrifices" of life as a cultivator, particularly the problem of coping with the steep slopes of the volcano Malinche. At the urging of an interviewer, he turns to a discussion of the female spirit of the mountain:

3. *Mihtahulia in nēca Malīntzīn, cmopialia in nēca* **arete**, *huān*      1
it is said of that Malinche that she has those earrings, and

   *nēca, nēca, nēca* **collares**. *In tehhuān tquiliah,* '*īcolālex in*      2
those, those, those necklaces. As for us we say, 'her necklaces the

   *Malīntzīn.' Quin-, quinmopialia, cualtzīn, mopetlānaltia, in nēca*      3
Malinche. Them-, she has them, beautiful, she shines, that

   *Malīntzīn. Cualtzīn quinmopialihticah, in nēca īcolālexhuān, huān*      4
Malinche. Beautiful she is having them, those her necklaces, and

   *nēca īpīpilōlhuān cualtztīn.*      5
those her earrings beautiful.

Here, at the beginning of the passage we see a wholly characteristic use of Spanish loans, *arete* (earring[s]) and *collares* (necklaces). The variation in pluralization of inanimate nouns is typically Mexicano, and the use of the Spanish suffix *-es* on *collares* illustrates one of the rare instances of a borrowed affix; *-s, -es* have been added to the Mexicano repertoire of plural suffixes for use on Spanish loan nouns. However, the speaker suddenly changes his approach to these words, noting that *tehhuān* (we) would say a different form—*īcolālex* (her necklaces)—which exhibits a Mexicano possessive marker and phonological nativization of the loan word, including the plural marker [*īkolāleš*]. In line 4, he further nativizes the form by adding the Mexicano plural suffix for possessives, *-huān*. In line 5, *arete* is replaced by a fully Mexicano form, root and all, *īpīpilōlhuān* (her earrings). These nativized forms are clearly not simply referential "direct words." Instead, they establish a Mexicano "semantic position." In Bakhtin's system, they are double-voiced words of the "active" type, uttered by the Mexicano voice with what Bakhtin called a "side-long glance" at their Spanish alternatives. This passage is not simply a description of the beautiful and seductive Malinche, but a translinguistic battlefield, upon which two ways of speaking struggle for dominance. Bakhtin comments on this capacity for words to shift their position in mid-speaking:

> the interrelationships . . . in a concrete living context have a dynamic, not a static character: the interrelationships of voices within the word can change drastically, a single-directed word can transform itself into a hetero-directed one, the inner dialogization can be intensified or weakened, a passive type can become activated, etc. [Bakhtin 1973 (1929):165].

A second kind of evidence, in addition to the kind of backtracking and reframing seen in example 3, of the representation of the practices of peasant consciousness in speaking can be found in hesitations, stammering, and other failures of fluency, and in violation of systemic constraints on code-switching proposed by Gumperz (1982). An example of this type can be seen in example 4. Here, an elderly cultivator, a full *principal* of his town of San Lorenzo Almecatla on the edge of the Malinche region, discusses how his son was attracted into a shady business deal, which was in conflict with his community responsibilities and which eventually led to his murder.

4. *Huán ōquinōtzqueh de . . . ser tesorero īmināhuac, neh acmo ōniccāhuaya*
   and when they called him . . . to be treasurer with them, I no longer gave permission

   *porque lo mismo ōyec presidente.*
   because that same person was (municipal) president.

   (He was invited to be treasurer of the local community bus lines, a sure route to gaining wealth through embezzlement.)

In this passage, we see a code switch, between the verb *ōquinōtzqueh* (they called him) and its complement, *de ser tesorero* (to be treasurer), violating Gumperz's Verb-Verb Complement Constraint (1982:88), which states that code switching will not take place between the two. In general in Malinche usage, this constraint makes an excellent test for assigning a Spanish complement phrase to the category of fully incorporated "borrowing." However, we know that Malinche speakers always emphatically reject Spanish infinitives such as *ser* as "not Mexicano"; this kind of form is particularly accessible to sanction as "mixing." In Bakhtin's terms, we can analyze this example as a struggle (and note the hesitation represented by the ellipses) between a "voice" of corrupt local politicians, speaking in the Spanish of civil government and profit-making commerce, and the Mexicano, peasant, communitarian voice of the narrator. Here, the "Spanish" voice is powerful enough to break through systemic constraints on its appearance, and we see Spanish *ser* instead of Mexicano *yēz* (to be).

If cultivators such as Don Otilio in example 3 and Don Gabriel in example 4 face a struggle with the ambivalent place of the Spanish they have turned to the purposes of Mexicano, we might imagine that the struggle would become particularly acute in the usage of factory workers. Factory workers face a number of problems in the successful presentation of a "Mexicano" identity that will warrant their access to community resources. These resources, distributed through the community ritual sector, are a vital backstop to factory-worker participation in a particularly oppressive and insecure wage labor market, which often denies them legally mandated benefits and minimum wages, and in which they experience frequent layoffs. During layoffs (and even when employed) they are hard-pressed for basic subsistence, and they maintain themselves and their families through the loans that circulate among *compadres*, and the redistribution of high-quality food that takes place in the system of feasting organized through the *mayordomías*. But the identity of factory workers is ambivalent. They can often devote little time to cultivation, relegating these tasks largely to women, children, and the elderly in their families. They find it almost impossible to participate fully in the *mayordomía* system. Since they spend most of their time out of town, they have less opportunity than do cultivators to keep their political fences mended within the town. While the towns value endogamy, factory workers often meet and marry the sisters and daughters of workmates who come from other towns; these women often do not even speak Mexicano (although they usually try very hard to learn it). Such wealth as they have, which comes through wages, is wealth acquired in a "universalistic" sector; the wealth of a cultivator, acquired on his lands (even though lands are privately held, the towns consider the lands "their own" and fiercely defend against acquisition of land by outsiders), is "particularistic"—his access to land and water is possible because he is a *mexicano*, a *campesino*, a *puebleño* (member of the town). The increasing permeability of the towns, because of improved transportation and the penetration of mass media, is a matter of great concern; members of the towns are often quite hostile to outsiders (a hostility that culminated in the murder of three students from Puebla by men of San Miguel Canoa in 1968).[3] Thus, factory workers, in contrast to cultivators, face special problems in authenticating their identity as "member of the town."

The ability to use the Mexicano language is an important badge of such an identity, and here as well factory workers face special problems. Education, particularly for boys, is held to be very important in the towns, and parents often speak in Spanish to children during the school years in order to help them succeed. This means that in late adolescence and early adulthood, many young men are relearning Mexicano as a "first-and-a-half" language. However, a young man who goes to work in a factory spends an enormous amount of time outside the town arena where he might consolidate his Mexicano competence, in an environment—the workplace—where Indian identity is often fiercely stigmatized. Mexicano is used in the workplace only for teasing and joking at the expense of the butt, who is temporarily assigned the identity of a *cuāx-epoh* (stupid Indian, literally "grease-head," perhaps related to American English *greaser*, "Mexican"). Thus, workers experience intense pressure toward the local vernacular Spanish norm and are not exposed to as many counterpressures from Mexicano as are cultivators. The two groups exhibit different patterns of bilingualism. Cultivators are likely to exhibit Mexicano interference in Spanish, while workers exhibit the opposite pattern. In example 5 we see this in the speech of a 30-year-old factory worker:

5. *Amo nicpia **pleito, siempre** niviviroa **en paz** ica in notahtzin huan*
   Not I have lawsuits, always live in peace with my father and

---

[3] No Malinche people seem to be involved in collective class action. The sort of sporadic violence represented by the Canoa incident, wars over land between towns, and a high level of interpersonal violence are the major manifestations of the structural contradictions facing Malinche people. Like Mexicano-speaking people elsewhere in Mexico, they do not see themselves as "tribal," and have not formed an "Indian Council," the kind of organization that has emerged among some other indigenous groups with the blessing of the ruling PRI party. Very few Malinche factory workers are members of unions, and many people who have been involved in factory work see their major political outlet as being the official national peasant organization, the CNC.

*nonantzin huan ica nos-, nopilhuan.*
my mother and with my-, my children.

Here, the frequency of Spanish borrowings is not particularly unusual. However, a Spanish systemic voice dominates. For instance, this speaker does not exhibit contrastive vowel length, as in Mexicano, but has simply a pattern of stress alternation borrowed from Spanish. We also see lexical and morphological penetration. The form *ica* (usually *īca* [with]) is the Mexicano instrumental, not the form for marking accompaniment, which is *īnāhuac*. In the last word, we can see the Spanish agreement pattern appear as the speaker adds *-s*, the Spanish plural, to the Mexicano possessive prefix *no-* (my), in order to make it agree with *pilhuan* (children); he immediately corrects this slip.

Assimilation to Spanish in the usage of young factory workers is also apparent in the syntax of complex sentences, illustrated in example 6 in the usage of a 26-year-old factory worker from the same town as that of the speaker in the previous example.

6. *Pues neh niquimati de que Malintzin cah—como se dice* **vivo?**—*yoltoc!*
   Well I I know that Malinche is—how does one say alive?—alive!

   *Yoltoc, huan cerro non, cah sagrado según no imaginación, verdad, de que*
   alive, and mountain that, is, sacred according to my imagination, right, that

   *personas que yahueh ompa quinequi mohuetziz di ipan de que ipan tepetl*
   people who go there she wants him to fall from on it who on the mountain

   *yahui, zan yenon.*
   goes, just that.

Here, again, we notice the absence of vowel-length contrast, and the obvious problem with lexical resources faced by such speakers. In addition the speaker uses the Spanish *que* to form embedded, rather than adjoined, complement and relative clauses. *Que* embeds the complement of the expression of propositional attitude, *según no imaginación* (according to my imagination [understanding, belief]). *Que* also forms the relative clauses, *personas que yahueh* (people who go), and *que ipan tepetl yahui* (who go on the mountain). This speaker is also having difficulty keeping verb number agreement straight, changing from plural *yahueh* (go) to singular *mohuetziz* (will fall) and singular *yahui* (goes). A hispanicized use of Mexicano *cah* (to be in a place) also occurs: here, it is calqued (loan-translated) on Spanish *está*, which can be used for "is in a place," but can also be used to link nouns and predicate adjectives. In Mexicano, we would find in *Malīntzīn, yōltoc* or *yōltoc in Malīntzīn* (the Malinche is alive), without *cah*. Note also that the speaker in example 6 has failed to use the Mexicano adjunctor *in* before the noun *Malintzin* in the first line, as Mexicano would require. This is almost certainly due to the pressure of stigmatization of the use of *in* in Mexicano-ized Spanish.

The pattern in example 6, of interference from Spanish into Mexicano syntax, can be contrasted with the opposite pattern, seen in example 7, a Spanish utterance by Don Otilio, the cultivator of examples 1, 2, and 3.

7. *Como ejemplo ahorita yo, yo es mi tio este señor, ya para mis hijos*
   For example now I, I is my uncle this man, now for my children

   *ya se ve ihcōn cē su abuelito.*
   now is seen thus one their grandfather.

Here, we find Mexicano lexical interference in *ihcōn* (thus) and *cē* (one). We see interference from Mexicano possessive morphology in the expression *cē su abuelito* (one their grandfather), calqued on Mexicano *cē īncohcoltzīn* (or *cē īmiabuelito*) [one their grandfather]). Perhaps most interesting, however, is the calqued relative clause *yo es mi tio este señor* (this man who is my uncle), a loan translation from Mexicano *neh notio nin señor*, with the addition of the Spanish copula *es* to adjoin *neh* and *notio*.

These examples show the intrusion of Spanish ways of speaking into the Mexicano usage of young wage laborers. While both cultivators and factory workers exhibit Spanish loan words, the Mexicano voice of most cultivators, while struggling with the ambivalence of Spanish loans, has at least the syntactic and morphological tools to dominate the loan words and turn them to its own purposes. In the usage of most factory workers, however, particularly the young, the Spanish voice has clearly moved into a more dominant position, occasionally penetrating even the morphological system of Mexicano. A highly hispanicized and calqued Mexicano is an inadequate filter for the pressure toward relexification and language shift that young factory workers face.

Members of the community, including factory workers themselves, see the Spanish in the Mexicano speech of such young men as "refunctionalized." Instead of serving as an elegant metonym of authority and prestige, it is seen as a symptom of pollution from the Spanish-speaking world. That is, this Spanish is seen as "Spanish," and a threat to Mexicano identity. In the face of this problem, factory workers often become ferociously purist, particularly as they reach middle age and come into competition with men who in their adult careers have taken the cultivator-ritual participation route to the control of community resources. While all Malinche speakers are capable of purism (as seen in example 3), I have encountered the fully developed purist repertoire only among middle-aged factory workers, who subject other speakers to vocabulary tests, challenge their usage as "mixed" in conversation, focus very self-consciously on selected syntactic phenomena such as noun-number agreement, and argue that no Mexicano usage which now occurs in the communities has any validity, because it is not *legítimo mexicano*. Many factory workers have developed their purism as a weapon to be deployed in a struggle for power; they challenge as "mixed" the hispanicized usage even of prestigious *principales*. Such challenges are often successful, even when the grammar of the challenger is of the type seen in examples 5 and 6 or 8 below, because people are, in general, self-conscious about lexical items, but are not attuned to (or at least do not have an appropriate set of discourses for commenting upon) grammatical structures.[4]

Space does not allow illustration of all of the different kinds of purist discourse, so I illustrate only one type, the challenge of "mixed" usage, as shown in example 8. The challenger is a 60-year-old factory worker, who has lived most of his life in Mexico City, visiting his home town only on weekends. Now retired in the town, he has invested capital saved from wages in political contributions which have brought him the CONASUPO (the national farm-product purchasing agency) maize brokerage for his town. While this is not a "traditional" route to power in these communities, Don Leobardo has become a figure to be reckoned with. In order to work in his town, my husband and I had to seek his permission, even though he held no official position other than the corn brokerage. An American graduate student working in the town asked Don Leobardo's permission to record our conversation with him, and it was given. We went to his house with our Mexicano-speaking interviewer. Don Leobardo was drinking with his cronies, all important men. In conversation, he exhibited purism as a tool of dominance, challenging the identity of the young interviewer by attacking even such seemingly innocent hispanisms as place names and personal names. This is seen in the following brief excerpt:

8.  DL: *In teh, ticmah, quenin motoca, non, non tlatzintli, campa titlacat?*
    As for you, do you how your name, that, that land, where you are born?
    *Ticmah? Tlen, tlen motoca?*
    Do you know? What, what your name?
    I: *Quēnin ītōca in tlālticpac?*
    How its name the earth?
    DL: *Quen itoca in ca-, campa tiviviroa in teh?*
    How its name where, where you live you?
    I: *Pos ihcōn ītōca, San Miguel Canoa.*
    Well thus its name, San Miguel Canoa.
    DL: *Entonces ye morrevolveroh.*
    Then now it is mixed up.
    I: *Ah.*
    DL: *Entonces yocmo igual.*
    Then it's no longer the same.

---

[4] Both Sapir and Whorf addressed the question of what kinds of categories in language might become the object of conscious consideration; Boas, of course, believed that patterning in language was generally inaccessible to consciousness. However, Sapir noted that both scholars and bilinguals were often quite conscious of linguistic categories of all types. The degree of "consciousness" of a linguistic category is quite possibly related to the kinds of social use that are made of that category. While in general lexical usages seem to be particularly accessible to stereotyping, phonological usages and grammatical usages have also become sociolinguistic markers (as in r-less and negative-concord versus r-ful and negative-polarity varieties of American English).

In this passage, it is evident that Don Leobardo's Mexicano has become a virtual pidgin. He calques even routine expressions on Spanish, saying, for instance, *quenin motoca* (How your name) instead of universal Mexicano *tlen motōca* (What your name). In the first utterance, he does not, in fact, mean *motōca*, (your name), but *ītōca* (its name). He has forgotten to prefix the antecessive marker *ō-* to the past tense verb *-titlacat* (you were born). The form *morrevolveroh* (it is mixed up) should be *morevolveroa*, or perhaps *ōmorevolveroh* (it was mixed up). Don Leobardo, like the speakers in examples 5 and 6, lacks the long-short vowel contrast. His Mexicano is so bad that the interviewer has some difficulty understanding him, and requests clarification. However, his performance is received with complete seriousness by his fellow townsmen, and also by the interviewer, who is fully aware of his power. Fortunately, after scoring several purist points, Don Leobardo grew friendly and eventually became one of our most helpful supporters.

Confronted with the possibility of this kind of linguistic terrorism, many young people prefer not to speak Mexicano, except in contexts where it is absolutely required. The interviewer stood up to Don Leobardo's attack because it was his job to speak in Mexicano, even to hostile strangers to whom one would normally speak Spanish. Thus, purist rhetoric joins other pressures in driving Mexicano into an underground, often secret, solidarity code. Don Leobardo is "speaking Mexicano," but the Spanish origin of his purist voice is clearly apparent in the form of his usage, and its result, discouraging the use of Mexicano, is entirely in line with national policy. And, of course, Don Leobardo is in no position to tell anyone how to say "San Miguel Canoa" in *legítimo mexicano*; as far as we know, there is only one native speaker of Mexicano on the Malinche, the scholarly Don Amado Morales of Santa Catarina Ayometitla, who owns dictionaries and grammars of this language. The Spanish voice that uses Don Leobardo as its mouthpiece can also be heard in the cities, where we were often told that there was no point in studying Malinche Mexicano because it was so broken down and hispanicized. The failure of this purist voice to provide an alternative derives also from a national policy that provides no indigenous-language educational materials in the Malinche region.

The debate over the structural position within the world system of populations like that of the Malinche Volcano has been conducted almost exclusively in materialist terms. Only Arturo Warman has seen the importance of studying the "symbolic flow"—the "words and ideas [which] actually connect the modes of production and shape their relations toward the inside and toward the outside" (Warman 1980:304). In this paper, I hope I have shown that attention to language can shed important light on the nature of consciousness, the symbolic practice of a structural position. Close examination of usage and structure in the speech of the people of the Malinche reveals several points of interest. First, it shows that the peasant use of Mexicano, far from being conservative, is a dynamic and highly creative endeavor which draws widely on the symbolic resources of its environment. Second, it shows that there are important differences between different kinds of people who all "speak Mexicano." These differences in linguistic practice suggest that the delicate balancing act of "peasant autonomy" is beginning to fail; the contradictions within the material sphere, as well as the contradictions within the symbolic sphere, seem to be yielding a shift in which the capitalist sector and its Spanish voice are gaining the upper hand. Interestingly, the linguistic data are easier to interpret than the economic data. While Bartra (1978) proposes that Mexican "peasant" populations are in fact a rural proletariat, in contrast to the argument of Warman and Stavenhagen that they constitute a "peasant mode of production," it is in fact very difficult to test whether or not an institution like the stewardship of the saints has been refunctionalized and brought under domination by the capitalist sector, or whether it is still structurally shaped within an autonomous peasant mode.[5] But the structuralist tools of the linguist give a much clearer picture of the relative dominance of "Mexicano" and "Spanish" voices, and provide access to a structural index that might be consulted with profit by political economists.

---

[5] Perhaps the most detailed treatment of this problem is found in Greenberg (1982), where data from homicide are used to explore the structural function of the *cargo* system among the Chatino of Oaxaca.

## REFERENCES

Bakhtin, Mikhail M.
1968[1940] Rabelais and His World. Cambridge, MA: MIT Press.
1973[1929] Problems of Dostoevsky's Poetics. Ann Arbor, MI: Ardis.
1980[1935] The Dialogic Imagination. Austin: University of Texas Press.
Bartra, Roger
    1978    Capitalism and the Peasantry in Mexico. Latin American Perspectives 9:36–47.
Brown, Roger, and A. Gilman
    1960    The Pronouns of Power and Solidarity. In Style in Language. T. Sebeok, ed. pp. 253–276. Cambridge, MA: The Technology Press.
Diebold, A. Richard
    1961    Incipient Bilingualism. Language 37:91–110.
Greenberg, James
    1982    Santiago's Sword. Berkeley: University of California Press.
Gumperz, John
    1982    Discourse Strategies. Cambridge: Cambridge University Press.
Jaulin, Robert
    1979    Del Folklore. In La Des-Civilización. R. Jaulin, ed. pp. 85–90. México: Editorial Nueva Imagen.
Karttunen, Frances, and James Lockhart
    1976    Nahuatl in the Middle Years. University of California Publications in Linguistics 85.

Lastra de Suárez, Yolanda, and Fernando Horcasitas
1979    El Náhuatl en el Estado de Tlaxcala. Anales de Antropología 16:275–323.
Lukács, Georg
1968    History and Class Consciousness. Cambridge, MA: MIT Press.
Markey, Thomas L.
1983    Change Typologies: Questions and Answers in German. Studies in Language and Literature in Older Germanic Dialects. B. Brogyany and T. Krommelbein, eds. (forthcoming)
Nutini, Hugh G.
1984    Ritual Kinship: Ideological and Structural Integration of the Compadrazgo System in Rural Tlaxcala. Princeton: Princeton University Press.
Nutini, Hugo G. and Betty Bell
1980    Ritual Kinship: The Structure and Historical Development of the Compadrazgo System in Rural Tlaxcala. Princeton: Princeton University Press.
Nutini, Hugo G., and Barry L. Isaac
1974    Los Pueblos de Habla Náhutal de la Región de Puebla y Tlaxcala. México: Instituto Nacional Indigenista.
Olivera, Mercedes
1967    Tlaxcalancingo. Instituto Nacional de Antropología e Historia, Departamento de Investigaciones Antropológicas, Publicación No. 18. México.
Rothstein, Frances
1974    Factions in a Rural Community in Mexico. Ph.D. dissertation. University of Pittsburgh.
Todorov, Tzvetan
1981    Mikhaíl Bakhtine, Le Principle Dialogique Suive de Écrits du Cercle de Bakhtine. Paris: Editions du Seuil.
Voloshinov, V. N.
1973[1930] Marxism and the Philosophy of Language. New York: Seminar Press.
Warman, Arturo
1980    "We Come to Object": The Peasants of Morelos and the National State. Baltimore: Johns Hopkins University Press.

# Whorf's View of the Linguistic Mediation of Thought

## John A. Lucy

The proposal that a semiotic system mediates, that is, enables or shapes, some other aspect of human activity is of perhaps greatest interest and significance when the semiotic system is natural language and the human activity is conceptual thought. One of the more controversial aspects of this issue is whether differences among the various natural languages shape different patterns of thought among speakers of these languages. Discussion of this problem (especially in the United States) has centered on the proposals developed in the late 1930s by Benjamin Lee Whorf, a student of native American Indian languages. One reason for the enduring interest in Whorf's ideas lies in the surprisingly small amount of subsequent theoretical or empirical research produced on this topic; we know little more today than we did 40 years ago about the relation of language diversity to thought, or even about how to address this issue productively. Thus, despite their flaws, Whorf's writings remain the single most important theoretical and empirical contribution in this area and should constitute the starting point for any current research.

Ironically, given their importance, Whorf's writings have been widely misunderstood both as to their actual content and as to their historical position and significance. These misunderstandings have resulted from a complex interaction of underlying disciplinary assumptions, transient historical factors, and, in not a few cases, a simple failure to read the original texts with care. Thus, Whorf's view of language has been seen as limited to a superficial analysis of a few isolated surface forms that he mistakenly believed varied without constraint across languages. He has been portrayed as arguing that these forms absolutely determine human abilities such as reason and perception, hence assuring a complete linguistic relativity to which he himself must be victim. In line with these interpretations, any subsequent discovery of either linguistic or cognitive universals has been seen as refuting his views. Whorf's own empirical work has been presented as being confined to linguistic data that serve to establish both the language patterns and the associated thought patterns. Thus subsequent direct attempts to test his ideas have concentrated on drastic reformulations of his views in order to generate an "acceptable" nonlinguistic variable, that is, one which would be readily susceptible to experimental investigation. (Most have looked at whether color vocabulary has an influence on perceptual recognition memory of standardized

**415**

color samples.) Other empirical approaches have also tended to ignore Whorf's actual arguments by concentrating on detailed restudies of his specific linguistic examples or by looking at special (and thus very problematic) cases such as multilinguals. These misconceptions and associated empirical approaches have had great impact on subsequent debate (certainly more than Whorf's own ideas), and the absence of serious contemporary research can be directly attributed to them.

In contrast, a careful consideration of Whorf's writings reveals a complex and sophisticated view of language and its relation to thought which deserves renewed attention as a basis for research. This reading takes a first step toward correcting prevailing misunderstandings of Whorf by presenting in brief form the most important of his views. It highlights the assumptions he accepted from his immediate predecessors Boas and Sapir in developing a view of how language represents an implicit analysis of experience, it outlines the logical structure of his argument that this analysis of experience influences thought, and it analyzes the nature of the evidence he provided in support of his argument. The final section assesses Whorf's work and the prospects for further research along the lines he suggested.


## THE LINGUISTIC ANALYSIS OF EXPERIENCE

From his predecessors Franz Boas and Edward Sapir, Whorf inherited the view that language contains an implicit classification of experience which varies from language to language. Boas (1911) observed that such classification was essential in language if an infinite variety of experience was to be expressed by a finite set of phonetic groups and their combinations. An implicit classification emerges, then, when elements of experience are bound together by giving them similar lexical or grammatical treatment. The individual speaker tends to be unaware of these classifications because their use is so highly automatic. Boas emphasized that linguistic classifications vary widely across languages both in the formal apparatus by which experiences are represented and in the experiences that must be obligatorily expressed. He gave examples of how a similar idea or experience might be rendered by a single word in one language, multiple words in another; by lexical form in one language, grammatical form in another. Further, he showed that simple descriptive utterances referring to events would differ radically from language to language as to the concepts which must be obligatorily involved in the descriptions.

Sapir (1924, 1929, 1931) argued that a language consists of a formally complete, self-contained system of such classifications which as a whole is capable of referring to all aspects of experience. This systematic, formal aspect of linguistic phenomena makes them particularly resistant to folk analyses because the latter tend to deal primarily with isolated elements, rather than with the place of elements within a system. Sapir stressed that languages differ from each other as *systems*, and not merely in the form or content of their individual elements; in fact, such systems may represent "incommensurable analyses of experience." Although his theoretical arguments provide some of the analytic tools necessary to explore such systemwide differences, Sapir's actual examples follow the same general pattern as those of Boas: illustration of how a given idea or experience would be differently expressed, either formally or substantively, in two or more languages.

Whorf (1956a [1927–1941]) shared these views about the systematic, classificatory nature of language, about the difficulty of bringing these language classifications into critical awareness, and about the variability of these classifications (both individually and as systems) across languages, and he built upon them in important ways. Drawing out the implications of Sapir's views concerning the importance of formal systematicity in language, Whorf emphasized the critical importance of pattern in language—the structural relations among lexical and morphological elements—in contributing to meaning and, in particular, to reference (e.g., 1956a:67–68, 258–260). In studying these patterns, he advanced beyond Boas and Sapir in three ways which merit further discussion here: He developed the notion of underlying or "covert" categories; he showed the systematic coordination and interdependence among language categories; and he attacked the problem of developing frameworks for the comparison of language categories which would be independent of any particular language.

First, Whorf formally distinguished two types of categories[1] in language: *overt* and *covert*. Overt and covert categories differ from each other in their ubiquity of formal marking as a function of structural occurrence:

> An overt category is a category having a formal mark which is present (with only infrequent exceptions) in every sentence containing a member of the category. The mark need not be part of the same word to which the category may be said to be attached in a paradigmatic sense; i.e. it need not be a suffix, prefix, vowel change, or other "inflection," but may be a detached word or a certain patterning of the whole sentence. (1956a:88)

> A covert category is marked, whether morphemically or by sentence-pattern, only in certain types of sentence and not in every sentence in which a word or element belonging to the category occurs. The class-membership of the word is not apparent until there is a question of using it or referring to it in one of these special types of sentence, and then we find that this word belongs to a class requiring some sort of distinctive treatment, which may even be the negative treatment of excluding that type of sentence. This distinctive treatment we may call the REACTANCE of the category. (1956a:89)

---

[1] Whorf (1956a:87–101; also 67–83 and 104–111) drew a number of formal distinctions among kinds of grammatical categories of which overt versus covert was only one. These discussions show the influence of and in some ways extend and improve upon Bloomfield (1933, Chapters 10, 12, and 16).

For example, nominal gender in Latin or Spanish is an overt category since it is almost always marked—by the nominal ending and frequently in accompanying articles and adjectives as well. Gender in English, by contrast, is a covert category since it is not routinely marked for each occurrence of a noun, but is only revealed by rules of concord in coreferential pronouns and by certain minor patterns of lexical agreement. It should be stressed that covert categories are always marked by linguistic forms in a language, but that these markings are relatively infrequent relative to the occurrence of the category and emerge only in certain linguistic contexts (i.e., marking is contingent on context). Further, note that the substantive content of the category is not an issue in deciding whether it is covert or overt: what is overt in one language may be covert in another, and vice versa (1956a:69–70, 90–91).

Overt and covert categories operate together in a linguistic system so that the full understanding of the nature of a given overt category depends on understanding the related covert categories (1956a:109). This amounts to asserting that a correct understanding of any classification of experience implicit in a given grammatical category depends on an analysis of the position of that category in the overall patterning of grammatical categories in the language. While it might be difficult for speakers to become aware of such patterns, they are sensitive to them as evidenced by their speech (1956a:69–70), and their exact nature can be made explicit by the linguistic analyst, as Whorf demonstrated repeatedly through his illustrative analyses (e.g., 1956a:68–70, 90–91, 102–111). It is crucial to Whorf's subsequent arguments that the cognitive influences he traced to language patterns need not derive solely from the most obvious and systematically marked overt categories in a language, but may involve large numbers of underlying, covert linkages which function along with the overt patterns.[2] A linguistic classification need not be simple and obvious to be significant.

Second, Whorf (1956a:134–156) tried to show how languages could differ from one another *qua system* in their interpretations of experience. Rather than merely presenting a series of isolated examples of linguistic differences in the pattern of Boas and Sapir (although he did this too [e.g., 1956a:233–245]), Whorf tried to develop detailed case studies to show how several specific differences in classifications between two languages could work together cumulatively to signal quite general, often major, differences in fundamental approach to the interpretation of experience. In these case studies, Whorf worked to show that the categories in a language are semantically integrated in two senses: (1) The same distinction appears consistently in more than one category (one could perhaps call them the same category with multiple

---

[2] Whorf did not explicitly use the overt-covert distinction in his later (i.e., post-1938) writings on the language and thought problem, although its influence is clear. For an attempt to reword some of these later arguments using this distinction (and related ones) see Silverstein (1979).

manifestations), and (2) some category distinctions depend on the logically prior acceptance of others.

For example, Whorf identified in English a tendency to treat imaginary entities in the same way as concrete objects for the purposes of reference. This "objectification," as Whorf called it, emerges in the patterns of English pluralization, quantification, time expressions, and so forth. Further, other patterns are conceptually dependent on this treatment of temporal cycles as if they were concrete objects: the treatment of temporal duration as if it were a spatial entity (e.g., *a length of time*) and as if it were a combination of a form (e.g., a year) and a formless item (i.e., time—hence, *a year of time*). By contrast the Hopi language fails in each instance to exhibit such a pattern of classificatory treatment (i.e., shows no objectification). Thus, a given series of semantic decisions work together to indicate a single significant underlying pattern operative in each language and which may be said to be characteristic of the language. Further, these semantic differences are carried in, or marked by, a whole range of formal devices—morphological, syntactic, and lexical. Whorf summarized his position by noting that such classificatory or conceptual patterns

> do not depend so much upon ANY ONE SYSTEM (e.g., tense, or nouns) within the grammar as upon the ways of analyzing and reporting experience which have become fixed in the language as integrated "fashions of speaking" and which cut across the typical grammatical classifications, so that such a "fashion" may include lexical, morphological, syntactic, and otherwise systemically diverse means coordinated in a certain frame of consistency. (1956a: 158)

Essentially, then, Whorf presented a new kind of analysis and evidence which was crucial in making more explicit Sapir's arguments about the systemic, interlocking nature of the linguistic analysis of experience. In particular, Whorf showed that differences of the sort identified by Boas and Sapir may have deep roots in the overall semantic structure of a language and cannot be brushed aside as being superficial or easily changeable aspects of the grammar. In doing so, he moved toward being able to characterize the implicit points of view or "fashions of speaking" typical of a given language. It is these "fashions of speaking" that Whorf attempted to relate to thought and not, as some have supposed, isolated, individual classifications.

Third, Whorf realized that the very variety among languages posed serious problems for the comparison of linguistic classifications. Contrary to the popular image of Whorf as an absolute relativist, he firmly believed in the possibility of meaningful comparison of and generalization across languages. However, he insisted that the frames of reference used in such comparisons be independent of the particularities of any given language (1956a:162). He proposed nonlinguistic approaches to the description of experience as one route toward the unbiased understanding of the conceptual content of categories. And he proposed linguistic approaches to the comparison of grammatical categories based heavily on an analysis of the configurative patterns of each language and on a careful comparison of many languages as a route toward the unbiased characterization of the forms (or formal properties) of categories.

Whorf felt that it was important to have frames of comparison for the description of experience based on nonlinguistic grounds: "In describing differences between [languages] . . . we must have a way of describing phenomena by non-linguistic standards, and by terms that refer to experience as it must be to all human beings, irrespective of their languages or philosophies" (1956b:6). The principal such standard explicitly suggested by Whorf lay in the laws of visual perception discovered by Gestalt psychology (1956a:158, 163). Whorf illustrated what he had in mind in a comparison of the relative modes of expressing figure and ground relations in English and Hopi (1956b:7–9), in his characterizations of the semantic content of Hopi and Aztec word classes (1946a: 164–165, 168, 173–174; 1946b:376), and in his use of Gestalt concepts in a description of Shawnee stem composition (1956a:160–172).[3] At times, especially in his early works, Whorf implicitly endorsed other nonlinguistic standards such as modern physical science (e.g., 1956a:55–56, 85), but in the last pieces which he wrote, he indicated that he had come to distrust these as being linguistically conditioned as well (e.g., 1956a:246–270).

For the comparison of grammatical categories as such, Whorf advocated building a vocabulary or frame of reference directly from the study of languages. Unfortunately, the grammatical terms and concepts developed in the study of Indo-European languages he regarded (following Boas and Sapir) as inadequate, because the close historical relationship among these languages limited their range of variation (1956a:214). To remedy this problem, Whorf urged a wide-scale survey of languages to provide the basis for an adequate understanding of the true range of variation among languages (1956a:76–78, 81, 87, 239, 244–245; 1956b:3). Such a contrastive linguistics would be able to plot "the outstanding differences among tongues—in grammar, logic, and general analysis of experience" (1956a:240). Whorf realized that such a contrastive survey would of necessity involve the use of traditional, inadequate terminology, at least initially, but he felt that with an awareness of the problems involved, new conceptual frames could eventually be developed (1956a:59, 87, 162, 242). By a process of iterative reformulation, a vocabulary adequate to the task of unbiased linguistic description could be built.

Whorf went beyond exhortation on this issue. He developed new conceptualizations of grammatical categories (e.g., overt versus covert, selective

---

[3] Whorf also refers, on occasion, to speakers' subjective awareness or basic perceptions of reality (e.g., 1956a:139–144). Such references represent either further attempts on Whorf's part to frame his comparison or attempts to account for some invariant conceptual structure. They should not be taken as claims by Whorf for the ontological reality of the categories, but rather as claims about possible universals of human perceptual experience. As such, they remain problematic, but on different grounds.

versus modulus) suitable for the general comparison of languages, and he indicated his view of the proper approach to the development of generic taxonomic categories for grammatical comparisons (1956a:87–101). He also provided the detailed beginnings of a format for the systematic survey of languages founded both on his own theoretical insights and on the experience of the Boas-Sapir group more generally (1956a:125–133; 1956b). Too often, Whorf's concern with pressing the significance of linguistic variation has led to the neglect of his interest in the development of cross-linguistically valid descriptions, comparisons, and generalities.

In sum, the linguistic analysis of experience as understood by Whorf is complex. Utterances in two languages referring to similar experiences may contain striking differences as to the classifications which are obligatorily and overtly specified. But beyond this, many covert categories will be involved that are important not only in their own right as classifications of experience but also as contributors to the meanings of the overt categories. Such categories (both overt and covert) can interrelate with others in a language, reinforcing and complementing one another, so as to constitute large-scale patterns that may differ as a system from patterns in other languages. When considered as classifications of experience, such systems may represent fundamentally different interpretations of, or points of view about, the nature of experience. In the languages with which he was most familiar, Whorf pushed to uncover and explore such large-scale patterns, and it was these interlocking patterns of classifications that he saw as so important in influencing thought. But Whorf went beyond merely complicating the picture in these ways. He pointed the way toward the comparative analysis of such linguistic classifications by proposing approaches to their cross-linguistic taxonomy and interpretation. For it was in the comparison of and generalization across languages that Whorf sought awareness and understanding of the true nature of our own language as a route toward transcending its influences on our thinking (1956a:239).


## THE INFLUENCE OF LANGUAGES ON THOUGHT

In considering the relation between language and thought, Whorf again revised and extended the ideas of Boas and Sapir. Boas saw language as reflecting thought: Variations among languages reflected the divergent historical experiences of groups of speakers, and the universal occurrence of certain "fundamental grammatical concepts" showed the "unity of fundamental psychological processes" (1911:67). There are exceptions to this general position such as the following remark: "The categories of language compel us to see the world arranged in certain definite conceptual groups which, on account of our lack of knowledge of linguistic processes, are taken as objective categories and which, therefore, impose themselves upon the form of our thoughts" (Boas 1920:320). And late in his life Boas (1942:181–183) gave a very cautious endorsement of ideas similar to those adopted by Whorf. In no case, however, did he give detailed discussion or exhibit much enthusiasm or conviction about the possibility of language influencing thought.

Sapir, by contrast, argued persuasively that language, as a formally complete system, gives rise to a systematic reconstruction of reality:

> Language is . . . a self-contained, creative symbolic organization, which not only refers to experience largely acquired without its help but actually defines experience for us by reason of its formal completeness and because of our unconscious projection of its implicit expectations into the field of experience. . . . [Language] categories . . . are, of course, derivative of experience at last analysis, but, once abstracted from experience, they are systematically elaborated in language and are not so much discovered in experience as imposed upon it because of the tyrannical hold that linguistic form has upon our orientation in the world. (Sapir 1931:578)

It only remains to add the observation that these categories vary across languages to be able to reach the conclusion that the form of thought is relative to the language spoken:

> It would be possible to go on indefinitely with such examples of incommensurable analyses of experience in different languages. The upshot of it all would be to make very real to us a kind of relativity that is generally hidden from us by our naive acceptance of fixed habits of speech as guides to an objective understanding of the nature of experience. This is the relativity of concepts or, as it might be called, the relativity of the form of thought. (Sapir 1924:155)

This "relativity of the form of thought" arises, then, because speakers accept their linguistic categories (formally systematized abstractions from experience) as guides in the interpretation of experience, even though those categories are highly variable across languages.

Whorf, following Sapir, felt that language classifications influenced thought and, therefore, that the diversity of those classifications insured a certain diversity of thought among speakers of different languages:

> Users of markedly different grammars are pointed by their grammars toward different types of observations and different evaluations of externally similar acts of observation, and hence are not equivalent as observers but must arrive at somewhat different views of the world. (Whorf 1956a:221)

Unlike Sapir, however, Whorf took up in some detail just how speakers are "pointed by their grammars." His central treatment of the problem is given in his paper "The Relation of Habitual Thought and Behavior to Language" (1956a:134–159) which serves as the principal basis for the following discussion.[4]

---

[4] Whorf's other writings on the relation of language and thought are either early manuscripts which he never published or later popularizations with the simplifications and orientations one would expect. While consistent with the piece emphasized here, they are not as detailed, sophisticated, or authoritative as this work prepared for publication by Whorf for a professional audience.

Whorf began by laying out the scope of his research project:

> That portion of the whole investigation here to be reported may be summed up in two questions: (1) Are our own concepts of 'time,' 'space,' and 'matter' given in substantially the same form by experience to all men, or are they in part conditioned by the structure of particular languages? (2) Are there traceable affinities between (a) cultural and behavioral norms and (b) large-scale linguistic patterns? (1956a:138)

Embedded within this statement are clear indications of the aspects of language and thought that were of concern to Whorf in his study. On the linguistic side, he was interested in the pervasive structural (or grammatical) patterns that are characteristic of particular languages, along the lines reviewed in the first section of this reading. On the cognitive side, he was interested in the fundamental conceptual ideas habitually used by speakers. The focus on the conceptual aspect of thought appears throughout Whorf's writings although often with different labels such as "abstractions," "categories and types," and "grand generalizations" (1956a:58–59, 213–216). Also consistent with this interpretation are his many references to the influence of language on an individual's or people's "Weltanschauung," "metaphysics," "unformulated philosophy," "cosmology," "world view," "ideology of nature," and "picture" (or "description" or "view") of the universe (1956a:58–61, 221, 241–242). It should be clear, then, that Whorf was not primarily concerned either with perception or with what might be called cognitive processes, but with conceptual content. Further, Whorf was not primarily concerned with the more removed, specialized notions of philosophy or science, but rather with the habitual thought characteristic of ordinary speakers of a language: "the microcosm that each man carries about within himself, by which he measures and understands what he can of the macrocosm" (1956a:147). Specialized conceptual systems such as those of science and philosophy are built upon such a system of everyday concepts by a specialization of the same linguistic patterns that gave rise to the more widespread habitual thought patterns (1956a:152–153, 221, 263–266).[5] Although Whorf was concerned with the impact of language on these specialized fields, they were, in his view, a subset of the larger problem.

Whorf did not present a fully developed, explicit theory about how language structure influences concepts but rather a programmatic discussion based on the comparative analysis of selected, interrelated aspects of English and Hopi

---

[5] Cf. Bloomfield:

> The categories of a language, especially those which affect morphology (*book : books, he : she*), are so pervasive that anyone who reflects upon his language at all, is sure to notice them. In the ordinary case, this person, knowing only his native language, or perhaps some others closely akin to it, may mistake his categories for universal forms of speech, or of "human thought," or of the universe itself. This is why a good deal of what passes for "logic" or "metaphysics" is merely an incompetent restating of the chief categories of the philosopher's language. (1933:270)

grammar. Before turning to a consideration of these analyses, it is useful to highlight briefly the essential arguments implicit in his approach. Through its categories a language can unite (i.e., classify together) demonstrably different aspects of experience as "alike" for the purposes of speech. Such grouping of aspects of experience Whorf sometimes called *linguistic analogy* to indicate both its specifically linguistic nature and its meaningful (versus purely formal) character (1956a:135–148).[6] Linguistic analogies which vary from language to language are not "necessary," that is, they cannot simply be constructed as "given" by experience prior to language, and, further, are distinctive from analyses of experience based on nonlinguistic criteria. Linguistic analogies are meaningful for speakers in two senses: (1) The grouping of elements in a category is usually made on the basis of *some* similarity of content, and (2) the interpretation of any given element in such a grouping is influenced by the meanings of other elements with which it is seen as analogically the same, including aspects of those meanings which might be quite distinct from the original basis of the classification. Such analogical equivalences then are used in thought as guides in the interpretation of and behavioral response to experienced reality. Whorf has no single term for this process of appropriating linguistic analogies for cognitive ends, referring variously to language "conditioning" or "shaping" thought (1956a:135–137), to thought "marching in step with purely grammatical facts" (1956a:211), to language as a "program and guide for the individual's mental activity" (1956a:212), to thought being "pointed by . . . grammars toward different types of observation" (1956a:221), and to thinking following "a network of tracks laid down in the given language" (1956a:256). In most cases, however, there is a suggestion that the linguistic analogies become involved as sources of structure in an autonomously constituted cognition (i.e., there is no attempt to reduce all thought to language, 1956a:66–68). Typically, speakers are not aware that they are appropriating linguistic analogies in this way, because language patterning itself is an out-of-awareness, background phenomenon for speakers (1956a:137, 209–214), and because language is generally conceived of solely as a vehicle for the expression of thought which precedes it (1956a:207–208). Thus, speakers routinely and unwittingly accept much of the suggestive value of the linguistic analogies present in their language even though, upon reflection, they might recognize that they are "non-necessary" or even, in some cases, misleading.

Whorf first[7] analyzed the grammatical category of number, that is, singular

---

[6] The term analogy may come from Bloomfield:

A grammatical pattern . . . is often called an *analogy*. A regular analogy permits a speaker to utter speech-forms which he has not heard: we say that he utters them *on the analogy* of similar forms which he has heard. (1933:275)

[7] Whorf provided a number of lexical examples in several of his articles which show that his argument is by no means confined to grammatical categories. Because of limitations of space, they will be passed over here in order to devote more time to his grammatical arguments which he regarded as more important (1956a:137) and which are more distinctive of his approach.

versus plural, and enumeration by cardinal numbers. He described the English[8] pattern as follows:

> In our language . . . plurality and cardinal numbers are applied in two ways: to real plurals and imaginary plurals. Or more exactly if less tersely: perceptible spatial aggregates and metaphorical aggregates. We say 'ten men' and also 'ten days.' Ten men either are or could be objectively perceived as ten, ten in one group perception—ten men on a street corner, for instance. But 'ten days' cannot be objectively experienced. We experience only one day, today; the other nine (or even all ten) are something conjured up from memory or imagination. If 'ten days' be regarded as a group it must be as an "imaginary," mentally constructed group. Whence comes this mental pattern? . . . , from the fact that our language confuses the two different situations, has but one pattern for both. When we speak of 'ten steps forward, ten strokes on a bell,' or any similarly described cyclic sequence, "times" of any sort, we are doing the same thing as with 'days.' CYCLICITY brings the response of imaginary plurals. But a likeness of cyclicity to aggregates is not unmistakably given by experience prior to language, or it would be found in all languages, and it is not. (1956a:139)

Thus, the plural category applies to both immediately perceptible spatial aggregates of objects as in the case of *men* and mentally constructed (i.e., not immediately perceptible) aggregates of cycles (i.e., non-objects) as in the case of *days*. But only the former can actually be united in a single time and place as a spatial grouping. The pattern of cardinal numbers reinforces this pattern by quantifying objective and imaginary entities in the same way, leading speakers to assume "that in the latter the numbers are just as much counted on 'something' as in the former" (1956a:140). Whorf called this "objectification"—the treatment of intangibles such as time and cyclic sequences as if they were concrete, perceptible objects.

Whorf then showed the non-necessary nature of this linguistic analogy by comparing the English pattern with that of Hopi:

> In Hopi there is a different linguistic situation. Plurals and cardinals are used only for entities that form or can form an objective group. There are no imaginary plurals, but instead ordinals used with singulars. (1956a:140)

> Time is mainly reckoned "by day". . . or "by night". . . , which words are not nouns but tensors,[9] . . . The count is by ORDINALS. This is not the pattern of counting a number of different men or things, even though they appear successively, for, even then, they COULD gather into an assemblage. It is the pattern of counting successive reappearances of the SAME man or thing, incapable of forming an assemblage. The analogy is not to behave about

---

[8] Whorf used English as a representative of Standard Average European (SAE) and meant to emphasize by the use of the latter label that all the languages of Europe bear sufficient similarity to one another that they may be taken as one in his comparisons with Hopi.

[9] Tensors are a distinct part of speech in Hopi and are somewhat like our adverbs (1956a: 143, 146; 1946a:179–180).

day-cyclicity as to several men ("several days"), which is what WE tend to do, but to behave as to the successive visits of the SAME MAN. (1956a: 148)

Thus, the grammatical pattern by which Hopi handles the phenomenon of duration is substantially different from English. The pattern "ordinal number + singular mark" is applied both to tensors and to nouns that refer to cases of repeated appearance, creating a grammatical bridge quite different from the link in English between perceptible and imaginary aggregates.

It is useful to examine two more of Whorf's analyses which will illustrate more clearly how related analogies can fit together to form a larger structure linking together diverse elements of experience. He next analyzed the distinction between *individual* and *mass* nouns in English, (a distinction more commonly referred to by others as the "count-mass distinction"):

> We have two kinds of nouns denoting physical things: individual nouns, and mass nouns, e.g., 'water, milk, wood, granite, sand, flour, meat.' Individual nouns denote bodies with definite outlines: 'a tree, a stick, a man, a hill.' Mass nouns denote homogeneous continua without implied boundaries. (1956a:140)

The two kinds of nouns admit of different grammatical possibilities: Mass nouns do not take plurals or the singular indefinite article whereas individual nouns do (1956a: 140). (The count-mass dichotomy conceived of as a word category in this way is covert, although Whorf did not label it as such.) Whorf noted that the distinction between individual and mass is more widely and uniformly drawn in English grammar than in the actual physical objects referred to, thus there are many circumstances in which speakers are forced to make the grammatical distinction when it makes little sense or is awkward. The language compensates for this deficiency:

> The distinction . . . is so inconvenient in a great many cases that we need some way of individualizing the mass noun by further linguistic devices. This is partly done by names of body-types: 'stick of wood, piece of cloth, pane of glass, cake of soap'; also, and even more, by introducing names of containers though their contents be the real issue: 'glass of water, cup of coffee, dish of food, bag of flour, bottle of beer.' (1956a:141)

Thus, the (covert) individual-mass distinction has given rise to a secondary (overt) pattern in the language.

Notice that two distinct kinds of experience—containers and body types— are brought together under a single grammatical pattern. As usual, Whorf argued that this has consequences:

> The formulas are very similar: individual noun plus a similar relator (English 'of'). In the obvious case this relator denotes contents. In the inobvious one it "suggests" contents. Hence the 'lumps, chunks, blocks, pieces,' etc., seem to contain something, a "stuff," "substance," or "matter" that answers to the 'water,' 'coffee,' or 'flour' in the container formulas. (1956a:141)

So the pattern "individual noun + *of* + mass noun" covers two meanings, one with a readily interpretable perceptible correlate, that is, a container and its contents, and another without such a correlate but which, Whorf argued, is interpreted in the same way. Thus bodies are thought of as being like containers which hold contents—substance or matter. Whorf concluded:

> So . . . the philosophic "substance" and "matter" are also the naive idea; they are instantly acceptable, "common sense." It is so through linguistic habit. Our language patterns often require us to name a physical thing by a binomial that splits the reference into a formless item plus a form. (1956a: 141)

We have then, in his view, an everyday basis for philosophical notions such as form and matter (or, accident and substance) which are so common in Western culture. Whorf continued with a third argument that this binomial pattern

> is implicit for all nouns, and hence our very generalized formless items like 'substance, matter,' by which we can fill out the binomial for an enormously wide range of nouns. (1956a:142)

Whorf is not explicit here about the nature of the grammatical bridge, but it appears to be the filling of a noun phrase slot in the grammar. He probably meant to restrict this argument to nouns referring to physical objects since his next remarks deal with the extension to nouns with more elusive referents:

> But even these [very generalized formless items like 'substance' and 'matter'] are not quite generalized enough to take in our [temporal] phase nouns. So for the phase nouns we have made a formless item, 'time.' We have made it by using 'a time,' i.e. an occasion or a phase, in the pattern of a mass noun. . . . Thus with our binomial formula we can say and think 'a moment of time, a second of time, a year of time.' (1956a:142–143).

Here the container-like portion is a "phase" and the content-like portion is "time." Thus, one part of our objectification of temporal notions involves their inclusion in the general binomial pattern for physical object nouns with attendant interpretational implications.

So step by step Whorf has built up an analysis of a series of three interrelated analogies: Body-type relator noun phrases are analogous to container-type relator noun phrases; syntactically simple physical object noun phrases, in turn, are analogous to syntactically more complex physical object noun phrases (= relator noun phrases—especially the body-type formulas); and phase noun phrases, finally, are analogous to physical object noun phrases. This nesting of interpretive analogies is clearer if we read Whorf's sequence in reverse: Phase noun phrases are interpreted like physical object noun phrases, syntactically simple physical object noun phrases are interpreted, in turn, like syntactically complex physical object noun phrases, and syntactically complex physical object noun phrases, finally, are interpreted like container-type relator noun phrases. Thus, phase nouns participate indirectly in the interpretive schema "container + contents." By showing how the treatment of "time" in English as a homogeneous continuum which is segmentable and measurable is grounded in a very complex series of grammatical equivalence relations, Whorf illustrated graphically the more general point that linguistic structures can link together in a coherent and semantically potent way apparently diverse elements of experience.

Whorf refers to habitual thought in these analyses, most often when he is specifying the implications he believes speakers draw from the linguistic patterns. However, as many critics have noted, Whorf does not seem to provide any independent evidence for the existence of these cognitive patterns or of their influence. There is some merit to this criticism, especially if we look for nonlinguistic behavioral evidence derived from observations of individuals.[10] But such a view fails to take into account the overall structure of Whorf's argument. He presents a series of five interrelated grammatical comparisons, three of which we have just described, in order to show how the patterns work together to provide a systematic, coherent, yet non-necessary construal of experience. References along the way to habitual thought help the reader understand the semantic implications and see the potential cognitive significance of the linguistic patterns rather than "prove" the existence of such thought. At the end of the series he draws together the overall implications (1956a:147–148) to make a unified statement about the habitual thought worlds of English and Hopi speakers as suggested by their language patterns. Concrete observable evidence for the existence, nature, and significance of the habitual thought worlds is presented in the following two sections (1956a: 148–152, 152–156) wherein he tries to show the tangible cultural connections (or affinities) with the hypothesized patterns of thinking. Thus, these "cultural and behavioral norms" (which were referred to at the outset in the statement of research problem) are meant not only to show the broad significance of these habitual thought worlds, but also to confirm both the view that they exist and the claim that they take the form presented in Whorf's analysis.

To illustrate briefly the kind of cultural evidence that Whorf presented, we continue with the analysis of the objectification of time by English (and other European) speakers. Objectification joins with other patterns (some of which have been discussed earlier) to yield a characteristic view of time as composed of a *linear* array of *formally equivalent discrete* units (i.e., like a row of identical objects). From such a view, Whorf believes, arise in part many of our cultural patterns involving time. The *discreteness* of temporal units leads to a propensity for historicity (viewing events as discrete happenings rather than as artificially segmented from other events, including the events of remembering, recording, or anticipating) and to a view that periods of time are somewhat like a series of equal containers to be filled as in record keeping by fixed units of time. The

---

[10] Whorf does provide anecdotal data suggesting an influence of language on individual behavior in some of his lexical examples (e.g., 1956a:135–137, 261–262). These have not been taken up here for reasons mentioned in Note 7.

*formally equivalent* nature of these discrete units leads to a view that they are in fact of equal value. Hence, the notion of the equivalent monetary value of time units as with rent, interest, depreciation, insurance, and time wages. Also related to this view of time are the attempts to measure time more precisely and to do things more quickly. Finally, the *linearity* of time allows us to project into the future by imagining an unending sequence of such formally equivalent discrete units; hence our attention to the budgeting, programming, and scheduling of time and our view of time as monotonous with the attendant attitudes of complacence about future events (the future will be like the past). Most of these patterns are observable cultural practices, and in his discussion Whorf describes observable correlates of the few which have been mentioned here as attitudes.

Hopi cultural patterns, by contrast, are quite different and in ways which appear to relate to their linguistic treatment of time. Recall that in Hopi, cycles are treated like repeated visits of the same man, hence, "it is as if the return of the day were felt as the return of the same person, a little older but with all the impresses of yesterday, not as 'another day,' i.e. like an entirely different person" (1956a:151). With past events essentially "present" in the present, there is less incentive to be concerned with detailed recording of past events; this is supported by a more general tendency not to regard events as discrete and well bounded (1956a:153). As a consequence, in Whorf's view, the Hopi fail to exhibit our tendency toward historicity. Conversely, one can act in the present to influence the future:

> One does not alter several men by working upon just one, but one can prepare and so alter the later visits of the same man by working to affect the visit he is making now. This is the way the Hopi deal with the future—by working within a present situation which is expected to carry impresses, both obvious and occult, forward into the future event of interest. (1956a:148)

Whorf provides descriptions of a large number of observable correlates of this view in the form of various, culturally distinctive activities of preparing: "announcing," inward and outward preparations for future events, and an emphasis in many activities on the cumulative value of persistent, incremental accumulations of effort and energy toward a goal. Note that these are not like our activities of budgeting and scheduling which frame and allow for future contingencies, but rather are activities in the immediate present with presumed actual future effect.

Thus, Whorf's full argument contained three elements: the meaningful language patterns, the individual habitual thought worlds which are influenced by them, and the cultural and behavioral norms which give evidence of the existence and significance of the individual thought worlds. Although Boas and Sapir rejected the notion of language *forms* as such having an influence on culture, Whorf was able to argue for an *indirect* influence in some cases via the shaping role of the meaningful implications of language forms on the individual thought worlds of the members of a culture. Whorf in no way intended to support traditional attempts to show a direct correlation between formal properties of language as such (e.g., inflected or not) with some general cultural description (e.g., agricultural, pastoral) (1956a:138–139). The introduction of the intermediate level, the individual microcosm, was crucial to his argument because it allowed him to show how the *meaningfulness* of integrated linguistic patterns could be effective in indirectly shaping *particular* cultural patterns. Further, he argued that these indirect influences ran in both directions so that culture also influenced language; but in the interaction of the two, language, which Whorf regarded as being more systematic, played the more conservative role (1956a:156). And finally Whorf was cautious, asserting that this relationship obtained only when a language and culture were in long association and, more generally, need not necessarily be universally true. He brought these arguments together in the following concluding remark:

> There are connections but not correlations or diagnostic correspondences between cultural norms and linguistic patterns. Although it would be impossible to infer the existence of Crier Chiefs [a Hopi institution involving announcing, or preparative publicity, which he has discussed] from the lack of tenses in Hopi, or vice versa, there is a relation between a language and the rest of the culture of the society which uses it. There are cases where the "fashions of speaking" are closely integrated with the whole general culture, whether or not this be universally true, and there are connections within this integration, between the kind of linguistic analyses employed and various cultural developments. Thus the importance of Crier Chiefs does have a connection, not with tenselessness itself, but with a system of thought in which categories different from our tenses are natural. These connections are to be found not so much by focusing attention on the typical rubrics of linguistic, ethnographic, or sociological description as by examining the culture and the language (always and only when the two have been together historically for a considerable time) as a whole in which concatenations that run across these departmental lines may be expected to exist, and, if they do exist, eventually to be discoverable by study. (1956a:159)

It is just such an integrated, cross-cutting study of language, thought, and culture which Whorf's essay presents and which has been so little emulated since.

Thus, when we take in to account Whorf's entire argument, there is no shortage of nonlinguistic evidence; his argument is not circular. By connecting the language patterns to broad cultural patterns in this way, Whorf undoubtedly intended to demonstrate more clearly the great significance he felt language had. However, the chain of reasoning from language pattern to cultural pattern is long and complex—long and complex enough to have escaped many readers entirely (hence the claim that there is no nonlinguistic evidence) and to have left unconvinced some of those who in fact understood the argument.

## ASSESSMENT OF WHORF'S VIEWS

As Whorf's writings became more widely available during the 1950s, they sparked widespread discussion in several disciplines about the relation of language to thought. However, despite this interest, few undertook the empirical and theoretical tasks necessary to seriously investigate and develop his ideas.[11] Given this historical situation, it seems worthwhile, while summarizing Whorf's most significant contributions to our understanding of the linguistic mediation of thought, to mention the more important research problems left unsolved in his approach but which must be addressed by any adequate theory and to indicate, without complex justification, some directions toward their solution. The discussion is divided into four parts which treat, respectively, Whorf's contributions to our understanding of language, of thought, of the relation between them, and of how to explore their relation empirically.

Whorf's first contribution lay in his approach to language. His emphasis, following Boas and Sapir, was not on purely formal differences between languages (e.g., whether they were inflected or not) nor on content differences as such (e.g., potential referential equivalence) but on how each language represents a particular formal structuring of meanings, an implicit way of classifying experience, wherein the selection and structuring themselves are the significant factors. Whorf's particular achievements were to demonstrate the complex nature of such structures and to elucidate the implicit linguistic analogies underlying them. Apparently simple linguistic classifications may have complex connections with other grammatical categories; apparently identical classifications may be embedded in quite different underlying configurations; and some classifications may only be evidenced by patterns of structural interaction rather than by overt morphology. It is the analogical suggestiveness of such structural differences in grammars, Whorf's "fashions

---

[11] The sheer volume of secondary discussion somewhat obscures the absence of actual research. Despite keen interest within Whorf's own field of anthropological linguistics, there has been almost no empirical work (but see Hoijer 1951 for one example). In the new field of psycholinguistics, which arose during the 1950s partly as a response to interest in Whorf's ideas, some research was also done, although this tradition bore little relation to what Whorf wrote, as has been pointed out by Alford (1978), and was short lived for reasons having little to do with the findings of the research itself, as has been shown by Lucy and Shweder (1979). Perhaps the most insidious development, now evidenced in nearly every discussion, is the division of the linguistic relativity hypothesis into a strong ("language determines") form which is unacceptable to all, and a weak ("language influences") form which is acceptable to all. (Of course, the construal of the strong and weak arguments varies dramatically by discipline, and any apparent agreement is an illusion.) Acceptance or rejection of Whorf's views, in this way of thinking, then hinges on which form of the argument one believes he *intended* to endorse, rather than on any analysis of his specific ideas. Drawing this strong-weak dichotomy also effectively undercuts the motivation for and the reception of new research since the hypothesis is prejudged as either "obviously true" or "obviously false" depending on how the question is formulated.

of speaking," which are at the heart of his theory: meanings of elements formally classed together may influence each other and, therefore, may also influence interpretations of reality based on them. Subsequent treatments of the language and thought problem fail to understand or profit from Whorf's work to the extent they have attended only to formal patterns in languages (i.e., attempted to avoid considering meaning), have devolved into arguments about whether it is possible to say such and such in a given language (i.e., disregarded the psychological significance of differences in formal structure), have isolated a single lexeme or small set of lexemes from their structural positions to represent "language," or have failed to compare the linguistic structures at issue with those in other languages.

There are, however, some critical linguistic issues that remain undeveloped in Whorf's work. First, a fuller account of linguistic analogy is needed that articulates its distinctively linguistic (or semiotic) nature, that is, shows how it is not reducible to cognitive, cultural, or other principles. At the same time, such an account must be able to characterize linguistic analogy as a cohesive phenomenon, that is, show that it is not so highly variable or arbitrary as to be impervious to systematic investigation. Such an account will necessarily deal with the interaction of form and meaning, whether semantic or pragmatic, in language. Examples of distinctively semiotic regularities include "laws" of phonological and morphological change which, although undoubtedly involving general cognitive tendencies, must both respond to semiotic functional limitations (i.e., forms, whether phonological or morphological, must remain distinctive for communication to be successful) and operate on historically specific linguistic configurations (e.g., Kurylowicz 1945–1949). Still more relevant are those attempts to characterize the structure of linguistic forms, and grammatical categories in particular, as products, in part, of the pragmatic nature of speech as contextualized social communication (e.g., Jakobson's 1957 notion of "shifters," Kurylowicz's 1964 and 1972 studies of the deictic framework of speech, and Silverstein's 1981b investigations of the role of pragmatic factors and metapragmatic forms in the regimentation of grammar).[12]

Second, there is a need to investigate whether the particular formal instantiation of a category (e.g., whether a category is covert rather than overt, selective rather than modulus, or, in traditional terminology, lexical rather than grammatical) has effects on thought. This should not be confused with a concern about form itself, but rather addresses the significance (both language

---

[12] Also in need of serious revision (Hymes 1968, Silverstein 1976b) are the assumptions held by many and perhaps by Whorf that language is monofunctional, that is, serves only a referential function, and that it is isofunctional, that is, serves everywhere the same ends. Note, however, that theories arguing for the existence of a characteristically linguistic structure (i.e., one that is not reducible to something else) usually depend on claims about the universal centrality of the referential function in human speech.

internally and comparatively) of a given meaning having a particular type of formal representation. Thus, within psychology it has been suggested that cognitive processing is enhanced if a concept is "codable" into lexical form (e.g., Brown and Lenneberg 1954), and within linguistics it has been suggested that the potential for native awareness of a linguistic pattern is enhanced if it is formally "segmentable" (Silverstein 1981a).

On the cognitive side Whorf's major contribution was to emphasize habitual concepts—not what *can* be thought, but rather what typically *is* thought. Thus, he stressed the importance of the structure of the acquired content of thought as opposed to its purportedly innate potentials, and he directed attention to everyday individual thought and not just to the abilities or concerns of unusual, culturally specific groups of specialists. Critics who concern themselves exclusively with the implications of language for perceptual or cognitive potential or who maintain that Whorf's view of linguistic relativity makes study of the issue logically impossible, ignore this emphasis on habitual concepts.

Absent from Whorf's account, though, is a detailed view of cognition. (Cognition here should be understood to include perception.) There must be some account of the nature of thought or cognition in terms of its own functions such as attention, categorization, reasoning, and memory, as they shape and are shaped by experience.[13] Only on such a foundation can an understanding of language's role in cognition be developed. Whorf is not alone in his weakness on this issue. For example, nearly all experimental studies testing Whorf's views have used recognition memory as the dependent variable, even though psychological research on memory (Baddeley 1976) suggests that language factors play a much greater role in recall memory than in recognition memory.

In addition to these first two contributions which direct our attention to more appropriate aspects of language and of thought, Whorf also gave us the beginnings of a genuine theory of their linkage, rather than a mere assertion of relationship. Formal equivalences in the language, following analogical patterns, lead to the association of meanings which are not *necessarily* related. When cognition relies on or utilizes language forms, these associations may be activated and influence the interpretation of experience.

However, Whorf did not articulate the functional basis for this appropriation: When and why does cognition appropriate language structure? This problem has two aspects. On the one hand, it raises the question of whether there is some cognitive function for natural language whereby it facilitates or enables certain kinds of thought which would otherwise be difficult or impossible.

---

[13] The use of the expression "its own functions" here should not be taken as a call for a view of a completely autonomous "cognition." However, for the present, it seems best to entertain the idea that some nonlinguistic cognitive functions exist even as we question their integration into a distinctive whole cognition and their autonomy from other human activities.

Theories of this sort have been proposed both by those directly concerned with Whorf's claims, such as those who suggest the utility of the linguistic "coding" of information in facilitating memory (Brown and Lenneberg 1954, Lantz and Stefflre 1964), and by those concerned with other theories of the relation between language and thought wherein the internalization of speech serves to transform thought, enabling the distinctively human forms of higher mental functioning (e.g., Vygotsky 1962—discussed by Wertsch).[14] On the other hand, there is no guarantee that language is everywhere and always used in cognition to the same degree or in the same way (Hymes 1968, Lucy 1981). In Hymes's (1968) terminology, there is a second level of relativity, which might be called a functional relativity, implicated in the Whorfian question and which has yet to receive much attention, namely that there may be cultural constitutions of the way language is used in thought (e.g., whether the language is the primary or only language used by a group, whether there is a tendency to give verbal accounts of cultural phenomena, whether language forms are believed to represent reality, and how much information is acquired purely through linguistic channels). From this perspective, Whorf's own views may have been shaped by the way language is used, or ideologically conceived of, in our own society.

A related problem is the need to articulate the reverse connection, that is, the extent to which and the ways in which cognition shapes language. Failure to recognize such effects will lead to the spurious identification of linguistic influences when, in fact, language is merely reflecting cognitive patterns. Of course, some cognitive or conceptual abilities are presupposed in the very formation of language categories and hence cognitive factors constrain, to some degree, the range and types of linguistic variation. This highlights again the need to identify a characteristically linguistic, or semiotic, pattern of organization that can be distinguished from a characteristically cognitive one. Further, the extent to which cognitive factors influence language structure and use differentially as a function of cultural system is another unexplored issue.

Finally, Whorf provided the first real empirical case study of the relation of language variation to thought. Boas and Sapir discussed the classificatory nature of language, and Sapir speculated on the significance of linguistic categories for the interpretation of experience, but Whorf tackled the difficult problem of actually trying to demonstrate empirically a relation between language and some nonlinguistic domain with firsthand materials, and he succeeded in showing one way to do so. Critics of Whorf's evidence often fail to recognize or acknowledge this contribution. All contemporary empirical research, imitative or corrective, presupposes Whorf's approach.

---

[14] There are, of course, an abundance of psychological and cultural theories that use language structures as a model for cognitive representations. In light of the issues of concern in this reading, these approaches beg the question.

Of course, there is a need for further empirical work involving a wide range of evidence—experimental, naturalistic, and interpretive—to properly understand the relation of language variation to thought. Since it is highly likely that many, if not most, of the important influences of language on thought will not be amenable to controlled study, their proper interpretation will depend heavily on the few cases that are. Hence the most pressing immediate need is for some carefully controlled nonlinguistic evidence for the cognitive "reality" of the individual linguistically conditioned habitual thought worlds in a number of languages. Earlier experimental attempts to assess Whorf's views from a psychological perspective (e.g., Brown and Lenneberg 1954, Lenneberg and Roberts 1956, Carroll and Casagrande 1958, Stefflre, Castillo Vales, and Morley 1966, Heider 1972, Lucy and Shweder 1979, and Lucy 1981) can be instructive in designing such controlled studies, but much more must be done to make these empirical approaches applicable to Whorf's theory and consistent with contemporary theories of language and of thought. Likewise, accumulated research on linguistic universals that focuses on systematic cross-linguistic patterns in the formal-functional structuring of meanings underlying the observed variation among languages (e.g., Berlin and Kay 1969, Friedrich 1974, Silverstein 1976a) will be especially useful in designing controlled studies. Further, we need to examine under what conditions linguistic configurations or linguistically constituted thought worlds in fact connect with broader cultural patterns which may not be, as Whorf claimed, "just an assemblage of norms" (Hoijer 1953). Here too, the element of controlled comparison of multiple cases is essential to building a firm theory.

Through his linguistic and cultural analyses, Whorf showed clearly the interdisciplinary perspective research on the significance of linguistic diversity must take. It is a major task to fuse diverse theories and methodologies into a cohesive approach. Yet to be combined in any study are a comparative analysis of a distinctively linguistic (preferably grammatical) pattern, a controlled exploration of the effects of such a pattern on individual, functionally conceived, nonlinguistic conceptual organization, and a detailed demonstration of (rather than vague allusion to) the broader cultural significance of such conceptual patterns. The epistemological significance of the claims for an influence of linguistic diversity on thought is likely to keep these problems before us for many years. But the intrinsic difficulty of such a coordinated attack depending as it does on sustained theoretical, methodological, and empirical progress in several fields assures that our understanding will advance slowly. It is within the context of these difficulties, of our present scant knowledge, and of the failure of others to make progress that the achievement represented by Whorf's account of the linguistic mediation of thought becomes clear.

# REFERENCES

Alford,D.
1978    The Demise of the Whorf Hypothesis (A Major Revision in the History of Linguistics). *Proceedings of the Fourth Annual Meeting of the Berkeley Linguistics Society* 4:485–499.

Baddeley, A. D.
1976    *The Psychology of Memory.* New York: Basic Books.

Berlin, B., and P. Kay
1969    *Basic Color Terms: Their Universality and Evolution.* Berkeley: University of California.

Bloomfield, L.
1933    *Language.* New York: Holt.

Boas, F.
1911    Introduction. In *Handbook of American Indian Languages* (Bureau of American Ethnology Bulletin 40, Part 1), ed. F. Boas, pp. 1–83. Washington, D.C.: Smithsonian Institution.
1920    The Methods of Ethnology. *American Anthropologist* 22:311–321.
1942    Language and Culture. In *Studies in the History of Culture: The Disciplines of the Humanities*, American Council of Learned Societies Devoted to Humanistic Studies, Conference of the Secretaries of the Constituent Societies, pp. 178–184. Menasha, WI: George Banta.

Brown, R., and E. H. Lenneberg
1954    A Study in Language and Cognition. *Journal of Abnormal and Social Psychology* 49:454–462.

Carroll, J. B., and J. B. Casagrande
1958    The Function of Language Classifications in Behavior. In *Readings in Social Psychology* (3rd ed.), eds. E. Maccoby, T. Newcomb, and E. Hartley, pp. 18–31. New York: Holt.

Friedrich, P.
1974    *On Aspect Theory and Homeric Aspect* (Indiana University Publications in Anthropology and Linguistics; Memoir 28 of the *International Journal of American Linguistics*). Bloomington: Indiana University.

Heider, E. R.
1972    Universals in Color Naming and Memory. *Journal of Experimental Psychology* 93:10–20.

Hoijer, H.
1951    Cultural Implications of Some Navaho Linguistic Categories. *Language* 27:111–120.
1953    The Relation of Language to Culture. In *Anthropology Today*, ed. A. L. Kroeber, pp. 554–573. Chicago: University of Chicago.

Hymes, D.
1968    Two Types of Linguistic Relativity. In *Sociolinguistics, Proceedings of the UCLA Sociolinguistics Conference* (1964), ed. W. Bright, pp. 114–165. The Hague: Mouton.

Jakobson, R.
1957    *Shifters, Verbal Categories, and the Russian Verb.* Cambridge: Harvard University Russian Language Project.

Kurylowicz, J.
1945–1949 La Nature des Procès dits "analogiques." *Acta Linguistica* 5:15–37.
1964     *The Inflectional Categories of Indo-European.* Heidelberg: Carl Winter Universitätsverlag.
1972     The Role of Deictic Elements in Linguistic Evolution. *Semiotica* 5:174–183.

Lantz, D., and V. Stefflre
1964     Language and Cognition Revisited. *Journal of Abnormal and Social Psychology* 64:472–481.

Lenneberg, E. H., and J. M. Roberts
1956     *The Language of Experience: A Study in Methodology* (Indiana University Publications in Anthropology and Linguistics; Memoir 13 of the *International Journal of American Linguistics*). Bloomington: Indiana University.

Lucy, J. A.
1981     Cultural Factors in Memory for Color: The Problem of Language Usage. Paper presented at the 80th Annual Meetings of the American Anthropological Association, Los Angeles.

Lucy, J. A., and R. A. Shweder
1979     Whorf and His Critics: Linguistic and Nonlinguistic Influences on Color Memory. *American Anthropologist* 81:581–615.

Sapir, E.
1924     The Grammarian and His Language. *American Mercury* 1:149–155.
1929     The Status of Linguistics as a Science. *Language* 5:207–214.
1931     Conceptual Categories in Primitive Languages. *Science* 74:578.

Silverstein, M.
1976a     Hierarchy of Features and Ergativity. In *Grammatical Categories in Australian Languages* (Australian Institute of Aboriginal Studies, Linguistic Series, No. 22.), ed. R. M. W. Dixon, pp. 112–171. Canberra: Australian Institute of Aboriginal Studies.
1976b     Shifters, Linguistic Categories, and Cultural Description. In *Meaning in Anthropology*, eds. K. Basso and H. Selby, pp. 11–55. Albuquerque: University of New Mexico.
1979     Language Structure and Linguistic Ideology. In *The Elements: A Parasession on Linguistic Units and Levels*, eds. P. Clyne, W. Hanks, and C. Hofbauer, pp. 193–247. Chicago: Chicago Linguistic Society.
1981a     The Limits of Awareness. *Working Papers in Sociolinguistics*, No. 84. Austin: Southwestern Educational Laboratory.
1981b     Case-Marking and the Nature of Language. *Australian Journal of Linguistics* 1:227–244.

Stefflre, V., V. Castillo Vales, and L. Morley
1966     Language and Cognition in Yucatan: A Cross-Cultural Replication. *Journal of Personality and Social Psychology* 4:112–115.

Vygotsky, L. S.
1962     *Thought and Language*, eds. and trans. E. Hanfmann and G. Vakar. Cambridge, MA: MIT Press. (Condensed from the 1934 original.)

Whorf, B. L.

1946a    The Hopi Language, Toreva Dialect. In *Linguistic Structures of Native America*, ed. H. Hoijer, pp. 158–183. New York: Viking Fund. (Written in 1939.)

1946b    The Milpa Alta Dialect of Aztec, with Notes on the Classical and the Tepoztlan Dialects. In *Linguistic Structures of Native America*, ed. H. Hoijer, pp. 367–397. New York: Viking Fund. (Written in 1939.)

1956a    *Language, Thought, and Reality, Selected Writings of Benjamin Lee Whorf*, ed. J. B. Carroll. Cambridge, MA: MIT Press. (Written from 1927 to 1941.)

1956b    Report on Linguistic Research in the Department of Anthropology of Yale University for the Term September 1937-June 1938 (incomplete) (Written in part with G. Trager). In *Microfilm Collection of Manuscripts on Middle American Cultural Anthropology*, No. 51: (Miscellanea), pp. 1–9. Chicago: University of Chicago Library. (Written in 1938.)

# Ethnoecology: The Relevance of Cognitive Anthropology for Human Ecology

Eugene Hunn

Anthropologists have defined culture variously in their pursuit of diverse theoretical goals. Keesing (1974) distinguishes two fundamentally distinct perspectives on the study of culture, the adaptational (or materialist) and the ideational. Examples of the first approach include cultural ecology and cultural materialism. They are characterized by a focus on the adaptive value of culturally patterned behaviors. In cultural materialism "culture" reduces to learned behaviors (Harris 1979). Ideational theories define cultures as semiotic systems. The relations between such systems of signs and the realities of behavioral adaptation is of only peripheral interest. Keesing contrasts ideational theories associated with Lévi-Strauss, Geertz, Schneider, and Goodenough, the last of which is cognitive anthropology, the guiding perspective of this reading.

Keesing, as an ideational theorist, like Harris on the materialist side, reflects the widely held view that adaptational and ideational perspectives are fundamentally incompatible. I would like to argue to the contrary—that our best hope of developing an effective theory of culture is to bridge the chasm separating adaptationist and ideational positions. The synthesis I propose here may be called "ethnoecology" (but not as described by Fowler 1977). This synthesis should combine the strengths of modern ecological anthropology with those of cognitive-semiotic anthropology while avoiding the weaknesses of both.

The strength of the adaptational approach is its recognition that human behavior both affects and is affected by a complex environment, the social and ecosystems of which humans are but one part. This strength becomes a weakness if it is not clearly recognized that social and ecosystems are composed of individual organisms, each of which is pursuing its own "selfish" plans (Dawkins 1976). The functionalist fallacy results from attributing goal direction to systems rather than to individual actors (Richerson 1977). This problem is avoided by more recent models based on evolutionary ecology, in which adaptation is interpreted in terms of the effect traits have on the individuals who express them, rather than the effect such traits might have on the encompassing system *qua* organism (Smith 1984).

The strength of ideational approaches lies in their focus on symbolic thought and communication. Learning may take place in the absence of symbolic means of expression. Thus culture, defined as learned behaviors, may also exist without such communication. However, such learning is limited in quantity and adaptive flexibility, and thus nonsymbolic culture remains rudimentary. The fact that humans possess a highly elaborated, species-specific, and universal capacity for language should be sufficient motivation to give symbolic expression a central role in our theories of human adaptation.

Some adaptational theories, such as Harris's cultural materialism, treat the symbolically coded information by which human behavior is planned, evaluated, replicated, and manipulated as if it served primarily as an ideological smoke screen that it is the analyst's task to dispel. Other adaptationists perceive only a quantitative difference between nonsymbolic social learning (by imitation) and symbolically mediated cultural transmission (Richerson and Boyd, 1989). On the other hand, ideational theorists of culture have often devoted inordinate attention to expressive, in preference to instrumental, aspects of culture (Hunn 1982). This emphasis on the noninstrumental may then be combined with a radical relativism and/or a virulent antipositivism (positivism being used loosely as an epithet for modern science) that borders on a rejection of the possibility of a science of human culture. Such ideational theorists define the proper goal of cultural analysis as interpretation rather than explanation. Ideational theorists are also prey to the same functionalist fallacy that waylaid early cultural ecology, subordinating the individual actor to the controlling influence of the encompassing system, whether social, cultural, or ecological.

## COGNITIVE DEFINITIONS OF CULTURE

Cognitive anthropology among the ideational theories seems best suited to propose a theoretical marriage of ideational and adaptationist approaches. Cognitive anthropology seeks to develop a scientific approach to ethnography, one that can produce systematic and replicable descriptions of particular cultures (or segments thereof) as a first step toward valid cross-cultural generalizations (Kay 1970). Cognitive anthropology focuses on the individual as the bearer and creative user of culture. The cognitivist culture concept was first clearly articulated by Goodenough, who defined culture as that which one needs to know to act appropriately in all the normal social contexts of the society in question (1957:167). Culture is thus information, not behavior, a point of agreement with leading cultural evolutionary theorists such as Cloak (1975) and Boyd and Richerson (1985). This definition was inspired by a reaction to the positivistic excesses of behaviorist psychology and descriptive linguistics. This same reaction gave impetus to the Chomskyan revolution in linguistics (Chomsky 1959) and led to the development of cognitive psychology (Neisser 1975). Mental phenomena were not to be ignored as impenetrable and insubstantial, but were to be explained by reference to testable cognitive models. Observed behavior was seen as a superficial phenomenon generated by underlying cognitive processes interacting with—not simply reacting to—

external reality. For anthropologists this meant that the seemingly infinite variety of human behavior could be understood in terms of cultural rules learned by individuals in society. Systems of such cultural rules, or cultural grammars on the linguistic model, were necessarily finite and otherwise constrained by the limits of human mental capacity.

This notion of culture as a grammar for behavior—derived from the equation CULTURE : BEHAVIOR :: LANGUAGE : SPEECH—is flawed, for grammars define what is the appropriate form of a sentence, saying nothing of what is its appropriate content. Chomsky's famed nonsensical sentence, "Colorless green ideas sleep furiously," is grammatically correct but "ecologically" absurd. An ecologically appropriate culture concept must address not only what is formally appropriate, but also what is ecologically effective. We should therefore amend Goodenough's definition of culture as follows: Culture is what one must know to act effectively in one's environment. (The environment is understood to include both natural and social components from the individual actor's point-of-view.)

This definition retains an essential ambiguity. What do we mean by "effective"? In Goodenough's original definition there was no question: appropriateness of behavior was to be judged by the native, just as the grammaticality of a sentence must be judged by a native speaker, through introspection. The standard of cultural appropriateness may be equated with Freilich's "proper culture" (1980). But cultural effectiveness includes as well Freilich's "smart culture." Both are emic standards, relevant to culturally defined goals, the one social, the other individual. Alternatively we might adopt an etic standard of effectiveness, that is, by reference to culturally external standards. To a human ecologist effectiveness may refer to the efficiency of energy conversion or ultimately, in evolutionary ecology, to maximizing inclusive fitness. I suggest that ethnoecology adopt as a working hypothesis the assumption that, other things being equal, the effective pursuit of culturally defined goals is the proximate mechanism for realizing the ultimate goals imposed by the biological and cultural evolutionary systems of which the human individual is a part (cf. Durham 1979, 1982).

Thus ethnoecology provides a framework for understanding the mechanisms of human cultural evolution, mechanisms that have only recently been seriously considered by cultural adaptationists (Ruyle 1973; Cavalli-Sforza and Feldman 1981; Cloak 1975; Dawkins 1976; Durham 1979; Pulliam and Dunford 1980; Boyd and Richerson 1985). I believe the analogy CULTURE : BEHAVIOR :: GENOTYPE : PHENOTYPE is more productive than the original Goodenough formulation, promoting a view of a culture as a system of information that serves as a blueprint for a way of life and that is ultimately judged by how well it sustains and promotes that way of life.[1]

---

[1] Geertz entertained this analogy briefly in his essay on "Religion as a Cultural System" in *The Interpretation of Cultures*, pp. 92–93, but has not, to my knowledge, capitalized upon it.

In this view, behavior is the result of culture, the product of cultural plans. It is my view that such cultural plans are frequently conscious, that is, symbolically coded in and thus accessible through the native language of the culture bearer. Though learned behaviors and thus culture are not necessarily governed symbolically or consciously, conscious, linguistically encoded plans constitute a very large and highly invested segment of human cultural life, the analysis of which should yield substantial progress toward an understanding of the more general phenomenon of the evolution of learning.

It needs to be stressed that such cultural plans are context sensitive, in that the behaviors they call for will vary depending on the conditions of the environment at the time and place the plans are expressed, as biological phenotypes vary depending on the environment of gene expression. Furthermore, such plans serve as blueprints, and a blueprint of a house is not the same thing as the house it describes, though it contains the information required to organize the material means necessary for the house's construction and thus embodies the material need for shelter the house is designed to satisfy. This shift of emphasis from models of cultures as autonomous formal structures to processual models of cultures as adaptive systems parallels the shift toward pragmatics in linguistic analysis (Silverstein 1976) and toward praxis in Marxian theory (Ortner 1984).

## IMAGE AND PLAN

If culture consists of the information necessary for effective action, what is the nature of that information and how is it organized, stored, acquired, and passed on? Such questions with regard to genetic information have received a great deal of attention from scientists analyzing biogenetic evolutionary mechanisms. Similar efforts will be needed in the study of cultural evolution.

At one level cultural information is coded neurophysiologically, but among humans it is most often transmitted and manipulated symbolically via language. Thus, a substantial core of human cultural information will be manifested in the language of the culture bearer. Cognitive anthropology is concerned primarily with the form and content of cultural information as it is expressed linguistically. This strategic focus on natural language as the medium of culture is shared by Schank and Abelson, leading artificial intelligence (AI) theorists, who note that "a great deal of the human scene can be represented verbally" (1977:5).

A primary distinction relevant to understanding how cultural information is encoded is that between systems of information organized by similarity and those organized by contiguity (cf. iconicity versus indexicality). The former focus on features intrinsic to the "things"[2] classified and relevant to their

---

[2] By "things" I mean to include not only material objects but also events and relationships.

identification regardless of context. The latter refer to extrinsic features of things, i.e., relationships between things and their contexts, which are primarily relevant to understanding how things function, their roles in events.

Models of human knowledge and memory based on abstract similarity have dominated cognitive theorizing in cognitive psychology and cognitive anthropology into the mid-1970s. Concept formation by reference to similarity has traditionally been judged a more "mature" mode of thought than that based on functional association (Bruner, Goodnow, and Austin 1956:6–8), being characterized as "abstract" (because context free), as opposed to the "concrete" associations of contiguity. Semantic theories of memory conceive of memory as "organized in a hierarchical fashion using class membership as the basic link" (Schank and Abelson 1977:18), with class membership typically defined in terms of shared similarity. Cognitive anthropology has viewed cultural knowledge similarly, defining as the primary units of analysis "semantic domains" by reference to shared similarity (cf. Sturtevant 1964). Culture in this view is an Image of the world (cf. Boulding 1956) that includes cultural "maps," "taxonomies," and "paradigms" as particular organizational forms. The Image is analogous to the lexicon in models of natural language. It consists of "models of," not "models for," a way of life (Geertz 1973:93).

Relations of contiguity have recently been emphasized in models of the conceptual organization of human behavior, that aspect of cultural knowledge more directly involved in interpreting events and selecting courses of action than in describing what the world looks like (Randall 1977, 1987). I will contrast such models of the cultural Plan (cf. Miller, Galanter, and Pribram 1960) with those of the Image. A cultural Plan includes "information processing rules" (Geoghegan 1973); "scripts, plans, goals" (Abelson 1976, 1981; Schank and Abelson 1977); and "routine action plans" (Randall 1977, 1987) as particular organizational forms. It involves episodic rather than semantic memory (Schank and Abelson 1977:18). "Hierarchical decision trees" (Gladwin 1980) may be incorporated as required.

Cognitive anthropologists have made substantial progress in the analysis of the cultural Image, of Image domains such as color, kinship relations, folk biological taxonomies, and folk anatomy. Considerable progress is also evident in the study of decision trees, cultural rules, and routine planning. What is lacking is an effective integration of our models of Image and of Plan (see Figure 1). I will discuss below several cases of cognitive anthropological research that suggest the direction such an integration of Image and Plan might take. Each illustrates how cognitive anthropologists have addressed the ecological relevance of cultural knowledge.

## Preliminary Illustrations

### Case 1. "Cultural Ecology and Ethnography," Charles Frake (1962)

In this brief note Frake illustrates how a local settlement pattern of scattered homesites in the southern Philippines could be "generated" from just three

FIGURE 1    A Model of Image and Plan

**Natural Environment**

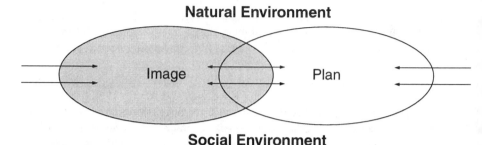

**Social Environment**

cultural "rules." The rules were the bases on which individuals selected sites preferred for constructing their houses. They sought simultaneously to minimize the distance between home and fields and to maximize the distance to their nearest neighbor's house, while also minimizing the labor of fence construction around the periphery of their fields. The rules were readily elicited in the native language and clearly define appropriate choices of action in terms of social and ecological variables. Thus the observed settlement pattern is the collective behavioral expression of many individual culturally and environmentally governed choices. The behavioral pattern may change, that is, we may observe cultural evolution, without change in the cultural rule, if environmental parameters, such as population density, should change.

*Case 2. "Residential Decision Making among the Eastern Samal,"*
*William Geoghegan (1970)*

In this classic study Geoghegan constructs an "information-processing model" of residence mode selection in a Philippine Island community. The rule is graphically represented as a flow-chart—a popular convention in cognitive anthropological studies of choice—each node of which represents an environmental assessment relevant to the choice of "appropriate" residence mode. The validity of the model is tested against census data from the original community as well as from a population of war refugees. Predictions were 98 percent and 94 percent confirmed for the two populations. Marvin Harris (1974), in a critique of this and similar cultural accounts of behavior, argues that this demonstrates that etic outputs require etic inputs. However, Harris redefines etic here as "real" versus "imagined." This is a distortion of Pike's (1956) original formulation of the emic-etic contrast. Furthermore, the inputs required by Geoghegan's model are emic in the proper sense of that term, being distinctions relevant to the actor's cultural frame of reference. That cultural rules incorporate information—linguistically encoded—about the "real" world does not make them etic. Clearly, if cultural Images of reality were not more or less faithful to that reality, cultural Plans based on such information would be ecologically ineffective. So Harris is right to demand that cultural systems effectively link objective environmental states (his "etic inputs") to behavioral practice (his "etic outputs"). He is wrong only in suggesting that cognitive anthropologists believe otherwise.

### Case 3. "Ice and Travel among the Ft. Norman Slave," Keith Basso (1972)

Basso shows how an elaborate Slave Indian ice taxonomy, incorporating thirteen named varieties of ice of three major types, is relevant to subsistence and survival in the boreal forest environment. The well-worn example of the elaboration of Inuit snow terminology is presumed to illustrate how cultural knowledge reflects adaptive requirements, though no one has actually demonstrated such a relationship. Basso does so for his Ft. Norman Slave case. The thirteen named ice varieties are associated with seven contrasting combinations of mode of travel (on foot, on snowshoes, by sled) and strategies of approach to water barriers (cross at full speed, test before crossing, circumnavigate) encountered by hunters during winter travel. These relationships between named environmental conditions and behavioral options are explicitly taught to the younger generation by means of a word game in which the child is given two of the three conditions and must select the appropriate third element. In this case the Image is an efficient repository of information about the environment essential to ecologically effective choices of action. The importance of language in cultural transmission is also clear in this example.

### Case 4. "Talking About Doing: Lexicon and Event," Michael Agar (1974)

Agar argues that the specialized terminology of the heroin addict subculture in the United States is better represented in terms of events characteristic of the addict's life-style rather than in terms of semantic domains defining an Image of the addict's world. In other words, relations of contiguity regarding actors, actions, means, and locations provide a more meaningful characterization of this subculture than do relations of similarity defining, for example, taxonomies of such actors, means, and locations, as had been traditional in ethnoscience. The terms characteristic of the addict subculture, when arranged as in an English sentence, with terms filling slots in the sentence representing actions (verbs), agents (subjects), objects of actions, and means and locations of the labeled actions succinctly summarized "what one needed to know to act appropriately" within the addict subculture.

The possibility that all human languages are built upon an underlying universal "case grammar" (Fillmore 1968, 1977) suggests that the human understanding of events may be as regularly structured as human semantic memory. Schank's Conceptual Dependency Theory (1975) and the various computer simulations of how people understand natural language accounts of human events represent parallel efforts by psychologists and AI researchers to develop a theory of human knowledge of "the world of psychological and physical events occupying the mental life of ordinary individuals . . . [of] the common sense . . . assumptions which people make about the motives and behavior of themselves and others—and also a kind of 'naive physics,' or primitive intuition about physical reality" (Schank and Abelson 1977:4). From this theoretical perspective the cultural Image (as well as the Plan) is primarily structured by functional relations of contiguity; thus the Image, the Plan, and the grammatical structure of human language share a common analytical framework.

*Case 5. "Making Plans to 'Make a Living' in the Southern Philippines," Robert Randall (1977)*

Randall's analysis of Linungan fishing plans is an ambitious attempt to describe what one must know to "make a living" in this particular ecological setting. His analysis adds a dimension of ethnographic reality to the efforts of AI theorists to account for human understanding of everyday life. Randall stresses the significance of having or acquiring the means necessary for successful action, an environmental constraint on the selection of culturally appropriate behaviors. Randall carefully distinguishes how routine choices of action are implemented, in contrast to the selection of exceptional or marked alternative actions when unusual obstacles or opportunities are encountered (Randall 1987). His analysis describes some microevolutionary changes in Linungan subsistence plans.

These studies are but a sample of cognitive anthropological research relevant to cultural ecology. Basso demonstrates that cultural knowledge has adaptive significance. Frake, Geoghegan, and Randall show the ecological relevance of cultural plans. Geoghegan, Agar, and Randall propose general models of such cultural plans. I will now describe in greater detail an ethnobiological case from my own research to suggest the form an ethnoecological ethnography might take.

*Sahaptin Root Digging*

This example begins with a traditional ethnoscientific analysis that organizes terminologically labeled elements of the Image as a taxonomic domain structured by relations of perceptual similarity (Kay 1971; Berlin, Breedlove, and Raven 1973; Hunn 1976). The elements of the Image are analyzed in terms of their role in the cultural Plan. The two perspectives are then contrasted.

I have recorded over 200 basic plant taxa for the Columbia River dialects of the Sahaptin language of the Plateau of northwestern North America.[3]

---

[3] Sahaptin is a Penutian language spoken today by several hundred Indians in south central Washington and north central Oregon. My research pertains most directly to the dialects of that language spoken by Columbia River Indians whose ancestral winter villages were located on the Columbia River between Celilo Falls and the Umatilla River.

A basic category is distinguished from more or less inclusive categories in the same domain by a characteristic combination of features, including high information content, an unmarked name, and a cognitive representation as a prototypical image (Hunn 1976; Berlin 1978; Rosch 1978). The fact that most of these 200-odd categories correspond to scientific species or closely approximate them demonstrates that perceptual similarity is the primary basis for the classification of individual plants into basic level categories. In this respect Sahaptin resembles other folk biological classification systems. However, Sahaptin is unusual in comparison with other well-known folk biological systems in its minimal hierarchical structure. Morphologically based "life form" taxa and folk specific taxa are virtually nonexistent. (Life forms are defined by Berlin, Breedlove, and Raven [1973] as taxa inclusive of a range of "folk generic" or basic-level taxa, while specifics are defined as subdivisions of folk generics characteristically labeled by names of binomial form.) The Sahaptin taxonomic hierarchy thus reduces to a nearly unstructured list of basic level categories.

I would like to be able to say more than this about Sahaptin ethnobotany. To do so I must consider more than the perceptual basis of Sahaptin folk classification. I must consider not only relations of similarity among plant taxa but also relations of contiguity between plant taxa and other conceptual elements of the Sahaptin Image. One way to approach this task is to describe what I call the "activity signature" of each plant (Hunn 1982), which is the set of Sahaptin sentences incorporating each plant name. Activity signatures are lists of admissible predications for which the plant serves as an argument. Those sentences delimit a set of contexts that collectively define the plant's cultural relevance.

Context-defining sentences may be compared among a set of plants to appreciate the contrasting relevance of each plant. As an initial step in this ethnographic program I have drawn from open-ended, native language texts on gathering activities that I recorded from several Sahaptin elders. From these texts I have abstracted an outline of a root gathering plan, a cultural context central to the meaning of the Sahaptin ethnobotanical category *xni-t*, "plants that are dug, roots." I then asked my Sahaptin teacher, James Selam, to review and correct my interpretations.

The basic plant categories grouped under the heading *xni-t* correspond closely to scientific species. Nineteen of the twenty-six roots, or 73 percent, correspond perfectly to scientific species, while the remaining seven are near misses. The perceptual basis for these basic-level taxa is thus clear. However, the collectivity of roots represents a diverse assortment of plants from several plant families. This category includes the edible species of some scientific genera and families while excluding other very similar but inedible species of the same genus or family. Clearly, the category *xni-t* is not based on perceptual similarity. Rather it reflects the common role each such species plays in the cultural Plan. All roots, for example, are appropriate as objects of the transitive verb *xni-* "to dig [something]." The similarity here is a functional equivalence;

TABLE 1   A Sahaptin Root Digging Plan XNI-T

I. Primary goal: to eat *tkʷáta-sha*
   A. Have means to eat, e.g., is there food? *i-wá tkʷáta-t*
      1. If yes, go to B. If not, select means, e.g., option 1d.
         a. Fish *np'íwi-sha*: select means, for example,
            1) Fish by hook-and-line *wac'ílak-sha*
            2) Fish by bone choker *shapáʔaxch-sha*
            3) Spear fish *tayxáy-sha*
            4) Dip-net fish *twalúu-sha*
            5) Set-net fish *tapatúk-sha*
            6) Fish by weir *shapá-xaluu-sha*
         b. Hunt *tkʷáynp-sha*
         c. Pick fruit *á-tmaani-sha*
         d. Dig roots *á-xni-sha*
         e. Use stored foods *yáxaynakt-pamá*
      2. Enact root digging plan *wishushuwa-sha xnít-atash*
         a. Have means to dig roots *wás-nas xnit-pamá*, e.g., digging stick *kápin*, twined bag *wápas?*
         b. If not, acquire means. if yes, initiate plan.
            1) Plan trip *wishushuwa-sha wína-tash*
            2) Pack up gear *i-wiwalakʷ'ik-sha kutkut'áwas-na*
            3) Go for roots *máana-sha*
            4) Travel to camp *wishána-sha wáwtukash-kan*
            5) Go around [looking for a camp site] *waqit-sha wáwtuk-awas*
            6) Camp overnight *wishwáwtuk-sha*
            7) Find digging site *á-yax-sha xnit-pamá-na*
            8) Look around for roots *q'inuq'inú-sha xnit-pamá-na*
            9) Select root species, e.g., bitterroot *pyaxí*, camas *wáq'amu*, Indian potato *anipásh*
            10) Dig roots *á-xni-sha*
            11) If bitterroot, strip skin *á-chapyax-sha*
            12) Put in twined bag *á-nich-sha wápas-pa*
            13) Repeat 10) & 12) until bag is full *káakim*, then go on
            14) Collect in large bag *á-yakta-sha ánpsh-pa*
            15) Repeat 14) until full, then continue
            16) Pack roots back to camp *kʷnáyti-sha*
      3. Prepare roots, select means, e.g., option 3b.
         a. Store underground *á-tamki-sha*, go to I, A, 1, e.
         b. Eat them now *áw tkʷáta-sha*, go to A4.
         c. Keep them for winter *á-nich-sha ánwich-tash*, initiate sequence
            1) Wash roots *áw-iix-sha*
            2) Peel roots *á-miik-sha*
            3) If bitterroot, go to C6
            4) If camas, bake underground *á-tamaych-sha*
            5) If *luksh*, make root cakes *áwiʔani-sha sap*  , *initiate sequence*
               *a) Pound roots á-tut-sha*
               *b) Mix dough shapátwa-sha*
               *c) Form cakes áwiʔani-sha sap*
            *6) Dry in sun áwilaxyawi-sha ichú-pa*
            7) Pack them home *áwishapashap-sha túxna-t*
            8) Put them away in the cellar *á-nich-sha wulchí-pa*
      4. Cook roots *á-shapaʔat'i-sha xnít-na:* select means, e.g.,
         a. boil them *á-shapa-lamulayt-sha*
   B. Eat *tkʷáta-sha*

Note relationships of goals, activities, and means; of options and sequences; of special selection and identification subplans.

the members of the category may substitute for one another in a particular role within a characteristic activity, in this case an ecologically fundamental one.

If all twenty-six kinds of roots are functionally equivalent, why bother to name each separately? This seems wasteful of mental effort and of memory capacity. Why not call them all simply *xni-t?* Such a strategy is, in fact, adopted with regard to two categories of useless plants in Sahaptin, *latít* (flower) and *c'ic'k* (grass) (Randall and Hunn 1984). However, all roots on closer inspection are not precise functional equivalents. Though all roots may be harvested with the same digging movement, in the larger context of using these roots, highly salient contrasts appear. To appreciate the cultural need for naming so many roots we must describe root digging in more detail.

The actual act of digging the root from the ground is but one step—albeit the conceptually central one—in a sequence of connected activities. Applying ethnoscientific elicitation techniques in this case is useful. If we ask *táynam-chi á-xni-sha kʷˑáaman?* (why one digs this root or that), the answer will be, *tkʷátat-yaw* (to eat it). One doesn't just dig roots and then discard them! Root digging is a goal-directed activity. If we ask *míshniki-nam á-xni-xa kʷˑáaman?* (how does one dig roots), we are likely to receive as an answer a description of a sequence of activities. To dig a root requires that one first go root digging *máana-*, on arrival look around for the specific root(s) sought *q'inuq'inú-*, dig them *xni-*,[4] peel them *miik-*, collect them in a bag *yákta-*, pack them back to camp *kʷnáyti-*, wash them *iix-*, pound them *tut-*, dry them *láxyawi-*, cook them *shapá-ʔat'i-*, and finally eat them *tkʷáta-*.[5] Eating is the culmination of the process as well as its motivating goal.

At each step of this sequence one may ask again, how? For example, "How do you 'cook' them?" *míshniki-nam á-shapaʔat'i-xa?* The answers reveal a set of alternative cooking techniques differentially appropriate to various roots. Camas (*Camassia quamash*, liliaceae), for example, must be baked underground *tamáych-*,[6] while *pank'ú* (*Tauschia hooveri*, umbelliferae) is eaten raw *xapít*. [The cooking step of the sequence is deleted.] The Sahaptin recognition of two distinct varieties of Canby's lomatium (*Lomatium canbyi*, umbelliferae) makes sense when we discover that the first variety is ground, made into dough, then sun-dried as finger cakes *saⱡtɬ*, while the other is baked underground. Other ecologically relevant distinctions are revealed by asking "where?" "when?" or "by whom?" the roots are dug.

---

[4] Note the polysemy of *xni-t* used to describe both the action of digging roots and the sequence of activities of which that is the focal segment. It is a nomenclatural pattern with close parallels elsewhere (Agar 1974; Berlin 1976).

[5] The verbs are cited in their unmodified stem form. Transitive stems such as these would be inflected to indicate impersonal subject and plural object by adding the prefix *á-* and for continuing action in the present by the suffix *-sha*, thus *á-xni-sha* "you are digging [roots]."

[6] The adaptive value of such processing has been demonstrated by Konlande and Robson's nutritional analyses (1972).

Asking how? to do something does not always produce a description of a sequence of activities involved in completing the action. At some point the answer will be a slightly annoyed "You just do it." This response suggests the limits of conscious planning have been reached (or the limits of one's informant's patience). For example, eating ultimately involves a complex sequence of jaw motions, the control of which is largely outside of conscious awareness. Chewing is an atomic activity at the conscious level. Digging likewise involves such atomic physical actions as grasping the digging stick, bending, lifting, and twisting. Such atomic units may be incorporated into a variety of molar activities and are thus not particular to an ethnographic account of activities. Our ethnoecological description need not proceed beyond this level of detail.

In other situations the question how? may generate a list of alternatives requiring a decision as to which is preferred. For example, "How should one fish?" in the Sahaptin Plan is a question that implies alternative technologies appropriate to the time and place and to the species sought. One fishes by hook-and-line or bone choker; with a spear, dip net, or set net; by weir or trap. To accomplish the task of fishing one must first select an appropriate way to fish. A "hierarchical decision tree" (Gladwin 1980) may be required to describe this segment of the Plan.

As should now be clear, a discussion of folk classification restricted to aspects of perceptual similarity will be woefully incomplete as an account of the Sahaptin Image of their natural environment. The Image includes not only the cultural knowledge of what a plant or animal looks like (which is put to use in identification subplans), but also a representation of the plant or animal in its characteristic cultural contexts. The Sahaptin Image of camas would call to mind not only a collectivity of similar plants but also a scene in which camas plays a central role. We would see in our mind's eye a vernal meadow in summer, full of mature camas, with Indian women actively engaged in uprooting the plants with their digging sticks. In the background of the picture would be other plants and animals characteristic of meadows, ecological associates of camas. We would imagine the underground ovens being prepared. We would be reminded of the firewood, the heating stones, and the various plants used to cover and flavor the baking camas, things that are characteristically part of these activities.

An appropriate data structure for representing this knowledge is an "event" (Agar 1974) or an "episode," as in theories of episodic memory preferred by Shank and Abelson (1977:17–19), a kind of "schema" (Neisser 1975; Casson 1983) rather than a taxonomy. We would, of course, also recall the camas plant itself, its spike of large blue flowers, its sheathing cluster of leaves, its onionlike bulb pulled fresh from the ground. While a taxonomic structure may be abstracted from such information, such information is also required by the Plan whenever an identification is required to select or enact a Plan segment. We might be reminded of the death camas (*Zigadenus spp.*, liliaceae), a deceptively similar plant. Perceptual similarity is important in this instance because it implies contrasting functional patterns for the two similar items; eat one, carefully avoid the other. Thus similarity and contiguity both play important roles in the Image. Even our plans are reflected in our Image of the environment, as our own activities take place in that environment and are thus incorporated reflexively in the Image.

A cultural Plan is a complex entity, a hierarchical organization of subplans each dominating either a sequence of subsidiary activities or a set of alternatives from which a choice of action must be made (Randall 1977). It is possible to move around in the cultural Plan by systematic questioning, using basic question frames, which are probably linguistic universals. For example, why? moves "the cursor" upward; how? moves it downward through the Plan hierarchy. Each subplan, whether step or alternative, may be expressed as a natural language sentence in which the action or state is indicated by a verbal predicate, the arguments of which include associated actors, objects, implements, and settings indicated by nominal elements marked for case— candidates for status as linguistic universals (Fillmore 1968).

## CONCLUSIONS

I have argued for an ethnoecology that unites cognitive anthropology and cultural and evolutionary ecology. I believe this approach answers the most important criticisms that have been raised against each field. Cognitive anthropology's focus on the individual actor who, guided by cultural knowledge, designs a plan for living, is joined with the ecologists' appreciation of the complex web of mutual influence linking individuals and the elements of their natural and social environments. Ecology may also contribute a vision of the encompassing evolutionary processes that govern all life. Cognitive anthropology contributes a method and conceptual framework for understanding the powerful role of culture in evolution. Culture is seen to be an evolutionary mechanism in its own right, capable of independent replication and subject to selection processes distinct from those governing genetically coded information (Dawkins 1976; Durham 1982; Boyd and Richerson 1985), transformed by the power of human language as a medium of symbolic communication.

I have offered a series of examples to illustrate the application of this view of culture to phenomena of ecological significance. In these examples I have sketched the outline of a theory of culture as a symbolic means for adapting to a changing environment. The theory is closely related to models of human understanding developed in the study of artificial intelligence and in cognitive psychology but is informed by the wider perspective of ethnography. I believe we cannot hope to understand cultural evolution adequately without such a theory of human understanding based in human language use, for that is the locus of the cultural analog of DNA.

The model of culture sketched here is an organization of ideas. The ideas are concatenated in a variety of data structures in memory, both semantic and episodic. Episodic structures, called variously "scripts" or "plans," are stressed here, as they reflect in the Image our experience of significant events as well as the cultural plans that we use to construct our behavior. There is a necessary parallel between the structure of such plans and the structure of sentences in natural language, as human language is the primary means we have of representing to ourselves the reality to which we must adapt.

Detailed and particularistic ethnographic description will be necessary as the basis for generalizations about the effectiveness of cultural practices. The analysis of specific cultural plans should also reveal recurrent patterns of form and content relevant to our understanding of cultural evolutionary processes. Cultural evolution is ultimately the result of changes in the way individuals choose to pursue the goals set by their cultural Plan, changes that may subsequently alter the goals themselves. Cultural evolution is a process sensitive to nuances of environmental variation continuously reflected in the cultural Image. By such a process our ancestors may have been led to substitute—step-by-step—agricultural strategies for those of hunting and gathering, as Pacific Northwest Indians substituted the white man's potatoes for the native camas and planting of crops for the care of stands of wild plants (Suttles 1951). Likewise, market production superseded subsistence production, and wage labor in cities overcame household production. In sum, I believe our comprehension of the course of human history requires that we first understand cultural adaptation in terms of human individuals engaged in the familiar routines of everyday life.

## REFERENCES

Abelson, Robert P.
  1981    "Psychological Status of the Script Concept." *American Psychologist* 36:715–29.
  1976    "Script Processing in Attitude Formation and Decision Making." In *Cognition and Social Behavior*, J. S. Carroll and L. W. Payne, eds. Hillsdale, NJ: Lawrence Erlbaum.
Agar, Michael
  1974    "Talking About Doing: Lexicon and Event." *Language in Society* 3:83–89.
Basso, Keith
  1972    "Ice and Travel among the Ft. Norman Slave: Folk Taxonomies and Cultural Rules." *Language and Society* 1:31–49.
Berlin, Brent
  1978    "Ethnobiological Classification." In *Cognition and Categorization*, E. Rosch and B. Lloyd, eds. Hillsdale, NJ: Lawrence Erlbaum.
  1976    "The Concept of Rank in Ethnobiological Classification: Some Evidence from Aguaruna Folk Botany." *American Ethnologist* 3:381–99.
Berlin, Brent, Dennis E. Breedlove, and Peter H. Raven
  1973    "General Principles of Classification and Nomenclature in Folk Biology." *American Anthropologist* 75:214–42.

Boulding, Kenneth E.
1956    *The Image: Knowledge in Life and Society.* Ann Arbor: University of Michigan Press.
Boyd, Robert, and Peter J. Richerson
1985    *Culture and the Evolutionary Process.* Chicago: University of Chicago Press.
Bruner, Jerome S., Jacqueline J. Goodnow, and George A. Austin
1956    *A Study of Thinking.* New York: Wiley.
Casson, Ronald W.
1983    "Schemata in Cognitive Anthropology." *Annual Review of Anthropology* 12:429–62.
Cavalli-Sforza, Luigi, and Marcus Feldman
1981    *Cultural Transmission and Evolution.* Princeton, NJ: Princeton University Press.
Chomsky, Noam
1959    "A Review of *Verbal Behavior* by B. F. Skinner." *Language* 35:26–58.
Cloak, F. T., Jr.
1975    "Is a Cultural Ethology Possible?" *Human Ecology* 3:161–82.
Dawkins, Richard
1976    *The Selfish Gene.* New York: Oxford University Press.
Durham, William H.
1982    "Interactions of Genetic and Cultural Evolution: Models and Examples." *Human Ecology* 10:289–323.
1979    "Toward a Co-Evolutionary Theory of Human Biology and Culture." In *Evolutionary Biology and Human Social Behavior*, N. Chagnon and W. Irons, eds. North Scituate, MA: Duxbury.
Fillmore, Charles J.
1977    "The Case for Case Reopened." In *Syntax and Semantics.* Vol. 8, *Grammatical Relations*, P. Cole and J. Sadock, eds. New York: Academic.
1968    "The Case for Case." In *Universals in Linguistic Theory*, E. Bach and R. Harms, eds. New York: Holt, Rinehart & Winston.
Fowler, Catherine
1977    "Ethnoecology." In *Ecological Anthropology*, D. Hardesty, ed. New York: Wiley.
Frake, Charles O.
1962    "Cultural Ecology and Ethnography." *American Anthropologist* 64:53–59.
Freilich, Morris
1980    "Smart-Sex and Proper-Sex: A Paradigm Found." *General Issues in Anthropology* 2:37–51.
Geertz, Clifford
1973    *The Interpretation of Cultures.* New York: Basic.
Geoghegan, William H.
1973    *Natural Information Processing Systems. Monographs of the Language-Behavior Research Laboratory.* Berkeley: University of California.
1970    "Residential Decision Making among the Eastern Samal." Paper presented to the Symposium on Mathematical Anthropology, 69th Annual Meeting of the American Anthropological Association, San Diego.

Gladwin, Christina H.
1980   "A Theory of Real Life Choice: Applications to Agricultural Decisions."
In *Agricultural Decision Making: Anthropological Contributions to Rural
Development*, P. Barlett, ed. New York: Academic.

Goodenough, Ward H.
1957   "Cultural Anthropology and Linguistics." In *Report of the Seventh
Annual Round Table Meeting on Linguistics and Language Study*, P. L.
Garvin, ed. Georgetown University Monograph Series on Languages and
Linguistics, No. 9. Washington, DC.

Harris, Marvin
1979   *Cultural Materialism: The Struggle for a Science of Culture*. New York:
Random House.
1974   "Why a Perfect Knowledge of All the Rules One Must Know to Act Like
a Native Cannot Lead to the Knowledge of How Natives Act." *Journal
of Anthropological Research* 30:242–51.

Hunn, Eugene S.
1982   "The Utilitarian Factor in Folk Biological Classification." *American
Anthropologist* 84:830–47.
1976   "Toward a Perceptual Model of Folk Biological Classification." *American
Ethnologist* 3:508–24.

Kay, Paul
1971   "Taxonomy and Semantic Contrast." *Language* 47:866–87.
1970   "Some Theoretical Implications of Ethnographic Semantics." In *Current
Directions in Anthropology*, Bulletins of the American Anthropological
Association 3(3, part 2).

Keesing, Roger
1974   "Theories of Culture." *Annual Review of Anthropology* 3:73–98.

Konlande, J. E., and J. R. K. Robson
1972   "The Nutritive Value of Cooked Camas as Consumed by Flathead
Indians." *Ecology of Food and Nutrition* 2:193–95.

Miller, George A, Eugene Galanter, and Karl H. Pribram
1960   *Plans and the Structure of Behavior*. New York: Holt, Rinehart &
Winston.

Neisser, Ulrich
1975   *Cognition and Reality: Principles and Implications of Cognitive
Psychology*. San Francisco: Freeman.

Ortner, Sherry B.
1984   "Theory in Anthropology since the Sixties." *Comparative Studies in
Society and History* 26:126–66.

Pike, Kenneth
1956   "Towards a Theory of the Structure of Human Behavior." In *Estudios
Publicados en Homenaje al Doctor Manuel Gamio*. Mexico, D.F.: Sociedad
Mexicana de Antropologia.

Pulliam, H. Ronald, and C. Dunford
1980   *Programmed to Learn: An Essay on the Evolution of Culture*. New York:
Columbia University Press.

Randall, Robert A.
1987    "Plans and Planning in Cross-Cultural Settings." In *Blueprints for Thinking: The Role of Planning in Psychological Development*, S. L. Friedman, E. K. Scholnick, and R. R. Cocking, eds. New York: Cambridge University Press.
1977    "Change and Variation in Samal Fishing: Making Plans to 'Make a Living' in the Southern Philippines." Ph.D. diss. University of California, Berkeley.
1976    "How Tall Is a Taxonomic Tree? Some Evidence for Dwarfism." *American Ethnologist* 3:543–53.
Randall, Robert A, and Eugene S. Hunn
1984    "Do Life Forms Evolve or Do Uses for Life? Some Doubts About Brown's Universals Hypotheses." *American Ethnologist* 11:329–49.
Richerson, Peter J.
1977    "Ecology and Human Ecology: A Comparison of Theories in the Biological and Social Sciences." *American Ethnologist* 4:1–26.
Richerson, Peter J., and Robert Boyd
1989    "A Darwinian Theory for the Evolution of Symbolic Cultural Traits." In *The Relevance of Culture*, M. Freilich, ed. New York: Bergin & Garvey, pp. 121–141.
Rosch, Eleanor
1978    "Principles of Categorization." In *Cognition and Categorization*, E. Rosch and B. Lloyd, eds. Hillsdale, NJ: Lawrence Erlbaum.
Ruyle, Eugene E.
1973    "Genetic and Cultural Pools: Some Suggestions for a Unified Theory of Biocultural Evolution." *Human Ecology* 1:201–15.
Schank, Roger
1975    *Conceptual Information Processing.* Amsterdam: North Holland.
Schank, Roger, and Robert Abelson
1977    *Scripts, Plans, Goals, and Understanding.* Hillsdale, NJ: Lawrence Erlbaum.
Silverstein, Michael
1976    "Shifters, Linguistic Categories, and Cultural Description." In *Meaning in Anthropology*, K. Basso and H. Selby, eds. Albuquerque: University of New Mexico Press.
Smith, Eric A.
1984    "Anthropology, Evolutionary Ecology, and the Explanatory Limitations of the Ecosystem Concept." In *The Ecosystem Concept in Anthropology*, E. F. Moran, ed. American Association for the Advancement of Science Selected Symposia Series. Boulder, CO: Westview Press.
Sturtevant, William C.
1964    "Studies in Ethnoscience." In *Transcultural Studies in Cognition*, A. K. Romney and R. G. D'Andrade, eds. *American Anthropologist* 66 (3, part 2): 99–131.
Suttles, Wayne
1951    "The Early Diffusion of the Potato among the Coast Salish." *Southwestern Journal of Anthropology* 7:272–88.

# Biocultural Implications of Systems of Color Naming

Paul Kay
Brent Berlin
William Merrifield

This article presents a brief report on some recent findings of the World Color Survey (WCS) and more generally on the implications of those findings for larger questions involving the relation of biological and cultural systems.

The field procedures employed by the WCS involve assessing the color naming systems of 25 speakers from each language in an interview that takes about two hours per speaker. The experimental session includes eliciting the speaker's judgment regarding the most appropriate simple name of 329 distinct color chips as well as eliciting the favored designation of the focal chip or chips for each of the basic color terms employed. The present report represents the preliminary analysis of data from 111 languages. We must emphasize that these analyses are not final and that additional checking may change some details of the overall picture. The main lines are, however, established with sufficient clarity to warrant this report. Unfortunately, there will be no time to discuss analytical procedures and problems, of which there are many, nor to consider other methodological issues.

## BIOLOGICAL AND CULTURAL SYSTEMS: THE FRAMEWORK OF THE RESEARCH

Cultural anthropology is afflicted with two opposing and unyielding dogmas. Radical cultural relativism holds that cultures are not comparable and that culture is entirely independent of biology. Radical biological determinism holds that all the phenomena we unreflectingly call cultural or social can be reduced to biology. Each dogma has a more polite version, which eschews crude quantifiers like "all" and talks instead about "the more interesting phenomena," or "currently pressing research priorities," but this kind of rhetorical patina does not, nor is it really intended to, disguise the narrow and monolithic character of the two doctrines.

Ideology aside, what do we know of the relevant facts? First, we know that behavior across human groups is underlain by a common biological substrate. Except for certain geographically circumscribed medical pathologies, there is virtually no evidence linking important cultural variation to differences in biology. On the other hand, substantial intercultural and intersocial variation exists: ethnography was born as the attempt of science to deal with this brute fact.

In the perspective adopted here, it is unproductive to point either to the common biology of humankind or to the variability of human culture in an attempt to deny the existence of the other. Rather, anthropology can make a contribution to science by attempting to discover what limits common human biology sets on possible intercultural variation, what the dimensions of that variation are, and what the possible parameters on those dimensions may be. When the anthropologist can go beyond this and discover which biologically exogenous factors determine the particular parameters of cultural variation in particular times and places our subject will be contributing significantly to scientific understanding.

What does work on the tightly circumscribed topic of color naming have to do with such grand issues? Briefly, this is an area in which (1) constraints on intercultural variation have been discovered (for example, Berlin and Kay 1969), (2) much has been discovered independently of anthropology regarding the *prima facie* relevant biological substrate: color vision (for example, De Valois et al. 1966), and (3) some reasonably precise generalizations have been proposed relating (1) and (2) (for example, Kay and McDaniel 1978). The current, tentative findings of the World Color Survey support and explain some parts of the Berlin-Kay-McDaniel model and challenge other parts of it. We have today some new data, some explanations of existing generalizations, and some new questions to consider.

The data presented here will be oriented toward two related though distinguishable issues. The first, covered in the section immediately following, is concerned with establishing the inventory of possible composite color categories and with explaining, insofar as possible, just why these composite categories and no others are to be found in the world's languages. The next section will be concerned specifically with the recently demonstrated, albeit long-known, existence of composite categories that associate yellow and green and with the implications of color systems containing yellow-green categories for the early stages in the evolution of basic color vocabulary.

## WHAT ARE THE POSSIBLE COMPOSITE COLOR CATEGORIES AND WHY DO ONLY THESE OCCUR?

Kay and McDaniel (1978) introduced the term "composite" to refer to named color categories that comprise more than one of the colors that have been established by neurobiologists, independently of language, to correspond to fundamentally distinct neural response processes (De Valois et al. 1966). These fundamental neural response categories (hereafter FNRs) correspond quite closely to the denotations of the English words *black, white, red, yellow, green,* and *blue* and to their translations into many other languages. Berlin and Kay

(1969) recognized the existence of composite categories implicitly, for example in their positing the category RED, comprising red, yellow, and other warm hues. The phenomenon in question was of course recognized much earlier, being reflected in an extensive 19th-century literature dealing with the so-called color confusions of so-called primitives. Of the principal 19th-century writers on this subject, only the German ophthalmologist, Hugo Magnus, seems to have entertained clearly the possibility that a language might give a single name to two fundamental colors even though the speakers' color vision were identical to his own (see Berlin and Kay 1969:139). Although the 19th-century literature was neglected in American anthropology of the first half of this century, anthropologists concerned with language and field linguists in the New World and elsewhere nonetheless frequently documented color names for categories comprising more than one of the six basic FNR categories.

The specific contribution of Kay and McDaniel in this area was to note that the named categories which lump fundamental sensations always comprise (the fuzzy union of) some subset of the six FNR categories. Kay and McDaniel did not, however, attempt to explain why, out of the 63 logically possible, non-null subsets of the six fundamentals, only a small number of actual composite categories occur empirically. With the new World Color Survey data, we have reason to suspect that we may be getting close to documenting all the composite categories that can in principle be denoted by a basic color term of a human language. . . .

Consider Figure 1. The six nodes represent the six FNR categories. The horizontal and vertical lines connecting these nodes represent adjacency in perceptual color space. On the horizontal dimension of the diagram are represented the sequential, pairwise subjective adjacencies of hue. Subjectively, red shades gradually, through orange into yellow. Similarly, yellow shades gradually, through chartreuse or lime, into green, and green shades gradually, through turquoise, into blue.

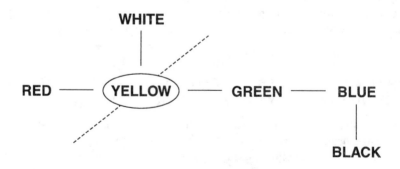

FIGURE 1
Visual and Linguistic Relations among FNR Categories

The vertical dimension of the diagram represents the subjective dimension of lightness. The privileged association of yellow with white is justified, since perceptual yellow is not only defined as a certain hue but also as the bright colors of that hue. As the array shows, in contrast to red, green, and blue, yellow is an inherently light color. With regard, however, to the association shown on the diagram between blue and black, we have as yet found no comparable justification in vision science. That is, the semantics of the world's languages show a privileged association of black and blue, in contrast to red, yellow, and green, for which we would like to find independent warrant in the vision literature.

There remains to be explained the significance of the oblique, dotted line through yellow. This indicates, at the semantic level, that while yellow may be associated in a composite category with, on the one hand, either red or white or both and, on the other hand, with green and through green to colors extending to the right in the diagram, no composite category has been found that crosses the dotted line. For example, there is no attested basic color term in any language that includes green, yellow, and red or that includes green, yellow, and white. This finding strikes many people as intuitively natural: yellow may either be grouped with red or white or both as a warm, arousing color or it may be grouped with green and other cool, soothing colors, but not both simultaneously. However, despite this intuitive plausibility we are not aware of any concrete evidence in the vision literature to justify, independently of our semantic findings, the dotted line through yellow. Until such justification is discovered this aspect of the diagram, like the blue-black association, remains arbitrary with regard to our knowledge of the visual system.

The preceding discussion has implicitly covered the interpretation of Figure 1. The diagram indicates subjective pairwise associations of the neurologically defined fundamental neural color responses at the level of color vision, that is, at a level of neural organization shared by all higher primates, at least. Our interpretation of the diagram derives from these language independent associations of color sensations a rule that predicts which composite basic color categories can be encoded in the lexicon of a language.

**Composite Category Rule:** A possible composite category is any fuzzy union of a subset of fundamental neural response categories which, in Figure 1, forms an unbroken associational chain not crossing the diagonal line.

This rule sets an empirical limit of 9 on the 63 logically possible composite categories, that is, those that might be formed from all possible subsets of the six FNRs. In Table 1, each row corresponds to one of these nine. Of the nine possible composite categories now predicted to occur, Kay and McDaniel recognized four empirically and did not attempt any theoretical explanation of that inventory. The four recognized by Kay and McDaniel are given in the second column of the table: red/white/yellow and green/blue each contain three FNRs; red/yellow and green/blue each contain two FNRs.

| No. of FNR CATs included | In Kay and McDaniel 1978 | Not in Kay and McDaniel 1978 | Now attested |
|---|---|---|---|
| 4 | | Y/G/Bu/Bk | No |
| 3 | R/W/Y | | Yes |
| 3 | G/Bu/Bk | | Yes |
| 3 | | Y/G/Bu | Yes |
| 2 | R/Y | | Yes |
| 2 | G/Bu | | Yes |
| 2 | | W/Y | Yes |
| 2 | | Y/G | Yes |
| 2 | | Bu/Bk | Yes |

TABLE 1
Categories Predicted to Occur by Composite Category Rule

In addition to the four composite categories recognized by Kay and McDaniel, four more of the nine predicted by the Composite Category Rule are attested in the WCS data. These are the three-FNR category yellow/green/blue and the three two-FNR categories white/yellow, yellow/green and blue/black. No other composite color categories are attested in the WCS data. That is, there are no attested composite categories that do not conform to the Composite Category Rule. There is, however, exactly one composite category that does not conform to the rule which is not attested in the WCS data. That is the unique four-FNR category: yellow/green/blue/black.

A *posteriori*, it is easy enough to provide a theoretical rationale for the nonattestation of yellow/green/blue/black. One might suppose, for example, that four FNRs is somehow too many for a psychologically computable composite category to contain. It is also plausible that no composite category can include both yellow, which is inherently light, and black.[1] In any case, in our current state of ignorance it is impossible to make a reasoned choice whether the four-FNR composite should be ruled out on theoretical grounds or simply considered sufficiently rare empirically as to have escaped getting into our sample. In support of the latter hypothesis is the fact that any color system that contained such a category would necessarily be at a very early stage of evolution and such systems are almost certainly, perhaps by definition, less frequent today than they once were. On the other side is the observation that a system that contained a category of this type would, according to the hypotheses embodied in the diagram and rule, have to consist of three terms: red, white, and yellow/green/blue/black. But we have no hint in our data of an observed system that shows traces of this kind of history. Many documented systems show vestiges that provide clues to their past, but nothing of this

---

[1] A similar comment, however, might be registered about the attested three-FNR composite category yellow/green/blue, which contains the opponent categories blue and yellow.

sort in the data suggests an earlier system consisting of a white category, a red category, and a yellow/green/blue/black category.

To summarize this section, the diagram in Figure 1 is largely, if not entirely, motivated by known properties of the visual system. Our rule for predicting from this diagram the possible composite color categories of the world's languages yields nine types of composite color category. Eight of these nine are now empirically attested and, significantly, no composite category outside of these nine is empirically attested. The one predicted but unattested type is the unique four-FNR composite. The vagueness of the current model on whether this nonattestation should be interpreted as an impossible versus a low probability event does not seem a serious embarrassment. The more serious lacunae in the story concern the blue-black association and the pivotal role of yellow. Modulo the latter two unresolved problems, we can go a substantial way in predicting the composite color categories of the world's languages from properties of color vision that are independent of culture and of language, biological properties which are in fact independent of human experience per se, being widespread in genera other than *Homo*.[2]

## YELLOW-GREEN CATEGORIES AND THE EARLY STAGES OF BASIC COLOR TERM EVOLUTION

Categories including yellow and green did not show up in the original Berlin and Kay data report in 1969. Shortly thereafter, however, communications were received from field linguists, in particular Mary Haas and Dale Kinkade, attesting to the existence of such categories in languages they had studied (specifically in Muscogean and Salishan languages, respectively). Some of the possible implications for the evolutionary sequence of basic color vocabularies that include such categories were considered in Kay (1975) and mentioned in Kay and McDaniel (1978). The first full documentations of systems with a yellow/green category in studies using controlled stimuli were reported by MacLaury in 1986 (see also MacLaury 1987) for several Salishan and Wakashan languages of the Northwest Coast. The data of the WCS add several new cases of yellow/green categories to these. It is now indisputable that composite categories comprising yellow and green exist. It is equally clear that they are rare. Many mysteries surround the evolution of systems displaying this distinctly minority choice in category composition.

Figure 2 displays a summary of the languages in the World Color Survey having five or fewer basic color terms, that is, belonging to the first four evolutionary stages. Each column in the figure corresponds to a stage.

With regard to the principal new findings of the WCS about later stages (that

---

[2] The attestation of the yellow/green/blue category, as mentioned in note 1, must also be registered as a surprise, since it comprises the two opponent colors yellow and blue.

is, those not shown), these can be briefly summarized by saying (1) that green/blue may persist, undissolved, even after brown, purple, or both have been accorded basic color terms and (2) that there appears to be no fixed ordering to the temporal appearance of brown and purple.

In Figure 2, the top two rows represent those WCS data that conform to, but do not extend, the Kay and McDaniel model. At stage I, with two composite terms—white/red/yellow and green/blue/black—the parentheses indicate that the WCS data per se do not contain any attestation of this or any other type of two-term system. That such systems exist is, however, not in doubt. Several cases have been reported elsewhere, including the Dani of New Guinea, extensively documented by E. Rosch (Heider 1972a, b).

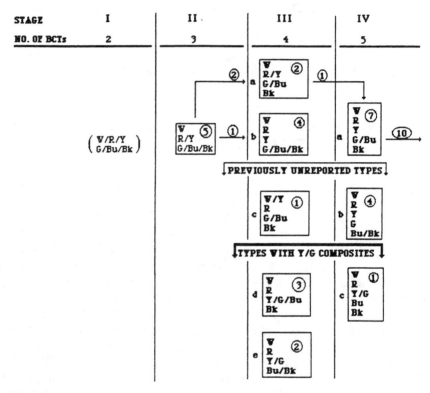

FIGURE 2
Early Stages of Basic Color Term Evolution

Circled numerals denote the number of languages of the boxed type attested in the WCS data. For example, there is only one type of stage II language—white, red/yellow, and green/blue/black; five languages of this type are attested in the data.

Headed arrows connecting two types indicate languages in transition between the two types. Briefly, a language is in transition between two types if some of the speakers are of one type and some of the other. Thus there were two languages for which the WCS sample included both speakers of stage II and speakers of stage IIIa, the latter containing terms for white, red/yellow, green/blue, and black. There is no need to discuss here stages IIIb and IVa, as they have been discussed in earlier literature.

We are now ready to consider types of early-stage color terminologies that occur in the WCS data which were previously undocumented. The third row of Figure 2 shows two types of system, one four-term and one five-term. Neither involves a yellow-green association and therefore they need not detain us long. Type IIIc is notable for being the only instance of a reported white/yellow composite, excluding red. Type IVb is notable for clearly documenting the previously undiscovered blue/black composite, of which, incidentally, we will see further instances presently.

We are now in a position to consider language containing a term associating yellow and green. These are displayed in the bottom two rows of Figure 2. The WCS data contain six languages with the yellow-green property. There are no yellow-green languages that are transitional between two types (i.e., there are no arrows). This is unfortunate in that transitional languages, if we had them, could give us important information on the evolutionary trajectory of yellow-green systems.

There are two types of four-term systems containing a category associating yellow and green. Type IIId contains, along with terms for white, red and black, a composite category comprising yellow, green, and blue. This pattern is attested in three languages. The other four-term, yellow-green system, type IIIe, contains the yellow/green composite and the blue/black composite discussed earlier, as well as terms for white and for red. This type is attested twice.

Also attested in the WCS data is one stage IV or five-term system, type IVc, with terms for white, red, blue, black, and yellow/green. An earlier attestation of this type of system is given by MacLaury's (1987) description of Shuswap.

## THE PUZZLE OF THE YELLOW-GREEN ASSOCIATION

Since there are six FNRs, composite terms must occur in any language with five or fewer basic color terms (BCTs). In fact composite terms also occur in languages with as many as seven basic color terms. But composites associating yellow and green occur only in languages with four or five basic color terms. That is, only the three yellow-green types shown in Figure 2 occur. Even among languages of four or five basic color terms, yellow-green systems constitute a distinct minority: 7 out of 37, or less than 20%. Yet there is no question that the phenomenon is real: the WCS has six clear cases (with many speakers for each language). In addition we have experimentally based accounts of at least four languages of the Northwest Coast already cited (MacLaury 1986, 1987). Moreover, Kinkade (1988) states, "Yellow and green are expressed by a single term (opposed to blue) in at least the following Salishan languages. Sechelt, Chilliwack Halkomelem, Northern Straits, Nooksack, Lushootseed . . . Quinalt, Lower Chehalis, Upper Chehalis, Cowlitz, Lillooet, Thompson, and Shuswap, and probably also in Comox and Pentlach."

In the simplest terms, this is the puzzle: how can yellow and green be associated in a single composite at stage III when they are not so associated at stage II? That is, how do yellow and green come to be associated in languages with four basic color terms, when we have no direct evidence of a language with three or fewer basic color terms that contains a term associating yellow and green? There seem to be three possibilities, *a priori*. None of them is particularly plausible, yet it would seem that one of them has to be right.

## Simultaneous Splitting and Recombining

Let us consider what would have to happen for a type such as II to evolve directly into a type such as IIIe. Since yellow and green are associated in a single composite category at IIIe, in the transition from II to IIIe the red/yellow and green/blue/black categories of type II would have to split, liberating yellow and green respectively. Yellow and green would then have to recombine into yellow/green as it appears in IIIe. This scenario is unlikely, since we have no evidence of this kind of split-plus-recombination ever happening in cases that do not involve a yellow-green association. For that matter, even if we set splitting aside, outside of languages with a yellow-green association there is not even indirect evidence of combining alone ever taking place (that is, of composite categories being formed from separately established FNR categories). The entire thrust of basic color term evolution seems to consist of two movements: (1) the progressive splitting of composite categories into the FNR categories and (2) the formation of derived or compromise categories from established FNR categories: for example, the formation of orange from previously established red and yellow.

Note that the formation of a compromise category like orange, which denotes not red *or* yellow but red *and* yellow, and whose existence presupposes that red and yellow continue as named categories, is unlike the hypothetical formation from separately established yellow and green of a yellow/green composite category, which would cover all of yellow and green and by definition henceforth preclude the separate existence of basic yellow and green categories. The creation of derived categories does not involve lumping or neutralization of contrast; it consists in naming the intersection of two overlapping, gradient categories, each of which continues to be separately recognized.

Categories that are gradient and overlapping, as color categories often are, permit a possibility for the formation of new categories which nongradient, mutually exclusive categories do not. For a pair of psychologically adjacent categories, whether or not they are overlapping there is always the hypothetical possibility of simply lumping them, that is, neutralizing the distinction between them. In this case a new category would be recognized which comprehended everything that was previously included in either of the two prior categories, while these would no longer be recognized or would be recognized only at a lower level of generalization. (Whether or not this actually occurs outside the domain of color we are not in a position to speculate on, but in the color domain we have recorded no evidence of it.) With overlapping categories, however, there is a distinct possibility: that of recognizing the area of overlap as a new category at the same level of generality as the originals. Such is the case, for example, with the recognition of a derived basic color category such as orange. Since red and yellow overlap in a gradient fashion, we can form the category orange—that is, red and yellow—while maintaining the categories and yellow exactly as before.

Available information on color category formation shows no direct evidence of new categories arising through neutralization or lumping but it does show substantial evidence of formation of new categories through recognition of overlap. If lumping occurs in the development of color systems, we should by now have observed some direct evidence of it. We have no such direct evidence, but instead only some quite tenuous, indirect evidence, specifically involving yellow/green categories, to which we will return presently.

## Missing Data

Given both the rarity of composite categories associating yellow and green and the rarity of three- and two-term systems in general, it is possible that we have just by chance failed to run across a system representing the intersection of these two rare events: a two- or three-term system with a composite category associating yellow and green.

Yet even if we permit ourselves to imagine any data we like, there can be no simple story based on missing data, since yellow and green are dissociated not only in all the attested stage II data but also in all attested stage I data. That is, as far as existing data go, yellow and green are dissociated from the start. If missing data are to be the explanation for the origin of yellow/green categories, those data will have to go back to stage I: there will have to be a system with no previous history that associates yellow and green. But, if the Composite Category Rule is to survive this hypothetical discovery, there is no possible two-term system that can associate yellow and green in the same term, since white and red are linked only through yellow and so must each constitute a separate category if yellow is associated with green. Hence, the only possible precursor to the attested four-term yellow-green types IIId and IIIe would be a hypothetical type we discussed briefly in the beginning of this article, when we considered the theoretically possible but empirically absent four-FNR composite: yellow/green/blue/black. Specifically, the only theoretically possible precursor to IIId and IIIe which does not involve recombination would be a three-term system consisting of a red term, a white term, and a single term comprising green, yellow, blue and black. If such a system could be found it would thus solve two mysteries: first, why just one of the nine theoretically possible composite categories does not figure in the attested data and, second, where yellow-green systems come from.

## No History for Types IIId and IIIe

The Just-So Story we have told, ending with the stage I, three-term system consisting of red, white, and yellow/green/blue/black, acknowledges as possible that not all basic color lexicons trace ultimate ancestry to a two-term system but rather may have a three-term system as their ultimate ancestor. This line of thinking might be extended to eliminate all the hypothetical data by assuming simply that the problematical IIId and IIIe systems themselves had no histories. This seems implausible for a variety of reasons, but must be admitted as a logical possibility. Nothing guarantees that every observed color system descends ultimately from one having only two BCTs. On the other hand, given the orderliness of the evolutionary data in all respects other than those having to do with yellow/green categories, positing that systems of types IIId and IIIe simply have no history seems more a confession of bewilderment than a solution to the mystery.

## Splitting and Lumping Again

We return now to the suggestive, indirect data for the splitting and relumping hypothesis, discussed at the end of the section on simultaneous splitting and recombining. MacLaury (1986), MacLaury and Galloway (1988) and MacLaury (personal communication) report evidence that some of the five-term, IVc systems they have observed (with terms for white, red, blue, black, and yellow/green) may have evolved, not from either the four-term types with a yellow/green category documented in the WCS (IIId, IIIe) but rather from IIIa systems, which contain terms for white, black, red/yellow, and green/blue (notably lacking yellow/green composites). The evidence is that some older speakers of these languages in fact currently display such IIIa systems. The data are not extensive and other conjectures are possible. Kinkade (1988), for example, reconstructs a yellow/green/blue category for proto-Salish, while MacLaury claims that (1) in Halkomelem an original green/blue term was extended to yellow and simultaneously retracted from blue (MacLaury and Galloway 1988; MacLaury personal communication) while (2) in Shuswap an original red/yellow term was extended to green and simultaneously retracted from red (MacLaury 1986).

A careful look at Indo-European might be rewarding in this regard, although finely tuned semantic reconstruction at such a time depth is fraught with peril. It seems reasonably well established that one of the few basic color terms of ancient Greek, *khlôros*, probably denoted a yellow/green category, while Latin *uiridis* undoubtedly denoted a blue/green category. The implications of these facts, if they are facts, would be that whether proto-Indo-European (PIE) associated green with yellow à la Greek or with blue à La Latin, if it did not associate all three in a single category as IIId languages do, there must have been splitting and relumping between PIE and either Latin or Greek. There is, however, troubling methodological indeterminacy in the fixing precisely the colors denoted by reconstructed color terms, even when one knows with fair certainty their denotations in attested daughter languages. Thus, modern English *black* and *blue* share a common etymon with each other and with modern French *blanc(he)* "white." There is a story about this, but it is a long one. An essential methodological problem with looking to PIE in the yellow/green case is that a guiding theory of what is a reasonable semantic reconstruction from known glosses in daughter languages is required for accurate semantic reconstruction, but the effort here is precisely to derive a theory of plausible semantic change from the "facts" of inheritance from the reconstructed protolanguage.

The role of yellow/green categories in the early stages of color term evolution is not yet well understood.

## CONCLUSION

The wider range of data in the WCS has confirmed the main lines of the original hypotheses of Berlin and Kay regarding the existence of semantic universals in basic color lexicons and a system of partial constraints on the evolutionary development of basic color vocabularies. With regard to the Kay and McDaniel model, which attempts to relate these generalizations to visual physiology, the WCS data enable us to take further steps toward a comprehensive account of why we find in the languages of the world just the inventory of composite categories that we do find.

The existence of composite categories associating yellow and green FNRs, claimed very early by Haas and by Kincade, has now been documented experimentally by MacLaury and associates and in six independent cases in the WCS data. The phenomenon is unquestionably rare but also unquestionably real.

How yellow/green composites and the systems that contain them arise in the evolutionary sequence remains a mystery and one to which color term research should devote energy in the future. Some of the possibilities this research might pursue have been discussed.

More broadly, we may observe that the cultural construction of simple color categories is in several respects constrained by biology. We have seen that the semantics of basic color words in the straightforward expression of visual experience is partially constrained by parameters of the visual system. No comparable demonstration exists, however, regarding the semantics of color words in the kinds of ritual, symbolic, and metaphorical contexts with which much of contemporary cultural anthropology primarily concerns itself. And even in the relatively concrete semantic area that we have considered, it is clear that the color system of a given language at a certain moment can assume a large number of forms while remaining within the limits set by biology.

The evolutionary sequence, of which we have considered in this article only the early stages, gives a certain degree of welcome structure to the latter area of variation. We have also acquired some knowledge relating parameters of the visual system to the shape of possible stages in that sequence; the constraints on possible composite categories that we have discussed exemplify the latter advances in knowledge. Nevertheless, gaps, anomalies, and perplexities abound.

It is perhaps in showing a measure of *detail* regarding both the correspondence and the noncorrespondence of cultural to biological variables that research on color semantics may throw light on broader issues regarding the relation between biology and culture. To the extent that we may judge from the present state of research on color term meanings and their biological basis, sweeping conclusions of any kind in the area of culture and biology appear unwarranted by currently available facts.

## REFERENCES

Berlin, B., and P. Kay
  1969    Basic Color Terms: Their Universality and Evolution. Berkeley: University of California Press.
De Valois, R. L., I. Abramov, and G. H. Jacobs
  1966    Analysis of Response Patterns of LGN Cells. Journal of the Optical Society of America 56:966–977.
Heider, E. R. [E. H. Rosch]
  1972a  Probabilities, Sampling, and Ethnographic Method: The Case of Dani Colour Names. Man (n.s.)7:448–466.
  1972b  Universals in Color Naming and Memory. Journal of Experimental Psychology 93:10–20.
Kay, P.
  1975    Synchronic Variation and Diachronic Change in Basic Color Terms. Language in Society 4:257–270.
Kay, P., and C. K. McDaniel
  1978    The Linguistic Significance of the Meanings of Basic Color Terms. Language 54:610–646.
Kinkade, D.
  1988    Proto Salishan Colors. In In Honor of Mary Haas: From the Haas Festival Conference on Native American Linguistics. W. Shipley, ed. Berlin: Mouton de Gruyter.
MacLaury, R. E.
  1986    Color Categorization in Shuswap, Chilcotin, Kwak'wala, and Makah: A Description. Proceedings of the 21st International Conference on Salish and Neighboring Languages. Seattle, Washington.
  1987    Color-Category Evolution of Shuswap Yellow-with-Green. American Anthropologist 89(1):7–124.

MacLaury, R. E., and B. Galloway
1988    Color Categories and Color Qualifiers in Halkomelem, Samish, Lushootseed, and Yakima. Proceedings of the 23rd International Conference on Salish and Neighboring Languages. Eugene, Oregon.

# Language Acquisition and Socialization: Three Developmental Stories and Their Implications

Elinor Ochs
Bambi B. Schieffelin

This selection addresses the relationship between communication and culture from the perspective of the *acquisition of* language and socialization *through language.* Heretofore the processes of language acquisition and socialization have been considered as two separate domains. Processes of language acquisition are usually seen as relatively unaffected by cultural factors such as social organization and local belief systems. These factors have been largely treated as "context," something that is *separable* from language and its acquisition. A similar attitude has prevailed in anthropological studies of socialization. The language used both *by* children and *to* children in social interactions has rarely been a source of information on socialization. As a consequence, we know little about the role that language plays in the acquisition and transmission of sociocultural knowledge. Neither the forms, the functions, nor the message content of language have been documented and examined for the ways in which they *organize* and *are organized* by culture.

Our own backgrounds in cultural anthropology and language development have led us to a more integrated perspective. Having carried out research on language in several societies (Malagasy, Bolivian, white-middle-class American, Kaluli [Papua New Guinea], and Western Samoan), focusing on the language of children and their caregivers in three of them (white middle-class American, Kaluli, Western Samoan), we have seen that the primary concern of caregivers is to ensure that their children are able to display and understand behaviors appropriate to social situations. A major means by which this is accomplished is through language. Therefore, we must examine the language of caregivers primarily for its socializing functions, rather than for only its strict grammatical input function. Further, we must examine the prelinguistic and linguistic behaviors of children to determine the ways they are continually and selectively affected by values and beliefs held by those members of society who interact with them. What a child says, and how he or she says it, will be influenced by local cultural processes in addition to biological and social processes that have universal scope. The perspective we adopt is expressed in the following two claims:

1. The process of acquiring language is deeply affected by the process of becoming a competent member of a society.
2. The process of becoming a competent member of society is realized to a large extent through language, by acquiring knowledge of its functions, social distribution, and interpretations in and across socially defined situations, i.e., through exchanges of language in particular social situations.

In this reading, we will support these claims through a comparison of social development as it relates to the communicative development of children in three societies: Anglo-American white middle class, Kaluli, and Samoan. We will present specific theoretical arguments and methodological procedures for an ethnographic approach to the development of language. Our focus at this point cannot be comprehensive, and therefore we will address developmental research that has its interests and roots in language development rather than anthropological studies of socialization. For current socialization literature, the reader is recommended to see Briggs 1970; Gallimore, Boggs, & Jordon 1974; Geertz 1959; Hamilton 1981; Harkness & Super 1980; Korbin 1978; Leiderman, Tulkin, & Rosenfeld 1977; LeVine 1980; Levy 1973; Mead & MacGregor 1951; Mead & Wolfenstein 1955; Montagu 1978; Munroe & Munroe 1975; Richards 1974; Wagner & Stevenson 1982; Weisner & Gallimore 1977; Whiting 1963; Whiting & Whiting 1975; Williams 1969; and Wills 1977.

## APPROACHES TO COMMUNICATIVE DEVELOPMENT

Whereas interest in language structure and use has been a timeless concern, the child as a language user is a relatively recent focus of scholarly interest. This interest has been located primarily in the fields of linguistics and psychology, with the wedding of the two in the establishment of developmental psycholinguistics as a legitimate academic specialization. The concern here has been the relation of language to thought, both in terms of conceptual categories and in terms of cognitive processes (such as perception, memory, recall). The child has become one source for establishing just what that relation is. More specifically, the language of the child has been examined in terms of the following issues:

1. The relation between the relative complexity of conceptual categories and the linguistic structures produced and understood by young language-learning children at different developmental stages (Bloom 1970, 1973; Bowerman 1977, 1981; Brown 1973; Clark 1974; Clark & Clark 1977; Greenfield & Smith 1976; Karmiloff-Smith 1979; MacNamara 1972; Nelson 1974; Schlessinger 1974; Sinclair 1971; Slobin 1979).

2. Processes and strategies underlying the child's construction of grammar (Bates 1976; Berko 1958; Bloom, Hood, & Lightbown 1974; Bloom, Lightbown, & Hood 1975; Bowerman 1977; Brown & Bellugi 1964; Brown, Cazden, & Bellugi 1969; Dore 1975; Ervin-Tripp 1964; Lieven 1980; MacWhinney 1975; Miller 1982; Scollon 1976; Shatz 1978; Slobin 1973).

3. The extent to which these processes and strategies are language universal or particular (Berman in press; Bowerman 1973; Brown 1973; Clancy in press; Clark in press; Johnston & Slobin 1979; MacWhinney & Bates 1978; Ochs 1982b, in press; Slobin 1981, in press; Asku & Slobin in press).

4. The extent to which these processes and strategies support the existence of a language faculty (Chomsky 1959, 1968, 1977; Fodor, Bever, & Garrett 1974; Goldin-Meadow 1977; McNeill 1970; Newport 1981; Newport, Gleitman, & Gleitman 1977; Piattelli-Palmarini 1980; Shatz 1981; Wanner & Gleitman 1982).

5. The nature of the prerequisites for language development (Bates et al. in press; Bloom 1973; Bruner 1975, 1977; Bullowa 1979; Carter 1978; de Lemos 1981; Gleason & Weintraub 1978; Golinkoff 1983; Greenfield & Smith 1976; Harding & Golinkoff 1979; Lock 1978, 1981; Sachs 1977; Shatz in press; Slobin 1973; Snow 1979; Snow & Ferguson 1977; Vygotsky 1962; Werner & Kaplan 1963).

6. Perceptual and conceptual factors that inhibit or facilitate language development (Andersen, Dunlea, & Kekelis 1982; Bever 1970; Greenfield & Smith 1976; Huttenlocher 1974; Menyuk & Menn 1979; Piaget 1955/1926; Slobin 1981; Sugarman 1984; Wanner & Gleitman 1982).

Underlying all these issues is the question of the *source* of language, in terms of not only what capacities reside within the child but the relative contributions of biology (nature) and the *social* world (nurture) to the development of language. The relation between nature and nurture has been a central theme around which theoretical positions have been oriented. B. F. Skinner's (1957) contention that the child brings relatively little to the task of learning language and that it is through responses to specific adult stimuli that language competence is attained provided a formulation that was subsequently challenged and countered by Chomsky's (1959) alternative position. This position, which has been termed nativist, innatist, rationalist (see Piattelli-Palmarini 1980), postulates that the adult verbal environment is an inadequate source for the child to inductively learn language. Rather, the rules and principles for constructing grammar have as their major source a genetically determined language faculty:

> Linguistics, then, may be regarded as that part of human psychology that is concerned with the nature, function, and origin of a particular "mental organ." We may take UG (Universal Grammar) to be a theory of the language faculty, a common human attribute, genetically determined, one component of the human mind. Through interaction with the environment, this faculty of mind becomes articulated and refined, emerging in the mature person as a system of knowledge of language. (Chomsky 1977:164)

It needs to be emphasized that an innatist approach does not eliminate the adult world as a source of linguistic knowledge; rather, it assigns a different role (vis-à-vis the behaviorist approach) to that world in the child's attainment of linguistic competence: The adult language presents the relevant information that allows the child to select from the Universal Grammar those grammatical principles specific to the particular language that the child will acquire.

One of the principal objections that could be raised is that although "the linguist's grammar is a theory of this [the child's] attained competence" (Chomsky 1977:163), there is no account of *how* this linguistic competence is attained. The theory does not relate the linguist's grammar(s) to processes of acquiring grammatical knowledge. Several psycholinguists, who have examined children's developing grammars in terms of their underlying organizing principles, have argued for similarities between these principles and those exhibited by other cognitive achievements (Bates et al. 1979; Bever 1970).

A second objection to the innatist approach has concerned its characterization of adult speech as "degenerate," fragmented, and often ill formed (McNeill 1966; Miller & Chomsky 1963). This characterization, for which there was no empirical basis, provoked a series of observational studies (including tape-recorded documentation) of the ways in which caregivers speak to their young language-acquiring children (Drach 1969; Phillips 1973; Sachs, Brown, & Salerno 1976; Snow 1972). Briefly, these studies indicated not only that adults use well-formed speech with high frequency but that they modify their speech to children in systematic ways as well. These systematic modifications, categorized as a particular speech register called baby-talk register (Ferguson 1977), include the increased (relative to other registers) use of high pitch, exaggerated and slowed intonation, a baby-talk lexicon (Garnica 1977; Sachs 1977; Snow 1972, 1977b) diminuitives, reduplicated words, simple sentences (Newport 1976), shorter sentences, interrogatives (Corsaro 1979), vocatives, talk about the "here-and-now," play and politeness routines — peek-a-boo, hi-good-bye, say "thank you" (Andersen 1977; Gleason & Weintraub 1978), cooperative expression of propositions, repetition, and expansion of one's own and the child's utterances. Many of these features are associated with the expression of positive affect, such as high pitch and diminutives. However, the greatest emphasis in the literature has been placed on these features as evidence that caregivers *simplify* their speech in addressing young children (e.g., slowing down, exaggerating intonation, simplifying sentence structure and length of utterance). The scope of the effects on grammatical development has been debated in a number of studies. Several studies have supported Chomsky's position by demonstrating that caregiver speech facilitates the acquisition of only language-specific features but not those features widely (universally) shared across languages (Feldman, Goldin-Meadow, & Gleitman 1978; Newport, Gleitman, & Gleitman 1977). Other studies, which do not restrict the role of caregiver speech to facilitating only language-specific grammatical features (Snow 1977b, 1979), report that caregivers appear to adjust their speech to a child's cognitive and linguistic capacity (Cross 1977). And as children become more competent, caregivers use fewer features of the baby-talk register. Whereas certain researchers have emphasized the direct facilitating role of caregiver speech in the acquisition of language (van der Geest 1977), others have linked the speech behavior of caregivers to the caregiver's desire to communicate with the child (Brown 1977; Snow 1977a, 1977b, 1979). In this perspective, caregivers simplify their own speech in order to make themselves understood when speaking to young children. Similarly, caregivers employ several verbal strategies to understand what the child is trying to communicate. For example, the caregiver attends to what the child is doing, where the child is looking, and the child's behavior to determine the child's communicative intentions (Foster 1981; Golinkoff 1983; Keenan, Ochs, & Schieffelin 1976). Further, caregivers often request clarification by repeating or paraphrasing the child's utterance with a questioning intonation, as in Example 1 (Bloom 1973:170):

Example 1*

| Mother | Allison (16 mos 3 wks) |
|---|---|
| (A picks up a jar, trying to open it) | more wídə̀/ə wídə̀/<br>ə wídə̀/ ə wídə̀/ |
| (A holding jar out to M) | up/ Mama/ Mama/<br>Mama ma ə wídə̀/<br>Mama Mama ə wídə̀/ |
| What, darling? | Mama wídə̀/ Mama/<br>Mama wídə̀/ Mama<br>Mama wídə̀/ |
| What do you want Mommy to do? | —/ ə wídə̀ ə wídə̀/ |
| (A gives jar to M) | —/here/ |
| (A tries to turn top on jar in M's hand) | Mama/Mama/ə wídə̀t/ |
| Open it up? | up/ |
| Open it? OK.<br>(M opens it) | |

*Examples 1–5 follow transcription conventions in Bloom and Lahey 1978.

In other cases, the caregiver facilitates communication by jointly expressing with the child a proposition. Typically, a caregiver asks a question to which the child supplies the missing information (often already known to the caregiver), as in Example 2 (Bloom 1973:153):

Example 2

| Mother | Allison |
|---|---|
| What's Mommy have (M holding cookies) | |
| (A reaching for cookie) | cookie/ |
| Cookie! OK. Here's a cookie for you<br>(A takes cookie; reaching with other hand toward others in bag) | more/ |
| There's more in here. We'll have it in a little while.<br>(A picking up bag of cookies) | bag/ |

These studies indicate that caregivers make extensive accommodations to the child, assuming the perspective of the child in the course of engaging him or her in conversational dialogue. Concurrent research on interaction between caregivers and prelinguistic infants supports this conclusion (Bruner 1977;

Bullowa 1979; Lock 1978; Newson 1977, 1978; Schaffer 1977; Shotter 1978). Detailed observation of white middle-class mother-infant dyads (English, Scottish, American, Australian, Dutch) indicates that these mothers attempt to engage their very young infants (starting at birth) in "conversational exchanges." These so-called protoconversations (Bullowa 1979) are constructed in several ways. A protoconversation may take place when one party responds to some facial expression, action, and/or vocalization of the other. This response may be nonverbal, as when a gesture of the infant is "echoed" by his or her mother.

> As a rule, pre-speech with gesture is watched and replied to by exclamations of pleasure or surprise like "Oh, my my!", "Good heavens!", "Oh, what a big smile!", "Ha! That's a big one!" (meaning a story), questioning replies like, "Are you telling me a story?", "Oh really?", or even agreement by nodding "Yes" or saying "I'm sure you're right". . . . A mother evidently perceives her baby to be a person like herself. Mothers interpret baby behavior as not only intended to be communicative, but as verbal and meaningful. (Trevarthen 1979a:339)

On the other hand, mother and infant may respond to one another through verbal means, as, for example, when a mother expresses agreement, disagreement, or surprise following an infant behavior. Social interactions may be sustained over several exchanges by the mother assuming both speaker roles. She may construct an exchange by responding on behalf of the infant to her own utterance, or she may verbally interpret the infant's interpretation. A combination of several strategies is illustrated in Example 3 (Snow 1977a: 12).

Example 3

| Mother | Ann (3 mos) |
|---|---|
| | (smiles) |
| Oh what a nice little smile! | |
| Yes, isn't that nice? | |
| There. | |
| There's a nice little smile. | (burps) |
| What a nice wind as well! | |
| Yes, that's better, isn't it? | |
| Yes. | |
| Yes. | (vocalizes) |
| Yes! | |
| There's a nice noise. | |

These descriptions capture the behavior of white middle-class caregivers and, in turn, can be read for what caregivers believe to be the capabilities and predispositions of the infant. Caregivers evidently see their infants as sociable and as capable of intentionality, particularly with respect to the intentional expression of emotional and physical states. Some researchers have concluded that the mother, in interpreting an infant's behaviors, provides meanings for those behaviors that the infant will ultimately adopt (Lock 1981; Ryan 1974; Shotter 1978) and thus emphasize the active role of the mother in socializing the infant to her set of interpretations. Other approaches emphasize the effect of the infant on the caregiver (Lewis & Rosenblum 1974), particularly with respect to the innate mechanisms for organized, purposeful action that the infant brings to interaction (Trevarthen 1979b).

These studies of caregivers' speech to young children have all attended to what the child is learning from these interactions with the mother (or caregiver). There has been a general movement away from the search for *direct* causal links between the ways in which caregivers speak to their children and the emergence of grammar. Instead, caregivers' speech has been examined for its more general communicative functions, that is, how meanings are negotiated, how activities are organized and accomplished, and how routines and games become established. Placed within this broader communicative perspective, language development is viewed as one of several achievements accomplished through verbal exchanges between the caregiver and the child.

## THE ETHNOGRAPHIC APPROACH

### Ethnographic Orientation

To most middle-class Western readers, the descriptions of verbal and nonverbal behaviors of middle-class caregivers with their children seem very familiar, desirable, and even natural. These descriptions capture in rich detail what goes on, to a greater or lesser extent, in many middle-class households. The characteristics of caregiver speech (baby-talk register) and comportment that have been specified are highly valued by members of white middle-class society, including researchers, readers, and subjects of study. They are associated with good mothering and can be spontaneously produced with little effort or reflections. As demonstrated by Shatz and Gelman (1973), Sachs and Devin (1976), and Andersen and Johnson (1973), children as young as 4 years of age often speak and act in these ways when addressing small children.

From our research experience in other societies as well as our acquaintance with some of the cross-cultural studies of language socialization (Blount 1972; Bowerman 1981; Clancy in press; Eisenberg 1982; Fischer 1970; Hamilton 1981; Harkness 1975; Harkness & Super 1977; Heath 1983; Miller 1982; Philips 1983; Schieffelin & Eisenberg in press; Scollon & Scollon 1981; Stross 1972; Ward 1971; Watson-Gegeo & Gegeo 1982; Wills 1977) the general patterns of white middle-class caregiving that have been described in the psychological literature are characteristic neither of all societies nor of all social groups (e.g., all social classes within one society). We would like the reader, therefore, to reconsider the descriptions of caregiving in the psychological literature as ethnographic descriptions.

By ethnographic, we mean descriptions that take into account the perspective of members of a social group, including beliefs and values that underlie and organize their activities and utterances. Ethnographers rely heavily on observations and on formal and informal elicitation of members' reflections and interpretations as a basis for analysis (Geertz 1973). Typically, the ethnographer is not a member of the group under study. Further, in presenting an ethnographic account, the researcher faces the problem of communicating world views or sets of values that may be unfamiliar and strange to the reader. Ideally, such statements provide for the reader a set of organizing principles that give coherence and an analytic focus to the behaviors described.

Psychologists who have carried out research on the verbal and nonverbal behavior of caregivers and their children draw on both methods. However, unlike most ethnographers, the psychological researcher *is* a member of the social group under observation. (In some cases, the researcher's own children are the subjects of study.) Further, unlike the ethnographer, the psychologist addresses a readership familiar with the social scenes portrayed.

That the researcher, reader, and subjects of study tend to have in common a white middle-class literate background has had several consequences. For example, by and large, the psychologist has not been faced with the problem of cultural translation, as has the anthropologist. There has been a tacit assumption that readers can provide the larger cultural framework for making sense out of the behaviors documented, and, consequently, the cultural nature of the behaviors and principles presented have not been explicit. From our perspective, language and culture as bodies of knowledge, structures of understanding, conceptions of the world, and collective representations are extrinsic to any individual and contain more information than any individual could know or learn. Culture encompasses variations in knowledge between individuals, but such variation, although crucial to what an individual may know and to the social dynamic between individuals, does not have its locus within the individual. Our position is that culture is not something that can be considered separately from the accounts of caregiver-child interaction; rather, it is what organizes and gives meaning to that interaction. This is an important point, as it affects the definition and interpretation of the behaviors of caregivers and children. How caregivers and children speak and act toward one another is linked to cultural patterns that extend and have consequences beyond the specific interactions observed. For example, how caregivers speak to their children may be linked to other institutional adaptations to young children. These adaptations, in turn, may be linked to how members of a given society view children more generally (their "nature," their social status and expected comportment) and to how members think children develop.

We are suggesting here that the sharing of assumptions between researcher, reader, and subjects of study is a mixed blessing. In fact, this sharing represents a paradox of familiarity. We are able to apply without effort the cultural framework for interpreting the behavior of caregivers and young children in our own social group; indeed, as members of a white middle-class society, we are socialized to do this very work, that is, interpret behaviors, attribute motives, and so on. Paradoxically, however, in spite of this ease of effort, we can not easily isolate and make explicit these cultural principles. As Goffman's work on American society has illustrated, the articulation of norms, beliefs, and values is often possible only when faced with violations, that is, with gaffes, breaches, misfirings, and the like (Goffman 1963, 1967; Much & Shweder 1978).

Another way to see the cultural principles at work in our own society is to examine the ways in which *other* societies are organized in terms of social interaction and of the society at large. In carrying out such research, the ethnographer offers a point of contrast and comparison with our own everyday activities. Such comparative material can lead us to reinterpret behaviors as cultural that we have assumed to be natural. From the anthropological perspective, every society will have its own cultural constructs of what is natural and what is not. For example, every society has its own theory of procreation. Certain Australian Aboriginal societies believe that a number of different factors contribute to conception. Von Sturmer (1980) writes that among the Kugu-Nganychara (West Cape York Peninsula, Australia) the spirit of the child may first enter the man through an animal that he has killed and consumed. The spirit passes from the man to the woman through sexual intercourse, but several sexual acts are necessary to build the child (see also Hamilton 1981; Montagu 1937). Even within a single society there may be different beliefs concerning when life begins and ends, as the recent debates in the United States and Europe concerning abortion and mercy killing indicate. The issue of what is nature and what is nurtured (cultural) extends to patterns of caregiving and child development. Every society has (implicitly or explicitly) given notions concerning the capacities and temperament of children at different points in their development (see, e.g., Dentan 1978; Ninio 1979; Snow, de Blauw, & van Roosmalen 1979), and the expectations and responses of caregivers are directly related to these notions.

## Three Developmental Stories

At this point, using an ethnographic perspective, we will recast selected behaviors of white middle-class caregivers and young children as pieces of one "developmental story." The white middle-class developmental story that we are constructing is based on various descriptions available and focuses on those patterns of interaction (both verbal and nonverbal) that have been emphasized in the literature. This story will be compared with two other developmental stories from societies that are strikingly different: Kaluli (Papua New Guinea) and Western Samoan.

A major goal in presenting and comparing these developmental stories is to demonstrate that communicative interactions between caregivers and young children are culturally constructed. In our comparisons, we will focus on three facets of communicative interaction: (1) the social organization of the verbal environment of very young children, (2) the extent to which children are expected to adapt to situations or that situations are adapted to the child, (3) the negotiation of meaning by caregiver and child. We first present a general sketch of each social group and then discuss in more detail the consequences of the differences and similarities in communicative patterns in these social groups.

These developmental stories are not timeless but rather are linked in complex ways to particular historical contexts. Both the ways in which caregivers behave toward young children and the popular and scientific accounts of these ways may differ at different moments in time. The stories that we present represent ideas currently held in the three social groups.

The three stories show that there is more than one way of becoming social and using language in early childhood. All normal children will become members of their own social group, but the process of becoming social, including becoming a language user, is culturally constructed. In relation to this process of construction, every society has its own developmental stories that are rooted in social organization, beliefs, and values. These stories may be explicitly codified and/or tacitly assumed by members.

*An Anglo-American White Middle-Class Developmental Story*

The middle class in Britain and the United States includes a broad range of lower middle-, middle middle-, and upper middle-class white-collar and professional workers and their families.[1] The literature on communicative development has been largely based on middle middle- and upper middle-class households. These households tend to consist of a single nuclear family with one, two, or three children. The primary caregiver almost without exception is the child's natural or adopted mother. Researchers have focused on communicative situations in which one child interacts with his or her mother. The generalizations proposed by these researchers concerning mother-child communication could be an artifact of this methodological focus. However, it could be argued that the attention to two-party encounters between a mother and her child reflects the most frequent type of communicative interaction to which most young middle-class children are exposed. Participation in two-party as opposed to multiparty interactions is a product of many considerations, including the physical setting of households, where interior and exterior walls bound and limit access to social interaction.

Soon after an infant is born, many mothers hold their infants in such a way that they are face-to-face and gaze at them. Mothers have been observed to address their infants, vocalize to them, ask questions, and greet them. In other

---

[1] This story is based on the numerous accounts of caregiver-child communication and interaction that have appeared in both popular and scientific journals. Our generalizations regarding language use are based on detailed reports in the developmental psycholinguistic literature, which are cited throughout. In addition, we have drawn on our own experiences and intuitions as mothers and members of this social group. We invite those with differing perceptions to comment on our interpretations.

words, from birth on, the infant is treated as a *social being* and as an *addressee* in social interaction. The infant's vocalizations and physical movements and states are often interpreted as meaningful and are responded to verbally by the mother or other caregiver. In this way, protoconversations are established and sustained along a dyadic, turn-taking model. Throughout this period and the subsequent language-acquiring years, caregivers treat very young children as communicative partners. One very important procedure in facilitating these social exchanges is the mother's (or other caregiver's) taking the perspective of the child. This perspective is evidenced in her own speech through the many simplifying and affective features of the baby-talk register that have been described and through the various strategies employed to identify what the young child may be expressing.

Such perspective taking is part of a much wider set of accommodations by adults to young children. These accommodations are manifested in several domains. For example, there are widespread material accommodations to infancy and childhood in the form of cultural artifacts designed for this stage of life, for example, baby clothes, baby food, miniaturization of furniture, and toys. Special behavioral accommodations are coordinated with the infant's perceived needs and capacities, for example, putting the baby in a quiet place to facilitate and ensure proper sleep; "baby-proofing" a house as a child becomes increasingly mobile, yet not aware of, or able to control, the consequences of his or her own behavior. In general, the pattern appears to be one of prevention and intervention, in which situations are adapted or modified to the child rather than the reverse. Further, the child is a focus of attention, in that the child's actions and verbalizations are often the starting point of social interaction with more mature persons.

Although such developmental achievements as crawling, walking, and first words are awaited by caregivers, the accommodations have the effect of keeping the child dependent on, and separate from, the adult community for a considerable period of time. The child, protected from those experiences considered harmful (e.g., playing with knives, climbing stairs), is thus denied knowledge, and his or her competence in such contexts is delayed.

The accommodations of white middle-class caregivers to young children can be examined for other values and tendencies. Particularly among the American middle class, these accommodations reflect a discomfort with the competence differential between adult and child. The competence gap is reduced by two strategies. One is for the adult to simplify her/his speech to match more closely what the adult considers to be the verbal competence of the young child. Let us call this strategy the self-lowering strategy, following Irvine's (1974) analysis of intercaste demeanor. A second strategy is for the caregiver to richly interpret (Brown 1973) what the young child is expressing. Here the adult acts *as if* the child were more competent than his behavior more strictly would indicate. Let us call this strategy the child-raising (no pun intended!) strategy. Other behaviors conform to this strategy, such as when an adult cooperates in a task with a child but treats that task as an accomplishment of the child.

For example, in eliciting a story from a child, a caregiver often cooperates with the child in the telling of the story. This cooperation typically takes the form of posing questions to the child, such as "Where did you go?" "What did you see?" and so on, to which the adult knows the answer. The child is seen as telling the story even though she or he is simply supplying the information the adult has preselected and organized (Greenfield & Smith 1976; Ochs, Schieffelin & Platt 1979; Schieffelin & Eisenberg 1984). Bruner's (1978) description of scaffolding, in which a caregiver constructs a tower or other play object, allowing the young child to place the last block, is also a good example of this tendency. Here the tower may be seen by the caregiver and others as the child's own work. Similarly, in later life, caregivers playing games with their children let them win, acting as if the child can match or more than match the competence of the adult.

The masking of incompetence applies not only in white middle-class relations with young children but also in relations with mentally, and to some extent to physically, handicapped persons as well. As the work of Edgerton (1967) and the recent film *Best Boy* indicate, mentally retarded persons are often restricted to protected environments (family households, sheltered workshops or special homes) in which trained staff or family members make vast accommodations to their special needs and capacities.

A final aspect of this white middle-class developmental story concerns the willingness of many caregivers to interpret unintelligible or partially intelligible utterances of young children (cf. Ochs 1982c), for example, the caregiver offers a paraphrase (or "expansion"; Brown & Bellugi 1964; Cazden 1965), using a question intonation. This behavior of caregivers has continuity with their earlier attributions of intentionality to the ambiguous utterances of the infant. For both the prelinguistic and language-using child, the caregiver provides an explicitly verbal interpretation. This interpretation or paraphrase is potentially available to the young child to affirm, disconfirm, or modify.

Through exposure to, and participation in, these clarification exchanges, the young child is socialized into several cultural patterns. The first of these recognizes and defines an utterance or vocalization that may not be immediately understood. Second, the child is presented with the procedures for dealing with ambiguity. Through the successive offerings of possible interpretations, the child learns that more than one understanding of a given utterance or vocalization may be possible. The child is also learning who can make these interpretations and the extent to which they may be open to modification. Finally, the child is learning how to settle upon a possible interpretation and how to show disagreement or agreement. This entire process socializes the child into culturally specific modes of organizing knowledge, thought, and language.[2]

[2] We would like to thank Courtney Cazden for bringing the following quotation to our attention: "It seems to us that a mother in expanding speech may be teaching more than grammar; she may be teaching something like a world-view" (Brown & Bellugi 1964).

## A Kaluli Developmental Story

A small (population approximately 1,200), nonliterate egalitarian society (Schieffelin 1976), the Kaluli people live in the tropical rain forest on the Great Papuan Plateau in the southern highlands of Papua New Guinea.[3] Most Kaluli are monolingual, speaking a non-Austronesian verb final ergative language. They maintain large gardens and hunt and fish. Traditionally, the sixty to ninety individuals that comprise a village lived in one large longhouse without internal walls. Currently, although the longhouse is maintained, many families live in smaller dwellings that provide accommodations for two or more extended families. It is not unusual for at least a dozen individuals of different ages to be living together in one house consisting essentially of one semipartitioned room.

Men and women use extensive networks of obligation and reciprocity in the organization of work and sociable interaction. Everyday life is overtly focused around verbal interaction. Kaluli think of, and use, talk as a means of control, manipulation, expression, assertion, and appeal. Talk gets you what you want, need, or feel you are owed. Talk is a primary indicator of social competence and a primary means of socializing. Learning how to talk and become independent is a major goal of socialization.

For the purpose of comparison and for understanding something of the cultural basis for the ways in which Kaluli act and speak to their children, it is important first to describe selected aspects of a Kaluli developmental story that I have constructed from various ethnographic data. Kaluli describe their babies as helpless, "soft" (*taiyo*), and "having no understanding" (*asugo andoma*). They take care of them, they say, because they "feel sorry for them." Mothers, the primary caregivers, are attentive to their infants and physically responsive to them. Whenever an infant cries, it is offered the breast. However, while nursing her infant, a mother may also be involved in other activities, such as food preparation, or she may be engaged in conversation with individuals in the household. Mothers never leave their infants alone and only rarely with other caregivers. When not holding their infants, mothers carry them in netted bags suspended from their heads. When the mother is

---

[3] This analysis is based on the data collected in the course of ethnographic and linguistic fieldwork among the Kaluli in the Southern Highlands Province between 1975 and 1977. During this time, E. L. Schieffelin, a cultural anthropologist, and S. Feld, an ethnomusicologist, were also conducting ethnographic research. This study of the development of communicative competence among the Kaluli focused on four children who were approximately 24 months old at the start of the study. However, an additional twelve children were included in the study (siblings and cousins in residence), ranging in age from birth to 10 years. The spontaneous conversations of these children and their families were tape-recorded for one year at monthly intervals with each monthly sample lasting from 3 to 4 hours. Detailed contextual notes accompanied the taping, and these annotated transcripts, along with interviews and observations, form the data base. A total of 83 hours of audio-tape were collected and transcribed in the village. Analyses of Kaluli child acquisition data are reported in Schieffelin 1981, in press-a, and in press-b.

gardening, gathering wood, or just sitting with others, the baby sleeps in the netted bag next to the mother's body.

Kaluli mothers, given their belief that infants "have no understanding," never treat their infants as partners (speaker/addressee) in dyadic communicative interactions. Although they greet their infants by name and use expressive vocalizations, they rarely address other utterances to them. Furthermore, a mother and infant do not gaze into each other's eyes, an interactional pattern that is consistent with adult patterns of not gazing when vocalizing in interaction with one another. Rather than facing their babies and speaking to them, Kaluli mothers tend to face their babies outward so that they can see, and be seen by, other members of the social group. Older children greet and address the infant, and the mother responds in a high-pitched nasalized voice "for" the baby while moving the baby up and down. Triadic exchanges such as that in Example 4 are typical (Golinkoff 1983).

Example 4

Mother is holding her infant son Bage (3 mos). Abi (35 mos) is holding a stick on his shoulder in a manner similar to that in which one would carry a heavy patrol box (the box would be hung on a pole placed across the shoulders of the two men).

| *Mother* | *Abi* |
|---|---|
| (A to baby) | Bage/ do you see my box here?/ |
| | Bage/ ni bokisi we badaya?/ |
| | Do you see it?/ |
| | olibadaya?/ |
| (high nasal voice talking as if she is the baby, moving the baby who is facing Abi): My brother, I'll take half, my brother. nao, hɛbɔ ni diɛni, nao. | |
| (holding stick out) | mother give him half/ nɔ hɛbɔ emɔ dimina/ mother, my brother here/here take half/ nao we/we hɛbɔ dima/ |
| (in a high nasal voice as baby): My brother, what half do I take? nao, hɛbɔ diɛni hɛh? | |
| What about it? my brother, put it on the shoulder! Wangaya? nao, kɛlɛnɔ wɛla diɛfoma! | |
| (to Abi in her usual voice): Put it on the shoulder. kɛlɛnɔ wɛla diɛfɔndo. | |
| (Abi rests stick on baby's shoulder) | |
| There, carefully put it on. ko dinafa diɛfoma. (stick accidently pokes baby) | |
| Feel sorry, stop. Heyɔ, kadɛfoma. | |

When a mother takes the speaking role of an infant she uses language that is well formed and appropriate for an older child. Only the nasalization and high-pitch mark it as "the infant's." When speaking as the infant to older children, mothers speak assertively, that is, they never whine or beg on behalf of the infant. Thus, in taking this role the mother does for the infant what the infant cannon do for itself, that is, appear to act in a controlled and competent manner, using language. These kinds of interactions continue until a baby is between 4 and 6 months of age.

Several points are important here. First, these triadic exchanges are carried out primarily for the benefit of the older child and help create a relationship between the two children. Second, the mother's utterances in these exchanges are not based on, nor do they originate with, anything that the infant has initiated—either vocally or gesturally. Recall the Kaluli claim that infants have no understanding. How could someone with "no understanding" initiate appropriate interactional sequences?

However, there is an even more important and enduring cultural construct that helps make sense out of the mother's behaviors in this situation and in many others as well. Kaluli say that "one cannot know what another thinks or feels." Although Kaluli obviously interpret and assess one another's available behaviors and internal states, these interpretations are not culturally acceptable as topics of talk. Individuals often talk about their own feelings (I'm afraid, I'm happy, etc.). However, there is a cultural dispreference for talking about or making claims about what another might think, what another might feel, or what another is about to do, especially if there is no external evidence. As we shall see, these culturally constructed behaviors have several important consequences for the ways in which Kaluli caregivers verbally interact with their children and are related to other pervasive patterns of language use, which will be discussed later.

As infants become older (6–12 months), they are usually held in the arms or carried on the shoulders of the mother or an older sibling. They are present in all ongoing household activities, as well as subsistence activities that take place outside the village in the bush. During this time period, babies are addressed by adults to a limited extent. They are greeted by a variety of names (proper names, kin terms, affective and relationship terms) and receive a limited set of both negative and positive imperatives. In addition, when they do something they are told not to do, such as reach for something that is not theirs to take, they will often receive such rhetorical questions such as "who are you?!" (meaning "not someone to do that") or "is it yours?!" (meaning "it is not yours") to control their actions by shaming them (*sasidiab*). It should be stressed that the language addressed to the preverbal child consists largely of "one-liners" that call for no verbal response but for either an action or termination of an action. Other than these utterances, very little talk is directed to the young child by the adult caregiver.

This pattern of adults treating infants as noncommunicative partners continues even when babies begin babbling. Although Kaluli recognize babbling (*dabedan*), they call it noncommunicative and do not relate it to the speech that eventually emerges. Adults and older children occasionally repeat vocalizations back to the young child (age 12–16 months), reshaping them into the names of persons in the household or into kin terms, but they do not say that the baby is saying the name nor do they wait for, or expect, the child to repeat those vocalizations in an altered form. In addition, vocalizations are not generally treated as communicative and given verbal expression except in the following situation. When a toddler shrieks in protest of the assaults of an older child, mothers say "I'm unwilling" (using a quotative particle), referring to the toddler's shriek. These are the only circumstances in which mothers treat vocalizations as communicative and provide verbal expression for them. In no other circumstances did the adults in the four families in the study provide a verbally expressed interpretation of a vocalization of a preverbal child. Thus, throughout the preverbal period very little language is directed to the child, except for imperatives, rhetorical questions, and greetings. A child who by Kaluli terms has not yet begun to speak is not expected to respond either verbally or vocally. As a result, during the first 18 months or so very little sustained dyadic verbal exchange takes place between adult and infant. The infant is only minimally treated as an addressee and is not treated as a communicative partner in dyadic exchanges. Thus, the conversational model that has been described for many white middle-class caregivers and their preverbal children has no application in this case. Furthermore, if one defines language input as language directed to the child then it is reasonable to say that for Kaluli children who have not yet begun to speak there is very little. However, this does not mean that Kaluli children grow up in an impoverished verbal environment and do not learn how to speak. Quite the opposite is true. The verbal environment of the infant is rich and varied, and from the very beginning the infant is surrounded by adults and older children who spend a great deal of time talking to one another. Furthermore, as the infant develops and begins to crawl and engage in play activities and other independent actions, these actions are frequently referred to, described, and commented upon by members of the household, especially older children, to each other. Thus the ongoing activities of the preverbal child are an important topic of talk among members of the household, and this talk about the here-and-now of the infant is available to the infant, though it is not talk addressed to the infant. For example, in referring to the infant's actions, siblings and adults use the infant's name or kin term. They say, "Look at Seligiwo! He's walking." Thus the child may learn from these contexts to attend the verbal environment in which he or she lives.

Every society has its own ideology about language, including when it begins and how children acquire it. The Kaluli are no exception. Kaluli claim that language begins at the time when the child uses two critical words, "mother" (*nɔ*) and "breast" (*bo*). The child may be using other single words, but until these two words are used, the beginning of language is not recognized. Once a child has used these words, a whole set of interrelated behaviors is set into motion. Once a child has begun to use language, he or she then must be "shown how to speak" (Schieffelin 1979). Kaluli show their children language in the form of a teaching strategy, which involves providing a model for what the child is to say followed by the word ɛlɛma, an imperative meaning "say like that." Mothers use this method of direct instruction to teach the social uses of assertive language (teasing, shaming, requesting, challenging, reporting). However, object labeling is never part of an ɛlɛma sequence, nor does the mother ever use ɛlɛma to instruct the child to beg or appeal for food or objects. Begging, the Kaluli say, is natural for children. They know how to do it. In contrast, a child must be taught to be assertive through the use of particular linguistic expressions and verbal sequences.

A typical sequence using ɛlɛma is triadic, involving the mother, child (20–36 months), and other participants, as in Example 5 (Schieffelin 1979).

Example 5

Mother, daughter Binalia (5 yrs), cousin Mama (3 1/2 yrs), and son Wanu (27 mos) are at home, dividing up some cooked vegetables. Binalia has been begging for some, but her mother thinks that she has had her share.

M→W→»B:*
Whose is it?! say like that.
Abɛnowo?! ɛlɛma.

    whose is it?!/
    abɛnowo?!/

Is it yours?! say like that.
Gɛnowo?! ɛlɛma.

    is it yours?!/
    gɛnowo?!/

Who are you?! say like that.
ge oba?! ɛlɛma.

    who are you?!/
    ge oba?!/

Mama→W→»B:
Did you pick?! say like that.
gi suwo?! ɛlɛma.

    did you pick?!/
    gi suwo?!/

M→W→»B:
My grandmother picked! say like that.
ni nuwɛ suke! ɛlɛma.

    My grandmother picked!/
    ni nuwɛ suke!/

Mama→W→»B:
This my g'mother picked! say like that
we ni nuwɛ suke! ɛlɛma.

    This my g'mother picked!/
    we ni nuwɛ suke!/

*→ = speaker→addressee
→» = addressee→intended addressee

In this situation, as in many others, the mother does not modify her language to fit the linguistic ability of the young child. Instead, her language is shaped so as to be appropriate (in terms of form and content) for the child's intended addressee. Consistent with the way she interacts with her infant, what a mother instructs her young child to say usually does not have its origins in any verbal or nonverbal behaviors of the child but in what the mother thinks should be said. The mother pushes the child into ongoing interactions that the child may or may not be interested in and will at times spend a good deal of energy in trying to get the child verbally involved. This is part of the Kaluli pattern of fitting (or pushing) the child into the situation rather than changing the situation to meet the interests or abilities of the child. Thus mothers take a directive role with their young children, teaching them what to say so that they may become participants in the social group.

In addition to instructing their children by telling them what to say in often extensive interactional sequences, Kaluli mothers pay attention to the form of their children's utterances. Kaluli correct the phonological, morphological, or lexical form of an utterance or its pragmatic or semantic meaning. Because the goals of language acquisition include the development of a competent and independent child who uses mature language, Kaluli use no baby-talk lexicon, for they said (when I asked about it) that to do so would result in a child sounding babyish, which was clearly undesirable and counterproductive. The entire process of a child's development, of which language acquisition plays a very important role, is thought of as a hardening process and culminates in the child's use of "hard words" (Feld & Schieffelin 1982).

The cultural dispreference for saying what another might be thinking or feeling has important consequences for the organization of dyadic exchanges between caregiver and child. For one, it affects the ways in which meaning is negotiated during an exchange. For the Kaluli, the responsibility for clear expression is with the speaker, and child speakers are not exempt from this. Rather than offering possible interpretations or guessing at the meaning of what a child is saying, caregivers make extensive use of clarification requests such as "huh?" and "what?" in an attempt to elicit clearer expression from the child. Children are held to what they say and mothers will remind them that they in fact have asked for food or an object if they don't act appropriately on receiving it. Because the responsibility of expression lies with the speaker, children are also instructed with εlεma to request clarification (using similar forms) from others when they do not understand what someone is saying to them.

Another important consequence of not saying what another thinks is the absence of adult expansions of child utterances. Kaluli caregivers put words into the mouths of their children, but these words originate from the caregiver. However, caregivers do not elaborate or expand utterances initiated by the child. Nor do they jointly build propositions across utterances and speakers except in the context of sequences with εlεma in which they are constructing the talk for the child.

*Language Acquisition and Socialization* **487**

All these patterns of early language use, such as the lack of expansions and the verbal attribution of an internal state to an individual, are consistent with important cultural conventions of adult language usage. The Kaluli avoid gossip and often indicate the source of information they report. They make extensive use of direct quoted speech in a language that does not allow indirect quotation. They use a range of evidential markers in their speech to indicate the source of speakers' information, for example, whether something was said, seen, heard or gathered from other kinds of evidence. These patterns are also found in a child's early speech and, as such, affect the organization and acquisition of conversational exchanges in this face-to-face egalitarian society.

## A Samoan Developmental Story

In American and Western Samoa, an archipelago in the southwest Pacific, Samoan, a verb-initial Polynesian language, is spoken.[4] The following developmental story draws primarily on direct observations of life in a large, traditional village on the island of Upolu in Western Samoa; however, it incorporates as well analyses by Mead (1927), Kernan (1969), and Shore (1982) of social life, language use, and childhood on other islands (the Manu'a islands and Savai'i).

As has been described by numerous scholars, Samoan society is highly stratified. Individuals are ranked in terms of whether or not they have a title, and if so, whether it is an orator or a chiefly title—bestowed on persons by an extended family unit (*aiga potopoto*)—and within each status, particular titles are reckoned with respect to one another.

Social stratification characterizes relationships between untitled persons as well, with the assessment of relative rank in terms of generation and age. Most relevant to the Samoan developmental story to be told here is that caregiving is also socially stratified. The young child is cared for by a range of untitled persons, typically the child's older siblings, the mother, and unmarried siblings

---

[4] The data on which this analysis is based were collected from July 1978 to July 1979 in a traditional village in Western Samoa. The village, Falefa, is located on the island of Upolu, approximately 18 miles from the capital, Apia. The fieldwork was conducted by Alessandro Duranti, Martha Platt, and Elinor Ochs. Our data collection consisted of two major projects. The first, carried out by Ochs and Platt, was a longitudinal documentation, through audio- and videotape, of young children's acquisition of Samoan. This was accomplished by focusing on six children from six different households, from 19 to 35 months of age at the onset of the study. These children were observed and taped every five weeks, approximately three hours each period. Samoan children live in compounds composed of several households. Typically, numerous siblings and peers are present and interact with a young child. We were able to record the speech of seventeen other children under the age of 6, who were part of the children's early social environment. A total of 128 hours of audio and 20 hours of video recording were collected. The audio material is supplemented by handwritten notes detailing contextual features of the interactions recorded. All the audio material has been transcribed in the village by a family member or family acquaintance and checked by a researcher. Approximately 18,000 pages of transcript form the child language data base. Analyses of Samoan child language are reported in Ochs 1982a, 1982b, and in press.

of the child's mother. Where more than one of these are present, the older is considered to be the higher ranking caregiver and the younger the lower ranking caregiver (Ochs 1982c). As will be discussed in the course of this story, ranking affects how caregiving tasks are carried out and how verbal interactions are organized.

From birth until the age of 5 or 6 months, an infant is referred to as *pepemeamea* (baby thing thing). During this period, the infant stays close to his or her mother, who is assisted by other women and children in child-care tasks. During this period, the infant spends the periods of rest and sleep near, but somewhat separated from, others, on a large pillow enclosed by a mosquito net suspended from a beam or rope. Waking moments are spent in the arms of the mother, occasionally the father, but most often on the hips or laps of other children, who deliver the infant to his or her mother for feeding and in general are responsible for satisfying and comforting the child.

In these early months, the infant is talked *about* by others, particularly in regard to his or her physiological states and needs. Language addressed *to* the young infant tends to be in the form of songs or rhythmic vocalizations in a soft, high pitch. Infants at this stage are not treated as conversational partners. Their gestures and vocalizations are interpreted for what they indicate about the physiological state of the child. If verbally expressed, however, these interpretations are directed in general not to the infant but to some other more mature member of the household (older child), typically in the form of a directive.

As an infant becomes more mature and mobile, he or she is referred to as simply *pepe* (baby). When the infant begins to crawl, his or her immediate social and verbal environment changes. Although the infant continues to be carried by an older sibling, he or she is also expected to come to the mother or other mature family members on his or her own. Spontaneous language is directed to the infant to a much greater extent. The child, for example, is told to "come" to the caregiver.

To understand the verbal environment of the infant at this stage, it is necessary to consider Samoan concepts of childhood and children. Once a child is able to locomote himself or herself and even somewhat before, he or she is frequently described as cheeky, mischievous, and willful. Very frequently, the infant is negatively sanctioned for his or her actions. An infant who sucks eagerly, vigorously, or frequently at the breast may be teasingly shamed by other family members. Approaching a guest or touching objects of value provokes negative directives first and mock threats second. The tone of voice shifts dramatically from that used with younger infants. The pitch drops to the level used in casual interactions with adult addressees and voice quality becomes loud and sharp. It is to be noted here that caregiver speech is largely talk directed *at* the infant, and typically caregivers do not engage in "conversations" *with* infants over several exchanges. Further, the language used by caregivers is not lexically or syntactically simplified.

The image of the small child as highly assertive continues for several years and is reflected in what is reported to be the first word of Samoan children: *tae* (shit), a curse word used to reject, retaliate, or show displeasure at the action of another. The child's earliest use of language, then, is seen as explicitly defiant and angry. Although caregivers admonish the verbal and nonverbal expression of these qualities, the qualities are in fact deeply valued and considered necessary and desirable in particular social circumstances.

As noted earlier, Samoan children are exposed to, and participate in, a highly stratified society. Children usually grow up in a family compound composed of several households and headed by one or more titled persons. Titled persons conduct themselves in a particular manner in public, namely, to move slowly or be stationary, and they tend to disassociate themselves from the activities of lower status persons in their immediate environment. In a less dramatic fashion, this demeanor characterizes high ranking caregivers in a household as well, who tend to leave the more active tasks, such as bathing, changing, and carrying an infant to younger persons (Ochs 1982c).

The social stratification of caregiving has its reflexes in the verbal environment of the young child. Throughout the day, higher ranking caregivers (e.g., the mother) direct lower ranking persons to carry, put to sleep, soothe, feed, bathe, and clothe a child. Typically, a lower ranking caregiver waits for such a directive rather than initiate such activities spontaneously. When a small child begins to speak, he or she learns to make his or her needs known to the higher ranking caregiver. The child learns not to necessarily expect a direct response. Rather, the child's appeal usually generates a conversational sequence such as the following:

Child appeals to high-ranking caregiver (A→B)
High ranking caregiver directs lower ranking caregiver (B→C)
Lower ranking caregiver responds to child (C→A)

These verbal interactions differ from the ABAB dyadic interactions described for white middle-class caregivers and children. Whereas a white middle-class child is often alone with a caregiver, a Samoan child is not. Traditional Samoan houses have no internal or external walls, and typically conversations involve several persons inside and outside the house. For the Samoan child, then, multiparty conversations are the norm, and participation is organized along hierarchical lines.

The importance of status and rank is expressed in other uses of language as well. Very small children are encouraged to produce certain speech acts that they will be expected to produce later as younger (i.e., low ranking) members of the household. One of these speech acts is reporting of news to older family members. The reporting of news by lower status persons complements the detachment associated with relatively high status. High status persons ideally (or officially) receive information through reports rather than through their own direct involvement in the affairs of others. Of course, this ideal is not always realized. Nonetheless, children from the one-word stage on will be explicitly instructed to notice others and to provide information to others as Example 6 illustrates.

Example 6

Pesio, her peer group including Maselino (3 yrs 4 mos) and Maselino's mother, Iuliana, are in the house. They see Alesana (member of research project) in front of the trade store across the street. Iuliana directs the children to notice Alesana.

| Pesio (2 yrs 3 mos) | Others | |
|---|---|---|
| | Iuliana: | Va'ai Alesana. |
| | | Look (at) Alesana! |
| ā?/ | | |
| Huh? | Iuliana: | Alesana |
| | Maselino: | Alesaga/ |
| ai   Alesaga/ | | |
| Look (at) Alesana | Iuliana: | Vala'au Alesana |
| | | Call (to) Alesana. |
| ((very high, loud)) | | |
| SAGA?/ | | |
| Alesana! | ((high, soft)) | |
| | Iuliana: | Mālō. |
| | | (Greeting) |
| ((loud)) | | |
| ALŌ! | | |
| (Greeting) | Iuliana: | (Fai) o Elegoa lea. |
| | | (Say) prt. Elenoa here. |
| | | (say "Elenoa [is] here.") |
| Sego lea/ | | |
| Elenoa here | | |
| (Elenoa [is] here.) | | |

The character of these instructions is similar to that of the triadic exchanges described in the Kaluli developmental story. A young child is to repeat an utterance offered by a caregiver to a third party. As in the Kaluli triadic exchanges, the utterance is designed primarily for the third party. For example, the high, soft voice quality used by Iuliana expresses deference in greeting Alesana, the third party. Caregivers use such exchanges to teach children a wide range of skills and knowledge. In fact, the task of repeating what the caregiver has said is *itself* an object of knowledge, preparing the child for his or her eventual role as messenger. Children at the age of 3 are expected to deliver *verbatim* messages on behalf of more mature members of the family.

The cumulative orientation is one in which even very young children are oriented toward others. In contrast to the white middle-class tendencies to accommodate situations to the child, the Samoans encourage the child to meet the needs of the situation, that is, to notice others, listen to them, and adapt one's own speech to their particular status and needs.

The pervasiveness of social stratification is felt in another, quite fundamental aspect of language, that of ascertaining the meaning of an utterance. Procedures for clarification are sensitive to the relative rank of conversational participants in the following manner. If a high status person produces a partially or wholly unintelligible utterance, the burden of clarification tends to rest with the hearer. It is not inappropriate for high status persons to produce such utterances from time to time. In the case of orators in particular, there is an expectation that certain terms and expressions will be obscure to certain members of their audiences. On the other hand, if a low status person's speech is unclear, the burden of clarification tends to be placed more on the speaker.

The latter situation applies to most situations in which young children produce ambiguous or unclear utterances. Both adult and child caregivers tend not to try to determine the message content of such utterances by, for example, repeating or expanding such an utterance with a query intonation. In fact, unintelligible utterances of young children will sometimes be considered as not Samoan but another language, usually Chinese, or not language at all but the sounds of an animal. A caregiver may choose to initiate clarification by asking "What?" or "Huh?" but it is up to the child to make his or her speech intelligible to the addressee.

Whereas the Samoans place the burden of clarification on the child, white middle-class caregivers assist the child in clarifying and expressing ideas. As noted in the white middle-class developmental story, such assistance is associated with good mothering. The good mother is one who responds to her child's incompetence by making greater efforts than normal to clarify his or her intentions. To this end, a mother tries to put herself in the child's place (take the perspective of the child). In Samoa good mothering or good caregiving is almost the reverse: A young child is encouraged to develop an ability to take the perspective of higher ranking persons in order to assist them and facilitate their well-being. The ability to do so is part of showing *fa'aaloalo* (respect), a most necessary demeanor in social life.

We cannot leave our Samoan story without touching on another dimension of intelligibility and understanding in caregiver-child interactions. In particular, we need to turn our attention to Samoan attitudes toward motivation and intentionality (cf. Ochs 1982c). In philosophy, social science, and literary criticism, a great deal of ink has been spilled over the relation between act and intention behind an act. The pursuit and ascertaining of intentions is highly valued in many societies, where acts are objects of interpretation and motives are treated as explanations. In traditional Samoan society, with exceptions such as teasing and bluffing, actions are not treated as open to interpretation. They are treated for the most part as having one assignable meaning. An individual may not always know what that meaning is, as in the case of an oratorical passage; in these cases, one accepts that there is one meaning that he or she may or may not eventually come to know. For the most part as well, there is not a concern with levels of intentions and motives underlying the performance of some particular act.

Responses of Samoan caregivers to unintelligible utterances and acts of young children need to be understood in this light. Caregivers tend not to guess, hypothesize, or otherwise interpret such utterances and acts, in part because these procedures are not generally engaged in, at least explicitly, in daily social interactions within a village. As in encounters with others, a caregiver generally treats a small child's utterances as either clear or not clear, and in the latter case prefers to wait until the meaning becomes known to the caregiver rather than initiate an interpretation.

When young Samoan children participate in such interactions, they come to know how "meaning" is treated in their society. They learn what to consider as meaningful (e.g., clear utterances and actions) procedures for assigning meaning to utterances and actions, and procedures for handling unintelligible and partially intelligible utterances and actions. In this way, through language use, Samoan children are socialized into culturally preferred ways of processing information. Such contexts of experience reveal the interface of language, culture, and thought.

## Implications of Developmental Stories: Three Proposals
### Interactional Design Reexamined

We propose that infants and caregivers do not interact with one another according to one particular "biologically designed choreography" (Stern 1977). There are many choreographies within and across societies, and cultural as well as biological systems contribute to their design, frequency, and significance. The biological predispositions constraining and shaping the social behavior of infants and caregivers must be broader than thus far conceived in that the use of eye gaze, vocalization, and body alignment are orchestrated differently in the social groups we have observed. As noted earlier, for example, Kaluli mothers do not engage in sustained gazing at, or elicit and maintain direct eye contact with, their infants as such behavior is dispreferred and associated with witchcraft.

Another argument in support of a broader notion of a biological predisposition to be social concerns the variation observed in the participant structure of social interactions. The literature on white middle-class child development has been oriented, quite legitimately, toward the two-party relationship between infant and caregiver, typically infant and mother. The legitimacy of this focus rests on the fact that this relationship is primary for infants within this social group. Further, most communicative interactions are dyadic in the adult community. Although the mother is an important figure in both Kaluli and Samoan developmental stories, the interactions in which infants are participants are typically triadic or multiparty. As noted, Kaluli mothers organize triadic interactions in which infants and young children are oriented away from their mothers and toward a third party. For Samoans, the absence of internal and external walls, coupled with the expectation that others will attend to, and eventually participate in, conversation, makes multiparty interaction far more common. Infants are socialized to participate in such interactions in ways appropriate to the status and rank of the participants.

This is not to say that Kaluli and Samoan caregivers and children do not engage in dyadic exchanges. Rather, the point is that such exchanges are not accorded the same significance as in white middle-class society. In white middle-class households that have been studied, the process of becoming social takes place predominantly through dyadic interactions, and social competence itself is measured in terms of the young child's capacity to participate in such interactions. In Kaluli and Samoan households, the process of becoming social takes place through participation in dyadic, triadic, and multiparty social interactions, with the latter two more common than the dyad.

From an early age, Samoan and Kaluli children must learn how to participate in interactions involving a number of individuals. To do this minimally requires attending to more than one individual's words and actions and knowing the norms for when and how to enter interactions, taking into account the social identities of at least three participants. Further, the sequencing of turns in triadic and multiparty interactions has a far wider range of possibilities vis-á-vis dyadic exchanges and thus requires considerable knowledge and skill. Whereas dyadic exchanges can only be ABABA . . . , triadic or multiparty exchanges can be sequenced in a variety of ways, subject to such social constraints as speech content and the status of speaker (as discussed in the Samoan developmental story). For both the Kaluli and the Samoan child, triadic and multiparty interactions constitute their earliest social experiences and reflect the ways in which members of these societies routinely communicate with one another.

*Caregiver Register Reexamined*

A second major proposal based on these three developmental stories is that the simplifying features of white middle-class speech are not necessary input for the acquisition of language by young children. The word "input" itself implies a directionality toward the child as information processor. The data base for the child's construction of language is assumed to be language directed *to* the child. It is tied to a model of communication that is dyadic, with participation limited to the roles of speaker and addressee. If we were to apply this strict notion of input (language addressed to the child) to the Kaluli and Samoan experiences, we would be left with a highly restricted corpus from which the child is expected to construct language. As we have emphasized in these developmental stories, the very young child is less often spoken to than spoken about. Nonetheless, both Kaluli and Samoan children become fluent speakers within the range of normal developmental variation.

Given that the features of caregivers' speech cannot be accounted for primarily in terms of their language-facilitating function, that is, as input, we might ask what can account for the special ways in which caregivers speak to their children. We suggest that the particular features of the caregiver register are best understood as an expression of a basic sociological phenomenon. Every social relationship is associated with a set of behaviors, verbal and nonverbal, that set off that relationship from other relationships. Additionally, these behaviors indicate to others that a particular social relationship is being actualized. From this point of view, the "special" features of caregiver speech are not special at all, in the sense that verbal modifications do occur wherever social relationships are called into play. This phenomenon has been overlooked in part because, in describing the language of caregivers to children, it is usually contrasted with a generalized notion of the ways in which adults talk to everyone else. The most extreme example of this is found in interviews with adults in which they are asked to describe special ways of talking to babies (Ferguson 1977). A less extreme example is found in the procedure of comparing caregiver speech to children with caregiver speech to the researcher/outsider (Newport, Gleitman, & Gleitman 1977). In the latter case, only one adult-adult relationship is used as a basis of comparison, and this relationship is typically formal and socially distant.

The social nature of caregiver speech has been discussed with respect to its status as a type of speech register. Nonetheless, the language-simplifying features have been emphasized more than any other aspect of the register. The dimension of simplification is significant with respect to the white middle-class caregiver registers documented; however, the notion of simplification has been taken as synonymous with the caregiver register itself. More to the point of this discussion is the apparent tendency to see simplification as a universal, if not natural, process. Ferguson's insightful parallel between caregiver speech and foreigner talk (1977) has been taken to mean that more competent speakers everywhere spontaneously accommodate their speech to less competent interactional partners, directly influencing language change in contact situations (pidgins in particular) as well as in acquisition of a foreign language. Ferguson's own discussion of "simplified registers" does not carry with it this conclusion, however. Further, the stories told here of Kaluli and Samoan caregiver speech and comportment indicate that simplification is culturally organized in terms of when, how, and extent. In both stories, caregivers do not speak in a dramatically more simplified manner to very young children. They do not do so for different cultural reasons: The Kaluli do not simplify because such speech is felt to inhibit the development of competent speech, the Samoans because such accommodations are dispreferred when the addressee is of lower rank than the speaker.

The cultural nature of simplification is evidenced very clearly when we compare Samoan speech to young children with Samoan speech to foreigners (*palagi*). As discussed by Duranti (1981), "foreigner talk" *is* simplified in many ways, in contrast to "baby talk." To understand this, we need only return to the social principle of relative rank. Foreigners typically (and historically) are persons to whom respect is appropriate—strangers or guests of relatively high status. The appropriate comportment toward such persons is one of accommodation to their needs, communicative needs being basic. The Samoan example is an important one, because we can use it to understand social groups for whom speaking to foreigners is like speaking to children. That is, we can at least know where to *start* the process of understanding this speech phenomenon; to see the phenomenon as expressive of cultural beliefs and values. Just as there are cultural explanations for why and how Samoans speak differently to young children and foreigners, so there are cultural explanations for why and how white middle-class adults modify their speech in similar ways to these two types of addressees. These explanations go far beyond the attitudes discussed in the white middle-class story. Our task here is not to provide an adequate cultural account but rather to encourage more detailed research along these lines. An understanding of caregiver or baby-talk register in a particular society will never be achieved without a more serious consideration of the sociological nature of register.

*What Caregivers Do with Words*

In this section we build on the prior two proposals and suggest that:

1. A functional account of the speech of both caregiver and child must incorporate information concerning cultural knowledge and expectations;
2. Generalizations concerning the relations between the behavior and the goals of caregivers and young children should not presuppose the presence or equivalent significance of particular goals across social groups.

In each of these developmental stories we saw that caregivers and children interacted with one another in culturally patterned ways. Our overriding theme has been that caregiver speech behavior must be seen as part of caregiving and socialization more generally. What caregivers say and how they interact with young children are motivated in part by concerns and beliefs held by many members of the local community. As noted earlier, these concerns and beliefs may not be conscious in all cases. Certain beliefs, such as the Kaluli notions of the child as "soft" and socialization as "hardening" the child, are explicit. Others, such as the white middle-class notions of the infant and small child as social and capable of acting intentionally (expressing intentions), are not explicitly formulated.

To understand what any particular verbal behavior is accomplishing, we need to adopt ethnographic procedures, namely, to relate particular behaviors to those performed in other situations. What a caregiver is doing in speaking to a child is obviously related to what she or he does and/or others do in other recurrent situations. We have suggested, for example, that the accommodations that middle-class (particularly American) caregivers make in speaking to young children are linked, patterned ways of responding to incompetence in general (e.g., handicapped persons, retardates). Members of this social group appear to adapt situations to meet the special demands of less competent persons to a far greater extent than in other societies, for example, Samoan society. We have also suggested that the heavy use of expansions by middle-class caregivers to query or confirm what a child is expressing is linked to culturally preferred procedures for achieving understanding, for example, the recognition of ambiguity, the formulation and verification of hypotheses (interpretations, guesses). In participating in interactions in which expansions are used in this way, the child learns the concepts of ambiguity, interpretation, and verification, and the procedures associated with them.

A common method in child language research has been to infer function or goal from behavior. The pitfalls of this procedure are numerous, and social scientists are acutely aware of how difficult it is to establish structure-function relations. One aspect of this dilemma is that one cannot infer function on the basis of a structure in isolation. Structures get their functional meaning through their relation to contexts in which they appear. The "same" structure may have different functions in different circumstances. This is true within a society, but our reason for mentioning it here is that it is true also across societies and languages. Although caregivers in two different societies may expand their children's utterances, it would not necessarily follow that the caregivers shared the same beliefs and values. It is possible that their behavior is motivated by quite different cultural processes. Similarly, the absence of a particular behavior, such as the absence of expansions among caregivers, may be motivated quite differently across societies. Both the Kaluli and the Samoan caregivers do not appear to rely on expansions, but the reasons expansions are dispreferred differ. The Samoans do not do so in part because of their dispreference for guessing and in part because of their expectation that the burden of intelligibility rests with the child (as lower status party) rather than with more mature members of the society. Kaluli do not use expansions to resay or guess what a child may be expressing because they say that "one cannot know what someone else thinks," regardless of age or social status.

Our final point concerning the structure-function relation is that the syntax of our claims about language acquisition must be altered to recognize variation across societies. The bulk of research on communicative development has presupposed or asserted the universality of one or another function, for example, the input function, the communicative function, and the illustrated verbal and nonverbal behaviors that follow from, or reflect, that function. Our three stories suggest that generalizations must be context-restricted. Thus, for example, rather than assuming or asserting that caregivers desire to communicate with an infant, the generalization should be expressed: "Where caregivers desire communication with an infant, then . . ." or "If it is the case that caregivers desire communication with an infant then . . ."

## A TYPOLOGY OF SOCIALIZATION AND CAREGIVER SPEECH PATTERNS

At this point, with the discussion nearing its conclusion, we have decided to stick our necks out a bit further and suggest that the two orientations to children discussed in the developmental stories—adapting situations to the child and adapting the child to situations—distinguish more than the three societies discussed in this reading. We believe that these two orientations of mature members toward children can be used to create a typology of socialization patterns. For example, societies in which children are expected to adapt to situations may include not only Kaluli and Samoan but also white and black working-class Anglo-Americans (Heath 1983; Miller 1982; Ward 1971).

The typology of course requires a more refined application of these orienting features. We would expect these orientations to shift as children develop; for example, a society may adapt situations to meet the needs of a very small infant, but as the infant matures, the expectation may shift to one in which the child should adapt to situations. Indeed, we could predict such a pattern for most, if not all, societies. The distinction between societies would be in terms of *when* this shift takes place and in terms of the *intensity* of the orientation at any point in developmental time.

Having stuck our necks out this far, we will go a little further and propose that these two orientations will have systematic reflexes in the organization of communication between caregivers and young children across societies: We predict, for example, that a society that adapts or fits situations to the needs (perceived needs) of young children will use a register to children that includes a number of simplifying features, for example, shorter utterances, with a restricted lexicon, that refer to here-and-now. Such an orientation is also compatible with a tendency for caregivers to assist the child's expression of intentions through expansions, clarification requests, cooperative proposition building and the like. These often involve the caregiver's taking the perspective of a small child and correlate highly with allowing a small child to initiate new topics (evidencing child-centered orientation).

On the other hand, societies in which children are expected to meet the needs of the situation at hand will communicate differently with infants and small children. In these societies, children usually participate in multiparty situations. Caregivers will socialize children through language to notice others and perform appropriate (not necessarily polite) speech acts toward others. This socialization will often take the form of modeling, where the caregiver says what the child should say and directs the child to repeat. Typically, the child is directed to say something to someone other than the caregiver who has modeled the original utterance. From the Kaluli and Samoan cases, we would predict that the utterances to be repeated would cover a wide range of speech acts (teasing, insulting, greeting, information requesting, begging, reporting of news, shaming, accusations, and the like). In these interactions, as in other communicative contexts with children, the caregivers do not simplify their speech but rather shape their speech to meet situational contingencies (Table 1).

TABLE 1
Two orientations toward children and their corresponding
caregiver speech patterns

| Adapt situation to child | Adapt child to situation |
| --- | --- |
| Simplified register features baby-talk lexicon | Modeling of (umsimplified) utterances for child to repeat to third party (wide range of speech act, not simplified) |
| Negotiation of meaning via expansion and paraphrase | |
| Cooperative proposition building between caregiver and child | Child directed to notice others |
| Utterances that respond to child-initiated verbal or nonverbal act | Topics arise from range of situational circumstances to which caregiver wishes child to respond |
| Typical communicative situation: two-party | Typical communicative situation: multiparty |

## A MODEL OF LANGUAGE ACQUISITION THROUGH SOCIALIZATION (THE ETHNOGRAPHIC APPROACH)

### Cultural Organization of Intentionality

Like many scholars of child language, we believe that the acquisition of language is keyed to accomplishing particular goals (Bates et al. 1979; Greenfield & Smith 1976; Halliday 1975; Lock 1978; Shotter 1978; Vygotsky 1962). As Bates and her colleagues (1979) as well as Carter (1978) and Lock (1981) have pointed out, small children perform communicative acts such as drawing attention to an object and requesting and offering before conventional morphemes are produced. They have acquired knowledge of particular social acts before they have acquired language in even the most rudimentary form. When language emerges, it is put to use in these and other social contexts. As Bates and her colleagues suggest, the use of language here is analogous to other behaviors of the child at this point of development; the child is using a new means to achieve old goals.

Although not taking a stand as to whether or not language is like other behaviors, we support the notion that language is acquired in a social world and that many aspects of the social world have been absorbed by the child by the time language emerges. This is not to say that functional considerations determine grammatical structure but rather that ends motivate means and provide an orienting principle for producing and understanding language over developmental time. Norman (1975), as well as Hood, McDermott, and Cole (1978), suggests that purpose/function is a mnemonic device for learning generally.

Much of the literature on early development has carefully documented the child's capacity to react and act intentionally (Harding & Golinkoff 1979). The nature and organization of communicative interaction is seen as integrally bound to this capacity. Our contribution to this literature is to spell out the social and cultural systems in which intentions participate. The capacity to express intentions is human; but which intentions can be expressed by whom, when, and how is subject to local expectations concerning the social behavior of members. With respect to the acquisition of competence in language use, this means that societies may very well differ in their expectations of what children can and should communicate (Hymes 1967). They may also differ in their expectations concerning the capacity of young children to understand intentions (or particular intentions). With respect to the particular relationship between a child and his or her caregivers, these generalizations can be represented as follows:

Social expectations and language acquisition

| Expectations | *Influence* | Participation in social situations | How & which intentions are expressed by child *Influences* How & which intentions are expressed by caregiver | Structure of child language *Influences* Structure of caregiver language |

Let us consider examples that illustrate these statements. As noted in the Samoan development story, Samoans have a commonly shared expectation that a child's first word will be *tae* (shit) and that its communicative intention will be to curse and confront (corresponding to the adult for *'ai tae* (eat shit). Whereas a range of early consonant-vowel combinations of the child are treated as expressing *tae* and communicative, other phonetic strings are not treated as language. The Kaluli consider that the child has begun to use language when he or she says "mother" and "breast." Like the Samoans, the Kaluli do not treat other words produced before these two words appear as part of "language," that is, as having a purpose.

Another example of how social expectations influence language acquisition comes from the recent work by Platt (1980) on Samoan children's acquisition of the deictic verbs "come," "go," "give," "take." The use of these verbs over developmental time is constrained by social norms concerning the movement of persons and objects. As noted in the Samoan story, higher ranking persons are expected to be relatively inactive in the company of lower ranking (e.g., younger) persons. As a consequence, younger children who are directed to "come" and who evidence comprehension of this act tend not to perform the same act themselves. Children are socially constrained not to direct the more mature persons around them to move in their direction. On the other hand, small children are encouraged to demand and give out goods (particularly food).

At the same developmental point at which the children are *not* using "come," they *are* using "give" quite frequently. This case is interesting because it indicates that a semantically more complex form ("give"—movement of object and person toward deictic center) may appear in the speech of a child earlier than a less complex form ("come"—movement of person toward deictic center) because of the social norms surrounding its use (Platt 1980).

Although these examples have focused on children's speech, we also consider caregiver speech to be constrained by local expectations and the values and beliefs that underlie them. The reader is invited to draw on the body of this reading for examples of these relationships, for example, the relation between caregivers who adapt to young children and use of a simplified register. Indeed, the major focus of our developmental stories has been to indicate precisely the role of sociocultural processes in constructing communication between caregiver and child.

## Sociocultural Knowledge and Code Knowledge

In this section we will build on our argument that children's language is constructed in socially appropriate and culturally meaningful ways. Our point will be that the process of acquiring language must be understood as the process of integrating code knowledge with sociocultural knowledge.

Sociocultural knowledge is generative in much the same way that knowledge about grammar is generative. Just as children are able to produce and understand utterances that they have never heard before, so they are able to participate in social situations that don't exactly match their previous experiences. In the case of social situations in which language is used, children are able to apply both grammatical and sociocultural principles in producing and comprehending novel behavior. Both sets of principles can be acquired out of conscious awareness.

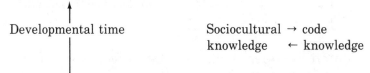

Developmental time          Sociocultural → code
                            knowledge    ← knowledge

In the case of infants and young children acquiring their first language(s), sociocultural knowledge is acquired hand-in-hand with the knowledge of code properties of a language. Acquisition of a foreign or second language by older children and adults may not necessarily follow this model. In classroom foreign-language learning, for example, a knowledge of code properties typically precedes knowledge of the cultural norms of code use. Even where the second language is acquired in the context of living in a foreign culture, the cultural knowledge necessary for appropriate social interaction may lag behind or never develop, as illustrated by Gumperz (1977) for Indian speakers in Great Britain.

Another point to be mentioned at this time is that the sociocultural principles being acquired are not necessarily shared by all native speakers of a language. As noted in the introduction, there are variations in knowledge between individuals and between groups of individuals. In certain cases, for example, children who are members of a nondominant group, growing up may necessitate acquiring different cultural frameworks for participating in situations. American Indian and Australian Aboriginal children find themselves participating in interactions in which the language is familiar but the interactional procedures and participant structures differ from earlier experiences (Philips 1983). These cases of growing up monolingually but biculturally are similar to the circumstances of second-language learners who enter a cultural milieu that differs from that of first socialization experiences.

## On the Unevenness of Language Development

The picture we have built up suggests that there is quite a complex system of norms and expectations that the young language acquirer must attend to, and does attend to, in the process of growing up to be a competent speaker-hearer. We have talked about this system as affecting structure and content of children's utterances at different points in developmental time. One product of all this is that children come to use and hear particular structures in certain contexts but not in others. In other words, children acquire forms in a subset of contexts that has been given "priority" by members.

Priority contexts are those in which children are encouraged to participate. For example, Kaluli and Samoan children use affect pronouns, for example, "poor-me," initially in begging, an activity they are encouraged to engage in. The use of affect pronouns in other speech acts is a later development. Similarly, many white middle-class children use their first nominal forms in the act of labeling, an activity much encouraged by caregivers in this social group. Labeling is not an activity in which Kaluli and Samoan caregivers and children engage. Each social group will have its preferences, and these, in turn, will guide the child's acquisition of language.

## On Lack of Match between Child and Caregiver Speech

Those who pursue the argument concerning how children acquire language often turn to correlational comparisons between children's and caregivers' speech strategies. Lack of match is taken as support for some input-independent strategy of the child and as evidence that some natural process is at work. We suggest that this line of reasoning has flaws.

If the reader has accepted the argument that societies have ideas about how children can and should participate in social situations and that these ideas differ in many respects from those concerning how more mature persons can and should behave, then the reader might further accept the conclusion that children may speak and act differently from others because they have learned to do so. Why should we equate input exclusively with imitation, that is, with a match in behavior? Of course there are commonalities between child and adult behavior, but that does not imply that difference is not learned. In examining the speech of young children, we should not necessarily expect their speech and the functions to which it is put to match exactly those of caregivers. Children are neither expected nor encouraged to do many of the things that older persons do, and, conversely, older persons are neither expected nor encouraged to do many of the things that small children do. Indeed, unless they are framed as "play," attempts to cross these social boundaries meet with laughter, ridicule, or other forms of negative sanctioning.

## A Note on the Role of Biology

Lest the reader think we advocate a model in which language and cognition are the exclusive product of culture, we note here that sociocultural systems are to be considered as *one* force influencing language acquisition. Biological predispositions, of course, have a hand in this process as well. The model we have presented should be considered as a subset of a more general acquisition model that includes both influences.

Social Expectations                                      Language over
                                                         developmental time
                          Influence
Biological
predispositions


## CONCLUSIONS

This is a reading with a number of points but one message: That the process of acquiring language and the process of acquiring sociocultural knowledge are intimately tied. In pursuing this generalization, we have formulated the following proposals:

1. The specific features of caregiver speech behavior that have been described as simplified register are neither universal nor necessary for language to be acquired. White middle-class children, Kaluli children, and Samoan children all become speakers of their languages within the normal range of development and yet their caregivers use language quite differently in their presence.
2. Caregivers' speech behavior expresses and reflects values and beliefs held by members of a social group. In this sense, caregivers' speech is part of a larger set of behaviors that are culturally organized.
3. The use of simplified registers by caregivers in certain societies may be part of a more general orientation in which situations are adapted to young children's perceived needs. In other societies, the orientation may be the reverse, that is, children at a very early age are expected to adapt to requirements of situations. In such societies, caregivers direct children to notice and respond to others'

actions. They tend not to simplify their speech and frequently model appropriate utterances for the child to repeat to a third party in a situation.

4. Not only caregivers' but children's language as well is influenced by social expectations. Children's strategies for encoding and decoding information, for negotiating meaning, and for handling errors are socially organized in terms of who does the work, when, and how. Further, every society orchestrates the ways in which children participate in particular situations, and this, in turn, affects the form, the function, and the content of children's utterances. Certain features of the grammar may be acquired quite early, in part because their use is encouraged and given high priority. In this sense, the process of language acquisition is part of the larger process of socialization, that is, acquiring social competence.

Although biological factors play a role in language acquisition, sociocultural factors have a hand in this process as well. It is not a trivial fact that small children develop in the context of organized societies. Cultural conditions for communication organize even the earliest interactions between infants and others. Through participation as audience, addressee, and/or "speaker," the infant develops a range of skills, intuitions, and knowledge enabling him or her to communicate in culturally preferred ways. The development of these faculties is an integral part of becoming a competent speaker.

## Coda

This reading should be in no way interpreted as proposing a view in which socialization determines a fixed pattern of behavior. We advocate a view that considers human beings to be flexible and able to adapt to change, both social and linguistic, for example, through contact and social mobility. The ways in which individuals change is a product of complex interactions between established cultural procedures and intuitions and those the individual is currently acquiring. From our perspective, socialization is a continuous and open-ended process that spans the entire life of an individual.

## REFERENCES

Aksu, A., & Slobin, D. I. In press. Acquisition of Turkish. In D. I. Slobin, ed., *The Crosslinguistic Study of Language Acquisition.* Hillsdale, NJ: Erlbaum.

Andersen, E. 1977. *Learning to speak with style.* Unpublished doctoral dissertation, Stanford University.

Andersen, E. S., Dunlea, A., & Kekelis, L. 1982. *Blind children's language: Resolving some differences.* Paper presented at the Stanford Child Language Research Forum, Stanford, CA.

Andersen, E. S., & Johnson, C. E. 1973. Modifications in the speech of an eight-year-old to younger children. *Stanford Occasional Papers in Linguistics,* No. 3:149–60.

Bates, E. 1976. *Language and Context: The Acquisition of Pragmatics.* New York: Academic Press.

Bates, E., Beeghly-Smith, M., Bretherton, I., & McNew, S. In press. Social bases of language development: A Reassessment. In H. W. Reese & L. P. Lipsitt, eds., *Advances in Child Development and Behavior,* vol. 16. New York: Academic Press.

Bates, E., Benigni, L., Bretherton, I., Camaioni, L., & Volterra, V. 1979. *The Emergence of Symbols.* New York: Academic Press.

Berko, J. 1958. The child's learning of English morphology. *Word* 14:150–77.

Berman, R. In press. Acquisition of Hebrew. In D. I. Slobin, ed., *The Crosslinguistic Study of Language Acquisition.* Hillsdale, NJ: Erlbaum.

Bever, T. 1970. The cognitive basis for linguistic structure. In J. R. Hayes, ed., *Cognition and the Development of Language.* New York: Wiley.

Bloom, L. 1970. *Language Development: Form and Function in Emerging Grammars.* Cambridge: MIT Press.

———. 1973. *One Word at a Time.* The Hague: Mouton.

Bloom, L., Hood, L., & Lightbown, P. 1974. Imitation in language development: If, when, and why? *Cognitive Psychology* 6:380–420.

Bloom, L., & Lahey, M. 1978. *Language Development and Language Disorders.* New York: Wiley.

Bloom, L., Lightbown, P., & Hood, L. 1975. Structure and variation in child language. *Monographs of the Society for Research in Child Development* 40(2, serial no. 160).

Blount, B. 1972. Aspects of socialization among the Luo of Kenya. *Language in Society* 1:235–48.

Bowerman, M. 1973. *Early Syntactic Development: A Cross-linguistic Study with Special Reference to Finnish.* Cambridge: Cambridge University Press.

———. 1977. Semantic and syntactic development: A review of what, when and how in language acquisition. In R. Schiefelbusch, ed., *Bases of Language Intervention.* Baltimore: University Park Press.

———. 1981. Language development. In H. Triandis & A. Heron, eds., *Handbook of Cross-cultural Psychology,* vol. 4. Boston: Allyn & Bacon.

Briggs, J. L. 1970. *Never in Anger: Portrait of an Eskimo Family.* Cambridge: Harvard University Press.

Brown, R. 1973. *A First Language: The Early Stages.* Cambridge: Harvard University Press.

———. 1977. Introduction. In C. Snow & C. Ferguson, eds., *Talking to Children: Language Input and Acquisition.* Cambridge: Cambridge University Press.

Brown, R., & Bellugi, U. 1964. Three processes in the child's acquisition of syntax. *Harvard Educational Review* 34:133–51.

Brown, R., Cazden, C., & Bellugi, U. 1969. The child's grammar from I to III. In J. P. Hill, ed., *Minnesota Symposium on Child Psychology,* vol. 2. Minneapolis: University of Minnesota Press.

Bruner, J. S. 1975. The ontogenesis of speech acts. *Journal of Child Language* 2:1–19.

———. 1977. Early social interaction and language acquisition. In H. R. Schaffer, ed., *Studies in Mother-Infant Interaction.* London: Academic Press.

———. 1978. The role of dialogue in language acquisition. In A. Sinclair, R. J. Jarvella, & W. J. M. Levelt, eds., *The Child's Conception of Language.* New York: Springer-Verlag.

Bullowa, M. 1979. Introduction: Prelinguistic communication: A field for scientific research. In M. Bullowa, ed., *Before Speech: The Beginnings of Interpersonal Communication.* Cambridge: Cambridge University Press.

Carter, A. L. 1978. From sensori-motor vocalizations to words. In A. Lock, ed., *Action, Gesture and Symbol: The Emergence of Language*. London: Academic Press.

Cazden, C. 1965. *Environmental assistance to the child's acquisition of grammar*. Unpublished doctoral dissertation, Harvard University.

Chomsky, N. 1959. Review of *Verbal Behavior* by B. F. Skinner. *Language* 35:26–58.

———. 1965. *Aspects of the Theory of Syntax*. Cambridge: MIT Press.

———. 1968. *Language and Mind*. New York: Harcourt Brace Jovanovich.

———. 1975. *Reflections on Language*. Glasgow: Fontana/Collins.

———. 1977. *Essays on Form and Interpretation*. New York: North Holland.

Clancy, P. In press. Acquisition of Japanese. In D. I. Slobin, ed., *The Crosslinguistic Study of Language Acquisition*. Hillsdale, NJ: Erlbaum.

Clark, E. V. 1974. Some aspects of the conceptual basis for first language acquisition. In R. L. Schiefelbusch & L. Lloyd, eds., *Language Perspectives: Acquisition, Retardation and Intervention*. Baltimore: University Park Press.

———. In press. Acquisition of Romance, with special reference to French. In D. I. Slobin, ed., *The Crosslinguistic Study of Language Acquisition*. Hillsdale, NJ: Erlbaum.

Clark, H. H., & Clark, E. V. 1977. *Psychology and Language*. New York: Harcourt Brace Jovanovich.

Corsaro, W. 1979. Sociolinguistic patterns in adult-child inter-action. In E. Ochs & B. B. Schieffelin, eds., *Developmental Pragmatics*. New York: Academic Press.

Cross, T. 1977. Mothers' speech adjustments: The contributions of selected child listener variables. In C. Snow & C. Ferguson, eds., *Talking to Children: Language Input and Acquisition*. Cambridge: Cambridge University Press.

de Lemos, C. 1981. Interactional processes in the child's construction of language. In W. Deutsch, ed., *The Child's Construction of Language*. London: Academic Press.

Dentan, R. K. 1978. Notes on childhood in a nonviolent context: The Semai case. In A. Montagu, ed., *Learning Non-aggression: The Experience of Nonliterate Societies*. Oxford: Oxford University Press.

Dore, J. 1975. Holophrases, speech acts and language universals. *Journal of Child Language* 2:21–40.

Drach, K. 1969. *The language of the parent*. Working paper 14, Language Behavior Research Laboratory, University of California, Berkeley.

Duranti, A. 1981. *The Samoan Fono: A Sociolinguistic Study*. Pacific Linguistic Series B, vol. 80. Canberra: Australian National University.

Edgerton, R. 1967. *The Cloak of Competence: Stigma in the Lives of the Mentally Retarded*. Berkeley: University of California Press.

Eisenberg, A. 1982. *Language acquisition in cultural perspective: Talk in three Mexicano homes*. Unpublished doctoral dissertation, University of California, Berkeley.

Ervin-Tripp, S. 1964. Imitation and structural change in children's language. In E. Lenneberg, ed., *New Directions in the Study of Language*. Cambridge: MIT Press.

Feld, S., & Schieffelin, B. B. 1982. Hard words: A functional basis for Kaluli discourse. In D. Tannen, ed., *Analyzing Discourse: Talk and Text*. Washington, DC: Georgetown University Press.

Feldman, H., Goldin-Meadow, S., & Gleitman, L. 1978. Beyond Herodotus: The creation of language by linguistically deprived deaf children. In A. Lock, ed., *Action, Gesture and Symbol*. London: Academic Press.

Ferguson, C. 1977. Baby talk as a simplified register. In C. Snow & C. Ferguson, eds., *Talking to Children: Language Input and Acquisition*. Cambridge: Cambridge University Press.

Fischer, J. 1970. Linguistic socialization: Japan and the United States. In R. Hill & R. Konig, eds., *Families in East and West*. The Hague: Mouton.

Fodor, J., Bever, T., & Garrett, M. 1974. *The Psychology of Language*. New York: McGraw-Hill.

Foster, S. 1981. The emergence of topic type in children under 2, 6: A chicken and egg problem. *Papers and Reports in Child Language Development*, No. 20. Stanford: Stanford University Press.

Gallimore, R., Boggs, J., & Jordan, C. 1974. *Culture, Behavior and Education: A Study of Hawaiian Americans*. Beverly Hills: Sage.

Garnica, O. 1977. Some prosodic and para-linguistic features of speech to young children. In C. Snow & C. Ferguson, eds., *Talking to Children: Language Input and Acquisition*. Cambridge: Cambridge University Press.

Geertz, C. 1973. *The Interpretation of Cultures*. New York: Basic Books.

Geertz, H. 1959. The vocabulary of emotion: A study of Javanese socialization processes. *Psychiatry* 22:225–37.

Gleason, J. B., & Weintraub, S. 1978. Input language and the acquisition of communicative competence. In K. Nelson, ed., *Children's Language*, vol. 1. New York: Gardner Press.

Goffman, E. 1963. *Behavior in Public Places*. New York: Free Press.

———. 1967. *Interaction Ritual: Essays on Face to Face Behavior*. Garden City, NY: Doubleday (Anchor Books).

Goldin-Meadow, S. 1977. Structure in a manual language system developed without a language model: Language without a helping hand. In H. Whitaker & H. A. Whitaker, eds., *Studies in Neurolinguistics*, vol. 4. New York: Academic Press.

Golinkoff, R., ed. 1983. *The Transition from Prelinguistic to Linguistic Communication*. Hillsdale, NJ: Erlbaum.

Goody, E. 1978. Towards a theory of questions. In E. Goody, ed., *Questions and Politeness*. Cambridge: Cambridge University Press.

Greenfield, P. 1979. Informativeness, presupposition and semantic choice in single-word utterances. In E. Ochs & B. B. Schieffelin, eds., *Developmental Pragmatics*. New York: Academic Press.

Greenfield, P. M., & Smith, J. H. 1976. *The Structure of Communication in Early Language Development*. New York: Academic Press.

Gumperz, J. 1977. The conversational analysis of interethnic communication. In E. L. Ross, ed., *Interethnic Communication*. Proceedings of the Southern Anthropological Society. Athens: University of Georgia Press.

Halliday, M. A. K. 1975. *Learning How to Mean: Explorations in the Development of Language*. London: Arnold.

Hamilton, A. 1981. *Nature and Nurture: Aboriginal Childrearing in North-Central Arnhem Land*. Canberra, Australia: Institute of Aboriginal Studies.

Harding, C., & Golinkoff, R. M. 1979. The origins of intentional vocalizations in prelinguistic infants. *Child Development* 50:33–40.

Harkness, S. 1975. Cultural variation in mother's language. In W. von Raffler-Engel, ed., *Child Language—1975, Word* 27:495–8.

Harkness, S., & Super, C. 1977. Why African children are so hard to test. In L. L. Adler, ed., *Issues in Cross Cultural Research: Annals of the New York Academy of Sciences* 285:326–331.

Harkness, S., & Super, C., eds. 1980. *Anthropological Perspectives on Child Development*. New Directions for Child Development, no. 8. San Francisco: Jossey-Bass.

Heath, S. B. 1983. *Ways with Words: Language, Life and Work in Communities and Classroom*. Cambridge: Cambridge University Press.

Hood, L., McDermott, R., & Cole, M. 1978. *Ecological niche-picking* (Working Paper 14). Unpublished manuscript, Rockefeller University, Laboratory of Comparative Human Cognition, New York.

Huttenlocher, J. 1974. The origins of language comprehension. In R. L. Solso, ed., *Theories of Cognitive Psychology*. Hillsdale, NJ: Erlbaum.

Hymes, D. 1967. Models of the interaction of language and social setting. *Journal of Social Issues* 23(2):8–28.

_____. 1974. *Foundations in Sociolinguistics: An Ethnographic Approach*. Philadelphia: University of Pennsylvania Press.

Irvine, J. 1974. Strategies of status manipulation in the Wolof greeting. In R. Bauman & J. Sherzer, eds., *Explorations in the Ethnography of Speaking*. Cambridge: Cambridge University Press.

Johnston, J. R., & Slobin, D. I. 1979. The development of locative expressions in English, Italian Serbo-Croatian and Turkish. *Journal of Child Language* 6:529–45.

Karmiloff-Smith, A. 1979. *A Functional Approach to Child Language*. Cambridge: Cambridge University Press.

Keenan, E., Ochs, E., & Schieffelin, B. B. 1976. Topic as a discourse notion: A study of topic in the conversations of children and adults. In C. Li, ed., *Subject and Topic*. New York: Academic Press.

Kernan, K. T. 1969. *The acquisition of language by Samoan children*. Unpublished doctoral dissertation, University of California, Berkeley.

Korbin, J. 1978. *Caretaking Patterns in a Rural Hawaiian Community*. Unpublished doctoral dissertation, University of California, Los Angeles.

Leiderman, P. H., Tulkin, S. R., & Rosenfeld, A., eds. 1977. *Culture and Infancy*. New York: Academic Press.

LeVine, R. 1980. Anthropology and child development. *Anthropological Perspectives on Child Development*. New Directions for Child Development, no. 8. San Francisco: Jossey-Bass.

Levy, R. 1973. *The Tahitians*. Chicago: University of Chicago Press.

Lewis, M., & Rosenblum, L. A., eds. 1974. *The Effect of the Infant on its Caregiver*. New York: Wiley.

Lieven, E. 1980. Different routes to multiple-word combinations? *Papers and Reports in Child Language Development*, no. 19, Stanford University, Stanford, CA.

Lock, A. 1981. *The Guided Reinvention of Language*. London: Academic Press.

_____. 1978. *Action, Gesture and Symbol*. London: Academic Press.

MacNamara, J. 1972. The cognitive basis of language learning in infants. *Psychological Review* 79:1–13.

McNeill, D. 1966. The creation of language by children. In J. Lyons & R. J. Wales, eds., *Psycholinguistic Papers*. Edinburgh: Edinburgh University Press.

_____. 1970. *The Acquisition of Language*. Harper & Row.

MacWhinney, B. 1975. Rules, rote and analogy in morphological formation by Hungarian children. *Journal of Child Language* 2:65–77.

MacWhinney, B., & Bates, E. 1978. Sentential devices for conveying givenness and newness: A cross-cultural developmental study. *Journal of Verbal Learning and Verbal Behavior* 17:539–58.

Mead, M. 1927. *Coming of Age in Samoa.* New York: Blue Ribbon Books.
———. 1975. *Growing Up in New Guinea.* New York: Morrow. Originally published, 1935.
Mead, M., & MacGregor, F. 1951. *Growth and Culture.* New York: Putnam.
Mead, M., & Wolfenstein, M. 1955. *Childhood in Contemporary Cultures.* Chicago: University of Chicago Press.
Menyuk, P. & Menn, L. 1979. Early strategies for the perception and production of words and sounds. In P. Fletcher & M. Garman, eds., *Language Acquisition.* Cambridge: Cambridge University Press.
Miller, G., & Chomsky, N. 1963. Finitary models of language users. In R. Bush, E. Galanter, & R. Luce, eds., *Handbook of Mathematical Psychology*, vol. 2. New York: Wiley.
Miller, P. 1982. *Amy, Wendy and Beth: Learning Language in South Baltimore.* Austin: University of Texas Press.
Montagu, A. 1937. *Coming into Being Among the Australian Aborigines: A Study of the Procreation Beliefs of the Native Tribes of Australia.* London: Routledge.
Montagu, A., ed. 1978. *Learning Non-aggression: The Experience of Nonliterate Societies.* Oxford: Oxford University Press.
Much, N., & Shweder, R. 1978. Speaking of rules: The analysis of culture in breach. In W. Damon, ed., *Moral Development.* New Directions for Child Development, no. 2. San Francisco: Jossey-Bass.
Munroe, R. L., & Munroe, R. N. 1975. *Cross Cultural Human Development.* Monterey, CA: Brooks/Cole.
Nelson, K. 1974. Concept, word and sentence: Interrelations in acquisition and development. *Psychological Review* 81:267–85.
Newport, E. L. 1976. Motherese: The speech of mothers to young children. In N. J. Castellan, D. B. Pisoni, & G. R. Potts, eds., *Cognitive Theory*, vol. 2. Hillsdale, NJ: Erlbaum.
———. 1981. Constraints on structure: Evidence from American sign language and language learning. In W. A. Collins, ed., *Minnesota Symposium on Child Psychology*, vol. 14. Hillsdale, NJ: Erlbaum.
Newport, E. L., Gleitman, H., & Gleitman, L. R. 1977. Mother, I'd rather do it myself: Some effects and non-effects of maternal speech style. In C. Snow & C. Ferguson, eds., *Talking to Children: Language Input and Acquisition.* Cambridge: Cambridge University Press.
Newson, J. 1977. An intersubjective approach to the systematic description of mother-infant interaction. In H. R. Schaffer, ed., *Studies in Mother-Infant Interaction.* London: Academic Press.
———. 1978. Dialogue and development. In A. Lock, ed., *Action, Gesture and Symbol.* London: Academic Press.
Ninio, A. 1979. The naive theory of the infant and other maternal attitudes in two subgroups in Israel. *Child Development* 50:976–80.
Norman, D. A. 1975. Cognitive organization and learning. In P. M. A. Rabbitt & S. Dornic, eds., *Attention and Performance V.* New York: Academic Press.
Ochs, E. 1982a. *Affect in Samoan child language.* Paper presented to the Stanford Child Language Research Forum, Stanford, CA.
Ochs, E. 1982b. Ergativity and word order in Samoan child language: A sociolinguistic study. *Language* 58:646–71.
——— 1982c. Talking to children in Western Samoa. *Language in Society* 11:77–104.

Ochs, E. In press. Variation and error: A sociolinguistic study of language acquisition in Samoa. In D. I. Slobin, ed., *The Crosslinguistic Study of Language Acquisition*. Hillsdale, NJ: Erlbaum.

Ochs, E., Schieffelin, B. B., & Platt, M. 1979. Propositions across utterances and speaker. In E. Ochs & B. B. Schieffelin, eds., *Developmental Pragmatics*. New York: Academic Press.

Philips, S. 1983 (reissued 1983). *The Invisible Culture*. Prospect Heights, IL: Waveland Press.

Phillips, J. 1973. Syntax and vocabulary of mothers' speech to young children: Age and sex comparisons. *Child Development* 44:182–5.

Piaget, J. 1955. *The Language and Thought of the Child*. London: Routledge & Kegan Paul. Originally published, 1926.

Piattelli-Palmarini, M., ed. 1980. *Language and Learning: The Debate Between Jean Piaget and Noam Chomsky*. Cambridge: Harvard University Press.

Platt, M. 1980. The acquisition of "come," "give," and "bring" by Samoan children. *Papers and Reports in Child Language Development*, no. 19. Stanford: Stanford University.

Richards, M. P. M., ed. 1974. *The Integration of a Child into a Social World*. Cambridge: Cambridge University Press.

Ryan, J. 1974. Early language development: Towards a communicational analysis. In M. P. M. Richards, ed., *The Integration of a Child into a Social World*. Cambridge: Cambridge University Press.

Sachs, J. 1977. Adaptive significance of input to infants. In C. Snow & C. Ferguson, eds., *Talking to Children: Language Input and Acquisition*. Cambridge: Cambridge University Press.

Sachs, J., Brown, R., & Salerno, R. 1976. Adults speech to children. In W. von Raffler Engel & Y. Lebrun, eds., *Baby Talk and Infant Speech*. Lisse: Riddler Press.

Sachs, J., & Devin, J. 1976. Young children's use of age-appropriate speech styles. *Journal of Child Language* 3:81–98.

Schaffer, H. R., ed. 1977. *Studies in Mother-Infant Interaction*. London: Academic Press.

Schieffelin, B. B. 1979. Getting it together: An ethnographic approach to the study of the development of communicative competence. In E. Ochs & B. B. Schieffelin, eds., *Developmental Pragmatics*. New York: Academic Press.

_____. 1981. A developmental study of pragmatic appropriateness of word order and case marking in Kaluli. In W. Deutsch, ed., *The Child's Construction of Language*. London: Academic Press.

_____. In press-a. Acquisition of Kaluli. In D. I. Slobin, ed., *The Crosslinguistic Study of Language Acquisition*. Hillsdale, NJ: Erlbaum.

_____. In press-b. *How Kaluli Children Learn What to Say, What to Do and How to Feel*. Cambridge: Cambridge University Press.

Schieffelin, B. B., & Eisenberg, A. 1984. Cultural variation in children's conversations. In R. L. Schiefelbusch & J. Pickar, eds., *Communicative Competence: Acquisition and Intervention*. Baltimore: University Park Press.

Schieffelin, E. L. 1976. *The Sorrow of the Lonely and the Burning of the Dancers*. New York: St. Martin's Press.

Schlesinger, I. M. 1974. Relational concepts underlying language. In R. Schiefelbusch & L. Lloyd, eds., *Language Perspectives—Acquisition, Retardation and Intervention*. Baltimore: University Park Press.

Scollon, R. 1976. *Conversations with a One Year Old*. Honolulu: University Press of Hawaii.

Scollon, R. & Scollon, S. 1981. The literate two-year-old: The Fictionalization of self. Abstracting themes: A Chipewyan two-year-old. *Narrative, Literacy and Face in Interethnic Communication.* vol. 7 of R. O. Freedle, ed., *Advances in Discourse Processes.* Norwood, NJ: Ablex.

Shatz, M. 1978. The relationship between cognitive processes and the development of communication skills. In C. B. Keasey, ed., *Nebraska Symposium on Motivation,* vol. 25. Lincoln: University of Nebraska Press.

――――. 1981. Learning the rules of the game: Four views of the relation between social interaction and syntax acquisition. In W. Deutch, ed., *The Child's Construction of Language.* London: Academic Press.

――――. In press. Communication. In J. Flavell & E. Markman, eds., *Cognitive Development,* P. Mussen, gen. ed., *Carmichael's Manual of Child Psychology,* 4th ed. New York: Wiley.

Shatz, M., & Gelman, R. 1973. The development of communication skills: Modifications in the speech of young children as a function of listener. *Monographs of the Society for Research in Child Development,* 152(38, serial no. 5).

Shore, B. 1982. *Sala' Ilua: A Samoan Mystery.* New York: Columbia University Press.

Shotter, J. 1978. The cultural context of communication studies: Theoretical and methodological issues. In A. Lock, ed., *Action, Gesture and Symbol.* London: Academic Press.

Sinclair, H. 1971. Sensorimotor action patterns as a condition for the acquisition of syntax. In R. Huxley & E. Ingram, eds., *Language Acquisition: Models and Methods.* New York: Academic Press.

Skinner, B. F. 1957. *Verbal Behavior.* New York: Appleton-Century-Crofts.

Slobin, D. I. 1973. Cognitive prerequisites for grammar. In C. Ferguson & D. I. Slobin, eds., *Studies in Child Language Development.* New York: Holt, Rinehart and Winston.

――――. 1979. *Psycholinguistics,* 2nd ed. Glenview, IL: Scott Foresman.

――――. 1981. The origin of grammatical encoding of events. In W. Deutsch, ed., *The Child's Construction of Language.* London: Academic Press.

――――. 1982. Universal and particular in the acquisition of language. In E. Wanner, & L. R. Gleitman, eds., *Language Acquisition: The State of the Art.* Cambridge: Cambridge University Press.

Slobin, D. I., ed. 1967. *A Field Manual for Cross-cultural Study of the Acquisition of Communicative Competence.* Language Behavior Research Laboratory, University of California, Berkeley.

――――. In press. *The Crosslinguistic Study of Language Acquisition.* Hillsdale, NJ: Erlbaum.

Snow, C. 1972. Mothers' speech to children learning language. *Child Development* 43:549–65.

――――. 1977a. The development of conversation between mothers and babies. *Journal of Child Language* 4:1–22.

――――. 1977b. Mothers' speech research: From input to inter-action. In C. Snow & C. Ferguson, eds., *Talking to Children: Language Input and Acquisition.* Cambridge: Cambridge University Press.

――――. 1979. Conversations with children. In P. Fletcher & M. Garman, eds., *Language Acquisition.* Cambridge: Cambridge University Press.

Snow, C., de Blauw, A., & van Roosmalen, G. 1979. Talking and playing with babies: The role of ideologies of child-rearing. In M. Bullowa, ed., *Before Speech: The Beginnings of Interpersonal Communication.* Cambridge: Cambridge University Press.

Snow, C., & Ferguson, C., eds. 1977. *Talking to Children: Language Input and Acquisition.* Cambridge: Cambridge University Press.

Stern, D. 1977. *The First Relationship: Infant and Mother.* Cambridge: Harvard University Press.

Stross, B. 1972. Verbal processes in Tzeltal speech socialization. *Anthropological Linguistics* 14:1.

Sugarman, S. 1984. The development of preverbal communication: Its contribution and limits in promoting the development of language. In R. L. Schiefelbusch & J. Pickar, eds., *Communicative Competence: Acquisition and Intervention.* Baltimore: University Park Press.

Trevarthen, C. 1979a. Communication and cooperation in early infancy: A description of primary intersubjectivity. In M. Bullowa, ed., *Before Speech: The Beginnings of Interpersonal Communication.* Cambridge: Cambridge University Press.

———. 1979b. Instincts for human understanding and for cultural cooperation: Their development in infancy. In M. von Cranach, K. Foppa, W. Lepenies, & D. Ploog, eds., *Human Ethology: Claims and Limits of a New Discipline.* Cambridge: Cambridge University Press.

van der Geest, T. 1977. Some interactional aspects of language acquisition. In C. Snow & C. Ferguson, eds., *Talking to Children: Language Input and Acquisition.* Cambridge: Cambridge University Press.

von Sturmer, D. E. 1980. *Rights in nurturing.* Unpublished master's thesis, Australian National University, Canberra.

Vygotsky, L. S. 1962. *Thought and Language.* Cambridge: MIT Press.

Wagner, D., & Stevenson, H. W., eds. 1982. *Cultural Perspectives on Child Development.* San Francisco: Freeman.

Wanner E., & Gleitman, L. R., eds. 1982. *Language Acquisition: The State of the Art.* Cambridge: Cambridge University Press.

Ward, M. 1971 (reissued 1986). *Them Children: A Study in Language Learning.* Prospect Heights, IL: Waveland Press.

Watson-Gegeo, K., & Gegeo, D. 1982. *Calling out and repeating: Two key routines in Kwara'ae children's language acquisition.* Paper presented at the American Anthropological Association meetings, Washington, DC.

Weisner, T. S., & Gallimore, R. 1977. My brother's keeper: Child and sibling caretaking. *Current Anthropology* 18(2): 169–90.

Werner, H., & Kaplan, B. 1963. *Symbol Formation.* New York: Wiley.

Whiting, B., ed. 1963. *Six Cultures: Studies of Child Rearing.* New York: Wiley.

Whiting, B., & Whiting, J. 1975. *Children of Six Cultures.* Cambridge: Harvard University Press.

Williams, T. R. 1969. *A Borneo Childhood: Enculturation in Dusun Society.* New York: Holt, Rinehart and Winston.

Wills, D. 1977. *Culture's cradle: Social structural and interactional aspects of Senegalese socialization.* Unpublished doctoral dissertation, University of Texas, Austin.

# Language and the Culture of Gender: At the Intersection of Structure, Usage, and Ideology

Michael Silverstein

The contemporary sociolinguistic dilemma of English pronoun usage—to "he" or not to "he"—illustrates a larger theoretical point about language as a semiotic system. It also suggests a practical lesson about how language is mobilized in political struggles. First, the theoretical point. The total linguistic fact, the datum for a science of language, is irreducibly dialectic in nature. It is an unstable mutual interaction of meaningful sign forms contextualized to situations of interested human use, mediated by the fact of cultural ideology. And the linguistic fact is irreducibly dialectic, whether we view it as so-called synchronic usage or as so-called diachronic change. It is an indifferently synchronic-diachronic totality, which, however, at least initially—in keeping with traditional autonomous divisions of scholarly perspective—can be considered from the points of view of language structure, contextualized usage, and ideologies of language.

From this, second, the suggested lesson. Attempts at the regimentation of language, the explicit formulation of standards bespeaking adherence to various larger social and political values, are part of such dialectical social processes played out over time. One component of the process is an ideological formation rationalizing some particular linguistic value; but it is the larger dialectic process that ultimately regiments language as an institution. Explicit views on acceptable language exert only one, generally indirect force on the process.

It is interesting that, concluding a 1979 survey of the social marker of gender in speech, Smith could write that "it seems unlikely that speech would ever become the focal point of popular concern over relations between the sexes, as it has for some ethnic and nationalist movements" (1979:138). Even given reasonable publication lag times, it is difficult to understand such a statement in light of a decade-long multimedia public discourse in virtually every area of quotidian or contemplative life. For English and other European standard languages, proposals about language reform abound, based on particular views and/or analyses of the constituted problem of language and gender. Governments and other official institutions meanwhile redo printed and spoken titles and status names, personal naming regulations, et cetera. Learned journals and textbook publishers as much as popular periodicals have explicitly reformulated stylistic guidelines about pronominal usage in attempts to please

**513**

everyone, or at least offend no one. Such phenomena certainly demonstrate that language is indeed a "focal point" of a social concern, the vehicle of an unfolding process that it behooves us to try to understand with as much dispassionate analytic rigor as we can.

To begin consideration of the matter, three perspectives can be identified that have generally been treated as distinct and independent, what we might call the structural, the pragmatic, and the ideological. I want to develop the argument that these analytically distinct realms seem to interact in the linguistic (and even sociolinguistic) fact of 'gender.' And more generally, this is a claim-by-example for *every* linguistic category related to our ability to refer and predicate, which, carefully examined, is situated at such a triple intersection. So let me briefly characterize these perspectives, at least as they traditionally present themselves, and then go on to examine 'gender' that way. In conclusion, I can return to the argument about the merely perspectival analytic distinctness of these realms, and make some proposals about what ought to replace them.

The *structural* realm defines a norm of categories of linguistic form as these interact in a system or grammar. This grammatical norm, Saussure's *langue*, is said to underlie, or to be implicit in, the actual usage of language as a behavioral vehicle of communication, Saussure's *parole*. Hence, categories of grammar in this sense are abstract, though they are traditionally abstracted from usage under assumptions about communication. Specifically, traditional views of linguistic structure assume that communication is propositional in value, that is, is organized so as to refer to things (pick out objects of reference or topics of discourse) and, in different gradient degrees and modalizations, to characterize or describe or predicate truths about them. If we take the most "concrete" of English grammatical categories, such as 'singular' vs. 'plural' *number*, this seems to be the set of formal regularities related to picking out or characterizing objects as one or many. If we take the most "abstract" of English grammatical categories, such as 'subjective' vs. 'objective' *case* (formally indicated mostly with order of certain words), even this seems to be the set of formal regularities ultimately related to certain directionalities of predicable relationships between objects (*Who* buys from/sells to *whom*, etc.). Virtually all of what both users and professional analysts (grammarians) of language call the structure of a language is abstracted from such assumptions about the propositional or representational value of linguistic communication.

There is a second perspective on language, here called *pragmatics*. This studies usage as discourse in actual situations of communication, looking for regularities of how "appropriate" linguistic forms occur as indexes of (pointers to) the particularities of an intersubjective communicative context and how "effective" linguistic forms occur as indexes of (pointers to) intersubjective consequences of communication. Such study of language as discourse, rather than as abstract propositional structure, includes principles of cohesion—and its specialization in poetic form—of discourse units when we consider previously instanced language forms as part of the shared ongoing context of communication. It includes so-called illocutionary and perlocutionary "speech acts"—"doing things with words" such as promising, insulting, warding off evil, et cetera, appropriately and effectively carried out when we use language forms. And very importantly, pragmatics includes the notion of how systematic variations in "saying the same thing" in discourse constitute social identity markers of participants in the communicative act. Several approaches to pragmatics are differentiated by whether or not they concern themselves with the problem of goal directedness or purposivity (or even individual intentions) in using language, as related to and implicated in the mere fact of happenstance or systematic indexical value of a particular language form. These two areas of concern are both sometimes called the "function(s)" of actual language use, so we should carefully distinguish purposive function(s) in the one sense from indexical function(s) in the other, as we do below.

But this suggests, then, a third perspective on language, particularly as we consider the distinctness of purposivity in language use from indexical value or meaningfulness. That the very users explicitly formulate language use as a means to an end in interaction indicates that their understanding of pragmatics (as of structure) can be at least implicitly reconstructed as rationalization in the paradigm of interested human social action. That is, conscious purposivity in language use entails a consideration of the ideologies about language form, meaning, function, value, et cetera that the users apparently bring to bear on the activity of using it. Such an ideological realm is thus a more institutionalized expression of the tendency to metalevel apprehension of language as behavior and structure. Any statements about language are indeed metalinguistic statements, since they take language as the very topic of discourse; ideological analysis studies to what extent such statements are rationalized, perhaps systematically, in culturally understandable terms as the socially emergent reflectivity of actors themselves. How are doctrines of "correctness" and "incorrectness" in language usage rationalized? How are they related to doctrines of inherent representational power, beauty, expressiveness, et cetera of language as a valued mode of action? Such questions can be studied from the point of view of ideological and cultural analysis.

It would appear that the phenomenon of gender in language can be approached initially from any of these points of view, Certainly, particular languages are said to have a gender system as an aspect of the norms of propositional linguistic structure. Certainly, particular language usages are said to belong to the realms of men's vs. women's speech, appropriate variations in saying otherwise "the same thing" indexing gender identities in the speech situation. Certainly, language users have views on how men and women should and/or do speak, how language structure and/or usage inherently and/or actually plays a role in defining what they perceive to be the social reality of gender identity. Just how bound up with each other all these facts are, however, has generally escaped notice in both popular and technical accounts. This I explore, using contemporary Modern English as the major exemplification.

The argument here is that for contemporary Modern English, the structural category of gender fits into an expected and universal typology of categories of noun phrases. It is one from among the set of different but consistent ways that certain semantic configurations are expressible in language form. The pragmatic expression of gender in English linguistic usage emerges from a quite widespread phenomenon, the pragmatics of social power asymmetries and similar hierarchical aspects of constituted social structure. In English, the pragmatic expression of gender has been only marginally related to the structural category. And the ideology of gender, including language, is now constituted in English as part of a political struggle. Views on various sides of the issues nevertheless show characteristic reflections of metalinguistic awareness of the users, as would be predicted: pragmatic characteristics are apprehended and analyzed in terms of an expectable misanalysis of the principles of structural gender categories. Native speaker metalinguistics assimilates pragmatic effects to an expected model of representational structure of the language, and seeks to rationalize usage (and structure) in terms of this, in a constant dialectic the reality of which emerges ultimately to analytic view in historical change.

## GENDER AS A CATEGORY OF REFERENCE AND PREDICATION

Let us begin with differentiating gender as a noun phrase category in the structural sense from the notion of gender in discourse usage. We can illustrate the independence of these two values of particular forms of language by ordering examples in a two by two array, as shown in Table 1. If linguistic structure comprehends the formal regularities abstractable from how one refers to and predicates about the gender of things with language (as ordered from left to right), and linguistic usage comprehends the formal regularities of how we index (point to) the social realities of gender in the speech situation (as ordered from top to bottom), for any example of a linguistic form, we can illustrate the presence (+) and absence (−) of these meanings by its placement in the correct cell.

The traditional grammatical category of gender, or gender classes of noun phrases, for example, is a formal distinction from the analytic perspective of reference and predication. Note that in many (perhaps all) languages, certain nouns, regardless of any grammatical category membership, refer to gendered entities; certain verbs also predicate states and activities of gendered entities, with a kind of implicit, semantic categorization represented. In many languages, for example, Hebrew, even the forms that refer to/predicate about the individuals in the roles of speaker and hearer at the time the speech is ongoing—that is, the so-called first person and second person pronouns and so-called first-person and second-person verb forms—also formally distinguish gender of speaker, gender of hearer. All these examples, presenting gender of objects of reference-and-predication, are in the left column.

TABLE 1

Categorical Codings of Gender Distinctions in Language

| | Gender forms in reference and predication | |
|---|---|---|
| Gender forms in discourse | + | − |
| + | First and Second Person pronouns and/or verb forms, e.g., Thai, Hebrew, Russian | "Men's and Women's speech," e.g., Koasati, Yana, Chukchee |
| − | "Gender" classes of regular noun phrases, e.g., English, French, Chinook, Djirbal<br><br>Gender reference of certain nouns/gender predication of certain verbs (most languages—all?) | All other features of languages |

The rows of Table 1, by contrast, plot the presence or absence of a formal system of discourse indexicals of the gender of at least one of the participants in the linguistic interaction (independent of any propositional message ongoing about some object(s) of reference and predication). So-called men's-and-women's speech in many languages is a phenomenon of this sort, whether the formal indication of gender of participants is a difference of phonology, morphology, et cetera. Observe that the indication of participant gender by distinct pronouns and/or inflections of the first and second persons, placed in the left upper cell in Table 1, participates in both systems simultaneously; such reference and predication is inherently deictic, or dependent upon discourse indexicality, in terms of which only can we define the roles of speaker, hearer, et cetera.

Thus, a gender system in the purely referential sense—a phenomenon placed in the left lower cell of Table 1—is just a formal categorization of nouns or noun phrases like any other such formal categorization, associated with certain semantic characteristics. What is called the gender system of English is a categorization of every basic singular noun stem in the language by what replacive anaphoric pronoun it selects in the syntactic system of reference maintenance. Thus, note that *man* goes together with *he*; *woman* goes together with *she*; *car* goes together with *it* (and of course *men*, *women*, or *cars*, the plurals, all go together with *they*). In English, unlike in many languages, there is nothing about the form of the noun itself that puts it into one or another of the gender categories, no local formal indication like a prefix or a suffix that always must accompany the stem in a full word to indicate gender class of the noun, though some few derivational suffixes do, in fact, have feminine gender regularly determined (*-ess*, for example).

In distinguishing the English system from among all possible systems of noun categorization, we should observe, as shown in Table 2, that there are really three levels of relevant phenomena. In the right column are shown FORMAL or grammatical labels for various commonly encountered noun categorizations in referential linguistic structure. These have the property of being more and more inclusive, the higher classes being formal specializations of the ones below. For example, any form in the PERSONAL category is in the ANIMATE category, but not vice versa; any form that is ANIMATE is also AGENTIVE, but not vice versa. In general, there are such relationships of implication of membership among the sets of nominal forms, when we view them in terms of specialization of their systematic formal attributes, their grammatical properties as linguistic elements. (The situation is sometimes more complex in particular languages, in that at some given level in this universal schema of possibilities there will be cross-cutting categorizations that jointly make up the equivalent of a formal class, but we will oversimplify for expository purposes.)

TABLE 2

Gender Systems in Reference Are Classificatory Distinctions that Form Part of Formal, Notional, and Referential Classes of Nouns

| Differential reference to | Notional | Formal |
|---|---|---|
| Woman | Female | FEMININE |
| Man | Male | MASCULINE |
| Social status/role | Human | PERSONAL |
| Beast | Large being | ANIMATE |
| Spirit, weather | Potent/Volitional | AGENTIVE |
| Small creature | Thing | NEUTER |
| Inanimate manipulables | Shape or other physical characteristics | SHAPE, MANIPULABILITY |
| Food, artifacts | Edibility, utility | THING |
| Segmentable wholes | Enumerability | COUNT |
| States-of-being, ideas | Abstract thing | ABSTRACT |

Now each of the FORMAL categories has what we can call a *notional core*, a definable class-specific property in a system of conceptual or notional categories associated with the FORMAL categorical distinctions. These notional categories permit us, in fact, to recognize which FORMAL categories we are dealing with in any specific language, as compared with other possible ones. As most people have probably observed in learning French or German or similar European languages, every noun has at least one FORMAL gender category, but some of the assignments cannot be justified to us English speakers in notional terms, that is, in terms of how we conceptualize the objects the

French words seem to refer to. Thus, we readily conceptualize tables as objects of utility, and appreciate the FORMAL classification of *table* in the THING class, with its associated notional category centered on this property. But in French the form (*la*) *table*, the closest translation equivalent, is in the FEMININE formal category. So again for *easy chair*, which in French is in the MASCULINE category (*le fauteuil*).

These kinds of disparities, from the point of view of our own English gender system, have frequently been incorrectly used to talk of the total arbitrariness of each language's formal categorizations. This is wrong. As is seen, the notional core of a true FORMAL gender system must differentiate notionally 'male' referents from notionally 'female' referents, whatever other referents are put into the same FORMAL classes as male vs. female. There are many languages with complicated systems of noun classification—like some of the native languages of the Pacific Northwest, or like Navajo and Apache—which have elaborate formal systems of noun categories, such as animacy, agency, shape, manipulability, et cetera. But since they show no formal separation of what we can see as a 'male' vs. 'female' notional core of referents, they do not have gender systems as such, just noun classification systems. The essence of the relationship is the separation of notionally male vs. notionally female properties by corresponding FORMAL categorizations, whatever else holds about the correspondence between FORMAL and notional systems.

So far we have been characterizing gender systems in terms of the relationship between forms and notional (or semantic) core properties. There is another kind of relationship to note. What object or entity does a user characteristically and differentially refer to when using the particular formally distinguished nominal category? Here, we are not dealing with the overall formal categorizations of linguistic forms as these emerge from the rules of grammar. Nor are we dealing with the categorizations of objects referred to as these can be given notional specification at least at the center or core of the category. We are dealing now with specific acts of referring, using language to pick out entities by applying particular grammatical forms in discourse. And the question at issue is how to characterize the typical (and differential) entity or thing in the real world the category as used is referring to, at its most specific.

We might think of the problem this way: The notional categorizations tend to be inclusive ones, the topmost categories in Table 2 being more highly specified subcategories of ones below; the differential reference categories, on the other hand, tell us what in particular the given formal category, but not any of the others, typically is used to refer to. So comparing the formal AGENTIVE and PERSONAL categories, by definition, we might note, the 'potent/volitional' core property of the AGENTIVE category is included in the notion 'human'; humans characteristically are conceptualized linguistically as though they had the power and will to act as agents. But the typical entity referred to with specifically AGENTIVE (as distinct from PERSONAL) grammatically coded category is not in fact 'human,' but is something like a spirit, force of weather, deity, or the like, spoken about with forms that indicate power and will to act as agent at the notional level, but understood as the differentially typical entity for which such a FORMAL category is used. So it is the spirit, force or weather, deity, et cetera that is coded with AGENTIVE rather than PERSONAL, characterizing how languages typically have their machinery applied in acts of differential reference. We would say that the kinds of objects to which we refer with AGENTIVE nominal categories *to the exclusion* of those we indicate with PERSONAL class are things like deities, spirits, weather, et cetera.

The schema in Table 2 is a kind of universally applicable maximal one, of which, with certain adjustments, the system of each particular language, like English, is a specialized subsystem. Characteristically, such adjustments consist of not making the totality of distinctions. But what distinctions we do make in our English gender system show that notionally masculine, feminine, and neuter genders have certain properties in keeping with their placement in the schema. They show what are called asymmetries of *markedness* as well as certain spread beyond the notional core in definable ways.

Sets of examples in Standard English such as *A passenger must have dropped his/her scarf,* demonstrate the asymmetries of markedness. The norm has been to use *his* as the pronoun maintaining reference to the passenger, about which referent we are not given any information in the subject of the sentence beyond human, volitional notional properties, that is, that it is a seemingly PERSONAL coding. This example and many similar ones would indicate that the MASCULINE formal gender category is applicable to any potential human referent, such as in indefinite human reference, and is therefore the so-called unmarked category vis-à-vis the FEMININE. As indicated in Figure 1, languages are quite regular in the way marked and unmarked categories pattern structurally and are implemented in discourse. If some whole universe of possibilities is exhaustively subcategorized by marked and unmarked categories, let us consider a diagram of the partition as here given. If the whole

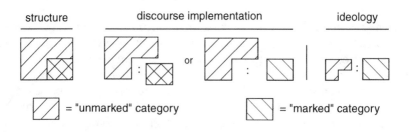

FIGURE 1
Properties of Marked and Unmarked categories in language

universe of possible notionally human (formally PERSONAL) referents is represented by the large rectangle, singly hatched, under "structure," this is the range of possible reference, all constructions taken into consideration, of the MASCULINE gender category. The range of possible reference with the FEMININE structural category is the smaller, doubly hatched rectangle enclosed: the FEMININE category, when it occurs, is more specific, more informative; it tells us something more definite about the referent(s) than the MASCULINE category, which indicates only notional personhood or humanness from a structural point of view.

By contrast, in discourse implementation, there are really two possibilities in the way MASCULINE and FEMININE categories occur. In such cases as the indefinite one cited previously, the occurrence of the one or the other preserves the asymmetry of inclusiveness of possible reference, shown in our diagram of discourse implementation by the opposed figures of singly and doubly hatched areas, the occurrence of the doubly hatched being the more informative as the means of giving more information. However, in many usages, particularly so-called definite ones, the referential range of the unmarked category MASCULINE is really being contrasted with that of the marked category FEMININE; the exclusive referential range of the one vs. the other is being signaled, as indicated in the mutually exclusive singly-hatched discourse implementation figures. It should be observed that this ambiguity of discourse implementation captures the distinction between the notional categorization on the one hand, and differential reference on the other. For it is only at the level of what we have termed typical reference that we can say that MASCULINE refers to or picks out male humans, FEMININE to female humans. MASCULINE typically is used to refer differentially to PERSONAL referents of the male sort, represented by the singly hatched remains of the large rectangle, once the small FEMININE rectangle of typical reference is differentiated.

Note that, at this level of typicality of referent of a FORMAL category, we feel queasy about the GENDER categorizations of *infant, baby,* that traditionally have governed agreement with *it* in formal markers; that is, these words are treated like those for small, impotent creatures. We tend to feel queasy also with large animals, especially PERSONALized ones such as pets and domesticated beasts, and so use *he* and *she* as their pronouns. In this usage, GENDER is sometimes assigned on a species basis, as a secondary of PERSONALization, so that *dogs* take *he* agreement, *cats* take *she*, in normal circumstances. *Ships* (and *ships* of the air) take *she* agreement in traditional usage, as do *automobiles*, though this has been rapidly changing as a sign of greater "thingness" of the once wondrous and affect-laden creatures. In the following, we can observe this contrast between the straightforward *it* usage in newspaper prose, and the excited, affect-laden *he-she* usage in the narrated drama of the framed quotation by an airline employee:

*Miami—A Boeing 727 airliner* carrying 67 passengers and 7 crew members made a successful emergency belly landing on a runway at Miami International Airport Tuesday night after *its* landing gear failed to retract fully after takeoff from Palm Beach International Airport. Seven persons suffered minor injuries. "He pulled all of his gear up and slid *her* in on *her* tummy—*her* belly," Eastern Airlines spokesman Jim Ashlock said. *The airliner*, Eastern Flight 194, was flying to John F. Kennedy International Airport in New York and then Albany, N.Y. Emergency equipment stood by as *the plane* skidded to a stop, sparks flying. (*Chicago Tribune*, 16 February 1983, Sec. 1, p. 5; italics added)

The queasiness we feel about these usages, at the conscious level, comes from *translating the FORMAL categories directly into terms of typical differential reference*, rather than from having conscious knowledge of the implicit and analyzable structure of gradually inclusive notional principles and FORMAL categories. As indicated to the right of Figure 1, this has profound consequences for the ideology of language, the way that speakers rationalize their structures. For at the level of ideological reflection about gender, MASCULINE vs. FEMININE is understood as equal and opposite differential "male" vs. "female," markedness asymmetry notwithstanding.

So observe that the English system of noun phrase categories relevant to pronominalization patterns something like Figure 2 at the FORMAL and notional levels. Starting from the innermost distinctions of the system, (marked) FEMININE is differentiated from (unmarked) non-feminine, the latter also called MASCULINE, and this whole category of (marked) ANIMATE is differentiated from (unmarked) non-animate, the latter also called NEUTER, and both ANIMATE and non-animate are included in the explicitly indicated (unmarked) non-plural, as opposed to the (marked) PLURAL category. Every English noun has at least one gender categorization as its basic formal affiliation in this system, with its associated notional or semantic connotation.

In English, the expression or signal of the category membership occurs elsewhere than on the noun itself, namely, as the particular pronoun that substitutes, under the correct circumstances, for the noun in reference maintenance. And the typical object of reference of the noun/pronoun is to be distinguished from the notional category of gender. The frequent disparity between the two, caused by the fact that this linguistic system, like virtually every other investigated, patterns according to the asymmetries of markedness (as diagrammed in Figure 1), makes us queasy in our usage at the conscious level. And the queasiness persists even in the formally PLURAL category, where the pronominal usage would be uniformly *they*, because of the fact that the notional and referential properties are associated with the noun itself, and persist communicatively even where no explicit pronominal indicator distinguishes them overtly:

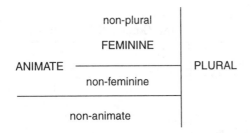

N.B.: MARKED vs. unmarked
non-plural is called "singular;
non-feminine is called "masculine";
non-animate is called "neuter"

FIGURE 2
Noun categories of Modern English (gender and number)

One of my pet peeves is the currently popular usage of the word "guys." You often hear a group of people described as "guys," even when the group includes women. In fact, it is quite common to hear women addressing a group of other women as "you guys." This strikes me as strange. Some people I have asked about it, however, have adamantly maintained that when "guy" is in the plural, it has lost all traces of masculinity. I was arguing with a woman about this, and she kept saying, "It may have retained some of the male flavor for *you*, but it has none in most people's usage." I was not convinced, but nothing I could say would budge her from her position. In the end I got lucky, because in a last-ditch attempt to convince me she said, "Why, I've even heard *guys* use it to refer to a bunch of women." Only after saying it did she realize she had just undermined her own claim. (Hofstadter 1982:30)

The doubly functioning unmarked category, under what is called "contrastive stress," can be used to emphasize differential referentiality; otherwise it is just as wide in possible reference as the notional categorization allows. (In this passage, by the way, the specificity achieved with the words *woman/women* should be observed.)

Consider another gender system for comparison, within a very different kind of formal system of noun classes. Djirbal (Dixon 1972:308–311), a language of northeastern Australia, shows a typical Australian Aboriginal linguistic system in this respect. As shown in Table 3, there are four FORMAL classes, marked by the kind of specifier (like German *der/die/das*) that occurs with the noun, each associated with a notional core. The specifically gender aspect of the system emerges in the contrast of Classes I and II, which preserves the distinction between notional 'male' and notional 'female,' whatever else they include. Class III includes 'edible fruits and vegetables' and Class IV is the 'everything else' class. Considering now Classes I and II, the notional principles for the first center on attributes or metonymic connections with 'animateness' and '(human) masculinity,' while those for the second center on '(human) femininity,' 'water,' 'fire,' 'fighting.' As Dixon observes, referents expectedly in Classes I or II occur in the opposite class when belief-derived attributes so

## TABLE 3
Djirbal (Australia) Noun Classes, Including Gender Reference, Illustrated[a]

| I. *bayi*-class | II. *balan*-class | III. *balam*-class | IV. *bala*-class |
|---|---|---|---|
| Men | Women | | Parts of body |
| Kangaroos | Bandicoots | | Meat |
| Possums | Dog | | |
| Bats | Platypus, echidna | | |
| Most snakes | Some snakes | | |
| Most fishes | Some fishes | | |
| Some birds | Most birds | | |
| Most insects | Firefly, scorpion, crickets | | Bees and honey |
| | Hairy mary grub | | |
| | Anything connected with fire, water | | |
| Moon | Sun and stars | | |
| Storm, rainbow | | | Wind |
| Boomerangs | Shields | | Yamsticks |
| Some spears | Some spears | | Some spears |
| Etc. | Some trees | All trees with | Most trees |
| | Etc. | edible fruit | |
| | | | Grass, mud, Stones, noises, Language Etc. |

[a]Adapted from Dixon 1972:307.

dictate. Thus, birds, spirits of dead human females, are classified in II, except willy wagtails, mythical male figures, which are in I; specially to-be-noted notional properties, especially 'harmfulness (to humans)' of a type of referent, also are indicated by opposite class membership.

It is clear that this system conforms to the general principles of classification set out previously. Class IV is the residual FORMAL class, with Class III a specialization of non-animates by the notional principle of '(flora with) edible parts.' We can further systematize by applying Dixon's own principles of class transfer: Class I is the basic 'animate' class, and Class II its specialization by several different kinds of further notional principles—including for 'humans,' 'femininity'—all of which differentiate specific examples of things either themselves animates with special characteristics, or associated with such special animates. Class II is the most specifically characterized notionally-based FORMAL class in this system. It is interesting to observe further that while 'male-female' are notionally distinguished classificatory principles for humans, regardless of the Class I vs. Class II membership of any non-human animate, just as in English, differential reference to a male vs. female referent of any species can be made by using the appropriate classifier on some particular occasion of use, thus *bayi* [Class I] *guda* ('MALE dog'), even though normal usage is *balan* [Class II] *guda* (an animate with very specific distinctness as a domesticated companion of humans, hence transferred from expected Class I into specialized Class II).

## INDEXING PARTICIPANT GENDER IN COMMUNICATION

Such gender systems within noun classifications contrast with gender indexicals. Here, the speaker uses a form in a discourse context, in which the specific form used indicates something about the gender of speaker and/or addressee (or even audience) of the relevant framing discourse context. In the simplest case, the framing context is the ongoing social situation in which speaker and addressee of the message are participants. It does not matter what is being said, nor whom or what is being referred to; the indexical forms mark something about the context in which they are used. As shown in Table 4, there are several typologically distinct ways in which this can and does occur. Koasati, an American Indian language originally of present-day Alabama, systematically indexes the gender of the speaker as either male or female (Haas 1944), regardless of the gender of the addressee, as represented in Row I. Row II constructs the case in which there is systematic indexing of the gender of the addressee as either male or female, regardless of the gender of the speaker; no pure example of this can be located in the literature, though some languages, for example, Tunica (Haas 1941), have gender distinctions systematic for so-called second-person pronouns, that is, when the referent and the addressee in a speech event are identical (hence mixing the plane of reference-and-predication with the plane of discourse-indexicals). The third type of case, as in Row III, systematically indicates that gender of *both* speaker and addressee are respectively either male or female, as opposed to any other combination of genders of participants. Yana, an American Indian language of California, systematically indexes male speaker communicating to male addressee with one form of words, and all other gender combinations with another (Sapir 1949 [1929]).

To illustrate how this phenomenon typically occurs, in Table 5 we show some of the inflected verb forms of Koasati, with translations. The basic regularity underlying this set of forms (and many others for this stem 'lift' as for all other verbs) is that the female-speaking form is the basic one, with its various inflections for person referred to, mood, tense, et cetera. To derive the male-speaking form, suffix an indexical marker -*s*, the sequence of sounds in whatever is already in inflection plus the additional -*s* frequently changing according to perfectly regular, though complex, rules of the language. So the -*s* indexical form appears clearly in 'he is lifting it [male speaking],' but it is masked when it at least structurally appears after the č sound (as in English *church*) of 'you are lifting it.' Yana has an even more complicated set of suffixes

TABLE 4
"Male vs. Female Speech" Codes Gender Identity of Speaker
and/or Hearer in Actual Situations of Discourse[a]

| Type | Speaker gender | Hearer gender | Example |
|------|----------------|---------------|---------|
| I. | m:f | m,f | Koasati |
| II. | m,f | m:f | (may not exist) |
| III. | m/f:*other* | m/f:*other* | Yana |

[a]Coding of chart: m=male; f=female; :='is distinct from'; ,='or (indifferently)'; /='is respectively distinct from'

TABLE 5
Koasati Verb Paradigms (Forms Excerpted from Relevant Indicative and Imperative Sets)

| Woman speaking | Man speaking | English glosses |
|----------------|--------------|-----------------|
| *lakáwč* | *lakáwč* | 'you are lifting it' |
| *lakawwą* | *lakawwá-s* | 'he will lift it' |
| *lakawwîl* | *lakawwís* | 'I am lifting it' |
| *lakáw* | *lakáws* | 'he is lifting it' |
| *lakawčin* | *lakawčî-s* | 'don't lift it!' |

and changes of sounds that differentiate its male-speaking-to-male forms.

We emphasize that it does not matter what is the topic of discourse; the gender indexicals are systematic distinctions of form that indicate who is doing the discoursing/to whom the discoursing is being done. And, in the maximally clear case, such as these, there is a distinct and systematic modification of forms, whether by affixation or changes of sound shapes, or whatever formal means, the sole "meaning" of which is indexical in this way. It should also be noted that (1) everyone in the language community knows and can produce these forms, though appropriateness of usage is defined by the indexical rules of speaker and/or addressee gender, for violations of which, for example, children are corrected by speakers of either gender; and that (2) when a speech situation between characters is set up in discourse as the topic of narration, quoted speech is used for the appropriate gender indexing of the narrated characters. These are metalinguistic usages that reach a high level of consciousness, obviously.

# GENDER AND STATISTICAL INDEXES
# OF SOCIAL STRATIFICATION

Such *categorical* (and *overt*) *gender-indexicals* contrast with what we might term *statistical indexes* (and especially *covert* statistical indexes) of women's vs. men's speech that have been discovered in urban areas of advanced, class-stratified societies such as those of Western Europe and America. In these societies, there is a high degree of explicit and codified standardization of the languages through institutional authority including especially the written channel. A tradition of so-called sociolinguistic study has emerged over the last 20 years (Labov 1972) that relates the frequencies of relatively Standard vs. non-Standard forms in samples of actual language production to the membership of speakers in any of a number of cross-cutting social groups and categories, and to the overall task demands of the contextual conditions of the produced samples. That is, frequencies of Standard/non-Standard linguistic forms can be seen as indexes of both social identities of the speaker and overall contextual "style," the strength of Standard-inducing demands made by various contexts of language production.

One repeated finding is that socioeconomic class position of language users in general varies directly as the frequency of production of Standard forms, and that there is a peak of contextual "style" effects on Standard-form production not at, but near the top of the stratification continuum. (We return to this later.) When we focus on particular social variables such as gender, a broad regularity seems to emerge, that, controlling for other variables, female speakers overall show significantly greater production of Standard forms (and lesser production of non-Standard) than male speakers, the effect interacting with the effects of social and/or socioeconomic class and contextual style. Thus, Table 6 shows findings summarizing data from Wolfram's (1969) study of Black English in Detroit (reproduced in Trudgill 1974:91). Scoring production data on the occurrence of non-Standard double negatives for four different socioeconomic classes, it was observed that females show characteristically *lower* non-Standard usages (and hence higher Standard usages) in all four groups, with the effect peaking as an absolute phenomenon (i.e., total absence of non-Standard for female speakers) in the lower middle class, here labeled "upper middle" for the Black English community by virtue of calibration techniques.

In effect, these are gradient or statistical indexes of male vs. female gender of speakers of English, though operating in terms of a cultural system of Standardization in a class-stratified society. There is no special formal marker the presence or absence of which we can associate exclusively with the gender identity of the speaker, as in Koasati, et cetera. Rather, the strength of productive realization of Standardization, yielding frequency effects in actual linguistic production, is what seems to differentiate the two gender categories of speakers.

TABLE 6
Gradient or "Statistical" Frequency Data on Male vs. Female Speech
in English: Example from Multiple Negation (. . . *Ain't* . . . *No* . . .)
in Detroit Non-Standard Speech[a]

| Gender | Percentage of multiple negation of total production[b] | | | |
|--------|------|------|------|------|
|        | UMC  | LMC  | UWC  | LWC  |
| Male   | 6.3  | 32.4 | 40.0 | 90.1 |
| Female | 0.0  | 1.4  | 35.6 | 58.9 |

[a]From Trudgill (1974:91).
[b]LMC=lower middle class; LWC=lower working class; UMC=upper middle class; UWC=upper working class.

A most revealing comparative case is presented by the participant pronominals ('I,' 'you') of Thai, where the indexicals of gender interact very regularly with gender in reference, since reference is to either speaker or addressee in the speech situation. As seen in Table 7 (summarizing data from Cooke 1970:11–15, 19–39), we can give the "meanings" of a sample of first-person pronominals—there are many more in the total repertoire of the language—in terms of the parameters defining specific speech situations in which they would be appropriately used. Note that they all refer to speaker, so in this gross referential sense are all "saying the same thing." But we must take into account the gender and age-status of both speaker and hearer, and certain further *relational* characteristics holding of the speaker-addressee dyad: the relative social status—akin to 'deference entitlement' (Shils 1982)—of addressee with respect to speaker (thus, addressee higher-than/same-as/lower-than speaker); the degree of intimacy presupposed between speaker and addressee (and, in the instance, the intimacy that can be effected, intersubjectively called up, by use of the particular form); (non)restraint of social interaction, the speaker's degree of adherence to the standards of social interaction for this contextual dyad.

So gender itself interacts with several other variables of the speech situation in a complex pattern of both referential and indexical regularities. Some of these can be noted for later comparison (see Table 8 for summary). It can be seen for any given form otherwise determined, in usage the higher the relative status of the addressee with respect to the speaker, the greater the intimacy between speaker and addressee; that is, there is an inverse relationship between status of the *speaker* and intimacy between speaker and addressee in the use of any given form. Note for the pair *dìchăn* and *chăn*, female speaking, that intimacy increases from 0 to +1 as relative addressee status goes from equal (/) to higher (+), and that intimacy similarly changes as relative addressee status goes from lower (-) to equal (/), other things remaining generally constant. So any particular form can be an index of high-status and intimate addressee, or low-status non-intimate addressee, relative to speaker. Looked at across forms, then, the indexicals reveal a system in which status is the inverse of intimacy, allowing the complementarity of indexical possibilities. For ʔàadtamaa, spoken by a Buddhist priest, the opposite is the case, since such a high-status speaker can only speak to status equals or status inferiors. Note also that the form chăn, male speaking, is used equivalently in indexing either of two situations, one where the addressee is of lower relative status, and the other where addressee is female. Finally, male speakers may use the same form, phŏm, in a neutral and standardized usage across all addressee relative statuses, while female speakers must switch forms in covering the dimension of addressee relative status; so female speakers must more elaborately and unambiguously mark hearer-status asymmetries.

Such data are representative of many similar first- and second-person forms. Taken all into account, on this basis there is a system of indexical values of the forms that demonstrates an inverse relationship between a person's status and the presumed intimacy with which communication takes place; Buddhist priests, at the absolute top of the status scale, confirm this complementarily. The unmarked or residual case is male adult speaker, in the middle of a pair of analogical distinctions: female is to male (is to Buddhist priest) as lower status is to neutral status (is to high status). There is, then, what we might term a *metaphorical* or *analogical* relationship between gender-indexing in Thai and relative status indexing of addressee, such that female speaking to male is as lower status speaking to higher status. Such a relationship indexed linguistically seems to correspond to a larger kind of relationship in society, on the one hand, and, most importantly, to a reality *referred to* by the pronoun *I*. It is thus the overlap of the two systems that reenforces the indexical values *in referring*.

Given such a categorical case illustrating clearly this principle of pragmatically (metaphorically) linked indexical systems involving the contextual dimension of gender, formally identical to a potent referential system, we can return to the kind of gender indexing found in languages such as English, et cetera, in which statistical frequency differentiation of forms goes along with gender-identity distinctions. In Thai, we saw an analogy between male:female (gender) indexed as higher:lower (relative status-ranking). Given what sociolinguists have discovered about variability of occurrence of Standardized forms, we might see that this analogy holds up for English and similar languages as well.

Figure 3 illustrates in schematic fashion—actual parameters and slopes differ from study to study—repeatedly found relationships. Considering an appropriate linguistic form relevant to Standardization, for each of a range of ranked social or socioeconomic categories/groups, we can plot the frequency of occurrence of relatively Standardized linguistic production as a function of the so-called contextual "style," the "formality" of the situation, including

## TABLE 7
### Gender-Sensitive Participant-Pronouns[a,b]

| Thai first-person (I) pronouns | Speaker | | Hearer | | Relation of hearer-to-speaker | | | |
|---|---|---|---|---|---|---|---|---|
| | Female | Adult | Female | Adult | Status | Intimate | Speaker n.r.[c] | Qualifications |
| ʔaatamaa | − | /+ | | /+ | − | +1 | 0 | Speaker Buddhist priest |
| | − | /+ | | /+ | / | 0 | 0 | Speaker, hearer Buddhist priests |
| dichǎn | + | + | | | + | +1 | 0 | |
| | + | + | | | / | 0 | 0 | |
| phǒm | − | /+ | | | (/+) | (0) | 0 | |
| chǎn | − | /+ | + | | − | (+1) | | |
| | − | /+ | | | | +1 | | |
| | + | | | | − | (0) | | |
| | + | | | | / | +1 | | |

Adapted from Cooke (1970:38, chart 10).

[a] Indicate gender of at least the referent (speaker, hearer, or both), and frequently of both referent and the other participant. In these pronouns, referent is always the speaker.

[b] Codings of chart: oo = no; negative; + = yes; positive; / = neutral; equal; numeral = degree; ( ) = "a connotative suggestion of."

[c] Speaker nonrestraint = a certain defiance of or nonconformity to underlying standards or more proper usage on the part of the speaker.

TABLE 8
Generalizations and Observations[a]

---

*Observations*

  a. Same form spoken to one of higher status increases intimacy value; except for Buddhist priest speaking, where inverse relationship is found.

  b. Same form is spoken to female as to lower-status hearer.

  c. Female speaker must switch forms in going from lower- to equal- to higher-status hearer.

*Generalization*

  a. Increase of status of speaker with regard to hearer is inverse of increase of intimacy between hearer and speaker.

  b. Analogical distinctions in Table 7 are female : male : Buddhist priest :: lower : neutral : high status.

---

[a]Observations are about the gender-sensitive participant-pronouns as presented in Table 7.

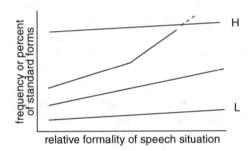

FIGURE 3
Sociolinguistic stratification of markers in usage

all those institutional and interpersonal factors that might be Standard-inducing for those with some allegiance to the Standard. Characteristically, lowermost groups show low Standardized production that remains low across increasingly Standard-demanding situations. At the opposite extreme, highest groups show relatively constant, though increasing, Standardization. In between, there are increasing degrees of Standardization of production with increase in ranked position, and, interestingly, increase in the slope of the frequency changes in going from the least to the most formal contextual conditions. For the group near, but not quite at the top, in particular, one characteristically finds that in the most extreme Standard-demanding situations, the produced frequencies surpass both the uppermost group and even surpass the structural norms ("hypercorrection").

In fluidly stratified societies in particular, Labov (1972) and others have discovered robust results of just this sort of statistical variability. Linguistically Standard vs. non-Standard forms occur such that their frequencies have identifiable indexical values of "Standardness" and its connotations about the social position of the speaker. There is a kind of "linguistic insecurity" before the Standard manifested most by the ranked groups that are not quite at the top of the stratification, as shown in the very pronounced shifts in linguistic production across the sample of formality conditions. Such linguistic insecurity, it has been found, goes together with several kinds of attitudinal and other evaluative results, such as rating the users of relatively Standard forms more highly on a great number of positive or desirable status-related and personality attributes; overreporting (even overscoring) one's own frequency of Standard usage (even as categorical), while underreporting one's own frequency of non-Standard; being easily induced to hypercorrection, the production of non-normal forms through an avoidance of only apparently, but not really, non-Standard ones (. . . *between you and I* . . .); being generally more sensitive to linguistic forms along the dimensions of Standard and non-Standard on all tests. In general, for socioeconomic stratification, the lower-to-mid middle class demonstrates such linguistic insecurity to the greatest degree, along with characteristic production curves as discussed previously.

It turns out also that when women vs. men are examined in this light, the same characteristics emerge independent of the other variables by which native speakers can be categorized. There is, in this sense, a characteristic "women's language," as it were, that is a socially real phenomenon in these kinds of societies. It is a statistically (not, as in Koasati, categorically) indexed orientation to the Standard language, the explicitly codified norm of society, with an indexically significant frequency of productive differentiation from men that almost makes us expect women to speak more "correctly" than men. It is also a covert (not, as in Thai, overt) phenomenon, in that only when we discover the statistical relationship between Standardization and stratification, does the place of women's language use and attitudes within *that* configuration allow us to see that there is an implicit identification of the type: women are to men as relatively lower is to relatively higher status group (along the dimension of socioeconomic class). Hence, we might say, it might be puzzling that those who speak "best"—and are more oriented to do so—do not also enjoy the power of those usually at the top in the conventional appreciation of the benefits of "Standardized" demeanor and behavior.

That this configuration is a culture-specific fact is seen comparatively along both dimensions of Standardization (and hence "correctness" in language use), gender identity and status position. For as Ochs (1974) has shown, the Merina (Malagasy) culture of good language is such that men speak correctly and even elegantly, while women (and children, and Frenchmen) do not, and ought not to. And as Irvine (1975, 1978) has shown, among the Wolof (Senegal) there are quasi-castelike distinctions between "nobles" and "*griots*" ('bards'), and for these social identities, the higher the noble, the less correct is his language;

for speaking correctly—and loudly, fluently, ornately—is left to the *"griots"* as work really unbecoming the inherent nature of nobility.

Such, let us say, is the pragmatic fact of usage. Note the contrast between two completely independent aspects of language. First, there is the referential gender system as an unmarked:marked categorical relationship between masculine and feminine structural and notional distinctions in noun phrases. Second, there is the pragmatic usage system, with its inherent value of indexing analogical links among various social distinctions manifested in— and hence relevant to understanding—social interaction. Let us turn now to ideology.

Feminist theory of language, and its analysis and prescription for linguistic reform, seems correctly and accurately to perceive the pragmatic metaphorical relationship between gender identity and status, though much is cast into the rhetoric of power in a more abstract and less culturally situated form. But the ideological location of the cause of this metaphorical relationship demonstrates perhaps the most characteristic "distorting" effects in the mode of operation of ideologies of social forms like language. For, writers on the subject have identified the cause of the analogy as the system of gender in the functional plane of reference and predication, the noun classification system, and related referential and predicational facts, and have seen the origin of the indexical facts in the existence of the referential ones. Moreover—and again, as we noted previously, quite characteristic of ideological perceptions of language—the referential categories, with all their autonomous formal structure, are perceived to be not formal categories, nor even notional ones, but as directly referential according to the specific, typical, and differential referentiality of the category in its most formally unconstrained occurrences.

Sometimes, writers see a "natural" basis for phenomena like the asymmetric markedness of gender categories, interpreted referentially, as in the following:

> Words with a particular application to the condition of women attract to themselves a "women only" quality, a precision of reference that limits their use to a notional "world of women" with which men need not concern themselves. In the recent past, this "world of women" had a perfectly real existence. . . . In this "world of women," one may find a kind of ur-language of sisterhood. (Carter 1980:229)

But, notwithstanding this expectable specialization—or markedness—of "women only" words, those of the feminine gender category, there is frequently a counter feeling that the categorical facts themselves are unjust:

> I leave the reader to draw *his* own conclusions. Please observe, from the above sentence, that the English language does indeed assume *everybody* to be male unless *they* are proved to be otherwise; and this kind of usage is, simply, silly, because it does not adequately reflect social reality, which is the very least one can expect language to do. (Carter 1980:234; italics added)

The crux of the matter turns on the view that Standard language both is and ought to be a *truthful* reference-guide to "reality," a basic fact about our own Standard Average European (SAE) anglophone culture's overall ideology of the nature of language. It is in these terms that the arguments on both sides of the issue have been played out. For proponents of a new linguistic Standard, the used of *his* vs. *her* in contexts such as the above quotation becomes the linguistic problem as diagnosed. The elimination of the older Standard usage from our pronominal (or, more precisely, reference-maintenance) system becomes the prescription, with a number of different alternatives being proposed in the varied literature on the subject.

This engagement of native user's ideology of linguistic expression of gender with the systems of referential structure and pragmatic structure is very much an ongoing issue, with some linguistic changes the probable outcome. The nature of the processes involved can perhaps be better grasped by historical comparison with an earlier linguistic change in English for which the results are "complete," to the extent we might use this term.

## A PARALLEL: PERSONAL DEICTICS IN ENGLISH

The linguistic change to be considered has resulted in the contemporary configuration of a different aspect of the structure of Modern English, that of so-called person and number. As shown in Figure 4, the Modern English system has a distinction of first, second, and third PERSON, which anchors some topic of discourse in relationship to the participants of the communicative situation. There is also a distinction of a singular and non-singular NUMBER in the first person, and one of plural and non-plural in the third person, the third person non-plural showing GENDER distinctions through the substitutive pronoun schema we characterized previously. It is observed that there is no apparent number distinction of second-person category, in the Standard language at least.

The English system is one of many different possibilities that are to be expected in referential-and-predicational language structures for person and number in noun phrases, as shown in Figure 5. The category of person allows a speaker to make reference to some person(s) or thing(s) relative to the contextual roles of speaker and addressee. This dimension is given along the top of the chart, with their common grammatical names, so that each column is a distinct category type. Three different degrees of numerosity are provided for in the rows (though they are labeled differently for the first three person columns vs. the fourth); these are ways of indicating something about the quantification of the referent(s).

It is seen that the INCLUSIVE category is always NON-SINGULAR in number, referring to both speaker and addressee at the minimum, the DUAL without, the PLURAL with, some other referent(s). The so-called EXCLUSIVE can refer to speaker uniquely in the SINGULAR, to speaker and one other

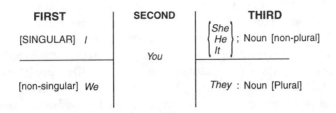

|  | FIRST | SECOND | THIRD |
|---|---|---|---|
| [SINGULAR] | *I* |  | $\begin{Bmatrix} She \\ He \\ It \end{Bmatrix}$ ; Noun [non-plural] |
|  |  | *You* |  |
| [non-singular] | *We* |  | *They* : Noun [Plural] |

**FIGURE 4**
Modern English referential categories of noun phrases
(Person, Number, Gender)

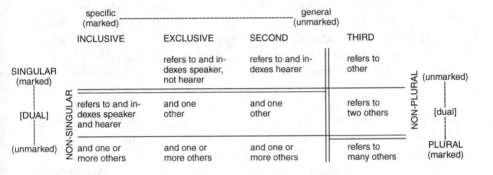

|  |  | specific — — — — — — — — — — — — — — — — general |  |  |  |  |
|---|---|---|---|---|---|---|
|  |  | (marked) | | | (unmarked) |  |
|  |  | INCLUSIVE | EXCLUSIVE | SECOND | THIRD |  |
| SINGULAR (marked) |  | refers to and in-dexes speaker, not hearer | refers to and in-dexes hearer | refers to other |  | NON-PLURAL (unmarked) |
| [DUAL] | NON-SINGULAR | refers to and in-dexes speaker and hearer | and one other | and one other | refers to two others |  | [dual] |
| (unmarked) |  | and one or more others | and one or more others | and one or more others | refers to many others |  | PLURAL (marked) |

**FIGURE 5**
Universal Possibilities of noun phrase categories of Person
and Number (with markedness relations)

referent in the DUAL, and to speaker and many other referents in the PLURAL. Similarly for the SECOND-PERSON, which communicates a reference to a set of persons centered about the addressee, uniquely so in SINGULAR and addressee plus other(s) in two forms of NON-SINGULAR. The THIRD PERSON categories do not necessarily create referential sets centered on the participant roles and, hence, in the familiar form of reasoning, seem differentially to refer to entities specifically excluding them; these are the "other(s)" of the communicative act, as it were. In the THIRD PERSON, the PLURAL is the marked number category, specifically communicating the notion of more-than-one of whatever is referred to (as distinct from PLURAL in the other persons, where the referents are inherently different, speaker and/or addressee with or without some other(s).) Within the NON-PLURAL, we can differentiate a marked DUAL and an unmarked SINGULAR. For where there is a grammatical contrast in number for THIRD PERSON forms, the SINGULAR is used to characterize not only a single thing, but also the abstract essence of things, the prototypical case of a kind of thing, the general case of any of the category of possible referents; as well, it is the category that lexically codes abstract and "non-count" entities of reference.

From this configuration, it would appear that the THIRD PERSON SINGULAR is the maximally unmarked category in the system, and indeed, a great number of entailed predictions about linguistic structure following from this are in fact observable in the way languages operate and change. One such will emerge later, insofar as the particular unmarked position of the THIRD PERSON NON-PLURAL vs. PLURAL in the referential-semantic system appears to be crucial to understanding the rise of the particular Modern English person and number system seen in Figure 4.

For, what strikes us immediately about the person-number system of modern English, is that from the referential-semantic point of view, there would seem to be an irregularity in the SECOND PERSON category, the absence of a SINGULAR/NON-SINGULAR distinction as found in the FIRST PERSON, or a PLURAL/NON-PLURAL distinction as found in the THIRD PERSON. Was this always the case in English? And if not, how has it arisen? If language structure is a purely referential-and-predicational semantic mechanism, we would expect that if there is a number distinction in the other two persons, there would be one for the SECOND PERSON, consistent with Figure 5. Or, we would ask, are there other factors that either can or must enter into the constitution of a linguistic structure in its categorical details that, as it were, override the straight referential-and-predicational constraints? Such, I argue, is the case here, in which a specific historical explanation is to hand involving the social history of England and the way it has operated as a determinate force on the emerging modern Standard English language. The SECOND PERSON pronominal categories have been forms swept up into a pragmatic system of indexicals of potent social value, and exposed to the shaping influence of ideological struggle and change.

Philological evidence indicates that Old English had a pronominal system that was more regular in the SECOND PERSON categories, showing SINGULAR, PLURAL, and, until perhaps into the thirteenth century, DUAL distinctions of NUMBER. The pronominal forms also showed distinctions of CASE, indicating their function in the syntactic organization of propositional clauses, NOMINATIVE for 'subject' function, ACCUSATIVE/DATIVE for 'object' functions of various sorts, et cetera. In the SINGULAR, the SECOND PERSON forms show NOMINATIVE *thu* (pronounced something like [θu·]) and DATIVE/ACCUSATIVE *the* ([θe·]), forms that survive into the modern period as *thou* and *thee* ([ðaw] and [ðɪy]) by fairly regular developments of their sounds. In the PLURAL, the counterpart Old English forms are *ge·* ([ɣe·]) and *e·ow*, surviving into the modern period as *ye* ([yɪy]) and *you* ([yUw]). We still recognize these four forms, though only *you* survives in contemporary Standard usage. What we outline here is the change in meaningfulness that led ultimately to the nonuse of all but one of these forms.

In the thirteenth century, it turns out, under the cultural domination of Anglo-Norman French, cultivated speakers of English took over the French distinctions between a so-called polite and a so-called familiar second person pronominal usage. This distinction of referring to a single addressee either with the categorically SECOND SINGULAR form or with the categorically SECOND PLURAL form, gives to the formal distinction *thou/thee* vs. *ye/you* a new set of social-indexical values overlain over the strictly referential distinction of NUMBER. The social practice of French usage, associated with upper-status position and good breeding, was simply transferred by translation of the appropriate categories, *thou/thee/thine* for (modern) *tu/te/ton/tien*, *ye/you/your(s)* for *vous/votre/vôtre* (to give the different CASE forms), with indexical values of a particular sort.

As Brown and Gilman showed in their classic article (1960) on the subject, we might, as in Figure 6 (where I have substituted English abbreviations), consider the indexical values of *thou*, et cetera ("T") vs. *ye*, et cetera ("Y") in terms of two social dimensions of the interpersonal context of communication— ones that we will recognize immediately from the Thai case discussed previously. First, there is the asymmetrical relationship of "power" (or status) superiority/inferiority of speaker with respect to addressee. One refers to a superior addressee with Y, speaking "up," as it were, and to an inferior

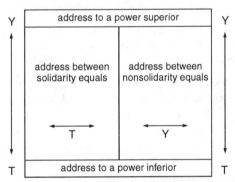

FIGURE 6
Discourse-situation relationships of participant Power and Solidarity (intimacy) indexed by *thee* (T) and *you* (Y) (After Brown and Gilman 1960.)

addressee with T, speaking "down," as it were. This is indicated in the figure by the directionality of arrows along the vertical dimension. Second, particularly operative for status equals, there is the symmetrical relationship of "solidarity" (or interpersonal identification, intimacy) between speaker and addressee. One refers to a solidary addressee with T, and to a nonsolidary addressee with Y.

It can be seen at once that this system, which became established for early Modern English down to the seventeenth century, demonstrates once again the inverse relationship between status ranking and intimacy, the very signal of speaking to a superior being that of speaking nonintimately. It is understandable why the public language, the language of communication dependent upon positional status identities, used a uniform Y in SECOND PERSON reference. It is also understandable why upper class persons, and persons of breeding in general, apparently used mutual Y as an index of their status as such, an important fact for the later history of the indexical system here. Certainly, by about 1600, the symmetrical Y was the usage of cultivation, with indexical value of such, and metonymically the value of the form itself (as opposed to T) was a reflection of the contextual parameters it indexed.

There is, then, a kind of double functional value of the SECOND PERSON pronouns, (1) to refer to and to index the addressee as individual (*thou/thee*) or as the defining member of a group (*ye/you*), and (2) to index the power (asymmetrical T/Y) and solidarity (symmetrical T/Y) relationships of speaker and addressee, according to a complex and interacting set of indexical meanings. Some formal readjustments took place, to be sure, such as the gradual loss in the sixteenth century of the grammatical distinction between *ye* [NOMINATIVE] and *you* [DATIVE/ACCUSATIVE] in favor of more homogeneous *you* in all CASE functions.

But the basic systematicity of indexical usage remained as such into the seventeenth century. Wyld reports, for example, that

> Sir Thomas More's [1478–1535] son-in-law, Roper, in his Life of that famous man, represents him as addressing the writer—'Sonne Roper'—as *thou, thee,* but himself as using *you* in speaking to Sir Thomas More. (Wyld 1920:330)

Brown and Gilman (1960), too, cite many examples that illustrate the social dimensions of usage, including the 1603 speech of the attorney general Sir Edward Coke addressing Sir Walter Raleigh (1552?–1618) at the latter's trial for treason: "All . . . was at thy instigation, thou viper; for I 'thou' thee, thou traitor!" Adding insult to injury, Coke not only repeats the downwardly directed T form, but uses a delocutionary construction (Benveniste 1966) with a verb derived from quoting the form *thou*, that is, 'to [say,] "thou" to someone,' pointing out that he is treating him as a *thou*, not a *you*, as would be expected both in ordinary cultivated (especially ennobled) society, and in the formal situation of a trial. Note that at the trial of Charles I in 1649, both the defendant and the Lord President of the court address each other with symmetrical *you* (Barber 1976:48–50). As Barber observes,

> The use of *you* between equals among the upper classes was imitated by those below them, and the usage spread down the social hierarchy. By 1600, *you* was the normal unmarked form of the singular pronoun in all classes with any pretensions to politeness, while *thou* was the form which carried special implications (e.g., of [speaker's] emotion, social superiority). (Barber 1976:210)

By 1700, however, the use of *thou*, the inherited SECOND SINGULAR pronoun, had run its course as a productive form. Why?

The seventeenth century in England, one of considerable political, religious, and intellectual upheaval, is, in a real sense, the formative period of modern anglophone culture. The central transformations we recognize for this period can be viewed from one or another of these institutional perspectives, but it is clear that there were no such distinctions at the time. It is interesting, for example, that political struggles were played out from the pulpits of the various Protestantisms, official and sect specific, engaging with the authority of the state. Intellectual life was characterized by a discourse of divines at the universities and elsewhere, as much as by anyone else.

Through all this, certain trends of the seventeenth century should be distinguished, relevant to our argument. (See, for example, Haller 1938, Jones 1953, Barber 1976.) First, the religious idiom made problematic the nature of "truth," whether Divine or otherwise, and how this truth was or could be represented, in language and similar symbolic systems in terms of which people engaged the world. To different degrees, various kinds of Protestant belief located Divine truths within each individual, whose personal experience, externalizable in language, et cetera, thus counted as much as or more than any formal doctrine elaborated through established church worship, through which individuals could be made subservient to the officially given 'truths' of institutions. Once this ideological stance emerged in the evolving anti-Church rhetoric, there was nothing to prevent its being taken beyond the phase of establishing an autochthonous and politically sanctioned Church of England (against "Romish" authority), to countering the very authority of any church/state as against the inspiration of individual religious—and, quite dangerously, civil—experience and belief. And the extreme "left," as we might now call it, pushed equalitarianism and voluntarism to its limits and beyond. The seventeenth century in England emerged as a series of constant struggles between the authority of institutions—Crown, Church, et cetera—and the authority of what we might term the empirical experience of individuals. Language, as the primary system of representational consciousness and interpersonal communication of such, was swept up into the politico-religious and intellectual transformations in several ways.

First, parallel to trends observable in Continental countries, there is the emergence of a consciousness of English as a "language," with an emblematic value as something representing the distinctness of the English nation. Grammar, style, rhetoric, et cetera become problems for English as a language as much as for Latin, Greek, Hebrew, et cetera (See Jones 1953:272–323, Michael 1970, Barber 1976:65–142). English is seen more and more as a vehicle that goes along with opposition to the received traditions of educational, intellectual, religious, civil authority represented by such classical languages and their rhetorical hypertropy.

Consequently, it is not surprising that the Baconians, in their struggle to fashion 'true' empirical science, or "natural philosophy," rejected Latin and Greek and furthered the cause of a plain English, unadorned by rhetorical embellishment, which was seen as an impediment to 'truth' and logic and the practical availability of the language-external world to all. As a kind of culmination of this movement, the founding of the Royal Society in 1660 focused issues of the relationship of linguistic and symbolic representation to external empirical truth, and authoritatively decided in favor of a plain English style of scientific discourse. As Bishop Thomas Sprat wrote of this group of natural philosophers in his *History of the Royal-Society of London* in 1667:

> They have therefore been most rigorous . . . to reject all the amplifications, digressions, and swellings of style: to return back to the primitive purity, and shortness, when men deliver'd so many *things*, almost in an equal number of *words*. They have exacted from all their members, a close, naked, natural way of speaking; positive expressions; clear senses; a native easiness: bringing all things as near the Mathematical plainness, as they can. (quoted from Barber 1976:132)

Observe Sprat's italicization of the problem of denotative representation: words for things, in which scientific discourse should strive for truth through a "mathematical" plainness, whereby English could become a transparent window to truths both formulable and communicable in it (cf. Jones 1953:310–311).

What is remarkable is that this same conceptualization about language emerges in the various "leveling" sects of Puritanism, who see classical learning as well as rhetorical ornamentation as evils of established, prideful religious authority that work against the true glory of personal belief, expressed in the so-called Plain Style of English. Haller observes about the role of such sects as over against the established Anglicanism or later Presbyterianism of a ruling establishment, that

> [t]hey are important chiefly as symptoms of the democratization of English society and culture which was steadily being advanced by Puritan preaching in general, by the translation and publication of the Bible, and by the spread of literacy. The end toward which the whole movement was tending was the reorganization of society on the basis of a Bible-reading populace. Calvinism helped this movement forward by setting up a new criterion of aristocracy in opposition to the class distinctions of the existing system. But there was also a concept of equalitarianism implicit in Calvinism which transcended aristocracy and which the necessity the preachers were under of evangelizing the people brought steadily to the fore. . . . It became difficult not to think that election and salvation by the grace of God were available to everyone who really desired them. Moreover, once the Calvinist preachers admitted that the only true aristocracy was spiritual and beyond any human criterion, they had gone a long way toward asserting that all men in society must be treated alike because only God knows who is superior. The main body of preachers, to be sure, professional intellectuals with their own positions and prestige at stake, held to the notion of a national church, reformed from within, and did their best to keep the disruptive implications of their doctrines from being pressed too far. But granted their premises, it was natural that

there should start up among them as well as about them many impatient individualists unwilling to wait upon the slow processes of reform. (Haller 1938:178)

The most radical theology implied secular equalitarianism along with a separatist notion of the congregation as a unit through which, by belief, an individual makes a commitment to be bound to God. Separatism from the national church, notes Haller,

> was the extreme expression of the religious individualism of Puritan faith and doctrine, the individualism which drastically leveled all men before God. The dissenting preachers, moreover, were happy to find converts wherever they could, and found them in greater and greater numbers among men who by any leveling process felt themselves likely to gain rather than lose. . . . Consequently, the notions of universal grace and free will, which the main body of Puritan preachers opposed so bitterly in the church but which were the natural expression in theological terms of some of the most important implications of Calvinism on the moral and social plane, these flourished among the sects. (1938:181)

And these flourished particularly among the Friends, or Quakers as they came to be called by midcentury, who wrapped themselves in Plain English language as an index of their Truth.

Indeed, one of the central attacks of George Fox (1624–1691), the founder of the Religious Society of Friends, was on the symbolism of such practices as the pronominal usage of *ye/you* in its acquired indexical values. For the Friends, the indexical values of saying *ye/you* for deference to the addressee, or for elegance of style, were the very opposite of the civil equality of all people before God. Early Quaker leaders delivered many explicit pronouncements on the subject, their ideological rationalizations about this system of indexicals, turning it into a matter of truth and falsity to the "natural," original, and holy order of things. Midcentury Quakers were using *thou/thee* exclusively for the SECOND SINGULAR form, never *ye/you*, a societally shocking, even insulting usage that was explicitly subversive in intent to "prideful" and "ambitious" authority, both religious and civil.

Quaker address with *thou/thee* played upon the fact that English scriptural prose was translated into this form, maintained as a distinct functional register from the T/Y usage in polite interpersonal usage: hence, these were people *truly* of The Book once more on earth, an indexically implied arrogation to the sect of a legitimacy beyond any others—indeed, of a legitimacy pointedly beyond the authorities of the Crown, to and from whom uniform Y (vs. T) usage was expected in the other functional system. "Thou and Thee was a sore cut to proud flesh," wrote George Fox in his *Journal*,

> and them that sought self-honour, who, though they would say it to God and Christ, could not endure to have it said to themselves. So that we were often beaten and abused, and sometimes in danger of our lives, for using those words to some proud men, who would say, "What! you ill-bred clown, do you

Thou me?" as though Christian breeding consisted in saying You to one; which is contrary to all their grammars and teaching books, by which they instructed their youth (1919) [1694]:381–382).

In 1660, Fox, along with followers John Stubs and Benjamin Furley, published *A Battle-Door for Teachers and Professors to Learn Singular and Plural*; You to Many, *and* Thou to One: *Singular* One, Thou; *Plural* Many, You. Addressed to the learned with righteous irony—for a *battledore* is a schoolchild's primer—the authors start from the premise "that the propriety of every language is kept in the Bible" (Fox, Stubs, and Furley 1660:20) from God. They survey the referential category of number in a large variety of then-known languages to derive the divine truthfulness of using *thou* exclusively in singular address, and also to oppose the degeneracy of the form *you*, usage of which is ultimately blamed on errant, established Protestants and, thence, on the pope.

This is a remarkable, though expectable form of rationalization, in which the referential category of number plays the decisive role in what we may call *literalizing the indexical usage of T/Y as a metaphor of it*. It is not merely a question of opposing the T/Y usage as such; it is a matter of the pure referential truth of the category of NUMBER. Note, then, that in effect the category of NUMBER is taken at the level of typicality of differential reference (cf. the book's subtitle), with no attention to the asymmetries of markedness that differentiate NUMBER in the second vs. third PERSONS (cf. Figure 5). As shown in Table 9, the configuration of NUMBER in the *unmarked* THIRD PERSON—the category of PERSON with which we can objectify an "other" in abstract terms for rationalizing processes—imposes itself on the T/Y differentiation through this literalizing effect. The *you* of power, as Brown and Gilman (1960) termed it, is rationalized as a *false* and pridefully arrogant "pluralization" of a basically and differentially singular *thou*: Thus, by what right and with what metaphorical truth does any *individual* other get referred to by a PLURAL form? The NON-SINGULAR of the SECOND PERSON is taken to be differentially equivalent in reference to the PLURAL of the THIRD PERSON.

Hence the indexical value of Quaker Plain Speech "T" in respect to the norms of the wider English society. As shown in Figure 7, to Friends the form *thou*, has the indexical-referential value of SECOND SINGULAR pronominal, at the same time as (1) used symmetrically, it indexes speaker and addressee membership in the particular ideological and religious group (i.e., their solidarity), or (2) used asymmetrically, it indexes speaker nonadherence to status marking as a function of formality (i.e., politeness, deference) in language.

To the larger society, by contrast, the symmetric usage of T is highly marked as informal solidarity, camaraderie or intimacy, while asymmetric usage is highly marked for unequivocal status differential, as we saw earlier. So there is a polarization of usage in which, as Table 10 schematizes, the older T/Y system is revaluated into indexicality of a new sort, that marking *speaker*

# TABLE 9
Literalizing the Metaphor of 'Power'—Analogy from the Unmarked Function of Reference

| | | | |
|---|---|---|---|
| THIRD PERSON "NUMBER": | "One" | vs. | "More than one" |
| (Speaking *of* others) | Unmarked interpreted ◄──────► Marked as specifically "not" marked | | |
| | | | |
| SECOND PERSON "NUMBER": | "One addressee" | vs. | "More than one addressee" |
| (Speaking *to/of* another) | (*thee*) | | (*ye/you*) |

identity. Asymmetric usage has exactly the opposite values for Friends and others, and is the cause of strife; for just those who might be *"thou"*ing Friends within the T/Y system, magistrates and other officers of the Crown speaking to such decided status inferiors, would use *you* in official situations, in which Friends would be *thou*ing them, expressing in their own system defiance of worldly pride and ambition! Friends use symmetric T, and hence others had to avoid it, lest they be mistaken for members of the sect; Friends avoid symmetric Y, and hence others must use it only. Consequently, a new system emerges, in which societal norms abandon T decisively as a usage indexing speaker as Quaker and take up the invariant usage of Y. A STRUCTURAL or FORMAL change in the norms of English has been effected.

$$\text{"T"} = \begin{cases} \text{reference to and index of addressee;} \\ \text{index of speaker and addressee member-} \\ \text{ship in group (i.e., solidarity);} \\ \text{non-adherence to status-marking as} \\ \text{a function of formality in language} \end{cases}$$

FIGURE 7
Indexical and referential values of Quaker Plain Speech

To recapitulate, a particular formal indexical distinction gets incorporated into English through borrowing, skewing usage of formal referential categories organized according to universal and particular structural constraints. In time, this usage is strengthened by an emerging ideology of formal, standard language as an instrument of public authority. Against this, an ideology of equality and private revelation takes up the question of this indexical distinction, finding in it the very antithesis of a (differential-)truth-in-category doctrine of the representational value of language—to which assertedly more

TABLE 10
Older and Innovative Systems Compared for Evolution of T/Y System

| Older, post-Norman system | Ideologically marked system | |
|---|---|---|
| | Quakers | Non-Quakers |
| Asymmetrical | | |
| Y "up"/T "down" | – | – |
| symmetric-solidary T | + | – |
| symmetric-nonsolidary Y | – | + |

fundamental standard all linguistic usage, including indexical conventions, is held. Such a view of language characteristically starts with the structure of unmarked categories of reference, literalizing indexicals as metaphors of such referential categories, and rationalizes usage in terms of the metaphor as analyzed. In this particular case, the nature of the now highly ideologized usage is such that the system of referential categories itself, as a structural norm, is changed decisively in a direction away from the innovative ideological view.

## INDEXICAL/REFERENTIAL IDEOLOGICAL METAPHORS AND PRESCRIPTIONS FOR REFORM

Ideological rationalization thus engaged with language at and through an intersection of structural form and indexical usage, producing tension in the then highly charged "metaphoricization" of indexical meanings of forms. The resolution of this tension seems to move the very structural system into new configurations, generally unforeseen by the users of the language.

The contemporary situation with language and gender has many parallels to the previous example. Ideologically informed perception correctly intuits the cultural parallelism between indexicals of speaker gender and status, and turns it into a metaphorical equivalence relationship by literalizing status asymmetry in terms of the *referential category* of gender, through which the *statistical indexicals* of gender are grasped in metalinguistic consciousness. To be sure, pointed Standardization in performance and in attitude is perceived as suggestively effeminate for men, and its opposite as suggestively masculinized for women. But, whatever its aims at dealing with such indexical values, the analysis and prescription for so-called nonsexist language has focused upon categorical reform of the semantico-referential system itself, as a means to reform of what we have seen is an indexical statistical tendency of language usage. Thus, the two basic routes of reform by the ideologically committed and convinced: lexical neutralization of various gender-indicating terms of role identity (e.g., *waiter* vs. *waitress* [feminine] neutralized as *server*), and neutralization of gender-indicating anaphoric pronouns (e.g., *he* vs. *she* [feminine] neutralized as some prescribed form) under certain conditions.

The first reform does not actually deal with the existence of a category of semantic gender as such, but only with some of its overt examples that have explicit, affixal expression of formal GENDER (cf. *-ess*, added or not to the stem *wait(e)r-*), the differential referential interpretation of which is ideologically perceived as irrelevant, or even inimical, to the assertible equality of individuals in this role. Such ideologically charged but merely lexical reform has both a certain potential for misfire and abuse, and a certain generative force reasserting categorical homeostasis. For, the innovating term can be incorporated in language as essentially a substitute for the marked FEMININE term, as for example *chairperson* (vs. older *chairman*), which can be used to indicate 'female' as opposed specifically to 'male.' Or, the innovating term can rapidly replace an older one as the stem for a derivational set, in effect reconstituting the category of GENDER, as for example *serveress*, an encountered nonce formation built on the new, intendedly GENDER-neutral *server*.

The second, pronominal reform attacks the very marking of the category in the grammatical system of the language. It does so through an ideological assault on the differentially referential "truth"-value of the structurally unmarked MASCULINE form *he/him/his* (henceforth, H) in certain anaphoric uses. Thus, note, that *categorical* (not the statistical) presence or absence of a clear, segmentable unit in linguistic usage, because someone uses H or not in these constructions, is turned into an index of a certain absence or presence of ideological solidarity with the reformers. An additional indexical polarity has been created in the language riding on the previous set of functions of the anaphoric or reference-maintenance system. As indicated in Figure 8, in such cases, to the ideologically committed reformers certain uses of H are not only a predictable consequence of the regular anaphoric system (*The student . . . He . . .*), they also refer unavoidably to a notional 'male' and differential man, and *thereby* index the speaker as not solidary with the equalitarian ideals (and hence "truth" in this normative sense) of the reform group. And in pragmatics, as we have seen with the T/Y distinction, there is no asymmetry of markedness that allows any user of the language to escape being susceptible to ideological location by an interested interlocutor.

But what is proposed as the alternative, solidarity-indexing form? Here, native speakers find themselves in something of a dilemma, from which the structural route out has not yet solidified as a categorical norm. Clearly, given the structural asymmetries of English grammatical categories, differentially referential truth-in-anaphoric-equality emerges as a problem. It emerges from the fact that SINGULAR MASCULINE category has been one of the basic means of indicating indefiniteness of information in a nominal construction communicating about a notional 'human' (see Table 2 and Figure 2). Thus the well-known *Man is mortal, but he . . .* which logicians quantify universally over humanity. So when, intending neutralization of GENDER, we use a lexical

$$"H" = \begin{cases} \text{anaphorizes (indexes) antecedent noun} \\ \quad \text{phrase;} \\ \text{refers to notional male, differential man;} \\ \text{indexes that speaker is without raised} \\ \quad \text{consciousness (or with hostility), etc.} \end{cases}$$

FIGURE 8
Indexical and referential values of Modern English anaphora He/Him/His for ideologically committed group

item, word, or standardized expression in the SINGULAR, or more specifically in the notional 'non-plural,' how can we maintain reference to the introduced topic—given our particular linguistic categories—in the face of the added indexical baggage of the H form? A great number of different solutions have been proposed and illustrated. These range from neological and channel-specific *s/he* anaphor, useful only for writing; to the referential nicety of the logician's disjunctive anaphor *he or she*; to the time-sequence alternation of *he* with *she* as construction demands an anaphor, which requires a realtime self-monitoring capacity beyond most and possibly all of us; to the blanket reversal of the markedness of GENDER by using *she* as both GENDER neutralized *and* notionally 'female' category; to the blanket reversal of NUMBER markedness for notional 'human' topics by using PLURAL nominals only for indefinites; through capitalizing upon the existence of indefinite *they* in colloquial usage.

The possibility of a structural norm compatible with so-called nonsexist usage is interesting. For as an engagement of ideologically informed usage with the language system, the discovery or diagnosis of the purported structural ailment—accomplished by literalizing a metaphor from categories of reference to categories of indexicals—is really a process of unambiguous creation of—or infectious inoculation with—the pragmatic disease. Such discovery/creation is a political process par excellence, in which language as it is available to its users' consciousness is the medium of practical struggle in now categorical indexical terms. This will clearly have repercussions on the nature of the structural norms of the semantico-referential system, but how is a complicated matter. We can see some of the complications by looking at perhaps the "best" nonsexist indexical, the last enumerated—best for the structural norm because it has already penetrated colloquial anaphoric usage and seems least to violate the universal constraints on systems.

Many languages have a categorically THIRD PLURAL pronominal form that is used for indefinite—that is, further unspecified—introduction of a 'human' or at least 'volitional' topic of discourse, generally in transitive or active subject position. Thus, in English, the paranoid's "*They* are out to get me!" Colloquial English for some time has shown the spread of similar categorical forms to nonsubject positions of reference maintenance (anaphora), especially possessive modifier of plural nominals, starting from the analogical point of entry with INDEFINITE subjects *everyone, everybody, every* [Noun], in which a differentially referential plurality is suggested by the modifier *every-*. Thus, *Everyone put on their scarves*, or even . . . *scarf—*which is perfectly acceptable colloquial usage, perhaps even Standard for many English speakers. From *every-* indefinites, the usage has spread to others, for example with *any-, some-,* emphasizing the indefiniteness of notionally 'human' or 'animate' reference more than the notion of 'plurality.' At this point, it is clear, *they/their* (and for some people *them*) has joined the SECOND PERSON *you/your* as a generalizing indefinite form, as witness in the transition from one to the other in the following passage from a user's bulletin that switches from report mode to directive by the shift of PERSON at the categorical level: "Once this feature was removed, the data disconnections stopped. Unfortunately, this means that *everyone* must make sure either to depress *their* data buttons or to turn off *your* terminal to make sure *your* connection is severed" (*Tele-Data* [University of Chicago], vol. 2, no. 5 [Dec., 1982], p. 4; italics added). Given the indefiniteness of the clause subject *everyone*, intended apparently to include writer, addressees, and any others in the local community of computer users, and given that the possessive modifiers do little more than specify ownership/location that can be presupposed, the writer might well have come up with: ". . . that everyone must make sure either to depress *the* data buttons or to turn off *the* terminal to make sure *the* connection is severed."

It is obvious, then, that THIRD PLURAL anaphors occur as grammatically dictated forms for reference maintenance where the specificity of categorical content is low, indeed, sometimes being nothing further than that of a definite article. And it is clear that the uses of H, the sexist anaphor, give maximally foregrounded offense to the ideologically committed precisely in such cases. Hence, these have been the foci for reform, *not* those cases where notions of 'male' and 'female' are definitely introduced in the antecedent nominal expression. Few would seem to propose *The woman put on their coat*, or even *A woman put on their coat* as a corrective to H; for recall that the attack has been grounded in a doctrine of presumptive masculinity in otherwise notionally 'human' topics of discourse. Hence, it does not seem to be the categorical obligatoriness of anaphoric agreement *tout court* that is at issue, though obviously one extreme and unworkable solution to the indexical offense of using H is to eliminate overt anaphoric reference maintenance. Rather, recalling Figure 2, we see that in structural terms, the problem is tantamount to using the machinery of the indefinite agent *they* and generic anaphor *their* [*/them*] to express a *new and distinct overt category*, ANIMATE SINGULAR, to which anaphoric reference maintenance is ideologically prescribed, whether 'definite' or 'indefinite,' whether 'specific and distributive' or 'generic.' The traditional system, with markedness asymmetries of (marked) PLURAL and (marked) FEMININE, uses H to achieve this. The proposed *they/their/them* anaphor for 'gender'-indefinite reference maintenance in effect attempts to override this, so that the overt form *they/their/them* would now have several distinct areas of usage, seen by category, with neutralizations forming a patchwork structure of explicit distinctions otherwise unattested in such reference-maintenance systems. TH. as we might relabel the prescribed index, would now be categorically sometimes specifically PLURAL, sometimes specifically ANIMATE SINGULAR, sometimes specifically INDEFINITE (AGENTIVE), in the face of its usual markedness position—a "local" morphological solution that quickly leads to "global" discourse confusion in complicated reference tracking.

We could examine various other proposals as well to see what effects they seem to have on the numerous semantically and pragmatically relevant functions of English language forms. Those attempting to devise so-called nonsexist discourse forms generally eliminate the maximally offensive H, only to find that this requires a number of readjustments of varying structural severity in order that, within a particular ongoing discourse context, they can keep definiteness distinct from indefiniteness, singular from plural, parties of first from those of the second from those of the . . . nth parts (all categorical THIRD PERSONS), and so forth. It is easier to proscribe H by declaring indexical offense than to prescribe a structurally stable solution to the entailed disruption. For multiple syntactic systems are at issue once the H form is no longer a possible category of neutralization. The case of H/TH or H/??? is not as simple in alternatives as the case of T/Y, because the former are of much greater structural centrality and functional ubiquity. And any stability reached will involve more profound effects on the structural norms of English.

What is common to the two cases, however, is that an ideology focuses upon a particular, structurally dictated indexical usage, finding it wanting as a vehicle of the ideology, and entailing a charged indexical contrast with some alternative, structurally dictated usage. These examples, like any others we might have chosen, show the fact of what Saussure (1960[1916]:30f.) called *parole*—and what contemporaneously we call "performance" (cf. Chomsky 1965:4)—is really a complex and bidirectional relationship played out in micro-realtime.

To different degrees, any linguistic *form*, a pragmatic realization of structure in use, has multiple indexical values for its users, whether or not these are explicitly recognized in conscious awareness (cf. Silverstein 1982). Most are not. But it is as analogues or metaphors of structure reconstructively seen through the *differential reference* value of use that indexical values more generally come to consciousness and inform interested ideologies of how language is and ought to be. In a sense, then, structure, though a theoretical abstraction, "determines" presupposable use-value, because in interpretation there is a tendency to project a prior structurally determined use-value (differentially referential structure) as at the basis—logically and/or temporally—of the apprehended, that is, imputed, analogues and metaphors of usage. The "truth" of indexicals is one such.

But contrariwise, any linguistic form in use is also an action, with consequences or entailments for its users of which it is a prospective index.

In implementation, there is a requirement for a metalinguistic consciousness of how such entailments are and ought to be accomplished, a consciousness that has its own linguistic externalization possible to different degrees. The degree to which such metalevel consciousness grasps indexical entailments, and to which such linguistic externalizations of consciousness are inseparable from the forms in use, determine the way a structural system of functionally semantico-referential value can be abstracted from the fact of conscious usage. Structural categories, then, are prospectively determined by the interaction of consciousness, frequently ideologically informed consciousness, with entailing use-value. In a sense, then, structure, though a theoretical abstraction, "is determined by" entailing use-value, to the extent that structural categories are precipitated by constancies of consciously informed entailments in the social action of language use.

And whether in micro-realtime, called synchrony, or, as we have here emphasized, in macro-realtime, called diachrony, such a bidirectional dialectic constitutes the minimalest total linguistic fact.

## REFERENCES

Barber, C.
1976    *Early Modern English*. London: Andre Deutsch.
Benveniste, E.
1966    Les Verbes Délocutifs. In *Problèmes de Linguistique Générale*, pp. 277–285. Paris: Gallimard.
Brown, R. and A. Gilman
1960    The Pronouns of Power and Solidarity. In *Style in Language*, ed. T. A. Sebeok, pp. 253–276. Cambridge: MIT Press.
Carter, A.
1980    The Language of Sisterhood. In *The State of the Language*, eds. L. Michaels and C. Ricks, pp. 226–234. Berkeley: University of California Press.
Chomsky, N.
1965    *Aspects of the Theory of Syntax*. Cambridge: MIT Press.
Cooke, J. R.
1970    *The Pronominal Systems of Thai, Burmese, and Vietnamese*. (University of California Publications in Linguistics, No. 52). Berkeley: University of California Press.
Dixon, R. M. W.
1972    *The Dyirbal Language of Northern Queensland*. (Cambridge Studies in Linguistics, No. 9). Cambridge: Cambridge University Press.
Fox, G.
1919 [1694] *George Fox, an Autobiography*, ed. R. M. Jones. Philadelphia: Ferris and Leach.
Fox, G. J. Stubs, and B. Furley
1660    *A Battle-door for Teachers and Professors to Learn Singular and Plural; You to Many, and Thou to One: Singular One, Thou; Plural Many, You.* London: Robert Wilson. (Facsimile reprint: [1968] English Linguistics 1500–1800, No. 115. Menston: Scolar Press.)

Haas, M. R.
1941    Tunica. Extract from *Handbook of American Indian Languages*, Vol. 4. New York: Augustin.
1944    Men's and Women's Speech in Koasati. *Language* 20:142–149.
Haller, W.
1938    *The Rise of Puritanism*. New York: Columbia University Press.
Hofstadter, D. R.
1982    Metamagical Themas. *Scientific American* 247(5): 18, 22, 26, 30, 36.
Irvine, J. T.
1975    Wolof Speech Styles and Social Status. *Working Papers in Sociolinguistics*, No. 23. Austin: Southwest Educational Development Laboratory.
1978    Wolof Noun Classification: The Social Setting of Divergent Change. *Language in Society* 7:37–64.
Jones, R. F.
1953    *The Triumph of the English Language*. Stanford: Stanford University Press.
Labov, W.
1972    *Sociolinguistic Patterns* (Conduct and Communication Series, No. 4). Philadelphia: University of Pennsylvania Press.
Michael, I.
1970    *English Grammatical Categories and the Tradition to 1800*. Cambridge: Cambridge University Press.
Ochs [Keenan], E.
1974    Norm-makers, Norm-breakers: Uses of Speech by Men and Women in a Malagasy Community. In *Explorations in the Ethnography of Speaking*, eds. R. Bauman and J. Sherzer, pp. 125–143. Cambridge: Cambridge University Press.
Sapir, E.
1949 [1929]    Male and Female Forms of Speech in Yana. In *Selected Writings of Edward Sapir in Language, Culture, and Personality*, ed. D. G. Mandelbaum, pp. 206–212. Berkeley: University of California Press.
Saussure, F. de
1960 [1916]    *Cours de Linguistique Générale* (5th ed.) eds. C. Bally and A. Sechehaye. Paris: Payot.
Shils, E.
1982    Deference. In *The Constitution of Society*, pp. 143–175. Chicago: University of Chicago Press.
Silverstein, M.
1981    The Limits of Awareness. *Working Papers in Sociolinguistics*, No. 84. Austin: Southwest Educational Development Laboratory.
Smith, P. M.
1979    Sex Markers in Speech. In *Social Markers in Speech*. (European Studies in Social Psychology), eds. K. R. Scherer and H. Giles, pp. 109–146. Cambridge: Cambridge University Press.
Trudgill, P.
1974    *Sociolinguistics: An Introduction*. Harmondsworth: Penguin.
Wolfram, W.
1969    *A Sociolinguistic Description of Detroit Negro Speech*. Washington, DC: Center for Applied Linguistics.
Wyld, H. C.
1920    *A History of Modern Colloquial English*. London: T. Fisher Unwin.

# Parental Speech and Language Acquisition: An Anthropological Perspective

## Ben G. Blount

The editorial to this issue mentions the contributions that anthropology has made to pre-natal and peri-natal studies (see also Laughlin 1989). Within that framework, the present article is focused on what anthropology might contribute to the study of children's first language acquisition. Anthropology, by virtue of its concept of culture and its descriptive, observational research methods, is well placed to address specific issues in child language acquisition research.

One major issue in child language research has been the role of speech addressed to young children in aiding or promoting language acquisition. The argument will be presented below that the issue has been clouded by lack of information about what parents, or their socialization surrogates, actually do when they direct speech to infants or young children. The absence of a strong data base pertaining to the contextual support and the nature of parent-child interaction severely limits our ability to understand how linguistic features of interaction may promote child language acquisition.

## THE CONCEPT OF CULTURE: METHODOLOGICAL CONSIDERATIONS

### Culture

The concept of culture has been central to anthropological inquiry since the nineteenth century, when it was developed more or less concurrently with academic anthropology. The individual largely responsible for the emergence of both the concept and the discipline was Edward B. Tylor, who provided a definition of culture that has informed anthropology for more than a century: "Culture . . . is that complex whole which includes knowledge, belief, arts, morals, law, custom, and any other capabilities and habits acquired by man as a member of society" (Tylor, 1871, p. 1).

Tylor's seminal definition of culture has been the starting point for many of the reconceptualizations the concept has undergone in the anthropological community, including the way that culture tends to be viewed in contemporary anthropology. Among the features proposed by Tylor were: (1) culture consists of knowledge; (2) culture is acquired; and (3) acquisition occurs within a societal framework. The same features can be seen in the definition that prevails in anthropology today, supplied by Ward Goodenough: "A society's culture consists of whatever it is that one has to know or believe in order to operate in a manner acceptable to its members, and do so in any role that they accept for any one of themselves (Goodenough, 1957, p. 167). In other words, culture is an information system that allows members of a society to interpret each other's behavior in meaningful ways. Behavior is viewed in broad terms. Even behavior that has clear biological bases, such as emotions, falls within the scope of culture, since societies have culturally defined frameworks within which they interpret emotionally-derived behavior as meaningful (see Lutz, 1988).

## Methodological Concerns

In research that involves anthropology and other disciplines, two points about the importance of the culture concept should be highlighted. One is that a focus on culture requires a methodological framework in which the notion or concept of an "individual" is contextualized. The focus is on a framework within which individuals can relate to each other. Moreover, the "relation" is in terms of meaning, which is shared and which is a constitutive part of any event in which behavior occurs. To state that point otherwise, a notion of a "natural" individual—an acultural one—requires that meaning not be assigned to his behavior. Although such a concept may be useful, it is difficult not to smuggle meaning into accounts of behavior. If meaning is ascribed to behavior, linguistic or otherwise, then a cultural framework must be present for adequate description of the behavior. Otherwise, culture can remain invisible, rendering description incomplete and even misinformative.

A second, methodological point is that since Tylor's time, anthropology has tended to be broad, even holistic, in research perspective. Anthropological inquiry tends to be exploratory and descriptive, and the cornerstone of inquiry has been to make culture visible, to explicate behavior in terms of patterns of meaning within a broader cultural framework. In anthropological research, culture is typically a critical variable. That methodological view is often contrasted to the more formal, experimental methods of psychology in which, for example, an "individual" may be defined as acultural. While the contrast has some merit and utility, it can easily be overdone. A better way, perhaps, to characterize the methodological differences is that descriptive research places priority on validity over reliability and on internal as opposed to external validity. Anthropological inquiry tends to be pre-operational and thus preparatory to hypothesis testing, although the caveat must be made that there are notable exceptions (see Thomas, 1986; Bernard, 1988). The anthropological emphasis on making culture visible lends itself to qualitative, conceptualizing research, in effect of producing a richer contextualization of behavior.

An example of making culture visible should be instructive. The cross-cultural studies on socialization undertaken by the Whiting team in the 1960s

(B. Whiting, 1963; B. Whiting and J. Whiting, 1975) led to several significant findings (see Laughlin's 1989 survey). One major finding was that one particular type of caretaking stood out as unusual among all of the other types surveyed. That type is characteristic of the United States. Its central, defining feature is that mothers tend to be in prolonged, close proximity with offspring in residences which isolate them from other individuals. That residential pattern, one nuclear family per housing unit, has fostered an isolation of one adult and offspring, clearly the exception in comparison with other societies where child caretaking responsibility is shared among several co-resident individuals. The point is that the pattern is not "natural" to human socialization, which is easily overlooked in the absence of cross-cultural research. The apparent "naturalness" of the isolated mother-child pattern of socialization to members of U.S. society is a cultural folk-model, and in fact a strong one. The current, hotly contested debates about two-track career women and about daycare as a substitute for mother-specific socialization are derived from that folk-model. That is not to say that the issues are not real, but that the socialization pattern is culturally motivated, and the set of issues and problems cannot be fully understood unless that fact is recognized.

## The Developmental Niche

Numerous efforts have been made to develop a model that would integrate a cultural approach to human behavior with more psychological, "individualized" approach (Broffenbrenner, 1979; Fishbein, 1976; Kessel and Siegel, 1983; also see Monroe, Monroe, and Whiting, 1981). One recent and promising effort in the area of human development is the idea of a developmental niche (Super and Harkness, 1986). Recognizing that research on child development has tended to be either on the socializer, who exemplifies cultural behavior, or on a decontextualized, acultural child, who reveals universal developmental processes, they propose an integrative perspective that includes the social settings of behavioral development, the customs of child care and rearing, and the psychology of the caretakers. Although each of the three components is related in different ways to the larger societal environment, they are interrelated and form a system. The important point is that culture is not hidden in that framework, and moreover, it is a vital part of the environmental input from which a child abstracts the knowledge which becomes part of his or her own cultural understanding.

One of the strong points of the developmental niche concept is that it accommodates change. The three sub-components must remain more or less in harmony, but each component can vary according to its own input. A child's physical maturation, for example, may lead to new or altered and culturally based expectations as to what the child's behavior should become, placing new pressures and priorities on them by their parents (see Blount, 1977). The interrelationship of the sub-components and the allowance for change in the system make the developmental niche a valuable framework for contextualizing research that may focus on only one or two components of the system but can, at least in theoretical terms, be related to the other components.

## PARENTAL SPEECH

### Preliminary Problems in Research

The developmental niche model has excellent potential to advance research on the role of parental speech in child development. The model can serve as a systematic framework to guide research, and it also can serve as a target against which research to date can be evaluated. In each instance, the model can provide direction for the description of linguistic features of parental speech and for the use of the parental speech register. As a target to aid assessment of work to date, the model can make explicit a number of obstacles and oversights that have arisen in this field of inquiry, as discussed below.

Numerous observers have noted that children's caretakers in many societies have a special speech register for addressing language-acquiring children, and a host of explanations have been proposed to account both for the phenomenon and for the contribution that it might make to language acquisition. Although our understanding of that speech register has been advanced by those observations, the research suffers in many instances by being "monotonic" (Pye 1988), i.e., based on only one language or one aspect of acquisition. For example, considerable discussion has been devoted in recent years to the role of "motherese" in children's first language acquisition (Wanner and Gleitman, 1982; Gleitman, Newport, and Gleitman, 1984), but the work has focused on simple linear relationships between the mean length of maternal utterances and the syntactic gain by children. The usefulness of that measure should be seriously questioned, since it constitutes a unidimensional, decontextualized approach to understanding parental speech (see Bohannon and Warren-Leubecker, 1988). While correlations between syntactic aspects of parental and child speech can be sought, failure to find significant and positive correlations cannot serve as a basis to reject any or all contributions of parental speech to child language acquisition. Further discussion on that point is given below.

Other efforts to clarify the contributory role of parental speech have frequently been on logical grounds, the thrust of the argument being that language acquisition cannot be fully explained by speech input and thus speech input must play only a minor, insignificant role, if any (Gleitman and Wanner, 1982). An argument has even been made that parental speech input to a language acquiring child could have a retarding effect on acquisition by limiting the range of grammatical constructions available to a child for his or her processing (Wexler, 1982). However logical that type of argument might appear, it is based on an unwarranted assumption that the availability of all of the grammatical forms of a language, *tout ensemble*, better facilitates language acquisition than grammatical forms adjusted, through time, to a child's level of comprehension and production. That assumption also allows for the conflation of all speech registers in the acquisition process, thereby removing social and contextual features from the acquisition process by fiat. Although a child obviously must learn his or her own language, it seems rather extreme to project that the learning is accomplished by a miniature automaton parsing and reassembling linguistic structure alone.

Understanding of the language socialization functions of parental speech has been impeded not only by premature conjectures about its marginal importance, but also by the piecemeal nature of research and a corresponding lack of standardization of concepts and measurements. A principal problem is the general lack of calibration of parental speech characteristics with the developmental phase or stage of children who receive the speech. These two general problems—premature judgment and lack of standardization—are in part consequences of the same phenomenon, a focus on the early emergence of grammar as the most important aspect of child language development and a view of parental speech that tended to restrict it to a single function, the enhancement of acquisition of grammar. "Motherese" thus has been defined as containing relatively short, syntactically simple utterances (usually a single clause) and assessed by the correlation, if any, between "motherese" and child syntax (Gleitman, Newport, and Gleitman, 1984). Critics of the "motherese" hypothesis, i.e., those who reject any role for it and thus support an innatist position, point to the absence of correlations as evidence for its marginality (Gleitman and Wanner, 1982). That view, however, is based on an exceptionally narrow, syntax-driven, conceptualization of parental speech and a small slice of the developmental period of language acquisition. In other words, it is unnecessarily restrictive and narrow to equate parental speech with "motherese" and to assess its supportive role in language acquisition only by the criterion of a direct, causal link between the syntax of the mother's speech and the child's speech. A broader conceptualization of parental speech seems advisable.

## Characterizations of Parental Speech

One of the earliest attempts to characterize parental speech broadly, but principally in linguistic terms, was Charles Ferguson's article on "baby talk" in six languages (1964). He identified several recurrent characteristics across cultures in the "baby talk" code. These included simple canonical structure of word-form, CVC and CVCV (consonant-vowel-consonant, etc.); basic consonants (stops and nasals) and common vowels; reduction of phonological clusters; phonological reduplication; absence of inflectional affixes (except for a diminutive suffix specific to the code); and lexical domains centered on kin terms, body parts, and animals. The descriptive catalogue was devoted principally to the segmental code, although a preference for high pitch and certain intonational contours, i.e., suprasegmentals, were mentioned. Special interactional processes such as imitation (mimicking) and repetition were not identified as part of the behavior. Ferguson also was not concerned with the age or developmental stage of the children who were the recipients of the special code, other than the global period of language acquisition. He left open the question of when given features might be used according to degree of acquisition.

Despite its limitations, Ferguson's work provided the first steps in a general characterization of the "baby talk," or parental speech, register. Two logical steps could be taken to continue the work: (1) the identification of further characteristics of the code; and (2) descriptions of usage patterns through examination of parent-child interaction.

Since Ferguson's initial work, considerable advances have been made in further identification of characteristics of the code. Ferguson expanded his comparative base and extended the list of segmental characteristics of the register (1977; 1978), and descriptive accounts of parental speech registers in specific societies have been produced, e.g., Berber (Bynon, 1977), Latvian (Ruke-Dravina, 1977) and Quiche Mayan (Pye, 1986). The characteristics were also extended to include suprasegmentals. Blount (1972a) discovered in a study of language socialization of Luo children in Kenya that the most distinctive characteristics of parental speech were suprasegmentals, especially intonation and intensity of speech. Garnica (1977) extended the list of prosodic and paralinguistic features to include fundamental frequency and duration of syllable nuclei in each utterance, sentence final pitch terminals, whispering, and primary stress. Garnica went on to demonstrate that the patterns of prosody (pitch, frequency, and duration) were different in speech to two-year-olds and five-year-olds.

Prosodic aspects of parental speech have, understandably, continued to be of interest. Penman, Cross, Milgrom-Friedman and Meares (1983), for example, found that prosodic features of maternal speech varied across age of infant and across mode of speech (informational versus affective).

The most extensive expansion of parental speech characteristics, in terms of number of identifiable features, was in a study of English-speaking and Spanish-speaking parents (Blount and Padgug, 1977; Blount, 1984). The study, exploratory in nature, identified prosodic, paralinguistic, and interactional features in parental speech to infants approximately nine to 22 months of age. A complete list of the features is given in Table 1.

A description of the features is given in Blount (1984) and need not be repeated here. The points to emphasize here are that a sizeable number of special features are present in parental speech and that interactional, language-usage features such as parental repetition of child utterances and prompters to talk are included. In one sense, all of the features are interactional, since they occur in parent-child face-to-face interaction, but some features constitute a part of the actual interactional structure beyond the characteristics of the vocalizations themselves. In other words, the parental speech features include not only how the speech is articulated but how the vocalizations "fit into" and function in the social interaction.

## TABLE 1
### Categories and features of parental speech

| | |
|---|---|
| I. Prosody | Tenseness |
|   A. Volume: air | Stress |
|     breathiness | Nasality |
|     Breath held | Rounding |
|   B. Volume: sound |   B. Segmental (phonetic) |
|     Whisper |     Alteration |
|     Lowered volume |     Substitution |
|     Raised volume | III. Lexical-Grammatical |
|   C. Pitch/Intonation |   A. Lexical |
|     Falsetto |     Special lexical items |
|     High pitch |     Nonsense forms |
|     Low pitch |   B. Grammar |
|     Exaggerated intonation |     Grammatical deviations |
|     Singing | IV. Interactionals |
|   D. Rate of speech |   A. Structural |
|     Slow rate |     Attentionals |
|     Fast rate |     Prompters |
|   E. Duration |     Tag questions |
|     Lengthened vowel |     Repetition |
|     Lengthened consonant |   B. Modeling |
|     Shortened vowel |     Imitation |
|     Shortened consonant |     Turn substitution |
| II. Paralinguistics |     Personal pronoun substitution |
|   A. Non-segmental |     Interpretation |
|     Creaky voice | |

Several of the results of the English and Spanish study are relevant to the discussion here. Comparison in frequency of feature usage across families, holding child age and language group constant, showed remarkable consistency. Exaggerated intonation and repetition (multiple expressions of an utterance by a parent), were the most common features, suggesting that they play a prominent role in parental speech. Language and culture differences also were observed. The English-speaking parents relied comparatively more on prosodic features—pitch, intonation, duration, breath, and tension—whereas Spanish-speaking parents relied comparatively more on interactional features—pronominals and attentionals (utterances designed to attract a child's attention)—and on different prosodic features—tempo and volume.

## Constraints on Parental Speech by Age of Child

The English and Spanish study also indicated that the most frequently used features in each language were not distributed differently across the age ranges of the children. Although some features were more likely to be used in speech to older children (post 18 months), they were relatively infrequent in occurrence in comparison to intonational and pitch features. In each language group, the features that showed increased usage to the older children were specifically interaction related, repetition and interpretation in English and fast rate and interpretation in Spanish (interpretation means that a parental utterance assigns lexical meaning to a child's utterance, even if the latter has no clear reference or sense). Only in the period beyond 18 months was there an apparent, concentrated effort by parents to make the interaction meaningful in a linguistic sense and to resemble verbal interaction. That suggests that the parental concerns were not principally with language development per se but were to foster and promote interaction in a proto-conversational form. Their extensive use of some two dozen special features in their speech appeared to be designed to attract a child's attention, to focus the attention, and use the attention to exchange vocalizations. The use of three or more features per parental utterance probably is a reflection of the elusiveness and fleeting nature of a child's attention.

Overall, as exploratory as it was, the anthropological study of English and Spanish parental speech suggests that the structural demands of capturing and engaging a child's attention during the latter part of the first and much of the second year of life promote the use of special, attention-getting features in the speech of parents. In terms of the developmental niche, the defining or limiting characteristic is the tenuous attentional and interactional capacity of the child, reflected in the parental "psychology" of special speech accommodation, but not devoid of cultural preferences that shape the frequency and the form of some of the special features. Culture is thus made visible within a framework in which its content can be seen as meaningful.

The English and Spanish study made culture visible in another way by illustrating that the common cultural definition of parental speech as built of special lexical items, such as "choo-choo" for train, and of simplified grammatical constructions, such as "baby like milk?", is erroneous. Those types of forms occurred only infrequently, as did all register-specific lexical and grammatical features. Any study that took for granted, on the basis of a cultural folk-model, that those types of features characterize parental speech would be very incomplete and misleading, no matter how careful the measurement of those features.

The emergence of meaning-related features in parental speech in English and Spanish at approximately 18 months set against a continuation of attention-related features from nine to 22 months indicates that parental speech is multi-functional. Moreover, the different functions may be related to the communicative capacity of the child. At 18 months, the children were more adept at the use of lexical items and had some concept of labelling and meaning. Meaning-related features began to appear in parental speech at that time. Other studies suggest a transition in parental speech of a different kind when infants first begin to use lexical items. A number of researchers have noted that the semantic and syntactic aspects of parental speech are more complex and less like "baby talk" prior to the onset of a child's first words (Brown, 1977; Cross and Morris, 1980; Phillips, 1973). The clear implication is that when a child begins to encode lexical meaning, the parental speech begins to adjust to that capacity.

Addressing the issue of age-related speech input directly and using data from Australian English, Robyn Penman et al. (1983) suggest that maternal speech in a child's prelinguistic stages has monologic and dialogic components, whereas once language begins to emerge, a dialogic component comes to the fore. The earlier, monologic component appeared to be more a commentary on the infant's behavior than speech addressed to him or her, a phenomenon also observed among the Luo (Blount, 1971). The Luo also report that efforts to engage infants in vocal communication prior to the onset of words is culturally prohibited.

Another type of transition was suggested by Roger Brown (1977), who proposed that the maternal speech register is shaped by two relatively independent interpersonal functions, the affective and the communicative. The results of more recent research indicate that considerably more is involved and that the different functions are reflective of infant interactive capacity. An affective component may be present throughout the first two years or so of a child's life, although it is likely to be concentrated in the first 4–6 months, when attracting and holding a child's attention is a major undertaking (see Stern, Spieker, Barnett, and MacKain, 1983). Prosodic and paralinguistic features are likely to predominate then, embedded in concentrated nonverbal cues such as vision (see Tronick, Als, and Adamson, 1979). In terms of meaning-related vocal behavior, the first nine months or so is likely to contain monologic parental speech, describing infant activities but not for proto-conversational exchange.

The prelinguistic phase of a child's development is thus likely to contain not one but two types of parental speech, monologic descriptions and heavily affective, attention-getting and attention-sustaining dialogic speech. As lexical meaning begins to emerge in an infant's vocal behavior, the monologic forms become less frequent, affective attentionals begin to predominate, and as vocabulary grows, meaning-related features appear more frequently in parental speech (see also Blount and Kempton, 1976, for a similar account).

The multifunctional model of parental speech described above is based on the notion of accommodation. An individual with developed, complex communicative skills modifies those in order to interact with an individual who has limited skills, severely limited in terms of referentiality, meaning, and sense (Blount, 1977; Bohannon and Warren-Leubecker, 1988). Affect is enhanced and reinforced throughout, serving as the "topic" in early stages, as a means of focusing on the topic at later stages (Tomasello, 1988), and sustaining verbal interaction as meaning becomes more and more central to the interaction.

## Universality of Parental Speech?

Since accommodation to the capacity of the child constitutes the basis of the parental speech model, and since infants appear to follow a relatively pre-set developmental model (Stern et al., 1983), it would be tempting to conclude that the model is universal. It is certainly widespread. Ferguson (1977, 1978) compared baby talk in 15 societies, representing language families as diverse as Siberian, Semitic, Yuman, and Dravidian. The list today could be considerably expanded, to the extent that universality might seem plausible. Universality, however, is a strong claim, and preliminary questions should be asked. Arethere societies in which investigations have failed to detect parental speech? In those societies which have parental speech, are there common forms and functions, or is there a high degree of variability that tend to render them culturally specific?

To the author's knowledge, there are no reports of societies totally devoid of parental speech. One society, Samoa, is reported to have almost no forms (Ochs, 1982). However, in that study, the youngest child observed was 19 months old, at the beginning of a twelve-month study. What occurs prior to 19 months is not clear. Ochs reported that infants and caregivers have considerable physical and social contact, but that the infants' behavior is not treated as social acts and that they are not engaged in communicative-like interactions, as widely reported for British and American infants. The text is not explicit, however, as to whether Ochs refers to infants pre-19-months of age or whether she refers to those in her sample at post-19-months of age. If it is the former, then no data base is reported, and if the latter, several interesting questions are raised.

One question is what happens during the prelinguistic phase, especially when contact between a Samoan mother and her infant is the most extensive. Are there prosodic, affective parental utterances? All that can be said here is that there is no evidence for Samoan to serve as a counter-example. A second question is what characterizes the parental speech to children who are already into lexical and early grammatical acquisition? Ochs' answer to that question is clear. Samoans ". . . do not use baby talk lexicon, special morphological modifications, simpler syntactic constructions . . . [nor do they] . . . expand children's utterances" (1982, p. 101). Moreover, only a minimum of cooperative utterance-building is reported between child and caregiver. Ochs interprets the general absence of interactional and language-supportive caregiver behavior as due to the cultural definition accorded to Samoan children, essentially a low-status position within a highly status-conscious society.

Ochs' main point is consistent with and supportive of one of the major themes of the current paper, namely that how parents interact with children is constrained in part by cultural definitions. Samoans represent a society in which the cultural constraints are especially strong once a child has the ability to communicate verbally. Speech to a child must be assessed in relation to the culturally defined status of the child. To expand that point even further,

Samoan socialization behavior can profitably be viewed in terms of the developmental niche concept. Caretaker psychology, cultural definitions, and social settings interrelate during the post-19-month development of children to socialize them, language-wise, toward Samoan social organization.

A question can still be raised as to what communicative support Samoans provide for young children. Although Samoan caregivers may minimize the overt language support given to children in language acquisition, some accommodation for the lesser capacity of children does appear to occur. Comparative analysis of parental speech to Samoan, Luo, and American children at the age of two and one-half years indicated a skewing of wh-questions toward the semantically simpler "what" and "who" forms as opposed to the more complex "when" and "why" forms (Blount, 1972b). Consistent, however, with Ochs' later study, analysis of the use of parental yes/no questions and of the distribution of imperatives, interrogatives, and declaratives in parental speech indicated that in Samoan and Luo, the children were not defined and viewed as social equals to adults. They were addressed with more imperatives than the American children and with almost no yes/no questions (which asks for an opinion or observation and thus implies a more equal status of the interlocutors).

In one sense, the form of Samoan and Luo parental speech behavior could also be viewed as accommodative, since it was selected to be consistent with and thus to model the appropriate language interaction with children, appropriate according to cultural expectations. In other words, the absence of salient linguistic markers in Samoan parental speech does not mean that no accommodation is made to the child's linguistic interactive capacity. To the contrary, the speech appears, in fact, to be tailored to the cultural definition of the child and thus consistent with the broader cultural parameters.

The research on Samoan indicates that parental speech may be patterned in subtle ways according to cultural definitions of personhood and status. Parental speech may thus have virtually no register-specific prosodic, paralinguistic, or interactional forms similar to those in Table 1, with the caveat that the children are likely to be beyond the prelinguistic stage where such features would be more likely to be interactively effective.

The importance of culture in the selection of linguistic features that constitute a parental speech register can be seen in another study on a non-Western language. Clifton Pye (1986) evaluated Quiche Mayan parental speech against the 17 register features identified in Ferguson (1978). He found that the Quiche speech contained only five of the 17 features: repetition, baby-talk forms for qualities, compound verbs, diminutives, and special sounds (all imitative of child speech). Pye also discovered forms in Quiche that were not included in Ferguson's inventory: whispering, initial syllable deletion, baby-talk forms for verbs, a register-specific verbal suffix, a more fixed word order with relatively fewer overt noun phrases, more imperatives, and a special interpretive routine. Pye concluded that like other societies, Quiche has a special register for talking with children and that the register is largely culturally defined. The choice of features to characterize parental speech is due to what the Quiche Mayan deem appropriate, constrained by the structure of the adult language.

Addressing the functionalist explanation of "motherese"—that the input is simplified and enhances acquisition—Pye points out that the Quiche parental speech register does not constitute simplification. In fact, some features make the register more complex, e.g., special sounds and a special verbal suffix, and Pye thus rejects the idea that motherese is designed as a language-teaching device. He sees the origin of the register in the cultural concepts about children and in the culturally defined ways that children and speech associated with them fit into a larger societal organizational and behavioral framework.

The conclusions reached in the Quiche Mayan study were similar to those of the Samoan studies in that speech was culturally defined and that language acquisition did not appear to be a function of the speech. The youngest age of the children in the samples was also similar, 22 months in Quiche and 19 months in Samoan. Unlike Samoan, however, which was viewed by Ochs as devoid of a parental speech register, Quiche clearly had one, even though Pye did not view it as language-acquisition supportive. A problem, however, arises here. Why do the features occur in speech to children well into the one-word stage of development if they are not supportive of acquisition? Do they mark affect, as is the case in English and Spanish? Are they merely attention-getting devices? No information is available to answer those questions, but perhaps the Quiche parental speech is marked with parental speech features merely as socially appropriate forms independent of questions of comprehension and acquisition. The latter is the explanation accepted by Pye.

Even in cases, however, where didactic or comprehension issues are not explicit, to rule out any instructional role seems premature. When children become aware that speech is directed to them and they attend to the speech, no clear basis exists for rejecting all roles that the speech might have in promoting understanding and acquisition. In other words, if there are interaction patterns that are routinely marked with special features of speech and a child is beginning to process lexical meaning, then the special features may at least have a role as attentionals in behavioral exchanges that promote language exchange and thus the acquisition of meaning.

A second consideration emerges in the Quiche study. What are the characteristics of parental speech in the prelinguistic stage of development? Pye indicated that Quiche mothers wait until their infants begin to use words before they begin to converse with them and that they lack any notion of talking with their infants to stimulate linguistic development. The Luo, however, also have the same ideas, including a strong cultural prohibition against conversing with a prelinguistic infant, but that does not prevent them from using a parental speech register to "address" infants. Do the Quiche Mayans (and the Samoans) report that they do not converse with their infants but in actual fact "speak" to them in a parental speech register laden with prosodic and paralinguistic features? English-speaking and Spanish-speaking mothers also will deny, sometimes vigorously, that they converse with their infants, but observations of their behavior will show that they almost always use highly stylized speech to attract the attention of their infants and engage in affect-laden proto-conversational exchanges. Quiche and Samoan may be different in that regard, but we cannot draw that conclusion from the evidence currently available.

## SUMMARY: CULTURE AND FUNCTIONS OF PARENTAL SPEECH

What functional role or roles in language acquisition does parental speech in fact play, if any? What has been suggested here is that parental speech may play a role in that it creates the behavioral framework and context out of which language acquisition emerges. A distinction probably should be made between parental speech to prelinguistic infants and to those who have embarked on the acquisition of lexical meaning. In the first instance, parental speech registers are clearly part of the attention-getting and attention-sustaining processes which underlie the emergent patterns of social interaction in which language will later play a role. Although societies may differ in the extent to which parents thus engage their infants, it is difficult to imagine, given the vocal and interactive capacities that prelinguistic infants manifest and the careful attention that they demand, that caretakers do not engage in some vocal exchanges with them. The chapter on that set of questions and issues is certainly not closed.

In the second instance, parental speech to infants who have embarked on vocabulary-acquisition, the evidence is clear that speech plays a role. Parents do call infants' attention, repeatedly, to the association, through modeling, of specific vocalizations and exemplars of the classes named by the vocalization (Ninio and Bruner, 1978; Bohannon and Hirsh-Park, 1984; Hoff-Ginsburg and Shatz, 1987). The suggestion is also presented here that parental speech supports acquisition through creation of contexts culturally appropriate for children's behavior. Children are provided the context in which to learn what meaning is associated with specific vocalization types (see Schieffelin and Ochs, 1986, for case studies of prompting routines in that regard). Not only lexical meaning but socially appropriate forms of talk are thus made available to children for learning.

Lastly, the suggestion has been made that the rejection of parental speech as instrumental in the acquisition of grammar is premature. As noted, that issue has been central in discussions about what "motherese" is and whether it is language-acquisition related. That issue has been heavily clouded by lack of clarity about what aspects of "motherese" may be relevant, what developmental age or age-range is involved, in effect by a general absence of any clear conceptualization as to what is appropriate to measure and what calibration should be used.

The issue about what should be measured depends, obviously, on what it is that is considered to be acquired. A child who has acquired concepts of plurality and past tense ultimately must learn for himself or herself how to encode those into the structure of the language, and it is clear that parents in no society provide explicit instructions in training sessions as to how that is to be accomplished. The observation that children must learn the encoding for themselves, and even that part of that "learning" may be based in some bioprogram, does not mean that children do not use environmental information, including parental speech, to arrive at the proper formulation of rules for encoding. Much of the problem seems to reside in a strict separation of rules to generate linguistic form from any principled contextual support for the discovery that the rules, however "learned," are expressed in a particular way. The important questions are what is the information that a child needs to make the discoveries necessary for the expression, say, of English plurals, and where does the child get that information. The place to begin to look is not merely at plurals in the adult language but at the routines in which parents and children participate and in which concepts such as plurality become salient and meaningful. The routines involve cultural definitions of what is possible and appropriate, and that type of information, given our present state of knowledge, must involve descriptive, exploratory studies that are sensitive to the importance of culture. Anthropological research is relevant and has contributions to make in those regards.


## REFERENCES

Bernard, H. R. (1988). *Research methods in cultural anthropology*. Newbury Park, CA: Sage Publications.

Blount, B. G. (1971). Socialization and pre-linguistic development among the Luo of Kenya. *Southwestern Journal of Anthropology* 27, 41–50.

Blount, B. G. (1972a). Aspects of Luo socialization. *Language in Society* 1, 236–248.

Blount, B. G. (1972b). Parental speech and language acquisition. *Anthropological Linguistics* 14, 119–130.

Blount, B. G. (1977). Ethnography and caretaker-child interaction. In C. E. Snow & C. A. Ferguson (Eds.), *Talking to children: Language input & acquisition*. Cambridge: Cambridge University Press.

Blount, B. G. (1984). Mother-infant interaction: features and functions of parental speech in English and Spanish. In A. Pellegrini & T. Yawkey (Eds.), *The development of oral and written language in social contexts*. Norwood, NJ: Ablex.

Blount, B. G. & Kempton, Willett. (1976). Child language socialization: parental speech and interaction strategies. *Sign Language Studies* 12, 251–277.

Blount, B. G. & Padgug, E. (1977). Prosodic, paralinguistic, and interactional features in English and Spanish. *Journal of Child Language* 4, 67–86.

Bohannon, J. N. & Hirsh-Park, K. (1984). Do children say as they are told? A new perspective on motherese. In L. Feagans, C. Carvey, & R. Golinkoff (Eds.), *The origins of growth of communication*. NY: Ablex.

Bohannon, J. N. & Warren-Leubecker, A. (1988). Recent developments in speech to children: We've come a long way, baby-talk. *Language Sciences* 10, 89–110.

Broffenbrenner, U. (1979). *The ecology of human development*. Cambridge, MA: Harvard University Press.

Brown, R. (1977). Introduction. In C. E. Snow & C. A. Ferguson (Eds.), *Talking to children: Language input & acquisition*. Cambridge: Cambridge University Press.

Bynon, J. (1977). The derivational processes relating Berber nursery words to their counterparts in normal inter-adult speech. In C. E. Snow & C. A. Ferguson (Eds.), *Talking to children: Language input and acquisition*. Cambridge: Cambridge University Press.

Cross, T. C. & Morris, J. E. (1980). Linguistic feedback and maternal speech: comparisons of mothers addressing infants, one-year-olds, and two-year-olds. *First Language 1*, 98–121.

Ferguson, C. A. (1964). Baby-talk in six languages. *American Anthropologist 66* (part 2), 103–114.

Ferguson, C. A. (1977). Baby talk as a simplified register. In C. E. Snow & C. A. Ferguson (Eds.), *Talking to children: Language input & acquisition*. Cambridge: Cambridge University Press.

Ferguson, C. A. (1978). Talking to children: A search for universals. In J. H. Greenberg (Ed.), *Universals of human language. Vol. 1, Method and theory*. Stanford: Stanford University Press.

Fishbein, H. D. (1976). *Evolution, development, and children's learning*. Pacific Palisades, CA: Goodyear.

Garnica, O. K. (1977). Some prosodic and paralinguistic features of speech to young children. In C. E. Snow & C. A. Ferguson (Eds.), *Talking to children: Language input & acquisition*. Cambridge: Cambridge University Press.

Gleitman, L. R. & Wanner, E. (1982). Language acquisition: the state of the state of the art. In E. Wanner & L. R. Gleitman (Eds.), *Language acquisition: The state of the Art*. Cambridge: Cambridge University Press.

Gleitman, L. R., Newport, E. L. & Gleitman, H. (1984). The current status of the motherese hypothesis. *Journal of Child Language 11*, 43–79.

Goodenough, W. (1957). Cultural anthropology and linguistics. In P. Garvin (Ed.), *Report of the seventh annual round table meeting on linguistics and language study*. Washington, DC: Georgetown University Press.

Hoff-Ginsburg, E. & Shatz, M. (1987). Linguistic input and the child's acquisition of language. *Psychological Bulletin 85*, 1104–1122.

Kessel, F. S. & Siegel, W. (Eds.) (1983). *The child and other cultural inventions*. NY: Praeger.

Laughlin, C. D. (1989). Pre- and perinatal anthropology: a selective review. *Pre- and Perinatal Psychology Journal 3*(4), 261–296.

Lutz, C. A. (1988). *Unnatural emotions: Everyday sentiments on a Micronesian atoll & their challenge to Western authority*. Chicago: University of Chicago Press.

Munroe, R. H., Munroe, R. L. & Whiting, B. B. (1981). *Handbook of cross-cultural human development*. NY: Garland Press.

Ninio, A. & Bruner, J. S. (1978). The achievements and antecedents of labelling. *Journal of Child Language 5*, 1–16.

Ochs, E. (1982). Talking to children in Western Somoa. *Language in Society 11*, 77–104.

Penman, R., Cross, T., Milgrom-Friedman, J. & Meares R. (1983). Mother's speech to prelingual infants: A pragmatic analysis. *Journal of Child Language 10*, 17–34.

Phillips, J. (1973). Syntax and vocabulary of mothers' speech to young children: Age and sex comparisons. *Child Development 44*, 182–185.

Pye, C. (1986). Quiche Mayan speech to children. *Journal of Child Language 13*, 85–100.

Pye, C. (1988). Towards an anthropology of language acquisition. *Language Sciences 10*, 123–146.

Ruke-Dravina, V. (1977). Modifications of speech addressed to young children in Latvia. In C. E. Snow & C. A. Ferguson (Eds.), *Talking to children: Language input & acquisition*. Cambridge: Cambridge University Press.

Schieffelin, B. B. & Ochs, E. (Eds.) (1986). *Language socialization across cultures*. Cambridge: Cambridge University Press.

Stern, D. N., Spieker, S., Barnett, R. K. & MacKain, K. (1983). The prosody of maternal speech: Infant age and related changes. *Journal of Child Language 10*, 1–15.

Super, C. M. & Harkness, S. (1986). The developmental niche: A conceptualization at the interface of child and culture. *International Journal of Behavioral Development 9*, 545–569.

Thomas, D. H. (1986). *Refiguring anthropology: First principles of probability & statistics*. Prospect Heights, IL: Waveland Press.

Tomasello, M. (1988). The role of joint attentional processes in early language development. *Language Sciences 10*, 69–88.

Tronick, E., Als, H. & Adamson, L. (1979). Structure of early face-to-face communicative interactions. In M. Bullowa (Ed.), *Before speech: The beginning of interpersonal communication*. Cambridge: Cambridge University Press.

Tylor, E. B. (1871). *Primitive culture*. London: John Murray.

Wanner, E. & Gleitman, L. R. (Eds.) (1982). *Language acquisition: The state of the art*. Cambridge: Cambridge University Press.

Wexler, K. (1982). A principle theory for language acquisition. In E. Wanner & L. R. Gleitman (Eds.), *Language acquisition: The state of the art*. Cambridge: Cambridge University Press.

Whiting, B. (Ed.) (1963). *Six cultures: Studies of child rearing*. NY: Wiley & Sons.

Whiting, B. & Whiting, J. M. W. (1975). *Children of six cultures: A psychocultural analysis*. Cambridge: Harvard University Press.

# Genre, Intertextuality, and Social Power

Charles L. Briggs
Richard Bauman

Why devote an article to the subject of genre? It must be admitted from the outset that genre engenders a number of possible objections when presented as an analytic tool for the study of speech. Like such notions as *text, genre* strikes some practitioners as too global and fuzzy a concept to be of much use to detailed formal and functional analysis. Its association with literary theory and critical practice may similarly suggest that it is not likely to be illuminating with respect to either "everyday conversation" or "ordinary" linguistic processes. It is generally used, after all, in *classifying* discourse; typological tasks are often rejected by empiricists and anti-positivists alike, and some researchers will find it difficult to believe that the use of broad empirical categories is likely to be of much use to fine-grained analysis of particular social interactions. Beyond these issues, all of us know intuitively that generic classifications never quite work: an empirical residue that does not fit any clearly defined category—or, even worse, that falls into too many—is always left over.

In defending our chosen topic, we could point out that the concept of genre (with or without the label) has played a role in linguistic anthropology since at least the time of Boas. Generic classifications helped set the agenda for research on Native American languages. The study of genre was later boosted by ethnoscience, structuralism, the ethnography of speaking, and the performance-centered approach to verbal art. The recent popularity of Bakhtin's translinguistics and new perspectives on emotion and gender have similarly accorded new cachet to generic investigation. The first part of our article will thus be devoted to a critical discussion of the place of genre within linguistic anthropology.

As will become apparent in the second part, our goal is not to defend the concept or to claim that it should occupy a more central role in linguistic anthropology. We will rather argue that its nature and significance have been misconstrued in certain fundamental ways by proponents and critics alike. Although the same could be said of research on genre in folkloristics and literary theory as well as in linguistic anthropology, these areas lie beyond the scope of this article. This misapprehension has contributed to the ambivalent reception that the concept has received and its periodic movements in and out of scholarly fashion. We will argue that grasping the complex intertextual relations that underlie genre, along with the way these relations are closely linked to social, cultural, ideological, and political-economic factors, can offer insight into why studies of genre have proved to be so problematic. We hope to be able not only to provide a more solid foundation for investigations of genre, but also to show how research on generic intertextuality can illuminate central issues in linguistic anthropology.

## THE BOASIAN TRADITION

As we have noted, genre—as term and as concept—has achieved currency in contemporary linguistic anthropology largely under the stimulus of the ethnography of speaking, performance-centered approaches to verbal art, and the work of Mikhail Bakhtin. To be sure, the foundations of this interest in genre were laid much earlier, principally at the points of convergence between linguistic anthropology and the adjacent discipline of folklore, in which the generic shaping and classification of oral forms has been a fundamental concern. In particular, generic issues (though not the term) played a certain operational role in the Americanist tradition of Boas and his intellectual heirs, although the concept was seldom the focus of critical examination in their work. Given the centrality of texts in the Boasian tradition, rooted in the philological foundations of Boasian anthropology, discrimination among orders of texts was at times seen to be a necessary task, at least for certain purposes.

The most prominent use of generic distinctions in the Boasian line occurs in the organization of text collections. Perusal of these collections, however, reveals that the grouping of texts within their pages is frequently quite ad hoc, without discussion of the conceptual basis of the respective sections. Sapir, for example, in his classic collection *Wishram Texts*, writes only that "the arrangement of the texts under the heads of Myth, Customs, Letters, Non-Mythical Narratives, and Supplementary Upper Chinookan Texts, is self-explanatory and need not be commented upon" (1909:xii). The distinction between myths and tales or historical narratives attributed by Boas to North American cultures generally had some effect in shaping text collections (see, e.g., Reichard 1947), but other sorting principles, such as grouping by informant (see, e.g., Reichard 1925), may also be found. One noteworthy feature of Americanist text collections in the Boasian tradition is the frequent inclusion of a corpus of "ethnological narratives" (e.g., Sapir and Hoijer 1942) or "ethnographic texts" (e.g., Jacobs 1959), generic rubrics that reflect the Boasian predisposition toward cultural information in entextualized packages. This genre brings into special relief the way in which generic categories and textual forms are co-created by the ethnographer and the consultant (see Briggs 1986).

Boas's own work displays a marked ambivalence about the usefulness of generic categories. On the positive side, he does suggest the need to record the full array of verbal genres because of their varying "stylistic peculiarities" (1940c[1917]:200), in tacit recognition that discourse form is a significant patterning principle in the organization and distribution of linguistic structure, and he does direct attention to the presence or absence of particular verbal genres in a culture's repertoire as a means of testing (generally, debunking) universalistic theories of the origin and development of literature (1940c[1917]:209). Overall, however, Boas treats generic distinctions with varying degrees of care and precision. In certain instances, he displays a tendency to use generic designations rather casually. In the opening paragraphs of "The Development of Folk-Tales and Myths" (1940b[1916]:397), for instance, folktales and myths are first separated terminologically, then (apparently) merged under the general rubric of *tales*, after which (again apparently) *folk-tales* becomes the cover term.

If this is an instance of casual sliding across a range of terms, there are other points at which the absence of clear generic distinctions in Boas's writings rests on a more principled foundation. In his comparative investigations of the narrative repertoires of North American peoples, Boas discovered that particular themes and motifs might diffuse, with some degree of independence, to combine and recombine with other elements in a variety of shifting ways. In larger scope, by whatever criteria one might employ to make generic distinctions between myth and folktale, for example, Boas perceived that there is "a continual flow of material from mythology to folk-tale and *vice versa*" (1940b[1916]:405). Boas's distrust of various attempts to discriminate between narrative genres was further bolstered by his perception that such distinctions did not remain consistent for specific narratives across group boundaries; once again, by whatever criteria the distinction was attempted, narratives that were clearly genetically related might appear in one group's repertoire to belong to one class, and in the neighboring group's repertoire, to another. Hence, Boas attributed the "somewhat indefinite" use of the terms *myth* and *folk-tale* to "a lack of a sharp line of demarcation between these two classes of tales" (1940a[1914]:454). Boas's critique of generalized, a priori, analytical genre definitions rests on a substantive test of a particular kind: it is not their productiveness in delimiting categories of cultural forms within cultures that is at issue, but their inconsistency in capturing genetically related cultural items across cultures that renders them of questionable usefulness for Boas's purposes.

There is, however, one basis for discriminating between myths and folktales to which Boas is prepared to accord a degree of legitimacy and productiveness—this is a distinction purportedly "given by the Indian himself" (1940a[1914]:454). "In the mind of the American native," Boas writes,

> there exists almost always a clear distinction between two classes of tales. One group relates incidents which happened at a time when the world had not yet assumed its present form, and when mankind was not yet in possession of all the arts and customs that belong to our period. The other group contains tales of our modern period. In other words, tales of the first group are considered as myths; those of the other as history. [1940a(1914):454–455]

Concerning this purportedly local distinction, Boas reminds us that here, too, historical and comparative investigations reveal movement between the two classes, and thus from his "analytical" point of view, this way of sorting out narrative genres is no better founded than those devised by scholars. It does, however, have the advantage of corresponding "to concepts that are perfectly clear in the native mind. Although folktales and myths as defined in this manner must therefore still be studied as a unit, we have avoided the introduction of an arbitrary distinction through our modern cultural point of view, and retained instead the one that is present in the minds of the myth-telling people" (1940a[1914]:455).

Several elements are significant here. First, observe that Boas attributes the distinction between myth and folktale that he outlines to American Indians generally; he never finds it necessary or useful to explore the distinction directly and in detail in any given Native American culture. Rather, he generalizes broadly and summarily, remaining far more centrally interested in those particularistic historical and comparative investigations that require that "folk-tales and myths . . . still be studied as a unit" (1940a[1914]:455).

A further point that is especially worthy of attention is Boas's repeated insistence on how "perfectly clear in the mind of the Indian" is the distinction between myths and historical tales. One wonders at the basis for Boas's assurance in this regard, especially in light of his observation that "historical tales may in the course of time become mythical tales by being transferred into the mythical period, and that historical tales may originate which parallel in the character and sequence of their incidents mythical tales" (1940a[1914]:455). Apparently, Boas did not encounter—or chose to disregard—instances in which his consultants saw particular narratives as generic hybrids or as categorically ambiguous. Nevertheless, the distinction drawn by Boas between analytical genres and local categories represents an early invocation of a persistent issue in linguistic anthropology and adjacent disciplines.

Among Boas's students, one who stands out for his considered attention to the problematics of genre is Paul Radin. Radin's most significant contribution is his "Literary Aspects of Winnebago Mythology" (1926), which takes its opening frame of reference from Boas but departs from Boas's approach in markedly important ways. Radin begins by observing that "it has been frequently pointed out that many Indian tribes divide their myths into two groups, one coinciding in the main with our category of myth proper, and the other with that of our semi-historical legend or novelette," noting that "the two types are set off from one another by objective differences in style," some of which are defined in terms of linguistic elements and structures (1926:18). Noting that "this distinction between myth (*waika*) and the tale (*worak*) is very strong and every tale is classified by them in one or another category" (1926:18), Radin might seem to be casting his account in the mold provided by Boas. Even here, however, the Winnebago case demands qualification of the general schema, as being "at variance with all conventional ethnological classifications: an origin story, being regarded as accounting for true happenings, must fall into the category of the 'tale'" (1926:21). Radin is thus clearly concerned, as Boas and others appeared not to be, with locally defined generic discriminations, adding to the preceding one still others, having to do with occasions of use and dramatis personae.

The most striking discovery that flows from Radin's attentiveness to Winnebago bases for discriminating among orders of narrative is the availability of a third classificatory possibility, "a mixed category, the 'myth-tale'" (1926:18). So much for Boas's "perfect clarity." Radin goes on to elaborate:

> The differentiation between a myth and a tale can be made, then, for the Winnebago on several counts, none of them mutually exclusive, and the proper classification of any one story is sometimes therefore a question of the weighting of several factors. . . . In any case it is clear that whenever we encounter a story of what might be called a mixed type, we can never be certain what weighting of the various factors will seem proper to the Winnebago, and, in consequence, to what category the story will be assigned. [1926:21–22]

Now, although Radin might seem to be conceding an inability to disentangle the various bases employed by the Winnebago for assigning a given narrative to one or another category, his insight is far stronger than that. What he is saying, rather, although in preliminary and partial terms, is that generic categories represent flexible social resources in two senses: (1) the selection of one or another basis for categorization will depend upon situational factors, and (2) the generic calibration of a narrative, by combining within it features characteristic of contrasting types, will likewise depend upon situational and strategic factors, such as clan politics. To the best of our knowledge, however, this remarkable insight was never significantly exploited beyond this essay, by Radin or anyone else, for the next half-century.

## FORMAL DEFINITIONS OF GENRE

Outside the Boasian tradition of linguistic anthropology, but convergent with it in certain respects, was a small line of scholarship devoted to the formulation of structural definitions of oral genres. Thomas Sebeok, in his classic article, "The Structure and Content of Cheremis Charms" (1964[1953]), cites the stylistic analysis of folklore texts of Boas and some of his students (e.g., Radin, Reichard) among other lines of structural analysis, but identifies his own analysis most centrally with symbolic logic and the morphological analysis of the Russian formalist folklorist, Vladímir Propp. Propp's influential study is well known and has been the subject of much critical discussion; there is no need to recapitulate his argument here, beyond noting that Propp offers his analysis of fairy tale morphology as the basis of a hypothetical *definition* of the genre (1968[1928]:99), an element missing from the Americanist line of formal stylistic analysis. "Much in the sense in which Vladímir Propp argued that all fairy tales are uniform in structure," Sebeok argues, "one is compelled to recognize that every Cheremis incantation belongs to the same structural type" (1964[1953]:363).

Sebeok describes his analytical strategy as follows: "Our analytical procedure will be an application of binary opposition as a patterning principle: that is, we shall repeatedly divide sequences dichotomously until the ultimate constituents are reached" (1964[1953]:360). The charm is thus divided by sections, sentences, clauses, and actor-action phrases, the ultimate contrastive constituents, the relationships between which are rendered in symbolic logic notation to yield the defining structure of the genre.

In a supplement to the original version of the article, published in 1964, Sebeok adds to his morphological analysis of the Cheremis charm an examination of its poetic style. Although charm structure is invariant in defining the genre, "each text is marked by a unique set of features which impart to it a certain particularity and concreteness or—to borrow a label from literary criticism—texture. An extremely interesting fact about the data is this: that striking symmetries are found to characterize each message no less than the work itself" (1964[1953]:363). The contrast is thus between "general structure" and "individual texture." Sebeok goes on to analyze the structure of a charm text in terms of syllabic patterns and phonological and syntactic parallelism. There is structure at both levels, but morphological structure defines the entire genre, whereas textural structures organize individual texts. The assignment of priority to morphological structure over textural patterns has significant implications: it is an analytical, not an ethnographic, operation. How Cheremis people conceive of the genre, what features define or characterize it in their understanding and practice, remains outside the purview of Sebeok's analysis.

Like Sebeok, Alan Dundes draws his inspiration from the work of Propp in insisting on the primacy of morphological analysis in the study of folklore genres. For Dundes, the determination of morphological structure opens the way to the investigation of many folkloristic problems of which one is genre definition (Georges and Dundes 1963:111). Again, like Sebeok (and Propp), Dundes sees morphological structure as the locus of invariance in folklore forms, but although he acknowledges the variant nature of style or texture, he places more emphasis on content as a variant element: "Content may vary, but form is relatively stable" (1965:127; see also 1964:25, 53). Dundes's focus on "variability within a given frame" (1964:25) leads him to employ such linguistic models as Pike's tagmemic analysis (Dundes 1964) and Hockett's topic-comment analysis (Georges and Dundes 1963) in his structural explorations.

There is a certain ambiguity in Dundes's writings on the structural definition of genre. At times, he advances structural analysis as the basis of genre definition itself: "An immediate aim of structural analysis in folklore is to define the genres of folklore" (Georges and Dundes 1963:111; see also Dundes

1964:105). At other times, however, he points up the inadequacy of a reliance on morphological structure alone. Among the conclusions he draws in *The Morphology of North American Indian Folktales* (1964), for example, is the following:

> Another conclusion suggested by the present analysis is the confirmation of the notion that myth and folktale are not structurally distinct genres. In fact, morphologically speaking, myths and folktales are one and the same. This means that the distinction between them is wholly dependent upon content criteria or totally external factors, such as belief and function. [1964:110]

In general, then, Dundes's writings raise another persistent problem in regard to genre definition, namely, what feature(s) constitute a sufficient or adequate basis for defining a genre: morphological structure, content, belief, function, and so on?

Much the same problem arises in Charles T. Scott's *Persian and Arabic Riddles: A Language-Centered Approach to Genre* (1965), another attempt at the formal definition of genre. Scott goes to striking lengths—even contortions—to confine his analysis within the disciplinary boundaries of linguistics, but is ultimately forced to concede the inadequacy of this approach. At the end of his monograph Scott essays a "definition of the riddle genre that is recognized as being incomplete":

> The riddle is defined as a grammatical unit of discourse, externally distributed within a matrix of longer discourse or of nonverbal behavior, and internally composed of two obligatory utterance-level units, between which there obtains a partially obscured semantic fit. [1965:74]

What makes the definition incomplete is that the matrix of longer discourse, or of nonverbal behavior in which the genre occurs, is left undescribed because that is the province of anthropology. Scott concludes then, that

> linguistic units alone are not sufficient to provide a complete definition of a literary genre. They are relevant to a description of the internal composition of a genre, which is a necessary component of a definition. However, a description of the nonverbal matrix within which the genre is distributed is a further necessary component of a definition, and linguistics cannot provide this description. It is in these terms that we support an earlier assertion . . . that the linguist, within the restrictions of his discipline, is compelled to take an incomplete and unsatisfactory position with respect to literature. [1965:74]

## GENRE IN THE ETHNOGRAPHY OF SPEAKING

With the emergence of the ethnography of speaking in the early 1960s, as we have suggested at the beginning of this article, genre assumes a significant place in the repertoire of concepts in linguistic anthropology (Philips 1987).

Neither the term nor the concept figures in Dell Hymes's pioneering essay, "The Ethnography of Speaking" (1962), although the significance of genre is anticipated in Hymes's considerations of speech events and linguistic routines. Genre is mentioned only in passing in Hymes's "Toward Ethnographies of Communication" (1964), but this article likewise adumbrates the later frames of reference in terms of which Hymes locates genre within the conceptual and analytical framework of the ethnography of speaking. In the 1967 article, "Models of the Interaction of Language and Social Setting," genre achieves a clear place in the program, which is subsequently expanded and elaborated in a range of further programmatic essays. In general terms, Hymes's writings offer three complementary perspectives on genre: (1) genre as category or type of speech act or event; (2) genre as a nexus of interrelationships among components of the speech event; and (3) genre as a formal vantage point on speaking practice. Taken all together, Hymes's writings (1967, 1972a, 1972b, 1974, 1975a, 1975b) offer a rich and ramified framework for the exploration of genre, but the scope and focus of this article require that we limit our discussion to selected points.

One significant issue addressed by Hymes has to do with the scope or comprehensiveness of genre as an organizing factor in the speech economy of a community. At first, Hymes suggests that "it is heuristically important to proceed as though all speech has formal characteristics of some sort as manifestation of genres; and it may well be true" (1972a:65). Elsewhere, it is genres and speech acts that jointly constitute the domain of ways of speaking (1972b:50). Later, in "Ways of Speaking" (1974), this position is hedged: "It is tempting to generalize the [category] of genre . . . so that all verbal material is assignable to some genre. . . . My own hunch is that communities differ in the extent to which this is true, at least in the sense of tightly organized genres" (1974:443–444). From this vantage point, then, the task becomes one of discovering what portion of the speech economy is generically organized, what portion escapes generic regimentation, and why.

This question is further underscored in substantive terms through the juxtaposition of related ethnographic accounts by Gary Gossen and Brian Stross. Consistent with the perspective of the ethnography of speaking, Gossen (1972, 1974) approaches the speech genres of the Chamula people of highland Chiapas as locally constituted and systemically interrelated, in powerful contrast to the scholarly tradition of reliance on a priori, universalistic, Western-based analytical genres, atomistically defined and etically applied.[1] Some Chamula genres may be analogous to Western ones, but the categories and their organization are ultimately fundamentally different. In

---

[1] The way that a number of anthropologists approached ethnographically situated genres converged with work in folkloristics; the distinction drawn by Ben-Amos (1976[1969]) between "analytical types," the etic categories used by scholars in comparative research, and "ethnic genres," the emic categories used by members of particular speech communities, was highly influential.

discriminating the Chamula system of generic categories, Gossen employs the structural-semantic analytical techniques of ethnoscience, which encouraged the exploration of lexicalized category systems, to discover the comprehensive taxonomic organization of the Chamula domain of *sk'op kirsano* 'people speech,' from the everyday to the most highly formalized and densely meaningful genres. As speaking is a cultural focus in Chamula, the cultural organization of this generic taxonomy is complex and resonant, encompassing interrelated and isomorphic formal, functional, situational, social organizational, axiological, ethical, and cosmological principles. The categorical elucidation of Chamula ways of speaking thus offers a powerful vantage point on Chamula culture and society in general. Gossen's analysis underscores the productiveness of a systemic ethnographic perspective as against a focus on selected or privileged genres (e.g., myth) alone, or on mere generic inventories (as in Shimkin 1964[1947]).

As illuminating as Gossen's analysis may be, though, it also displays the limitations of a rigorously taxonomic classificatory perspective on genre. Some of the most salient limitations may be highlighted by comparing Gossen's work and that of Brian Stross on the neighboring Tenejapa Tzeltal (1974). Gossen's taxonomy of Chamula genres of verbal behavior carries the taxonomic organization down to fifth level taxa. In discussing his methodology, Gossen acknowledges that first, second, and third level taxa represent "general agreement" among his six male informants, who ranged in age from 18 to 60. Informants did not agree with the same degree of consistency on fourth and fifth level taxa, although if fewer than half did not agree on the definition of a category and its placement in the system, it was not included in his considerations. The resultant schema yields an organizing framework of great order and powerful integration, a succinct view of Chamula language, society, and culture as an integrated system. But what of the kinds of people's speech concerning which there was only limited agreement or consistency—or none at all?

This messy underside of people's speech is what draws the attention of Brian Stross in his analysis of Tenejapa Tzeltal labels for kinds of speaking (1974). The Tenejapa Tzeltal, as noted, are neighbors of the Chamula in highland Chiapas, speakers of a related Mayan language. Stross finds a four-level taxonomy of kinds of *k'op* 'speech' that is quite similar to the one discovered by Gossen. He goes on, however, to record 416 additional terms in the Tzeltal metalinguistic lexicon—not an exhaustive and finite list, but simply as many terms as he managed to collect before giving up the elicitation process. Moreover, he gives us some of the rules for generating additional acceptable terms within this highly productive metalinguistic system. The important point is that his informants could not agree upon the assignment of these terms to superordinate categories. Stross, then, offers us a category system that is open, ambiguous, flexible, disorderly: "The Tzeltal domain of speaking is in fact an open system with fuzzy boundaries. . . . As such it is highly adaptable to change in the social environment and must be seen as constantly evolving" (1974:213).

Taken together, Gossen's and Stross's explorations reveal genre systems in their contrasting capacities as spheres of order and as open-ended spheres of expressive possibility. The counterposition of the two investigations must also raise questions concerning the isomorphism of generic systems and other aspects of culture. Whereas Gossen's analysis highlights strong structural correspondences, the amorphous openness and flexibility revealed by Stross calls into question what the overall fit might be.

In establishing the place of genre in the conceptual repertoire of the ethnography of speaking, one important task has been to articulate the relationship between genre and other core concepts and units of analysis, such as speech act, speech event, and speech style. This task represents another prominent concern in Hymes's programmatic essays. Like many other issues, this one emerged into focus in stages. In one early formulation, Hymes blurs distinctions in stating that "by Genres are meant categories or types of speech act and speech event" (1967:25). Elsewhere, however, he articulates several bases for distinguishing among these units of analysis. As early as 1964, Hymes suggests that "from one standpoint the analysis of speech into acts is an analysis of speech into instances of genres. The notion of genre implies the possibility of identifying formal characteristics traditionally recognized" (1972a:65). That is to say, in these terms, the notion of speech act focuses on speaking in its guise as social action, whereas the concept of genre directs attention to the routinized, conventionalized organization of formal means, on the formal structure of language beyond the sentence (1972b:48). This is not merely an analytical distinction; local conceptions of the organization of the domain of speaking may be articulated in terms of categorical systems of speech acts as well as of genres (see Abrahams and Bauman 1971).

If genre affords a formal vantage point on speech acts, speech styles offer a formal vantage point on genre. Building upon the work of Susan Ervin-Tripp (1972), Hymes (1974) develops a concept of speech styles as organized in terms of relations of co-occurrence and alternation:

> One can characterize whatever features go together to identify a style of speech in terms of rules of co-occurrence among them, and can characterize a choice among styles in terms of rules of alternation. The first concept gives systematic status to the ways of selecting and grouping together of linguistic means that actually obtain in a community. The second concept frees the resulting styles from mechanical connection with a particular defining situation. [1974:434]

Significant speech styles may be associated with social groups (varieties), recurrent types of situations (registers), persons (personal style), specific situations (situational styles), and genres (genre styles). Genre styles, then, are constellations of co-occurrent formal elements and structures that define or characterize particular classes of utterances. The constituent elements of genre styles may figure in other speech styles as well, establishing indexical resonances between them. Additionally, particular elements may be abstracted from recognized generic styles and employed in other discursive settings to endow them with an indexical tinge, a coloration, of the genres with which they are primarily associated and the social meaning that attaches to them, as when students perceive an instructor to be "preaching at them" in a classroom lecture. In a related manner, a subset of diacritical generic features may be combined with those that characterize another genre to effect an interpretive transformation of genre, a phenomenon that Hymes terms "metaphrasis" (1975a). Finally, elementary or minimal genres—irreducible generic structures—may combine in a variety of ways into complex, incorporative genres, as is widely noted of African oratory, for example, or riddle ballads. Considered in these terms, genres may be seen as conventionalized yet highly flexible organizations of formal means and structures that constitute complex frames of reference for communicative practice.

Greg Urban, in his study, "The Semiotics of Two Speech Styles in Shokleng" (1984a), develops this line of analysis in especially suggestive ways. The two speech styles featured in Urban's essay are in fact generic styles, one associated with origin-myth narration and the other with ritual wailing. Extending the principle of co-occurrence, Urban notes that "speech styles are inherently indexical, since their use co-occurs with some other entity, namely, the context or subject matter" (1984a:313). He goes on to offer a close semiotic analysis of origin-myth narration and ritual wailing that elucidates the webs of interrelationship that link them to other ways of speaking in Shokleng and to explore the communicative capacities of generic speech styles more broadly.

Hymes's observation that attention to rules of alternation organizing choices among speech styles "frees the resulting styles from mechanical connection with a particular defining situation" (1974:434) implicates the relationship between genres and speech events. The casual merger of genres and speech events in the early literature of the ethnography of speaking soon yielded to the documentation and analysis in the field-based literature of the transferability of genres from their primary situational contexts of use to other speech events as well as to the differential mobilization of particular genres in a range of events. Joel Sherzer, for example, traces the various contexts in which *ikarkana*, or curing texts, figure in San Blas Kuna culture, from the primary magical uses for curing, disease prevention, improving abilities, and general control of the spirit world to the rehearsal of an *ikar* by specialists, the teaching and learning of an *ikar*, and the chanting of an *ikar* for entertainment on festive occasions, each of which is marked by formal and functional differences (Sherzer 1983:118–120). In a similar vein, Alessandro Duranti explores the formally and functionally contrastive uses of the Samoan genre of oratory, called *lauga*, in ceremonial events (especially rites of passage) and in a type of political meeting called *fono*. Sherzer's and Duranti's analyses establish that the generic specification of the *ikar* or *lauga* cannot be accomplished by the examination of texts alone, but resides rather in the interaction between the organization of the discourse and the organization of the event in which it is employed; the ways and degrees to which a genre is grounded in, or detachable from, events is to be discovered.

The Kuna and Samoan examples raise one further point, also adumbrated by Hymes in various writings. The most salient difference identified by Duranti between *lauga* in the *fono* and *lauga* in other ceremonial events has to do with performance. The ceremonial *lauga* "is the socially recognized domain of 'performance' par excellence" (1984:235), in the sense of a display of verbal virtuosity, whereas the *lauga* in the *fono* is delivered and received in a very different, more instrumentally oriented mode. Likewise, the *ikar* as featured in festive occasions is framed primarily as virtuosic performance, in practicing as rehearsal, in teaching as demonstration, and so on. These cases, then, highlight the variable relation of genres to performance and to other frames. That this line of inquiry has been pursued most fully in relation to performance (Bauman 1977b; Hymes 1975a) is understandable in light of the long-standing centrality of artistic "literary" forms in the study of genre more generally. Most significant here is the recognition that not every doing of even the most poetically marked genres is framed as performance, or as full performance, in the sense of the assumption of accountability to an audience for a display of virtuosity, subject to evaluation for the skill and effectiveness with which the display is accomplished.

Of recent work in the exploration of genre in linguistic anthropology William Hanks's essay, "Discourse Genres in a Theory of Practice" (1987), stands out as the most direct and critical attempt to synthesize a conception of genre and to offer a comprehensive framework for its investigation. Although the contributions of the ethnography of speaking are fundamental to Hanks's treatment of genre, his analytical framework is most immediately a synthesis of Mikhail Bakhtin's sociological poetics and Pierre Bourdieu's theory of practice. In marked contrast to conceptions of genre—formalist and otherwise—in which genre is a structural property of texts, Hanks conceives of genre as an orienting framework for the production and reception of discourse. In Hanks's perspective, "The idea of objectivist rules is replaced by schemes and strategies, leading one to view genre as a set of focal or prototypical elements, which actors use variously and which never become fixed in a unitary structure" (1987:681). Generic structures and functions, which are normatively specified in formalist and eufunctional approaches, "become problematic achievements in a practice-based framework" (1987:681). More specifically, Hanks defines genres as "the historically specific conventions and ideals according to which authors [in Bakhtin's sense of authorship as the production of utterances] compose discourse and audiences receive it. In this view, genres consist of orienting frameworks, interpretive procedures, and sets of expectations that are not part of discourse structure, but of the ways actors relate to and use language" (1987:670).

The principle of historic specificity is especially important; it builds into the notion of genre the recognition of historical emergence and change (see also Hymes 1975a), again in radical contrast to treatments of genres as timeless, fixed, unitary structures. In Hanks's framework, genres occupy a dual relationship to historically situated action. Genres are at the same time the ideational outcomes of historically specific acts and among the constituting, transposable frames of reference in terms of which communicative action is possible; they are thus open to innovation, manipulation, and change (1987:671, 677). Hanks goes on to offer a penetrating elucidation in terms of form-function-meaning interrelationships of the emergence and transformation of genres of 16th-century Maya discourse as part of the emergence of new, hybrid forms of discourse under rapidly changing colonial conditions. Here, the "stylistic, thematic, and indexical schemata" (1987:668) that constitute a range of available generic orienting frameworks become resources for the shaping of new discursive practice.

## THE PROBLEMATICS OF GENRE

On the basis of the foregoing survey of perspectives on genre in linguistic anthropology, let us attempt to abstract and summarize the principal issues, problems, and ways of thinking about them that have characterized the field in order to establish a frame of reference for the discussion that follows.

One of the most central and persistent approaches to genre is from the vantage point of classification. Here, in its most basic terms, genre serves as a way of making categorical discriminations among discursive forms, which may be conceived of in textual terms, as verbal products, or in practice-based terms, as ways of speaking (and writing). The scope of genre, its range of applicability, varies among approaches. The term may be limited to "literary" forms, as forms of verbal art, or it may be extended to encompass a broader range of discursive forms, including, potentially, the entire domain of verbal production. Likewise, genre may be reserved for named categories of discourse, or, alternatively, all discursive forms may be taken to be generically regimented. The latter view, that there is no speaking without genre, may be stated axiomatically, as given, or hypothetically, as to be discovered.

The use of genre as a classificatory concept does not necessarily imply self-conscious attention to classification itself as an intellectual problem. Indeed, much work in the field tends to treat each generic category atomistically. Some significant work, however, has been devoted to the systemic organization of generic classifications, from the vantage point of either scientific taxonomy or the ethnographic investigation of locally constructed classification systems. The former, it is worth noting, fosters a conception of generic categories as necessarily mutually exclusive, consistent with the canons of scientific taxonomy, while the latter more often reveals generic categories that overlap and interpenetrate in a range of complex ways, or aspects of verbal production that are resistant to orderly categorization. Implicated here as well, of course, is the etic-emic distinction—a priori, analytical, universalistic categories, usually labeled in Western terms, versus locally constituted classification systems, employing local labels, which are to be discovered.

The criteria employed to define genres have included a wide range of features, ultimately taking in everything that people have considered significant about discourse: form, function or effect, content, orientation to the world and the cosmos, truth value, tone, social distribution, and manner or contexts of use. Definitional efforts in linguistic anthropology, however, are distinguished by the centrality of formal patterns, whether as the sole basis of definition or in relation to function, content, or context. The most significant dimension of contrast among formal perspectives on genre distinguishes those approaches that identify the formal organization of genre as an immanent, normative, structuring property of texts from those that view generic form as a conventionalized but flexible and open-ended set of expectations concerning the organization of formal means and structures in discursive practice. The latter view tends to raise the emergent properties of discursive organization to parity with the socially given, normative dimensions of generic structure.

Finally, we would register the very broad contrast between those approaches to genre that treat genre as a problem in its own right and those that explore the interrelationships that link genre to other terms, concepts, and sociocultural factors. Within linguistic anthropology in particular, one line of inquiry has concerned itself with the relationship between genre and other sociolinguistic organizing principles, especially speech acts, speech events, speech styles, and frames. In broader anthropological compass, investigators have analyzed dimensions of interrelationship between genres or genre systems and other cultural domains, such as ethics and cosmology, or other social structures, such as institutions or systems of social relations.

Whatever the focus of inquiry may be, however, the broadest contrast that characterizes understandings of genre in linguistic anthropology (and, we might add, in adjacent disciplines) sets off those approaches that constitute genre as an orderly and ordering principle in the organization of language, society, and culture from those that contend with the elements of disjunction, ambiguity, and general lack of fit that lurk around the margins of generic categories, systems, and texts. In the section that follows, we offer in exploratory terms a perspective on genre that brings the fuzzy fringes of genre to the center of the intellectual enterprise.

## GENERIC INTERTEXTUALITY

The preceding discussion suggests that genre has been under-theorized in linguistic anthropology. Beyond the fact that it has been put to a wide range of analytic and descriptive uses, practitioners have generally simply assumed that they and their audiences know what genres are and what makes them work. We suggest that this general failure to examine critically the nature of genres and to devote sufficient attention to their limitations as tools for classifying discourse is motivated in part by the persistence of the orientation toward genre laid out by Aristotle in the *Poetics*. Aristotle (Telford 1961:1–2) suggested that to distinguish such types as epic or tragedy we must discern three elements of "the composite whole" of a given work: (1) the formal means by which an object is imitated, (2) the objects which are imitated, and (3) the manner of imitation (first-person narration, third-person narration, or acting). Although a great deal of discussion has centered on questions of mimesis and representation and on the *differentia specifica* of particular genres, Aristotle's emphasis on genre as dealing with works in terms of the way that features of their global construction place them within poetic types has endured.

We noted above that Bakhtin's work has stimulated a rethinking of, and a new emphasis on, genre in linguistic anthropology and other fields. His characterization of genre is particularly rich in that it sees linguistic dimensions of genres in terms of their ideologically mediated connections with social groups and "spheres of human activity" in historical perspective (1986:65). By drawing attention to "complex" genres that "absorb and digest" other generic types, Bakhtin challenged the notion that genres are static, stylistically homogeneous, and nonoverlapping units (of which more later). In spite of the many advances he made in this area, however, Bakhtin's own definitions of genre are strikingly similar to Aristotle's: An early work, *The Formal Method in Literary Scholarship*, suggests that "genre is the typical totality of the artistic utterance, and a vital totality, a finished and resolved whole" (Bakhtin and Medvedev 1985[1928]:129), while one of his last essays, which focused specifically on "speech genres," suggests that genres are "certain relatively stable thematic, compositional, and stylistic types of utterances" (1986:64). Like Aristotle and his followers, Bakhtin laments the failure of researchers "to meet the fundamental logical requirement of classification: a unified basis" (1986:64). In spite of the profound shift he effects in the theoretical placement of genre, Bakhtin thus casts genre as a tool for both classifying texts and grasping their textual structure by looking in each case for a "unified" set of generic features.

The basic question here concerns the manner in which discourse is seen as "containing" structure, form, function, and meaning. Since Jakobson has played such a key role in shaping how linguistic anthropologists (inter alia) approach poetics, let us examine what he considers to be the proper analytic focus. In concluding his classic "Concluding Statement: Linguistics and Poetics," Jakobson (1960:365) argues for a strict distinction between the study of invariants and variables in poetic patterning, on the one hand, and concern with variability in the "recitation" of a particular poetic work, on the other. He cites the "sage memento" of Wimsatt and Beardsley in arguing that "there are many performances of the same poem—differing among themselves in many ways. A performance is an event, but the poem itself, if there *is* any poem, must be some kind of enduring object" (1960:365–366, emphasis in original). Jakobson makes it clear that the study of performance will not inform our understanding of the "enduring object," and it is accordingly not useful "for the synchronic and historical analysis of poetry" (1960:365).

To be sure, the last 20 years have witnessed a shift in orientation from *text* to *performance*, with the latter term drawing researchers' attention to both social and poetic dimensions of the assumption of accountability to an audience for a display of virtuosity, subject to evaluation (Bauman 1977b; Hymes 1975a). Although concern with performance has helped shift researchers' focus from the "enduring object" to the process of poetic production and reception, this change runs the risk of simply drawing the analytic drawstrings wider—to encompass the relationship between linguistic and social or cultural dimensions of a given interaction—rather than questioning the equation of poetics with immanent features of particular discursive acts. Not only is the focus too narrow, but it lies in the wrong place as well.

## INTERTEXTUAL STRATEGIES AND GENRE

An initial clue that can help us build an alternative approach to the study of genre—and of poetics and performance in general—is provided by Bakhtin's view of intertextuality. Kristeva neatly captures the contrasting basis of Bakhtin's thinking along these lines:

> Bakhtin was one of the first to replace the static hewing out of texts with a model where literary structure does not simply *exist* but is generated in relation to *another* structure. What allows a dynamic dimension to structuralism is his conception of the "literary word" as an *intersection of textual surfaces* rather than a point (a fixed meaning), as a dialogue among several writings: that of the writer, the addressee (or the character), and the contemporary or earlier cultural context. [Kristeva 1980:64–65, emphasis in original]

Two facets of this characterization are crucial. First, structure, form, function, and meaning are seen not as immanent features of discourse but as products of an ongoing process of producing and receiving discourse. Second, this process is not centered in the speech event or creation of a written text itself, but lies in its interface with at least one other utterance.

Bakhtin's interest in a "translinguistics" that is vitally concerned with intertextuality has clearly provided part of the force that lies behind the recent interest in reported speech evident in linguistic anthropology and other fields.[2] A number of works have pointed to the way that intertextual relationships between a particular text and prior discourse (real or imagined) play a crucial role in shaping form, function, discourse structure, and meaning; in permitting

---

[2] See studies by Bauman (1986), Briggs (1990, 1992b), Goodwin (1990), Hymes (1981), Philips (1986), Silverstein (1985), Tannen (1989), Urban (1984b), and a volume edited by Lucy entitled *Reflexive Language: Reported Speech and Metapragmatics* (1992).

speakers (and authors) to create multiple modes of inserting themselves into the discourse; and in building competing perspectives on what is taking place.

We would argue, similarly, that genre cannot fruitfully be characterized as a facet of the immanent properties of particular texts or performances. Like reported speech, genre is quintessentially intertextual. When discourse is linked to a particular genre, the process by which it is produced and received is mediated through its relationship with prior discourse. Unlike most examples of reported speech, however, the link is not made to isolated utterances, but to generalized or abstracted models of discourse production and reception.[3] When genre is viewed in intertextual terms, its complex and contradictory relationship to discourse becomes evident. We suggest that the creation of intertextual relationships through genre simultaneously renders texts ordered, unified, and bounded, on the one hand, and fragmented, heterogeneous, and open-ended, on the other. Each dimension of this process can be seen from both the synchronic and the diachronic perspective.

Viewed synchronically, genres provide powerful means of shaping discourse into ordered, unified, and bounded texts. As soon as we hear a generic framing device, such as "once upon a time," we unleash a set of expectations regarding narrative form and content. Animals may talk and people may possess supernatural powers, and we anticipate the unfolding of a plot structure that involves, as Propp (1968[1928]) showed us long ago, an interdiction, a violation, a departure, the completion of tasks, failure followed by success, and the like. The invocation of genre thus provides a textual model for creating cohesion and coherence, for producing and interpreting particular sorts of features and their formal and functional relations all the way from particular poetic lines to the global structure of the narrative. We would like to call attention not simply to the structural effects but to the process itself—the generation of textuality or, as we referred to it in an earlier work, entextualization (Bauman and Briggs 1990).

When viewed in diachronic or, as Bakhtin put it, vertical perspective,[4] generic intertextuality provides a powerful means of ordering discourse in historical and social terms. Genres have strong historical association—proverbs and fairy tales have the ring of the traditional past, whereas electronic mail (E-mail) is associated with the ultramodern. Genres also bear social, ideological, and political-economic connections; genres may thus be associated with distinct groups as defined by gender, age, social class, occupation, and the like. Invoking a genre thus creates indexical connections that extend far beyond the present

---

[3] The qualifier here suggests the fact that there are important exceptions. Some types of reported utterances, such as proverbs, may be attributed not to a particular individual or speech event but to a category of speakers or simply to "tradition" (see Briggs 1988:101–135).

[4] In developing his notion of the spatialization of the word in dialogue, Bakhtin discussed an opposition between the *horizontal* characterization of a word's status, a relationship between a writing subject and an addressee, and a *vertical* one, in which the word is viewed in its relationship to a preceding utterance.

setting of production or reception, thereby linking a particular act to other times, places, and persons. To draw on the terminology we used earlier, generic features thus foreground the status of utterances as recontextualizations of prior discourse. Even when the content of the discourse lacks a clear textual precedent, generic intertextuality points to the role of recontextualization at the level of discourse production and reception. Genre thus pertains crucially to negotiations of identity and power—by invoking a particular genre, producers of discourse assert (tacitly or explicitly) that they possess the authority needed to decontextualize discourse that bears these historical and social connections and to recontextualize it in the current discursive setting. When great authority is invested in texts associated with elders or ancestors, traditionalizing discourse by creating links with traditional genres is often the most powerful strategy for creating textual authority (see Briggs 1988; Gossen 1974; Kuipers 1990). Building on Bourdieu (1977). We can say, thus, that generic intertextuality affords great power for naturalizing both texts and the cultural reality that they represent (see also Hanks 1987).

The variability that is evident in the way generic intertextual relationships are created points to an extremely important dimension of the diachronic dynamics of genre. We drew attention above to the fact that linguistic anthropologists, linguists, folklorists, and literary critics have largely followed Aristotle in viewing genre in empirical terms as involving a process through which rules or conventions impose structural and content-based constraints on textual production. Even writers who are particularly interested in the way speakers and hearers and writers and readers resist these rules and conventions generally see the nature of the entailed intertextual relations as relatively transparent and automatic. The fallacy of this assumption is evident when one realizes that genres are not road maps to particular texts. Invocations of genre rather entail the (re)construction of classes of texts. Specific features are then selected and abstracted, thus bringing into play a powerful process of decontextualization (see Bauman and Briggs 1990). As scholars in a number of fields have suggested, the power of genres emerges from the way they draw on a broad array of features—phonological, morphological, lexical, and syntactic, as well as contextual and interactive (see, for example, Ben-Amos 1976[1969]; Leitch 1991). By choosing to make certain features explicit (and particularly by foregrounding some elements through repetition and metapragmatic framing), producers of discourse actively (re)construct and reconfigure genres. Note the great similarity between the discourse practices associated with the use of genre in shaping extextualization, on the one hand, and the scholarly practices of linguistic anthropologists, literary critics, and the like, on the other: both entail creating classes of texts, selecting and abstracting features, and using this process in creating textual authority. (More later on the importance of this analogy.)

We have argued that the central role played by an active sociocultural and linguistic process of creating intertextual relations in genre renders it a powerful means of creating textual order, unity, and boundedness. The dynamic and constructed character of this relation is apparent in that the same text may be connected to the same genre to varying degrees, in highly contrastive ways, and for quite different reasons. We would now like to suggest that it becomes evident that these intertextual relations are not simply automatic effects of immanent properties of texts when the focus is shifted to the way that generic intertextuality simultaneously produces the *obverse* of these properties. Turning first to the synchronic dimensions of this problem, although generic intertextuality may help imbue texts with order, unit, and boundedness, it also draws attention to the *lack* of self-sufficiency and autonomy of the formal-functional configuration of the discourse at hand—recourse must be made to other discursive formations to interpret its patterning and significance. In Bakhtin's terms, genre points to the inherent dialogicality of the word. Just as genre can create order and sense in a text, it can render texts chaotic, fragmented, and nonsensical.

When viewed diachronically or vertically, the fit between a particular text and its generic model—as well as other tokens of the same genre—is never perfect; to paraphrase Sapir, we might say that all genres leak. Generic frameworks thus never provide sufficient means of producing and receiving discourse. Some elements of contextualization creep in, fashioning indexical connections to the ongoing discourse, social interaction, broader social relations, and the particular historical juncture(s) at which the discourse is produced and received. In short, other pragmatic and metapragmatic (cf. Silverstein 1976, 1992) frameworks must be brought into play in shaping production and reception.

The process of linking particular utterances to generic models thus necessarily produces an intertextual *gap*. Although the creation of this hiatus is unavoidable, its relative suppression or foregrounding has important effects. One the one hand, texts framed in some genres attempt to achieve generic transparency by *minimizing* the distance between texts and genres, thus rendering the discourse maximally interpretable through the use of generic precedents. This approach sustains highly conservative, traditionalizing modes of creating textual authority. On the other hand, *maximizing* and highlighting these intertextual gaps underlies strategies for building authority through claims of individual creativity and innovation (such as are common in 20th-century Western literature), resistance to the hegemonic structures associated with established genres, and other motives for distancing oneself from textual precedents.

## EXAMPLES OF STRATEGIES FOR MANIPULATING GENERIC INTERTEXTUALITY

One of the most interesting facets of the way genre enters into discourse production and reception is the great variation that is evident in strategies for manipulating such gaps. Although we cannot present even a schematic inventory of the means by which intertextual distance is suppressed and foregrounded, some examples may serve to illustrate both the range of possibilities and the profound linguistic and social impact of these intertextual differences.

Kuipers's (1990) analysis of Weyewa ritual speech in Sumba, Indonesia, provides a striking example of the process of minimizing intertextual gaps. Ritual specialists attempt to decrease the distance between the "words of the ancestors" and their invocation in ritual performances. The three types of "ritual speech" with which Kuipers is primarily concerned—"divination," *zaizo* rites of placation, and "rites of fulfillment"—involve progressively greater suppression of demonstrative and personal pronouns, locutives (which frame discourse as reported speech), and discourse markers, features that contextualize the performance in its unique social and historical setting. The process goes hand in hand with building greater textual authority—and narrowing intertextual gaps—by affording more prominence to dyadic parallelism and proper names.

Such strategies for minimizing intertextual gaps bear directly on recent discussions of the complex social processes involved in the construction of history, tradition, authenticity, ethnicity, and identity (see, for example, Appadurai 1981; Clifford 1988; Dorst 1989; Handler and Linnekin 1984; Hobsbawm and Ranger 1983; Kirshenblatt-Gimblett 1991). Invocations of genre provide powerful strategies for building what Anderson (1991[1983]) terms "imagined communities." As in the Weyewa case, the speech genres that comprise the "talk of the elders of bygone days" among Spanish speakers in New Mexico play a key role in this process; unlike Weyewa "ritual speech," however, their use in constructing history, tradition, and ethnicity differs from genre to genre in both practice and ideology (see Briggs 1988).

The spiritual efficacy and experiential intensity of Lenten performances of hymns and prayers is contingent upon the progressive displacement of any perceived separation between the words uttered by Christ and the Virgin Mary in the course of the crucifixion, their inscription in sacred texts, and their utterance in performance. Worshippers assert that the written texts used in Lenten rituals have been handed down verbatim through the generations. Unison recitation suppresses intertextual variation within performances by regulating the volume, pitch, rate, breath, syntax, lexicon, and rhetorical structure of each worshipper's discourse production to such a point that differences between individual voices are nearly erased. The ritual process symbolically strips away elements that contextualize performances in terms of the social, temporal, spatial, and historical parameters of contemporary society and renders the here and now an icon of the crucifixion tableau. In attempting to achieve symbolic unification with Christ and the Virgin, participants deny the intertextual gap to such an extent that they seek to overcome the opposition between signifier and signified itself, merging the experience of the worshipper and that of Christ and the Virgin (as textually constructed). The control over ritual intertextuality that this process confers on the "Brothers," particularly elderly officers in the confraternity, affords them a great deal of religious authority and social power in general in their communities.

*Mexicano* speech genres are organized along a continuum, from genres that emphasize entextualization to those in which overt contextualization is crucial (Briggs 1988). Whereas hymns and prayers are highly extextualized, oral historical discourse is the most contextualized. In oral historical discourse, elders attempt to maximize the gap between "the talk of the elders of bygone days" and the contemporary discursive settings in which it emerges. One way in which this process is undertaken involves avoiding direct discourse, recasting this "talk" as the speaker's own utterances and personal experience; direct intertextual links to the words of "the elders of bygone days" are thus avoided. The maximization of intertextual distance plays a central role in both the rhetorical patterning of the discourse and its explicit framing by virtue of the way it motivates point-by-point contrasts between life *antes* "in bygone days" and the present. This is not to say that the discursive *effect* of such strategies is to achieve some sort of complete separation of text and genre—any invocation of generic features creates both intertextual relations and intertextual gaps. Such maximization is rather a rhetorical strategy that foregrounds the latter dimension of generic intertextuality.

Unlike the Weyewa case, this strategy does not render the discourse any less powerful in social terms than attempts to minimize the intertextual distance. For Weyewa, the ability to silence all dissenting voices and impose "unity" by linking monologic utterances as directly as possible to the "words of the ancestors" provides the central means of investing speech genres and individual performances with ritual and social power. In the *Mexicano* case, on the other hand, both minimizing and maximizing strategies, as differentially distributed according to genre, are used in appropriating—and (re)constructing—"the talk of the elders of bygone days," thereby legitimating courses of action and positions of social power.

Although genres tend to be linked to particular sets of strategies for manipulating intertextual gaps, it is clearly not the case that selection of a particular genre *dictates* the manner in which this process will be carried out. Transformation narratives ("myths") told by Warao storytellers in eastern Venezuela present narrators with a wide range of possible ways of manipulating intertextual gaps between the powerful speech of characters who lived "when our world was still being formed," the individual who told the particular narrative to the present narrator, and the narrating event. Authoritative, semantically monologic performances attempt to reduce the intertextual distance to zero, merging primordial and contemporary realms by suppressing explicit contextualization and centering the discourse deictically in the narrated (rather than the narrating) events (see Briggs 1992a). Like *Mexicano* oral historical discourse, Warao dialogic performances point precisely to differences between the two textual planes, playfully recontextualizing quoted utterances in both primordial and contemporary realms. Pedagogically oriented performances create maximal intertextual distance by focusing on the storytelling process itself, thus rendering the time when "our world was still being formed" experientially inaccessible. Not only can tokens of the same genre be performed in these intertextually contrastive fashions, but the same individual also can tell the same narrative in these three ways (see also Hymes 1985).

A shift in key (see Hymes 1972a) can similarly produce highly contrastive types of intertextual relations for the same genre. Recall Sherzer's (1983, 1991) analysis of the way that Kuna *ikarkana* can be used for practice, display, and as entertainment at drunken gatherings as well as in curing rituals; each type of performance would seemingly be related to quite different strategies for treating intertextual gaps.

Another example of the use of highly contrastive intertextual strategies in different performances of the same genre is apparent in Duranti's (1984) Samoan data, as discussed above. When fully performed in ceremonial contexts, *lauga* foreground intertextual relations with generic precedents. In political meetings (*fono*), on the other hand, elaborating stylistic features in displaying one's competence, vis-à-vis the textual authority invoked by the genre, is far less important than using *lauga* in shaping the ensuing discussions. Thus, both the nature of the intertextual links to prior and subsequent discourse and the strategies that guide the reception of *lauga*, and evaluations of the manner in which it is performed, contrast radically between settings. As was the case in the Warao and Kuna examples, these differences in strategies for creating intertextuality lie at the heart of both formal and functional patterning as well as the social power of the discourse.

Strategies for maximizing and minimizing intertextual gaps can coexist even more intimately as they enter dialogically into constituting the same text or performance. In nightlong performances of nativity plays (termed *coloquios*) in the Mexican state of Guanajuato, intertextual gaps are necessarily created as the script is subjected to a series of transformations; this process of recentering the text in performance takes place as the script is copied out, learned, rehearsed, and performed (see Bauman 1992b). In a production in Tierra Blanca de Abajo studied by Richard Bauman and Pamela Ritch, all the actors save one accepted the authority of the written script, as mediated by the *primer encargado*, the individual who has overall control of the production, and the prompter; they accordingly attempted to memorize their lines and reproduce them *por pura frase* 'by exact phrases' (i.e., word-for-word). Although they acknowledged that such factors as limited literacy, imperfections in the script, difficulties in hearing the prompter, lapses in memory, and the like prevent exact reproduction of the script, they sought to reduce the intertextual gap to zero. Fidelity to genre and text entailed adhering to a number of formal constraints, particularly the production of octasyllabic lines with assonant endings on alternating lines; assonance alternated with other patterns, such as rhymed couplets. Similarly, the script was rendered in a highly conventionalized style of delivery that featured three or four regular stresses per line and a fixed intonational pattern that was repeated (by some actors) for each line.

The actor who plays the Hermitaño (Hermit) adopted a mode of creating intertextuality that was diametrically opposed to that taken by the other actors. Although the fact that he is illiterate augmented the "technical" limitations to intertextual transparency, his departure from the script was more squarely motivated by a carnivalesque and subversive stance. As the Hermitaño offered few of his lines directly from memory, the prompter fed him his lines one-by-one, in a manner audible to the audience. Unlike the other actors who required prompting for each line, however, the Hermitaño decided whether to remain faithful to the stylistic and content-based features of the text and genre—the dominant intertextual ideology—or to transform it. He linked his utterances to text and genre by creating three types of intertextual relations. First, he often repeated at least some of the lexical items in the line as spoken by the prompter, and the syntactic structure remained largely identical across the two renditions; he repeated some lines verbatim. Second, the Hermitaño matched the phonological features of the line-final words in his utterances to those of their counterparts in the script. Third, the Hermitaño retained the characteristic intonational style of the *coloquio*. This retention of octasyllabic lines, rhyming schemes, and intonational patterns thus created strong generic intertextuality both with the essential characteristics of the *coloquio* and with the lines as read by the prompter.

With the exception of the lines he repeated verbatim, however, the Hermitaño's discourse departed subversively from the types of generic constraints observed by the other actors. Although the language of the *coloquio* and of the prompter's recitation was archaic, elevated, pious, and often magniloquent, the Hermitaño's recasting of them was colloquial, debased, richly sexual, and coarse. He similarly displaced much of the semantic content of his lines; although the sexual and other allusions he substituted can be parsed individually through familiarity with community social relations and the actor's own biography, they were so poorly linked to each other semantically that the Hermitaño's speeches essentially added up to rich nonsense. Interestingly, the Hermitaño created his parody by transforming features of the phonological patterning associated with the genre—alliteration, assonance, and rhyme—through punning. The strategies he adopted go beyond the creation of comic effect to objectify and foreground the pragmatics of recentering the text in the production process, as undertaken by the other actors, the *primer encargado*, and the prompter. By subversively recasting the lines that were recited for him by the prompter (and are heard by much of the audience as well), the Hermitaño revealed the central role played by the suppression of intertextual gaps in the genre. The Hermitaño's dramatic anti-language (Halliday 1978:164–182) called attention to the possibility of creatively exploiting intertextual gaps rather than attempting to render them invisible. Yet the Hermitaño's burlesque creation and proliferation of such gaps is itself a generic convention of the *coloquio*; the Hermitaño is traditionally expected to take liberties with the scripted text. As performed, the *coloquio* genre exploits two strongly contrasting intertextual strategies.

The *coloquio* example points to the way that different strategies can be invested in different roles in the same performance. The tall tale provides a case in which different ways of approaching intertextual gaps are undertaken by the same participant and serve as constitutive features of the genre. Tall tales generally begin as personal-experience narratives; this framing entails a commitment to recounting episodes of the speaker's own life in a truthful manner. This told-as-true quality is signaled by metanarrative devices that assert the text's faithfulness, both to the events themselves and (through reported speech) to previous renditions of part or all of the narrative. A strategy used by a master Texas storyteller, the late Ed Bell, additionally involves directly addressing the audience's state of belief or disbelief and the credibility of the story itself: "And I don't blame y'all if you don't believe me about this tree, because I wouldn't believe it either if I hadn'ta seen it with my own eyes, I don't know whether I can tell ya how you could believe it or not, but that was a big tree" (Bauman 1986:99).

As the story progresses, however, it increasingly transcends the limits of credibility. Hyperbolic details and metanarrative indications of the decreasing believability of the events create a sort of generic static, as it were, that interferes with interpreting the discourse as the relation of personal experience. The unreal qualities eventually become sufficiently prominent to lead most audience members to reinterpret the story as a tall tale. The genre thus involves a transformational process in discourse reception that moves from accepting strategies that seek to minimize intertextual gaps to perceiving a growing gap between the discourse and its purported generic framing to embracing a different form of generic intertextuality, one that celebrates intertextual gaps as powerful creative tools (see Bauman 1986:78–111, 1987).

The movement evident in tall tales from one type of generic intertextuality to another points to the status of what Bakhtin (1986[1979]) refers to as *secondary* or *complex* genres as powerful means of creatively exploiting intertextual gaps. Here, possibilities for manipulating the gap between discourse and genre are multiplied as a text is linked to more than one set of generic features, to a genre that is itself mixed, or to both. Beyond opening up a range of possible interpretive relationships between generic precedents and the discourse being produced and received, mixing genres foregrounds the possibility of using intertextual gaps as points of departure for working the power of generic intertextuality backwards, as it were, in exploring and reshaping the formal, interpretive, and ideological power of the constituent genres and their relationship.

Let us turn to another type of Warao discourse in illustrating the role of intertextuality in mixed genres. When someone dies, female relatives compose and sing *sana* 'laments' until after the return from the graveyard (see Briggs 1992b). Beyond expressing the anger and sadness of the mourner, *sana* offer sharp criticism of actions seen as having contributed to the death or threatening the well-being of members of the community. One woman generally composes verses containing new material while the remaining wailers sing refrains—and listen. The other participants then either repeat the verses, changing both deictic elements and semantic content to reflect their own experience, or present their own verses.

*Sana* performances regulate intertextuality in three significant ways. First, wailers use reported speech in extracting discourse from a wide range of genres, including gossip, conversations, political rhetoric, arguments, and dispute mediation events. The intertextual reach of *sana* is thus quite impressive in that performers both create links with other lament performances and assimilate a broad range of other genres to the lament. Wailers exploit intertextual gaps to great effect by constantly reinterpreting this prior discourse in terms of the way its recontextualization is affected by the death and by juxtapositions with other reported utterances. Deictics and tense/aspect forms further manipulate the distance between reported and reporting speech. A second dimension of this intertextual regulation pertains to the carefully orchestrated polyphony that dominates performances. Extremely subtle features of the tempo, pitch, volume, and timbre of the women's voices, as well as the poetic interrelations between the verses they sing, foreground the emergence of both individual voices and a collective discourse (see Briggs 1989); the latter dimension shields individual wailers from retribution. Recall Urban's (1988) analysis of the way the iconic relations between the acoustic features of individual voices, other tokens of the genre, and the "natural icons" of crying constitute "meta-signals" regarding social solidarity and "adherence to a collective norm" in examples of ritual wailing recorded in other areas of South America. Warao women use the form, content, and performance dynamics of their laments in calling such social norms—and claims by others to adhere to them—into question. Third, these same features of *sana* regulate the intertextual relations between their laments and future discourse. *Sana* are seldom criticized or reinterpreted; although their content is subsequently recontextualized in narrative accounts of "what the women are crying," women sometimes specify in their *sana* how these stories should be told and to whom.

The interaction between gender and genre is crucial here. Outside of laments, Warao women have very little role in the production and reception of "mythic" narratives, political rhetoric, and shamanistic discourse. The ability of *sana* to incorporate other genres and, exploiting intertextual gaps, to question their authority provides women with frequently recurring opportunities to have a more powerful role in discourse production and reception. Research by Feld (1990a[1982], 1990b) and Seremetakis (1991) on the role of polyphony and intertextuality in, respectively, Kaluli (New Guinea) and Inner Maniat (Greek) laments points to the powerful role that generic intertextuality plays in constituting—and transgressing—gender roles. (We will have more to say about the relationship between gender, emotion, and genre below.)

## AXES OF COMPARISON

These examples point to the broad range of strategies that are used in minimizing and maximizing intertextual gaps. While we are still far from being able to present an exhaustive inventory of the forms of intertextuality associated with genre, we would like to adumbrate some of the principal loci in which variation is evident with respect to the nature of generic intertextuality and the means by which intertextual gaps are manipulated.

1. One axis of comparison is provided by the dimensions of the entextualization process that are exploited in creating and manipulating intertextual relations. Just as phonology, lexicon, morphosyntax, rhetorical structure, turn-taking, thematic content, prosody, gesture, participation roles, and other features can be used in linking discourse to generic precedents, strategies for minimizing and maximizing intertextual gaps can draw on an equally broad range of features. Dell Hymes (1981), Virginia Hymes (1987), and others have documented the recurrent use of rhetorical progressions of narrative action and patterns of versification in creating intertextual continuity and variation in Native American narratives. Bauman (1986:54–77) argues that West Texas oral anecdotes, which use reported speech in building a punch line, are more stable over time than those in which reported speech is not the point of the story. As evident in the *coloquio* example, one of the most common strategies is to use formal features in creating generic intertextuality, while disjunctions in semantic content, participant structures, metapragmatic frames, and the like are used in challenging generic precedents; clearly, these relations can also be reversed.

2. Another source of variability with respect to the degree to which generic relations create order, unity, and boundedness lies in the fact that all genres are not created equal—or, more accurately, equally empowered—in terms of their ability to structure discourse. While "ordinary conversation" affords much greater room for disorder, heterogeneity, and open-endedness, some genres of ritual discourse provide almost no room for these characteristics or for structural flexibility in general. The Weyewa and *Mexicano* examples illustrate the differential distribution of this ordering capability by genre within particular discursive economies.

3. The power of genre to create textual structure also varies in keeping with the degree to which the generic patterning is imposed on a particular body of discourse. Although connections between a particular text and its generic precedent(s) sometimes crucially shape the formal structure and social force of the discourse, in other cases generic intertextuality is simply one of the available interpretive options. The use of *lauga* in ceremonial and political contexts provides an example in which these two options are evident in the case of a single genre. Generic features may not be overtly marked, and features that do appear may be foregrounded to various degrees (through repetition, metapragmatic signaling, et cetera) (see Briggs 1988). As we will argue below, the fact that the capacity of genre to create textual order, unity, and

boundedness can be invoked to varying degrees is of profound interactive, ideological, and political-economic significance.

4. One of the most interesting loci of variation involves the extent to which intertextual strategies become, in Silverstein's (1992) terms, denotatively explicit, in the sense that the metapragmatic framing of intertextual relations is marked overtly through the denotative content of the entailed expressions. With regard to the preceding examples, Warao ritual wailing and Texan tall tales make extensive use of explicit framings, whereas the Hermitaño's subversive transformations are not explicitly signaled. The latter example will serve as a warning against jumping to the ready (and ethnocentric) conclusion that denotationally explicit signals will be more salient in every case; when semantic interpretability is greatly limited by auditory interference, the use of unintelligible lexicons or languages, and the like, implicit signals expressed through prosodic or visual features may be more accessible. Basso's (1984) analysis of Apache moral narratives similarly provides a telling example of the social power of implicit framings. These parsimonious narratives contain little explicit information on intertextual relations; the framing seems to be limited to a statement regarding the place in which the reported event took place ("it happened at") and its temporal locus ("long ago"). The point of the performance is to induce an individual who is present to link her or his recent behavior—and what community members are saying about it—to the moral transgression committed in the story. Interestingly, these narratives contain explicit statements of intertextual relations (provided by the opening spatial and temporal frames) as well as entirely implicit relations (the link to talk about a member of the audience). This case also points to the fallacy in assuming that intertextual relations are established by performers or authors alone: a crucial part of the process of constructing intertextual relations may be undertaken by the audience.

5. A similar note of caution should be sounded with respect to the use of oral versus written resources in creating intertextuality. The work of Goody (1977), Ong (1967, 1982), and other writers, who sharply distinguish between "orality" and "literacy" as distinct modes of discourse production and reception and cognitive orientations, would lead us to expect that intertextual gaps will be minimized when written texts are used. The written text is indeed regarded as authoritative—and intertextual gaps are highly constrained—in the case of the scripts used in Mexican *coloquios* and New Mexican notebooks containing hymns and prayers. Nonetheless, the (re)production of written texts, along with their reception and recontextualization (in either oral or written form), necessarily creates intertextual gaps. The Hermitaño example shows how these gaps can be creatively expanded in establishing intertextual relations. Heath's (1982) research on class differences in literacy practices suggests that learning to exploit intertextual gaps by linking "ways of taking information from books" to other types of discourse production and reception (such as providing descriptions of everyday objects and events) is a crucial prerequisite to success in school. (We will have more to say later about the connection between

intertextuality, language socialization, and social class.) Hanks (1987) and Lockhart (1991) similarly demonstrate the way that the production of written documents by, respectively, the Maya and Nahua of colonial Mexico drew on generic innovation as a key response for negotiating rapidly changing social and political relations.

6. A number of writers have argued for the need to examine how genre shapes the expression of emotions as well as the related question of the relationship between genre and gender. In an early extension of the ethnography of speaking to issues of gender and emotion, Keenan (1974) describes Malagasy men's control over speech styles and genres that minimize expressions of anger, criticism, and disagreement; women, on the other hand, use "unsophisticated" speech that expresses emotion in a direct and often confrontational manner. Feld (1990a[1982]) demonstrates the differing potential of contrastive genres for constructing emotions; in particular, women's ritual weeping provides a powerful means of expressing shared sentiments, whereas men's *gisalo* songs produce particular affective states in listeners. Schieffelin (1990) shows how Kaluli mothers develop teasing routines with sons yet discourage the same type of interactions—and the emotional expressions they occasion—with daughters. In a number of papers, Brenneis (1987, 1988, 1990) has pointed to the contrastive social values, patterns of social interaction, and emotional states that are evoked by different genres; he goes on to suggest that excluding women from participation in particular types of performances enacted by Hindi-speaking Fiji Indians largely prevents them from obtaining access to a number of culturally valued emotional experiences.

Naturalizing the connection between genre, gender, and emotional experience can in turn rationalize the subordinate status of particular social groups or categories of persons; Lutz's (1990) discussion of the association between "emotionality" and the female in Western society provides a case in point. On the other hand, individuals who enjoy less social power due to gender, age, race, or other characteristics may draw on particular genres in expressing the injustice of their situation or in attempting to gain a more active role in social and political processes; women's performances of ritual wailing provide a striking example (see Briggs 1992b; Seremetakis 1991; Tolbert 1990).[5]

7. The role of music in creating intertextuality is also fascinating. By virtue of its capacity for closely regulating pitch, timbre, tempo, volume, and other features, and its frequent use in regulating movement (through dance), music can provide a powerful resource in attempting to suppress intertextual gaps. The use of music in parody and satire (as in Brecht's plays) points contrastively to its potential for foregrounding intertextual gaps. Feld (1990a[1982]) shows

---

[5] Investigations of the relationship between genre and gender are currently providing a rich cross-disciplinary convergence of interests between linguistic and sociocultural anthropologists (see Appadurai et al. 1991; Gal 1991; Philips et al. 1987) and practitioners in such fields as ethnomusicology (see Herndon and Ziegler 1990; Koskoff 1989), folkloristics (Farrer 1975; Jordan and Kalčik 1985), and literary criticism (Miller 1986; Showalter 1985).

how musical features can simultaneously create intertextual links to generic precedents and to quite different types of discourse; the tonal characteristics of Kaluli "melodic-sung-texted weeping" stimulate powerful emotional responses by connecting a woman's performance with the weeping of other women and with the tremendously evocative call of the *muni* bird. The fascinating problem of sonic or acoustic icons, including onomatopoeias, sound symbols, vocables, and the like, can be fruitfully analyzed with respect to their functions as powerful means of naturalizing intertextual relations. The relationship between musical and verbal modalities, along with dance, costume, and the like, in creating and challenging generic intertextuality constitutes an area in which further research is needed.

8. A final axis of comparison pertains to the nature of generic intertextuality. The framing of some texts aligns them closely with a single genre; as we noted above, the link in other cases may be either to a number of different genres, to a mixed ("secondary") genre, or to both. Relations may be relatively fixed or emergent and open-ended. Warao ritual wailing, for example, affords a great deal of flexibility as to which genres are incorporated and how they enter into the performance. The routines performed by stand-up comics exhibit similar flexibility. In other examples, intertextual relations are established with two or more particular genres in relatively consistent ways.

Icelandic legends regarding magical poets, for example, embed recitations of verses imbued with magical efficacy into narratives (see Bauman 1992a). A number of types of intertextual relations play a central role in constituting these texts. First, narrators traditionalize texts, asserting their authenticity by recounting intertextual histories of the transmission of a particular example from narrator to narrator. This metanarrative framing both minimizes inter-textual distance by constructing narrative continuity and maximizes the gap by questioning the authority of other interpretations of the story. Second, the intertextual gap between the reported recitation of the magical verse and its presentation in the narrative is minimized through the poetic distinctiveness of the verse. A gap remains, however, in that the narrator is not composing but representing the magical verse; its performative potency for realizing supernatural violence is thus absent. Third, the narrative relates to the verse through content alone, describing the circumstances of its initial performance and reporting on its effects (e.g., a man cursed in a verse died in the brutal manner that it specified). Finally, the verse affects the narrative formally; magical verses extend beyond their textual confines to shape the lexical, grammatical, and rhetorical patterning of the narrative. Here the types of intertextual strategies that accrue to each genre as well as their dialogic inter-relations are relatively conventional.

## BROADER IMPLICATIONS FOR LINGUISTIC ANTHROPOLOGY

These examples suggest that generic intertextuality cannot be adequately understood in terms of formal and functional patterning alone—questions of ideology, political economy, and power must be addressed as well if we are to grasp the nature of intertextual relations. This discussion thus opens up a much larger theoretical and methodological issue that has emerged in linguistic anthropology and the study of discourse in general. At first glance, it seems as if the number of scholars who have aligned their work with the concept of discourse would have produced a fruitful integration or at least an articulation of a wide range of approaches and concerns. A closer look suggests that the highly divergent conceptualizations of the nature and significance of "discourse" have often *widened* the gap between research agendas. A great deal of recent work in linguistic anthropology resonates with Sherzer's call for a "discourse-centered" approach to the study of culture, one that focuses on detailed analyses of "actual instances of language in use," carefully documenting the relationship between formal and functional patterning and dimensions of social interaction, social structure, and cultural processes (1987:296). The concept of "discourse" used by other scholars draws on Foucault, Bourdieu, and other post-structuralists; here, discourse is located more in the general processes by which social groups and institutions create, sustain, and question social power than in particular "speech events." Such practitioners are generally more interested in the rhetorical and political parameters of scholarly writing, mediated communication, and institutional discourse than in the situated speech of ethnographic "Others."

Unfortunately, this hiatus has further divided linguistic from social-cultural anthropology. The rift emerges in competing strategies for establishing textual authority, with linguistic anthropologists often claiming the low ground of methodological and analytic precision, and social-cultural types staking out the higher ground of sensitivity to the theoretical and political issues that prevail in the postmodern world. This situation frequently gives rise to ignorance of complementary perspectives and a hardening of intradisciplinary and epistemological lines. We believe that the perspective we have outlined in this article suggests ways that linguistic anthropologists can draw on the theoretical and methodological strengths of their training in challenging this unproductive opposition.

The preceding section focused mainly on formal and functional dimensions of strategies for creating intertextual relations. As we believe the examples clearly show, however, the roots of intertextual practices run just as deeply into social, cultural, ideological, and political-economic facets of social life as they do into the minutiae of linguistic structure and use. We would like to suggest that relations between intertextuality and ideology can be read in both directions—in terms of the way that broader social, cultural, ideological, and political-economic formations shape and empower intertextual strategies and the manner in which ideologies of intertextuality and their associated practices shape society and history.

The long-standing association between genre and order in Western discourse provides a strong sense of the impact of changing ideologies and social relations on intertextuality. The existence of a purportedly clearly defined and elaborate system of genres has often been associated with the social, political, and communicative value of national languages and literatures. For example, one of the central foci in many areas of Europe during the Renaissance was the legitimation of national languages (particularly vis-à-vis Latin and Greek) through the development and inculcation of an extensive set of rules for the generic structuring of texts (see Dubrow 1982:58; Lewalski 1986). Like the establishment of a standard language, the production of a presumably fixed set of generic conventions played a role in the creation of "imagined communities" (see Anderson 1991[1983]). The potential utility of an orderly system of literary genres for the establishment of an orderly social system was made explicit by such figures as Hobbes and Pope. A highly rigid characterization of genres formed a central concern during the neoclassic era in view of the prevalent fear of disorder in individuals and in society as a whole (see Dubrow 1982).

The association of genre with order has similarly often prompted those interested in countering established social and literary orders to challenge established genres or even the role of genres in general. The Romantics' search for a "natural" order led them, accordingly, to read the association between conventional order and genre as a basis for distrusting genre. Feminist scholars have argued that women often appropriate and manipulate generic conventions as a means of gaining entrance into male-dominated discourses (see Miller 1986). The scholarly production of such "folk" genres as the epic, proverb, fable, fairy tale, and ballad assisted in the nostalgic creation of a "folk" culture, which could be used in advancing nationalist agendas by appropriating the past as well as establishing the cultural autonomy and superiority of literary genres (see Hall 1981; Handler and Linnekin 1984; Herzfeld 1982; Kirshenblatt-Gimblett 1991; Stewart 1991).

A number of writers have argued that individual genres are hierarchically ordered (see, for example, Bourdieu 1991:67; Kuipers 1990; Leitch 1992:87). By virtue of the profound social and ideological associations of genres, hierarchies of genres are tied to social hierarchies. Given the connection between genres and conventional order, as well as their hierarchical organization, it is far from surprising that developing competence in different generic frameworks is a major focus of educational systems. Following Bourdieu's (1977, 1991; Bourdieu and Passeron 1977) analysis of the cultural politics of education, it is evident that the hierarchical organization of discursive competences according to genre provides efficient means for both controlling access to symbolic capital and evaluating the discursive competence of individuals.

Recall Heath's (1982) analysis of the connection between "ways of taking information from books" and educational success. The middle-class white, working-class white, and working-class African-American communities she studied were characterized by distinctive "ways of taking." Although books were accorded great authority and reading was highly encouraged in both of the predominantly white communities, the working-class parents "do not, upon seeing an item or event in the real world, remind children of a similar event in a book and launch a running commentary on similarities and differences" (Heath 1982:61). Heath reports that although bedtime routines were not common in the working-class African-American community, participation in oral storytelling and other forms of verbal art afforded children great acuity in creating intertextual relations, particularly as based on metaphorical and fictionalized links.[6] Heath suggests, however, that classroom discourse discouraged these types of intertextuality "because they enable children to see parallels teachers did not intend, and indeed, may not recognize until the children point them out" (Heath 1982:70). She goes on to argue that the compatibility between the "ways of taking" inculcated by middle-class white parents—even before the children were reading—and those rewarded in the classroom fostered much greater success in school. Rejecting the genres that predominated in the African-American community and the narrow constraints on recontextualization that prevailed among white members of the working class constituted crucial means of controlling access to symbolic capital.

Bauman's (1977a, 1982) account of children's "solicitational routines"—speech acts (such as riddles and knock-knock jokes) in which a response is solicited—presents analogous data drawn from genres in which literacy practices are not central. He suggests that solicitational routines provide contexts in which such educationally crucial intertextual skills as asking and answering questions can be learned and strategies for using them in gaining interactional power can be mastered. In an interesting parallel to Heath's data, the Anglo children in Bauman's Austin, Texas, sample were interested in a broader range of solicitational routines than either Chicano or African-American children; similarly, much more extensive intertextual relations between solicitational routines and television shows, comic books, and other forms of popular culture were evident in the repertoire of the Anglo children. Both sets of data suggest that both race and class regulate access to socialization into the types of intertextual strategies that are rewarded by the dominant society; the studies we cited earlier on genre and gender suggest that gender plays a crucial role in shaping the relevant socialization practices as well. We would go on to suggest that such differential distribution of competence in intertextual strategies provides an important means of naturalizing social inequalities based on race and ethnicity, gender, and social class.

One of the thorniest issues that divides social-cultural anthropologists from their linguistically oriented colleagues is the keen interest that many members of the former subdiscipline take in the "poetics and politics" of ethnography (see Clifford 1988; Clifford and Marcus 1986). Linguistic anthropologists—and

---

[6] See also Labov (1972) on the sociolinguistic skills of inner-city African-American children; he similarly argues that the hegemony of sociolinguistic patterns associated with middle-class whites in schools thwarts the ability of African-American children to draw on their verbal abilities and sets them up for educational failure. Interestingly, Gates (1988) argues that intertextuality lies at the heart of African-American aesthetics.

more than a few social-cultural types as well—often regard their preoccupation with the writing of ethnography, both in "the field" and in the office, as a means of diverting scholarly energy away from the task of discovering the similarities and differences in the ways that people talk and act. Investigating intertextual strategies would seem to offer important possibilities for transcending this epistemological standoff. Fieldwork, analysis, and publication are just as dependent on intertextual strategies as are *coloquio* performances, ritual wailing, and the other forms we have discussed. Such techniques as interviewing draw on complex intertextual relations in creating discourse that is preconfigured for scholarly recontextualizations. As Paredes (1977) has so skillfully shown, ethnographers can be easily misled as to the types of generic intertextuality that their "informants" are using in framing their discourse. As in other types of discourse production and reception, what is negotiated is not just what types of intertextual links are being established, but who gets to control this process; race, class, gender, status, institutional position, and postcolonial social structures in general affect the production and reception of intertextual relations in fieldwork (see Briggs 1986; Mishler 1986).

A number of anthropologists have recently focused on literary intertextuality in ethnographic writing, illuminating the way that both fieldwork and its representation are shaped by intertextual relations; the generic parameters of ethnographies are shaped through intertextual links not simply with the discourse of Others, but with such literary genres as travel literature, autobiography, and colonial accounts (Clifford 1988; Clifford and Marcus 1986; Marcus and Fischer 1986; Taussig 1987, 1992). Although anthropological writing generally claims to derive its authority from knowledge gained "in the field," intertextual relations established through allegorical narratives and rhetorical tropes play a crucial role in creating authenticity and scientific authority. Examined from the perspective of the creation of generic intertextuality, these literary features are fascinating, both for the way they attempt to naturalize the ethnographer's control over intertextual processes and for the manner in which they seek to erase the monumental gap between the discourses they represent and their own textual representations. The extensive use of tape recorders in the field and side-by-side transcriptions/ translations by linguistic anthropologists (present company included) clearly play a role in this process.

This is not to say that anthropological research, linguistic or otherwise, is untenable and should be abandoned. It is to say that fieldwork and its representation provide no less interesting examples of generic intertextuality than other types of discourse and that they are no less in need of scholarly attention. Attempts to dismiss analysis of the intertextual relations that we construct in the course of research and writing would seem to deny us vital information regarding the scientific status of these materials. Such proscriptions simply add up to another set of strategies for minimizing intertextual gaps; as in all such cases, we must inquire into the ideologies that sustain them and the power relations that render them effective or ineffective.

## CONCLUSION

In this article we have critiqued views of genre that draw on purportedly immanent, invariant features in attempting to provide internally consistent systems of mutually exclusive genres. We presented an alternative view of genre, one that places generic distinctions not within texts but in the practices used in creating intertextual relations with other bodies of discourse. Since the establishment of such relations necessarily selects and abstracts generic features, we argued that generic intertextuality is not an inherent property of the relation between a text and a genre but the construction of such a relationship. A text can be linked to generic precedents in multiple ways; generic framings of texts are thus often mixed, blurred, ambiguous, contradictory. We accordingly suggested that generic links necessarily produce an intertextual gap; the strategies used for constructing intertextual relations can seek to minimize this gap, maximize it, or both. Choices between intertextual strategies are ideologically motivated, and they are closely related to social, cultural, political-economic, and historical factors.

Scholars have generally regarded systems of literary and speech genres as means of classifying or ordering discourse. Since intertextual relations produce disorder, heterogeneity, and textual open-endedness, as well as order, unity, and boundedness, scholarly strategies for creating generic links similarly involve arbitrary selections between competing intertextual relations and are affected by ideological, social, cultural, political-economic, and historical factors. Therefore, no system of genres as defined by scholars can provide a wholly systematic, empirically based, objective set of consistently applied, mutually exclusive categories.

One of the most interesting lines of inquiry in linguistic anthropology and folklore (see Ben-Amos 1976[1969], 1992) has located the study of speech genres in the ethnographic study of locally constructed classification systems rather than in a priori analytic categories. This shift has had a positive impact on research by drawing attention to the processes of discursive ordering undertaken by a broader range of producers and receivers of texts than those associated with scholarly practices alone. Unfortunately, it has also helped displace the reification of generic intertextuality from scholarly discourse to representations of ethnographic Others. Ethnographically based studies often portray the situated use of ethnic genres as a process of applying relatively stable, internally consistent, mutually exclusive, and well-defined categories in the production and reception of texts. In representing such an orderly process, scholars run the risk of doubly mystifying the problem by failing to discern the ideologies and power arrangements that underlie local impositions of generic order as well as by covering up their own rhetorical use of genres in ordering ethnographic data. In so doing, scholars collude with the members of the community in question who are deemed to have control over the production and reception of intertextual relations; they similarly often overlook the existence of marginalized and dissenting intertextual strategies (but see

Appadurai et al. 1991). While the research on speech genres conducted by the two of us over the years has attempted to analyze the social, political, and linguistic processes that shape the production and reception of verbal art, our work is hardly immune from this sort of reification.

Our goal in this article is thus not to "rescue" the category of genre from these difficulties or to assert its centrality to research in linguistic anthropology. Any attempt to champion—or to dismiss—the concept of genre would have strong ideological underpinnings. We have rather tried to use our discussion of genre as a means of raising some basic issues regarding discourse production and reception. In an earlier article (Bauman and Briggs 1990) we argued that discourse analysis cannot best proceed either by (1) studying (socio)linguistic elements and processes apart from the process of discourse production and reception or by (2) studying social interactions as analytic microcosms. We rather pointed to the fruitfulness of studying discourse vis-à-vis the way it is transformed in the course of successive decontextualizations and recontextual-izations and of exploring the process of entextualization that provides the formal and functional basis for such transformations.

We have attempted to advance this line of inquiry here by drawing attention to some of the ways that linguistic anthropologists have used the concept of genre in elucidating discourse processes; we have pointed to a number of problems in the theoretical underpinnings of these discussions that pose obstacles to progress along these lines. We went on to use the notion of generic intertextuality in analyzing particular strategies for decontextualizing and recontextualizing discourse, along with the ways that this process both reflects and produces social power. We hope that this discussion has demonstrated the value of integrating detailed formal and functional analysis, the sine qua non of linguistic anthropology, with attention to ideology, power, and scholarly practices. We also hope to have suggested some of the ways that such a critical synthetic approach can illuminate contrastive—and often competing—approaches to the study of discourse.

## REFERENCES

Abrahams, Roger D., and Richard Bauman
    1971    Sense and Nonsense in St. Vincent: Speech Behavior and Decorum in a Caribbean Community. American Anthropologist 73(3):262–272.
Abu-Lughod, Lila
    1986    Veiled Sentiments: Honor and Poetry in a Bedouin Society. Berkeley: University of California Press.
    1990    Shifting Politics of Bedouin Love Poetry. In Language and the Politics of Emotion. Catherine A. Lutz and Lila Abu-Lughod, eds. Pp. 24–25. Cambridge: Cambridge University Press.
Anderson, Benedict
1991 [1983] Imagined Communities: Reflections on the Origin and Spread of Nationalism. London: Verso.

Appadurai, Arjun
1981    The Past as a Scarce Resource. Man 16(2): 201–219.
Appadurai, Arjun, Frank J. Korom, and Margaret A. Mills, eds.
1991    Gender, Genre, and Power in South Asian Expressive Traditions. Philadelphia: University of Pennsylvania Press.
Bakhtin, M. M.
1986 [1979] The Problem of Speech Genres. In Speech Genres and Other Late Essays. Caryl Emerson and Michael Holquist, eds. Pp. 60–102. Austin: University of Texas Press.
Balditin, M. M., and P. M. Medvedev
1985 [1928] The Formal Method in Literary Scholarship: A Critical Introduction to Sociological Poetics. Albert J. Wehrle, trans. Cambridge: Harvard University Press.
Basso, Keith H.
1984 (reissued 1988) "Stalking with Stories": Names, Places, and Moral Narratives among the Western Apache. In Text, Play, and Story. Edward Bruner, ed. Pp. 19–55. Prospect Heights, IL: Waveland Press.
Bauman, Richard
1977a   Linguistics, Anthropology, and Verbal Art: Toward a Unified Perspective, With a Special Discussion of Children's Folklore. In Linguistics and Anthropology. Muriel Saville-Troike, ed. Pp. 13–36. Washington, DC: Georgetown University Press.
1977b (reissued 1984) Verbal Art as Performance. Prospect Heights, IL: Waveland Press.
1982    The Ethnography of Children's Folklore. In Children In and Out of School: Ethnographic Perspectives in Education. Perry Gilmore and Alan Glatthorn, eds. Pp. 172–186. Washington, DC: Center for Applied Linguistics.
1986    Story, Performance, and Event: Contextual Studies of Oral Narrative. Cambridge: Cambridge University Press.
1987    Ed Bell, Texas Storyteller: The Framing and Reframing of Life Experience. Journal of Folklore Research 24(3): 197–221.
1992a   Contextualization, Tradition, and the Dialogue of Genres: Icelandic Legends of the Kraftaskald. In Rethinking Context: Language as an Interactive Phenomenon. Alessandro Duranti and Charles Goodwin, eds. Pp. 77–99. Cambridge: Cambridge University Press.
1992b   Transformations of the Word in the Production of Mexican Festival Drama. In The Decentering of Discourse. Michael Silverstein and Greg Urban, eds. (in press).
Bauman, Richard, and Charles L. Briggs
1990    Poetics and Performance as Critical Perspectives on Language and Social Life. Annual Review of Anthropology 19:59–88.
Ben-Amos, Dan
1976 [1969] Analytical Categories and Ethnic Genres. In Folklore Genres. Dan Ben-Amos, ed. Pp. 215–242. Austin: University of Texas Press.
1992    Do We Need Ideal Types (in Folklore)? An Address to Lauri Honko. Turku, Finland: Nordic Institute of Folklore.
Boas, Franz
1940a [1914] Mythology and Folk-Tales of the North American Indians. In Race, Language and Culture. Pp. 451–490. New York: Free Press.

1940b [1916] The Development of Folk-Tales and Myths. In Race, Language and Culture. Pp. 397–406. New York: Free Press.
1940c [1917] Introduction to International Journal of American Linguistics. In Race, Language and Culture. Pp. 199–210. New York: Free Press.

Bourdieu, Pierre
1977      Outline of a Theory of Practice. Richard Nice, trans. Cambridge: Cambridge University Press.
1991      Language and Symbolic Power. Gino Raymond and Matthew Adamson, trans. Cambridge: Harvard University Press.

Bourdieu, Pierre, and Jean-Claude Passeron
1977      Reproduction: In Education, Society and Culture. Richard Nice, trans. Beverly Hills: Sage.

Brenneis, Donald
1987      Performing Passions: Aesthetics and Politics in an Occasionally Egalitarian Community. American Ethnologist 14(2): 236–250.
1988      Telling Troubles: Narrative, Conflict and Experience. Anthropological Linguistics 30(3/4): 279–291.
1990      Shared and Solitary Sentiments: The Discourse of Friendship, Play, and Anger in Bhatgaon. In Language and the Politics of Emotion. Catherine A. Lutz and Lila Abu-Lughod, eds. Pp. 113–125. Cambridge: Cambridge University Press.

Briggs, Charles L.
1986      Learning How to Ask: A Sociolinguistic Appraisal of the Role of the Interview in Social Science Research. Cambridge: Cambridge University Press.
1988      Competence in Performance: The Creativity of Tradition in Mexicano Verbal Art. Philadelphia: University of Pennsylvania Press.
1989      "Please Pass the Poison": The Poetics of Dialogicality in Warao Ritual Wailing. Paper presented at the Conference on Lament, Austin, TX.
1990      History, Poetics, and Interpretation in the Tale. In The Lost Gold Mine of Juan Mondragón: A Legend from New Mexico Performed by Melaquías Romero. Charles L. Briggs and Julián Josué Vigil, eds. Pp. 165–240. Tucson: University of Arizona Press.
1992a      Generic versus Metapragmatic Dimensions of Warao Narratives: Who Regiments Performance? In Reflexive Language: Reported Speech and Metapragmatics. John A. Lucy, ed. Pp. 179–212. Cambridge: Cambridge University Press (in press).
1992b      "Since I Am a Woman, I Will Chastise My Relatives": Gender, Reported Speech, and the (Re)production of Social Relations in Warao Ritual Wailing. American Ethnologist 19(2): 337–361.

Clifford, James
1988      The Predicament of Culture: Twentieth-Century Ethnography, Literature, and Art. Cambridge: Harvard University Press.

Clifford, James, and George E. Marcus, eds.
1986      Writing Culture: The Poetics and Politics of Ethnography. Berkeley: University of California Press.

Dorst, John D.
1989      The Written Suburb: An American Site, an Ethnographic Dilemma. Philadelphia: University of Pennsylvania Press.

Dubrow, Heather
1982      Genre. London: Methuen.

Dundes, Alan
1964    The Morphology of North American Indian Folktales. Folklore Fellows Communications, 195. Helsinki: Suomalainen Tiedeakatemia.
Dundes, Alan, ed.
1965    The Study of Folklore. Englewood Cliffs, NJ: Prentice-Hall.
Duranti, Alessandro
1984 (reissued 1991) *Lauga* and *Talanoaga*: Two Speech Genres in a Samoan Political Event. In Dangerous Words: Language and Politics in the Pacific. Donald L. Brenneis and Fred R. Myers, eds. Pp. 217–242. Prospect Heights, IL: Waveland Press.
Ervin-Tripp, Susan
1972    On Sociolinguistic Rules: Alternation and Co-Occurrence. In Directions in Sociolinguistics: The Ethnography of Communication. John J. Gumperz and Dell H. Hymes, eds. Pp. 213–250. New York: Holt, Rinehart & Winston.
Farrer, Claire R., ed.
1975 (reissued 1986) Women and Folklore: Images and Genres. Prospect Heights, IL: Waveland Press.
Feld, Steven
1990a [1982] Sound and Sentiment: Birds, Weeping, Poetics, and Song in Kaluli Expression. 2d ed. Philadelphia: University of Pennsylvania Press.
   1990b    Wept Thoughts: The Voicing of Kaluli Memories. Oral Tradition 5(2/3): 241–266.
Gal, Susan
1991    Between Speech and Silence: The Problematics of Research on Language and Gender. In Gender at the Crossroads of Knowledge: Feminist Anthropology in the Postmodern Era. Micaela di Leonardo, ed. Pp. 175–203. Berkeley: University of California Press.
Gates, Henry Louis, Jr.
1988    The Signifying Monkey: A Theory of African-American Literary Criticism. New York: Oxford University Press.
Georges, Robert, and Alan Dundes
1963    Toward a Structural Definition of the Riddle. Journal of American Folklore 76(300): 111–118.
Goodwin, Matiorie Harness
1990    He-Said-She-Said: Talk as Social Organization Among Black Children. Bloomington: Indiana University Press.
Goody, John Rankin
1977    The Domestication of the Savage Mind. Cambridge: Cambridge University Press.
Gossen, Gary H.
1972    Chamula Genres of Verbal Behavior. In Toward New Perspectives in Folklore. Américo Paredes and Richard Bauman, eds. Pp. 145–167. Austin: University of Texas Press.
1974 (reissued 1984) Chamulas in the World of the Sun: Time and Space in a Maya Oral Tradition. Prospect Heights, IL: Waveland Press.
Hall, Stuart
1981    Notes on Deconstructing "the Popular." In People's History and Socialist Theory. Raphael Samuel, ed. Pp. 227–240. London: Routledge.
Halliday, M. A. K.
1978    Language as Social Semiotic. London: Arnold.

Handler, Richard, and Jocelyn Linnekin
1984　Tradition, Genuine or Spurious. Journal of American Folklore 97(385): 273–290.
Hanks, William F.
1987　Discourse Genres in a Theory of Practice. American Ethnologist 14(4): 668–692.
Heath, Shirley Brice
1982　What No Bedtime Story Means: Narrative Skills at Home and School. Language in Society 11(1): 49–76.
Herndon, Marcia, and Susanne Ziegler, eds.
1990　Music, Gender, and Culture. Wilhelmshaven, Germany: Florian Noetzel Verlag.
Herzfeld, Michael
1982　Ours Once More: Folklore, Ideology, and the Making of Modern Greece. Austin: University of Texas Press.
Hobsbawm, Eric, and Terence Ranger, eds.
1983　The Invention of Tradition. Cambridge: Cambridge University Press.
Hymes, Dell H.
1962　The Ethnography of Speaking. In Anthropology and Human Behavior. Thomas Gladwin and William C. Sturtevant, eds. Pp. 13–53. Washington, DC: Anthropological Society of Washington.
1964　Introduction: Toward Ethnographies of Communication. In The Ethnography of Communication. American Anthropologist, Special Publication 66, Number 6, Part 2. John J. Gumperz and Dell H. Hymes, eds. Pp. 1–34. Washington, DC: American Anthropological Association.
1967　Models of the Interaction of Language and Social Setting. Journal of Social Issues 23(2): 8–28.
1972a　Models of the Interaction of Language and Social Life. In Directions in Sociolinguistics: The Ethnography of Communication. John J. Gumperz and Dell H. Hymes, eds. Pp. 35–71. New York: Holt, Rinehart & Winston.
1972b　The Contribution of Folklore to Sociolinguistic Research. In Toward New Perspectives in Folklore. Américo Paredes and Richard Bauman, eds. Pp. 42–50. Austin: University of Texas Press.
1974　Ways of Speaking. In Explorations in the Ethnography of Speaking. Richard Bauman and Joel Sherzer, eds. Pp. 433–451. Cambridge: Cambridge University Press.
1975a　Breakthrough Into Performance. In Folklore: Performance and Communication. Dan Ben-Amos and Kenneth S. Goldstein, eds. Pp. 11–74. The Hague: Mouton.
1975b　Folklore's Nature and the Sun's Myth. Journal of American Folklore 88(350): 346–369.
1981　"In Vain I Tried to Tell You": Essays in Native American Ethnopoetics. Philadelphia: University of Pennsylvania Press.
1985　Language, Memory, and Selective Performance: Cultee's "Salmon's Myth" as Twice Told to Boas. Journal of American Folklore 98(390): 391–434.
Hymes, Virginia
1987　Tonkawa Poetics: John Rush Buffalo's "Coyote and Eagle's Daughter." In Native American Discourse: Poetics and Rhetoric. Joel Sherzer and Anthony C. Woodbury, eds. Pp. 62–102. Cambridge: Cambridge University Press.

Jacobs, Melville
1959    Clackamas Chinook Texts. Part 2. Bloomington: Indiana University Research Center in Anthropology, Folklore, and Linguistics.
Jakobson, Roman
1960    Closing Statement: Linguistics and Poetics. In Style in Language. Thomas A. Sebeok, ed. Pp. 350–377. Cambridge: MIT Press.
Jordan, Rosan A., and Susan Kalčik, eds.
1985    Women's Folklore, Women's Culture. Philadelphia: University of Pennsylvania Press.
Keenan, Elinor
1974    Norm-Makers, Norm-Breakers: Uses of Speech by Men and Women in a Malagasy Community. In Explorations in the Ethnography of Speaking. Richard Bauman and Joel Sherzer, eds. Pp. 125–143. Cambridge: Cambridge University Press.
Kirshenblatt-Gimblett, Barbara
1991    Objects of Ethnography. In Exhibiting Cultures: The Poetics and Politics of Museum Display. Ivan Karp and Steven D. Lavine, eds. Pp. 386–443. Washington, DC: Smithsonian Institution Press.
Koskoff, Ellen, ed.
1989    Women and Music in Cross-Cultural Perspective. Westport, CT: Greenwood Press.
Kristeva, Julia
1980    Desire in Language. Leon S. Roudiez, trans. New York: Columbia University Press.
Kuipers, Joel C.
1990    Power in Performance: The Creation of Textual Authority in Weyewa Ritual Speech. Philadelphia: University of Pennsylvania Press.
Labov, William
1972    Language in the Inner City. Philadelphia: University of Pennsylvania Press.
Leitch, Vincent B.
1991    (De)Coding (Generic) Discourse. Genre 24(1): 83–98.
Lewalski, Barbara Kiefer, ed.
1986    Renaissance Genres: Essays on Theory, History, and Interpretation. Cambridge: Harvard University Press.
Lockhart, James
1991    Nahuas and Spaniards: Postconquest Central Mexican History and Philology. Stanford: Stanford University Press.
Lucy, John, ed.
1992    Reflexive Language: Reported Speech and Metapragmatics. Cambridge: Cambridge University Press (in press).
Lutz, Catherine
1990    Engendered Emotion: Gender, Power, and the Rhetoric of Emotional Control in American Discourse. In Language and the Politics of Emotion. Catherine A. Lutz and Lila Abu-Lughod, eds. Pp. 69–91. Cambridge: Cambridge University Press.
Marcus, George E., and Michael M. J. Fischer
1986    Anthropology as Cultural Critique: An Experimental Moment in the Human Sciences. Chicago: University of Chicago Press.
Miller, Nancy K., ed.
1986    The Poetics of Gender. New York: Columbia University Press.

Mishler, Elliot G.
1986    Research Interviewing: Context and Narrative. Cambridge: Harvard University Press.
Ong, Walter J.
1967    The Presence of the Word: Some Prolegomena for Cultural and Religious History. Minneapolis: University of Minnesota Press.
1982    Orality and Literacy: The Technologizing of the Word. London: Methuen.
Paredes, Américo
1977    On Ethnographic Work among Minority Groups. New Scholar 6(1): 1–32.
Philips, Susan U.
1986    Reported Speech as Evidence in an American Trial. In Languages and Linguistics: The Interdependency of Theory, Data, and Application. Deborah Tannen, ed. Washington, DC: Georgetown University Press.
1987    The Concept of Speech Genre in the Study of Language and Culture. *In* Working Papers and Proceedings of the Center for Psychosocial Studies, 11. Pp. 25–34. Chicago: Center for Psychosocial Studies.
Philips, Susan U., Susan Steele, and Christine Tanz, eds.
1987    Language, Gender and Sex in Comparative Perspective. Cambridge: Cambridge University Press.
Propp, Vladímir
1968 [1928] The Morphology of the Folktale. Laurence Scott, trans. Austin: University of Texas Press.
Radin, Paul
1926    Literary Aspects of Winnebago Mythology. Journal of American Folklore 39(151): 18–52.
Reichard, Gladys
1925    Wiyot Grammar and Texts. University of California Publications in American Archaeology and Ethnology, 22(1). Berkeley: University of California Press.
1947    An Analysis of Coeur D'Alene Indian Myths. Memoirs of the American Folklore Society, vol. 41. Philadelphia: American Folklore Society.
Sapir, Edward
1909    Wishram Texts. Publications of the American Ethnological Society, vol. 2. Leiden: E. J. Brill.
Sapir, Edward, and Harry Hoijer
1942    Navaho Texts. Iowa City: Linguistic Society of America and University of Iowa.
Schieffelin, Bambi B.
1990    The Give and Take of Everyday Life: Language Socialization of Kaluli Children. Cambridge: Cambridge University Press.
Scott, Charles T.
1965    Persian and Arabic Riddles: A Language-Centered Approach to Genre Definition. Bloomington: Indiana University Research Center in Anthropology, Folklore, and Linguistics.
Sebeok, Thomas A.
1964 [1953] The Structure and Content of Cheremis Charms. In Language in Culture and Society. Dell H. Hymes, ed. Pp. 356–371. New York: Harper & Row.
Seremetakis, C. Nadia
1991    The Last Word: Women, Death, and Divination in Inner Mani. Chicago: University of Chicago Press.

Sherzer, Joel
1983 Kuna Ways of Speaking. Austin: University of Texas Press.
1987 A Discourse-Centered Approach to Language and Culture. American Anthropologist 89(2): 295–309.
1991 Verbal Art in San Blas. Cambridge: Cambridge University Press.
Shimkin, Demitri
1964 [1947] Wind River Shoshone Literary Forms: An Introduction. In Language in Culture and Society. Dell H. Hymes, ed. Pp. 344–355. New York: Harper & Row.
Showalter, Elaine, ed.
1985 The New Feminist Criticism: Essays on Women, Literature, and Theory. New York: Pantheon.
Silverstein, Michael
1976 Shifters, Linguistic Categories, and Cultural Description. In Meaning in Anthropology. Keith Basso and Henry A. Selby, eds. Pp. 11–55. Albuquerque: University of New Mexico Press.
1985 The Culture of Language in Chinookan Narrative Texts; or, on Saying that . . . in Chinook. In Grammar Inside and Outside the Clause. Johanna Nichols and Anthony Woodbury, eds. Pp. 132–171. Cambridge: Cambridge University Press.
1992 Metapragmatic Discourse and Metapragmatic Function. In Reflexive Language: Reported Speech and Metapragmatics. John A. Lucy, ed. Pp. 33–58. Cambridge: Cambridge University Press.
Stewart, Susan
1991 Notes on Distressed Genres. Journal of American Folklore 104(411): 5–31.
Stross, Brian
1974 Speaking of Speaking: Tenejapa Tzeltal Metalinguistics. In Explorations in the Ethnography of Speaking. Richard Bauman and Joel Sherzer, eds. Pp. 213–239. Cambridge: Cambridge University Press.
Tannen, Deborah
1989 Talking Voices: Repetition, Dialogue, and Imagery in Conversational Discourse. Cambridge: Cambridge University Press.
Taussig, Michael
1987 Shamanism, Colonialism and the Wild Man: A Study in Terror and Healing. Chicago: University of Chicago Press.
1992 The Nervous System. New York: Routledge.
Telford, Kenneth A.
1961 Aristotle's Poetics: Translation and Analysis. South Bend, IN: Gateway.
Tolbert, Elizabeth
1990 Magico-Religious Power and Gender in the Karelian Lament. In Music, Gender, and Culture. Marica Herndon and Suzanne Ziegler, eds. Pp. 41–56. Berlin: Institute for Comparative Music Studies.
Urban, Greg
1984a The Semiotics of Two Speech Styles in Shokleng. In Semiotic Mediation. Elizabeth Mertz and Richard J. Parmentier, eds. Pp. 311–329. Orlando: Academic Press.
1984b Speech about Speech in Speech about Action. Journal of American Folklore 97(385): 310–328.
1988 Ritual Wailing in Amerindian Brazil. American Anthropologist 90(2): 385–400.